Research Design in Clinical Psychology

THIRD EDITION

Research Design in Clinical Psychology

Alan E. Kazdin

Yale University

Allyn and Bacon

Boston   London   Toronto   Sydney   Tokyo   Singapore

Series editor: Carla F. Daves
Series editorial assistant: Susan Hutchinson
Manufacturing buyer: Suzanne Lareau

 Copyright © 1998, 1992, 1980 by Allyn & Bacon
A Viacom Company
Needham Heights, MA 02194

Internet: www.abacon.com
America Online: keyword: College Online

Library of Congress Cataloging-in-Publication Data

Kazdin, Alan E.
   Research design in clinical psychology / Alan E. Kazdin.
—3rd ed.
    p.   cm.
   Includes bibliographical references and index.
   ISBN 0-205-26088-8
   1. Clinical psychology—Research—Methodology. I. Title.
RC467.8.K39 1998
616.89'0072—dc21   97-37711
                              CIP

Printed in the United States of America
10 9 8 7 6 5 4 3 2   01 00 99 98

To Nicole and Michelle

Contents

Preface

The purpose of this book is to describe and explain methodology and research design in clinical psychology. The focus is on clinical psychology but the issues and methods are also relevant to other areas, such as counseling, education, school psychology, psychiatry, and social work, to mention a few. The topics within each of these areas span theory, research, and application. Consequently, many of the methodological challenges are shared. This book elaborates the methods of conducting research and the broad range of practices, procedures, and designs for developing a sound knowledge base.

Many available texts on methodology elaborate fundamental practices and methods of research design. Often research methods are presented by describing idealized conditions of laboratory studies or in abstract discussions removed from investigations within the field. In clinical psychology, as well as related areas, a great deal of research is conducted outside of the laboratory. Essentials of research design are no less important. Indeed, an in-depth understanding of methodology is of even greater importance because of the range of influences in clinical research that can obscure the results. These influences cannot be used as an excuse for poorly designed research. On the contrary, the subject matter requires grasp of the underpinnings and nuances of design so that special arrangements, novel control conditions, and methods of statistical evaluation can be deployed to maximize the clarity of our findings. Research design in clinical work requires rigor and ingenuity as a defense against the multitude of influences that can obscure the relations among variables.

The scope and challenges of the field have made research design in clinical psychology a rich topic. Traditionally, clinical psychology has embraced a variety of topics, such as the study of personality, assessment and prediction of psychological functioning and adjustment, etiology, course and outcome of various forms of psychopathology, the impact of interventions (treatment, prevention, education, and rehabilitation), and cross-cultural studies of personality and behavior. Many issues of contemporary life have added to the range of topics, as witnessed by the strong role that clinical psychology now plays in research on health, violence, crime, homelessness, and substance abuse. Also, family life and demographic characteristics of the population have changed (e.g., increases in teenage mothers, single-parent families, and blended families, more elderly who are physically active) and have spawned rich areas of study (e.g., child care and elderly care arrangements). Diversity of cultural and ethnic issues and understanding the bases of cultural variation further add to the richness of the field.

The topical breadth of clinical psychology also has been accompanied by a diversity of research methods. Consider a few of the dimensions that convey the methodological diversity of the field. Research in clinical psychology encompasses both large-scale, multisite investigations involving groups of subjects and experiments with the single case (individual subject); methods of data evaluation that use inferential statistical techniques as well as nonstatistical and clinical criteria to assess change; and experiments conducted in laboratory settings and observational studies in hospitals, clinics, schools, and in the community. The diversity of topics and types of research requires coverage and appreciation of the full range of methodological weapons that can be deployed to combat ambiguity.

This book is designed to address methodology in the contexts in which clinical psychologists are called on to work and in relation to the very special demands that these contexts may place on them. Although specific methodological practices and procedures are covered in detail, the book also focuses on the underpinnings, rationale, and purposes of these practices. After all, methodology is not merely a compilation of practices and procedures. Rather, it is an approach toward problem solving, thinking, and acquiring knowledge. An investigator in clinical psychology frequently is called on to resolve questions related to evaluation when the usual practices cannot be used and to maximize the knowledge yield from the demonstration.

The content of the book encompasses experimental design, assessment, sources of artifact and bias, data evaluation and interpretation, and ethical and professional issues raised by research. Issues are traced as they emerge in the planning and execution of research: developing the research idea; selecting methods, procedures, and assessment devices; analyzing and interpreting the data; and preparing the written report of the results. At each stage of research, the principles, pitfalls, artifacts, biases, alternative strategies, and guidelines are presented. Attention also is devoted to quasi-experiments, case-control studies, case studies and single-case experiments for clinical use, qualitative research, assessment methods, and diverse approaches to data evaluation.

A few key themes pervade the chapters. First, methodology not only encompasses a number of design options and practices but also a way of approaching problems and substantive questions. Indeed, the practices central to methodology (e.g., random assignment, use of control groups) are only important in relation to the issues they are intended to address. Understanding these issues can greatly expand the options for designing research and the quality and creativity of the products. Second, methodology cannot be divorced from substance or content. The ways in which we design and evaluate our studies include and embrace substantive positions about how the phenomena we study are conceived. Our selection of levels of the independent variable, of subjects, and especially statistical analyses says something important, even if implicit, about how we view the world, our theories, and hypotheses. These connections are important to draw to encourage novel methods as a way of developing or testing theories. Also, methodology is not merely a tool to evaluate ideas but in many ways shapes the ideas. Third, methodology is evolving. Already there is great diversity in the methods used in clinical research. Appreciation of this evolution and drawing on different research traditions can contribute to our development as investigators and to the findings in our programs of research. These themes, stated nebulously here, become more concrete throughout the text.

The revised edition of the book includes a number of additions to reflect the evolving nature of methodology and the proliferation of clinical research into many topic areas. Among the changes, three new chapters have been added. A chapter on case-control designs and cohort designs conveys research strategies when intact groups are identified and evaluated. A great deal of research in clinical psychology utilizes these designs, but their special demands, sources of artifact, and methods of control are rarely elaborated. A chapter was also added on qualitative research, a method that has not been used commonly within psychology in the United States. Qualitative research is covered in light of its special substantive contribution to clinical psychology, its increased use within the field, and its relation to more traditional methods of research. A brief closing chapter was added to place methodology in perspective and to encourage use and exploration of novel methods.

Apart from additions, each chapter was revised and updated. Core areas such as designs, their applicability to clinical situations, statistical considerations, ethical and professional responsibilities of the investigator, and preparation of manuscripts for publication have been elaborated in this revision. Throughout the book examples are provided to illustrate key points. The examples draw from classic (old) and new studies and from clinical and other areas of psychology. Also, I have tried to draw from other disciplines, especially public health and medicine, to convey points with which we are already familiar in these other contexts and also to underscore that many of the issues with which our field struggles are common problems. Examples are also drawn from everyday experience and topics in the news. (I realize that such examples risk making the book interesting, but that was a chance I wanted to take.)

The present edition includes teaching aids for the reader. First, outlines are provided at the beginning of each chapter to help organize the content and scope of the issues that each topic entails. Second, at the end of each chapter, a short list of readings is provided (For Further Reading) that directs the interested reader to more in-depth presentations of topics raised in the chapter. Finally, a Glossary is included at the end of the book to centralize and define briefly terms introduced throughout the chapters. Special terms italicized within the text are usually covered in the glossary. Although the book is not overabundant in terminology, there is value to providing a quick reference to terms and practices.

Several persons have contributed to the thrust and focus of this book during the past several years. It is gracious at this point to convey to the reader that any errors that remain in the book after extensive input from others is my responsibility alone. This is a useful point to depart from tradition. Unlike authors of most other books, I hold the people who contributed to this book personally responsible for limitations, errors, and oversimplifications. Of course to the extent that anything in the pages that follow is helpful, interesting, or inspired, I am pleased to share the credit.

Actually, the list of mentors, colleagues, and graduate students who deserve credit would be lengthy; the net effect of enumerating them all would be to diffuse the special gratitude I feel toward each person. Although many years have passed since my dissertation, I owe a special debt of gratitude to my dissertation committee. Many of their comments at my dissertation orals linger in their influence on me and on the topic of this book (e.g., "Alan, find another career." "Research isn't for everyone." "A 50% rate of attrition in a control group starting with 2 subjects is problematic." "When we said, 'use a pretest,' we did not mean omit the posttest.") These pithy comments raised the prospect that understanding methodology may be rather important. (Not wanting to be identified with my study, all my committee members entered the Dissertation Committee Witness Protection Program immediately after my oral exam and, unfortunately, cannot be identified by name. I am grateful to them wherever they are.)

Several sources of research support were provided during the period in which this book was written. A Research Scientist Award (MH00353) and research grant (MH35408) from the National Institute of Mental Health provided support for research, educational, and training opportunities directly related to methodology, assessment, and design. Support from the John D. and Catherine T. MacArthur Foundation is also gratefully acknowledged. Participation in the Network on Psychopathology and Development of the John D. and Catherine T. MacArthur Foundation has been enormously educational and influential because colleagues in the Network have shaped my views about science and evaluation more generally. Needless to say, the views expressed in this book do not reflect the views of any agency that has provided research support nor, for that matter, the agencies that have not provided support.

My appreciation extends to the following reviewers for their comments on the manuscript: Kathleen M. Schiaffino, Fordham University; Philip C. Kendall, Temple University; Lee Sechrest, University of Arizona; and Timothy Stickle, University of Arizona. The author is also extremely grateful to Carla Daves and Sue Hutchison of Allyn and Bacon and Marilyn Rash of Ocean Publication Services, for their special roles in bringing this project to fruition.

About the Author

Alan E. Kazdin (Ph.D., Northwestern University, 1970) is Professor and Chairman in the Department of Psychology and Professor in the Child Study Center at Yale University. He is also Director of the Yale Child Conduct Clinic, an outpatient treatment service clinic for children and families. Prior to coming to Yale, Professor Kazdin was on the faculty in Psychology at The Pennsylvania State University and in Psychiatry at the University of Pittsburgh School of Medicine. His research focuses primarily on the evaluation of factors that contribute to the development, treatment, and clinical course of antisocial behavior in children and adolescents and on factors that influence child, parent, and family participation in psychotherapy. He has been the editor of the *Journal of Consulting and Clinical Psychology, Psychological Assessment, Behavior Therapy*, and *Clinical Psychology: Science and Practice*. Currently, he is editor of the *Encyclopedia of Psychology* (American Psychological Association and Oxford University Press) and of the book series on *Developmental Clinical Psychology and Psychiatry* (Sage Publications). His professional awards include receipt of the Distinguished Scientific Contribution and Distinguished Professional Contribution Awards from the American Psychological Association (Division of Clinical Psychology) and a MERIT Award and a Research Scientist Award from the National Institute of Mental Health. He has authored, co-authored, or co-edited more than 30 books on the topics of research design, clinical psychology, child and adolescent psychopathology, psychotherapy, and cognitive–behavioral therapy.

*Research Design
in Clinical
Psychology*

Chapter 1

Introduction

The general purpose of science is to establish knowledge. Although many areas of scientific investigation, such as the study of the stars, weather, plants, and animals, are familiar to us, the systematic methods of investigation in scientific research and how these methods improve on casual observation are not widely appreciated. Indeed, occasionally the public is skeptical about scientific research and frustrated with the yield. For example, the seemingly frequent findings that various foods or food additives may cause cancer in animals has raised public disenchantment with scientific research. Products and materials present in everyday life (e.g., asbestos, radon) continue to be shown in research to contribute to cancer risk in humans. The disenchantment is reflected in the quip that "the only thing that causes cancer is scientific research!"

The disenchantment also belies frustration with research findings that often conflict with each other. For example, various foods (e.g., eggs, butter, meat, coffee) have been shown at various points in time to be harmful, helpful, and neutral in relation to particular health outcomes (e.g., forms of cancer, heart disease). Moreover, the simple findings or rules we would like (e.g., X is "bad" for us) are often sabotaged by nuances and qualifiers. Thus, we have learned that a little wine is good for us but a lot is bad and that some wines (e.g., red) more than others seem to be better. Interpretation of such findings and trying to act on them could lead one to drink!

When the scientific verdict seems relatively clear and has broad consensus (e.g., cigarette smoking contributes to many untoward health outcomes), many of us seem to know someone who is an exception (e.g., a 90-year-old uncle who is very healthy and smokes two packs a day immediately after eating his favorite breakfast—lard soufflé). Inconsistencies in scientific findings and counter-instances of a given finding in everyday life are not part of the problem of scientific research. Rather, they reflect the complexities of empirical relations. It is not the scientist's fault, for example, that high cholesterol is associated with an increased risk for heart disease but a decreased risk for cancer (West, 1995). Even though many findings are incomplete and there are complexities with incomplete knowledge, enormous advances have been made that we take for granted in everyday life (e.g., vaccines for diseases, predictions of weather, dangers of pollutants in the drinking water, medications, psychotherapies for depression).

Scientific research is essential for understanding natural phenomena and for making advances in knowledge. Although a number of research methods are available, they have in common careful observation and systematic evaluation of the subject matter under varying conditions. The diverse methods constitute special arrangements and plans of observation that are designed to uncover relations between variables in a relatively unambiguous fashion. The relations may seem apparent in nature when a particular phenomenon is observed casually. Yet, many relations are obscured by the complex interrelations and combinations of many variables as they normally appear. The task of identifying relations is compounded by the characteristics and limits of our perception. Among complex relations, it is easy and natural for us to connect variables perceptually and conceptually and to then integrate them into our belief systems. The relations can be firmly entrenched independently of whether the variables genuinely go together or are related in fact.

Scientific research attempts to simplify the complexity of nature and to isolate a particular phenomenon for careful scrutiny. The phenomenon is examined by manipulating or varying values of the variable of interest while controlling extraneous factors that might otherwise influence the results. By controlling or holding constant sources of influence that might vary under ordinary circumstances, the relation between the variables of interest can be examined. In addition to arranging features of nature, science also provides methods to aid perception. The methods consist of diverse practices, procedures, and decision rules to aid in drawing conclusions and in reaching a consensus about relations observed in research. Among the interesting features of scientific research is that the methods used to reveal nature can contribute significantly to the results. That is, how a study is conducted, the measures that are used, and how the data are analyzed are just a few of the aspects of methodology that influence the specific conclusions the investigator will draw. Consequently, the study of methodology and the underpinnings of decision making is essential.

In the present book, we discuss several research methods that are designed to address specific concerns, potential problems, artifacts, and biases and that serve as impediments to knowledge. It is important to understand these impediments because they foster an appreciation of the rationale of methods and encourage one to handle difficult situations in novel ways. In areas of research such as clinical psychology, psychiatry, counseling, social work, educational and school psychology, and other disciplines that span theory, research, and application, major challenges derive from addressing questions outside the laboratory. Drawing valid inferences is not sacrificed when one leaves the methodological comforts of the laboratory. However, thoughtful and creative application of design strategies assumes greater importance to ensure that valid inferences can be identified.

METHODOLOGY AND RESEARCH DESIGN

Methodology refers to the diverse principles, procedures, and practices that govern research. Within that general domain is the concept of *research design,* which refers to the plan or arrangement that is used to examine the question of interest. These terms tend to focus on the specific practices and options that characterize research. The focus of this book is on methodology and research design and hence covers diverse practices and procedures. Yet, the focus on concrete methods and practices has the danger of emphasizing ingredients of research and perhaps conjuring up a cookbook for the design of experiments. Research design is not a compilation of specific practices, procedures, or strategies. Even highly revered practices (e.g., random assignment of subjects or participants, use of large sample sizes) may be unnecessary to reach valid inferences in a given study.[1] The issue is one of understanding both the rationale for methodological practices and the practices themselves.

Methodology refers to a *way of thinking* and, as such, it is beneficial to avoid overemphasis of concrete practices involved in research process. Design and methodology alert us to the issues that affect how we examine and interpret phenomena. Consider an example of the type of thinking that methodology fosters. Sir Francis Galton (1822–1911), the British scientist, investigated the extent to which prayer increases longevity. Specifically, he was interested in whether praying for the health and longevity of other persons in fact added years to the lives of those persons. The hypothesis would be one of great theoretical and applied interest, to say the least. Galton reasoned that if prayer were effective, then kings, queens, and other royalty would live longer than others. After all, their health and longevity are consistently the objects of prayer (as attested to by frequent exhortations, "Long live the Queen," in contrast to the rare and less familiar, "Long live the beggar").

Galton selected and compared different groups who were presumed to vary in the extent to which people prayed for their health and longevity (Galton, 1872). The results indicated that royalty died at an earlier age than that of non-royalty. Specifically, the mean (average) age at the time of death for royalty was 64.0 years, a number lower than that for other groups including men of literature and science (67.6 years) and the gentry (70.2 years). Clearly, royalty died at a younger age. Does this study show that prayer was ineffective in increasing the longevity of royalty? Of course not.

Methodology teaches us ways to think about the relations between variables, about causes and effects, and about conclusions drawn from theory, research, and experience. In the case of Galton's study, methodology draws our attention to the hypothesis, findings, how the phenomenon was studied, and alternative explanations of the data. Consider the following. It might be that at the time of Galton, royalty without the benefit of other people's prayers would have died at an earlier age than the mean of 64.0 years. Perhaps the sedentary schedule, rich food, weighty responsibility, frequent guest appearances, and tight fitting, heavy, jewel-laden clothes of royalty would have conspired to produce a much earlier death. Let us say, for hypothetical purposes, that royalty during the time of Galton normally lived to be 55 years of age, on average. It is quite possible that prayer did in fact increase longevity from, say, 55 to 64 years for the royalty included in Galton's study. The data show only that royalty died at a younger age than that of comparison samples. Yet, the hypothesis was not whether royalty live *longer* than nonroyalty but whether prayer increases longevity. It is quite possible that prayer increases longevity (number of years of living) without making one group of persons actually live longer than another group. The original hypothesis remains unscathed and in need of further testing.

All sorts of research possibilities might be generated to clarify the results. We might, for example, wish to examine the extent to which royalty are prayed for and their longevity. Presumably "more might be better"; perhaps all royalty are not prayed for equally. Groups within the overall royal class might be matched on health characteristics related to longevity (e.g., age, sex, blood pressure, family history of disease and family longevity) but vary in the extent to which they are the objects of prayer. To ensure that they differed in the extent to which they were prayed for, perhaps we could survey the public to identify the persons for whom their prayers are directed. Also, it is possible that members of royalty themselves engage in more (or less) praying than others. Perhaps praying rather than being prayed for is critical. In general, we would wish to control for or assess several variables that plausibly relate to longevity to ensure that these variables did not vary between groups and were taken into account when comparing groups. It is important not to belabor the example. At the same time, how a study is conducted very much determines the extent to which the conclusions can be interpreted. Methodology is a way of thinking about phenomena because it alerts us to the types of questions to ask and, as importantly, to the practices designed to obtain enlightened answers.

Incidentally, there has been other testing of the relation of prayer to longevity and to physical and mental health. One controlled study that has received considerable public attention found that being prayed for improved recovery of hospitalized patients in a coronary care unit, even though the patients were not aware of prayers in their behalf (Byrd, 1988). The results have been subject to many different interpretations (Dossey, 1993). More well-documented is the role of religion on physical and mental health. Among the findings are studies showing that participation in religion (e.g., belief in god, attending church regularly, and being committed to religion) is associated with reduced rates of suicide, death from heart disease, depression, and higher levels of overall well-being (Levin, 1994; McCullough, 1995).

Designing research often is presented as a straightforward enterprise. At the most rudimentary level, in an experiment the design includes an experimental and a control group. The experimental group receives a form of the experimental condition or intervention and the control group does not. Differences between groups are considered to reflect the effect of the experimental manipulation. Although the basic comparison is well intentioned in principle, it greatly oversimplifies the bulk of contemporary research and the type of control procedures required in most studies in clinical psychology. Research design is a fascinating topic because of the many different ways in which investigations are completed, the advantages and disadvantages associated with the available design options, and the contribution of different designs to the results.

Scientific hypotheses are attempts to explain, predict, and explore specific relations. When hypotheses are formulated, they represent "if–then" statements about a particular phenomenon. The "if" portion of the hypothesis often refers to the independent variable that is manipulated or varied in some other way; the "then" portion refers to the dependent variable or resulting data. Findings consistent with an experimental hypothesis do not necessarily prove the hypothesis. Data can only be taken as proof of a hypothesis if no conceivable alternative hypothesis can account for the results or if the predicted relations would be obtained if and only if the hypothesis were true. Yet, these requirements are more likely to be met by logic and deductive reasoning than by scientific research. Whether another hypothesis conceivably could account for the results may be a matter for future investigators to elaborate. Also, whether a finding would result only from a particular hypothesis cannot be known with certainty. The confidence of certainty provided in logical deductions is not available in science. Of course, this fact refers to the logical bases of scientific conclusions. As scientists, we often *feel* quite certain about our conclusions. The experience or feeling of certainty is quite separate from the logical status and truth value of scientific propositions.

Not all experiments are conducted to test a particular prediction or an "if–then" relation. Many experiments explore the relations of variables and are not formulated as tests of hypotheses. Yet, the tenuous nature of the conclusions still applies. The findings, however systematic, do not necessarily reflect the effects of the independent variables. The findings may be a function of unspecified factors extraneous to the experimental manipulation itself. A number of these factors may be uncontrolled variables within or outside of the experiment and serve as explanations of the findings.

Although many extraneous factors can be recognized and controlled in advance of an experiment, others cannot. It may take years of research to recognize that something in the experiment other than the variable of interest contributed to the original findings. For example, in human drug research, a routine practice is to keep the hospital staff or investigators naive so that they do not know who is receiving the experimental (treatment) drug and who is receiving a placebo. Keeping staff naive is now recognized to be important because their beliefs and expectancies can influence patients' behavior independently of the effects of the drugs. In years past, many drug studies lacking this precaution were completed and can now be only regarded as inconclusive.

Methodology is directed at planning an experiment in such a way as to rule out or to make implausible competing explanations of the results. The better an experiment is designed, the fewer the alternative plausible explanations that can be advanced to account for the findings. Ideally, only the effects of the independent variable can be advanced as the basis for the results. Several methodological features we discuss are designed to maximize clarity of the findings.

PHILOSOPHY OF SCIENCE, RESEARCH METHODOLOGY, AND STATISTICAL INFERENCE

Experimentation encompasses three broad interrelated topics: philosophy of science, research methodology, and statistical inference. Philosophy of science considers the logical and epistemological underpinnings of the scientific method in general. Historically, experimentation has been closely tied to philosophical thought. Topics such as the basis of knowledge, the organization and limitations of perception, the nature and perception of causal relations, methods and limitations of inductive reasoning, the conditions required for testing and verifying predictions, and indeed the very notion of a hypothesis all revert to philosophy. The philosophy of science reveals, among other things, fundamental limitations in the logical underpinnings of observational and experimental methods. Experimental methods rely on several presuppositions and assumptions about the nature of the world and our knowledge of that world, and they cannot be logically justified. The philosophical challenge points to the tenuous nature of empirical knowledge. Yet, the challenge has not deterred research from progressing to elaborate natural phenomena.

The day-to-day business of the researcher requires planning investigations so that conceptual, interpretive, and practical problems are minimized. Research methods, rather than philosophy of science, enter at this point to provide options that maximize the clarity of the results. Broadly conceived, methodology encompasses the procedures and practices of conducting and designing research so that lawful relations can be identified. Results of research by their very nature are tentative because any particular finding may depend on unique features of the setting and experimental arrangement in which the finding was obtained. Findings may also be ambiguous because the relations might be due to influences that the investigator did not know, acknowledge, or identify. Tentativeness and ambiguity of research findings can never be completely eliminated. At the same time, the accumulation of multiple investigations can increase the clarity of the findings.

Statistical inference is integrally related to experimentation because of the extensive reliance on statistical tests in research to draw conclusions from data. Also, statistical techniques can be used to focus the interpretation of the findings of a particular study. Statistical controls or analyses of variables within the study that might contribute to or be confounded with the independent variable can help to reduce the plausibility of rival interpretations of the results. For example, socioeconomic disadvantage (e.g., poverty, receipt of social assistance) is related to many variables of interest in psychological research (e.g., physical and mental health, child-rearing practices, stress). Data-analytic strategies can play a major role in examining the separate and combined influences of socioeconomic disadvantage and these other variables and hence play a major role in drawing inferences about substantive issues. Thus, statistical analyses often work in concert with methodology.

Statistical evaluation provides agreed-on decision rules so that there is some uniformity in the criteria used to draw conclusions. Ironically, the criteria for making statistical inferences themselves often are based on arbitrary decisions. For example, the precise point that a finding is called statistically reliable or significant is purely a matter of convention, rather than being a statistically or logically justifiable criterion or, in a given situation, well advised. The manner in which experimental data ought to be analyzed statistically and the advantages and disadvantages of different analyses are widely discussed and debated. Developments in mathematics and statistics have made the area of statistical inference extremely important in its own right in understanding how data are to be interpreted and how experiments are to be designed to maximize interpretability.

The philosophy of science, research methodology, and statistical inference overlap considerably. This book generally focuses on research methods. The focus requires excursions to issues related to the basis of knowing and interpretation, but clearly not into epistemological discussions. Similarly, we address selected statistical issues in which research design is inextricably bound but eschew the underpinnings of data analysis. The excursions into other topics are all designed to serve the central goal, namely, to examine research methodology.

CHARACTERISTICS OF RESEARCH IN CLINICAL PSYCHOLOGY

Clinical psychology embraces standard features of scientific research, such as defining the research idea, generating hypotheses, designing investigations, collecting and analyzing data, and so on. Yet, in clinical psychology and other disciplines in which laboratory, clinical, and applied studies are conducted, the basic steps of research and methodological acumen of the investigator are challenged. The special demands for understanding research methods can be suggested by highlighting the substantive and methodological diversity of the field.

Substantive diversity refers to the content areas that clinical psychology encompasses. The content areas of the field are vast and would be difficult even to enumerate fully, much less describe. Consider for a moment just a few of the domains. Clinical psychology includes the study of diverse populations as illustrated by investigations of all age groups from infancy through the elderly; indeed, the field extends beyond these age limits by studying processes before birth (e.g., prenatal characteristics of mothers and families) and after death (e.g., the impact of death on relatives, treatment of bereavement). Also, a variety of special populations are studied, such as those with special experiences (e.g., the homeless, divorced, prisoners of prior wars), with psychological or psychiatric impairment (e.g., children, adolescents, or adults with depression, anxiety, post-traumatic stress disorder, autism, schizophrenia, to mention only a few), and with medical impairment and disease (e.g., cancer, acquired immunodeficiency syndrome [AIDS], spinal cord injury, diabetes). Persons in contact with special populations themselves are often studied (e.g., children of alcoholics, spouses of depressed patients, siblings of physically handicapped children).

Examples of a few of the populations in clinical research merely begins to convey the breadth of foci. Consider a few other dimensions that might be mentioned. Research in clinical psychology is conducted in diverse settings (e.g., laboratory, clinics, hospitals, prisons, schools, industry) and in the absence of structured settings (e.g., runaway children, homeless families). Clinical psychology research is also conducted in conjunction with many other areas of research and different disciplines (e.g., criminology, health psychology, neurology, pediatrics, psychiatry, public health). In addition, central areas of research within the field have remarkable breadth in the topics they encompass. For example, the study of personality characteristics; the assessment, diagnosis, treatment, and prevention of clinical dysfunction; and cross-cultural differences in personality, adjustment, and maladjustment are rich and broad areas of research.

Understandably, diverse methods of study are required to meet the varied conditions in which clinical psychologists work and the special challenges in drawing valid scientific inferences from situations that are often complex. The methodological diversity of clinical research, as the substantive diversity, can be illustrated in many different ways. Studies vary in the extent to which the investigator can exert control over the assignment of cases to conditions or administration of the intervention (e.g., true experiments and quasi-experiments) and the selection of preexisting groups and how they are followed and evaluated (e.g., case-control designs, cross-sectional and longitudinal studies). Also, designs (e.g., group vs. single case), methods of data evaluation (e.g., statistical and nonstatistical), and approaches to the study of clinical phenomena (quantitative vs. qualitative) further convey the methodological richness of the field. The book details diverse methodological practices and options.

The purpose in highlighting the diversity and richness of clinical psychology is to underscore the importance of facility with the methods of research. Special demands or constraints are frequently placed on the clinical researcher. Ideal methodological practices (e.g., random assignment) are not always available. Also, restrictions (e.g., a control group might not be feasible, only small sample sizes are available) may limit the researcher's options. The task of the scientist is to draw valid inferences from the situation and to use methodology, design, and statistics toward that end. In clinical psychology and related areas of research, the options in methodology, design, and statistics must be greater than in more basic research areas to permit the investigator to select and identify creative solutions. Clinical research is not in any way soft science; indeed, the processes involved in clinical research reflect science at its best precisely because of the thinking and methodological ingenuity required to force nature to reveal its secrets. Deploying strategies to accomplish this requires an appreciation of the purposes of research and the underpinnings of research strategies that serve as the means to achieve these purposes.

THE "PSYCHOLOGY" OF RESEARCH METHODOLOGY

In detailing the research practices and goals toward which they are aimed, it is easy to depersonalize the research enterprise. At the outset, it is critical to underscore that research design, and science more generally, is basically a human enterprise. This does not mean that the methods and findings are subjective or that science is guided by whim. Yet, researchers are people first. This obvious statement has broad implications for our subject matter. As people, we have ideas, beliefs, ambitions, individual histories and experiences, and so on. These natural human characteristics do not seep into science; they are central to it.

Consider, for example, the goal of research, namely, to draw clear inferences about the relations among variables. In subsequent chapters, we spend a great deal of time on ways to design investigations to maximize the clarity of the findings. Yet, "clarity of the findings" is not a property of the results of a study. Rather, it has to do with the consensus among those who read the report of the study. Reaching a consensus extends beyond epistemology or the branch of philosophy that addresses how we come to know things. Of relevance also is the substantive information from psychology (e.g., perception, learning, attitudes, beliefs, persuasion).

In most research, findings are not unequivocally clear. Usually, research must accumulate for years to elaborate a phenomenon and to clarify the circumstances in which the effects are evident. In such circumstances, our individual thresholds for stating that the findings are established or clear assume an important role. At what point shall we believe that a particular finding is sound or true? The threshold varies as a function of the specific area of research, strength of our beliefs, prior training and experiences, and no doubt many other factors. A finding may more readily be embraced as "clear" or "valid" to the extent it is compatible with these factors.

Our thresholds for believing may vary for our own research versus the research of others. The language with which we refer to our own research and the research of others may belie our varied thresholds for believability. For example, when *I* use weak measures in my studies and have an inadequate control group, I may regard and refer to the study as "somewhat weak," the "best that could be done under the circumstances," and clearly "better than prior work" in the area. When *you* conduct an experiment with identical characteristics, I may view this a bit more harshly. Your measure may be "homemade" and "not validated"; the lack of essential controls may represent a "serious or fatal flaw" in the design and "preclude conclusions" about the phenomenon of interest. We need not lament the different standards that individuals may apply to a given area of research or pattern of results. I mention the point here to provide an important context for methodology and research design.

Methodology has to do in part with the persuasiveness of findings. We engage in specific strategies and practices to persuade ourselves and the scientific community at large. Often findings are so clear and repeated so frequently that consensus is great. Even here, clarity is a matter of degree and individual preference. For example, for years data on the dangers of cigarette smoking varied in their credibility to scientists and the public. At first, individuals may have doubted the main finding that cigarettes are hazardous to one's health. As the evidence accumulated and entered the mass media, more people were persuaded and acknowledged the hazard as "true." Some still are not persuaded; others are persuaded but retain their original belief by stating that for themselves there are special circumstances that mitigate the dangers of smoking. Their belief is retained not by denying the finding (a main effect) but by noting that the danger is not applicable to their special circumstances (an interaction). The specific hypothesis under which such persons operate might be accurate, namely, that in their situations some other variable may reduce the danger. It may be untrue, is unlikely to be well tested, and probably is inadvisable to believe from the standpoint of physical health. (Of course, nonmethodologically based interpretations of why people completely ignore the smoking and health findings could be advanced by noting defense mechanisms—remember "Denial is not just a river in Egypt.")

The example is mentioned here to convey crucial aspects about beliefs and how they influence the clarity and impact of research findings. The task for both an individual study and for the field as a whole is to develop tests of hypotheses that are convincing. "Convincing" in this context does not mean that the results show a particular pattern, prove the hypotheses, or demonstrate that the investigator is right. Rather, "convincing" relates to the quality of the research design and the features that permit sound inferences to be drawn. A well-designed study provides a convincing test so that the results, whatever their pattern, are persuasive to the investigator and to others in the scientific community.

The fact that research depends on beliefs and persuasion is not a weakness of the enterprise. It is, however, important to accept this as a given and as a critical point of departure. The task before us is to uncover the secrets of nature. We adopt strategies of all sorts—theory construction, research methodology, and statistical evaluation—to aid in our task. Each strategy involves decision points that may affect the clarity of the conclusions we draw. Reasonable people not only can disagree about the conclusions of individual studies but do so routinely. Thus, there are inherent limits to what we can expect from an individual study, not merely from the complexity of the subject matter, but because of the diversity of human characteristics on which inferences and interpretation depend. At the same time, there is much that we can do to maximize the information from research and to accumulate knowledge in spite of these limitations.

OVERVIEW OF THE BOOK

Research methodology can be viewed as a decision-making process. Decisions are made at all stages of the process of an investigation, beginning with the decision of what to study and how to move from the idea to the investigation and end with interpretation of the findings. It is not always possible to specify how each decision should be made before considering a particular study. Each decision has its own implications and trade-offs in terms of the final product. Also, the decisions may depend on how the phenomenon examined in the experiment is conceptualized. The present text describes and evaluates different methodological, design, and assessment options and the rationale for their use. The book focuses on many of the complexities of design by emphasizing the problems that arise in experimentation and techniques designed for their control. Advantages, limitations, and other considerations in using particular design practices are elaborated.

The purpose of research is to draw valid inferences about the relations between variables. Methodology consists of practices that help to arrange the circumstances so as to minimize ambiguity in reaching inferences. Many of the factors that can interfere with drawing clear conclusions from research can be readily identified. These factors are referred to as *threats to validity* and serve as the basis for why and how we conduct research. Types of experimental validity and the factors that interfere with drawing conclusions are the basis for Chapters 2 and 3.

The investigation begins with an idea that becomes translated into a specific question or statement. A particular subset of variables is selected for manipulation or scrutiny. Sources of research ideas, types of variables, diverse questions, and the conditions under which these factors are investigated are described in Chapter 4.

An initial decision in research is selecting among many different design options. The range of questions, topics, and foci of research in clinical psychology has led to use of a large variety of designs. Advantages and potential limitations of several types of designs, problems that are likely to arise in their use, and control techniques to improve the designs are presented. Group designs used in experimental research in which variables are manipulated by the investigator are detailed in Chapter 5. Questions that are addressed in experimental research depend heavily on the control and comparison groups that are included in the design. In Chapter 6, several types of control and comparison groups are discussed along with the considerations that dictate their use.

A crucial aspect of experimental research is ensuring that the manipulation of the independent variable was effectively achieved. Checking on the experimental manipulation can greatly enhance the conclusions that can be drawn from research. The procedures to assess the implementation of the experimental manipulation, the interpretation of the results of these techniques, and the problems that may arise are elaborated in Chapter 7.

A great deal of research is based on understanding variables that cannot manipulated directly, for example, in the study of individuals with different characteristics (e.g., disorders, experiences, exposure to events). Observational designs (case-control designs and cohort designs) in which individuals are selected and evaluated concurrently or longitudinally are presented in Chapter 8. Single-case research designs and their use in clinical work are discussed in Chapter 9. The chapter examines the anecdotal case study briefly and focuses on experimental and quasi-experimental single-case designs for research and clinical application. Special design and data evaluation strategies that characterize single-case designs are also presented.

The vast majority of research within psychology is within the quantitative tradition involving group designs, hypothesis testing, assessment on standardized scales and inventories, and statistical evaluation. From a different tradition and approach, qualitative research methods are enjoying increased use in psychology. The topic is not usually covered in research-design books within the quantitative tradition. Chapter 10 provides an overview of the approach, conditions to which the designs are suited, and illustrations to convey the contribution to developing the knowledge base.

Selection of the measures to use in research raises a number of conceptual and assessment issues. The requirements for appropriate and useful measures in a particular investigation are manifold. Different modalities of assessment may be selected and, within these, vast options are available for specific measurement techniques. Usually more than one assessment modality is incorporated into the design. Chapter 11 discusses basic assessment considerations that dictate selection and use of measures in research and also highlights commonly used assessment modalities. Special topics in assessment, the focus of Chapter 12, include reactivity of assessment, the methods and use of unobtrusive measures, and expansion of criteria to evaluate interventions. This chapter raises a number of issues especially pertinent to treatment research including client-, treatment-, and consumer-related measures of outcome and the issues, problems, and procedures of follow-up assessment.

Many sources of artifacts and bias can interfere with drawing valid inferences from an experiment. They may derive from the investigator who designs and analyzes the experiment, the experimenter who actually runs the subjects, the demand characteristics of the experimental situation, the roles that subjects adopt as they participate in the study, and subject-selection biases prior to and during the experiment. Chapter 13 examines these influences, the manner in which they are likely to affect the results, and methods to minimize, assess, or eliminate their impact.

Evaluating the results of an experiment raises many options in clinical psychology. Clearly, statistical methods of data evaluation, particularly significance testing, are commonly used in empirical research. Chapter 14 focuses on the rationale and requirements of statistical evaluation and controversies associated with testing for statistical significance. Recommendations for replacing or supplementing significance testing are also provided. The chapter also presents methods of evaluating the clinical significance of changes in the context of treatment research. Although evaluation of clinical significance of change uses statistical methods, the goal is to identify changes that are important in everyday life.

Analyzing the data quantitatively is only part of the task of making sense of the results. Data interpretation and factors that facilitate and impede interpretation are no less significant. Special topics related to data evaluation and interpretation are covered in Chapter 15. Different types of effects produced by independent variables, negative results (no-difference findings), and replication of research are presented.

Conducting psychological research raises ethical issues that bear directly on design considerations. The manner in which a hypothesis is examined may entail the use of deception, invasion of privacy, and violation of confidentiality. One reason ethical issues are essential to consider is that they frequently specify the confines in which design options must be selected. Ethical issues in relation to the protection of subject rights, dilemmas of clinical research, guidelines for research, and responsibilities of the investigator in relation to the research enterprise and the scientific community are presented in Chapter 16.

Completion of an experiment is often followed by preparation of a written report which may be intended for publication. Communication of the results is not an ancillary feature of research methodology. The thought and decision-making processes underlying the design of a study and the specific methods that were used have direct implications for the conclusions that can be drawn. Preparation of the report is the investigator's opportunity to convey the interrelation of the conceptual underpinnings of the study and how the methods permit inferences to be drawn about those underpinnings. Chapter 17 discusses the written report and its preparation in relation to methodological issues presented in previous chapters. The special role that methodological issues and concerns play in the communication and publication of research is highlighted. The book ends with closing comments (Chapter 18) that discuss the interplay of substantive and conceptual issues and methodology and how advances in the latter enrich the former.

NOTE

[1]Throughout the book, the terms *subjects, participants,* and *clients* are used to delineate persons whose affect, cognition, or behavior is being studied, that is, those who participate in research and provide the data. The usage warrants comment because there has

been a change in recommended terminology to use the term *participants* instead of "subjects" (e.g., American Psychological Association, 1994). The change is intended in part to recognize that the participant is not merely an "object" of study without special rights and privileges and that the participant has more than a passive role in research (e.g., as represented by providing informed consent). The term subject(s) is retained but used interchangeably with the other terms (participant, client, patients). The term is also important because it has been adopted in key topics related to methodology (e.g., subject selection, subject artifacts). Also, participants in research include investigators (who design the study), experimenters (who administer the conditions), and, in an important sense, consumers of research (other professionals, the public at large). The distinctions are elaborated later; nevertheless, it is important to be clear at all times about who provides the data (i.e., subjects).

FOR FURTHER READING

Klee, R. (1997). *Introduction to the philosophy of science: Cutting nature at its seams*. New York: Oxford University Press.

Nagel, E. (1961). *The structure of science*. New York: Harcourt.*

Polkinghorne, J. (1996). *Beyond science: The wider human context*. New York: Cambridge University Press.

Popper, K. (1959). *The logic of scientific discovery*. New York: Basic Books.

Scheffler, I. (1967). *Science and subjectivity*. Indianapolis: Bobbs-Merrill.

*The early works (1959 and 1960s) cited here are among classics in scientific method and philosophy of science.

Chapter 2

Drawing Valid Inferences I

Internal and External Validity

CHAPTER OUTLINE

The purposes of empirical research are to uncover among variables relations that otherwise could not be readily detected and to verify relationships that have been hypothesized. Without research, potential relations among variables must be viewed in their full complexity as they appear in nature. Research design and statistical evaluation help simplify the situation in which the influence of many variables, often operating simultaneously, can be separated from the variable(s) of interest to the investigator. Without such simplification and isolation of variables, many, if not an unlimited number, of interpretations could explain a particular phenomenon. The special contribution of research is that it helps rule out or make implausible different factors that might explain a particular phenomenon. An experiment does not necessarily rule out all possible explanations, and the extent to which it successfully rules out alternative explanations is a matter of degree. From a methodological standpoint, the better the design of an experiment, the more implausible competing explanations of the results.

TYPES OF VALIDITY

The purpose of research is to reach well-founded (i.e., valid) conclusions about the effects of a given intervention and the conditions under which it operates. Four types of experimental validity address these purposes in different ways: internal, external, construct, and statistical conclusions (Cook & Campbell, 1979). These types of validity serve as a useful way to present several key facets of research methods and the rationale for many practices that are used. Table 2.1 lists each type of validity and the general type of questions to which each is addressed. Research design and its constituent methods and procedures, as well as methods of data analysis, are utilized to address these questions. Each type of validity is pivotal. Together they convey the multiple considerations that investigators have before them when they design an experiment.

TABLE 2.1.   Types of Experimental Validity and the Questions They Address

Type of Validity	Questions Addressed
Internal validity	To what extent can the intervention, rather than extraneous influences, be considered to account for the results, changes, or group differences?
External validity	To what extent can the results be generalized or extended to people, settings, times, measures, and characteristics other than those in this particular experimental arrangement?
Construct validity	Given that the intervention was responsible for change, what specific aspects of the intervention or arrangement was the causal agent, that is, what is the conceptual basis (construct) underlying the effect?
Statistical conclusion validity	To what extent is a relation shown, demonstrated, or evident, and how well can the investigation detect effects if they exist?

It is not difficult to argue in any given instance that one type is the most important. Indeed, we provide examples that show how the very nature of the investigator's interest dictates the priority of one type over another. In designing an experiment, it is critical for investigators to identify their purposes and specific questions clearly and to emphasize validity issues within the design that these questions entail because it is impossible to design and execute an experiment that addresses each type of validity perfectly. Investigators prioritize types of validity and management of threats where decisions are needed to ensure that their hypotheses are well tested. A weak experiment is one in which the type of inferences the investigators wish to draw are not carefully addressed. This chapter discusses internal and external validity. These types are presented first because they are relatively straightforward and reflect the logic of experimentation rather well. Also, failures to consider internal and external validity often represent the most blatant flaws in research.

INTERNAL VALIDITY

An investigation cannot determine with complete certainty that the independent variable accounted for change. However, if the study is carefully designed, the likelihood that the independent variable accounts for the results is high. When the results can be attributed with little or no ambiguity to the effects of the independent variable, the experiment is said to be internally valid. *Internal validity* refers to the extent to which an experiment rules out alternative explanations of the results. Factors or influences other than the independent variable that could explain the results are called *threats to internal validity*.

Threats to Internal Validity

Several types of threats to internal validity have been identified (Cook & Campbell, 1979). An investigation ought to be designed to make implausible the influences of these threats. To the extent that each threat is ruled out or made relatively implausible, the experiment is said to be internally valid.

History   This threat to internal validity refers to any event occurring in the experiment (other than the independent variable) or outside the experiment that may account for the results. History refers to the effects of events common to all subjects in their everyday lives (e.g., at home, school, or work). The influence of such historical events might alter performance and be mistaken for an effect resulting from the intervention or treatment. In an experiment it is important to be able to distinguish the effect of specific events occurring in the life of the subjects from the effect of the experimental manipulation or intervention. Although history usually refers to events outside the experiment, it may also include events that take place during the experiment. When participants are run in a group, unplanned events (e.g., power blackout, medical emergency of one of the participants, fire drill) may disrupt administration of the intervention and reduce or enhance the influence that the intervention normally would produce. Insofar as such events provide plausible explanations of the results, they threaten the validity of the experiment.

Maturation   Changes over time may result not only from specific events but also from processes within the subjects. Maturation refers to processes changing over time and includes growing older, stronger, wiser, and more tired or bored. Maturation is a problem only if the design cannot separate the effects of maturational changes from the intervention.

History and maturation often, but not invariably, go together as threats to internal validity. Although in any given case, it may not be easy to determine whether historical events or maturational processes accounted for change, it may not be essential to make the distinction in pointing out flaws in a study. For example, the problem of history and maturation can be seen in a study designed to evaluate the effects of training courses on childbirth for expectant mothers (Klusman, 1975). The purpose was to examine whether the two different training courses reduced self-reported anxiety. One of the courses trained expectant mothers to engage in special exercises that would facilitate delivery (Lamaze method); the other course merely provided information about labor, delivery, and child care (Red Cross course). In general, both groups reduced anxiety of expectant mothers and were not different from each other.

The findings would be very important if they provided clear information about treatment because another facet of this study demonstrated that the level of maternal anxiety is related to the amount of pain experienced during labor. Unfortunately, there is no clear basis for asserting that either training program was responsible for change. Quite possibly and quite plausibly, historical events occurring over time in the life of expectant mothers (e.g., reading about children, labor, and delivery; chatting with other expectant or new mothers about their experiences) or maturational processes (e.g., becoming less concerned about the anxieties of delivery over time) could explain the results. Special training programs may not be necessary for reductions in anxiety during the course of pregnancy. To help rule out the possible influence of history and maturation, the investigator could have evaluated mothers who did not undergo training (i.e., a no-treatment group). The latter group would have helped to separate treatment effects from naturally occurring events or processes extraneous to treatment.

One does not have to sift heavily through the literature to identify examples in which history and maturation are plausible explanations for the results. As another example, cognitive behavior therapy and a control condition (discussion of activities and one's "mental state") were compared for the treatment of depression in clinically referred children and adolescents (Vostanis, Feehan, Grattan, & Bickerton, 1996). By the end of treatment, both groups showed significant improvements on a variety of measures (e.g., mood, anxiety, social adjustment) but were not different from each other. It might be that both interventions were effective. However, history and maturation are plausible explanations of these findings.

Testing   This threat to internal validity refers to the effects that taking a test one time may have on subsequent performance on the test. In an experiment, pre- and postintervention tests might be given to evaluate how much an individual improves or deteriorates over time on a particular measure. Performance at the second testing may be influenced by practice or familiarity with the test because of the first testing. Changes at the second testing might not be due to an experimental manipulation or intervention but to the effects of repeated testing. In the examples for treatment of anxiety related to childbirth (Klusman, 1975) and for child and adolescent depression (Vostanis et al., 1996), improvements with repeated testing alone might also account for the pattern of results. We have known for some time that merely repeating the assessments without an intervention can be associated with significant improvements on measures of adjustment and personality (Frank, Nash, Stone, & Imber, 1963; Windle, 1954). A group that receives repeated testing without the intervention, such as a no-treatment control group, can help rule out testing as an explanation of changes evident in the intervention group. The no-treatment group would be expected to show the effects of testing; the treatment group shows the impact of the intervention beyond any effects of testing alone.

Instrumentation   This refers to changes in the measuring instrument or measurement procedures over time. For example, in many clinical studies, ratings of client improvement or observations of overt behaviors are made. The standards or scoring criteria that the therapists or clients use in rating or observing behaviors may change over time. Changes in the dependent variable during the course of treatment may result from changes in scoring criteria, rather than from changes in actual behavior.

Instrumentation can greatly affect conclusions about changes over time. For example, a major social concern is teenage substance use; annual surveys track changes over time. A difficulty is that the survey (measurement instrument) changes periodically as questions are reworded, dropped, and otherwise refined. Some of the significant changes—increases or decreases—in teenage drug use can be shown to be the result of changes in the measure, that is, instrumentation, in light of studies comparing old and new variations of the instrument in a given year (Moss, 1996). Data gathered longitudinally are often especially subject to instrumentation because investigators, administrators, or those responsible for policy make refinements and major changes in the instruments.

The problem of instrumentation does not usually arise when standardized paper-and-pencil tests are administered or when automated devices are used to score a response. The measuring devices, instruments, and scoring procedures are the same for each administration. Even so, it is conceivable that casual remarks by the experimenter at the time of the test administration might affect the subject's response and effectively alter the nature of the test and how the responses are obtained. For example, in a laboratory experiment on the reduction of arousal, stress, and anxiety, the experimenter might say, "I'll bet you're really relieved now that the film (story, task) is over. Please complete this measure again." It is conceivable that the different instructions preceding the measure alters the assessment in systematic ways and leads to the report of less anxiety. The reduction may result from assessment changes rather than from the experimental manipulation.

Statistical Regression   As a threat to internal validity, regression refers to the tendency for extreme scores on any measure to revert (or regress) toward the mean of a distribution when the measurement device is readministered. If individuals are selected for an investigation because they have had an extreme result on a given measure, one can predict on statistical grounds that at a second testing their scores will tend to revert toward the mean. That is, the scores will tend to be less extreme at the second testing. A less extreme score is, of course, one closer to the mean.

For example, in the investigation on child and adolescent depression noted earlier, youths were selected because they met criteria for depression (Vostanis et al., 1996). Both groups improved and did not differ from each other on outcome measures at the end of the treatment phase. The authors suggested that both conditions were effective. Yet, statistical regression could also have explained the results. Both groups, initially extreme on the measure of dysfunction, could have merely regressed toward the mean, that is, in the direction of improvement and may have done so without any treatment. A no-treatment or waiting-list control group would have helped in this study because we could then discern whether the changes in the two treatment conditions were any greater than changes without treatment (when regression artifacts would also have been evident in the no-treatment group). In general, regression is a is a threat to internal validity if the change due to the intervention cannot be distinguished from the effect of scores reverting toward the mean. (Regression is discussed in greater detail in Chapter 5.)

Selection Biases   The use of different methods for selecting subjects for experimental conditions is a threat to internal validity familiar to virtually all researchers. A selection bias refer to systematic differences in groups on the basis of the selection or assignment of subjects. Obviously, the effects of an independent variable among groups can be unambiguously inferred only if there is some assurance that groups do not systematically differ before the independent variable was applied. Random assignment of subjects is the procedure commonly used to minimize the likelihood of selection biases.

The threat of selection to the internal validity of an experiment often arises in clinical, counseling, and educational research in which intact groups are selected with patients from separate hospital wards, students from different classes, or samples from different schools. Groups are preformed and cannot be rearranged for research purposes. Even when groups are not already formed, practical demands may interfere with randomly assigning subjects to groups. For example, in a classic study designed to evaluate processes and outcomes of client-centered therapy, clients were assigned either to a treatment group or a control group (Rogers & Dymond, 1954). The treatment group received client-centered therapy; the control group initially was a waiting-list control group. Waiting-list clients received no treatment for 60 days and were measured before and after the waiting period to provide comparison data for the treatment group. If clients were assigned randomly to these conditions, initial subject selection would not serve as a threat to internal validity. Yet subjects were assigned on the basis of whether it seemed that they could wait for treatment (i.e., be in the waiting-list control group) without serious harm or discomfort. Thus, clients assigned to treatment and control groups might differ in terms of severity of their psychological state and also in many other variables. Group composition changed further once treatment began. Clients assigned to the waiting-list group occasionally were reassigned to the treatment group if, during the waiting period, they became anxious or were advised by someone else (e.g., the student's college advisor) to receive treatment. The main findings were that therapy was superior to no treatment. There is some ambiguity about the findings because selection is a threat to internal validity. It is plausible that subjects in treatment and waiting-list groups were very different to begin with or differed in their expected rate of improvement. Differences attributed to treatment effects may be confounded with subject characteristics, that is, selection.

Attrition   Attrition or loss of subjects may serve as a threat to internal validity. Loss of subjects does not refer to their veritable demise in most psychological experiments, although this too would present the same threat to validity. Attrition usually refers to participants dropping out of the study over time. If a single group of subjects is tested at different points in time, changes in overall group performance might be due to the gradual loss of subjects who scored in a particular direction rather than to improvements in the scores as a function of an intervention. If the experiment is conducted over a long period or includes a follow-up period to assess the long-term effects of treatment, attrition almost is inevitable and may obscure the conclusions that can be drawn.

Attrition is a threat to internal validity if there is a differential loss of subjects among groups or if the number of subjects lost is similar but there is reason to believe that the type of subjects or the standing of the subjects on a given measure differs among groups. Attrition can introduce selection biases into the study even though the investigator may have randomly assigned all cases to conditions at the beginning of the study. As subjects drop out, the remaining subjects cannot be assumed to represent the original sample that was recruited and assigned nor can the groups within the study (e.g., treatment, control) be assumed to be equivalent. Differential attrition across conditions within a study is likely in investigations in which conditions are differentially attractive or effective. Subjects are more likely to remain available and cooperative during and after treatment if they are receiving a treatment that is interesting, has little or no cost or adverse side effects, seems plausible, and is effective than if they are receiving a condition that is less desirable on these and related dimensions.

For example, one study compared the effects of drug therapy (imipramine) with cognitive therapy for the treatment of depression in adults (Rush, Beck, Kovacs, & Hollon, 1977). Cognitive therapy was found to be more effective. Interestingly, drug therapy led to significantly greater attrition during treatment than the cognitive therapy. This was an important finding at the time because it was the first randomized study to show that cognitive therapy was more effective than a standard medication treatment for depression. Yet the differential effects of treatment on outcome measures of depression might be the result of comparing groups of subjects at posttreatment that are no longer comparable in the way they were prior to treatment. Differences between groups might be due to the different treatments or to the different types of subjects remaining in each of the groups. From this study, there remains ambiguity about the relative effectiveness of cognitive therapy and medication. Because attrition has implications for each type of experimental validity, we return to the topic later.

Combination of Selection and Other Threats   Most prior threats refer to conditions that apply to all groups within the study (e.g., history, maturation, testing, regression) and that could explain the pattern of findings. Yet, it is possible that influences affect one group rather than or more than another. Group differences might be accounted for by different histories or maturation for the treatment versus control group. Whenever threats to internal validity vary for the different groups within the study, these are referred to as combinations of selection and that other threat. Another way to refer to this is to say that the threat interacts with (differentially applies to) groups (e.g., experimental and control conditions). An example is selection *x* history, which means that one of the groups has a historical experience (exposure to some event in or outside the investigation) that the other group did not have and that experience might plausibly explain the results. The threat is referred to selection *x* history because the threat (history) was selective in the bias it introduced (to one or more groups).

For example, one study was designed to compare the effects of behavioral-milieu therapy with routine ward care for the treatment of chronic psychiatric patients (Heap, Boblitt, Moore, & Hord, 1970). The behavioral-milieu therapy consisted of providing an incentive system on the ward for developing individualized self-care and social behaviors (behavioral part of the program). Patients were assigned either to the experimental ward or the control ward that received routine custodial care. Interestingly, the experimental group was moved to a special ward that was made available especially for this study. The ward included amenities such as drapes, bedspreads, rugs, clocks, and similar improvements not available in the control ward. Both the move and the addition of amenities to the ward constituted historical events within the experiment that were provided to experimental but not to control subjects. These events, provided to only one group, constituted a combined selection *x* history threat to internal validity; the histories for the different groups varied.

Concern with the historical events and related experiences may seem picky and purely academic. Indeed, to be threats at all, threats to validity must be plausible alternative hypotheses that could reasonably explain the pattern of results. How much can a move to another ward with more livable household conditions alter the behavior of seriously impaired psychiatric patients? Actually, quite a lot. Other studies have shown that merely moving to another ward, independently of whether a new treatment is given, can lead to durable therapeutic improvements in psychiatric patients (Gripp & Magaro, 1971; Higgs, 1970). Thus, historical differences (experiences, events) between groups could plausibly account for the differences the authors attributed to treatment.

Selection *x* history and selection *x* maturation are likely to be the most frequent confounds involving selection, but other combinations are possible. For example, if the participants in different groups are not tested at the same time, the results might be due to changes in the assessment procedures or criteria for scoring behavior over time (i.e., selection *x* instrumentation). As a general statement, if any single influence (e.g., history, testing) applies to only one group or applies in different ways to all the groups, the threat involves selection as an interaction.

Diffusion or Imitation of Treatment   It is possible that the intervention given to one group may be also provided accidentally to all or some subjects in a control group. The administration of treatment to the control group may be inadvertent and opposite from what the investigator has planned. Nevertheless, the effects will be to diffuse what the investigator concludes about the efficacy of treatment. Rather than comparing treatment and no-treatment conditions or two or more distinct treatments, the investigator is actually comparing conditions that are more similar than intended. As a threat to internal validity, the effect of a diffusion of treatment is to equalize performance of treatment and control groups.

An example of a diffusion of treatment as a threat to internal validity was reported in an investigation that compared two treatments for psychiatric patients in a day (rather than residential) hospital program (Austin, Liberman, King, & DeRisi, 1976). One treatment was a behaviorally oriented program in which patients received a wide range of techniques (e.g., incentive program, social-skills training) to develop adaptive behaviors that would facilitate community adjustment. The other program, conducted at a different facility, had an eclectic-milieu therapy approach in which group interaction, patient–staff planning meetings, and other forms of therapy were offered. The results, evaluated 3 and 6 months after treatment, showed a slight but nonsignificant superiority of the behavioral program in the extent to which patients improved on their individualized treatment goals.

At the end of the study, it was discovered that one of the therapists in charge of the eclectic-treatment condition used behavioral techniques extensively in her group, that is, techniques of the other treatment condition. The therapist had a close friend who was a behavioral psychologist and had taken workshops for further professional training in behavior therapy during the course of the project. Because the patients treated by this therapist did not actually receive eclectic-milieu treatment, their data were withdrawn so the results could be reanalyzed. The results then showed a significant difference between behavioral and eclectic-milieu treatments and favored the former. The threat to internal validity in this example is clear only because the authors were able to detect that the treatment for subjects in one group was inadvertently provided to some subjects in the other group. Because the treatments were not as distinct as originally planned, the net effect was to diffuse the apparent treatment effect on subsequent statistical analyses.

Diffusion of treatment is not a trivial or infrequent problem and affects a range of areas. For example, years ago a special program was designed to decrease heart attacks among men (N = 13,000, ages 35–57) at risk for coronary disease (Multiple Risk Factor Intervention Trial Research Group, 1982). The intervention included personal dietary advice, drugs to control hypertension, advice to stop smoking, and exercise. Random assignment permitted comparison of this group with the a control group that received testing (physical exams) but no special intervention (routine care). A follow-up 6 years after the program showed that the intervention had reduced risk factors for heart disease, but death rates due to heart disease were not statistically different between intervention and control groups. The absence of group differences has been interpreted to reflect a diffusion of treatment because the control group adopted many health-promoting practices on their own, which also decreased their risk factors (Farrington, 1992).

In many psychotherapy studies, the impact of interventions has been underestimated or inestimable because participants in the intervention group were unwittingly treated like controls or the controls received some interventions (Feldman, Caplinger, & Wodarski, 1983; Land, McCall, & Williams, 1992; Patterson, Chamberlain, & Reid, 1982). Another facet of diffusion, no less significant, is that some cases do not receive the intervention. In this situation, diffusion of the no-treatment condition occurred, that is, no treatment spread to cases (e.g., individuals in a therapy study, classes in a prevention study) assigned to receive the intervention. The net effect is the same, namely, when there is a diffusion of the conditions, the conclusions at the end of treatment are likely to be misleading.

Special Treatment or Reactions of Controls   In an investigation in which the intervention, treatment, or program is administered to the experimental group, the no-treatment control group may also be accorded special attention. This is likely to occur in applied settings such as schools, hospitals, and industry rather than in laboratory studies with college students. One group receives the special program that is viewed as generally desirable. Participants in the no-treatment control group may not receive the specific intervention of interest, but they may receive other services such as more money, more monitoring of their well-being, or special privileges. The services provided to the control group are usually intended to redress the apparent inequality and to compensate for not providing the intervention. From the standpoint of internal validity, however, the no-treatment group may be receiving an "intervention" in its own right that obscures the effect of the program provided to the experimental group.

Even if no special compensation in attention or money is provided to no-treatment control subjects, the absence of treatment may lead to special performance. When participants are aware that they are serving as a control group, they may react in ways that obscure the differences between treatment and no treatment. Control subjects may compete with the intervention subjects in some way. For example, teachers at control schools who learn they are not receiving the intervention may become especially motivated to do well to show they can be just as effective as those who receive the special treatment program. On the other hand, rather than trying extra hard, controls may become demoralized because they are not receiving the special program. The controls may have experienced initial enthusiasm when the prospect of participating in the special intervention was announced, but their hopes may have been dashed by the fate of random assignment. As a consequence, their performance deteriorates. By comparison, the performance of the intervention group looks better regardless of whether the intervention led to change.

Awareness of participating in an experiment can influence both intervention and control groups. From the standpoint of internal validity, a problem arises when this awareness differentially affects groups so that the effects of the intervention are obscured. At the end of the study, differences between treatment and control subjects or the absence of such differences may be due to atypical responses of the control group rather than to the effects of the intervention. Atypical responses could exaggerate or attenuate the apparent effects of treatment.

General Comments

Ideally, it would be instructive to select a single study that illustrated each threat to internal validity. Such a study would have failed to control for every possible threat and would not be able to attribute the results to the effects of the independent variable. A study committing so many sins would not be very realistic or represent most research efforts; there are generally only one or a few flaws at a time. Thus, detailing such an ill-conceived, sloppy, and uncontrolled study would have little purpose. (It would, however, finally give me a place to report the design and results of my dissertation in detail.)

In most research, the minimal experimental conditions include one group that receives an intervention or experimental condition with another group that does not. The purpose of using a no-intervention (manipulation) control group is to rule out as possibilities the threats to internal validity. History, maturation, testing, and so on could not account for group differences because both groups presumably would share the effects of these influences. Any group differences due to the intervention are superimposed on changes occurring for these other reasons. One might hypothesize that groups differed systematically in history, maturation, regression, and so on. But this is the combined threat of selection x history (or selection x some other factor). However, if participants were assigned randomly to groups, it may be difficult to explain how there were differences between groups on one of these dimensions. (Possible differences arising from random assignment are discussed in Chapter 5.)

In the course of an investigation, groups that are initially similar might become different for other reasons than the effects of the intervention. For example, it may be that subjects in a no-treatment group of a psychotherapy study drop out in higher numbers than subjects who are in treatment. If one group loses more subjects than another group and those subjects have scores that are better or worse than the rest of the sample in that group, subsequent group differences might be a function of who dropped out of the study rather than a function of the independent variable. Similarly, participation in a control condition may generate reactions such as compensatory performance or demoralization. Treatment and control group differences emerge from reasons other than the intervention provided to the treatment group.

Threats to internal validity are the major categories of alternative explanations of the conclusion that the intervention (manipulation or experimental condition) was responsible for group differences or changes. If a threat to internal validity is not ruled out or made implausible, it becomes a plausible rival explanation of the results. That is, whether the intervention or particular threat to validity operated to cause group differences cannot be decided; thus, the conclusion about the intervention becomes tentative. The tentativeness is a function of how plausible the threat is in accounting for the results given the specific area of research. Some threats may be dismissed on the basis of findings from other research that a particular factor does not influence the results. The degree to which a rival interpretation can be dismissed may be a matter of debate and may require subsequent research to resolve.

From a practical standpoint, it is important and useful for an investigator to decide in advance whether the investigation, when completed, will possibly be open to criticism to any of the threats and, if so, to decide what to do to rectify the situation. For example, in the examples cited in which history, maturation, and regression were plausible, a no-treatment condition to rule out each threat might have been included. However, not all threats to internal validity can be considered and completely averted before a study. Problems that arise during the study may later turn out to be threats (e.g., instrumentation or attrition). Even so, with many problems in mind prior to the study, specific precautions can be taken to optimize the clarity of the results.

EXTERNAL VALIDITY

External validity refers to the extent to which the results of an experiment can be generalized beyond the conditions of the experiment to other populations, settings, and conditions. External validity encompasses all the dimensions of generality of interest. Characteristics of the experiment that may limit the generality of the results are referred to as *threats to external validity.*

Threats to External Validity

Threats to external validity constitute questions that can be raised about the limits of the findings. It is useful to conceive of external validity as questions about the boundary conditions of a finding. Assume that a study has addressed the issues of internal validity and establishes a relation between an intervention and outcome. One is then likely to ask, Does this apply to other groups of persons (e.g., the elderly, nonhospitalized persons, diverse ethnic or racial groups), to other settings (e.g., clinics, day-care centers), or to other geographical areas (e.g., rural, other countries)? What are the boundaries or limits of the demonstrated relationship? Stated another way, one can discuss external validity in terms of statistical interactions. The demonstrated relation between the independent and dependent variables may apply to some people but not others or to some situations but not others, that is, the independent variable is said to interact with (or operates as a function of) the other conditions.

The factors that may limit the generality of an experiment usually are not known until subsequent research expands the conditions under which the relationship was originally examined. The manner in which experimental instructions are given; the age, ethnicity, race, and sex of subjects; whether experimenters are from the general population or are college students; the setting in which the experiment is conducted; and other factors may contribute to whether a given relationship is obtained. The generality of experimental findings may be a function of virtually any characteristic of the experiment. Some characteristics or threats to external validity that might limit extension of the findings can be identified in advance of a particular study.

Sample Characteristics The results of an investigation is demonstrated with a particular sample. A central question is the extent to which the results be generalized to other who vary in age, race, ethnic background, education, or any other characteristic. In research, there are different types or levels of concern in generalizing from one sample to another.

Concerns over characteristics of the sample and the implications for generalizing the results emerges in research with animals. For example, studies with mice and rats have elaborated the nature and basis for obesity. Special receptors for fat regulation in the brain (hypothalamus) and the genes responsible for these receptors have been identified. Extension of this work to humans has suggested that these receptors and genes are *not* implicated in human obesity (Considine et al., 1996). The animal research may still have critical implications for human obesity (e.g., drawing attention to related processes, identification of possible interventions), but biological differences in mice and rats compared with humans restricts the generality of these particular findings.

Concern over the generality of findings from animal research to humans often emerges when the intervention (e.g., consumption of soft drinks or a particular food) is provided to subjects (e.g., laboratory rats) and is shown to cause cancer. Many others (e.g., nonlaboratory rats, humans) no doubt would like to know whether these results generalize to them and their everyday diets. Apart from species differences, the results may not generalize to subjects whose diets, activities, metabolism, longevity, and other factors differ. It is possible, if not likely, that critical features of the subjects (rats) made them differentially responsive to the intervention and thus restricted generality across species. Medical researchers are well aware of this threat and often select species in which the mechanism or process of interest parallels the species to which one would like to generalize. It is important to note that characteristics of the sample may limit generality but not imply that animal research is not applicable to humans. Just the opposite, many major advances in psychology (e.g., learning), biology (e.g., genetic transmission, understanding human immunodeficiency virus [HIV]), and medicine (e.g., vaccination effects) have derived from the considerable generality across species.

In psychology, the most frequently voiced concern about generalizing results from one sample to another is based on the extensive use of college students as subjects. Within clinical psychology, college students are often participants in studies to evaluate treatment, correlates of a clinical or subclinical disorder (e.g., depression), or who have a particular traumatic experience (e.g., date rape). The research questions, samples, and findings are of interest in their own right. Will the findings from such research extend to others whose age, education, motivation, and other characteristics differ? The use of college student samples does not necessarily restrict generality of a finding. However, college students represent a very special sample in terms of subject and demographic characteristics, socioeconomic class, level of intelligence, experience, and other attributes. It may be plausible that some of these special characteristics relate to the independent variable of interest. Hence, the findings may be limited to samples with these features.

More attention about generality of sample characteristics has been expressed in the context of underrepresented and minority groups. Women and various ethnic groups have not been extensively studied in the context of many topics within the social sciences. Hence, central lines of work focus on the extent to which results generalize across groups. When the study of the generality of findings across groups or samples is the basis for research, it is important to go beyond the basic question of whether or the extent to which prior results also apply to a new group. As a basis for new research, it is very useful to identify theoretical issues or to propose mechanisms or processes that would lead one to expect differences in the findings across previously studied and to-be-studied samples. For example, if differences are expected as a function of sex, race, social class, country of origin, or type of personality style, it is advisable for the investigator to specify *why* a particular factor would be expected and to measure the processes or hypothesized basis for group differences in the investigation. This type of study is a much more significant contribution than merely assessing whether effects of prior research generalize to a new set of subjects who vary in some way from the original sample.

Stimulus Characteristics and Settings   Although the usual concern in generality of results has to do with sample characteristics and whether the findings extend across different subjects, equally relevant but less commonly discussed is the extent to which the results extend across the stimulus characteristics of the investigation (Brunswik, 1955). The stimulus characteristics refer to features of the study with which the intervention or condition may be associated and include the setting, experimenters, interviewers, or other factors related to the experimental arrangement. Any of these features may restrict generality of the findings (Maher, 1978a).

Consider a number of examples in which generality of findings from one setting or context to the next has been questioned. Reviews of psychotherapy research consistently conclude that treatment is effective for a variety of clinical problems (Lambert & Bergin, 1994; Roth & Fonagy, 1996). Other analyses suggest that the effectiveness of treatment in controlled studies is greater than that obtained in clinical settings (Weisz, Weiss, & Donenberg, 1992).[1] Clearly, generality of results from controlled clinic/laboratory settings to "real-life" clinics raises a critical issue. A recent review suggests that treatment effectiveness is similar in controlled studies and in clinical work (Shadish et al., 1997). The discrepant conclusions and paucity of treatment outcome research in clinic settings make this an area ripe for further research.

In medicine, we occasionally consider interventions as less related to setting and context influences that might affect generality. Yet, the concern is no less relevant. As an example, consider the effectiveness of vaccinations for pertussis (whooping cough). This disease is a highly contagious respiratory condition that affects more than 50 million people worldwide and kills approximately 350,000 people annually (Winslow, 1995). In the United States, vaccination is effective in 70–95 percent of the cases, that is, those vaccinated who do not contract the disease. In randomized controlled trials in other countries, testing the effectiveness of the vaccination showed the effects as much less (36 percent in Italy, 48 percent in Sweden). Thus, there are different conclusions about the effects of the vaccination. One explanation is that, compared to people in the United States, people in other countries have much higher exposure to the bacteria causing the disorder and hence require much stronger protection than the usual vaccination provides. In any case, the results from studying the effectiveness of vaccinations in the United States do not automatically generalize to the other countries.

These examples convey that generality across settings cannot be automatically assumed. A difficulty in research is identifying what facets of the different settings may be responsible for (moderate, interact with) the intervention to account for the different effects. For example, in the case of psychotherapy as conducted in research versus clinical practice, there are many differences in who is seen in treatment, what types of problems the clients present, who provides treatment, and so on (Kazdin, 1995b). One source of research hypotheses is identifying why an effect does not generalize and what can be done to promote generalization.

The setting is only one example of the stimulus conditions that may be relevant. The general concern that some feature of the stimulus conditions within the investigation may restrict generality. From the standpoint of designing an investigation, it is hazardous to use *one* experimenter or therapist, to show *one* videotaped vignette to present stimuli to the subjects, or to embed the manipulation in any *one* set of stimuli because the narrow range of stimuli may contribute to the findings and the results may not extend beyond these stimuli. The implications of including a narrow range of stimuli in an investigation extend beyond a threat to external validity. We address and elaborate the issue again in the context of construct validity in the next chapter. At this point, it is important to note that the stimulus conditions of the experiment and settings in which research is conducted may very much relate to and limit generality of the results.

Reactivity of Experimental Arrangements   As a threat to external validity, reactivity of an experimental arrangement refers to the influence of the subjects' awareness that they are participating in an investigation. The results of an experiment may be influenced by the fact that subjects know they are being studied or that the purpose is to examine a particular outcome. The external validity question is whether the results would be obtained if subjects were not aware that they were being studied.

In evaluating treatment in an outpatient clinic, the results may differ depending on whether subjects know they are participating in an experiment. Participation in an experiment may elicit reactions such as trying to please the experimenter, avoiding responses that might lead the experimenter to evaluate the subject adversely, and so on. These influences presumably would not be present in an experiment in which subjects were unaware of their participation.

Not all aspects of reactivity may be of interest to investigators wishing to explore the external validity of a given finding. For example, subjects' awareness that they are receiving treatment may not be important. Regardless of whether subjects are in an investigation, they invariably are aware that treatment is being administered. However, superimposed on this general awareness might be that they are being evaluated for scientific purposes, and this aspect of reactivity might alter the subjects' responses in some way. (The effects of awareness of participating in experiments and the resulting roles that subjects may adopt are discussed in Chapter 11.)

Multiple-Treatment Interference   In some experimental designs, subjects are exposed to more than one experimental condition. Subjects might receive two or more interventions or alternate between intervention and no-intervention conditions. Multiple-treatment interference refers to drawing conclusions about a given treatment when it is evaluated in the context of other treatments. The conclusion drawn about one treatment or intervention might be restricted by the administration of prior treatments.

The problem of multiple-treatment interference can be illustrated in a study designed to treat marital discord (Azrin, Naster, & Jones, 1973). Twelve married couples interested in marital counseling were seen for treatment. The purpose was to examine a technique referred to as reciprocity counseling, which consists of a multifaceted program that helps spouses express mutual appreciation, provide feedback about areas of behavior that could be improved, and fulfill each other's fantasies to increase marital satisfaction, along with other procedures designed to enhance communication and sensitivity to the needs of the partner. Prior to receiving 4 weeks of reciprocity counseling, all couples received 3 weeks of catharsis counseling in which the couples met with a therapist and talked about their problems and feelings.

The results showed that reciprocity counseling was associated with marked improvements in marital satisfaction, but catharsis counseling did not improve satisfaction. Does reciprocity counseling work in improving marital satisfaction? From the study one can infer that this treatment, when preceded by the opportunity to discuss problems in a more traditional therapy format (catharsis), produces change. The external validity of the reciprocity counseling may be restricted to individuals who receive catharsis counseling. That is, the context or prior history of the catharsis treatment may be critical for reciprocity counseling to be effective. The results may not be applicable to participants who do not have a similar history or set of prior experiences within the experiment.

Novelty Effects   As a threat to external validity, novelty effects refer to the possibility that the effects of an intervention may in part depend on their innovativeness or novelty in the situation (Bracht & Glass, 1968). It is possible that the effects of the intervention depend on the fact that intervention is administered under conditions in which it is particularly salient, infrequent, or otherwise novel in some way. Consider an example of novelty effects outside clinical psychology. In the United States, thousands of accidents between fire trucks and other vehicles occur each year. Recent research has shown that yellow fire trucks, compared to more traditional red fire trucks, have significantly fewer accidents with cars (Christian, 1995). The primary interpretation of this finding is that the human eye has greater difficulty in perceiving red relative to many other colors, including yellow. Because the yellow trucks are more easily discriminated by drivers, fewer accidents are likely.

Nevertheless, after this research was completed (and continuing today), most fire trucks remain red. It is possible that the reduced accident rates associated with yellow fire trucks was due in part to the fact that yellow trucks are quite novel; that is, they depart from the majority of red trucks that still dominate the United States. The reduced accident effect could be restricted to the *novelty* of introducing a new color truck. It is quite possible that if most fire trucks were yellow, the benefits would be lost. Indeed, against a sea of yellow trucks, it might be that red trucks would be associated with reduced accidents because of *their* novelty. As a matter of safety, it may be prudent to change the color of fire trucks to yellow with the hope that there is no novelty effect. As part of this change, it would be important to investigate to ensure that the reduced accident rates are maintained. This research would be easy to do in naturalistic studies;

many fire houses refuse to change the color of their trucks because red is the traditional color.

The presence of novelty effects is difficult to evaluate. Thus, a new treatment when first proposed may seem to be very effective. Changes in the effects of an intervention over time might be due to the novelty of the early applications in the context of other available interventions. However, alternative explanations are available. For example, in the case of psychotherapy, early applications might prove to be more effective than later ones because over time interventions may be carried out less faithfully, may be diluted in their administration (e.g., when combined with other procedures), or may be applied to more complex cases. Alternatively, treatments that are novel to the public and are "new and improved" (very much like the soaps, cereals, automobiles, and shampoos we purchase) may be effective in part because of their novelty.

Reactivity of Assessment   Several different facets of assessment within a study may affect generality of the results. These facets can refer to any condition of assessment that differs from those to which the investigator may wish to generalize. For most measures used in psychological experiments, subjects or clients are aware that some facet of their functioning is assessed. The measures may include a variety of questionnaires or tests that subjects complete. If subjects are aware that their performance is being assessed, the measures are said to be *obtrusive*. Obtrusive measures are of concern in relation to external validity because awareness that performance is being assessed can alter performance from what it would otherwise be. If awareness of assessment leads persons to respond differently from how they would usually respond, the measures are said to be *reactive*.

In clinical research, the fact that clients are aware of the assessment procedures raises an important question about the generality of the findings. If the results of a treatment study are evident on paper-and-pencil inventories or on interviews by a therapist in the clinical setting, one might question the generality of treatment effects. That is, to what extent do treatment effects demonstrated on reactive measures within the laboratory or clinic setting extend to measures that are not reactive and are administered outside the setting? Treated clients may show great reductions in anxiety on various questionnaires, but has their anxiety decreased in their everyday lives? An exceedingly important question is whether the changes carry over to actual experience of the clients in their ordinary, everyday settings, a question of external validity of the results.

Test Sensitization   In many investigations, particularly in therapy research, pretests are administered routinely. The purpose is to measure the client's standing on a particular variable before receiving the experimental manipulation or treatment. Administration of the pretest may in some way *sensitize* the subjects so that they are affected differently by the intervention, a phenomenon referred to as *pretest sensitization*. Individuals who are pretested might be more or less amenable or responsive to an intervention (e.g., treatment, persuasive message) than individuals who are not exposed to a pretest merely because of the initial assessment.

As an example, consider an investigator who wishes to examine people's views toward violence. The hypothesis may be that viewing violent movies leads to an increase in aggressive thoughts and a positive evaluation of violence. The investigator may wish to evaluate views of people after they see a violent gangster film at a movie theater and ask patrons to complete a questionnaire before and after they see the film. As participants enter the lobby, they complete the measure right before viewing the film. It is possible that administration of a test before the film is shown, that is, the pretest, makes people view and react to the film somewhat differently from their usual reaction. Perhaps the questions heighten sensitivity to certain types of issues or to the entire topic of violence, which may not have otherwise been raised. At posttest performance, how subjects respond is not merely a function of their seeing the movie but also may be due in part to the initial pretest sensitization. Hence, a possible threat to external validity is that the results may not generalize to subjects who have not received a pretest. Administering a pretest does not necessarily restrict generality of the results. It does, however, raise the question of whether nonpretested individuals, usually the population of interest, would respond to the intervention in the same way as the pretested population.

Even when a pretest is not used, it is possible that assessment may influence the results. The posttest might sensitize subjects to the previous intervention that they have received and yield results that would not have been evident without the assessment. This effect, referred to as *posttest sensitization* (Bracht & Glass, 1968), is very similar to pretest sensitization in which test administration may crystallize a particular reaction on the part of the subject. With posttest sensitization, assessment constitutes a necessary condition for treatment to show its effect. Essentially, treatment effects may be latent or incomplete and appear only when a reactive assessment device is administered. As a threat to external validity, posttest sensitization raises the question of whether the results would extend to measures that subjects could not associate with the intervention or measures that were completely out of their awareness. The effect of posttest sensitization is slightly more difficult to assess than is pretest sensitization because it requires nonreactive assessment of treatment effects and a comparison of the results across measures varying in reactivity.

In passing, it is important to note that sensitization effects are not necessarily viewed as artifacts or threats to external validity. The effects suggest that a reactive forewarning may increase the impact of a subsequent intervention. For example, one study demonstrating the importance of sensitization evaluated the impact of a television-advertising campaign designed to reduce alcohol consumption among persons who had been identified as drinkers (Barber, Bradshaw, & Walsh, 1989). Large-scale media campaigns (via television, radio, newspapers) designed to reduce substance abuse are not regarded as very effective. The investigators evaluated whether sending a letter to persons before the campaign would sensitize community members to the television commercials that followed. The results indicated that persons who were sent the letter alerting them to the upcoming campaign and who then received the advertising on television showed significant reductions in alcohol consumption and were significantly lower in consumption than those who received the advertising campaign without the letter or the letter without the advertising campaign. Thus, in this study sensitization enhanced the impact of the intervention.

Timing of Measurement   The results of an experiment may depend on the point in time that assessment devices are administered. For example, an investigation may reveal that a particular type of psychotherapy surpassed no treatment or that one therapy was superior to another immediately after completion of treatment. An external validity question that can be raised is whether the same result would have been obtained had measurement been taken at another time, say, several months after treatment.

In psychotherapy outcome research, the effectiveness of treatment usually is evaluated immediately after the last therapy session (posttreatment assessment). It is possible that conclusions at this point in time would not extend to a later period. For example, in one study separate treatments were implemented at school to alter the behavior of maladjusted children (Kolvin et al., 1981). Two interventions (group therapy, behavior modification) yielded different effects depending on the point in time that assessment was completed. Immediately after treatment, relatively few improvements were evident. At follow-up approximately 18 months later, improvements in the groups, relative to controls who had not received treatment, were marked. The effects evident at one point in time (posttreatment) were different from those at another point in time (follow-up). Other treatment studies with adults and children can be identified to show that the conclusions reached about a particular treatment or the relative effectiveness of different treatments in a given study occasionally vary from posttreatment to follow-up assessment (Kazdin, 1988). In some cases, treatments are no different at posttreatment but are different at follow-up (Meyers, Graves, Whelan, & Barclay, 1996); in other cases, treatments are different at posttreatment but no different at follow-up (Newman, Kenardy, Herman, & Taylor, 1997).

General Comments

The previously discussed threats to external validity only begin to enumerate conditions that might restrict the generality of a finding. All conditions that are relevant to the generality of a finding cannot be specified in advance. In principle, any characteristic of the experimenters, subjects, or accouterments of the investigation might later prove to be related to the results. If one threat applies, some caution should be exercised in extending the results. The degree of caution is a function of the extent to which conditions introduced into the situation depart from those to which one would like to generalize and the plausibility that the specific condition of the experiment might influence generality.

One cannot simply discount the findings of a study as a very special case by merely noting that participants were pretested, that they were aware that they were participating in an experiment, or by identifying another characteristic of the experiment. Enumerating a list of threats that are possible in principle is insufficient to challenge the findings. The onus is on the investigator who conducts the study to clarify the conditions to which he or she wishes to generalize and to convey how the conditions of the experiment represent these conditions. The onus on those skeptical of how well the conditions have been achieved is to describe explicitly how a particular threat to external validity would operate and quite plausibly restrict the findings.

Many conditions might be ruled out as threats to external validity on seemingly commonsense grounds (e.g., hair or eye color of the experimenter, season of the year, birth weight of participants). In a given area, these seemingly remote factors might be important. The task of the reviewer or the consumer of research (e.g., other professionals, lay persons) is to provide a plausible account of why the generality of the findings may be limited. Only further investigation can attest to whether the potential threats to external validity actually limit generality and truly make a theoretical or practical difference. Of course, there is no more persuasive demonstration than several studies conducted together in which similar findings are obtained with some consistency across various types of subjects (e.g., patients, college students), settings (e.g., university laboratory, clinic, community), and other domains (e.g., different researchers, countries). Replication of research findings is important in part to help ensure that findings from an initial study are not likely to be due to various threats to internal validity or to chance. Replication is also important for external validity because all further studies after the original one are likely to vary some conditions (e.g., geographical locale, investigator, type of subject) that extend the generality of the findings.

INTERPLAY OF INTERNAL AND EXTERNAL VALIDITY

Internal and external validity convey critical features of the logic of scientific research. Internal validity is addressed by experimental arrangements that help rule out or make implausible factors that could explain the effects we wish to attribute to the intervention. Everyday life is replete with "demonstrations" that do not control basic threats to internal validity. For example, almost any intervention that one applies to oneself or a group may appear to cure the common cold. Consuming virtually any vitamin or potion from assorted animal parts or reading highly arousing material (e.g., on methodology and research design of course) may in a few days be associated with great improvement in the cold. Pre- and postassessments with one of the above interventions would, no doubt, reflect improvements. Did our intervention lead to improvement? Probably not. We can muse at the example because we know that colds usually remit without the above interventions. The example is relevant because maturation (immunological and recuperative processes within the individual) is a threat to internal validity and can readily account for changes. For areas we do not understand as well and in which the determinants and course are less clear, a host of threats can compete with the variable of interest in accounting for change. Control of threats to internal validity becomes essential.

As a priority, the internal validity of an experiment is usually regarded as more important, or at least logically prior in importance, than is external validity. One must first have an unambiguous finding before one can ask about its generality. Given the priority of internal validity, initial considerations of an investigation pertain to devising conditions that will facilitate demonstrating the relation between the independent and dependent variables. A well-designed experiment maximizes the opportunity to draw valid inferences about the intervention.

By emphasizing internal validity, there is no intention to slight external validity. For research with applied implications, as is often the case in clinical psychology, counseling, and education, external validity is particularly important. A well-conducted study with a high degree of internal validity may show what *can* happen when the experiment is arranged in a particular way. Yet it is quite a different matter to show that the intervention would have this effect or in fact does operate this way outside the experimental situation. For example, as mentioned already, experiments on cancer causes may show that a particular soft-drink or food additive caused cancer in laboratory animals fed high doses of the item. Internally valid experiments of this sort are informative because they show what can happen. The findings may have important theoretical implications for how and why cancers develop. Yet a major question in addressing the immediate utility of the findings for applied purposes is whether cancers develop in this way outside the laboratory. Do the findings extend from mice and rats to humans? To lower doses of the suspected ingredients? To diets that may include may other potentially neutralizing substances (e.g., water and assorted vitamins and minerals)? All these questions pertain to the external validity of the findings.

The goal of research is to understand phenomena of interest. Internal validity is obviously relevant because it pertains to many potential sources of influence, bias, or artifact that can interfere directly with demonstration and the validity of the inferences that are drawn. In the context of understanding phenomena, external validity has a very important role that goes beyond merely asking, Do the findings generalize to other people, places, settings, and so on? When findings do not generalize, there is a very special opportunity to understand the phenomenon of interest. Failure to generalize raises the question Why? For example, excessive corporal punishment seems to lead to aggressive behaviors in boys but not in girls (Lefkowitz et al., 1977). This prompts very interesting theory and research. What factors about boys and girls or about variations in parent–child interactions might account for the failure of the finding to generalize across sexes? The question prompts theory about sex differences and specific hypotheses that might explain the mechanisms or processes involved in development of sex differences. In the process, a deeper level of understanding of the phenomenon of interest is possible.

A contemporary example from public health also conveys the importance of external validity issues in relation to understanding a phenomenon of interest. As we know, contracting HIV through sexual contact or injection of infected needles leads to acquired immunodeficiency syndrome (AIDS) and death. This finding is has broad external validity insofar as it generalizes across people, places (countries), settings, and so on. However, a small proportion of individuals who contract the infection do not progress to AIDS. In the context of the present discussion, the finding that HIV leads to AIDS does not generalize to everyone. The importance of external validity does not end in noting that the finding is not universal. Rather, the failure to generalize immediately prompts questions about why; in this case, the questions focus on characteristics of individuals to whom the finding does not apply. This has led to important work on immune systems and genetics to understand the mechanism(s) that stop HIV from progressing to AIDS (Balter, 1996; Waldholz, 1997). Identification of a protective inborn gene mutation, the suspected mechanism, has led to interventions that can mimic the inborn protective factor and stop the progression from HIV to AIDS. In short, failure of a finding to generalize is critically important to progress in research and application because it promotes questions about the mechanisms involved and hence fosters a much deeper understanding of the phenomenon.

Occasionally in psychological research, failures to replicate a finding are viewed as reasons to be suspicious about the original finding—either the original finding was an artifact or the finding was veridical but restricted to very narrow conditions of the original investigation. Yet, it is possible that some other variable provides the boundary conditions under which a finding can be obtained. Theory and research about the variable(s) can promote highly valuable and sophisticated research. In our studies, we often search for or believe we are searching for general principles that have widespread, if not universal and intergalactic, generality. Yet the value of a finding does not necessarily derive from its generality. Knowledge of a phenomenon entails identifying the conditions under which the findings may not apply and the reasons for seeming exceptions to what we thought to be a general rule. External validity issues are not mere afterthoughts about whether the findings generalize, but get at the core of why we do research at all.

Considerations pertaining to external validity often serve as the initial attraction of persons beginning in psychological research. Students early in their research careers often wish to study something relevant, or at least something more obviously relevant than the experiments with college sophomores whose performance is evaluated under laboratory conditions. Thus, research questions in such settings as a treatment clinic, psychiatric hospital, or the home may be very enticing because of their obvious relevance to applied questions that may motivate research. As one becomes involved in research, sometimes one moves into more narrowly framed questions and away from the applied settings or problems that were initially enticing. Perhaps part of the influence is due to the obstacles that research in applied settings often raises and the difficulties in drawing valid inferences. Another part of the influence no doubt is realization that the goal is to understand and that some of the best applications can come from understanding. Consequently, lines of research develop and laboratory paradigms are devised to study a phenomenon in a very special way. All of this is to the good. In addition, direct tests of generality of the findings remain important to ensure that what we understand is not completely restricted in its applicability to the situations about which we wish to speak.

SUMMARY AND CONCLUSIONS

The purpose of research is to investigate specific relations between independent and dependent variables. The value of research derives from its capacity to simplify the situation in which variables may operate so that the influence of many variables can be separated from the variable of interest. Stated another way, an investigation helps rule out or to make implausible the influence of many alternative variables that might explain changes on the dependent measures.

The extent to which an experiment rules out as explanations factors that otherwise might account for the results is referred to as *internal validity*. Factors or sources of influence other than the independent variables are referred to as *threats to internal validity* and include history, maturation, testing, instrumentation, statistical regression, selection biases, attrition, selection in combination with other threats (e.g., selection x history), diffusion of treatment, and special treatment or reactions of controls.

Aside from evaluating the internal validity of an experiment, it is important to understand the extent to which the findings can be generalized to populations, settings, measurement devises, and experimenters other than those used in the original experiment. The generality of the results is referred to as the *external validity*. Although the findings of an investigation could be limited to any particular condition or arrangement unique to the demonstration, a number of potential limitations on the generality of the results can be identified. These potential limitations are referred to as *threats to external validity* and include characteristics of the sample, the stimulus conditions or setting of the investigation, reactivity of the experimental arrangement, multiple-treatment interference, novelty effects, reactivity of assessments, test sensitization, and timing of measurement.

Internal and external validity address central aspects of the logic of experimentation and scientific research more generally. The purpose of research is to structure the situation in such a way that inferences can be drawn about the effects of the variable of interest (internal validity) and to establish relations that extend beyond the highly specific circumstances in which the variable was examined (external validity). There often is a natural tension between meeting these objectives. Occasionally, the investigator arranges the experiment in ways to increase the likelihood of ruling out threats to internal validity. In the process, somewhat artificial circumstances may be introduced (e.g., videotapes to present the intervention, scripts that are memorized or read to the subjects). This means that the external validity may be threatened. The purposes of the investigation, both short and long term, ought to be clarified before judging the extent to which the balance of threats is appropriate. Yet, discussion of these matters first requires addressing other types or experimental validity. The next chapter turns to the notions of construct and statistical conclusion validity and then discusses the interrelations and priorities of all four kinds of validity.

NOTE

[1]Contemporary discussions of psychotherapy outcome research make a distinction between efficacy and effectiveness (Hoagwood, Hibbs, Brent, & Jensen, 1995). *Efficacy* refers to treatment outcomes obtained in controlled psychotherapy studies that are conducted under laboratory and quasi-laboratory conditions (e.g., treatment is specified in manual form, recruited subjects are homogeneous and may show a narrow range of problems, treatment delivery is closely supervised and monitored). *Effectiveness* refers to treatment outcomes obtained in clinic settings in which the usual control procedures are not implemented. Efficacy and effectiveness studies can be conceived as on a continuum or multiple continua because several dimensions that affect generality of the results can vary across clinic and laboratory settings (Hoagwood et al., 1995; Kazdin, 1978a). I use effectiveness here generically to mean "having impact on the problem that has been treated."

FOR FURTHER READING

Cook, T.D. (1990). The generalization of causal connections: Multiple theories in search of clear practice. In L. Sechrest, E. Perin, & J. Bunker (Eds.), *Research methodology: Strengthening causal interpretations of nonexperimental data* (pp. 9–31). DHHS Publication No. PHS, Rockville, MD: Department of Health and Human Services.

Cook, T.D., & Campbell, D.T. (Eds.) (1979). *Quasi-experimentation: Design and analysis issues for field settings*. Skokie, IL: Rand McNally.

Mook, D.G. (1983). In defense of external invalidity. *American Psychologist, 38*, 379–387.

Reichardt, C.S., & Gollob, H.F. (1989). Ruling out threats to validity. *Evaluation Review, 13*, 3–17.

Shadish, W.R. (1995). The logic of generalization: Five principles common to experiments and ethnographies. *American Journal of Community Psychology, 23*, 419–428.

Chapter 3

Drawing Valid Inferences II

Construct and Statistical Conclusion Validity

Internal and external validity are fundamental to research and nicely convey the underpinnings for many methodological practices. Two other types of validity, referred to as construct validity and statistical conclusion validity, must also be addressed to draw valid inferences. These types of validity are no less central to research design. Yet, they are less familiar to researchers and consumers of research and reflect slightly more complex concepts and design considerations than do internal and external validity. This chapter considers construct and statistical conclusion validity and the interrelations and priorities of the different types of validity. As in the previous chapter, the goal is to describe the nature of these types of validity and the threats they raise. Subsequent chapters focus on strategies to address these threats.

CONSTRUCT VALIDITY

Construct validity has to do with interpreting the basis of the causal relation demonstrated within an experiment. The meaning requires careful delineation of construct from internal validity. Internal validity, as you recall, focuses on whether some intervention is responsible for change or whether other factors (e.g., history, maturation, testing) can plausibly account for the effect. Assume for a moment that these threats have been ruled out by randomly assigning subjects to treatment and control groups, by assessing both groups in the same way and at the same time, and so on. We can thus presume that the group differences are not likely to have resulted from threats to internal validity but from the intervention. At this point the discussion of construct validity can begin. What is the intervention and why did it produce the effect? Is the reason for the relation between the intervention and behavior change due to the construct (explanation, interpretation) given by the investigator? *Construct validity* addresses the presumed cause or the explanation of the causal relation between the intervention or experimental manipulation and the outcome.[1]

Several features within the experiment can interfere with the interpretation. These are often referred to as *confounds*. We say an experiment is confounded or that there is a confound to refer to the possibility that a specific factor varied (or covaried) with the intervention that could in whole or in part be responsible for the change. In an experiment, some component other than the one of interest to the investigator may be responsible for change. Features associated with the intervention that interfere with drawing inferences about the basis for the difference between groups are referred to as *threats to construct validity*.

Threats to Construct Validity

Attention and Contact with the Clients   Attention and contact accorded the client in the experimental group or differential attention across experimental and control groups may be the basis for the group differences and threaten construct validity. The intervention may have exerted its influence because of the attention provided, not because of special characteristics unique to the intervention. A familiar example from psychiatric research is the effect of placebos in the administration of medication. Suppose investigators provide a drug for depression to some patients but no drug to other patients. Assume further that groups were formed through random assignment and that the threats to internal validity were all superbly addressed. At the end of the study, patients who had received the drug are greatly improved and significantly different from patients who did not receive the drug. The investigator may then discuss the effect of the drug and how the particular medication affects critical biological processes that control symptoms of depression. We accept the fact that the intervention was responsible for the outcome (internal validity). Yet the intervention consists of all aspects associated with the administration of the medication in addition to the medication itself. We know that taking any drug might decrease depression because of expectancies for improvement on the part of the patients and on those administering the drug. Indeed, such expectancies can exert marked therapeutic effects on a variety of psychological and medical dysfunctions (White, Tursky, & Schwartz, 1985). The intervention might have been effective because of such expectations and the change they generate. In the present example, these effects were not examined; thus, the investigator cannot identify the explanation of the effect.

To examine the basis for the effects (construct validity), it would be essential to include a third group that received a placebo on the same schedule of administration. A *placebo* is a substance that has no active pharmacological properties that would be expected to produce change. A neutral substance that is known to be inactive in relation to the clinical problem is used. Administration of a placebo to another group would be extremely useful in this example to address construct validity. A placebo might be a pill, capsule, or tablet of the same size and shape (and perhaps share other characteristics of the active medication). Those who administer the drug (physicians or nurses) and those who receive the drug should be naive (blind) to the conditions to which subjects are assigned. Thus, expectations for improvement might be constant between drug and placebo groups. With a placebo-control group, attention and contact with the client and expectations on the part of experimenters of clients become less plausible constructs to explain the effects the investigator wishes to attribute to the medication.

In a somewhat parallel fashion, treatment and no-treatment are often compared in psychotherapy research. The treatment may, for example, focus on cognitive processes that the investigator believes to be critical to the clinical problem. Assessment completed after treatment may reveal that the treatment group is significantly better than the no-treatment group on various outcome measures. If the investigator explains the finding as support for the importance of altering cognitions or using this particular treatment, there is a problem in construct validity. We must question whether plausible features associated with the intervention ought to be ruled out.

In fact, the treatment and no-treatment groups differ on several dimensions, such as providing regular meetings with a therapist, generating patient expectations for improvement, and providing a palpable effort to resolve or address the client's problems. Might these dimensions plausibly improve symptoms even if cognitions are not the focus of treatment? Some writers about psychotherapy answer affirmatively (Eysenck, 1995; Frank & Frank, 1991); in addition, evidence suggests that when control subjects are led to expect improvement, they often improve irrespective of whether they received a veridical treatment (Bootzin, 1985). Hence, in a psychotherapy study, if the investigator wishes to explain the findings in terms of specific mechanisms or processes of the treatment (e.g., changes in cognitions, therapeutic alliance), attention and expectations associated with the treatment ought to be controlled. Otherwise, other constructs could plausibly explain the findings. We discuss this further when control groups are examined (Chapter 6).

In general, there is a threat to construct validity when attention, contact with the subjects, and their expectations might plausibly account for the findings and have not been controlled for or evaluated in the design. A design that does not control for these factors is not necessarily flawed. The intention of the investigator, the control procedures, and the specificity of the conclusions the investigator wishes to draw determine the extent to which construct validity threats can be raised. If the investigator wishes to discuss why the intervention achieved its effects, attention and contact ought to be ruled out as rival interpretations of the results.

Single Operations and Narrow Stimulus Sampling   In any study, the investigator is usually interested in some general way in a phenomenon, variable, intervention, and its effects. For example, the investigator may believe that a particular intervention will reduce anxiety. The investigator develops procedures to test the idea. In moving from the idea to the specific procedure, we know that decisions may raise concerns over external validity, that is, whether the procedures used will produce results that generalize to the situations we have in mind. The way in which the idea is operationalized may also affect construct validity, that is, our ability to decide whether the treatment of interest or some feature associated with the intervention is responsible for the results.

In many studies, the intervention is operationalized so that it is associated with and is inseparable from features that are assumed to be irrelevant by the investigator. These irrelevancies may contribute to the results and help explain the basis of the intervention effect. For example, two different treatments might be compared. Let us say we recruit therapists expert in treatment A to administer that treatment and other therapists skilled in treatment B to administer that treatment. Thus, different therapists provide different treatments. This is reasonable because we may wish to use experts who practice their special techniques. At the end of the study, assume that therapy A is better than B in the outcome achieved with the patient sample. Because therapists were different for the two treatments, we cannot really separate the impact of therapists from treatment. We might say that treatment A was better than treatment B. Yet, a colleague obsessed with construct validity might propose that therapists who administered treatment A may have simply been much better therapists than those who administered treatment B and that therapist competence may account for the results. The confound of treatment with therapists raises a significant ambiguity.

There is a more subtle variation that may emerge as a threat to construct validity. Suppose we are comparing two treatments and we use one therapist. This therapist provides both treatments and sees clients in each of the treatment conditions. At the end of the investigation, suppose that one treatment is clearly more effective than the other. The investigator may wish to discuss how one technique is superior and explain on conceptual grounds why this might be expected. We accept the finding that one intervention was more effective than the other. In deference to construct validity we ask what the intervention was. The comparison consisted of the therapist giving treatment A versus the same therapist giving treatment B. With one therapist, it is possible that the different outcomes are somewhat due to the treatment and somewhat to how the therapist administered the treatments (e.g., enthusiasm, expectancies, fidelity). We cannot separate the influence of the therapist combined with the treatment in accounting for the results.

One might say that the therapist was "held constant" because he or she was used in both groups. But it is possible that the therapist was more credible, comfortable, competent, and effective with one technique than with the other. Perhaps the therapist believed in the efficacy of one technique more than another, performed one technique with greater fidelity than the other, or aroused patients' expectancies for improvement with one technique. The differential effects of treatment could be due to the interaction of the therapist x treatment, rather than a main effect of treatment. The study yields somewhat unambiguous results because the effect of the therapist was not separable in the data analyses from the different treatment conditions. In the history of psychotherapy outcome research, there are many examples in which one therapist administered two or more treatments (Ellis, 1957; Lazarus, 1961; Shapiro, 1989). In these cases, the more or most effective treatment was the one developed by the therapist—investigator and predicted to be more effective. We tend to be skeptical of the results until they are replicated because the particular therapist in combination with one of the treatments (therapist x treatment effect) may have been responsible for the effects, rather than the treatment alone.

Construct validity could be improved by sampling across a wider range of conditions associated with treatment delivery (i.e., therapists) so the effects of treatment can be evaluated in the design. Two or more therapists could be included, each of whom would administer both treatments. At the end of the study, the impact of therapists could be separated from the impact of treatment (e.g., by an analysis of variance). If the effectiveness of treatment varied between the therapists, this could be detected in the interaction (treatment x therapist) term.

As another example, consider a laboratory experiment designed to evaluate opinions held about mental illness. The purpose is to see whether people evaluate the personality, intelligence, and friendliness of others differently if they believe the other persons have been mentally ill. College students are the subjects and are assigned randomly to one of two conditions. In the experimental condition, the students see a slide of a 30-year-old man. They then listen to a tape that describes him as holding a factory job and living at home with his wife and two children. The description also includes a passage noting that the man has been mentally ill, experienced strange delusions, and was hospitalized 2 years ago. In the control condition, students see the slide and hear the same description except for the passages that talk about mental illness and hospitalization. At the end of the tape, participants rate the personality, intelligence, and friendliness of the person in the slide. Alas, the hypothesis is supported—subjects who heard the mentally ill description showed greater rejection of the person than subjects in the control group.

The investigator wishes to conclude that the content of the description that focused on mental illness is the basis for the group differences. After all, this is the only part of the content of the slide and description that distinguished experimental and control groups. Yet, there is a construct validity problem here. The use of a single case in the slide (i.e., the 30-year-old man) is problematic. It is possible that rejection of the mental illness description occurred because of special characteristics of this particular case presented on the slide. The difference could be due to the manipulation of the description of mental illness or to the interaction of the description with characteristics of this case. One would want slides of different persons varying in age, sex, and other characteristics so that mental-illness status could be separated from the specific characteristics of the case. In general, it is important to represent the stimuli in ways so that potential irrelevancies (e.g., the case, unique features of the task) can be separated from the intervention or variable of interest. Without separating the irrelevancies, the conclusions of the study are limited (Maher, 1978a).

The use of a narrow range of stimuli and the limitations that such use imposes sound similar to external validity. Actually, sampling a narrow range of stimuli as a threat can apply to both external and construct validity. If the investigator wishes to *generalize* to other stimulus conditions (e.g., other therapists or types of cases in the above two examples), then the narrow range of stimulus conditions is as a threat to *external validity.* To generalize across stimulus conditions of the experiment requires sampling across the range of these conditions if it is plausible that the conditions may influence the results (Brunswik, 1955). If the investigator wishes to explain *why* a change occurred, then the problem is one of *construct validity* because the investigator cannot separate the construct of interest (e.g., treatment or types of description of treatment) from the conditions of its delivery (e.g., the therapist or case vignette).

Experimenter Expectancies   In both laboratory and clinical research, it is quite possible that the expectancies, beliefs, and desires about the results on the part of the experimenter influence how the subjects perform?[2] The effects are sometimes referred to as *unintentional expectancy effects* to emphasize that the experimenter may not do anything on purpose to influence subjects' responses. Depending on the experimental situation and experimenter–subject contact, expectancies may lead to changes in tone of voice, posture, facial expressions, delivery of instructions, and adherence to the prescribed procedures and hence influence how participants respond. Expectancy effects are a threat to construct validity if they provide a plausible rival interpretation of the effects otherwise attributed to the intervention.

Expectancy effects received considerable attention in the mid-1960s, primarily in the context of social psychological research (Rosenthal, 1966, 1976). However, it is not difficult to imagine their impact in clinical research. In treatment research, the expectancy effects might be suspected in situations in which the experimenter has a strong investment in the outcome and has contact with subjects in various treatment and control conditions. For example, in therapy outcome studies (Ellis, 1957, Lazarus, 1961; Shapiro, 1989), the treatment developed by the investigator surpassed the effectiveness of other conditions to which the treatment was compared. In each case, the investigator was the therapist for all conditions. It is plausible that expectancies of the investigator might be quite different for the treatments, and perhaps these were conveyed to the individuals during the course of treatment or assessment. Expectancies might be much less plausible if the treatment was not preferred by the investigator or was less effective than one of the other treatments. Because of the investigator's position, expectancy as a possible threat to construct validity cannot be easily dismissed. We would very much want to see the study replicated with more and different therapists and perhaps even assess therapist expectancies at the beginning of the study to see whether they correlated with outcome.

The notion of experimenter expectancies as a threat to validity is infrequently invoked for at least two reasons. First, both the construct and the ways through which it achieves its effects are unclear. Second and related, many more parsimonious interpretations may serve as confounds before the notion of expectancies needs to be invoked. For example, differential adherence of the experimenter to the conditions, explicit and differential instructions to subjects, and changes in the measurement criteria (instrumentation) for subjects in different conditions might reflect more concretely why two conditions differ in their effects. Nevertheless, in a given situation, expectations on the part of the experimenter may plausibly serve as a source of ambiguity and threaten the construct validity of the experiment.

Cues of the Experimental Situation   Cues of the situation refer to the seemingly ancillary factors associated with the intervention that may contribute to the results. These cues have been referred to as the *demand characteristics of the experimental situation* (Orne, 1962). Demand characteristics may include sources of influence such as information conveyed to prospective subjects prior to their arrival to the experiment (e.g., rumors about the experiment, information provided during subject recruitment), instructions, procedures, and any other features of the experiment that may seem incidental to the overall manipulation.

The influence of cues in the experiment distinct from the independent variable was dramatically illustrated in a study that examined the role of demand characteristics in a sensory-deprivation experiment (Orne & Scheibe, 1964). Sensory deprivation consists of minimizing for the subject as many sources of sensory stimulation as possible. Isolating individuals from visual, auditory, tactile, and other stimulation for prolonged periods has been associated with distorted perception, visual hallucinations, inability to concentrate, and disorientation. These reactions usually are attributable to the physical effects of being deprived of sensory stimulation. Orne and Scheibe suggested that cues from the experimental situation in which sensory deprivation experiments are conducted might contribute to the reactions. They completed an experiment in which subjects were exposed to the accouterments of the procedures of a sensory-deprivation experiment but actually were not deprived of stimulation. Subjects received a physical exam, provided a short medical history, were assured that the procedures were safe, and were exposed to a tray of drugs and medical instruments conspicuously labeled Emergency Tray. Subjects were told to report any unusual visual imagery, fantasy, or feelings, difficulties in concentration, disorientation, or similar problems. They were informed that they would be placed in a room to work on an arithmetic task. If they wanted to escape, they could do so by pressing a red "emergency alarm." In short, subjects were given a variety of cues to convey that strange experiences were in store.

The subjects were placed in the room with food, water, and materials for the task. No attempt was made to deprive subjects of sensory stimulation. They could move about, hear many different sounds, and work at a task. This arrangement departs from true sensory-deprivation experiments in which the subjects typically rest, have their eyes and ears covered, and cease movement as much as possible. A control group in the study did not receive the cues preparing them for unusual experiences and were told they could leave the room by merely knocking on the window. At the end of the isolation period, the experimental group showed greater deterioration on a number of measures, the reporting of symptoms characteristically revealed in sensory-deprivation experiments. Although sensory deprivation was not administered, the cues usually associated with deprivation studies may have contributed to or accounted for the results.

Demand characteristics can threaten the construct validity if it is plausible that extraneous cues associated with the intervention could explain the findings. The situation described here conveys the potential impact of such cues. Whether demand characteristics can exert such impact in diverse areas of research is not clear. Also, in many areas of clinical research, the independent variable may include cues that cannot be so easily separated from the portion of the manipulation that is considered to be crucial. For example, different variations of treatment or levels of an independent variable (e.g., high, medium, and low) may necessarily require different cues and hence be intertwined with different demand characteristics. The cues that may give subjects hints on how to perform may not be considered as extraneous but as part of the manipulation itself. In such cases, it may not be especially meaningful to note that demand characteristics accounted for the results.

On the other hand, when several conditions are different from control conditions (e.g., a no-treatment control group), one might weigh the plausibility of demand characteristics as an influence. It may be that an implicit demand conveyed to control subjects is that they are not expected to improve from one test occasion to another. Presumably if cues were provided to convey this expectation, treatment and no-treatment differences might be due to different demand characteristics across the assessment conditions. The means of evaluating demand characteristics are discussed further in Chapter 13.

General Comments

The discussion has noted common threats to construct validity. However, construct validity threats are not easily enumerated because the threats have to do with interpretation of the reason for the outcome in an experiment. Thus, theoretical views and substantive knowledge about how the experimental manipulation works or the mechanisms responsible for change are also at issue, apart from the issue of experimental confounds. The questions of construct validity are twofold: What is the intervention? and Why did this intervention lead to change? The first question emphasizes that the intervention may be embedded in or confounded by other conditions that influence and account for the outcome. The second question emphasizes the related issue of the interpretation of what led the intervention to change performance. Here we do not speak of confound as much as better understanding of the mechanism, process, or theory to explain the change. The questions encompass construct validity because they affect interpretation of the basis for a given finding.

STATISTICAL CONCLUSION VALIDITY

Internal, external, and construct validity and their threats codify many of the concerns to which methodology is directed. The list of concerns is already long; what more can remain? Actually, a great deal. Assume we have designed our wonderful experiment to address the bulk of the threats already highlighted. Shall we find reliable differences between the groups? Even if the intervention and control conditions would produce differences in their outcomes, whether we find such differences depends on multiple considerations. *Statistical conclusion validity* refers to the facets of the quantitative evaluation that influence the conclusions we reach about the experimental condition and its effect.

Statistical evaluation often is viewed and taught from two standpoints. The first pertains to understanding the tests themselves and their bases. This facet may emphasize what the tests accomplish and the formulae and derivations of the tests. The second and complementary standpoint pertains to the computational aspects of statistical tests. Here application of the tests to data sets and their interpretation are emphasized. There is another facet that might be considered as a superordinate level, namely, the role of statistical evaluation in relation to research design and other threats to validity. Statistical conclusion validity reflects this level of concern with quantitative evaluation and is often the Achilles' heel of research. Because this type of validity is often neglected, failure to consider statistical issues commonly undermines the quality of an investigation. There are several facets of the results and statistical evaluation that can obscure interpretation of the experiment. These are referred to as *threats to statistical conclusion validity*.

Overview of Essential Concepts

Statistical Tests and Decision Making   Before discussing threats to validity, it is important to review a few of the essential concepts of statistical evaluation. In most psychological research, the conclusions in an experiment depend heavily on hypothesis testing and statistical evaluation. The null hypothesis specifies that there are no differences between groups (e.g., treatment vs. control group). Statistical tests are completed to evaluate whether the differences that are obtained are reliable or beyond what one is likely to find due to chance fluctuations. We can reject the null hypothesis of no difference if we find a statistically significant difference or accept the null hypothesis if we do not. The rejection and acceptance of hypotheses are weighty topics, only part of which we can treat here. The decision-making process is based on selecting a probability level that specifies the degree of risk of reaching a false conclusion. If the statistical differences between groups passes this probability level, we state that the difference is reliable and represents an effect of the intervention. If the difference fails to pass the threshold, we say that the difference is not statistically significant and that the groups are not different.

It is important to note at this point that the present discussion makes critical assumptions that are not fully agreed on in science generally or psychological research in particular. The utility of statistical tests and probability levels (alpha) as a basis for drawing inferences, at least as currently practiced, is a matter of debate (Schmidt, 1996b; Thompson, 1996). Many of these issues are addressed in Chapter 14. In our present discussion, these issues are skirted in recognition of the fact that the bulk of research in psychology is based on drawing inferences from statistical evaluation. As such, there are common weaknesses of research that can be identified under the rubric of statistical conclusion of validity.

Figure 3.1 notes the outcomes of an investigation on the basis of conclusions we might draw from statistical evaluation. The four cells represent the combination of *our decision* (there is a difference vs. there is no difference) and the *true state of affairs in the world* (there really is a difference or there is no difference). Our goal in experimentation is to draw conclusions that reflect the true state of affairs in the world. That is, if there are differences between two or more conditions (i.e., if the intervention is truly effective), we wish to reflect the differences in our decision (Cell B). If there is no difference between the conditions in the world, we would like to conclude that fact also (Cell C). Occasionally, there is a clear effect in our study when there actually is no effect in the world (Cell A) or there is no effect in our study when in fact there is one in the world (Cell D). We specify our probability level (alpha) for concluding the differences are significant. By doing so, we also fix the risk of concluding erro-

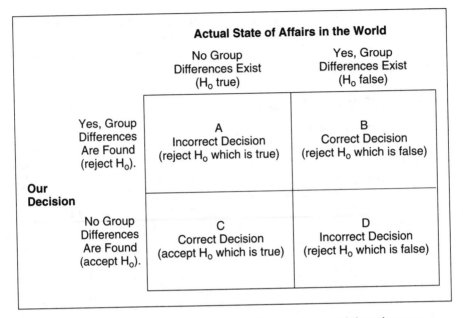

FIGURE 3.1.   A 2 *x* 2 matrix that conveys the decisions we reach based on our statistical evaluation of the results and in relation to the true state of affairs in the world. If H_0 (the null hypothesis) is true, there really are no group differences in the world. If H_0 is false, there really are group differences. (The cells have other names as discussed in the text.) In particular, it is worth noting here that Cell A is also known as alpha (α) or Type I error; Cell D is known as beta (β) or Type II error.

neously that there are differences when in fact there are none in the world and of concluding that there are no differences when in fact there are. The cells in Figure 3.1 have established names that reflect critically important statistical concepts to refer to the decision-making process, outcomes of our experiment, and risk of reaching a false conclusion. Table 3.1 lists these and other concepts that we draw on to elaborate the threats to statistical conclusion validity and to discuss statistical evaluation more generally later.

Effect Size   Among the concepts listed in Table 3.1, effect size is especially critical because it underlies several issues we shall consider. *Effect size* (ES) refers to the magnitude of the difference between two (or more) conditions or groups and is expressed in standard deviation units. When two groups are in a study, effect size equals the difference between means, divided by the standard deviation:

$$ES = \frac{m_1 - m_2}{s}$$

TABLE 3.1. Important Concepts in Relation to Statistical Conclusion Validity

Concept	Definition
Alpha (α)	The probability of rejecting a hypothesis (the null hypothesis) when that hypothesis is true. This is also referred to as a Type I error (Cell A).
Beta (β)	The probability of accepting a hypothesis (the null hypothesis) when it is false. This is also referred to as a Type II error (Cell D).
Power	The probability of rejecting the null hypothesis when it is false or the likelihood of finding differences between conditions when, in fact, the conditions are truly different. This probability is $1 - \beta$ (Cell B).
Effect size	A way of expressing the difference between conditions (e.g., treatment vs. control) in terms of a common metric across measures and across studies. The method is based on obtaining the difference between the means of interest on a particular measure and dividing this by the common (pooled) standard deviation.
Standard deviation	A measure of variation or variability about a mean. The standard deviation (also the square root of the variance) of a sample is given by the formula:

$$ S = \sqrt{\frac{\Sigma(X_i - \overline{X})^2}{N - 1}} \text{ or } \frac{SS}{df} $$

where X_i = an observation of Subject i
         $\overline{X}$ = mean of the sample
         N = sample size
         SS = sum of squared deviation
         df = degree of freedom

where m_1 and m_2 are the sample means for two groups or conditions (e.g. treatment and control groups), and s equals the pooled standard deviation for these groups.

For example, in a two-group study that evaluates treatment for clients experiencing anxiety, assume clients are assigned to treatment or no-treatment conditions. After the study, clients complete a measure of anxiety in which higher scores equal higher levels of anxiety. Suppose that treated subjects show a posttreatment mean of 10 on the scale, but control subjects show a score of 16. We shall also suppose that the standard deviation is 8. Effect size equals .75 (derived from 10 minus 16 divided by 8). This means that in standard deviation units, the mean of the treatment group was .75 higher than the mean of the control subjects.

Effect size is often assumed to reflect the magnitude of the difference as that difference exists in nature. Thus, if an investigator is exploring a truly effective technique or variable, this will produce a marked effect size and significant results. However, effect size is very much dependent on the design and methodology of the study. A poorly planned or executed study can produce small or nondetectable effects even when the effect size in nature is rather large. Flagrant methodological flaws, sloppiness, and error within the experiment as well as more subtle nuances related to heterogeneity of procedures, subjects, and conditions can increase variation (the standard deviation) and dilute, diminish, and negate any differences between groups.

We can influence effect size by considering the relation between different levels of the variable of interest and the outcome and selecting those levels (e.g., very high vs. very low) that are likely to show the greatest difference between groups. In testing a particular set of hypotheses, it is not only fine to select conditions that will maximize the likelihood of showing effects, it is also prudent to do so. With a very strong test, positive or negative results may then be more likely to be interpretable.

Assuming a given or fixed effect size in nature, we can do much to determine whether it is detected within our experiment. We can greatly influence effect size by reducing variability in the procedures to minimize the error term (standard deviation) that is used in the effect size equation. Many efforts to control features of the experiment are designed to minimize error variance, that is, variability in the formula for ES. The larger the variability (denominator), the smaller the effect size for a constant difference between means (numerator).

Threats to Statistical Conclusion Validity

Low Statistical Power   Central to statistical evaluation is the notion of statistical power, which refers to the extent to which an investigation can detect differences between groups when differences exist within the population (see Table 3.1). *Power* is the probability of rejecting the null hypothesis (i.e., there are no differences) when that hypothesis is false. Stated differently, power is the likelihood of finding differences between conditions when, in fact, the conditions are truly different in their effects. Certainly, if there is a difference between groups and if the intervention or experimental manipulation is effective, we wish to detect this difference in our statistical tests.

The central threat to statistical validity in studies is relatively weak power or a low probability of detecting a difference if one truly exists. When power is weak, the likelihood that the investigator will conclude there are no differences between groups is increased. There might be no differences in the world and the intervention may in fact be no different in the effects it produces from those of a control condition. However, the conclusion of "no difference" might be due to low power, rather than to the absence of differences between groups. The study must be designed to detect a difference if there is one.

Power is not an esoteric concept of relevance only to researchers in the confines of their studies; it can also affect decision making about practices that affect physical and mental health. For example, studies of treatments for cancer occasionally have been unable to demonstrate differences due to weak statistical power (Freiman, Chalmers, Smith, & Kuebler, 1978). More central to clinical psychology, the majority of comparisons of different psychotherapy techniques show no differences in treatment outcome. This could easily be due to the weak power of studies, given the relatively small samples and small effect sizes that characterize this research (Kazdin & Bass, 1989).

Statistical power of an experiment is a function of the criterion for statistical significance (alpha), the size of the sample (N), and the differences that exist between groups (effect size). Although the most straightforward method of increasing power is to increase sample size, alpha and effect size are under the control of the investigator in significant ways. We address these matters in more detail in Chapter 14.

Variability in the Procedures   The notion of effect size is useful as a way of introducing other threats to statistical conclusion validity. Consider as a hypothetical experiment, a comparison of two treatments, A and B, administered to different groups. Ordinarily, effect size is considered to be a function of the true differences in the effects of the treatments. That is, if treatment A is more effective than treatment B in the real world, this will be evident in our experiment and be shown in our statistical evaluation. Reconsider the formula for effect size. The denominator includes a measure of variability (standard deviation). Thus, whatever difference between treatment A and B in our study, that difference will be in part a function of the variability in our experiment. This variability includes individual differences among the subjects, random fluctuations in performance on the measures, differences in experimenters or therapists in how they administer the intervention, and other sources, not all of which are easily specifiable.

One source of variance has to do with how the interventions or experimental procedures are carried out. Ideally, the procedures will be held relatively constant and implemented in a way to minimize variation among subjects. This means that the procedures will be applied consistently and experimenters will be highly trained to administer the instructions and other procedures in a constant way. Rigor in the execution of the procedures is not a methodological nicety for the sake of appearance. Consistency in execution of the procedures has direct bearing on statistical conclusion validity. A given difference between groups may or may not be regarded as reliable. Variation cannot be eliminated, especially in relation to aspects of research involving human participants (e.g., as subjects, clients, experimenters, therapists) and in settings outside the laboratory. However, in any experiment, extraneous variation can be minimized by attention to details of how the study is actually executed. If variability is minimized, the likelihood of detecting a true difference between the treatments or treatment and control conditions is increased. In terms of our formula for effect size, the differences between groups will be divided by a measure of variability; this measure will be larger when there is uncontrolled variation than if the source of variation is minimized. The larger the variability, the lower the effect size that will be evident for a given difference between groups.

Sometimes one can tell from the way an experiment is designed that there will be relatively high levels of variability and consequently great difficulty in demonstrating differences between conditions. For example, several years ago, a now-classic study compared behavior therapy and psychotherapy for the treatment of adults who came for treatment (Sloane et al., 1975). Clients were assigned to behavior therapy, psychotherapy, or a waiting-list control group. The way in which the two treatments were designed and implemented provided the opportunity for relatively large variability. Specifically, treatment guidelines were provided to behavior therapists and psychotherapists, but the guidelines were quite general and allowed remarkable latitude in what was actually done in the sessions. Each therapist was selected because of special expertise in the practice of one of the two approaches. Consequently, considerable latitude was given to therapists so they could treat the clients as they wished within the broad guidelines. The individual characteristics of the therapists and what they actually did in treatment varied greatly within a given condition. In seeing this feature of the design, one might suspect on a priori grounds that there would be a great deal of within-group variability. Such variability could diminish the obtained effect size and the likelihood of obtaining statistical significance between conditions.

In general, the results showed few or no differences in the outcomes between behavior therapy and psychotherapy. It would be an oversimplification to state that one aspect of the study, namely, high within-treatment variability, led to no differences. There were other sources of variation that were also rather broad including heterogeneous subject characteristics (e.g., very diverse clinical problems, wide age range). Yet, on the basis of the results, we are hard pressed to tell whether the absence of differences was due to the equivalent effects of treatment or the manner in which the treatments were implemented. The latter point might always be raised in a study in which few or no differences are found. However, the design of this study heightens the concern because variability, usually controlled by specifying and administering treatment in a relatively standardized way, was given relatively free reign.

Subject Heterogeneity   Subjects in an investigation can vary along multiple dimensions and characteristics such as sex, age, background, marital status, race and ethnicity, and others. In general, the greater the heterogeneity or diversity of subject characteristics, the less likelihood of detecting a difference between conditions. Critical to the statement is the assumption that subjects are heterogeneous on a characteristic that is related to (or correlated with) the effects of independent variable. For example, clients recruited for a psychotherapy study may vary widely (and "lengthily") in shoe size. Is this heterogeneity of great concern? Probably not. It is unlikely for most forms of psychotherapy that treatment effectiveness and performance on the outcome measures would be correlated with shoe size. On the other hand, clients may vary widely in the severity or duration of their clinical problem and in employment, socioeconomic class, and the presence of other problems (e.g., substance abuse, depression, chronic medical disease) not of interest in the study. The impact of treatment and performance on the dependent measures might be influenced by these factors. That these factors influence outcome is not inherently problematic nor undesirable; however, heterogeneity of the sample means that there will be greater variability in the subjects' reactions to the measures and to the intervention. This variability will be reflected in the denominator for evaluating effect size. The greater the variability (denominator), the less likely a given difference between means will be found to be statistically significant.

Consider treatment research in which individuals are recruited for a particular type of clinical problem. Screening criteria are invoked to ensure that cases included meet criteria for a psychiatric diagnosis of major depression. Some subjects may also meet criteria for other psychiatric disorders (e.g., anxiety disorder, antisocial personality disorder). (Comorbidity is the term used to refer to instances in which the individual meets criteria for two or more disorders.) One source of heterogeneity of the subjects is whether they meet criteria for multiple disorders. At the end of the study, treatment A may be compared with no treatment or with another treatment and the effects may appear weak or nonexistent (ES is small or zero). One possible reason for this result might be that all subjects were considered as representing a single group that included both subjects with depression and those with depression and a comorbid disorder. Treatment may have worked only for subjects with depression; hence, the effect size will be diluted by including all subjects in one overall comparison. Variation among subjects in relation to comorbidity enters into the denominator as within-group variability and attenuates the likelihood of showing group differences.

A way to address this problem is to evaluate the effects of treatment separately for subjects with and without a comorbid disorder to see whether the effect sizes are different for the two groups. Although the example is stated hypothetically, treatment research has shown that individuals with comorbid disorders often respond less well to treatment than those without a comorbid disorder (Kazdin, 1995a; Ryan et al., 1986). Taking into account comorbidity in the data analyses is helpful on methodological grounds by analyzing a source of variance that can influence effect size. Comorbidity also raises important conceptual, research, and clinical issues.

Heterogeneity of the subjects as a threat to statistical conclusion validity can be addressed in different ways. The first is to choose homogeneous samples. Homogeneity is a matter of degree. One might wish to limit the age range, type of clinical problem, educational level, and other variables within reasonable boundaries. Ideally, the decision of what variables to consider and how to limit the variation in the sample is based on theory or research on the effects of these and related variables on the measures of interest. If in doubt, one might select a relatively homogeneous set of subjects on diverse factors as a conservative way of addressing the threat.

A second alternative is to choose heterogeneous samples but to ensure that the impact or effect of selected subject characteristics can be evaluated in the design. For example, subjects of different ages and type of depression can be included. In the design of the study and the data analysis, the effects of age (above vs. below the median) and type of depression (those diagnosed as clinically depressed vs. those experiencing bereavement) can be evaluated. When these factors are analyzed as separate effects in the analysis, they no longer become within-group or error variances, and they do not increase the denominator in evaluating treatment differences. In principle and practice, it is possible to analyze the data endlessly to explore an indefinite set of characteristics that might contribute to the results. Psychological studies typically have too few subjects to analyze very many factors and such fishing expeditions have other problems (e.g., an increase in the likelihood of chance findings). If a heterogeneous sample is selected, it is useful to begin the study with specific hypotheses about the subanalyses that will be completed and to ensure that the subanalyses can be conducted with adequate power. We return to these points later in Chapter 14.

Unreliability of the Measures   Reliability refers to the extent to which the measures assess the characteristics of interest in a consistent fashion. Reliability is a matter of degree and refers to the extent of the variability in responding. Performance on the measure may vary widely from item to item within the measure because items are not equally clear or consistent in what they measure and performance may vary widely from occasion to occasion. To the extent that the measure is unreliable, a greater portion of the subject's score is due to unsystematic and random variation. This variation means that in statistical evaluation, relatively large variability can be introduced. In studies with relatively unreliable measures, the obtained effect size is likely to be lower. Selection of assessment devices in designing a study is more than a quick shopping trip to the literature (see Chapter 11). Selection of poorly designed measures in which reliability and validity are in doubt can threaten statistical conclusion validity.

Multiple Comparisons and Error Rates   Not all threats to statistical conclusion validity pertain to variability. Statistical evaluation of the results can be hindered by other problems that directly influence whether the investigator concludes that groups differed. In an investigation, several different measures are likely to be used to evaluate the impact of the intervention. For example, in a treatment study, the clients, clinician, and perhaps relatives of the client are likely to complete a few measures (e.g., depression, symptoms in diverse areas, social functioning). At the end of the investigation, treatments A and B will be compared on each of the measures. The familiar *t* test may be used given that there are two groups and parametric data.

There are separate but interrelated problems that reflect a threat to statistical conclusion validity. The main problem to note at this point pertains to the number of statistical tests that will be completed. The more tests performed, the more likely a chance difference will be found, even if there are no true differences between conditions. Thus, the investigator may conclude mistakenly that there is a difference between groups and a true effect of the intervention (Type

I error). The possibility of this occurring is evident in any experiment. The risk of a Type I error is specified by alpha or the probability level that is used as a criterion for statistical significance. Yet this risk and its probability level applies to an individual test. When there are multiple comparisons, alpha is greater than 0.05, depending on the number of tests. The risk across several statistical tests, sometimes referred to as experiment-wise error rate, is much greater. The number of comparisons that are made within a study can lead to misleading conclusions about group differences. Strategies to address statistical issues in the execution of research are detailed in Chapter 14.

General Comments

The threats to statistical conclusion validity refer to the features of the study that affect the quantitative evaluation of the results. When the threats are made explicit, they may appear obvious. Yet, they often serve as the tacit downfall of an experiment. Excellent ideas conducted in carefully controlled tests routinely have weak power. Perhaps even more pervasive is the hidden variability that can emerge in all facets of experimentation and obscures differences between conditions.

When first introduced into the discussion of research, the notion of experimental control is usually raised in the context of control groups and threats to internal validity. However, a deeper understanding of the notion of control stems in part from its relation to statistical conclusion validity. The control and evaluation of variability in research, to the extent possible, are critical. The initial question of interest in designing a study is, Are the groups or conditions different? This question emphasizes the means on some measure or set of measures. The next question usually guides statistical conclusion validity, namely, If there is a difference, will this study be able to detect it? This question greatly influences several features of the design (e.g., selection, sample size) and procedures (e.g., implementation of the intervention, experimenter training). Many facets of research including recruitment of subjects, preparation and delivery of experimental instructions, and methods of scoring and checking data become potential sources of uncontrolled variation and can introduce ambiguity into the results.

We have discussed variability and variation as if it were the enemy. In some sense this might be true, but great care is needed in making this point. The goal of our research is not to eliminate variability but to understand it, which means we wish to elaborate the full range of factors that influence personality and behavior including our interventions (e.g., a new treatment), interventions of "nature" not under our experimental control (e.g., child-rearing practices, stress associated with bereavement, chronic disease, war), and individual differences (e.g., temperament, generic predispositions, personality style). When any one or more of these is the basis of our investigations, we need to control other sources of variation because the source of variation that is of interest in our study may be obscured by allowing free fluctuation of all other sources of variation. Experimental design and statistical evaluation separate and evaluate different sources of variation.

EXPERIMENTAL PRECISION AND ITS PRICE

In the present and previous chapters, we have covered internal, external, construct, and statistical conclusion validity. At the design stage, each type of validity needs to be considered along with their individual threats. Not all problems that can interfere with valid inferences can be predicted or controlled in advance (e.g., loss of subjects over time). However, most can be addressed in planning the experiment and its execution. Also, even problems that cannot be resolved in advance are worth considering at the design stage. It is worth reiterating that addressing each threat to validity perfectly well is not possible because addressing one type of validity often compromises another type of validity.

Threats to internal validity generally can be ruled out by allocating subjects randomly to conditions and controlling potential sources of bias (e.g., instrumentation, attrition) that might arise during the experiment. Yet, in designing experiments, researchers usually are interested in more than ruling out threats to internal validity; they also are interested in providing the most sensitive test of the independent variable possible. Maximizing the likelihood of detecting the relationship raises issues of statistical conclusion validity. The investigator wishes to minimize extraneous influences and sources of variation in how subjects respond in the experiment.

Increased precision is achieved by holding constant the potential sources of influence on subjects' behavior other than the independent variable. Conditions are held constant if they are identical or very close to that across subjects and experimental conditions. Of course, one cannot realistically expect to implement an experiment in which all conditions are the same except for the independent variable. To cite an obvious problem, all subjects in the study vary because of their differences in genetic makeup, childhood experiences, physical capabilities, intelligence, age, ethnic background, and familiarity with experiments. Each factor and many others introduce variation into the experiment in terms of how subjects respond to the intervention.

The manner in which the independent variable is implemented may introduce extraneous variation into the experiment. Ideally, the conditions of administration among subjects within a given condition do not vary at all. Some features of the experimental manipulation might be held constant, such as administering instructions or showing materials to the subjects by using audio or video tapes. If an experimenter interacts with the subjects, the interaction may vary slightly across different subjects; if several experimenters are used in the study, even greater variation may be introduced. Other extraneous factors of the experiment, such as the time of the day, weather, how the independent variable is implemented, and so on, may contribute to sources of variation. These factors can be *controlled* by having them vary unsystematically across groups. If there is no systematic bias with these sources of variation, the experiment is controlled. However, these factors can be *held constant,* which may be better from the standpoint of demonstrating the relationship between the independent and dependent variable. By reducing or removing sources of variation, one can provide a more sensitive (powerful) test of the independent variable.

At first glance, it may seem that experimenters should automatically maximize the sensitivity of all experimental tests by making the experiment as precise as possible in terms of minimizing extraneous sources of variation. Yet, experimental precision has its cost in the generality of the experimental results. As a general rule, *design features that make an experiment more sensitive as a test of the independent and dependent variables tend to limit the generality of the findings. Conversely, features of an experiment that enhance generality of the results tend to increase variability and to decrease the sensitivity of the experimental test.*

Careful experimental control does not always restrict the generality of a finding in clinical research, but there seems to be a relationship that a gain in either experimental precision or generality may be associated with a sacrifice in the other. Once a finding has been established through well-controlled and internally valid studies, research emphasis can extend to external validity. External validity is evaluated by systematically broadening samples of subjects, the type of settings in which treatment is administered, variations of treatment that are attempted, and the type of measures and constructs used to evaluate outcome.

In psychotherapy research, there is concern about the relevance of research for clinical practice. Salient among the issues is that in research, several practices are conducted to minimize variability, such as selection of homogeneous subjects, selection of therapists, and careful control and monitoring of treatment administration. The investigator is wise to carry out these and related practices to provide a sensitive test. In addition, a question is raised regarding the extent to which the effects, once demonstrated in well-controlled research, can be extended to situations in which many of the controls over variability are not easily carried out (Hoagwood & Hibbs, 1995). In other words, the control over the intervention and extraneous sources of variability (e.g., homogeneous subject sample) may bear a cost in terms of the external validity of the results. Conditions of tightly controlled research may deviate so markedly from the ordinary situation that the plausibility of producing generalizable findings is commensurately decreased. Research is required to address the matter by extending studies to other situations and by evaluating their impact.

SUMMARY AND CONCLUSIONS

Construct validity pertains to interpreting the basis for the causal relation that has been demonstrated. The intervention or the variable of interest may be one of many factors that distinguishes intervention and control conditions or two or more intervention conditions. Factors that may interfere with or obscure valid inferences about the basis for the effect are *threats to construct validity.* Major threats include attention and contact with the clients, single operations and narrow stimulus sampling, experimenter expectancies, and cues of the experimental situation.

Statistical conclusion validity refers to aspects of the experiment that affect the quantitative evaluation of the study and can lead to misleading or false conclusions about the intervention. Several concepts basic to statistical evaluation are mentioned because of their role in statistical conclusion validity. These concepts included the probability of accepting and rejecting the null hypothesis, the probability of making such decisions when they are false, and the notion of effect size. Major factors that commonly serve as threats to statistical conclusion validity operate by influencing one or more of these concepts and include low statistical power, variability in the procedures of an investigation, subject heterogeneity, unreliability of the measures, and multiple statistical comparisons and their error rates.

All four types of validity, internal, external, construct, and statistical conclusions validity, need to be considered at the design stage of an investigation. It is not possible in one experiment to address all threats well or equally well, nor is this necessarily a goal toward which one should strive. Rather, the goal is to address the primary questions of interest in as thorough a fashion as possible so that clear answers can be provided for specific questions. At the end of the investigation, new questions may emerge or questions about other types of validity may increase in priority. The need for further information is not necessarily a flaw, but rather the continued line of inquiry to which an important study invariably leads.

The obstacles in designing experiments emerge not only from the manifold types of validity and their threats but also from the interrelations of the different types of validity. Factors that address one type of validity might detract from or increase vulnerability to another type of validity. For example, factors that address statistical conclusion validity might involve controlling potential sources of variation in relation to the experimental setting, delivery of procedures, homogeneity of subjects, and so on. In the process of maximizing experimental control and making the most sensitive test of the independent variable, the range of conditions included in the experiment becomes increasingly restricted. Restricting the conditions, such as the type of subjects or measures and standardization of delivering the intervention or independent variable, may commensurately limit the range of conditions to which the final results can be generalized.

In this and the previous chapter we discussed different types of validity and their threats. The purpose has been primarily to describe the threats and how they operate. In remaining chapters, we address several of these areas again more concretely and discuss strategies that directly affect inferences drawn from research.

NOTES

[1]Construct validity is a more familiar term in the context of test development and validation (Wainer & Braun, 1988). For example, investigators may develop a psychological test that they believe measures anxiety. Several types of studies are completed to establish the construct validity, that is, that the scale measures anxiety rather than some other construct (e.g., intelligence, deviance, honesty, altruism) (see Chapter 11). Thus, in the use of test development, construct validity refers to the explanation of the measure or the dimension that it assesses. In a parallel way, construct validity of an experiment refers to the explanation of the outcome (Cook & Campbell, 1979).

[2]For purposes of discussion, we consider the *investigator* as the person who has responsibility for planning and designing the study and the *experimenter* as the person who is actively running the subjects and carrying out the procedures. This distinction is helpful despite the fact that the investigator and experimenter are occasionally the same person and that many persons in a project may vary in the extent to which they share these roles. We focus here on the experimenter to emphasize the person in direct contact with the subjects.

FOR FURTHER READING

Lipsey, M.W. (1990). *Design sensitivity: Statistical power for experimental research*. Newbury Park, CA: Sage.

Schmidt, F.L. (1996). Statistical significance testing and cumulative knowledge in psychology: Implications for training of researchers. *Psychological Methods, 1*, 115–129.

Wampold, B.E., Davis, B., & Good, R.H. (1990). Hypothesis validity of clinical research. *Journal of Consulting and Clinical Psychology, 58*, 360–367.

Chapter 4

Selection of the Research Problem and Design

Selection of the research problem refers to the idea that serves as the impetus or focus for investigation and the question that is to be addressed. Perhaps the general idea expresses the relation to be studied or specific hypotheses of what will happen when certain conditions are varied. However, the general idea must be reexpressed in concrete terms that specify the precise way in which the general concepts will be studied. The concrete terms refer to what will be done in the investigation and how performance will be measured. This chapter discusses the initiation of research and specification of the idea. The chapter also previews many design options from which the investigator can select.

RESEARCH IDEAS AND OPERATIONS

Sources of Ideas

The research investigation begins with an idea. How the idea is derived may be more appropriately discussed in the context of creativity rather than methodology. Nevertheless, some comments can be made in passing about the source of research ideas because this is the beginning of the research design process. Presumably a scientist might be equipped with excellent research design skills and knowledge of how to execute the design. Yet, in the absence of a specific research idea, he or she would be all dressed up with no place to go. Where one decides to go in research, that is, the question or problem that will be addressed, may arise from many sources.

First, many ideas arise from simple curiosity about a phenomenon. Curiosity is no explanation of why a particular course of research is pursued, but it helps convey that the motive for asking particular questions in the context of experimentation need not always germinate from complex or highly sophisticated theoretical notions. The research may seek to describe how people are or perform in a particular situation and then expand to generate ideas about why this occurs.

Second, a great deal of research in clinical psychology stems from the observations of clinical dysfunctions or human behavior more generally. A particular clinical problem (e.g., posttraumatic stress disorder), style of functioning (e.g., Type A personality, risk taking), or population (e.g., first-born children, spouses who are violent with each other) may be of interest, and the investigator asks what are the key and associated characteristics. The correlates (e.g., in personality style, family background) and similarities and differences among varied clinical problems encompass a wide range of investigations.

Third, theory is often devised to explain a phenomenon and the tested in research. In an effort to understand phenomena, investigators propose concepts to integrate different ideas and variables in an orderly fashion. The theory or model may explain different constructs and how they relate to each other and to other events. Research is completed to test predicted relations and other conditions that explain how the variables or processes operate. For example, theory might propose that there are certain personality styles or beliefs that account for behavior. An investigation might be devised to place persons in a situation to see whether the expected type of performance is evident.

Fourth, research sometimes is stimulated by efforts to operationalize or measure various constructs. Developing assessment devices is central because measurement is a precondition for other research. An investigator may be interested in studying empathy, risk taking, hopelessness, adjustment, or other constructs. Research is begun to develop a new measure and to establish various types of reliability and validity of the measure. In the process of the research, the relations of the measure and underlying construct to other domains of functioning are elaborated.

Fifth, research is often stimulated by other studies. Research may evaluate the interpretation of a relation provided by the original investigator or test the generality of conditions across which the relation holds. A very large portion of the published research is directed at building on, expanding, or reexplaining the results of other studies. The study may redress ambiguities from prior research or elaborate a relation that has been proposed.

Finally, in clinical psychology, a prominent source of hypotheses has been the case study. A case study usually consists of the intensive evaluation of an individual over time. Close contact with an individual case provides unique information because of observation of many variables, their interactions over time, and views about the bases of personality and behavior. Cases can generate many hypotheses about all facets of functioning (e.g., impact of special events in childhood, why one relates to others in particular ways). Because the case study has played a special role in clinical psychology and in research, it is treated further in a separate discussion (Chapter 9).

The source of an idea for psychological experimentation is not restricted to the above options. The value of the idea is determined by the empirical and conceptual yield. Ideas that are derived from everyday experience, common cultural wisdom, or stereotypic notions about behavior may be as useful in generating hypotheses as more complex psychological theories. The quality of the idea is ultimately evaluated. It is difficult to judge what a good research idea is because that judgment is based on subjective evaluation, theoretical predilection, and ultimately by its empirical yield. Despite the difficulty in judging the quality of ideas, professionals are called on to make these judgments in the context of reviewing research reports for possible journal publication or grant applications that seek funding. Professionals are asked to determine whether a completed or proposed study addresses an important question, adds to existing knowledge, and focuses on an agreed-on problem in an area of research.

An idea that may be viewed as a contribution to the literature often involves focusing on a problem area or unresolved issue in the specific research area of interest to the investigator. To develop a study on a problem or unresolved aspect of a given literature, detailed knowledge of the literature is extremely helpful. There is simply no substitute for knowing the area thoroughly. Reading incisive reviews and individual studies from the relevant literature is helpful; writing such a review may be better. Although there is no substitute for expertise to generate a research idea that takes an important "next step," mastery of the literature can also be delimiting. The literature in a given area reflects a set of agreed-on assumptions and methods, many of which are accepted on faith. Drawing on areas outside the content area to be researched frequently adds new dimensions that might not have been pursued otherwise. Thus, the advantage of novice researchers often is, paradoxically, that their thinking is not confined by the standard topics and procedures for investigation.

Levels of Understanding and the Focus of the Study

The overall goal of research is to understand the phenomenon of interest, which means that we know its characteristics, the factors with which it is associated, how it operates, and how it can be controlled. Sometimes the goal of research is stated to identify causal relations, a useful point of departure. Once causal relations are known, we know a great deal. However, there is more to know about relations among variables than their causal connection and also a great deal of important information to know even if we do not know about cause. Levels of understanding of the phenomena can better be described as a process moving from description to explanation; both description and explanation can vary in how much is known. In both description and explanation, there is an interplay between theory and evidence.

Key Questions and Concepts Several key concepts that may underlie the focus of an investigation help to convey different levels of understanding and different design issues and strategies. Table 4.1 presents key questions and con-

---

TABLE 4.1. Sample Questions and Concepts That Are the Impetus for Research

1. What is the relationship among the variables of interest?

Correlate—Two (or more) variables associated at a given point in time with no direct evidence that one variable precedes the other.

Risk factor—A characteristic antecedent to and that increases the likelihood of an outcome of interest. A correlate in which the time sequence is established.

Cause—One variable influences, either directly or through other variables, the appearance of the outcome. Changing one variable leads to a change in another variable (outcome).

2. What factors influence the relationship among variables, that is, the direction or magnitude of the relation?

Moderator—A variable that influences the relationship of two variables of interest. The relationship between the variables (A and B) changes or is different as a function of some other variable (e.g., sex, age, ethnicity).

3. How does the phenomenon work, that is, through what relation or mechanism or through what process does A lead to B?

Mediator—The process, mechanism, or means through which a variable produces a particular outcome. Beyond knowing that A may cause B, the mechanism elaborates precisely what happens (e.g., psychologically, biologically) to explain how B results.

4. Can we control or alter the outcome of interest?

Intervention—Something we can do to decrease the likelihood that an undesired outcome will occur (prevention) or decrease or eliminate an undesired outcome that has already occurred (treatment). These questions are usually framed as focusing on some undesirable outcome, but they often promote positive, prosocial outcomes to achieve their end.

Note: The terms and the relations they reflect are detailed elsewhere (Baron & Kenny, 1986; Kazdin et al., 1997; Kraemer et al., 1997).

cepts that pertain to the relations among variables of interest and that often serve as the impetus for an investigation. Research in clinical psychology often focuses on identifying *correlates* among variables. Subjects are tested on several measures at a particular point in time to relate such variables as symptoms (e.g., depression, anxiety), cognitive processes, personality, stress, family functioning, or physical health; correlations predicted from theory or another source are examined. Identifying characteristics of affect, cognition, behavior, and the contextual environment (e.g., characteristics of others) that are or are not correlated with a particular problem can be important for elaborating the nature of a problem and for testing or developing theories about the onset or course of a problem.

Other types of relations may be studied. The notion of *risk factor* represents a deeper level of understanding. Risk factor, as a concept, emerged from public health in the context of studying disease (morbidity) and death (mortality). The term and common foci in that context refer to "risky" practices (e.g., eating high-fat diets, cigarette smoking) and deleterious outcomes (e.g., heart disease, death). However, in research more generally, the term refers to events, experiences, or practices that increase a particular outcome of interest (Kraemer et al., 1997). The experiences (e.g., meditating, exercising) and the outcomes (e.g., coping well with stress, donating to charity) can be quite positive. Consequently, the term is used to reflect characteristics that are correlated with and antecedent to a later outcome, no matter what the outcome is. For a risk factor, the time line is established, namely, one event or experience (e.g., abuse, exposure to religion) is correlated with a later characteristic (e.g., marital happiness). The early experience may not be a cause, but we know that the experience, for whatever reason, increases the likelihood that the later outcome will occur. Demonstrating *cause* means that we have established the relation as not merely part of a temporal ordering of events but rather as a direct influence. Demonstration of causality is a high level of understanding and, as noted previously, a goal of research.

Research often focuses on *moderators*, that is, variables that influence the direction and nature of the relation. We may show, for example, that the relation holds for women but not for men, for individuals with a particular history, and so on. Identification of moderators is an important advance in understanding because knowing other factors that influence the relation between variables often prompts theory and research to explain why the moderator has an influence. We know, for example, that the rate of sudden infant death varies greatly (is moderated by) another variable (whether anyone in the home is a cigarette smoker). This finding does not mean that sudden infant death is caused by cigarette smoking. It could be that something about homes in which cigarette smoking occurs accounts for or contributes to the relation (e.g., more abuse of the child, poor child nutrition). However, knowing that smoking plays a role prompts further theory and research.

The focus on *mediators* or *mechanisms* represents a deeper level of understanding beyond the relations noted here before because this means we know *how* the problem unfolds, through what *processes*, and precisely the *ways* in which one variable leads to another. For example, research on the relation of cigarette smoking and lung cancer spans the range of concepts included in Table 4.1. That is, studies involving both human and animal research have shown that cigarette smoking is correlated with, a risk factor for, and a cause of lung cancer. This still leaves open the question of how cigarette smoke leads to the disease. Recent research has elaborated the mechanism involved in the causal relation. A chemical (benzo[*a*]pyrene) found in cigarette smoke induces genetic mutation (at specific regions of the gene's DNA) that is identical to the damage evident in lung cancer cells (Denissenko, Pao, Tang, & Pfeifer, 1996). This finding is considered to convey precisely how cigarette smoking leads to cancer at the molecular level. Thus, beyond the demonstration of a causal relation, a fine-grained analysis of mechanisms is also important. Knowing the mediator of a relation between variables obviously does not require knowing the biological substrates. The mechanism or process through which two variables are related may involve all sorts of psychological constructs, as illustrated with later examples.

Knowing the cause or a cause of a phenomenon can reflect different levels of understanding because precision of the knowledge may vary. In the usual case in clinical research, cause refers to knowing how to change a phenomenon. For example, a great deal of research focuses on interventions (treatment, prevention, and educational programs) to reduce clinical dysfunction, to prevent the onset of dysfunction, and to promote well-being or adaptive functioning. These studies focus on causal relations, that is, for example, making a change at the level of the individual, school, or community will lead to change in the outcome(s) of interest. Causal relations can refer to may different types of cause and to causes that bear varied temporal relations to an outcome (Haynes, 1992). Intervention research focuses on causes of change, which may be different from, and not necessarily related to, the original causes that led to the development of the problem. For example, psychotherapy and surgery can "cause" change and eliminate a problem (e.g., anxiety and cancer, respectively) although obviously absence of psychotherapy or surgery was not the cause of the dysfunctions to which they were applied. Related, in referring to a causal relation, it is important to bear in mind that there may be many causes. For example, to say that one causal relation has been shown between smoking and lung cancer is not the same thing as saying that smoking is the only cause of lung cancer. There may be many causes of lung cancer; smoking is only one of them.

We may know how to produce change even if we are not sure of the mechanisms involved. For example, successful prevention programs (e.g., for young children at risk for school failure and behavior problems) often rely on multimodal interventions, that is, programs that entail several techniques (e.g., counseling and medical care for the parents, special day care for the child, changes at home for the child such as reading, etc.) (Meisels & Shonkoff, 1990). If such an intervention produces reliable change, we can say that a causal relation was demonstrated even though we may not know how change was produced, precisely what facet of the intervention produced change, or what intervening steps (e.g., affect, cognition, behavior) led to the change in the target domain.

Table 4.1 presents key concepts that often implicitly serve as the basis for many research topics. The study of *subtypes or variations of a problem* is one area that stimulates research. An investigator may believe that what seems to be one type of person or clinical problem misses an important distinction. The goal of research is to show that there are subtypes and that characteristics of the subtypes (i.e., correlates, risk factors) vary. For example, children who are antisocial engage in behaviors such as fighting, stealing, lying, running away. Years of research has suggested that it is meaningful to delineate subgroups of these children, for example, those who are aggressive (engage in fighting) and those who are primarily delinquent (engage in stealing, vandalism). Correlates, risk factors, histories, and long-term outcomes vary as a function of these subtypes (Moffitt et al., 1996; Stanger, Achenbach, & Verhulst, 1997). Essentially, research on subtypes focuses on a moderating variable, namely, a key characteristic that influences the relations obtained among other variables.

Another type of research focuses on *paths* or *course of a problem*. In this case, the investigator is interested in the order, unfolding, phases, or course of a particular problem or phenomenon. The investigator identifies individuals in a particular stage or state and then hypothesizes how changes occur. As an example, we have learned from psychotherapy research that there are phases through which individuals go as they improve in psychotherapy. Clients tend to change first in their subjective well-being, followed by reductions in symptoms, followed by changes in life functioning or other more enduring characteristics (Howard, Lueger, Maling, & Martinovich, 1993). Research has shown that one type of change is likely to occur before the other and that a later phase of change is not likely to occur unless changes in a prior phase have occurred. Needless to say, this is not the way all changes occur, nor phases through which all patients pass, nor necessarily the only way of characterizing phases or stages of psychotherapy. A broader lesson we have learned from much research is that there are often many paths (progressions, causal relations) that lead to a particular outcome. In the context of phases of psychotherapy, research can begin to identify the persons and situations to which the phase model applies (moderators) and the reasons or bases for movement within the phases (mediators). In any case, impetus for research may stem from hypotheses about how the phenomenon of interest unfolds or progresses over time.

Some Brief Examples   Our understanding, of course, is optimal when we know great detail about a particular phenomenon of interest, i.e., correlates, risk factors, moderators, mediators, and causes. There are several lines of work in which one can see the progression in level of understanding. Consider briefly two examples from clinical psychology (on parenting and child-rearing) and one example from public health on human immunodeficiency virus (HIV) and acquired immunodeficiency syndrome (AIDS).

The first illustration focuses on parenting practices and the development of aggressive and antisocial behavior in children. Research has shown that inept parental discipline practices foster aggressive and antisocial behavior at home

(Dishion, Patterson, & Kavanagh, 1992; Patterson, Reid, & Dishion, 1992). Inept discipline practices include parental attention to deviant behavior, interactions in which increasingly aggressive child behavior is reinforced, inattention to prosocial behavior, coercive punishment, poor child supervision, and failure to set limits. Initial studies showed that inept discipline practices correlated with child antisocial behavior, as measured by parent, teacher, and peer ratings, in both community and clinic samples of boys and girls (Dishion et al., 1992; Forgatch, 1991). Cross-sectional and longitudinal studies helped to establish the time line of inept child-rearing practices and child antisocial behavior. In addition, randomized controlled clinical trials were conducted in which parents were randomly assigned to various treatment and control conditions.

A *randomized controlled clinical trial* is a frequently used term that spans multiple disciplines. It is useful to be familiar with this term because of its widespread use and because this type of study is recognized to be the best and most definitive way of demonstrating that an intervention is effective. The term refers to an outcome study in which clients with a particular problem are randomly assigned to various treatment and control conditions. In clinical psychology, these are usually referred to as treatment outcome studies, the vast majority of which are based on random assignment. Yet, the term randomized controlled clinical trial leaves no doubt that the study uses random assignment and that the treatment or intervention is evaluated in the context of a clinical sample. In this example, conditions involving direct alteration of parent discipline practices, compared to treatment and control conditions without this focus, led to decreases in child antisocial behavior (Dishion & Andrews, 1995; Dishion et al., 1992). Several randomized controlled trials have shown similar results, namely, changes in parenting skills led to changes in child behavior (Kazdin, 1997). From multiple studies, we know that adverse (especially harsh) parenting practices lead to aggressive and antisocial child behavior, even though this finding does not imply such practices are the only cause of these behaviors or even a necessary or sufficient cause of the behaviors. Yet, from the progression of research, we know a great deal about parenting practices, their impact, and what we can do about these situations.

A second example also illustrates the progression of understanding and pertains to the relationship between reading among children (ages 6–8) and subsequent school attainment. In an initial set of three studies, Hewison and Tizard (1980) interviewed parents to identify home background factors (e.g., attitudes toward play, discipline, activities, use of leisure time, and school) that were associated with reading achievement of the children. Reading achievement is one of the best measures of current school achievement and the best single predictor of subsequent attainment for this age group. The first study showed that among many characteristics examined, child reading in the home emerged as a significant influence (correlate) of reading achievement. Specifically, parents who reported that they listened regularly to their children read at home had children who were significantly higher in reading and school achievement, as measured by standardized tests. Similarly, in a second and larger-scale study, listening to children read at home on a regular basis, in relation to a number of other family characteristics, was the best predictor of child reading achievement and standardized intelligence test performance. This finding was robust across boys and girls, multiple samples, and schools; it could not be explained by several potentially confounding influences (e.g., child IQ, parental attitudes, mother's language ability). A third study replicated the finding but also examined whether there was a dose–response relation between reading at home and reading attainment.[1] Parents were classified by the extent to which they listened to their child read (e.g., 3-point scale—regular, occasional, none). The results supported a dose–response relation; more frequent reading was associated with higher levels of achievement.

The prior studies, however interesting, were correlational, so the antecedent relation of listening to children read on a regular basis and a later outcome (reading and school achievement) was not demonstrated. A randomized controlled trial was conducted to evaluate whether there was a causal relation between reading and academic achievement (Tizard, Schofield, & Hewison, 1982). A home-reading program was evaluated in which parents listened to their children read. Classrooms from several schools (with multiracial, inner-city children ages 6–7) were randomly assigned to one of three conditions: (1) parent intervention in which parents were available to assist and to listen to their children read on a regular basis; (2) teacher-reading condition (reading at school to control for increased exposure to reading materials), and (3) no special intervention (classroom practices as usual). In the parent-intervention condition, reading by the child at home was directly monitored, and teachers sent reading material home for the child to read. After 2 years of the intervention, reading achievement of the children in the parent-intervention condition improved on standardized measures of reading and school achievement, was significantly higher than the other two conditions, and surpassed the reading achievement level of their respective schools in prior years before the intervention. The effects were maintained at a 1-year follow-up after the intervention had been terminated. Overall, the results demonstrated that a parent's listening to the children read at home plays a causal role in subsequent school achievement. The sequence of studies conveys the progression from correlate to causal factor and the interplay of research strategies in this progression.

Another example can be drawn from research on HIV and AIDS. Early research identified several correlated features of contracting HIV. For example, one factor was intravenous drug use, that is, individuals who engaged in such use had higher rates of HIV. This was an important but early step in terms of levels of understanding. One hypothesis about the mediator, that is, the process relating drug use to HIV, was that drug use impaired one's immune system and led to increased vulnerability to the virus. From years of research, we know much more about HIV; among other things, we know that the basis for the relation of drug use and HIV lies elsewhere. The mechanism relating these variables is sharing of needles for intravenous injection, which spreads the virus directly. This level of understanding is obviously greater than the mere connection of the two variables. Knowledge of the mechanism can therefore enable us to alter the spread of AIDS by decreasing the sharing of needles or by making "clean" needles available.

As we now know, research has elaborated other paths for contracting HIV (direct sexual contact, contact with blood) and has shown rather clearly that the virus plays a direct role in relation to disease and death (i.e., the higher the level of the virus in the body, the shorter the period of survival) (e.g., Mellors et al., 1996). Further research has shown that not everyone exposed directly to HIV becomes infected or progresses to AIDS. The HIV virus is a necessary but not sufficient condition for contracting AIDS. Substances found within human cells influence the likelihood that an exposed person will contract HIV and AIDS (Cohen, 1996). Obviously, although much remains to be known about HIV, the level of understanding about the disease is considerable.

Importance of Theory   These examples do not answer the full range of questions of interest to us (e.g., identify all moderators, mechanisms), but they show important movement from merely establishing a relation to elaborating critical features about that relation. The progression of research from description to explanation and from correlation to cause, as described to this point, may inadvertently imply a crass empiricism, that is, one merely tests different types of relations among variables to see what role, if any, they play. Underlying the concepts that guide research (see Table 4.1) is the investigator's theory, which focuses the research idea.

Theory, broadly defined, refers to a conceptualization of the phenomenon of interest. The conceptualization may encompass views about the nature, antecedents, causes, correlates, and consequences of a particular characteristic or aspect of functioning. Also, the theory may specify the relations of various constructs to each other. There are different levels of theory. In clinical psychology, theories of personality have been a central topic in which diverse facets of human functioning are explained. Psychoanalytic theory illustrates this well by posing a variety of constructs, mechanisms that are designed to explain intrapsychic processes and performance in everyday life, psychopathology, development, and so on. More circumscribed theoretical views characterize contemporary research in an effort to develop specific models (integrated sets of findings and relations among variables). The models may explain the relation between specific characteristics and a disorder (e.g., hopelessness and helplessness in relation to depression) and how these characteristics lead to other features of dysfunction.

A goal is to understand human functioning; to achieve this understanding we do not merely accumulate facts or empirical findings. Rather (or in addition), we wish to relate these findings to each other and to other phenomena in a cohesive way. For example, an investigator may demonstrate that there are sex differences regarding a particular disorder, personality characteristic, or cognitive style. However, by itself, sex differences are not necessarily inherently interesting. A theoretical understanding would pose how the difference develops or what implications the difference may have for understanding biological or psycho-social development. Inevitably, there will be many exceptions to the theory and they will require posing moderators and new lines of work. From the standpoint of research, theoretical explanations guide further studies and the data generated by the studies require emendations of the theory. This is an important exercise because theory moves us to implications beyond the confines of the specific relations that have been demonstrated and the restricted conditions in which these relations may have been demonstrated.

Defining the Research Idea

Operational Definitions   Whatever the original idea that provides the impetus for research, it must be described concretely so that it can be tested. It is not enough to have an abstract notion or question. For example, one might ask at a general level such questions as: Do anxious people tend to withdraw from social situations? Are college students put to sleep by the lectures of their instructors? These and similar notions are adequate for initial leads for study but require considerable work before empirical research could be executed.

The concepts included in the abstract notion must be operationalized, that is, made into operational definitions. *Operational definitions* refer to defining a concept on the basis of the specific operations used in the experiment. For example, an operational definition of anxiety could be physiological reactions to a galvanic skin-response measure of skin resistance to an individual's self-report of being upset, nervous, or irritable in several situations. Greater specificity than merely noting the measure may be required. For example, the question about anxious people requires operational criteria for designating anxious and nonanxious individuals and for defining social withdrawal. "Anxious" may be operationalized by having the term refer to persons who attain relatively high scores (e.g., at or above the 75th percentile) on a standardized measure of anxiety. "Nonanxious" or low anxious persons might be defined as those who attain relatively low scores (e.g., at or below the 25th percentile) on the same scale. Specifying the measure and the cutoff criteria to define anxious and nonanxious groups would clearly satisfy the requirements of an operational definition. Similarly, for defining social withdrawal, the specific measure must be identified.

Although operational definitions are essential for experimentation, there are limitations that such definitions bear. To begin with, although the investigator may start with an abstract notion that is to be operationalized, the use of an operational definition may be incomplete or may greatly simplify the concept of interest. For example, an operational definition of love might be based on the expression of love on a self-report measure or overt physical expressions of affection. Although each measure is part of what people often mean by love, the measures, either separate or combined, are not the full definition that people usually have in mind when they talk about or experience love. From the standpoint of research, the purpose is to provide a working definition of the phenomenon. Yet, the working definition may not be all encompassing or even bear great resemblance to what people mean in everyday discourse.

A second limitation is that the operational definition may include features that are irrelevant or not central to the original concept. For example, anxiety might be operationalized by including persons who attend a clinic and complain of various symptoms. Yet, this definition includes components of interest other than anxiety and can thus influence the conclusions of the study. Attending a clinic is determined by many factors other than experiencing a problem, including the availability of clinic facilities, ethnic or cultural views about treatment, concern over possible stigma, and encouragement by relatives and friends. There may be many other persons in the community who are equally or more anxious than those who seek treatment. In general, there is always a concern that any single operation used to define a construct will be inadequate or incomplete or include components irrelevant to the original concept.

A third limitation of operational definitions pertains to the use of single measures to define a construct. There are limitations to all measurement devices due to special features of the device itself. Performance of the subject on a single measure is determined by more factors than the construct that is being measured. For example, although self-report of anxiety on a questionnaire is likely to be related to the experience of anxiety in everyday life, the extent to which anxiety is reported is likely to be a function of other factors such as the purposes for which the test will be used (e.g., receiving free therapy vs. obtaining a job), how the subject feels on that day, how the questions are worded, the characteristics of the individual administering the test, and the subject's general likelihood of admitting socially undesirable characteristics. Simply stated, any one method of operationalizing is fallible because it may depend on specific and unique characteristics of the measure.

Investigators usually wish to describe general relationships that go beyond single and narrowly circumscribed operations. For example, if possible, it is important to be able to make general statements about anxiety and its relation to other phenomena independently of the many different ways in which anxiety can be operationalized. Using a single measure to define a construct may impede drawing general relationships among concepts.

Multiple Operations to Represent Constructs   The inadequacies of defining a concept with a single measure or operation (referred to as *single operationism*) had led to use of multiple measures or operations (*multiple operationism*). Although a concept may be imperfectly measured by individual operations, the commonalties among several measure may converge on the concept of interest. Thus, self-report of anxiety, physiological responsiveness in anxiety-provoking situations, and overt behavioral performance together may help estimate a person's anxiety. Combined measures that attempt to explore a concept with different operations may allow an investigator to place more confidence in assessing the concept of interest.

Most investigations in clinical psychology utilize a set of measures to operationalize different constructs. For example, an effective treatment might be expected to improve three domains of client functioning: client symptoms, work adjustment, and family interaction. Each domain of interest represents a construct. Each construct would be represented by two or more measures because individual measures are fallible and unlikely to capture the construct of interest. The investigator looks for consistency among measures of a given construct.

Advances in design and statistical analyses have expanded the methods of evaluating constructs and combining multiple measures. Within a given study, multiple measures (two or more) can be used to define a construct. The relations of the measures to each other, to the overall construct, and to other measures or outcomes can be examined. The notion of *latent variable* has been used to reflect the idea of a construct represented by several measures. The specific measures are referred to as *observed variables* and represent the construct of interest. Correlational analyses can evaluate the associations among observed variables and the extent to which they represent a single latent variable of interest. Because the latent variable is defined by several different measures, it is not confounded by the measurement error of a single measure.

Consider an example of the methods of operationalizing latent variables in the context of research on adolescent drug use (Newcomb & Bentler, 1988). The investigators were interested in identifying critical paths toward deviance during the course of adolescence and young adulthood, with particular focus on the role of early drug use. They assessed youths for a period of 4 years to understand the factors that predict outcomes in young adulthood and to identify causal paths toward deviance. Several constructs or domains of functioning (latent variables) during adolescence were assessed, each represented by multiple measures. The domains included drug use, social conformity, criminal activity, deviant peer networks, and others. Three separate measures were used to operationalize drug use: frequency of alcohol use (beer, wine, liquor), cannabis use (marijuana and hashish), and hard-drug use (tranquilizers, sedatives, barbiturates, heroin, cocaine, and several others). The three measures were assumed to reflect a general tendency toward drug use, that is, an overall latent variable or construct. Specific data-analytic techniques (e.g., confirmatory factor analyses) demonstrated that the observed variables were highly related and reliably reflected the construct of interest. It is worth noting that during adolescence, teenage drug use was significantly related to lower levels of social conformity, greater criminal activity, and having a deviant friendship network. Early drug use was related years later to reduction in academic pursuits (less involvement in college), job instability (unemployment, being fired), and increased psychoticism (e.g., disorganized thought processes). Although the latent variable, drug use, was associated with untoward long-term outcomes, the analyses permitted separate evaluation of different observed variables or operational definitions. That is, the different measures and types of drug use were analyzed separately. As might be expected, among drug-use measures in adolescence, hard-drug use had particularly untoward outcomes in young adulthood.

Generally, use of multiple measures to operationalize a construct (both the independent variable and dependent variable) is to be encouraged. (The advantage relates to the earlier discussion of construct validity of an experiment.) If our study shows that the predicted relation between two constructs (e.g., anxiety and social behavior) holds when each is measured in more than one way, this greatly strengthens our demonstration. When the finding holds for more that one measure, we have greater assurance that the finding is not unique to one special type of measure (e.g., a self-report questionnaire). The advantages of using multiple measures stem from overcoming the problems of narrow stimulus sampling.

There are some measures in psychology (e.g., Minnesota Multiphasic Personality Inventory 2, Wechsler Adult Intelligence Scale) that have been studied extensively and their relation to other measures and many other facets of behavior are well known. When one of these measures is used by itself to define a construct, there is less objection than would be the case if a less well-established measure or questionnaire were used. The underlying principle is that if the construct validity of a measure is well established, greater faith can be placed in subsequent research that invokes the construct when interpreting the results of that measure. Yet, any measure, however well-established, is restricted by using a particular assessment method (e.g., self-report, other report, or direct observation) and the results may be restricted to that method. A good guideline for research is to use multiple measures and few constructs, rather than vice versa.

Discrepancies among Definitions   Although it is useful to operationalize a construct in more than one way, investigators who do this may subsequently feel they were punished by an unwanted dose of reality. Different operational definitions can lead to different conclusions about the phenomenon of interest. For example, an area of active research within clinical psychology is the nature of depression among children. Depression has been operationalized with use of many different measures and different raters (child, parent, teacher, peers) to define depression of the child. Three commonly used ways consists of child or parent ratings of the child's depression on a standardized scale (e.g., Children's Depression Inventory) and psychiatric diagnosis (derived from separate interviews that draw on parent and child information). When all three methods are compared for the same sample, there is little overlap among the children who are identified as depressed (Kazdin, 1989). That is, children defined as depressed by one operational criterion were not the same children as those defined as depressed by another criterion. In addition, the differences between depressed and nondepressed children on measures of cognitive processes, social behavior, and self-esteem varied as a function of the method of operationalizing depression. This is not to suggest that every different method of operationalizing a construct leads to a specific and unique result; the point here is that differences are quite possible among varied ways of operationalizing constructs and they need to be examined.

One might challenge the entire research enterprise if different ways of defining a construct lead to different findings. Yet, different definitions do not invariably lead to differences. Also, we wish to understand discrepancies that might emerge. For example, one investigator may operationalize happiness on the basis of the number of smiles and positive statements a person makes in an interview; another investigator may operationalize the construct by having persons complete a scale in which they report the degree to which they are happy. Differences or discrepancies in these methods of operationalizing the construct are not "problems." We wish to understand as part of the elaboration of human functioning what accounts for the fact that all persons who smile frequently do not report themselves to be happy and all persons who say they are happy do not smile frequently.

General Comments   Research usually begins with an abstract notion or concept that reflects the construct of interest. For purposes of experimentation the concept is operationalized through one or more procedures or measures. The constructs that constitute both the independent and dependent variables are translated into specific procedures and measurement operations. The experiment demonstrates a relation between the independent and dependent variables, which are specified very concretely. After the experiment, the investigator usually wishes to go beyond the specific operations to the more abstract level of concepts. Thus, an experiment may demonstrate a particular relation under specific environmental conditions with concrete operational definitions of the independent and dependent variables; however, to go beyond the very specific demonstration requires assuming a broader relation. There are an infinite number of ways that a construct might be operationalized. In a given study, it is valuable to utilize multiple measures of the construct of interest to evaluate the generality of findings among different concrete measures or operations and sources of measurement error.

VARIABLES TO INVESTIGATE

Types of Variables

Defining the research idea in operational terms is an important step in moving toward the investigation itself. Another way to consider the initial stage of the research process is in terms of the types of variables that are studied. The specific idea or hypothesis is expressed in such a manner that some independent variable can be altered and evaluated. The independent variable of a study refers to the conditions that are varied or manipulated to produce change or, more generally, to the differences among conditions that are expected to influence subject performance. Three types of independent variables discussed here are environmental or situational variables, instructional variables, and subject variables.

Environmental or Situational Variables   Many variables of interest consist of altering the environmental or situational conditions of an experiment. An *environmental variable* consists of varying what is done to, with, or by the subject, that is, a given condition or task may be provided to some subjects but not provided to others (e.g., treatment vs. no treatment, medication vs. no medication). Alternatively, different amounts of a given variable may be manipulated (e.g., more treatment to some subjects than to others). Finally, the environmental variable may consist of providing qualitatively different conditions to the subjects (e.g., one type of feedback or message vs. another type within the experiment). The following questions illustrate the type of manipulations that would require varying an environmental or situational variable.

1. Does recording one's calorie consumption and weight after each meal alter eating habits? The environmental variable here would be the task of self-observation, which might be invoked for some subjects but not for others.

2. Does a prenatal care program for pregnant women increase the birth weight and decrease the birth complications of their newborns? Here the special intervention (e.g., home visits, counseling in diet, monthly physical exams) is an environmental variable.

3. Are some forms of psychotherapy more effective than others with depressed clients? Here the type of treatment given is the environmental variable.

Instructional Variables These variables refer to a specific type of environmental or situational manipulation. *Instructional variables* refer to variations in what the participants are told or are led to believe through verbal or written statements about the experiment and their participation. In the simplest situation, when instructional variables are manipulated, other environmental variables are held constant. Instructional variables usually are aimed at altering the participant's perception or evaluation of a situation or condition. The following experimental questions consists of manipulations of instructional variables.

1. Does telling clients that they are participating in a "treatment project that should alter their behavior" enhance the effects of a veridical treatment technique relative to telling clients they are participating in an "experiment that is not expected to alter their behavior"? Here, the treatment procedure is constant across groups. However, different instructions are compared to examine the influence of client expectancies on treatment outcome.

2. Do therapists interpret psychological test results differently when they are told that the test responses were produced by disturbed patients rather than by people functioning adequately in everyday life? The sample test responses given to different therapists might be identical, but the instructions to the therapists about who completed them would vary.

3. Does telling participants that their responses on psychological tests will be anonymous rather than identifiable influence their admission of socially undesirable behaviors? The task presented to the subject consists of a set of questions or items. Completion of the test is preceded by instructions that lead subjects to believe that their scores will or will not be anonymous.

Subject or Individual Difference Variables *Subject variables* refer to attributes or characteristics of the individual subjects. The way in which the term is used in psychology also encompasses characteristics to which subjects may be exposed (e.g., environmental contexts, living conditions). Subject variables are not usually manipulated directly. Rather, they are varied in an experiment by selecting subjects with different characteristics, experiences, attributes, or traits. Subject variables may include such obvious characteristics as age, education, social class, sex differences, exposure to trauma, or scores on some personality measure. In clinical psychology, special samples are frequently studied (e.g., depressed adults, physically or sexually abused children, families of patients with a diagnosis of schizophrenia, couples in conflict, twins, only children, individuals who are identified as intellectually gifted, persons of various cultural or ethnic background). In such studies, persons with or without the characteristic of interest or persons with varying degrees of that characteristic are compared.

The fact that the variables usually are called subject variables does not mean that only the attributes of individuals who are subjects are studied. Characteristics of therapists, interviewers, and experimenters also are subject variables and may be studied as such in experiments. Research on subject variables may seek to elaborate differences and similarities among varied groups. For example, depressed and nondepressed parents may be identified and then compared in the manner in which they interact with their newborn infants or with their children or spouses. Research on subject variables may also evaluate the differential responsiveness or reactions of some persons to other variables (e.g., psychotherapy, efforts to manipulate mood). The following questions illustrate the subject-variable research approach.

1. Do clients with more formal education gain more from verbal psychotherapy than do clients with less education? Here education is the subject variable. Participants may be categorized in the study as college degree versus no college degree or baccalaureate versus postbaccalaureate education.

2. Do persons who have tested positive for AIDS have increased stress compared with untested persons or persons who have tested negative? Here groups are selected to evaluate the potential impact of diagnostic information.

3. Does birth order of the individual (position of birth among one's siblings) influence professional accomplishments achieved in later life? Here adults who have, say, two siblings will be included. The adults might be placed into one of three groups according to whether they were born first, second, or third in relation to their two siblings.

Investigation of Multiple Variables

The discussion thus far may imply that a given investigation is restricted to studying only one type of variable. However, an investigation can examine multiple variables of a particular type or different types of variables within a single study. Indeed, combining variables across categories in a given study is an excellent research strategy and may address a host of important questions. For example, for research in psychotherapy, we do not merely wish to examine the effectiveness of varied treatments (an environmental variable). It is likely that the effects of a given treatment depend on a variety of other factors such as client characteristics (e.g., diagnosis, severity of problems) and therapist characteristics (e.g., competence, experience, warmth) (subject variables). To understand treatment and to identify optimally effective applications, studies that evaluate environmental variables in the context of subject variables can make a special contribution.

In general, a study that manipulates a single variable or single class of variables addresses a rudimentary question. This does not mean that the question is trivial. The importance of the question cannot be evaluated in the abstract; it is determined by the relation of the study to the existing literature, theory, practice, and other considerations. However, the complexity of the question is increased by combining variables and variables from separate classes (e.g., subject and environmental variables). The question addresses the impact of a given manipulation under varied conditions and hence represents a deeper understanding of how the variables of interest operate.

RESEARCH DESIGN OPTIONS

The initial stages of research entail development of the research idea and operationalization and selection of the specific variables of interest, as already highlighted. There remain a variety of options for research related to how the idea is evaluated and the conditions in which the study is conducted. The options have implications for diverse threats to validity and hence the conclusions that can be drawn. Although the different ways in which the study might be designed are detailed in subsequent chapters, an overview is useful to consider major design options in which the variables of interest may be evaluated.

Types of Research

Research in clinical psychology actively draws on three major types of studies: true experiments, quasi-experiments, and case-control designs. *True experiments* consist of investigations in which the arrangement permits maximum control over the independent variable or manipulation of interest. The investigator is able to assign subjects to different conditions on a random basis, to vary conditions (e.g., treatment and control conditions) as required by the design, and to control possible sources of bias within the experiment that permit the comparison of interest. As mentioned already, when true experiments are conducted in the context of a treatment study, they are referred to as randomized controlled clinical trials. True experiments is the more generic term to apply to studies with an intervention or experimental manipulation and random assignment of subjects to conditions. From the standpoint of demonstrating the impact of a particular variable of interest, true experiments permit the strongest basis for drawing inferences.

Occasionally the investigator cannot control all features that characterize true experiments. Some facet of the study, such as the assignment of subjects to conditions or of conditions to settings, cannot be randomized. *Quasi-experiments* refers to designs in which the conditions of true experiments are approximated (Campbell & Stanley, 1963). For example, an investigator may be asked to evaluate a school-based intervention program designed to prevent drug abuse or teen pregnancy. The investigator wishes to use a nonintervention control group because the passage of time and course of development (e.g., history, maturation, testing, and other internal validity threats) can lead to change. However, for practical reasons, a control condition is not permitted within the school that wishes the program. The investigator seeks other schools that will be non-intervention control groups and will be tested over time for comparison purposes. These other schools might be similar (e.g., in population, size, geography). However, some features of true experiments have already been lost. Assignment of children or schools to conditions is not random, and a host of factors (e.g., motivation for change among administrators) may differ greatly across conditions. Already the design is less ideal than one would like. Yet, there are many design options and methods of drawing valid inferences.

True and quasi-experiments refer primarily to studies in which an independent variable is manipulated by the investigator, for example, by providing treatment or an experimental condition to some persons but not to others. A great deal of clinical research focuses on variables that nature has manipulated in some way. *Case-control designs* refer to studies in which the variable of interest is studied by selecting subjects (cases) who vary in the characteristic or experience of interest. Case-control designs, as a term, is used frequently in epidemiology and public health but much less frequently in psychology. Nevertheless, the type of research to which this term is applied has been used frequently and has a long history in psychology. In psychology, the terms related to case-control studies are correlational research (Cronbach, 1957, 1975) or passive–observational studies; the relations among variables are observed but not manipulated. These designs are distinguished from experimental research in which variables are manipulated directly by the investigator.

As an example of a case-control design, the investigator might wish to study differences between cigarette smokers and nonsmokers in relation to particular personality traits or background characteristics; between marital partners who are in the same occupation versus those who are not; between males and females; between persons who were former prisoners of war and those who were not. Of course, the investigator does not manipulate the independent variable but does identify groups that vary in the characteristic of interest. A comparison group or groups are also identified to control for factors that may interfere with drawing conclusions. Case-control studies can provide critical insights about the nature of a problem, characteristic, or experience.

True experiments, as compared to case-control studies, are often considered as the only firm basis for drawing causal inferences in science, a clear demonstration that the independent variable led to the effects on the dependent variable. The strength of true experiments is without peer in demonstrating the impact of an independent variable, given the control afforded and the ways in which that control rules out a variety of explanations that might account for the results. Even so, true experiments are not flawless. A true experiment, however well-controlled, does not provide the basis for certainty of the finding. Also, case-control studies are not diluted experiments, invariably flawed, nor inherently incapable of yielding causal information. Ingenuity of the investigator in relation to selecting cases and advances in methodology and statistics (e.g., path analyses, causal modeling, structural equation modeling, cross-lagged panel correlations) permit strong inferences to be drawn from case-control studies. Interests of clinical research involve many questions about nature's interventions. Theory, methodology, and experimentation can be used to separate the impact of different variables when less than ideal experimental controls are available.

Design Strategies

Research in clinical psychology draws upon different types of designs. Group designs and single-case designs highlight the diversity of methods employed in clinical research. In *group designs,* several subjects are studied. Usually groups are formed by the investigator who assigns subjects to conditions and each group receives only one condition. Occasionally, the general class of designs is called *between-group research* because separate groups of subjects are used and each group receives only one condition of interest. A between-group design includes at least as many groups as there are experimental conditions or treatments. In addition, depending on the precise question or hypothesis of interest, control groups add to the number of groups in the study.

The effects of different experimental and control conditions across groups are evaluated statistically by comparing groups on the dependent measures. Preliminary assignment of subjects to groups is usually determined randomly to produce groups equivalent on factors possibly related to the independent variable (intervention) or that might also account for group differences on the measures (dependent variables). If groups are equivalent on such factors *before* the experimental manipulation or treatment, any differences among groups *after* the manipulation are assumed to result from the effects of different experimental conditions. In clinical research, a wide range of group designs are used and the diversity of this general type of research alone raises a plethora of methodological issues.

In addition to group designs, the field also entails *single-case experimental designs.* These designs are characterized by investigation of a given individual, a few individuals, or one group over time. The underlying approach toward research for group and single-case designs is identical, namely, to implement conditions that permit valid inferences about the independent variable. However, in single-case research, this is accomplished somewhat differently. Typically, one or a few subjects are studied. The dependent measures of interest are administered repeatedly over time (e.g., days or weeks). The manner in which the independent variable is implemented is examined in relation to the data pattern for the subject or group of subjects over time. Single-case designs play a special role in the field because in clinical work a central concern is the treatment of individual clients. Single-case designs can be used to experimentally evaluate the impact of a given intervention or multiple interventions. As with group designs, there are many different single-case designs, each with its own requirements, advantages, and obstacles.

Conditions of Experimentation

The conditions under which the investigation is conducted to test the ideas of interest can vary widely. In clinical psychology and related areas, the conditions-of-research distinction most frequently is that of *laboratory research* versus *applied research*. For example, laboratory research may consist of evaluation of the performance of college students who receive instructions designed to alter their mood, perform a task, or evaluate a video tape of another person. In contrast, research in an applied setting may be at a clinic in which patients are seen for treatment. The research may evaluate different types of treatment or evaluate different populations (e.g., persons referred for one type of problem vs. another type of problem). In laboratory and clinic-based research, the differences encompass more than the settings. Characteristics of the subjects, the nature of the dependent variable, and the research problems that emerge can also vary greatly. In the context of psychotherapy and counseling research, studies that evaluate treatment under conditions that only resemble or approximate the clinical situation have been referred to as *analogue research*. An analogue study usually focuses on a carefully defined research question under well-controlled conditions. The purpose of the research is to illuminate a particular process or to study treatment that may be important in clinical applications. The difficulty in controlling or isolating variables in clinical settings makes laboratory research more feasible.

Analogue research can refer to a wide range of studies. For example, one might conduct animal laboratory research to study the development or elimination of fears. Animal analogues are critical to clinical research and have been the basis for establishing the underpinnings of varied treatments for various clinical problems (e.g., anxiety). Analogue research has also consisted of interpersonal interactions in laboratory studies in which interviews or personal exchanges resemble in varying degrees the interactions of a therapist and patient in psychotherapy. The analogue conditions most widely discussed have been in relation to laboratory studies compared with clinic studies of different treatments. In this context, an analogue experiment means a study in which the conditions of the experiment depart from conditions of clinical work. Yet, in a sense, virtually all experimental research with human subjects is analogue research insofar as it constructs a situation in which a particular phenomenon can be studied. Informing participants that they are participating in research, evaluating controlled and time-limited interventions or experimental manipulations, using as outcome measures specific psychological assessment devices (e.g., questionnaires), and similar conditions make the situation analogous to one to which the investigator might wish to generalize. Rather than using laboratory research versus applied research, one might find it useful to consider in a more analytic fashion the many conditions of research and how these conditions may depart from conditions to which the investigator wishes to generalize.

Table 4.2 conveys several conditions or dimensions that the investigator may select for research in the context of understanding a particular intervention (e.g., treatment, prevention, education). A given study can vary along the different dimensions. The closer one moves toward the *right side* of the table (where conditions of the experiment do not well resemble clinical or applied settings), the greater the ability of the investigator to control facets of the investigation and hence rule out many threats to internal validity. The closer one moves toward the *left side* of the table (where conditions resemble applied settings), the greater the external validity, but also the more difficulty in controlling many facets of the study. The extent to which a study has generalizable results cannot be decided by merely looking at Table 4.2. Many dimensions listed in the table may not influence external validity, even though the study departs from the conditions of applied settings.

External validity is not the only issue to consider in deciding what experimental conditions to use. In some cases, there is no interest in generalizing to other settings, for example, when basic research is conducted to test theory or to understand a particular process (e.g., communication between couples, changes in cognitions as a function of special kinds of communication). Rather than being the setting in which research is done, external validity draws attention to the many ways generality can be discussed and whether the generality is likely to be restricted in light of how hypotheses about the phenomenon are investigated in the study.

Time Frame for Research

Research often varies in the time frame for investigation. The bulk of research is conducted in a concurrent time frame in which the independent variables of interest and the measures to evaluate them are administered and completed within a relatively brief period. An example is a laboratory experiment in which subjects are exposed to an independent variable and complete the measures within one or two laboratory sessions. In contrast, the investigation may be conducted over an extended period of, say, several years. Frequently a distinction is made between cross-sectional and longitudinal studies. *Cross-sectional studies* usually make comparisons between groups at a given point in time. *Longitudinal studies* make comparisons over an extended period, often several years. The results can be quite different even when similar questions are addressed.

For example, research has indicated that during the course of child development many behaviors bothersome to children or parents (e.g., stuttering, anxiety, destroying objects, lying) are common. Among nonclinic samples, the different problems wax and wane during the course of development, peak at

TABLE 4.2. Select Dimensions along Which Studies May Vary and Degree of Resemblance to the Clinical Situation

Dimension	Resemblance to the Clinical or Nonresearch Situation		
	Identity with or Great Resemblance	Moderate Resemblance	Relatively Low Resemblance
Target problem	Problem seen in the clinic, intense or disabling	Similar to that in clinic but less severe	Nonproblem behavior or experimental task
Population	Clients in outpatient treatment	College students with nontreatment interest	Infrahuman subjects
Manner of recruitment	Clients who seek treatment	Individuals recruited for available treatment	Captive subjects who serve for course credit
Therapists	Professional therapists	Therapists in training	Nontherapists or nonprofessionals
Client set	Expect treatment and improvement	Expect "experimental" treatment with unclear effects	Expect experiment with nontreatment focus
Selection of treatment	Client chooses therapist and specific treatment	Client given choice over few alternative procedures in an experiment	Client assigned to treatment with no choice for specific therapist or condition
Setting of treatment	Professional treatment facility	University facility that may not regularly offer treatment	Laboratory setting
Variation of treatment	Treatment as usually conducted	Variation to standardize treatment for research	Analogue of the treatment as in infrahuman equivalent of treatment
Assessment methods	Direct unobtrusive measure of the problem that the client originally reported	Assessment on psychological devices that sample behaviors of interest directly	Questionnaire responses about the behaviors that are a problem

different periods, and usually diminish to a very low rate. The pattern of behavior can be assessed concurrently by evaluating children of different ages (Achenbach, 1991). This is a cross-sectional study showing a pattern of behavior at different ages. This type of study *suggests* a developmental pattern, that is, how behaviors change in frequency over time. This is not the same as the yield from a longitudinal study in which a group is identified in infancy or childhood and then repeatedly assessed (e.g., every few years) during the course of childhood, adolescence, and adulthood (Werner & Smith, 1992). A longitudinal study portrays how behaviors actually *change* in a given sample because the same children are studied over time.

Neither type of study is inherently superior. Indeed, they have different strengths and limitations. For example, a cross-sectional study may suggest that children show different characteristics at different ages. Yet, there is a possible *cohort effect*, the possibility that different age groups of subjects (cohorts) may have unique characteristics because of their different histories. For example, when they mature, the 2-year-olds may not have the pattern of behavior of the 8-year-olds in the study, something about how the 2-year-olds are growing up (e.g., nutrition, different parenting styles, more or fewer parents in the home) influences their performance in ways not evident in the other group(s). Thus, in 6 years, when they are 8 years old, they will not look like the 8-year-olds included in the cross-sectional study.

In a longitudinal study, differential history of the group is controlled because one group or more than one group is followed over time. We know that the 2-year-olds matured into 8-year-olds with a particular pattern. There may also be a cohort effect within the longitudinal study because the 2-year-olds, who were followed over time, might differ from other 2-year-olds who were selected at a different point in time. Also, in longitudinal studies it is often difficult to follow the subjects. Attrition or loss of subjects over time can limit the conclusions because of selection biases if the sample is increasingly depleted. Longitudinal and cross-sectional design strategies are often combined by selecting a few groups (e.g., 4-, 6-, and 8-year-olds), assessing them cross-sectionally, and then following them for a few years (e.g., 2–4 years). The strategy speeds up the design a bit from merely following one sample and permits one to assess whether cohorts differ when they reach a given age (discussed further in a later chapter).

Evidence from different time frames can be used to address different questions or even the same question differently. For example, the investigator may be interested in the correlates among children of viewing violence on television, a topic that has received considerable attention. Within a current time perspective, the investigator might compare children who view violent television with those who watch as much television but who do not view violent programs. Children might be matched on diverse subject (e.g., age, sex, IQ) and demographic characteristics (e.g., socioeconomic status, type of neighborhood). Comparisons might then be made on other measures, such as personality characteristics of the child, the child's parents, or aggressive behavior of the child at home or at school. The purpose would be to elaborate the features associated with television viewing. As an alternative, a more longitudinal focus might include following (assessing) children over time. One question that might be asked is What are the correlates of early television viewing later in life? Both cross-sectional and longitudinal studies indicate that viewing violence on television is associated with aggressive behavior and that the relation is influenced by a variety of factors (e.g., sex of the child, success of children in school) (Strasburger, 1995). In general, the time frame is important to consider in designing research because, as we see later, conclusions often vary as a function of *when* the assessment is conducted over time.

SUMMARY AND CONCLUSIONS

The research idea that serves as a basis for experimentation may be derived from any of several sources, such as curiosity about a particular phenomenon, interest in an applied problem, unresolved of issues raised by previous research, predictions derived from psychological theory, and so forth. Research also may seek to illuminate how variables or characteristic are related as reflected in such concepts as correlates, risk factors, causes, moderators, and mediators. Whatever the initial idea, ultimately it needs to be specified in operational terms. Specific experimental operations, procedures, and measures define the independent and dependent variables. When the experiment begins, it is not the overall concept that is manipulated but the specific, operationally defined variable.

The variables that comprise clinical investigations usually include environmental, instructional, and subject variables. *Environmental variables* usually consist of manipulating what is offered, presented, or done to the client. *Instructional variables*, actually a subcategory of environmental variables, refer to what the client is told. *Subject variables* consist of attributes, traits, or characteristics of the subjects, experimenters, or therapists, or others. Subject variables are examined by selecting subjects with specific characteristics rather than by manipulating specific conditions.

Developing the research idea, operationalizing, and selecting the specific variables are initial stages of the study. A variety of design options emerge in relation to how the effect of the variables is actually examined. *True experiments*, *quasi-experiments*, and *case-control studies* were highlighted to define major types of research. Varied design strategies were noted by distinguishing *group* and *single-case research*. The conditions of experimentation can vary and include laboratory and applied or clinical settings. *Analogue research* was discussed to illustrate the issue of testing in the context of therapy research. Finally, the time frame of research was discussed as a condition that can vary among experiments. *Cross-sectional and longitudinal research* were noted to convey strategies that vary in the time frame. Design and method options vary in the advantages and disadvantages they provide. In the next chapters, we elaborate designs in clinical research and the issues they address and raise in relation to drawing valid inferences.

NOTE

[1]Dose–response relation is a term frequently used in epidemiology and public health and is designed to show a gradient in the relation between a proposed antecedent and outcome (Kazdin et al., 1997). For example, there is a dose–response relation between cholesterol and heart disease, cigarette smoking and cancer, ingestion of lead and child hyperactivity, and severity of accidental head injury and rates of later psychiatric impairment. Each finding comes from longitudinal studies in which the antecedent (e.g., cholesterol levels, smoking) occurred before the outcome. Demonstrating a dose–response relation between an antecedent variable and a later outcome is consistent with a causal relation between the antecedent and outcome. The relation makes less plausible that some other antecedent variable is responsible for the outcome, but does not firmly establish a causal role per se.

FOR FURTHER READING

Baron, R.M., & Kenny, D.A. (1986). The moderator-mediator variable distinction in social psychological research: Conceptual, strategic, and statistical considerations. *Journal of Personality and Social Psychology, 51,* 1173–1182.

Cattell, R.B. (1988). The principles of experimental design and analysis in relation to theory building. In J.R. Nesselroade & R.B. Cattell (Eds.), *Handbook of multivariate experimental psychology* (2nd ed., pp. 21–67). New York: Plenum.

Haynes, S.N. (1992). *Models of causality in psychopathology: Toward dynamic, synthetic, and nonlinear models of behavior disorders.* Needham Heights, MA: Allyn & Bacon.

Kazdin, A.E., Kraemer, H.C., Kessler, R.C., Kupfer, D.J., & Offord, D.R. (1997). Contributions of risk-factor research to developmental psychopathology. *Clinical Psychology Review, 17,* 375–406.

Kraemer, H.C., Kazdin, A.E., Offord, D.R., Kessler, R.C., Jensen, P.S., & Kupfer, D.J. (1997). Coming to terms with terms of risk. *Archives of General Psychiatry, 54,* 337–343.

Serlin, R.C. (1987). Hypothesis testing, theory building, and the philosophy of science. *Journal of Counseling Psychology, 34,* 365–371.

Wicker, A.W. (1985). Getting out of our conceptual ruts: Strategies for expanding conceptual frameworks. *American Psychologist, 40,* 1094–1103.

Chapter 5

Experimental Research

Group Designs

By far the most common method within clinical psychology is to compare groups of subjects who are exposed to different conditions that are controlled by the investigator. This strategy constitutes an experiment and typically includes two or more groups or conditions (e.g., intervention vs. control condition). The general strategy can entail a variety of different arrangements depending on the groups included in the design, how assessment is planned, and when and to whom the intervention is presented. In this chapter, we consider group design strategies in which the investigator manipulates or systematically varies conditions and controls the assignment of subjects to different conditions.

SUBJECT ASSIGNMENT AND GROUP FORMATION

A fundamental issue in group designs is assignment of participants to groups. Group differences after the experimental manipulation is invoked become the basis for inferring a causal relationship between the manipulation and performance on the dependent measures. Hence, there must be some assurance that groups would not have differed without the experimental manipulation or intervention. The manner in which subjects are assigned to groups influences the confidence that one can place in the initial equivalence of groups and, consequently, the likelihood that subsequent group differences reflect the effects of the manipulation rather than various threats to internal validity.

Random Selection

When investigators discuss randomization in experimentation, they usually are concerned with one of two concepts, namely, random selection of subjects from a population and random assignment of subjects to experimental conditions. In group designs within psychology, random assignment and related procedures to form groups are the central topics. Random selection is an independent issue that is not necessarily related to the particular design but warrants mention.

Random selection of subjects refers to the equal probability that subjects within the population can be selected. That is, on the basis of all subjects from which the sample might be drawn, there is no bias in who is selected. Random selection pertains to the generality (external validity) of experimental results among subjects. If we wish to generalize results from a sample of subjects in the experiment to a population of potential subjects, usually it is essential to select a representative sample of the population. For example, if we wish to draw conclusions about depressed patients in general, we would not want to restrict selection to patients in a particular hospital or clinic, in a particular city, state, or country; we would want to sample from all available persons. If subjects can be drawn from the entire population, it is more likely that the sample will represent the entire population. Generality of experimental results depends on the representativeness of the participants in the experiment to individuals who were not included, that is, the rest of the population. Random selection refers to drawing from the total population of interest in such a way that each member of the population has an equal probability of being drawn. If that is accomplished and the sample is relatively large, one can assume there is no special bias.

There is an obvious restriction to random selection in both principle and practice. Subjects in an experiment cannot be selected from a population unless that population is very narrowly defined. For example, for a population defined as "all introductory psychology students currently enrolled in a given term at this university," a random sample might be obtainable. However, a random sample of "introductory psychology students in general" could not be readily obtained. To sample the latter population would require being able to select from all individuals who have already taken introductory psychology, including persons no longer living, all students currently enrolled, and all who are yet to enroll (including unborn individuals) across all geographical settings. Sampling from all subjects in the population including persons who are deceased or yet to be born is obviously not possible. If generality of the experimental results to a population depends on having randomly sampled from a population, conclusions would seem to be restricted to the narrowly confined groups of subjects.

Random selection from a population is often central to research. For example, epidemiological research identifies the distribution of various conditions (e.g., diseases, mental disorders) within a population. In such studies, special sampling procedures are used to ensure that the sample represents the current population of interest. Usually, different segments or subgroups of a population (e.g., households, blocks within a neighborhood) are identified to reflect demographic variables of interest such as geography, social class, ethnicity, and religion. Within such groups, persons are selected randomly so that the final sample reflects this distribution. In survey and opinion-poll research, sampling from the population in this way is also critically important to ensure generality to that population, within some margin of error.

In clinical research, whether involving patient, college student, or community samples, random sampling from a population is not usually invoked. There are exceptions. For example, one study was designed to evaluate and to treat cigarette smokers and to sample from two communities in a way that the results would represent the population within these communities (Killen et al., 1996). The selection began by calling segments of the population to represent the larger communities; this included random-digit dialing (because many residents had unlisted phone numbers). Once a home was called, all adults who were smokers were identified and asked to be interviewed, and they were eventually invited (with a opportunity to win $100) for treatment. This is a complex procedure and includes several hurdles in obtaining the final sample; therefore, the final sample (e.g., who agrees to participate) may not represent the population. Even so, the effort is likely to represent the community much better than a study that recruits a sample from one or two sources.

In most psychological studies, a representative sample is not considered essential, nor is its absence viewed as an issue. Also, sometimes very special populations are selected by the investigator because they are available for another purpose and are thus convenient. Special characteristics of the sample may raise concerns. However, a general operating assumption is that lawful relationships from experiments with a given sample are likely to hold for other individuals who are similar. Results obtained with college students at one university would be expected usually to hold for similar students at another university. Of course, many variables that would be assumed to be unimportant across samples, including geography, could lead to differences in experimental results.

Many variables across which one wishes to generalize may be irrelevant to the lawful relation discovered in the initial experiment. For example, assume we have developed an effective psychotherapy to treat agoraphobia (fear of open spaces) among young adults. It is parsimonious to assume initially that the treatment will be effective for males and females, young and old adults, and various ethnic and racial groups. The justification of generalizing results can come from direct experimental extensions to these other samples or from inferences about the likelihood that basic processes demonstrated in research vary as a function of different subject or other variables. It is quite possible (and in a given case, maybe even likely) that generality might not hold. As a general rule, the variables across which the results of a given finding can be extended must be determined empirically. However, we do not want to study whether the relation generalizes across *all* possible conditions. Theory is very relevant as a way of suggesting what dimensions might influence generality of the finding and generating hypotheses about why the phenomenon would be evident in one set of circumstances or for some subjects but not others.

Random Assignment

The central issue in group research is the assignment of participants to groups. Once a sample of subjects has been specified, individual members can be assigned to groups in an unbiased fashion. *Random assignment* consists of allocating subjects to groups in such a way that the probability of each subject's appearing in any of the groups is equal. This is usually accomplished by determining from a table of random numbers the group to which each subject is assigned. For example, if there are three groups in the experiment, a random-numbers table can be consulted to draw numbers 1, 2, and 3, corresponding to each group several times in random order. The numbers are listed in the order in which they are drawn from the table (e.g., 1, 1, 3, 2, 3, 3, etc.). (Numbers other than 1, 2, or 3 in the table are ignored.) As the subjects arrive to the experiment, they are assigned to the groups in order according to the number that was drawn. Thus, the first two subjects in our study would be assigned to group 1, the third to group 3, and so on in order. With such assignment, subjects are effectively assigned to groups randomly according to the predetermined schedule.

Drawing random numbers to determine group assignment does not guarantee that an equal number of subjects would be assigned to each group. In the above example, the number 3 may be drawn from the table more times than the numbers 1 and 2; thus, more subjects would be assigned to this group than the other groups. For power of statistical tests (statistical conclusion validity) and convenience in conducting several statistical analysis, it is better to have equal rather than unequal group sizes. This can be accomplished without violating random assignment by grouping subjects into blocks. Each block consists of the number of subjects that equals the number of groups in the experiment. If there are three groups, the first three subjects who appear in the experiment can be viewed as one block. One subject from this block of three would be assigned to each of the three groups. Of importance, the group to which any individual is assigned within a block is random. Assignment is accomplished by drawing numbers 1, 2, and 3 in any order as long as each block encompasses each number

(1, 2, 3) only once. Assigning subjects on the basis of numbers drawn in this way ensures that, as the experiment progresses, groups will not differ in size and that subjects in each group run through the course of the experiment.

Random assignment is obviously important and seems too basic to warrant comment. However, the simplicity of random assignment as a procedure, that is, how it is accomplished, belies greater complexities. Random assignment does not necessarily guarantee that groups are equivalent. Even so, random assignment is the best guarantee of making implausible various threats to internal validity (e.g., selection x history, selection x maturation) and for addressing the range of unintended influences (e.g., different subject characteristics in the groups) that might contribute to group differences.

Random assignment is important on a priori grounds, but does it make a difference in any palpable way? A recent analysis of marital and family-therapy research compared studies in which cases were randomly assigned to conditions with those in which they were not (Shadish & Ragsdale, 1996). The strength of the effects were greater and less variable for studies that used random assignment. This is interesting because few studies have looked at the impact of random assignment on results. Yet, the primary rationale for using random assignment is to facilitate interpretation of the effects we obtain, apart from any impact that assignment may have on the results themselves. Although randomly assigning cases to conditions is the preferred method of assigning subjects, in many situations in which researchers work (e.g., clinics, hospitals, schools), doing this is not possible. This does not in any way doom the study to weak inferences. Indeed, one's knowledge of principles and practices of methodology becomes more important in this context to ensure that valid and strong inferences can be reached.

Group Equivalence

Random assignment is important as a means of distributing characteristics of the sample among groups. There are several subject characteristics (e.g., age, sex, current historical events, motivation for participation), circumstances of participation (e.g., order of appearance, entry into the study), and other factors that might, if uncontrolled, interfere with interpretation of group differences. In some studies, evaluating the impact of these variables may be the central purpose. In other studies, they might be regarded as "nuisance" variables that, if uncontrolled, will obscure interpretation. Random assignment is a way of ensuring that nuisance variables will be distributed unsystematically across groups. An advantage of random assignment is that it does not require the investigator to be aware of all important variables that might be related to the outcome of the experiment. Over a sufficient number of subjects, the many different nuisance variables can be assumed to be distributed evenly among groups.

Random assignment sometimes is viewed as a dependable way of producing equivalent groups. Yet, random assignment refers only to the method of allocating subjects to groups and in a given experiment has no necessary connection with a particular outcome. Randomly assigning subjects can produce groups that differ on all sorts of measures. Group differences are more likely when sample sizes are small and when there are extreme scores in the sample. As an extreme example, if there are 15 subjects to be allocated to three groups and the subjects vary widely in age, level of anxiety, and other subject variables, it is quite possible that groups may differ significantly on these variables even after random assignment.

It is important to underscore that random assignment does not necessarily produce equivalent groups. With random assignment, the likelihood that groups are equivalent increases as a function of the sample size. This means that with small samples, group equivalence cannot be assumed. This is especially relevant to clinical research, for example, in studies of psychotherapy in which sample sizes may be relatively small (e.g., 10–20 subjects per group) (Kazdin & Bass, 1989). When the total sample (N) is in this range (e.g., 20–40 subjects total in a two-group study), the likelihood that groups are not equivalent across a number of nuisance variables is relatively high (Hsu, 1989). The net effect is that, at the end of the study, the difference between groups due to the intervention may be obscured or misrepresented because of the nonequivalence of groups.

Investigators wish to establish that the groups are equivalent by comparing groups after their random assignment on such variables as age, sex, IQ, years of institutionalization, and pretest performance on the measure of interest. The absence of differences (by nonsignificant t tests or analyses of variance) may provide false comfort that the groups are equivalent. When the samples are relatively small, statistical power (sensitivity) to detect differences is weak. Thus, the situation in which random assignment is least likely to obtain equivalence (small samples) is also one in which such differences may be the most difficult to detect. Investigators may feel that the absence of significant differences will satisfy others (e.g., reviewers, advisors). However, the systematic variation that was not detected between groups can still obscure the findings and lead to misleading results. With larger samples, the absence of differences between groups on subject variables and pretreatment measures provides greater assurance of group equivalence. Even so, such results do not establish absolutely that the groups are equivalent. Groups still may differ on some variable, relevant or irrelevant to the experimental manipulation, and in performance on the dependent measures that the investigator did not assess. In general, random assignment remains vitally important as a concept and procedure. However, there is a belief that the procedure guarantees group equivalence in situations in which this is not likely, that is, when the sample size is relatively small (Hsu, 1989; Tversky & Kahneman, 1971). Use of larger than usual sample sizes (e.g., > 40 subjects in each group) can increase the confidence in the equivalence of groups.

Matching

Often the investigator does not wish to leave to chance the equivalence of groups for a given characteristic of the sample. If a specific subject variable is known to relate to scores on the dependent measure, it is important to take this variable into account to ensure that groups do not differ prior to treatment. For example, it is possible that randomly assigning clients seeking treatment for anxiety could result in one of the treatment groups having participants who were more anxious prior to treatment than those in one of the other groups. Group differences after treatment could be directly influenced by severity of anxiety of the groups before treatment began. It is undesirable prior to the intervention to allow groups to differ on a variable that is highly related to performance on the dependent measure. This is especially obvious if the difference is on the pretest measure of the treatment problem. Even with random assignment, groups might differ in level of anxiety prior to treatment. Obviously, such initial differences can obscure conclusions. The best way to ensure equivalence of groups on a particular dimension is to match subjects on the dimension and then assign subjects randomly to groups. *Matching* refers to grouping subjects together on the basis of their similarity on a particular characteristic or set of characteristics. By matching, subjects at each level of the characteristic appear in each group and the groups do not differ on that characteristic prior to treatment.

Matching can be accomplished in different ways. Consider, for example, a two-group experiment that is designed to investigate the effectiveness of treatments for depression. Prior to treatment, the subjects complete a measure of depression. One way to match subjects is to look for pairs of subjects with *identical pretreatment scores*. When two subjects with the same scores are found, each is assigned to one of the two groups in an unbiased fashion (e.g., using a random-numbers table or coin toss). This is continued with all pairs of subjects with identical scores. If enough pairs of subjects are available and are assigned to groups, pretreatment mean depression scores for the groups would be identical. Yet, looking for sets of identical scores to match subjects is usually prohibitive because it means that most subjects who did not have a score identical to another subject's score would not be used. Thus large numbers of subjects would need to be assessed to find enough subjects to fill the groups.

A more commonly used procedure is to *rank all the subjects*, in this case from high to low depression scores. If there are three groups in the experiment, the first three subjects with the highest scores form the first block. These three subjects are assigned randomly so that one member of this block appears in each group. The three subjects with the next highest scores form the next block and are assigned randomly to each group, and so on until all subjects are used. This method of assignment utilizes all subjects by drawing them from the ranks in blocks of three (or whatever number of groups there are) and assigning them randomly to each of the groups. Matching followed by random assignment can equalize groups on the characteristic of interest. The advantage of this procedure is that it does not leave to chance the equivalence of groups on the characteristic(s) of interest.

In some cases, the investigator may wish to ensure that the groups are equivalent on a categorical variable, such as subject sex or ethnicity. Random assignment may not ensure that the proportion of subjects assigned to each group will be the same. One way to avoid this problem is to develop the random order of assignment of subjects to conditions (as already discussed) but to have separate lists for, say, males and females. Thus, if the first two subjects who arrive at the experiment are males, they are assigned (randomly) to each of the two groups (e.g., treatment, control) of the experiment. If the next person to arrive is a female, she is assigned randomly to the first condition on a separate list for female subjects. Assignments continue in this fashion by separate lists. Since each list includes a long stream of 1s and 2s (to indicate assignment to group 1 or 2), the proportion of subjects of each sex will be equal or close to equal no matter how many males or females come into the study. If the overall ratio of males to females who participate in the study is 3:1, the ratio will be reflected in each group. One refers to this in describing the procedure as random assignment with the restriction that an equal number of cases of each sex were assigned to each condition.

Implicit in the discussion is interest in the nature of the variables that are used for purposes of matching. Subjects are matched on the variables that are either known or assumed to be related to performance on the dependent measure. For example, in a treatment study, matching on initial severity of dysfunction, as measured by a pretest, is reasonable because pretest performance is likely to be related to posttest performance, and one may not want to leave group equivalence to chance (i.e., assume that random assignment will take care of equivalence). Other variables may be expected to relate to the outcome (e.g., diagnosis, age, birth order, and self-concept) and be the basis of matching. Matching is not essential or inherently valuable in its own right. An investigator matches groups when he or she knows or suspects that the characteristic relates to performance on the dependent measures.

Mismatching

The critical component of matching is random assignment. Subjects are matched first and then randomly assigned to groups. Occasionally, matching has been used in an attempt to equalize groups in which random assignment is not possible. For example, consider a treatment study in which the investigator wishes to compare two forms of psychotherapy administered to clients who come for outpatient treatment. Two different clinics are used in a particular city, and each clinic receives one or the other form of treatment. Clients referred to the clinics are not under the control of the investigator, that is, they cannot be randomly assigned. Therefore, it is possible that, at the end of the study, treatment A (at clinic 1) and treatment B (at clinic 2) will appear differentially effective because groups at the different clinics were not similar to begin with. The investigator might reasonably wish to evaluate treatment on clients who are equal in severity of impairment. Assume that the investigator assesses severity of symptoms from intake clinician ratings or from a self-report measure from the clients. Assume further that the scores on the measures can vary from 0 to 100, with a higher score indicating greater severity of symptoms.

The clients at the two clinics may differ in overall severity of symptoms be-cause they come from somewhat different populations (e.g., segments of the city). Yet, there is likely to be some overlap of scores. The scores of clients from each clinic in this hypothetical example are illustrated in Figure 5.1. Each nor-mal distribution in the figure represents the distribution of scores for one clinic. Note that clients at clinic 2 generally have higher scores. However, the distribu-tion of scores from the clinics overlap, as reflected in the scores that fall within the shaded area that crosses both distributions. The investigator may equalize severity of the cases in the study by drawing cases with similar scores (only the cases within the shaded area). In some sense, the clients have been matched be-

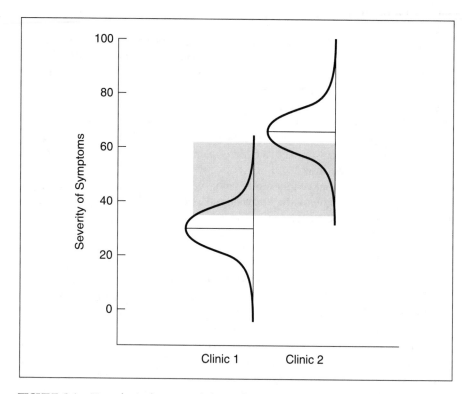

FIGURE 5.1   Hypothetical scores of clients from two different clinics. The two distributions represent all scores for the clients at the respective clinics. The *shaded* area reflects cases with similar scores across the two clinics and cases that might be matched across the clinics. At clinic 1, the cases are individuals with the highest scores (more symptoms, above their group mean); at clinic 2 the cases are individuals with the lowest scores (few symptoms, below their group mean). To the extent there is error in measurement, at a second assessment the cases will regress to the means of their respective distributions.

cause in each clinic the clients have equal or approximately equal mean symptom severity scores. Unfortunately, this matching procedure is problematic.

Each client's score is made up of a true level of symptoms plus error associated with factors such as the unreliability of the assessment device and daily fluctuations in client behavior. The error in measurement is reflected in the fact that scores from one testing to another are imperfectly correlated. Scores that are extremely high on one day are likely to be slightly lower on the next. Conversely, scores that are extremely low one day are likely to be slightly higher on the next testing. As a general rule, the more extreme the score, the more likely it is to revert in the direction of the group mean on subsequent assessment. Not every high score will become lower and not every low score will become higher, but on the average the scores at each extreme will revert or regress toward the mean.

Regression toward the mean is a statistical phenomenon that is related to the correlation between initial test and retest scores. *The lower the correlation, the greater the amount of error in the measure and the greater the regression toward the mean.* The problem with matching subjects who are in preassigned groups is that scores in each group may regress toward a different mean. Even if subjects across groups are selected because their scores are equal, the groups may come from populations with different means and be at different places in the distribution of scores in their respective groups. Hence, subsequent testing might lead to group differences merely because the groups regress toward their respective means.

Regression can lead to posttreatment differences even when treatment has no effect. In the present example, the clients selected for the experiment from the two different clinics might be reassessed at some later point. One would expect merely on the basis of regression that certain changes would take place in symptom scores. Clients from clinic 1 would be expected to show a *decrease* in their scores on reassessment because clients from this group were above their group mean of symptom severity. In contrast, clients from clinic 2 would be expected to show an *increase* in severity of symptoms because their scores tended to be below their group mean. In short, on reassessment, each sample will revert toward its group mean. If different treatments were administered at the clinics, the investigator might conclude that the treatment at clinic 1 really helped the clients (reduced symptoms), whereas the treatment at clinic 2 made clients worse (increased symptoms). Unfortunately, this change on reassessment may have occurred independently of the interventions merely on the basis of regression.

In general, regression is of concern when subjects are selected because of their extreme scores. In such cases, depending on the test–retest correlation, subjects at the extreme levels are likely to revert toward the mean. The error that contributed to their extreme scores on one occasion is less likely to operate in the same direction on the next assessment occasion. Thus, on retesting, their scores are likely to revert toward the mean.

There are two problems to bear in mind, both of which are threats to internal validity. The first regression problem is differential regression (selection x regression), that is, subjects in different groups show regression but they regress to different means. This is a possibility in situations in which intact groups are used and, by definition, random assignment to conditions is not possible. When random assignment *is* possible, differential regression is not likely to be a plausible explanation for group differences at the end of the study. The second regression problem was presented in the discussion of threats to internal validity. In this variation, all groups show an improvement from pre- to posttreatment, and no differences are evident between groups or in the amount of improvement a the second assessment. In such cases, regression might explain why everyone improved; namely, cases were selected because they were extreme (screening criterion) and assigned randomly to groups. However, all subjects as a group were likely to regress (show lower scores); when they do, it could be a result of treatment or simply statistical regression. This version of regression is relatively common among studies in which two or more interventions are compared and no control group is included in the design (Ouimette, Finney, & Moos, 1997; Vostanis et al., 1996).

SELECTED GROUP DESIGNS

Assigning subjects to groups in an unbiased fashion is one of the major defining characteristics of group experiments. Again, by "experiments" we are referring to studies in which the investigator is manipulating conditions, that is, controls the delivery of some procedure, intervention, or experimental manipulation. Subject allocation refers to how the groups are formed, not to the experimental design. Several different experimental designs commonly used in clinical psychology are discussed here along with their strengths and weaknesses. To illustrate the designs, the sequence of events in the design (assessment, intervention) for each group is presented symbolically using the following notation: R, random assignment of subjects to conditions; O, observation or assessment; and X, experimental manipulation or treatment (Campbell & Stanley, 1963). The symbols are presented in temporal order so that, for example, $O_1 X O_2$ signifies that the first observation or pretest (O_1) was followed by an intervention (X) followed by the second observation or posttest (O_2).

Pretest–Posttest Control Group Design

The pretest–posttest design consists of a minimum of two groups. One group receives treatment and the other does not. The essential feature of the design is that subjects are tested before and after the intervention. Thus, the effect of the intervention is reflected in the amount of change from pre- to postintervention assessment. In this design, subjects are assigned randomly to groups either prior to or after completion of the pretest. (Again, R denotes that subjects are assigned randomly; O an observation or assessment, and X the intervention.) The design can be diagrammed as follows:

$$R \quad O_1 \quad X \quad O_2$$
$$R \quad O_3 \qquad O_4$$

This design enjoys wide use in clinical psychology. The administration of a pretest and posttest allows assessment of the amount of change as a function of the intervention. Although all experimentation is interested in change, assessment of the amount of change is particularly important in treatment research. Treatment research is devised to determine how much change was made and how many clients made a change of a particular magnitude. Also, severity of impairment prior to treatment may be an important source of information for predicting whether clients are likely to profit from certain kinds of treatment. For these reasons, a pretest is essential.

Considerations in Using the Design The design has several strengths. To begin with, the design controls for the usual threats to internal validity. If intervening periods between pre- and posttreatment assessment are the same for each group, threats such as history, maturation, repeated testing, and instrumentation are controlled. Moreover, random assignment from the same population reduces the plausibility that group differences have resulted from either selection bias or differential regression (i.e., to different means). Loss of subjects is not an inherent problem with the design, although, as in any experiment, differential loss of subjects could interfere with drawing a conclusion about the intervention.

The use of a pretest provides several advantages. First, the data obtained from the pretest allow the investigator to match subjects on different variables and to assign subjects randomly to groups. Matching permits the investigator to equalize groups on pretest performance. Second and related, the pretest data permit evaluation of the effect of different levels of pretest performance. Within each group, different levels of performance (e.g., high and low) on the pretest can be used as a variable in the design to examine whether the intervention varied in impact as a function of the initial standing on the pretested measure. Third, the use of a pretest affords statistical advantages for the data analysis. By using a pretest, within-group variability is reduced and more powerful statistical tests of the intervention, such as analyses of covariance or repeated measures analyses of variance, are available than if no pretest were used (see Chapter 14). Fourth, the pretest allows the researcher to make specific statements about change, such as how many clients improved. In clinical research, in which individual performance is very important, the pretest affords information beyond mere group differences at posttreatment. One can evaluate the persons who did or did not change and generate hypotheses about the reasons. The pretest permits identification of the persons who changed. Finally, by using a pretest, we can look at attrition in a more analytic fashion than would be the case without a pretest. If subjects are lost over the course of the study, a comparison can be made among groups by looking at pretest scores of those who dropped out versus those who remained in the study. If only a few subjects dropped out, a comparison of dropouts and completers may not be very powerful statistically. Yet, the comparison may show differences, may generate hypotheses about who drops out and why, or may suggest that even with very lenient criteria (e.g., $p < .20$) dropouts and completers do not seem to differ on the variables evaluated. The pretest allows examination of the plausibility of these alternatives.

There are some weaknesses to the pretest–posttest treatment control group design. The main restriction pertains to the influence of administering a pretest. A simple effect of testing, that is, repeatedly administering a test, is controlled in the basic design. What is not controlled is the possibility of an interaction of testing x treatment or a pretest sensitization effect. Possibly the intervention had its effect precisely because the pretest sensitized subjects to the intervention. A pretest sensitization effect means that the results of the study can be generalized only to subjects who received a pretest.

Whether there is a pretest sensitization effect cannot be assessed in this design. The likelihood of sensitization depends on several factors. If assessment and the intervention are not close together in time or are unrelated in the perceptions of the subject, sensitization probably is less likely. Therefore, a pretest administered immediately prior to an intervention in the context of the experiment is more likely to lead to sensitization than is assessment in a totally unrelated setting (e.g., in class or in a door-to-door survey at the subject's home) several weeks prior to treatment. Yet, the more remote the pretest from the posttest in time and place, the less adequate it may be as a pretest. Intervening events and processes (e.g., history, maturation) between pretest and posttest obscure the effects that can otherwise be more readily attributed to the experimental manipulation. In general, the strengths of the design clearly outweigh the threat that pretest sensitization will obscure the findings. The information about subject status prior to intervening, the use of this information to match cases and to evaluate change, and the statistical advantages are compelling.

Posttest-Only Control Group Design

The posttest-only design consists of a minimum of two groups and is essentially is the same as the previous design except that no pretest is given. The effect of the intervention is assessed on a postintervention measure only. The design can be diagrammed as follows:

$$R \quad X \quad O_1$$

$$R \qquad O_2$$

The absence of the pretest makes this design less popular in clinical research for at least two reasons. First, in clinical research, it is often critical to know the level of functioning of persons prior to the intervention. For example, in studies designed to treat or prevent various disorders, it is important to establish that the clients were dysfunctional or at risk for dysfunction prior to the intervention. In cases in which screening criteria are used to identify subjects, pretest assessment is critical to examine whether clients begin at the intended level of functioning. Second, the lack of a pretest raises the discomforting possibility that group differences after the intervention might be the result of differences between groups prior to the intervention. Of course, random assignment of subjects, particularly with large numbers of subjects, is likely to equalize groups, and there is no more likelihood that random assignment will produce different groups prior to treatment with this design than in the previous design. Admittedly, however, there is no assurance that groups are similar on specific measures prior to treatment, a luxury afforded by the previous design.

Considerations in Using the Design   The design controls for the usual threats to internal validity in much the same way as the previous design. The absence of a pretest means that the effect of the intervention could not result from initial sensitization. Hence, the results could not be restricted in their generality to only subjects who have received a pretest.

Often a pretest may not be desirable or feasible. For example, in brief laboratory experiments, the investigator may not wish to know the initial performance level or to expose subjects to the assessment task before they experience the experimental manipulation. Also, large numbers of subjects might be available and randomly assigned to different conditions in such experiments. With large numbers of subjects and random assignment to the groups, the likelihood of group equivalence is high. Assurances of equivalent performance on premeasures may be of less concern to the investigator.

Certainly another feature that must be considered is that a pretest is not always available in clinical research. In many cases the assessment effort is very costly, and a pretest might be prohibitive. For example, an extensive battery of tests might serve as the outcome measures. The time required to administer and interpret an assessment battery may be several hours, which might make the pretest not worth the cost or effort. Indeed, from a practical standpoint, there may be no alternative but to omit the pretest. Ethical considerations also may argue for omission of the pretest, if, for example, a pretest might be stressful to the subjects.

The weaknesses of the posttest-only control group design derive from the disadvantages of not using a pretest. Thus, the inability to ensure that groups are equivalent on the pretest, to match subjects on pretest performance prior to random assignment, or to study the relation between pretest standing and behavior change; the lack of pretest information to evaluate differential attrition across groups; and reduced statistical power are all consequences of foregoing a pretest. Apart from these disadvantages, demonstration of the equivalence of groups at pretest and prior to any intervention is often comforting both to the investigator and to those who examine or review the work. As already noted, with small samples "no differences" on pretreatment performance may not mean that the groups are equivalent. Even so, it is more assuring to have data in favor of equivalence than to omit a pretest altogether. In general, several of the advantages of a pretest may not be of interest to the investigator. The statistical advantage of repeated observations that the pretest provides remains a decided advantage of the pretest–posttest design.

Solomon Four-Group Design

The effects of pretesting (pretest sensitization) were discussed in each of the above designs. The purpose of the Solomon four-group design is to evaluate the effect of pretesting on the effects obtained with a particular intervention (Solomon, 1949). That is, does administering a pretest influence the results? To address this question, a minimum of four groups is required. The four groups in the design are the two groups in the pretest–posttest control group design plus the other two groups of the posttest-only control group design. The Solomon four-group design can be diagrammed as follows:

$$
\begin{array}{ccccc}
R & O_1 & X & O_2 \\
R & O_3 & & O_4 \\
R & & X & O_5 \\
R & & & O_6
\end{array}
$$

Considerations in Using the Design   The design controls for the usual threats to internal validity. The effects of testing per se can be evaluated by comparing two control groups that differ only in having received the pretest (i.e., comparison of O_4 and O_6). More important, the interaction of pretesting and the intervention can be assessed by comparing pretested and unpretested groups (i.e., comparison of O_2 and O_5). The data can also be analyzed to evaluate the effects of testing and the testing x treatment interaction. To accomplish this, the posttreatment assessment data for each group are combined into a 2 x 2 factorial design and analyzed with a two-way analysis of variance. Only the following observations are used: O_2, O_4, O_5, and O_6. The factors in the analysis are testing (pretest vs. no pretest) and treatment (treatment vs. no treatment). Other methods of analyzing the data from the design are also available (Braver & Braver, 1988).

Another feature of the design is that it includes replication of treatment and control conditions. The effect of treatment (X) is replicated in several different places in the design. The effect of treatment can be attested to by one within-group comparison (O_2 vs. O_1) and several between-group comparisons (e.g., O_2 vs. O_4; O_5 vs. O_6; O_5 vs. O_3 or O_1). If a consistent pattern of results emerges from these comparisons, the strength of the demonstration is greatly increased over designs that allow a single comparison. Yet, there is a price for the gain in elegance and strength of inferences this design provides. As noted earlier, the experiment can be conceptualized as two smaller experiments. Twice the effort and costs are involved in the number of subjects run, the amount of data collected, and so on. To justify the extra effort the investigator usually would want to be primarily interested in evaluating pretest sensitization.

The design may appear to be somewhat esoteric because sensitization effects rarely enter into theoretical accounts of clinical phenomena. Yet, sensitization occasionally has important implications beyond design considerations. For example, in one study, a Solomon four-group design was used to evaluate the impact of a suicide awareness program for high-school students (Spirito et al., 1988a). The intervention consisted of a school curriculum designed to increase knowledge about suicide and to prevent or decrease the likelihood of suicide. Some students received the curriculum; others did not. Within these groups, some were pretested on measures related to knowledge about and attitudes toward suicide and hopelessness. The curriculum increased positive attitudes and reduced hopelessness. The finding is noteworthy because hopelessness is related to suicide; altering hopelessness may affect the likelihood of suicide. The effects of the intervention in this study were more marked for those who received the pretest (i.e., a pretest sensitization effect). Replication of the findings would be very important because they suggest a way to augment the effects of intervention programs.[1]

Additional research efforts probably should be directed at studying the effects of pretesting. The pretest–posttest control group design is used extensively and the influence of pretesting is rarely studied in the contexts of clinical research. A few studies using the Solomon four-group design in well-researched areas might be very valuable. Demonstrations across dependent measures might establish that, in clinical research with widely used measures or interventions, pretest sensitization is restricted to a narrow set of conditions or may not occur at all.

Factorial Designs

The above designs consist primarily of evaluating the impact of a single independent variable. For example, the independent variable (e.g., treatment) may be given to one group but withheld from another group. Alternatively, different versions of treatment might be provided across several groups. Whatever the variations, the studies basically evaluate one independent variable.

The main limitation of single-variable experiments is that they often raise relatively simple questions about the variable of interest. The simplicity of the questions should not demean their importance. In relatively new areas of research, the simple questions are the bedrock of subsequent experiments. However, more complex and refined questions can be raised. For example, a single-variable experiment might raise the question of which treatment works better for a particular clinical problem or whether experienced therapists exert more impact than nonexperienced therapists. A more complex question might be raised by including more than one variable. For example, are certain treatments more effective with certain types of therapists or clients? This type of question is somewhat more specific and entails evaluation of the separate and combined effects of two or more variables.

Factorial designs allow the simultaneous investigation of two or more variables (factors) in a single experiment. Within each variable, two or more conditions are administered. In the simplest factorial design, two variables (e.g., therapist experience and type of treatment) each consist of two different levels (e.g., experienced vs. inexperienced therapists and treatment A vs. treatment B). In this 2 x 2 design, there are four groups that represent each possible combination of the levels of the two factors (Figure 5.2).

Of course, a factorial design is not a single design but a family of designs that vary in the number and types of variables and the number of levels within each variable. The variation of factorial designs also is influenced by whether a pretest is used. If a pretest is used, testing can become one of the variables or factors (time of assessment) with two (pretest vs. posttest) or more levels. The data can be analyzed to assess whether subjects changed with repeated assessment independently of a particular intervention.

In single-variable experiments, one manipulation is of interest; all other variables that might influence the results are controlled. In a factorial experiment, multiple variables are included to address questions about separate and combined effects of different variables. The variables that are included in the factorial design are not merely controlled, their effect is evaluated as distinct variables in the design. For example, a factorial design might evaluate the influence of

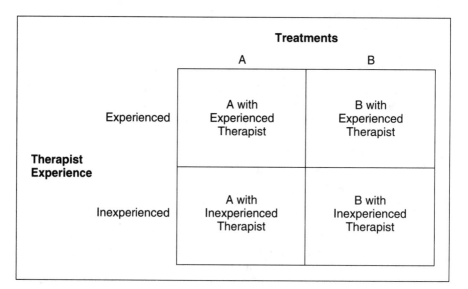

FIGURE 5.2   Hypothetical factorial design comparing two independent variables (factors), therapist experience and type of treatment. Each factor has two different levels of conditions, which makes this a 2 x 2 factorial design.

characteristics of the subject (e.g., sex of the client), the therapist (e.g., degree of warmth during the therapy session), variations of treatment (e.g., treatments A, B, or C), and duration of therapy (e.g., number of sessions). These general classes of variables may be combined in a single study to ask pointed questions about the conditions under which variables exert their effects.

A major reason for completing a factorial experiment is that the combined effect of two or more variables may be of interest, that is, their interaction. An *interaction* means that the effect of one variable (e.g., treatment A or B) depends on the level of one of the other variable (e.g., sex of the patient). Earlier we discussed interactions in terms of external validity. In this light, the interaction means that the effect of one variable may or may not be generalized across all conditions. Rather, the impact of that variable occurs only under certain conditions or operates differently under those conditions (e.g., with men rather than women, with younger rather than older persons).

Considerations in Using the Design   The strength of a factorial design is that it can assess the effects of separate variables in a single experiment. The feature includes one of economy because different variables can be studied with fewer subjects and observations in a factorial design than in separate experiments for the single-variable study of each variable one at a time. In addition, the factorial design provides unique information about the combined effects of the independent variables.

The importance of evaluating interactions cannot be overestimated in conducting research. Essentially, interactions provide the boundary conditions of independent variables and their effects. For example, in the context of treatment, a given intervention may not simply be effective or ineffective but instead may depend on a host of qualifiers such as who administers treatment, the scope of client problems, and the conditions of treatment administration. These qualifiers refer to variables with which treatment is likely to interact. Another way to refer to these qualifiers is to raise the notion of moderators, mentioned earlier. Interactions identify variables that moderate (influence) the effect of other variables. Results that reveal a significant interaction may be of interest because of the information about both the generality of the effect across conditions and the theoretical implications.

The concerns about using the factorial designs are both practical and interpretive. On the practical side, one must remember that the number of groups in the investigation multiplies quickly as new factors or new levels of a given factor are added. For example, a design in its conceptual stages might begin as a 2 x 3 design looking at type of treatment (meditation training vs. biofeedback) and severity of anxiety (high, moderate, and low). This design already includes 6 (i.e., 2 x 3) groups. Yet it also might be interesting to study whether the treatment is administered by a therapist or given by prerecorded taped instructions. The third variable, manner of administering treatment, includes two levels; thus, the overall design is now 2 x 2 x 3 and has 12 groups. One could also explore a fourth variable, instructions to the subjects. This variable might have two levels—half the subjects would be told that the treatment was "discovered by a guru" and the other half told that the treatment was "discovered by a scientist engaged in basic laboratory research." We might expect meditation subjects who receive the "guru instructions" and biofeedback subjects who receive the "scientific researcher instructions" to do better than their counterparts. This would be a $2 \times 2 \times 2 \times 3$ design with 24 groups (a formidable doctoral dissertation, to say the least—instead of a study, we have a career). As a general point, the number of groups in a study may quickly become prohibitive as factors and levels are increased. This means that the demand for subjects to complete each combination of the variables will also increase. In practice, there are constraints in the number of subjects that can be run in a given study and the number of factors (variables) that can be easily studied.

A related problem is interpreting the results of multiple-factor experiments. Factorial designs are optimally informative when an investigator predicts an interactive relationship among two or more variables. Simple interactions involving two or three variables often are relatively straightforward to interpret. However, when multiple variables interact, the investigator may be at a loss to describe the complex relationship in a coherent fashion, let alone offer an informed or theoretically plausible explanation. A factorial design is useful for evaluating the separate and combined effects of variables of interest when the variables are conceptually related and predicted to generate interactive effects. The inclusion of factors in the design is dictated by conceptual considerations of those variables and the interpretability of the predicted relations.

Quasi-Experimental Designs

The previous designs constitute basic between-group experimental designs and are true experiments because several facets of the study can be adequately controlled to eliminate threats to internal validity. The strength of the designs derives from the investigator's ability to control what treatment is administered to whom and at what point in time. Most important, subjects can be assigned randomly to conditions, thereby reducing the plausibility of potential threats to validity. There are, however, many situations in which the investigator cannot exert such control over subjects and their assignment or the administration of treatment to particular groups. In clinical, counseling, and educational research investigators often are unable to shuffle clients or students to meet the demands of a true experiment and must work within administrative, bureaucratic, and occasionally antiresearch constraints. As noted earlier, research designs in which the investigator cannot exert control required of true experiments have been referred to as *quasi-experimental designs* (Campbell & Stanley, 1963). For investigators who are genuinely bothered by less well-controlled studies, these can also be called *queasy-experimental designs.*

Pretest–Posttest Design   There are many between-group quasi-experimental designs, the most common of which parallel the pretest–posttest and posttest-only experimental designs. For each quasi-experimental equivalent of these designs, the control group is not demonstrably equivalent to the experimental group, usually because subjects have been assigned to groups prior to the inception of the investigation. Because the groups are already formed, they may differ before the intervention, which explains why the designs have also been referred to as *nonequivalent control group designs* (Campbell & Stanley, 1963).

The most widely used version of a nonequivalent control group design is the one that resembles the pretest–posttest control group design. The design may be diagrammed as follows:

$$nonR \quad O_1 \quad X \quad O_2$$
$$nonR \quad O_3 \qquad O_4$$

In this version, nonrandomly assigned subjects (e.g., subjects who already may be in separate hospitals, clinics, or classrooms) are compared. One group receives the treatment and the other does not. The strength of the design depends directly on the similarity of the experimental and control groups. The investigator must ask how the assignment of subjects to groups originally might have led to systematic differences before the intervention. For example, two high schools might be used to evaluate a drug-abuse prevention intervention in which the intervention is provided at one school but not at the other. Youths in the schools may vary on factors such as socioeconomic status, IQ, or other measures. Possibly, initial differences on the pretest measures or different characteristics of the groups, regardless of whether they are revealed on the pretest, account for the findings. The similarity of youths across schools can be attested to partially on the basis of pretest scores and on various subject variables. Pretest equivalence on a measure does not mean that the groups are comparable in all dimensions relevant to the intervention, but it increases the confidence one might place in this assumption.

In the version of the design diagrammed, the results could not easily be attributed to history, maturation, testing, regression, mortality, and similar factors that might occur across both groups. However, it is possible that the threats might differ *between* groups (i.e., selection x history interaction or selection x maturation interaction). These interactions mean that particular confounding events may affect one group but not the other and, hence, might account for group differences. For example, one group might experience historical events (within the school) or differ in rate of maturation (improvements without treatment). These influences might account for group differences even if the subjects were equivalent on a pretest. Differential regression toward the mean also might account for group differences if either group was selected because of its extreme scores on a measure related to posttest performance. Often differential regression might be caused by what the investigator does rather than occur as an inadvertent effect of an uncontrollable situation, as mentioned earlier in the discussion of mismatching. At the same time, the design can yield strong inferences depending on efforts the investigator makes to make implausible threats that random assignment normally handles.

As an illustration of a nonequivalent quasi-experimental design, Fisher et al. (1989) evaluated the effects of participating in an awareness-training group. Such training includes experiences that individuals sought to improve their daily life, personal effectiveness, decision-making skills, and interpersonal awareness. Adults ordinarily seek such training on their own and cannot easily be assigned to a control group. Thus, the authors began with the task of evaluating the impact of an intervention in which treatment and control groups cannot easily be formed by random assignment of cases to groups. The investigators devised a nonrandomly assigned control group to assist in reducing the plausibility of various threats to internal validity. The authors used a peer-nominated, nointervention group. Specifically, persons who sought and participated in awareness training (intervention group) were asked to nominate other persons not in their household who were the same sex, approximately the same age, from the same community, and whom they considered to be like themselves. The nominated persons (control group) were recruited and asked to complete the assessment battery at different points in time to coincide with the pre- and posttest intervals for subjects who received awareness training.

This control group clearly is not equivalent to a group comprised from random assignment of subjects to intervention and nonintervention groups. Was the group equivalent to the group that received awareness training? Data analyses revealed that at pretest, experimental and control subjects were no different in age, education, sex, income, and a variety of psychological measures of interest (e.g., social functioning, self-esteem). There was one initial preintervention difference on a measure of perceived control—training subjects attributed more internal control to themselves than did nonintervention subjects. However, across a very large number of variables and statistical tests, the groups were not different prior to the intervention. There might have been differences on some variables related to self-selection and interest in group awareness training in addition to the initial difference in perceived control on one of many measures. Yet, the onus is on us to pose a relevant difference that might plausibly influence the results. This nonequivalent group controls reasonably well for threats to internal validity (e.g., testing, history), even though confidence would have been augmented with equivalent and randomly comprised groups. In passing, the results indicated that the awareness-training group and the control group were not different on virtually all measures at posttreatment and at 1-year follow-up.

Posttest-Only Design   A nonequivalent control group design need not use a pretest. The posttest-only quasi-experimental design can be diagrammed as follows:

$$\text{nonR} \quad \text{X} \quad O_1$$
$$\text{nonR} \qquad\quad O_2$$

The problem with this design, as with its true experiment counterpart, is that the equivalence of groups prior to the intervention cannot be assessed. In the posttest-only experimental design discussed earlier, absence of a pretest was not necessarily problematic because random assignment increased the likelihood of group equivalence, particularly for large sample sizes. However, in a posttest-only quasi-experiment, the groups may be very different across several dimensions prior to treatment. Hence, attributing group differences to the intervention may be especially weak. Aside from problems of probable group nonequivalence prior to treatment and the absence of a pretest to estimate group differences, this version of the nonequivalent control group design suffers from each of the possible threats to internal validity of the same design with a pretest. As with the experimental designs, the nonequivalent control group designs share the same relationship to pretest sensitization effects and their control depending on whether a pretest is used. Also, by comparison with the other problems of quasi-experimental designs, pretest sensitization is of relatively less concern.

Although the posttest-only quasi-experiment is weak, occasionally this may be the most viable design available. For example, one study focused on the evaluation of an inpatient treatment program for chemically dependent adolescents (dependent primarily on alcohol, marijuana, speed, downers, and cocaine) (Grenier, 1985). The intervention consisted of a multidisciplinary program in the hospital (e.g., individual, group, and family therapy; an Alcoholics Anonymous model toward complete abstinence, and other procedures). The investigator examined whether those who completed the program were more improved than those who had not received the program. Random assignment was not possible. Consequently, the investigator completed an assessment of former patients and of persons on the waiting list. The abstinence rates of the groups were 65.6 percent for the youths who received the program and 14.3 percent for those who had yet to receive the program. The results are compatible with the view that the program improves outcome. Clearly, several questions remain unanswered, but this initial test provides critical information to suggest that the program may offer some benefit. A quasi-experiment provides an excellent beginning, particularly when compared with the alternative of little or no evaluation, which characterizes most institutional programs.

Variations Variations of these designs might also be used. One variation of the nonequivalent control group design with a pretest can be diagrammed as follows:

$$\text{nonR} \quad O_1 \quad X \quad O_2$$
$$\text{nonR} \quad \quad O_3 \quad \quad O_4$$

(The version of the design without the pretest can be illustrated by omitting O_1 and O_3.) The diagram indicates that groups received the pre- and posttreatment assessments at different points in time. Obviously, such a design has more problems than do designs in which measures are administered to groups at the same time. With this version, pretest equivalence of groups cannot really be determined because after one group is tested, there is no basis to infer the standing of the other group on the same measures at that time. In addition, different historical events, maturation, and instrument decay across groups become increasingly plausible as rival hypotheses of the results as the time of assessment of different groups becomes disparate.

Occasionally, the experimental and treatment groups are assessed at different times, but staggering the conditions does not necessarily compete with the conclusions that can be drawn. Treatment and control conditions in institutional experiments are often staggered to keep patients in different conditions from interacting. For example, one quasi-experiment of this sort evaluated the effects of teaching problem-solving skills to male hospitalized alcoholic patients (Intagliata, 1978). Treated patients received ten 1-hour group therapy sessions during which the patients were trained to recognize and define problems, to generate solutions, and to select alternatives. The purpose was to train persons to handle real-life problems after discharge. The assignment of subjects was staggered; groups were not run or assessed at the same time. The first 32 admissions were assigned to the control group. The next 32 admissions were designated as the treatment group. This violation of random assignment was made because of the author's interest in keeping controls (patients receiving routine ward treatment) from having direct contact with experimental patients. Indeed, the experimental patients did not begin their treatment until control patients had been discharged. The results showed that training in problem solving enhanced the skills on paper-and-pencil measures and in helping individuals plan for their postdischarge community adjustment.

Given the design it is possible to raise rival hypotheses such as the nonequivalence of groups or differential history, maturation, or instrumentation. However, these hypotheses are not very plausible despite the quasi-experimental nature of the study, in part because pretest information showed the groups did not differ in age, verbal IQ, marital status, and other variables and because the assignment to groups differed only by 3 or 4 weeks. Hence, this quasi-experiment staggered assessment and evaluation of the different groups, but the plausibility of resulting rival interpretations was minimal. Despite the disadvantages of using control groups that are assessed at different points in time from the experimental group, the addition of the control group makes these designs better than using only one group that receives the intervention. If only one group were used with pre- and postintervention assessment—or, even worse, only the postintervention assessment—not much more than an uncontrolled case study would remain, and most threats to internal validity could not be ruled out.

General Comments   Although the nonequivalent control group designs mentioned constitute the most frequently used variations, all possible quasi-experimental designs cannot be enumerated here. (Indeed, very unusual designs can be devised, sometimes inadvertently. For example, I pioneered a rather unique design variation, a pretest-only quasi-experimental design, in my dissertation.

However, the variation was an inadvertent result of a rather embarrassing over-sight—I forgot to administer the posttest. Although omission of a posttest pre-cluded evaluation of the experimental manipulation, there was absolutely no possibility of any bias due to posttest sensitization with my design.)

The general characteristics of these designs is that constraints inherent in the situation restrict the investigator from meeting the requirements of true experiments. This usually means that the investigator cannot assign subjects randomly to conditions and that many threats to internal validity will compete with the experimental manipulation in explaining the results.

The inability to meet the demands of true experiments does not invariably sentence the demonstration to ambiguity. Thus, quasi-experimental designs are not inherently flawed. The issue that raises concern pertains to the plausibility that rival hypotheses could explain the findings. Plausibility might vary greatly in a given study. In the examples discussed earlier, treatment was arranged in a way that made rival threats to internal validity not particularly strong contenders for explaining the results. This is not always the case. For example, in one quasi-experiment using a pretest–posttest experimental design, different doses (12 vs. 18 sessions) of a cognitively based treatment were compared (Lochman, 1985). The goal of the intervention was to control classroom behavior of aggressive boys. The group that received 12 sessions was run approximately 1 year before the group that received 18 sessions. The latter treatment was found to be more effective. However, comparisons revealed that subjects in the second treatment group were younger and more well behaved. It is to the author's credit to note that these differences might have accounted for or contributed to the different outcomes at posttreatment and hence rival the explanation accorded to the different amounts of treatment.

Often constraints limit the investigator to quasi-experimental designs. In such cases, ingenuity is required to mobilize methodological weapons against ambiguity. The threats to internal validity may be handled by various control groups that can be used in the situation. These groups may help weaken one or more threats to internal validity and patch up an otherwise imperfect design. Indeed, groups added to designs to rule out various rival explanations of the results have been referred to as *patched-up control groups* (Campbell & Stanley, 1963) and are discussed in the next chapter.

MULTIPLE-TREATMENT DESIGNS

The defining characteristic of the multiple-treatment design is that each different treatment under investigation is presented to each subject. Although the evaluation of treatments is "within subjects," separate groups of subjects are usually present in the design. In most multiple-treatment designs in clinical research, separate groups are used so that the different treatments can be balanced across subjects, that is, so that treatments can be presented in different orders. Because separate groups are used in the multiple-treatment designs, points raised about random assignment and matching are relevant for constructing different groups for multiple-treatment designs.

There are different versions of multiple-treatment designs depending on the number of treatments and the manner in which they are presented. All designs might be called *counterbalanced designs* because they try to balance the order of treatment across subjects. However, it is worth distinguishing the commonly used version of the multiple-treatment design from the general method for balancing treatments.

Crossover Design

A specific multiple-treatment design that is used in treatment research is referred to as the *crossover design*. The design receives its name because partway through the experiment, usually at the midpoint, all subjects "cross over" (i.e., are switched) to another experimental condition. The design is used with two different treatments. Two groups of subjects are constructed through random assignment. The groups differ only in the order in which they receive the two treatments. The design can be diagrammed as follows:

$$R \quad O_1 \quad X_1 \quad O_2 \quad X_2 \quad O_3$$
$$R \quad O_4 \quad X_2 \quad O_5 \quad X_1 \quad O_6$$

The diagram may appear complex because of the numbering of different interventions (X_1 and X_2) and the different observations (O_1 through O_6). However, the design is relatively straightforward. Essentially, each group is formed through random assignment (R). A pretest may be provided to assess performance prior to any intervention. The pretest (designated in the diagram as O_1 and O_4) is not mandatory but is included because it is commonly used and provides the benefits of a pretest, as discussed earlier. The crucial feature of the design is that the groups receive the interventions (X_1, X_2) in different order. Moreover, the subjects are assessed after each intervention. Thus there is an assessment halfway through the study at the crossover point and again after the second (final) treatment is terminated.

The design is used frequently in evaluating the effects of medication on various symptoms or disorders. For two (or more) medications, a comparison can be made within the same patients if there is an intervening "washout" period during which all medication is stopped. The second medication can then be administered with little or no concern over lingering effects of the first medication. In psychological experiments, this design is used less frequently, but there are instances of its use. As a case in point, a crossover design was used to compare two different treatments for eliminating obsessions in 10 patients with obsessional rituals and thoughts (Hackmann & McLean, 1975). Thought stopping and flooding were the two treatments. Thought stopping consisted of having the individual patient imagine situations that provoked an obsessional ritual or thought. As the patient signaled (by raising a finger) that the image or thought was clear, the therapist hit the desk with a ruler and shouted "Stop!" The purpose of treatment was gradually to interfere and thwart completion of the thought. Eventually control was transferred to the client, who could then state "stop" aloud and later subvocally to control his or her own thoughts. Flooding consisted of exposing patients to the feared situations that precipitated anxiety and that apparently led to obsessions. Patients were exposed to actual events (e.g., handling objects that the patient thought were contaminated) in the flooding condition. The 10 patients were divided into two groups of five patients. The first group received flooding followed by thought stopping; the second group received the treatments in the opposite order. Each treatment was given for four sessions. Assessment of the obsessions was completed by ratings and inventories before treatment, after the first treatment, and again after the second. During each treatment there were within-group improvements from the previous assessment period. Both treatments were associated with change, and there were no differences between the treatments.

The crossover design need not include two or more active treatments. In some cases, one of the interventions is a control condition. For example, a crossover design was used to evaluate the impact of exposure to light for the treatment of seasonal affective disorder among children and adolescents (ages 7–17). The youths were diagnosed with the disorder because of their repeated episodes of depression during winter months (Swedo et al., 1997). The treatment condition was exposure to light (exposure to 2 hours of simulation of the dawn plus 1 hour of bright-light) and was compared to a placebo condition (exposure to 5 minutes of simulation of the dawn and 1 hour of wearing clear glasses while doing a sedentary activity such as reading or watching television). Cases were assigned to receive the treatment or placebo condition first followed by the other condition. Treatment led to significant reductions in depression, based on weekly parental ratings of symptoms. This is an important demonstration in showing that light can lead to change. A logical next step would be to provide treatment in a between-group design, for a longer or more intense period, to see if depression can be influenced in ways that do not reverse as soon as the treatment is withdrawn, that is, nontransient effects of treatment.

Multiple-Treatment Counterbalanced Designs

The crossover design as discussed here is simple, usually two treatments in which each client receives both treatments but in a different order; that is, the treatments are counterbalanced. With an increase in the number of treatments, however, counterbalancing becomes more complex and the order in which the treatments are given is more difficult to balance. For example, consider the hypothetical experiment in which four treatments (A, B, C, D) are to be compared. Each subject will receive each treatment. An important issue is deciding the order in which the subjects should receive treatment. One method is to determine the sequence of treatments randomly for each subject. Thus, the sequence for each subject will vary according to chance. This procedure would be adequate with a large number of subjects. However, it is possible, particularly with a small number of subjects, that one of the four treatments may appear at some point in the sequence (e.g., the first treatment) but not at the other points. More likely, the different treatments will not appear at each point in the sequence for an equal or approximately equal number of times. This inequality could interfere with the conclusions about treatment effects. For example, one treatment may appear to be more effective because it happened to appear more often as the first treatment given to subjects. Obviously, if multiple treatments are evaluated within subjects, the order of the individual treatments must be distributed or varied (i.e., the first, second, or third treatment) across subjects.

A useful procedure to ordering the treatments in a multiple-treatment design is to select a set of sequences in advance and to assign subjects randomly to the sequences as they arrive to the experiment. For example, suppose that there are four groups of subjects and each subject receives each of the four treatments. A few specified arrangements or sequences of treatments could be preselected to which the subjects are randomly assigned. If there were four arrangements of the treatments, the design might be summarized as presented in Table 5.1. The characteristic of this ordering is that each group has a different sequence that includes each treatment. Moreover, each treatment is administered once in each available position. The arrangement of treatments in such a way that each occurs once and only once in each position and in each group is called a *Latin Square*. In a Latin Square, the number of groups (represented by rows in the table), orders or positions (represented by columns), and treatments (represented by A through D) are equal. (The table represents only one way of ordering the treatments. For a given number of treatments, there are actually several Latin Squares.) At the end of the investigation, analyses can compare dif-

TABLE 5.1. Order of Four Treatments in a Latin Square Design

Sequence	ORDER			
	1	*2*	*3*	*4*
I	A	B	C	D
II	B	A	D	C
III	C	D	A	B
IV	D	C	B	A

Each subject is assigned randomly to one of four groups (I, II, III, or IV), which constitutes a different sequence of the four treatments. Sequence refers to the set of treatments in a given order (i.e., the rows in the table); order refers to the position of a given treatment or whether it appears 1st, 2nd, 3rd, or 4th (i.e., the columns).

ferent treatments and can assess whether any effects were due to groups (rows), to order (columns), or to treatment (A vs. B vs. C vs. D).[2]

One effect that is still left uncontrolled is the particular sequence in which the treatment appears. The sequence of treatments in Table 5.1 (the rows) does not represent all possible sequences. Not every treatment is preceded and followed by every other treatment. For example, treatment B never immediately follows treatment D, nor does treatment C follow treatment A, and so on. Hence, it is not really possible with the above design to rule out the influence of different sequences as a contributor to the data for a given treatment. There may be an interaction between the effects of treatment and where treatment appears in the sequence. This interaction can be avoided as a source of confound by using all possible orders of treatment with separate groups of subjects. In a completely balanced design, each treatment occurs equally often in each order and each treatment precedes and follows all others. The problem with such a design is that the number of groups and subjects required may be prohibitive. The number of subjects for complete counterbalancing would be *k* factorial, where *k* equals the number of treatments in the experiment.

In general, the administration of multiple treatments to the same subject is rare. When treatment studies use multiple-treatment designs, two treatments are more commonly compared, as illustrated with the crossover design. Conducting additional treatments may require a relatively long period of continuous treatment so that each treatment has an opportunity to influence behavior. Moreover, the problem of reflecting change with multiple treatments (discussed below) makes testing for effects of several treatments a dubious venture. Consequently, several treatments are evaluated within subjects infrequently; when they are, the designs usually are not completely balanced to include all possible sequences of treatment.

Considerations in Using the Designs

The utility of multiple-treatment designs depends on several factors, such as the anticipated effects of juxtaposing different treatments, the type of independent and dependent variables that are studied, and the measurement of cumulative treatment effects with the same subjects.

Order and Sequence Effects Perhaps the most important consideration in using a multiple-treatment design relates to the problem of ordering treatments. Actually, different problems can be distinguished. To begin with, if an experiment consisted of one group of subjects who received two different treatments (A and B) in a particular order, the results would be completely uninterpretable. For example, if treatment B led to greater change than did treatment A, it would be impossible to determine whether B was more effective because of its unique therapeutic properties or because it was the second treatment provided to all subjects. Treatment B may have been more effective because continuation of treatment, independent of what the treatment was, may have led to greater change. Thus, the order in which the treatments appeared in this single-group study might have been responsible for treatment differences and hence is a plausible alternative explanation of the results.

When the order of treatments might account for the results, it is called *order effect.* The effect refers to the fact that the point in time in which treatment occurred, rather than the specific treatment, might be responsible for the pattern of results. In most multiple-treatment designs, order effects are not confounded with treatments because of counterbalancing, as illustrated in the discussion of crossover and Latin Square designs. Although order is not confounded with treatment when counterbalancing is used, it still may influence the pattern of results. We have known for some time that order effects may be important. Usually, treatments presented earlier in the sequence are more effective independent of what the treatment is (Crowe et al., 1972; Hackmann & McLean, 1975) quite possibly because this is related to ceiling and floor effects (discussed later) in that by the time the final treatment is provided in a series of treatments, the amount of change that can be reflected on the dependent measures is attenuated.

There is another way that the specific order of treatments may influence the results. Specifically, the transfer from one treatment to another is not the same for each treatment. Receiving treatment A followed by treatment B may not be the same as receiving treatment B followed by treatment A. The order in which treatments appear may partially dictate the effects of each treatment. When the arrangement of treatments contributes to their effects, it is called *sequence effects.* The nature of the problem is also conveyed by other terms, such as *multiple-treatment interference* or *carryover effects.* The importance of the sequence in which different events appear in dictating their effects is obvious from examples of everyday experience. For example, the taste of a given food depends not only on the specific properties of the food but also on what food or liquid immediately preceded it.

As a general statement, multiple-treatment designs are quite susceptible to the influence of sequence effects. Whether these effects are viewed as nuisances depends on the purposes of the investigator. Sequence effects represent complex interactions (e.g., treatment x order of appearance) and may be of interest in their own right. All events in one's life occur in the context of other events. Hence, sequence effects embrace questions about the context in which events occur and the effects of prior experience on subsequent performance. Depending on one's purpose, the fact that sequence effects occur may be central. However, for treatment evaluation, sequence effects are rarely sought. The purpose is to produce therapeutic change and to determine which among alternative treatments effectively accomplishes the change.

Restrictions with Various Independent and Dependent Variables   Considerations pertaining to the variables that are to be studied may dictate whether a multiple-treatment design is likely to be appropriate or useful for the experiment in question. Certain variables of interest to the investigator are not easily studied in a multiple-treatment design. For example, the experimental instructions or subject expectancies may present particular problems, depending on the precise experimental manipulations. The problem is in providing to the subject separate interventions that may present conflicting information or procedures. For example, individual therapy and family therapy may be difficult to compare within a particular set of subjects. The respective treatment rationales may present conflicting information to the subjects about the appropriate focus of intervention (either on the individual or family). The second treatment might seem odd if it would contradict the theoretical basis and actual operations of the first treatment. Hearing the rationale and receiving one of the procedures first might influence the client's belief in the other one. The problem of potentially conflicting information among the different treatments can sometimes be resolved. The solution may lie in the intricacy of the rationales that the experimenter provides so that the different treatments will not appear to conflict. Thus, the creativity of the investigator argues against any absolute rules about which treatments can and cannot accompany another in a multiple-treatment design.

Discussing potentially conflicting interventions raises another side of the issue. It is possible to select interventions that are very similar. For example, the treatments presented to the subjects may differ only in subtle characteristics and thus may produce few detectable effects in a multiple-treatment design because clients do not distinguish different conditions. In other words, the first intervention may lead to a certain degree of change, but the second intervention, or variation, may not be perceived as different from the first one and hence may produce no differences within subjects because the second intervention was perceived as a continuation of the first. Although intervention differences would not be revealed by changes within subjects, a comparison between groups for the first treatment conditions administered might yield a difference.

Personality, demographic, physical, and other stable characteristics are not studied within subjects because they do not vary within the same subject for a given experiment, that is, participants are not both male and female or both a psychiatric patient and not a psychiatric patient within the same experiment. However, it is possible to provide experiences within the experiment to change how a subject reacts to certain variables. A participant could be given a success or failure experience in an attempt to assess the impact of these experiences on dependent measures. Stable subject characteristics can be readily studied in factorial designs that combine group and multiple-treatment features. For example, a subject can be classified by one variable (e.g., sex, age, level of anxiety) and receive each of the different levels of another variable (e.g., treatments A and B). This combined design can examine whether treatment effects differ according to subject characteristics.

Aside from restrictions on independent variables, there are restrictions on dependent measures that can be readily evaluated in a multiple-treatment design. Dependent measures involving skills such as cognitive or motor abilities may not readily reflect treatment effects within subjects. When one treatment alters a skill (e.g., bicycle riding or reading), the effects of other treatments are more difficult to evaluate than when transient changes in performance are made.

Ceiling and Floor Effects   A possible problem in evaluating different interventions within the same subjects is that ceiling or floor effects may limit the amount of change that can be shown. *Ceiling* and *floor effects* refer to the fact that change in the dependent measures may reach an upper or lower limit, respectively, and that further change cannot be demonstrated because of this limit. The amount of change produced by the first intervention may not allow additional change to occur.

Assume, for example, that two treatments are presented in a multiple-treatment design and evaluated on a hypothetical measure of adjustment ranging from 0 to 100—a score of 0 equals poor adjustment, which means the individual is constantly depressed, anxious, drunk, suicidal, and apathetic (on the good days) and 100 equals the paragon of adjustment, that is, the individual is perfectly adaptive, content, and self-actualizing even in the face of recent loss of family, possessions, job, fortune, and memory. In pretreatment assessment, subjects are screened and selected according to their poor adjustment on the scale, say, scores lower than 25. Then two treatments are provided in counterbalanced order to two groups of subjects. Suppose the initial treatment increases adjustment to a mean of 95. Because of this initial change, a second treatment cannot provide evidence of further improvements. For example, the data might show the pattern illustrated in Figure 5.3, in which it can be seen that the first treatment (A or B) led to marked increments in adjustment, and administering the second treatment did not produce additional change. The conclusion would be that the treatments are equally effective, one does not add to the other.

A different pattern might emerge if there were no ceiling on the measure. That is, if even higher scores were allowed and a greater amount of change could be shown, different conclusions might be reached. For example, if the adjustment scale allowed scores beyond 100 and additional degrees of adjustment, different results might have been obtained. The treatments might have been different at their first presentation. Treatment A might have led to a mean score of 95 but treatment B to a score of 150. In that case, when the other (second) treatment was applied to each group, additional changes may have been detected, at least from A to B.

In general, the problem of ceiling or floor effects is not restricted to multiple-treatment comparisons. The absence of differences between groups on a measure may result from limits in the range of scores obtained on that measure. If scores for the different groups congregate at the upper and lower ends of the scale, it is possible that differences would be evident if the scale permitted a greater spread of scores. For example, in a child treatment outcome study, we evaluated treatment acceptability, that is, the extent to which treatment was viewed as appropriate, fair, and reasonable (Kazdin, Siegel, & Bass, 1992). At the end of the study, parents and children rated the treatment they received. The three treatments in the study were rated quite positively and did not differ in

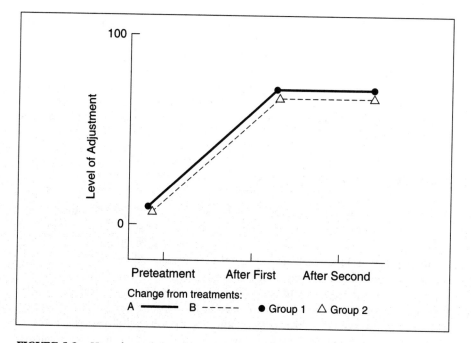

FIGURE 5.3 Hypothetical data for a crossover design in which each group of subjects receives treatments in a counterbalanced order.

level of acceptability. It is possible that the treatments were equally acceptable. Yet, the means for the treatments were close to the upper limit of possible scores on the scale. Thus, it remains possible that acceptability would differ if the ceiling of the scale had not been limited.

Although the problem of ceiling and floor effects can occur in any design, it is exacerbated by multiple-treatment designs because different treatments operate toward continued increases (or decreases) in scores. With repeated treatments, the limit of the scores may be approached with one or two treatments and not allow differentiation of later treatments. Thus, one consideration in using a multiple-treatment design is whether the different measures provide a sufficient range of scores to allow continued increments in performance from a measurement standpoint.

From multiple-treatment designs, ceiling and floor effects are readily avoided when change is transient. For example, interventions based on administration of drugs or incentives for performance may produce effects only while the interventions are in effect. Assessment can be made while these interventions are in effect. After withdrawal of the intervention, perhaps with an intervening period so that drug or incentive effects are completely eliminated, the second intervention can be implemented. If the effects of an intervention are transient and only evident when the intervention is in effect, the improvements resulting from one treatment will not limit the scores that can be achieved by the second treatment. The study of interventions with transient effects resolves the problem of ceiling and floor effects in the dependent measures. However, in areas of clinical or applied research, as in psychotherapy, counseling, and educational interventions, the purpose is to produce a nontransient change. It is not reasonable to select interventions with transient effects for purposes of design if the goal is protracted change.

SUMMARY AND CONCLUSIONS

In most research in clinical, educational, and counseling psychology, the intervention of interest is evaluated by making comparisons between groups. Careful attention must be given to the assignment of subjects to groups. In experimental research, subjects are assigned in an unbiased fashion so that each subject has an equal probability of being assigned to the different conditions. Typically, *random assignment* is employed. As an adjunctive procedure, subjects may be matched on a given variable at the beginning of the experiment and randomly assigned in blocks to conditions. *Matching* followed by random assignment is an excellent way to ensure equivalence of groups on a measure that relates to the dependent variable. Occasionally, matching is used with intact or preexisting groups as a way to identify across groups subjects who are equal on a measure prior to treatment. Although the intent of this matching procedure is well based, it may yield groups that regress to different group means. Independently of the intervention, groups may differ because of the regression effect. Because of the possible artifact in group differences, equalizing groups in this way is called *mismatching*.

Several different designs including *pretest–posttest control group design, posttest-only control group design, Solomon four-group design, factorial designs,* and *quasi-experimental designs* were discussed. The pretest–posttest control group was noted as particularly advantageous because of the strengths that the pretest provides for demarcating initial (preintervention) levels of functioning, evaluating change, and increasing power for statistical analyses. Factorial designs were also highlighted because they permit simultaneous study of the effects of two or more variables in a single experiment. In addition, these designs allow evaluation of *interactions* among variables, that is, whether the effects of one variable depend on different levels of another variable.

Multiple-treatment designs were also discussed. Although separate groups of subjects are included in these designs, their unique characteristic is the presentation of separate treatment or treatment and control conditions to the same subjects. In multiple-treatment designs, separate groups of subjects are used so that the different treatments can be counterbalanced. *Counterbalancing* is designed to ensure that the effects of the treatments can be separated from the order in which they appear. In the simplest multiple-treatment design, referred to as a *crossover design,* two treatments are given to two groups of subjects in different order. In more complex versions, several treatments may be delivered and presented either in a randomized or a prearranged order to randomly comprised groups of subjects. A *Latin Square* design refers to ways of arranging within subjects multiple treatments in which the number of treatments is equal to the number of groups and in which each treatment appears once in each position in the sequence in which treatments are arranged.

There are several considerations in using multiple-treatment designs. *Order* and *sequence effects* are controlled by ensuring that each treatment is administered at each point in the order of treatments (e.g., first, second, third, etc.). Sequence effects are more difficult to control unless each treatment precedes and follows all other treatments somewhere in the design, a balancing requirement prohibitive with multiple treatments. The problem with leaving sequence effects uncontrolled is that the effects of one treatment may be influenced by previous treatments. That is, there may be a carryover effect from one treatment to the next.

Another consideration pertains to restrictions in the use of various independent and dependent variables in multiple-treatment designs. Independent variables such as subject characteristics or treatments that appear to present conflicting information or procedures to the subject may be impossible or extremely difficult to study within subjects. Dependent variables that reflect abilities or skills may be difficult to evaluate in multiple-treatment designs if multiple treatments are presented. Unlike most transient measures of performance, ability and skill levels may not readily reflects the cumulative effects of multiple treatments on many measurement devices. Finally, studying multiple treatments may introduce problems of *ceiling* and *floor effects* that refer, respectively, to upper or lower limits on the response measure and that will not allow subsequent interventions to reflect further change in performance. There must be some assurance that the dependent measure(s) do not restrict the range of performance allowed in view of the subjects' responses to early treatments.

NOTES

[1]The Solomon four-group design calls for randomly assigning subjects to conditions. In the Spirito et al. (1988a) study, students who were absent on the day of the pretest were assigned to the no-pretest condition; those who were in school were assigned to the pretest condition. Thus, the effect of pretesting and the interaction with treatment effects is potentially confounded by selection bias, that is, the possibility that subjects who did not come to school are different. Replication is needed to demonstrate that pretesting rather than subject selection is clearly the basis for the finding.

[2]Although main effects of treatment, order, and groups can be extracted from Latin Square analyses, interactions among these effects present special problems that are beyond the scope of the present chapter. For a discussion of procedures to select or to form Latin Squares for a given experiment or for a table of various squares, the interested reader is referred to other sources (Fisher & Yates, 1963; Kirk, 1968); for a discussion of strategies for data analyses, the seminal paper on the topic (Grant, 1948) or more recent discussions (Winer, Brown, & Michels, 1991) are quite useful.

FOR FURTHER READING

Cook, T.D. & Campbell, D.T. (1979*). Quasi-experimentation: Design and analysis issues for field settings.* Chicago, IL: Rand McNally.

Hsu, L.M. (1995). Regression toward the mean associated with measurement error and the identification of improvement and deterioration in psychotherapy. *Journal of Consulting and Clinical Psychology, 63,* 141–144.

Rosenthal, R., & Rosnow, R.L. (1991). *Essentials of behavioral research: Methods and data analysis* (2nd ed.). New York: McGraw-Hill.

Shadish, W.R., & Ragsdale, K. (1996). Random versus nonrandom assignment in controlled experiments: Do you get the same answer? *Journal of Consulting and Clinical Psychology, 64,* 1290–1305.

Chapter 6

Control and Comparison Groups

In discussions of experiments, we are often taught that an experiment requires a control group. The notion of "a" control group is misleading because it implies that the addition of a single group to a design may provide a general control for diverse biases, artifacts, and rival hypotheses that might plague the research. In fact, there are all sorts of groups that may be added or included in a design, depending on the potential influences other than the intervention, that may account for the results (threats to internal validity) and the specificity of the statements the investigator wishes to make about what led to change or group differences (threats to construct validity). This chapter discusses control and comparison groups that are often used in clinical research, the design issues they are intended to address, and considerations that dictate their use.

CONTROL GROUPS

Control groups are usually used to address threats to internal validity such as history, maturation, selection, testing, and others. Control of these and related threats is accomplished by ensuring that one group in the design shares these influences with the intervention group but does not receive the intervention or experimental manipulation. If the intervention and control groups are formed by random assignment and assessed at the same point(s) in time, internal validity threats are usually addressed. In clinical research, several control groups are often used.

No-Treatment Control Group

Description and Rationale   In evaluating a particular therapy or experimental intervention, a basic question can always be raised, namely, to what extent would persons improve or change without treatment? The question can be answered by including a *no-treatment control group* in the experimental design. This group is so fundamental to intervention research that it was included in the basic descriptions and diagrams of the pretest–posttest control group and posttest-only control group designs discussed in the previous chapter. This is the group that is assessed but receives no other intervention. By including a no-treatment group in the design, the effects of history, maturation, and other threats to internal validity are directly controlled.

The performance of persons in a no-treatment control group can change significantly over time, which underscores the importance of this group in providing a baseline level for purposes of comparison when evaluating intervention effects. For example, in psychotherapy research, improvements often occur among clients who are in the no-treatment control condition. Historically, these improvements have been referred to as *spontaneous remission*. The term is not extremely informative because the reasons for the change ("spontaneous") and the extent to which change has improved client functioning ("remission") are arguable. Actually, spontaneous remission refers to changes made without receiving formal treatment in a given investigation. The term embraces history, maturation, and statistical regression but is usually not discussed as such in evaluations of therapy. In some cases, clear historical events are possible explanations. For example, people who are assigned to no treatment may seek other treatments at another clinic. Even if another type of treatment is not formally sought, clients may improve as a function of more informal means of "treatment," such as talking with relatives, neighbors, members of the clergy, or general-practice physicians. Improvements over time may also result from changes in the situations that exacerbated or precipitated the problem (e.g., adjustment after a death of a loved one) and other maturational influences that affect mood, outlook, and psychological status. Also, individuals who come for treatment may be at a particularly severe point in their problem. Hence, one would expect that reassessment of the problem at some later point would show improvement for many individuals. It may not be true that "time heals all wounds," but ordinary processes occurring with the passage of time certainly are strong competitors for many therapeutic techniques.

In view of the multiple influences that may impinge on clients who are in a no-treatment group, it is difficult to specify whether changes over time are spontaneous. From a methodological point of view, the important issue is to control for the amount of improvement that occurs as a function of the multiple, even if poorly specified and understood, influences. A no-treatment control group assesses the base rate of improvement for clients who did not receive the treatment under investigation.

Ideally, one would know in advance what the level of improvement is for clients with a particular problem so that treatment could be evaluated without using no-treatment control procedures. Yet even if improvement rates for various client disorders were well known, a no-treatment group is required in treatment research for other reasons. Changes in behavior may result from repeated assessment on the various dependent measures used to evaluate treatment. A no-treatment group is exposed to the same assessment procedures of the treatment group, thus making implausible the effects of testing and instrument decay as possible explanations of the results.

It is important to use as a no-treatment group clients who have been randomly assigned to this condition. Violation of random assignment reduces the confidence that can be placed in between-group differences after treatment has been completed. For example, for one reason or another, some individuals may choose not to participate in the program after pretreatment assessment or withdraw after a small number of treatment sessions. Persons who have withdrawn from treatment would not be appropriate to consider as part of or additions to the no-treatment control group. Although these clients might be considered to have received no treatment, they are self-selected for that status. Their subsequent performance on any measures might reflect variables related to their early withdrawal, not to the absence of treatment.

Special Considerations   Using a no-treatment control group presents obvious ethical problems. When clients seek treatment, it is difficult to justify withholding all attempts at intervention. Providing an experimental or exploratory treatment that is reasonable, even if unproved, is more ethically defensible than providing no treatment at all. When it comes to withholding treatment in a clinical situation, ivory-tower pleas for experimental elegance, control groups, and the importance of scientific research may be unpersuasive to prospective clients. Actually, the ethical issue is usually circumvented by conveying at the outset of a study that the subject could be assigned to a no-treatment condition and that individuals ought to participate in the study only if this possibility is acceptable. Solicitation of consent to participate before the study conveys the options to the prospective participants and allows them to decide whether participation is reasonable. However, for clients who are suffering significant impairment or dysfunction and who are indeed in crisis, it is unclear whether assignment to no-treatment would be ethically defensible even if the client agrees.

Aside from ethical issues, there are obvious practical problems in utilizing a no-treatment control group. Difficulties are encountered in explaining to clients who apply why treatment is unavailable or why there is a no-treatment condition. When the study begins, persons who are assigned to the no-treatment condition may seek treatment elsewhere or they may resent not receiving treatment and fail to cooperate with subsequent attempts to administer assessment devices.

If a no-treatment group of clients is successfully formed, it is likely that there will be time constraints on the group. As a general rule, the longer that clients are required to serve as no-treatment controls, the more likely they will drop out of the study. The investigator may wish to know the effects of the intervention over an extended period (e.g., 1, 5, or 10 years of follow-up). However, continuation of a no-treatment control group usually is not feasible over an extended period (e.g., months). Few no-treatment subjects are likely to remain in the study over an extended period; those who do may be a select group whose data are difficult to interpret. A partial solution to withholding treatment and meeting the requirements of a no-treatment control group is to use a waiting-list control group.

Waiting-List Control Group

Description and Rationale   A no-treatment group does not receive any treatment in the study. Rather than withhold treatment completely, one can merely delay treatment. A *waiting-list control group* withholds treatment for a period of time, but then treatment is provided. The period for which treatment is withheld usually corresponds to the pre- to posttreatment assessment interval of clients in the treatment condition. Thus, treatment and wait-list cases are assessed at the beginning of the study before any treatment is given and again at the point at which the treatment group has completed treatment. The waiting-list group will not have received the intervention during this period but will have completed all pre- and postassessments (it is really a second pretreatment assessment for them because they have not received treatment). As soon as the second assessment battery is administered, the wait-list subjects receive treatment.

When clients originally apply for treatment, they can be asked whether they would participate if treatment were delayed. Only subjects who agree would be included in the study. These clients would be assigned randomly to treatment or waiting-list control conditions. The control clients are promised treatment within a specified time period and in fact are called back and scheduled for treatment. Although it is tempting to assign clients who indicate they could wait for treatment to the control group and those who could not wait to the treatment group, circumventing random assignment in this way is methodologically disastrous. Treatment effects or the absence of such effects could be the result of subject selection in combination with history, maturation, regression, and other threats to internal validity.

A few rudimentary features characterize a waiting-list control group. First, if a pretest is used, there must be no treatment between the first and second assessment period for the waiting-list control group because during this period the wait-list group is functionally equivalent to a no-treatment control group. Second, the time period from first to second assessment of the waiting-list control group must correspond to the time period of pre- and posttreatment assessment of the treatment group. This may be easily controlled if treatment consists of a particular interval (e.g., 2 months) and the pre-to-posttreatment assessment period is constant across treated subjects. Waiting-list control subjects can return for reassessment after that fixed interval has elapsed. If treatment duration varies, a waiting-list subject might be reassessed at the same interval of the treatment subject to which he or she has been matched. For example, a waiting-list control subject can be scheduled for reassessment at the same time that a treated subject returns for posttreatment assessment. The waiting-list control and experimental subjects are grouped in this way on the basis of having taken the pre- and posttreatment assessment devices over the same time interval (e.g., within 1 week) or perhaps even on the same days. More simply stated, the assessment interval for a particular treatment client can correspond to the interval for a waiting-list control client. It is important to keep the time interval constant to control for history and maturation over the course of the assessment interval.

Waiting-list control clients complete pretest or posttest assessments and then receive treatment. An important practical question is how to have the waiting-list subjects return for reassessment immediately prior to providing them with treatment. Actually, this is not particularly difficult. Clients usually are required to complete the assessment again before receiving treatment. Essentially, reassessment is connected with the promise of scheduling treatment and serves as an immediate antecedent to the long-awaited intervention.

Special Considerations There is an obvious limitation of the waiting-list control condition, particularly in comparison to a no-treatment group. Because subjects in the waiting-list group receive treatment soon after they have served their role as a temporary no-treatment group, the long-term impact of processes such as history, maturation, and repeated testing cannot be evaluated. Even if waiting-list subjects did not change very much in the time interval in which they waited for treatment, they may have improved or deteriorated greatly by the time of follow-up assessment even without treatment. One can follow the treatment group to see how they are doing 1 or 2 years later. Yet, the waiting-list control group is no longer available for comparison because by this time the wait-list group will be another treatment group.

Although rare, in some instances, wait-list control cases are informed that they will receive treatment after an extended period. For example, in one study, two 12-week treatments were compared to a waiting-list control condition (Cunningham, Bremner, & Boyle, 1995). To their credit, the investigators wished to obtain 6-month follow-up data. Wait-list cases were told that they could begin treatment after the 6-month follow-up data were obtained. This was an excellent strategy from the standpoint of design, but would not be feasible in the vast majority of situations in which clients experience significant clinical impairment.

The use of a waiting-list control group has much to recommend it. From a practical standpoint, it usually is not as difficult to obtain waiting-list control subjects as it is to obtain no-treatment subjects. The difficulty partially depends on how long the controls are required to wait for treatment, the severity of the problem, their perceived need for treatment, and the availability of other resources. From the standpoint of experimental design, there is a decided advantage in the use of a waiting-list control group because having this group allows careful evaluation of treatment effects at different points in the design. Because treatment eventually is provided to the waiting-list control subjects, its effects can be evaluated empirically. Essentially, a waiting-list control study using a pretest can be diagrammed as follows:

$$R \quad O_1 \quad X \quad O_2$$
$$R \quad O_3 \qquad O_4 \quad X \quad O_5$$

The effect of treatment (X) is replicated in the design. Not only can the treatment be assessed by a between-group comparison (comparison of O_2 and O_4) but also by within-group comparisons (comparison of change from O_3 to O_4 with the change from O_4 to O_5). Of course, to accomplish this, waiting-list control group subjects must be reassessed after they finally receive treatment.

The waiting-list control group does not completely ameliorate the ethical problems of withholding treatment but may help somewhat. Now the issue is not withholding treatment from some of the clients. Rather, all clients receive treatment and differ only according to when they receive it. Ethical problems arise if clients request or require immediate treatment and if delaying treatment may have serious consequences (e.g., a waiting-list control group is not ethically defensible with acutely suicidal patients). Apart from such situations and as an alternative to the no-treatment control group, a waiting-list group offers a distinct advantage because clients eventually receive treatment.

No-Contact Control Group

Description and Rationale   The effects of participating in a study, even if only in the capacity of a no-treatment or waiting-list control subject, may have impact on the subjects because participation is reactive. In the context of treatment research, participating in a control group may exert a change and improvement. Indeed, it has been known for some time that clients who receive the initial assessment battery on separate occasions prior to treatment show marked improvements (Frank et al., 1963). Although regression alone might account for improvement on repeated testing, the anticipation of relief from participating in a treatment project may also be responsible.

Occasionally it is possible to evaluate the impact of participation by using as a control group individuals who have no contact with the project. These individuals constitute a *no-contact control group*. The requirements for a no-contact group are difficult to meet because the *subjects do not receive treatment and do not realize that they are serving in this capacity*. To obtain such a group of subjects, pretest information usually is needed for a large pool of subjects who are part of a larger assessment project. Some subjects, determined randomly, are selected for the no-contact group. To obtain the initial pretest information requires that assessment devices be administered under some other guise (e.g., part of routine class activities in an undergraduate course). Also, obtaining subsequent test information must be conveyed as part of a routine activity so it is not associated with a treatment project.

It is worth discussing this type of group even though it is used infrequently. As a classic example, Paul (1966) treated college students for speech anxiety and utilized several students who qualified for treatment as no-contact control subjects. Measures were administered under the guise of requirements for and a follow-up to ordinary college speech classes. No-treatment subjects, also a separate group in the study, received several assessment devices such as telephone contact, interviews, and other procedures related to the treatment project. The no-contact group received none of these assessments and had no basis to infer that they were in the study. Because the assessment before and after treatment was related to participation in the course, data were available without revealing use of the information as part of a treatment study. At the end, comparisons could be made assessing the effect of receiving contact with the program versus no contact. Among subjects who did not receive treatment, those who had no explicit contact with the study (no-contact controls) performed less well on various measures of anxiety and personality at the end of the study and at follow-up than did subjects (no-treatment controls) who knew they were part of the study. Thus, serving as a no-treatment subject explicitly connected with the study was associated with some improvements that may not otherwise have occurred.

Special Considerations   In outpatient research, a captive group of subjects analogous to college students is not usually available. In addition, administering measures under a guise other than treatment is likely to violate both the letter and spirit of current informed consent requirements for subjects who participate in research. Studies in institutional settings such as clinics, psychiatric hospitals, prisons, and schools might permit no-contact control groups. Assessment devices could be administered routinely on separate occasions and be used to provide data for comparisons with subsamples in the study. However, use of data as part of research requires informing subjects and obtaining consent. Thus, subjects would know they were in a study.

The main issue is not whether a no-contact group could be formed; the issue is the research question being addressed. In most studies, the investigator is not likely to be concerned with separating the effects of contact with the treatment or research project from no-contact; a no-treatment or waiting-list control group is likely to serve as the appropriate measure of improvement against which the effects of treatment can be evaluated. On the other hand, it might be important for conceptual reasons to evaluate whether serving in a project, even as a no-treatment subject, influences a particular set of measures or clinical problem.

An investigator may also wish to use no-contact procedures to avoid the influences associated with knowing that one is participating in an experiment. For example, in one program, over 500 seventh graders from 10 different schools were included in a study to control classroom discipline (Matthews, 1986). Children within each school were assigned randomly to experimental or control conditions. Teachers in the experimental condition were trained to conduct relaxation exercises in their classes; they did them daily for approximately 7 months. The objective was to calm the children and to develop a means for coping with tension. Control children did not receive the special program. Neither teachers nor students were aware that they were participating in a study; the intervention was provided as part of the curriculum for some students in their homerooms. The dependent measure consisted of discipline infractions at the school (e.g., fighting, cutting class) and the data were collected routinely and were not associated specifically with this study. The results indicated that experimental youth, when compared with controls, showed significantly fewer discipline infractions. The fact that persons in experimental and control group(s) were uninformed about their participation minimized the impact of potential threats to validity (e.g., special treatment or reactions of the control group, reactivity of the experimental arrangements, reactivity of assessment). In this study, the no-contact feature applied to both intervention and control conditions. In general, no-contact procedures or control groups may be useful to address the impact of serving in a study or to eliminate the potential reactivity of such an arrangement. Counsel is required to ensure that subjects' rights are protected and that the study meets ethical requirements of informed consent (see Chapter 16).

Nonspecific Treatment (Attention–Placebo) Control Group

Description and Rationale   No-treatment and waiting-list control groups are employed primarily to address threats to internal validity. In the context of treatment research, a nonspecific treatment control group addresses these threats but focuses on threats to construct validity. In any treatment there are many accouterments that may contribute to or be responsible for therapeutic change. Such factors as attending treatment sessions, having personal contact with a therapist, hearing a logical rationale that describes the genesis of one's problem, and undergoing a procedure directed toward ameliorating the problem may exert influence on client performance and generate therapeutic effects. These factors are referred to as *common* or *nonspecific factors* of psychotherapy because they are ingredients in most treatments. Moreover, when we consider specific therapy techniques (e.g., cognitive-behavioral treatment, structural family therapy), we do not consider the mechanisms of action or processes through which change is achieved to be due merely or solely to the common factors. Rather, additional processes are proposed to explain both the problem and the way(s) in which the problem will be resolved or addressed.

Actually, the common factors may not be trivial in the processes they mobilize within the individuals nor in the changes they produce. When clients participate in treatment, they are likely to believe in the procedures and have faith that some therapeutic change will result (Frank & Frank, 1991). We have learned from many years of medical research that the patient's belief in treatment is important. Placebos (inert substances such as sugar tablets) given under the guise of treatment can alter a variety of disorders ranging in severity from the common cold to cancer (Shapiro & Morris, 1978). Placebo effects, by definition, result from factors other than active ingredients in the substance itself. Hence, the belief of the patient in treatment and perhaps the belief in the physician who administers treatment and similar factors appear to be responsible for change.

Effects analogous to placebo reactions influence individuals who come to psychotherapy. Indeed, the history of psychological treatments can be traced by drawing attention to procedures and therapists (e.g., Franz Anton Mesmer [1734–1815] and Emile Coué [1857–1926]) whose effects we recognize to have been largely due to suggestion. Consequently, in an empirical investigation of psychotherapy, a simple comparison of treatment and no-treatment control groups does not establish what facet of "the intervention" led to change, that is, construct validity. To identify whether the specific intervention or the unique properties of a treatment are important in producing change in the clients, a nonspecific treatment group can be included in the design.

A nonspecific treatment control may include procedures in which clients meet with a therapist, hear a rationale that explains how their problem may have developed, and discuss something about their lives in sessions that are similar in number and duration to sessions in the treatment group. From the standpoint of the investigation, these subjects are considered to be receiving a psychological placebo. Although this procedure might be credible to the clients and appear to be effective, it is not based on theoretical or empirical findings about therapeutic change.

In developing a nonspecific control condition, the goal is to provide a form of pseudointervention that involves clients in some sort of experience. The goal is to control for factors common to coming to treatment without the putatively critical ingredient. Special care is needed to decide in advance what the investigators wish to control. As an illustration, a recent study evaluated an intervention to resolve unfinished emotional business, specifically, unresolved issues related to a significant other (Paivio & Greenberg, 1995). The treatment consisted of the Gestalt empty-chair dialogue in which a client engages in an imaginary dialogue with a significant other. The intervention is part of experiential therapy and is designed to access important feelings, to allow these feelings to complete their course, and to be restructured and allayed in the context of a safe therapy environment. Adults were recruited and screened for unfinished emotional business and assigned to the empty-chair treatment or to an attention–placebo control condition. The control condition included group sessions that discussed unfinished business but did not provide opportunities to experience and to access feelings by the empty-chair technique. The control condition was very good because the themes and topics were very similar to those used in the treatment condition. This would make this group more than just a group coming to treatment and seeing a therapist because, in the end, we might be able to say that merely raising the topic of unfinished business had not been enough (because the control group did this).

Unfortunately, the treatment and control groups differed in three ways (individual vs. group treatment, 12 vs. 3 sessions, approximately 10 vs. 6 hours of treatment), which raised a plausible rival interpretation of the results, namely, that multiple characteristics favored the treatment condition, apart from the manipulation of interest. Also, a critical issue for nonspecific treatment control groups is to control for level of expectations that are mobilized in the subjects. It is likely that the treatment group was much more credible than the control condition and these different expectations could account for or contribute to the outcome differences. As for the findings, at posttreatment the experimental group showed greater reduction in stress and resolution of unfinished business than did controls. Follow-up data did not permit comparison of the different conditions, but the treated subjects who were followed maintained their gains.

A nonspecific treatment control group is designed to control for common factors that are associated with participation in treatment. The goal is to reduce the plausibility that accouterments of treatment, such as coming to sessions and meeting with a mental health professional, account for change. It is important to note that once these accountrements are ruled out, the processes proposed by the investigator to characterize the treatment group (e.g., changes in cognitions, resolving conflict) are not necessarily supported. Nonspecific treatment groups rule out common factors, but they do not necessarily point to the construct that is responsible for change. If the investigator wishes to argue for the basis for change in the treatment group, evaluation of the processes considered to be central to change (e.g., cognitions, alliance) ought to be assessed directly and tested in relation to the amount of therapeutic change.

Special Considerations Several issues emerge in developing a nonspecific treatment control condition. First, the conceptual problems are not minor. What is an "inert" intervention that could serve as a control? A placebo in medicine, because of its pharmacological properties (e.g., salt or sugar in a tablet), is known to be inert, that is, not to produce effects through its chemical properties in relation to the clinical problem. In psychological treatment, one usually does not know whether the properties of the nonspecific treatment group are inert. Merely chatting with a therapist, engaging in activities that are related to one's problem, or merely relaxing with a therapist might be cast in theoretical language to make them seem plausible as genuine treatments. In therapy research, this is why one investigator's treatment group is another investigator's control group. It is difficult to devise an intervention that is both credible to the clients and one that could not also be construed by someone as a theoretically plausible treatment.

Another issue that emerges pertains to the credibility of the procedure. One ingredient in therapy is the client's belief that treatment will work. Presumably a plausible nonspecific treatment control group would also have this ingredient so that client expectations for improvement could not explain outcome differences between treatment and control conditions. However, devising a credible control condition requires a rationale about why the treatment is likely to be effective and why procedures in or outside the treatment sessions seem to be credible means toward therapeutic change. There is some evidence to suggest that highly credible control conditions are often as effective as treatment conditions (when compared to no treatment) (Lambert & Bergin, 1994). This finding has implications for conducting experiments (larger sample sizes are needed to detect small group differences) and for their interpretation (isolating the construct that accounts for change).

Ethical issues also emerge in providing nonspecific treatment conditions. This issue is not merely one of providing a treatment that may not be well based on theory or empirical findings. As with other control conditions, if clients are in need of care, this type of group may not be defensible. There is also a more subtle ethical issue. Participation in the present control condition might influence beliefs about therapy in general and have impact on client's subsequent use of treatment. If clients learn that treatment is not very credible, does not help, or does not focus on the problem, it might remove a possible resource from them. Conceivably, ordinary therapy might teach a given client such lessons; using a control condition without a veridical treatment merely increases the likelihood of such an effect.

Research to date tends to support the view that psychotherapy is more effective than nonspecific treatment control conditions and that nonspecific treatment control conditions are more effective than no treatment (Lambert & Bergin, 1994). In developing or evaluating a new treatment, it is critical to show that treatment effects surpass those achieved with the common factors that arise from merely participating in treatment. This can be accomplished by using a nonspecific treatment control group or another treatment that has already been shown to be effective. Routine treatment is also a viable comparison group and is discussed later.

Yoked Control Group

Description and Rationale Differences in procedures or events to which the subjects are exposed may arise during the investigation as a function of executing the study or implementing a particular intervention. The problem with these differences is that they are not random; they may vary systematically between groups. If the effect of the intervention is to be distinguished from differences that inadvertently arise across groups, the latter influences must be controlled.

One procedure to rule out or assess factors that may arise as a function of implementing a particular intervention is called the *yoked control group*. The purpose of the yoked control group is to ensure that groups are equal with respect to potentially important but conceptually and procedurally irrelevant factors that might account for group differences (Church, 1964). Yoking may require a special control group of its own. More likely in clinical research, yoking can be incorporated into another control group. In this case, yoking refers to equalizing the groups on a particular variable that might systematically vary across conditions.

Consider a hypothetical study designed to evaluate a specific therapy technique for the treatment of acrophobia (fear of heights). Three groups are used: (1) the "new and improved" treatment, (2) a nonspecific treatment control group that meets with a therapist but engages in a task not likely to be therapeutic (e.g., discussing the development of fears among people they know), and (3) no treatment. Suppose that clients in the treatment group are allowed to attend as many sessions as needed to master a set of tasks designated as therapeutic. For example, clients might have to complete a standard set of anxiety-provoking tasks in therapy to help them overcome anxiety. The number of sessions that clients attend treatment could vary markedly because of individual differences in the rate of completing the tasks. A nonspecific treatment control group might receive a bogus treatment in which group members merely discuss fears of their friends and relatives. One might raise the question of how many sessions the control group subjects should receive. It would be important to design the study so that any differences in effects of treatment cannot be due to the different number of sessions that the groups received. Yet the control subjects should not be given a fixed number of sessions because that would not guarantee equality of sessions across groups.

A solution is to yoke (match) subjects across groups by pairing subjects. The pairs might be formed arbitrarily unless matching was used to assign subjects to groups. A subject in the experimental group would receive a certain number of therapy sessions on the basis of his or her progress. Whatever that number turned out to be would be the number of sessions that would be given to the control subject to whom the subject was yoked. That is, the number of sessions for each control subject would be determined by the subject to whom he or she was paired or matched in the experimental group. Obviously, the yoking procedure requires running the experimental subject first so that the number of sessions or other variable on which yoking will be done is known in advance and can be administered to the control subject. The behavior of the experimental subject determines what happens to the control subject. At the end of treatment, the number of treatment sessions will be identical across groups. Hence, group differences could not be attributable to the number of sessions to which clients were exposed because yoking would have ensured that the number of sessions did not vary and would hold constant the number of sessions between the treatment and nonspecific control groups.

Yoking might be extended to address the other group in the design, namely, the no-treatment control group. If pre- and posttreatment assessments are provided, how long should the interval between these assessments be for the group that does not receive any treatment? Subjects in the no-treatment group could also be yoked to persons in treatment group in terms of the number of weeks between pretreatment and posttreatment assessment. Thus, at the end of the study, both treatment and nonspecific control groups would have received the same number of sessions and the time elapsed in weeks or days between pretreatment and posttreatment assessment would be the same for the all treatment and control conditions. Stated in a more quantitative way, the means and standard deviations would not differ in relation to the number of sessions (for the two treatment groups) or the number of days or weeks between pre- and posttreatment for all groups. As evident from this example, the yoked control procedure may not necessarily constitute a new control group. Yoking often can be added to a nonspecific treatment control group.

Special Considerations   Conceivably, an experimental and control group can be yoked on all sorts of variables that may differ between groups. Whether yoking is used as a control technique needs to be determined by considering whether the variables that may differ across these groups might plausibly account for the results. For example, in a given therapy study it might make sense to yoke on the number of treatment sessions because the amount of contact with a therapist and treatment may contribute to the differences between a treatment and nonspecific treatment control group, particularly if therapy subjects receive many more sessions. Stated differently, it may be plausible that the number of sessions, rather than the content of the sessions, is viewed as a threat to construct validity. The intervention confounds content and amount of treatment and hence raises ambiguities about why the intervention was more effective. On the other hand, it may be unimportant to yoke subjects in such a way that the time of the day that therapy sessions are held or the attire of the therapists is perfectly matched across groups. The variables that serve as the basis of yoking are often based on considerations of construct validity, that is, what the investigator wishes to say about the treatment and what facets of treatment, if allowed to vary systematically, might plausibly account for the results. By yoking, the investigator controls the variables that potentially can confound the results.

Nonrandomly Assigned (Patched-Up) Control Group

Description and Rationale   Many groups might be added to an experiment that utilize subjects who were not part of the original subject pool and not randomly assigned to treatment. These groups, referred to as *patched-up control groups,* help rule out specific rival hypotheses and decrease the plausibility of specific threats to internal validity. One use of nonrandomly assigned subjects is to help rule out specific threats to validity such as history, maturation, testing, and instrumentation. Such a group may be used when a no-treatment control group cannot be formed through random assignment. Although the purpose of this group is exactly the same as that of the randomly assigned no-treatment group mentioned earlier, there may be special interpretive problems that arise because of the way in which the group is formed. The control groups in the nonequivalent control design discussed in the context of quasi-experiments constitute patched-up groups. These groups are useful in helping to rule out threats to internal validity, but they may be weak for comparative purposes, depending on how they were formed.

For example, Rogers and Dymond (1954) used a patched-up control group in their classic study that evaluated the effects of client-centered psychotherapy. Clients who applied for treatment at a university counseling center were assigned either to treatment (individual client-centered therapy) or to waiting-list control conditions. Waiting-list control subjects waited 60 days before they were reassessed and given treatment. This group, though similar to the treatment subjects in motivation for treatment and various personality factors, did not completely control for such threats to internal validity as history, maturation, and testing because the interval before reassessment was only 60 days, a shorter than the average interval for therapy subjects to complete treatment. Technically, differences between these two groups might result from changes occurring during the different testing periods that elapsed, independent of treatment.

To help examine the plausibility of such threats to validity as history, maturation, and testing, the authors used a patched-up control group. Specifically, volunteers were solicited for an experiment on personality. These subjects had not applied for treatment and hence were different from treatment and waiting-list subjects in that regard. Yet, the patched-up controls were matched to subjects who had applied for treatment in terms of sex, student–nonstudent status, approximate age, and socioeconomic status. Half the patched-up controls were yoked to treatment subjects and the other half to control subjects in terms of the time that was allowed to elapse between testing periods. In other words, the patched-up group, although very different in subject composition, helped evaluate the effects of history, maturation, and testing on changes in the dependent measures. Moreover, this group assessed the influence of such threats during treatment and follow-up periods (6–12 months after treatment), by which time waiting-list subjects had long completed treatment. The patched-up control group was not comprised through random assignment among all subjects in the study and hence was not ideally comparable to the other groups. Yet the general failure of this group to show systematic improvements during the course of treatment helped diminish the plausibility of various threats in accounting for the changes that occurred in the therapy group.

Special Considerations   Patched-up control groups can vary widely and have to be evaluated on their individual merit. Their purpose is to reduce the plausibility that other influences (internal validity or construct validity) could explain the results. Because the group is not comprised randomly, the data may not be as persuasive as parallel data resulting from a randomly comprised control or comparison group. Yet, in any given case, the absence of randomness may not be a fatal limitation. The question is whether specific threat (e.g., selection x history or maturation) is as plausible as the interpretation the investigator wishes to place on the data. Although patched-up controls are less than perfect control groups, they can tip the balance of plausibility among alternative interpretations of data.

Not all patched-up or nonrandomly assigned groups in clinical research address threats to internal validity. Groups might be added to provide useful information and to expand the conclusions that can be reached about the outcome. In treatment research, a valuable use of nonrandomly selected subjects is to compare the extent to which clients in the study are distinguished from their peers who have not been referred for treatment. By comparing individuals who have been identified as a treatment population with their peers who apparently are functioning with little or no problem, one can assess whether treatment has brought the clients within a "normal" range of behavior. The use of normative data to evaluate treatment is part of a larger area of evaluating the clinical importance of changes made in treatment (see Chapter 14).

OTHER COMPARISON GROUPS

The notion of control groups is rudimentary. The familiar purpose of control groups is conveyed in a straightforward manner by discussing the no-treatment and waiting-list groups in which the threats to internal validity are controlled. A more in-depth understanding of research design might be pursued by discussing the broader concept of comparison groups. *Comparison groups* refer to any group included in design beyond the primary group or groups of interest. Comparison groups permit the investigator to draw various conclusions; the groups differ in the types of conclusions they permit. Control groups are merely one type of comparison group. Some control groups (e.g., no-treatment, waiting-list) primarily address the threats to internal validity; other types of control groups (e.g., nonspecific-treatment) also address concerns of construct validity in the sense that they aid in interpreting the basis for the impact of the intervention. The investigator may wish to make any number of statements about the intervention and what accounted for the change. Because the range of possible conclusions varies widely with content area and investigator interest, all comparison groups of interest cannot be catalogued. Nevertheless, comparison groups often used in clinical research can be identified and illustrated.

Routine or Standard Treatment

In clinical research, assigning individuals to no-treatment, waiting-list, and nonspecific-treatment control conditions may not be ethically defensible or feasible in light of presenting problems of the clients and the context in which treatment is provided. In such circumstances, the investigator may still wish to test whether a new treatment is effective. One alternative is to compare the new treatment with the standard one that is provided in the setting. For example, multisystematic therapy is an intervention that has been used to treat adolescent sexual offenders and juvenile offenders (Borduin et al., 1995; Henggeler, Melton, & Smith, 1992). The treatment combines multiple interventions (e.g., parent training, cognitive therapy) to address peer, school, adolescent, parent, and family problems. Because the youths have multiple offenses, they cannot be assigned to no-treatment or attention–placebo conditions. Consequently, the treatment studies evaluated the extent to which multisystemic therapy surpasses routine or standard care (individual therapy, "as-usual" procedures, such as probation). The random assignment of cases to these different conditions is feasible and addresses the question of interest without other control groups. In these studies, multisystemic therapy was much more effective than routine treatments were, as reflected on measures of emotional and behavioral problems and arrest and criminal behavior.

At least three advantages accrue to the use of standard treatment or routine care as a comparison condition. First, demands for service and ethical issues associated with many other control conditions are met. All persons in the study can receive an active treatment. No one receives a condition that is not designed to work (e.g., nonspecific-treatment control condition). Second, because everyone receives a veridical treatment, attrition is likely to be less than if various control conditions were used (e.g., no-treatment or waiting-list conditions). Third, routine treatment is likely to control for many of the common or nonspecific factors of therapy (e.g., contact with a therapist, participation in sessions). Thus, receipt of an intervention is not a viable rival interpretation of the results in most studies, although new therapies, when compared to standard treatments tend to have more enthusiasm, investigator hype, and therapist expectations than that of business as usual.

Standard and routine treatments or programs raise their own dilemmas. It is often difficult to know what these programs entail at a clinic, hospital, or school, no matter what the descriptions and brochures actually say. The investigator ought to monitor and assess carefully what is done as part of routine treatment. If possible, it is better from the standpoint of the design for the investigator to administer the condition so that integrity of the procedure and assessment before, during, and after treatment can be closely monitored. In addition, ethical dilemmas often arise after a study is completed and treatment is shown to be better than routine care. In such studies (e.g., multisystemic therapy cited above), routine care may become ethically indefensible because it is shown to be inferior to a new treatment.

The investigator may wish to compare the treatment of interest to another active treatment other than a standard or as-usual intervention that is routinely used. In a simple version of such a study, two active or viable treatments are compared and there is no control group in the usual sense. Assuming random assignment, the comparison group addresses the usual threats to internal validity (e.g., history, maturation). The only danger is that improvements in both groups and no outcome differences between groups could be explained completely by threats to internal validity. This is not a minor issue and has limited many studies.

The range of suitable or appropriate comparison groups is vast because they are likely to focus on theory and analysis of the key constructs underlying treatment rather than on many of the more specific threats to internal and construct validity to which more commonly used groups are aimed. The range of comparison conditions is illustrated later in the chapter by examining the progression of questions addressed in psychotherapy research.

Key Considerations in Group Selection

The previous discussion described control and comparison groups that are likely to be of use in experimental research, that is, studies in clinical psychology in which the investigator controls the manipulation through assignment of subjects to conditions. It is tempting to provide rules or guidelines for selecting a particular group in certain kinds of situations but not in others. Yet the precise groups that should be used in clinical research depend on at least three considerations: the interests of the investigator, previous research findings, and practical and ethical constraints.

The interests of the investigator refer to the claims that one would like to make at the end of the experiment. The interests embrace internal and construct validity. The investigator wishes to rule out the usual threats and at the same time to say something about why the effect was obtained. Addressing internal validity is relatively straightforward; addressing construct validity is more intricate because it depends on the investigator's view of what is critical to the intervention and the specificity of the desired conclusions.

The same collection of treatment groups would require different controls depending on what the investigator wishes to conclude when the study is completed. For example, consider a study that compared client-centered and cognitive therapy. If the investigator were interested only in discussing which of two treatments was better for a particular disorder, this design, without any of the familiar groups mentioned earlier, would be adequate. On the other hand, another investigator may be interested in asking whether either treatment exerts therapeutic effects beyond those that can be accounted for by nonspecific treatment effects. In this case, a control group that provided a nonspecific treatment experience would be critical. Thus, if the client-centered and cognitive treatments were equally effective, one could compare the groups to a nonspecific treatment condition to determine whether the treatment effects were likely to be the result of attending treatment per se. The latter design, with its addition of a nonspecific treatment control group, is not necessarily superior to the previous one in which only the two treatment groups were included. The issue of superiority of one design over another is not measured by how many control groups there are but by whether the question of interest to the investigator is adequately addressed. Both experiments appear to address their respective questions adequately. One could take a broader view of experimentation and note that the consumer of research may wish to draw more inferences from an experiment than did the investigator, in which case an extra control group might be useful. However, the main purpose of a given study should be to deploy resources to provide the best test of a limited question rather than to try to control for or anticipate all questions that might be asked, even though they were not of direct interest.

There are no rules for deciding specifically what control groups to include, and investigators probably proceed in different ways to reach the final decisions. In my own research, it has been useful to ponder the anticipated patterns of results to decide some groups that might be included. Specifically, this procedure involves plotting possible variations of results (e.g., differences between or among groups) that might come from the study while the study is still in the design stage. Initially, the ideal or expected results with respect to a particular hypothesis and prediction, if they can be specified, might be diagrammed; then more likely data patterns are considered. As variations of possible results are considered, the following question can be asked: What other interpretations can account for this pattern of results? The answer is likely to lead to changes in the experimental groups or to the addition of control groups to narrow the alternative interpretations that can be provided. Permutations of likely patterns or results and critical evaluation of rival interpretations of the findings are useful in generating additional comparison groups that are needed in a given study or bolstering the design by increasing the sample to ensure a strong test of the major comparisons of interest.

Previous research also may dictate the essential control groups for a given investigation. For example, in the study of a particular treatment, it is not always necessary to use a no-treatment or waiting-list control group. If there are consistent data that the absence of treatment has no effect, at least on the dependent measures of interest, these groups might be omitted. Of course, to justify exclusion of a no-treatment group, one would want convincing data about the likely changes over time without treatment. Relying on data from studies completed by other investigators at different research facilities might not provide an adequate basis to exclude a no-treatment group unless there is consensus that the problem is immutable without treatment. For example, "depressed clients" in one investigator's research may vary markedly from the "same" sample at another facility because of different measures used in screening and different locales. On the other hand, within a research program, continued studies may reveal that no treatment or nonspecific treatment groups lead to no change in the clients. In such a case, omitting these groups after several studies have been completed is somewhat more justifiable and also permits the investigator to move on to more sophisticated questions about the effects of treatment.

There is another way to view the elimination of particular groups such as no-treatment groups as a program of research progresses. As investigations build on one another, research questions become increasingly refined, and there may be no need for some of the control groups used early in the research. Again, it is difficult to specify when various groups can be abandoned; however, as noted earlier, experimental demonstrations vary in their persuasiveness to the scientific community depending on a host of factors. Hence, in cases of doubt, it is probably advisable to include a control group to augment the persuasiveness of the experimental test.

As a final consideration, the selection of control groups is limited greatly by practical and ethical constraints. Practical issues, such as procuring enough subjects with similar treatment problems, losing subjects assigned to control conditions for a protracted period, and related obstacles mentioned earlier, may dictate the types of groups that can be used. Ethical constraints such as withholding treatment, delivering treatments that might not help (or might even exacerbate) the client's problem, deception about ineffective treatments, and similar issues also limit what can be done clinically. In the context of clinical samples, both practical and ethical issues may make it impossible to perform the comparisons that might be of greatest interest on theoretical grounds.

PROGRESSION OF CONTROL AND COMPARISON GROUPS: EVALUATING PSYCHOTHERAPY

The use of various control and comparison groups isolated from an area of research is somewhat abstract. Also, the discussion does not convey the progression of research, which can be measured in the level of sophistication of the questions that are asked and the complexity of the conditions to which an experimental group is compared. Psychotherapy research usefully illustrates the progression of research and the role of various control and comparison groups.

A major task of psychotherapy research is to identify effective treatments, to understand the underlying bases of therapeutic change, and to elaborate the client, therapist, and other factors on which treatment effects depend. At the general level, the tasks to which research is devoted have been cast as a question, namely, "What treatment, by whom, is most effective for this individual with that specific problem, under which set of circumstances?" (Paul, 1967, p. 111). This question continues to be of keen interest in outcome research (Roth & Fonagy, 1996). The question can be translated into several more specific strategies that can guide individual studies. Table 6.1 presents major strategies and the questions they are designed to address.

Treatment Package Strategy

Perhaps the most basic question is to ask whether a particular treatment or treatment package is effective for a particular clinical problem. This question is asked by the treatment package strategy, which evaluates the effects of a particular treatment as the treatment is ordinarily used. The notion of a "package" emphasizes that treatment may be multifaceted and include several different components that could be delineated conceptually and operationally. The question

TABLE 6.1.   Treatment Evaluation Strategies to Develop and to Identify Effective Interventions

Treatment Strategy	Question Asked	Basic Requirements
Treatment package	Does treatment produce therapeutic change?	Treatment vs. no-treatment or waiting-list control
Dismantling strategy	What components are necessary, sufficient, and facilitative of therapeutic change?	Two or more treatment groups that vary in the components of treatment provided
Constructive strategy	What components or other treatments can be added to enhance therapeutic change?	Two or more treatment groups that vary in components
Parametric strategy	What changes can be made in the specific treatment to increase its effectiveness?	Two or more treatment groups that differ in one or more facets of the treatment
Comparative outcome strategy	Which treatment is more or most effective for a particular problem and population?	Two or more different treatments for a given clinical problem
Client and therapist variation strategy	What patient, family, or therapist characteristics does treatment depend on to be effective?	Treatment as applied separately to different types of cases, therapists, etc.
Process strategy	What processes occur in treatment that affect within-session performance and that may contribute to treatment outcome?	Treatment groups in which patient and therapist interactions are evaluated within the sessions

addressed by this strategy is whether treatment produces therapeutic change. To rule out threats to internal validity, a no-treatment or waiting-list control condition is usually included in the design.

As an example, a treatment package study was used to alleviate marital distress among couples with chronically ill children (Walker, Johnson, Manion, & Cloutier, 1996). Chronic illness in children can place special burden (financial, interpersonal) on the family and has been associated with increases in marital stress, conflict, poor communication, lack of intimacy, and ultimately marital break-up. In this study, couples whose child was receiving care for a chronic condition (e.g., cancer, diabetes, epilepsy, kidney disease, muscular dystrophy, etc.) agreed to participate and were assigned to treatment or a waiting-list group. Treated couples, seen individually rather than in a larger group, attended 10 sessions that focused on identifying sources of conflict, needs, and experiences and on efforts to promote acceptance and new interaction patterns and relationship issues in relation to the child's issues. Waiting-list participants were not treated during the study but were offered treatment when the study was completed. The results indicated that treated couples improved significantly on measures of marital adjustment at the end of treatment and at a 5-month follow-up assessment. Control cases tended to decrease in marital adjustment over time. The treatment was effective compared to no treatment in improving marital adjustment among families with a chronically ill child.

Strictly speaking, evaluation of a treatment package requires only two groups. Random assignment of cases to groups and testing each group before and after treatment controls the usual threats to internal validity. However, there has been considerable debate about the impact of nonspecific treatment factors and the effects they can exert on clinical dysfunction (Lambert & Bergin, 1994). Consequently, treatment package research is likely to include a group that serves as a nonspecific treatment control condition that requires clients to come to the treatment and receive some "control" type of active experience.

Dismantling Treatment Strategy

The dismantling treatment strategy consists of analyzing the components of a given treatment package. After a particular package has been shown to produce therapeutic change, research can begin to analyze the basis for change. To dismantle a treatment, individual components are eliminated or isolated from the treatment. Some clients may receive the entire treatment package; other clients receive the package minus one or more components. Dismantling research can help identify the necessary and sufficient components of treatment.

For instance, Nezu and Perri (1989) evaluated social problem-solving therapy for the treatment of depressed adults. Problem-solving treatment includes separate components: (1) a problem-solving orientation process which pertains to how individuals respond when presented with a problem or stressful situation; (2) a set of skills or goal-directed tasks that enable people to solve a potential problem successfully. The investigators evaluated whether the full package of training was superior to an abbreviated version in which only the skills component was provided. Clients were assigned to one of two groups to receive either the full treatment or only the skills component. A waiting-list control group was included in the design. At posttreatment and a 6-month follow-up, clients who received the full package (orientation and skills training) were less depressed than those who received the abbreviated treatment (skills training). The authors suggest that the orientation component provided a critical feature of the treatment. The findings suggest that the package offered more than orientation training alone. For present purposes, it is important to note that the specific question about treatment led to a comparison group that itself was a veridical treatment.

Constructive Treatment Strategy

The constructive treatment strategy refers to developing a treatment package by adding components to enhance outcome. In this sense, the constructive treatment approach is the opposite of the dismantling strategy. A constructive treatment study begins with a treatment that may consist of one or a few ingredients or a larger package to which are added various ingredients to determine whether the effects can be enhanced. The strategy asks the question, What can be added to treatment to make it more effective? A special feature of this strategy is the combination of individual treatments. Thus, studies may conceptually combine quite different treatments (e.g., verbal psychotherapy with pharmacotherapy).

There is a keen interest in testing treatment combinations because the scope of impairment of many clinical problems (e.g., depression, antisocial personality) affects many different domains of functioning (e.g., symptoms, social and work relations). Also, many contextual influences on the individual (e.g., parents, spouses) may need to be integrated into treatment to help promote change or to reduce influences that may contribute to or sustain dysfunction in the client. For example, some families of patients diagnosed with schizophrenia are highly critical, hostile, and overinvolved, a set of characteristics referred to as *expressed emotion*. Schizophrenic patients who leave the hospital after treatment and return home to families who are high in expressed emotion have a much higher relapse rate than patients who return home to families low in expressed emotion (Tarrier & Barrowclough, 1990). A single treatment (such as medication) that focuses on symptoms of schizophrenia (e.g., hallucinations, delusions) without attention to family interaction is limited. Several studies have shown that medication combined with a family-based component designed to address interpersonal communication significantly reduces relapse rates compared to treatment without the family component (Klerman et al., 1994; Lam, 1991).

Treatment combinations are often used both in clinical practice and research (Kazdin, 1996a). The obvious view is that combining treatments may overcome the limits of any individual treatment and at the very worst would not hurt. Occasionally a combined treatment is worse (less effective) than one of the constituent treatments presented by itself, that is, the whole is less than the sum of its parts. For example, in the treatment of antisocial behavior among adolescents, treatment that combined a parent program and teen-focused group *increased* behavioral problems and substance use in comparison to the parent group alone (Dishion & Andrews, 1995). Bringing problem youths together may introduce deleterious influences that compete with treatment effects. In any case, one cannot assume that combined treatments will automatically be neutral or better than their constituent treatments. In studies that combine treatments, it is obviously important to include as a comparison condition a group in which the most powerful constituent treatment or each of the treatments that comprise the package is evaluated alone.

Parametric Treatment Strategy

The parametric treatment strategy refers to altering specific aspects of treatment to determine how to maximize therapeutic change. Dimensions or parameters are altered to find the optimal manner of administering the treatment. These dimensions are not new ingredients added to the treatment (e.g., as in the constructive strategy) but are variations to maximize change within the technique. Increases in duration of treatment or variations in how material is presented are samples of the parametric strategy.

A basic parameter of treatment is duration. More treatment tends to produce greater change, although this is mediated by other variables such as type and severity of the problem seen in treatment (Steenbarger, 1994). Also, some domains (e.g., interpersonal and more enduring characteristics) require more time to change in therapy than do others (e.g., acute symptoms) (Kopta, Howard, Lowry, & Beutler, 1994). The impact of treatment duration on changes in different domains of functioning has not been tested directly in many studies. With this in mind, a study was completed to evaluate the effects of 8 versus 16 sessions of psychotherapy with clinically depressed adults (Barkham et al., 1996). Cases were randomly assigned to either cognitive-behavioral treatment or psychodynamically oriented therapy and to one of the two durations. The different durations reflect evaluation of parameters of treatment; the use of two different therapies is an example of comparative treatment evaluation (see below). The two treatments were not different in their effects, but duration effects proved to be interesting. In general, longer duration was associated with greater changes overall and with greater changes across characteristics of treatment that are likely to require more time (e.g., interpersonal spheres, views of oneself). Interestingly, by session 8, clients assigned to the shorter treatment showed greater changes than did those who were at the same session but were at the halfway point. That is, 8 sessions had different effects if clients were assigned to receive 8 instead of 16 sessions. Somehow being involved in the shorter treatment accelerated the rate of change. In any case, the results indicated that duration of treatment was an important parameter that contributed to outcome. The duration question was addressed without the need for special control or comparison groups because active treatment groups addressed the threats to internal and construct validity.

An interesting parametric variation of treatment pertains to the continuation of treatment or use of maintenance therapy. Maintenance therapy refers to the intervention that is provided after the initial (acute) treatment phase. Continuation of treatment has been evaluated in the context of adult depression because many patients may show a relapse or recurrence of depression after treatment (Frank, Johnson, & Kupfer, 1992). Outcome studies evaluating the use of continued, albeit tapered or reduced therapy, has shown that continuation of medication (imipramine) for a period of 3 years after the initial 2-year treatment course had a significant prophylactic effect on the recurrence of depression (Frank et al., 1993; Kupfer et al., 1992). Continuation of full-dose medication (imipramine) was more protective than continuation of half-dose medication and placebo. Interpersonal psychotherapy and cognitive therapy have also been effective in reducing relapse when continued as maintenance strategies, that is, after the initial treatment phase (Frank et al., 1992). As a general conclusion from multiple studies, adults with recurrent depression are very likely to profit from maintenance therapy and to experience much higher rates of relapse without such therapy. Preliminary evidence with adolescence also suggests that maintenance therapy (cognitive–behavioral treatment) following an acute treatment phase decreased relapse (Kroll et al., 1996). Maintenance therapy or continued therapy might be viewed as either a parametric variation of treatment (because it is more of the original treatment) or as a constructive treatment (because a slightly different variation of treatment is added).

Comparative Treatment Strategy

The comparative treatment strategy contrasts two or more treatments and addresses the question of which treatment is better (best) for a particular clinical problem. Comparative studies attract wide attention not only because they address an important clinical issue but also because they often contrast conceptually competing interventions. Classic battle lines that were the basis of comparative outcome studies included psychoanalysis versus behavior therapy, cognitive therapy versus medication, family therapy versus individual therapy, and many others. Such studies seem to draw much more attention, interest, and predictable controversy because they are cast as a contest for a gold medal. The yield (in my opinion) of such studies has been minor, except for mobilizing and sometimes clarifying particular positions. Clinical psychology now has moved away from narrow camps and approaches; hence, comparative studies are less of a battleground than they were during the past 20 years. Movement in the field toward integrative conceptual positions (e.g., integrationism in psychotherapy), emphasis on approaches with outcome evidence (e.g., so-called validated treatments), managed care pressures, and increased accountability in general have mobilized and unified factions and changed the nature of competing views of treatment.

Comparative studies are still important but often serve different purposes. One purpose is to evaluate the varied effects of different treatments. For example, Szapocznik et al. (1989) compared structured family therapy and psychodynamic therapy to treat Hispanic boys (6–12 years old) referred for a variety of different problems (e.g., conduct disorder, anxiety disorder, adjustment disorders). Families were seen in the family-therapy condition. Treatment emphasized modifying maladaptive interaction patterns among family members. Psychodynamic therapy consisted of individual therapy with the child. Treatment focused on play, expression of feelings, transference interpretations, and insight. Diverse outcome measures were included to reflect changes unique to the individual treatments. The results indicated that both groups attained equivalent reductions in behavioral and emotional problems at posttreatment and both groups were better at posttreatment than was a nonspecific treatment control condition in which recreational activities were provided. Family therapy was superior to psychodynamic therapy on a measure of family functioning at a 1-year follow-up. The main contribution of the study was in showing differential impact of the two treatments on family functioning. In passing, it is useful to mention that the control group in this study was very important. If the two treatment groups had been equally effective without this control, it is possible that the improvements for both groups could be attributed to history, maturation, retesting, and other threats to internal validity or to nonspecific treatment influences, which are a threat to construct validity. Evidence that the treatment conditions led to greater change than the control condition addressed these concerns.

Client and Therapist Variation Strategy

The previous strategies emphasized the technique as a major source of influence in treatment outcome and searches for main effects of treatment, that is, that treatment is better or worse for all individuals as a group. Yet it is much more likely that the effectiveness of treatments varies as a function of characteristics of the patients, the therapists, and, depending on the clinical problem, the context in which the patient functions (e.g., type of family, support system available). For example, we know that most individuals coming to treatment who meet diagnostic criteria for one psychiatric disorder are likely to meet criteria for at least one other disorder (Brown et al., 1995; Kazdin, 1995a; Wetzler & Sanderson, 1997). The effects of a given treatment may vary, depending on comorbidity (whether patients meet criteria for more than one disorder). Comorbidity is one client characteristic that would be a reasonable focus for a client and therapist variation treatment evaluation strategy.

The overall goal of this evaluation strategy is to examine factors that may *moderate* treatment effects, that is, whether attributes of the client, therapist, or context contribute to outcome. As noted previously, moderators refer to the variables that influence the effects of some other condition or variable (in this case, treatment). The strategy is implemented by selecting clients, therapists, or both on the basis of specific characteristics. When clients or therapists are classified according to a particular selection variable, the question is whether treatment is more or less effective with certain kinds of participants. For example, questions of this strategy might ask whether treatment is more effective with younger versus older clients or with certain subtypes of problems (e.g., depression) rather than with other subtypes. An example of a client variation study was reported in the treatment of alcoholic patients (Kadden, Getter, Cooney, & Litt, 1989). The investigators evaluated two treatments: coping skills training and interaction group therapy. Three subject variables were investigated—sociopathy, overall psychopathology, and neuropsychological impairment—each of which has prognostic significance in relation to alcoholism. The authors reasoned that higher-functioning patients (low on the three subject variables) would benefit from interaction experiences. Patients with greater impairment and relatively poorer prognosis would profit more from coping-skills training that emphasized relapse prevention. The findings indicated that patient characteristics interacted with type of treatment in outcome results, as reflected in days of drinking during the 6 months of treatment. Interaction-based treatment was more effective with higher-functioning patients;

coping-skills treatment was more effective for patients higher in sociopathy and psychopathology. This pattern of results was maintained at a 2-year follow-up assessment (Cooney, Kadden, Litt, & Getter, 1991).

The type of research illustrated by this example is more sophisticated in the sense of the type of predictions that are made. Rather than main effects of treatment (for all individuals in the experimental or treatment group), the question focuses on interactions (whether some individuals respond better to treatment than others or whether some individuals respond to one form of treatment and other individuals respond better to another form of treatment). Different types of variables (treatment, subject) are combined. Although the usual control conditions might be used, the question focuses on comparison groups that are comprised of combinations of treatment and subject characteristics. The main focus of the client and therapist variation strategy is to identify characteristics of the client that moderate treatment effects, that is, what works for whom (Roth & Fonagy, 1996). Occasionally a single variable (e.g., a particular characteristic of the client) is studied as a potential moderator. Finer-grained questions that incorporate multiple characteristics of the client (e.g., ethnicity, range or type of symptoms), therapist, and context (e.g., family factors of the client) can be asked. However, it is difficult to develop conceptual models to provide focused hypotheses and predictions about what combinations might be effective, with whom, and why. Nevertheless, the search for moderators represents a more sophisticated approach to treatment evaluation than does the search from main effects alone.

Process Research Strategy

The previously noted strategies emphasized outcome questions or the impact of variations of the intervention on clients at the end of or subsequent to treatment. The process research strategy addresses questions pertaining to the mechanisms of change of therapy by addressing manifold concerns of what transpires between the delivery of an intervention and the ultimate impact on the client. Topics may focus on the transactions between therapist and client and the impact of intervening events on moment-to-moment or interim changes during treatment. Many issues address questions of process, such as the sequence, stages, and progression of client or therapist affect, behavior, and cognition during the course of treatment or within individual sessions.

An example is provided in a study that examined the relation of therapy processes and outcome in the treatment of depression (Rounsaville et al., 1986). Patients (N = 35) received interpersonal psychotherapy for depression. Therapists (N = 11) who provided treatment were evaluated by their supervisors after observing tapes of several therapy sessions. Processes rated by the supervisors included therapist (exploration, warmth and friendliness, and negative attitude) and patient factors (participation, exploration, hostility, psychic distress) measured by the Vanderbilt Psychotherapy Process Scale. Treatment outcome was assessed with measures of psychiatric symptoms, social functioning, and patient-evaluated change. The results indicated that only one patient factor (hostility) was related to outcome on a measure of change completed by the patients. In contrast, therapist factors were much more strongly related to outcome. Therapist exploration was significantly and positively related to reductions in clinician evaluations of depression and patient-rated improvements. Therapist warmth and friendliness correlated significantly with improved social functioning and parent-rated improvements. These results convey the importance of specific therapist relationship characteristics in relation to treatment outcome. In this study, no control or comparison was used. The purpose was to correlate specific processes with specific outcomes within a particular technique. Here, too, this level of question is based on prior studies demonstrating that the treatment is effective when compared to various control conditions. After such demonstrations it becomes meaningful to ask the about the factors that contribute to change.

Treatment processes can be evaluated in the context of a larger-scale study that has multiple other purposes (e.g., other treatment evaluation strategies). For example, in a large-scale, multisite study for the treatment of depression, four different treatment and control conditions were compared (interpersonal psychotherapy, cognitive–behavioral therapy, imipramine with clinical management, and placebo with clinical management) (Krupnick et al., 1996). Clinical management consisted of meeting briefly with the patient to review medication or placebo. The therapeutic alliance was evaluated during the course of treatment and assessed by raters who viewed videotapes of selected sessions. The alliance reflects the quality of the bond between the therapist and the client. The results indicated that ratings of alliance during treatment significantly predicted treatment outcome, that alliance accounted for more outcome variance (magnitude of effect) than did treatment technique, and that alliance did not vary among the treatment and control conditions. This study shows the critical role of alliance in treatment outcome. Further research is needed to explain what alliance is, its correlates and predictors, and whether alliance or factors with which it is correlated account for the effect. Among the strengths of this study—the largest study of alliance—is the integration of multiple treatment evaluation strategies within the same study.

General Comments

The strategies noted reflect questions frequently addressed in current treatment research. The questions posed by the strategies reflect a range of issues required to understand fully how a technique operates and how it can be applied to achieve optimal effects. The treatment package strategy is an initial approach followed by the various analytic strategies based on dismantling, constructive, and parametric research. The comparative strategy probably warrants attention after prior work has been conducted that not only indicates the efficacy of individual techniques but also shows how the techniques can be administered to increase their efficacy. Frequently, comparative studies are conducted early in the development of a treatment, possibly before the individual techniques have been well developed to warrant such a test. A high degree of operationalization is needed to investigate dismantling, constructive, and parametric questions. In each case, specific components or ingredients of therapy have to be sufficiently well specified to be withdrawn, added, or varied in an overall treatment package.

The progression requires a broad range of comparison groups that vary critical facets of treatment. The usual control conditions (no treatment, attention–placebo control) may continue to play a role. However, the interest in evaluating change over time without treatment or factors common to treatment gives way to more pointed questions about specific facets of treatment that account for or contribute to change. Comparison groups are aimed to provide increasingly specific statements related to construct validity, that is, what aspects of the intervention account for the findings.

SUMMARY AND CONCLUSIONS

Control groups rule out or weaken rival hypotheses or alternative explanations of the results. The control group appropriate for an experiment depends on precisely what the investigator is interested in concluding at the end of the investigation. Hence all, or even most, available control groups cannot be specified in an abstract discussion of methodology. Nevertheless, treatment research often includes several specific control procedures that address questions of widespread interest.

The *no-treatment control group* includes subjects who do not receive treatment. This group controls for such effects as history, maturation, testing, regression, and similar threats, at least if the group is formed through random assignment. The *waiting-list control group* is a variation of the no-treatment group. Although the experimental subjects receive treatment, waiting-list control subjects do not. After treatment of the experimental subjects is complete, wait-list control subjects are reassessed and then receive treatment. A *no-contact control group* may be included in the design to evaluate the effects of participating in or having contact with a treatment program. Individuals selected for this group usually do not know that they are participating in a treatment investigation. Hence, their functioning must be assessed under the guise of some other purpose than a treatment investigation.

A *nonspecific treatment control group* consists of a group that engages in all the accouterments of treatments, such as receiving a rationale about their problem, meeting with a therapist, attending treatment sessions, and engaging in procedures alleged to be therapeutic. Actually, the purpose is to provide the generic ingredients of the treatment to the nonspecific treatment control group and to address the question of whether the effects of veridical treatment are due to its nonspecific treatment components.

A *yoked control group* controls for variations across groups that may arise during the course of the experiment. Implementing treatment procedures may involve factors inherent in but not relevant to the independent variables of interest to the investigator. *Yoking* refers to a procedure that equalizes the extraneous variables across groups by matching or pairing subjects in the control groups (or one control group) with subjects in an experimental group and using information obtained from the experimental subject to decide the conditions to which the control subject will be exposed. *Nonrandomly assigned control procedures* represent groups that are characterized by selection of subjects that are not part of random assignment. These groups are added to the design to address specific threats to validity (usually internal validity, such as history or maturation) that are not handled in the usual way (e.g., random assignment to experimental and no-treatment control groups). The group, by virtue of its selection, imperfectly controls these threats but still strengthens the plausibility of the conclusions that can be drawn.

Apart from control groups, the investigator may wish to include a wide range of comparison groups. They are usually included to address construct validity. Groups are selected to increase the specificity of the conclusions about the intervention or variable of interest. Frequently used comparison groups include *routine* or *standard conditions* provided to clients and *other treatments.* The addition of control and comparison groups to experimental designs usually addresses threats to internal and construct validity and hence adds precision to the conclusions that can be reached. The progression of research and the different control and comparisons groups that are used were illustrated in the context of psychotherapy research. Several different treatment evaluation strategies were discussed to convey various control and comparison groups and questions that do not require control conditions in the usual sense.

FOR FURTHER READING

American Psychiatric Association Commission on Psychotherapies. (1982). *Psychotherapy research: Methodological and efficacy issues.* Washington, DC: American Psychiatric Association.

Castonguay, L.G. (1993). "Common factors" and "nonspecific variables": Clarification of the two concepts and recommendations for research. *Journal of Psychotherapy Integration, 3,* 267–286.

Cook, T.D., & Campbell, D.T. (Eds.). (1979). *Quasi-experimentation: Design and analysis issues for field settings.* Chicago: Rand McNally.

O'Leary, K.D., & Borkovec, T.D. (1987). Conceptual, methodological, and ethical problems of placebo groups in psychotherapy research. *American Psychologist, 33,* 821–830.

Parloff, M.B. (1986). Placebo controls in psychotherapy research: A sine qua non or a placebo for research problems? *Journal of Consulting and Clinical Psychology, 54,* 79–87.

Chapter 7

Assessing the Impact of the Experimental Manipulation

CHAPTER OUTLINE

Checking on the Experimental Manipulation
Types of Manipulations
Utility of Checking the Manipulation

Interpretive Problems in Checking the Manipulation
Varied Data Patterns

Special Issues and Considerations
Assessment Issues
The Influence of Nonmanipulated Variables
Excluding Subjects in the Data Analyses

Establishing Potent Manipulations

Summary and Conclusions

For investigations in which some facet is varied by the investigator, the independent variable usually is manipulated by providing a particular condition to one group and omitting it from another group, providing varying degrees of a given condition to different groups, or presenting entirely distinct conditions to groups. Great care is required to ensure that the manipulation is a strong test of the hypothesis, that the variable or condition is manipulated as intended, and that the manipulation is consistent across cases within a group (e.g., all subjects intended to receive the manipulation actually do). Careful control and administration of the manipulation is required for interpretation of the findings (construct validity) and for a sensitive evaluation of the results (statistical conclusion validity). This chapter discusses the adequacy with which the independent variable is manipulated, the different ways in which the manipulation can be assessed, and the implications for interpreting the results of an experiment. The primary focus is on experimental research in which the independent variable is controlled or manipulated by the investigator.

CHECKING ON THE EXPERIMENTAL MANIPULATION

The hypothesis of interest in the investigation is based on the assumption that the independent variable was effectively implemented. It is quite possible that the investigator will not manipulate the independent variable effectively enough to demonstrate the relationship of interest or that those who implement the procedures (e.g., experimenters, therapists, parents, teachers) do not carry out the procedures as intended. It is extremely useful in clinical research to check whether the independent variable or intervention was implemented as intended. Providing a check on the manipulation refers to independently assessing the independent variable and its effects on the subjects. The assessment is designed to determine whether the subject is exposed to conditions as intended.

Assessment of the independent variable or a manipulation check is distinguished both procedurally and conceptually from dependent variables included in the study. The check on the independent variable assesses whether the conditions of interest to the investigator were altered. This may mean merely that the stimulus was presented as intended or that the intervention was perceived by the subject. For example, in a treatment study, a check on the independent variable would be achieved by ensuring that participants actually received the treatment, that the number of sessions was provided as intended, and that subjects in one group did not receive conditions appropriate for another group. These are checks on the independent variable or interventions and are quite separate from the dependent measures (e.g., therapeutic change, symptom reduction, improved adjustment). Manipulation checks are critical in all studies in which it is possible that the experimental condition is not faithfully rendered or presented.

In one sense, the best check on the effects of an independent variable is the dependent measure because the change in the independent variable is intended to alter the dependent measure. If the predicted results of an experiment are obtained, assessment of the independent variable to ensure that it has had the intended effect on the subject may not be essential. Presumably, the independent variable accounted for the results, barring obvious confounds. Even so, it is possible that the intervention produced the change by affecting a host of intervening processes in the individual and the construct of interest to the investigator was not the crucial one in the sense of being directly responsible for change. Also, it is possible that group differences at the end of the study support the prediction, albeit the independent variable was not manipulated well. Perhaps most misleading is the possibility that there are no differences between groups because the groups did not receive distinct conditions (diffusion of treatment) or the correct conditions as intended. Checking the extent to which the independent variable is effectively manipulated provides information that helps to rule out some of the different reasons that might account for the findings.

Types of Manipulations

The manner in which the success of the experimental manipulation can be assessed varies as a function of the type of manipulation. Manipulations vary in the precise conditions the investigator wishes to establish. Consider different types of variables and situations and the diverse manipulation checks that are relevant.

Variations in Information   In many experiments, the manipulation refers to different information given to subjects across experimental conditions. The initial question to be answered for the check on the success of the manipulation is whether the information was actually delivered. Assume that the information was provided by the experimenter (this is one of the easier aspects to control). The check on the manipulation is whether subjects received, attended to, and believed the information. Typically, a manipulation check consists of providing subjects with a questionnaire immediately after hearing the rationale or after exposure to the information. For example, the independent variable might consist of varying the instructions about when personality change would occur. If different treatment rationales mentioned that a change would not occur for several weeks and that it would occur almost immediately, a postmanipulation questionnaire could assess approximately when subjects believed that attitude changes would occur with the experimental manipulation. Presumably, if subjects respond to alternatives that reflect what they were told in their respective experimental conditions, the investigator could have more confidence that the independent variable was successfully manipulated.

When the manipulation relies upon information, self-report questionnaires are frequently used to assess the success of the manipulation. A few questions might be sufficient. These questions might be in multiple-choice, true–false, or open-ended (essay question) format. It is useful to include a multiple-choice or true–false format in most cases so that each question can be easily scored and answered. Open-ended questions such as What is likely to happen with this treatment? or Approximately when will behavior change? might be used. These questions are useful because they do not reveal the purpose of the experiment or what the correct answers are as readily as true–false or multiple-choice questions. On the other hand, it is very difficult to score the subjects' responses to open-ended questions. Many subjects do not answer them, reply with only one or two words, or write elaborate extended discussions that miss the point of interest to the investigator.

In general, when the independent variable involves variation of information to the subject, the manipulation check is relatively straightforward. There usually is a check to ensure that the information was delivered by the experimenter, that it was received or perceived by the subjects, and that experimental groups are distinguishable on a measure that assesses that information. Self-report measures are commonly used because they are readily adaptable to the experiment by constructing examination-type questions.

Variations in Subject Behavior and Experience   Many manipulations consist of having subjects do something, engage in a particular task, actually carry out the instructions, or experience a particular state. The experimental question of interest is whether a certain task facilitates or hinders some outcome. Assessment of the success of the manipulation can take many forms, depending on what it is that subjects are supposed to do.

An interesting manipulation was reported in a study of encounter groups (Dies & Greenberg, 1976). Years ago, encounter groups were part of a cultural movement in which individuals could become in touch with themselves and others, sometimes for self-enhancement and occasionally for treatment. In such groups, physical contact was considered important. This investigation set out to evaluate whether physical contact among participants in encounter groups contributed to various measures of affect and experience. The manipulation consisted of having three different levels of physical contact in encounter groups that performed similar activities. One group made no physical contact during the sessions, another engaged in moderate physical contact, and a final group engaged in a high amount of physical contact (e.g., hand holding, embracing, sitting together with knees or shoulders touching). The groups engaged in similar encounter group exercises but were instructed to maintain differences in the amount of physical contact. The investigators checked the manipulation to determine whether the groups really differed in the amount of contact. Several observers recorded the actual amount of physical contact they witnessed during the sessions. The conditions differed in the amount of physical contact and could be distinguished statistically. Incidentally, the results indicated that greater contact was associated with feeling of closeness, willingness to engage in risk-taking behaviors, and more positive attitudes towards oneself and others.

Not all tasks subjects are asked to perform are as readily observable as is physical contact. Subjects may be asked to engage in various activities in their everyday lives (e.g., think specific thoughts, perform various activities in public or in private). When subjects are given different tasks to perform, usually direct observation or self-report can assess whether they adhered to the task requirements. Unlike the assessment of the manipulation for independent variables on the basis of information, the manipulation check for task variables assesses what subjects do rather than what they know. It is important to provide a check because providing different task instructions is very different from carrying out the task.

The manipulation consists of instructions, activities, or tasks that are designed to induce a particular state in the subject. Exposure to the experimental manipulation or task alone is insufficient as a manipulation check. The investigator wishes the subjects to experience something in a particular way, and the experimental test depends on achieving this state. For example, the purpose of an experiment may be to induce high levels of euphoria or similar states in some subjects and moderate or low levels in other subjects. In these cases, it is useful to include items that allow participants to report the extent to which they experience a particular emotion. For example, an item might have participants rate on a 5-point scale how euphoric they feel (1 = not at all euphoric, 3 = moderately euphoric, 5 = very euphoric). The investigator could infer with some degree of confidence that the independent variable was successfully manipulated if groups differed in the extent of euphoria on their ratings according to the respective conditions to which they were assigned.

Variation of Intervention Conditions   Many interventions in clinical research consist of varying the conditions to which subjects are exposed. Actually, variation of information or experiences could be categorized here, but the present category is better as a way of covering a range of procedures provided to the subject. Primary examples of this type of manipulation are exposing subjects to different therapy, prevention, counseling, or remedial interventions. In this case, the success of the manipulation is out of the hands of the client. Rather, the onus is on the therapist or trainer to carry out the manipulation as intended.

In the simplest case, one group receives the intervention and the other group does not (treatment vs. no treatment or a waiting-list control). Specification of the experimental manipulation consists of how well treatment was delivered. Obviously, the implied hypothesis when the treatment is conducted appropriately (as intended, carefully, etc.) is likely to produce greater change than no treatment would. Of primary interest is an evaluation of the extent to which treatment was conducted as intended, a concept referred to as *treatment integrity* or *treatment fidelity.*

The importance of treatment integrity in relation to interpretation of the results can be conveyed by considering a well-designed study that evaluated various treatments for antisocial youth (ages 8–17) who attended a community activities setting in which the interventions were conducted (Feldman et al., 1983). The study evaluated treatments, experience of the therapist, and whether including in the groups peers without any dysfunction influenced treatment outcome. Consider for a moment the impact of three treatments: group social work (focus on groups processes, social organization, and norms within the group), behavior modification (use of reinforcement contingencies in the group, focus on prosocial behavior), and minimal treatment controls (sessions involving spontaneous interactions of group members, no explicit application of a structured treatment plan). The treatments were provided to different groups of subjects and were conducted for a period of a year in which the youths attended sessions and engaged in a broad range of activities and discussions (e.g., sports, arts and crafts, fund raising).

Few differences emerged as a function of treatment technique. Interestingly, checks on how treatment was carried out by direct observations of selected sessions revealed a breakdown in treatment integrity. Specifically, observations of treatment sessions indicated that only 25 percent of the observed sessions for the group social work condition and 65 percent of the sessions for the behavior modification condition were correctly implemented, that is, with procedures appropriate to their treatment. These percentages convey that for a substantial portion of time within a given treatment, the appropriate conditions were not administered. The minimal treatment condition, which was a control, also yielded interesting results. For approximately 44 percent of observed sessions, systematic interventions (treatment) were provided, even though interventions had not been planned to occur. This alone would lead one to expect a diffusion of treatment effects, a bias operating to reduce any treatment differences. On the basis of the treatment integrity data, it is difficult to draw conclusions about he relative impact of different treatments. It is still possible that there would be significant outcome differences and substantially different conclusions about individual treatment conditions if the treatments had been implemented as intended. It is to the original authors' credit to have assessed integrity, which greatly enhances interpretation of the findings.

Treatment integrity is relevant no matter what the final results of the study show. A study comparing two or more treatments, for example, may show that both treatments "worked" but were no different in their outcomes. A pattern of no difference might result from a failure to implement one or both treatments faithfully. Large variation in how individual treatments are carried out across patients within a given condition (within-group variability or "error" in the statistical analysis) and blending or mixing of treatment conditions that ought to be distinct (diffusion of treatment and reduction of between-group variability needed for statistical significance) could also lead to no differences. Ensuring treatment integrity can help avoid these pitfalls. Even when two treatments differ, it is important to rule out the possibility that the differences are due to variations of integrity with which each was conducted. One treatment, perhaps because of its complexity or novelty, may be more subject to procedural degradation and appear less effective because it was less faithfully rendered. Thus, integrity of treatment is relevant in any outcome study independent of the specific pattern of results (Waltz, Addis, Koerner, & Jacobson, 1993).

The breakdown of treatment integrity is one of the greatest dangers in intervention research. Occasionally, dramatic examples can be found in which the treatment integrity was sacrificed in the most extreme fashion, namely, the sessions were not actually held with the clients (see Sechrest, White, & Brown, 1979). The difficulty is that, until relatively recently, most intervention research did not include efforts to ensure or to assess the fidelity of treatment (Kazdin, Bass, Ayers, & Rodgers, 1990). This has left as a lingering question—whether weak or absence of treatment effects or the absence of differences between two treatments could be the result of how they were implemented (or not implemented). Current intervention research is more likely to include integrity checks and hence reflects an important methodological improvement with critical implications for interpreting the results.

There are several steps that can be performed to address treatment integrity. First, the criteria, procedures, tasks, and therapist and patient characteristics that define the treatment can be specified as well as possible. Many investigators have described treatment in manual form, which includes written materials to guide the therapist in the procedures, techniques, topics, themes, therapeutic maneuvers, and activities (Addis, 1997; Wilson, 1996). When treatment is explicitly described, it is easier to develop guidelines to decide when a session or treatment was or was not delivered as intended and what level or type departures are considered tolerable within the study.

Second, therapists can be trained carefully to carry out the techniques. It is useful to specify the requisite skills for delivering treatment and providing training experiences to develop these skills (e.g., role-playing, practice pilot cases with sessions that are videotaped for feedback and further training). For all or some treatments most of the skill components may not be specifiable as discrete behavioral acts and hence not be able to be taught as are skills in learning a motor skill or playing a musical instrument. Even teaching some of the fuzzy concepts can be explicit. Videotapes of good sessions can be used to convey the style and to provide guidelines regarding how the style is likely to be achieved. Years of experience in providing a treatment, often a criterion espoused in clinical work, is not an adequate criterion in research because experience alone does not ensure proficiency in adhering to a specific technique or set of techniques. Providing special and uniform training experiences for the therapists (experimenters, trainers) is useful and can have important implications for how faithfully treatment is likely to be rendered.

Third and related, when treatment has begun, it is valuable to provide continued case supervision. Listening to or viewing tapes of selected sessions, meeting regularly with therapists to provide feedback, and similar monitoring procedures may reduce therapist drift (departure) from the desired practices. If there are multiple therapists, group feedback and supervision sessions are especially valuable to help retain homogeneity in how treatment is implemented across a heterogeneous group of people.

Whether treatment has been carried out as intended can be evaluated definitively only after the treatment has been completed. The evaluation requires measuring the implementation of treatment. Audio- or videotapes of selected treatment sessions from each condition can be examined. Codes for therapist behaviors, patient behaviors, or other specific facets of the sessions can operationalize important features of treatment and help decide whether treatment was conducted as intended (DeRubeis, Hollon, Evans, & Bemis, 1982; Klosko et al., 1990). Checklists can be used to assess whether specific discrete tasks were performed; ratings can be used to assess more qualitative and stylistic features, if these are also relevant to integrity.

Treatment integrity is not an all-or-none matter. Hence, it is useful to identify what a faithful rendition of each treatment is and what departures fall within an acceptable range. For some variables, decision rules may be arbitrary, but making them explicit facilitates interpretation of the results. For example, to consider a relatively simple characteristic, treatment may consist of 20 sessions of individual psychotherapy. The investigator may specify that treatment is administered adequately (i.e., is reasonably tested) only if a client receives 15 (75 percent) or more sessions. For other variables, particularly within-session procedures that distinguish different treatments, specification of criteria that define an acceptable range may be more difficult. In some cases, the presence of select processes (e.g., discarding irrational beliefs, improving one's self-concept) might be sufficient; in other cases, a particular level of various processes (e.g., anxiety or arousal) might be required to denote that treatment has been adequately provided.

Utility of Checking the Manipulation

Data showing that the independent variable was manipulated as intended increase the confidence that can be placed on the basis for the results, that is, construct validity. Two situations are worth highlighting because manipulation checks provide particularly useful information, namely, when the experiment produced no significant differences between groups and when the experimental conditions may not have remained distinct.

No Differences between Groups   If the predicted results of an experiment are not obtained and, in fact, no significant group differences are evident, assessment of the independent variable may prove to be remarkably helpful in interpreting the results. As an example, consider an experiment that provides treatment to two groups that differ only in what the subjects are told about treatment. One group is told that the treatment is a well-established, effective therapeutic procedure for a wide range of clinical problems; the other group is told that the procedure is experimental and is not yet known to work in improving adjustment. At the end of a treatment period, there are no differences between groups on outcome measures. What can be said about the impact of the instructions on treatment outcome?

It is very important to ask whether the independent variable was manipulated adequately so that the different instructional sets were salient to the subjects. Certainly, we want to know whether subjects heard, knew, or believed the instructions about treatment. If the subjects did not hear or attend to the crucial instructions, the results of the study would be viewed differently than if the subjects fully heard and believed the instructions. If the subjects had not perceived the instructions, additional experimental research would be warranted to test the hypothesis under conditions in which the instructions were more salient.

On the other hand, if the subjects had perceived the instructions and the dependent measures reflected no group differences, this would suggest that the intervention was, in fact, manipulated and did not affect treatment outcome. In such a case, the investigator would be more justified in abandoning the original hypothesis. The results do not mean that all attempts to manipulate subjects' set or interpretations of treatment would produce no differences. However, the original hypothesis was tested and the adequacy of the test was partially demonstrated by showing that the subjects could distinguish the conditions to which they were assigned.

Keeping Conditions Distinct   Another way in which checking on the manipulation is useful is to ensure that the experimental conditions are, in fact, distinct. The investigator may intend to administer different conditions, instruct experimenters to do so, and provide guidelines and specific protocols of the procedures to ensure that this occurs. Yet the normal processes associated with the intervention may override some of the procedural distinctions envisioned by the investigator.

One place in which conditions may not remain distinct is the evaluation of different therapy techniques. Part of the problem may be inherent in the subject matter and the way in which it is studied. In therapy investigations, different techniques often are insufficiently specified; thus, the defining conditions and ingredients supposedly responsible for change are not distinguished across groups. Without sufficient specificity, nondistinct global procedures or loosely defined conditions (e.g., "supportive psychotherapy," "insight," "behavior therapy") are implemented. Such treatments are likely to overlap with another treatment that has some of the components of social interaction and interpersonal relationships. Indeed, in some classic therapy studies, general guidelines for applying different treatments led to considerable overlap among the procedures, which could readily explain the absence of outcome differences among the treatments (Sloane et al., 1975; Wallerstein, 1986). Overlap per se may not be detrimental as long as the areas that distinguish treatments are specified and corroborated by a manipulation check. Were the treatments implemented correctly? Did they remain distinct along the supposedly crucial dimensions specified by their conceptual and procedural guidelines?

Therapy studies have reported difficulty in keeping techniques distinct even though systematic observations of differences are not always reported. Therapists who administer different treatment conditions may include similar elements in both conditions despite efforts to keep treatments distinct. Also, clients assigned to specific treatments occasionally carry out on their own procedures that are included in other treatments. Comparisons of different treatments can be illuminated greatly by gathering information to ensure that the treatments are conducted correctly.

It is important to bear in mind that ensuring that the treatments were distinct (different on key characteristics) is somewhat different from ensuring that the treatments were administered as intended (treatment integrity). For example, in comparing interpersonal psychotherapy and cognitive–behavioral therapy, measures (e.g., ratings of audio- or videotapes of selected sessions, coding therapist verbal statements) of how much the therapist focused on interpersonal roles and relationships versus cognitions may show that the treatments were in fact different because of what the therapist did. That is, interpersonal therapy sessions may have had significantly more discussion, time, and therapist verbalizations of role-related topics than did the cognitive–behavioral treatment; the reverse pattern may also be evident and show that for time spent on cognitions the cognitive–behavioral treatment was higher. This is important, but it still possible that one or both treatments were not administered as intended. It may be that one or more therapies suffered a significant departure from the treatment manual, there was a diffusion of treatment, or sessions were omitted for some clients. Showing that treatments were distinct along predicted dimensions and showing that treatments were conducted as intended are both important and helpful in evaluating the study.

INTERPRETIVE PROBLEMS IN CHECKING THE MANIPULATION

Checking the effects of the manipulation can provide important information that not only aids in interpreting the findings of a particular investigation but also may provide important guidelines for further research. The increase in information obtained by checking on the manipulation and its effects is not without risk. Discrepancies between what is revealed by the check on the manipulation and the dependent measures may introduce ambiguities into the experiment rather than eliminate them. To convey the interpretive problems that may arise, it is useful to distinguish various simple patterns of results possible in a hypothetical experiment.

Varied Data Patterns

Consider a hypothetical experiment that checks whether the independent variable was in fact implemented as intended. After the manipulation check, subjects complete the dependent measures. When the results are analyzed, it is possible to infer whether the intervention was implemented effectively from two sources of information, namely, the assessment of the independent variable manipulation check and the dependent measures. These two sources of information may agree (e.g., both suggest that the intervention had an effect) or disagree (e.g., where one shows that the intervention had an effect and the other does not). Actually, there are four possible combinations, which are illustrated as different cells in Figure 7.1. For each cell, a different interpretation can be made about the experiment and its effects.

Effects on Manipulation Check and Dependent Measure   The first cell (Cell A) is the easiest to interpret. In this cell, the intervention had the intended effect on the measure that checked the manipulation (e.g., subjects believed the instructions, performed the tasks as intended, or the treatment was delivered as appropriate to the treatment condition). Moreover, the independent variable led to performance differences on the dependent measures (e.g., subjects improved). For present purposes, it is not important to consider whether the predicted relation was obtained but only that the independent variable was shown to have some effect on the dependent variable. In Cell A, the check on the manipulation is useful in showing that the procedures were executed properly but certainly is not essential to the demonstration. The positive results, particularly if

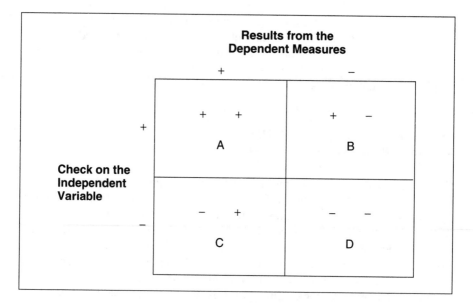

FIGURE 7.1 Possible agreement or disagreement between the manipulation check and dependent measures. A plus sign (+) signifies that the measure shows the effect of the manipulation or that experimental conditions differ on the dependent measures. A minus sign (–) signifies that the measure does not show the effect of the manipulation or that experimental conditions do not differ on the dependent measures.

they are in the predicted direction, attest to the effects of the independent variable. Because of the consistencies of the data for both the manipulation check and dependent measure, no special interpretive problems arise.

No Effect on Manipulation Check and Dependent Measure   In Cell D there also is no ambiguity in interpreting the results. However, the check on the manipulation greatly enhances interpretation of the investigation. In this cell, the check on the manipulation shows that the independent variable did *not* have the desired impact. The intervention was somehow missed by the subjects or was not sufficiently powerful to be perceived or noted by the subjects. The lack of changes on the dependent measures should be expected. The investigator anticipated change in the dependent measures on the presumption that the intervention was effectively manipulated. This pattern of results is instructive because it suggests that additional work is needed to perfect the experimental manipulation. The hypothesis of interest was not tested. The manipulation check clarified the results by showing that the absence of the predicted effects of the independent variable might have resulted from providing a very weak manipulation.

It is quite possible that the pattern of Cell D applies only to some of the groups in an experiment, that is, select groups did not show the effect of the independent variable on either the manipulation check or dependent measures. Other groups may have reflected important changes. Yet, when the independent variable shows no effects on the manipulation check and dependent measures for some groups, this may be extremely useful. In these cases, the manipulation check may reveal that select groups are not different on the independent variable despite the conditions to which they are exposed and may attest to the differential strength of the manipulation across conditions.

Effect on Manipulation Check but No Effect on the Dependent Measure

In Cell B, the manipulation check revealed that subjects were influenced by the intervention. On the other hand, the dependent variable did *not* reflect any effect. The conclusion that would seem to be warranted is that the intervention was well manipulated but that the original hypothesis was not supported. In fact, there may be no relation between the independent variable and the dependent measure, and perhaps this experiment accurately reflected this situation.

Failure to demonstrate an effect on the dependent measures despite the fact that the manipulation check reveals that the independent variable was successfully implemented does not prove the absence of a relation between the independent and dependent variables. It is possible that the manipulation was strong enough to alter responses on the measure of the manipulation but not strong enough to alter performance on the dependent measures. Some measures may be extremely sensitive to even weak interventions and others only to very strong interventions. For example, we have learned that prejudice is more readily reflected on verbal self-report measures than on measures of overt behavior (Kutner, Wilkins & Harrow, 1952; La Piere, 1934). When individuals are asked whether they will discriminate against or will not interact with others, they may readily express such negative intentions. Yet, when these same individuals are placed in a situation in which they have to exhibit an overt act to discriminate against others, they are much less likely to show prejudicial behavior. Indeed, the strength of the prejudice might be defined in part by the extent to which it is evident across different situations and measures. Weak prejudice might be shown across only a few situations and strong prejudice across diverse situations and measures.

In treatment research, one might view the strength of a given treatment in much the same way. A therapeutic technique that is relatively ineffective may change only the way an anxious individual talks about situations that arouse anxiety. After treatment, the clients may say on self-report inventories that they are less bothered yet continue to show physiological arousal and avoidance behaviors when placed in the actual anxiety-provoking situation. As a general statement, more potent interventions would be expected to effect broader and more consistent changes across a range of measures of anxiety.

The pattern of results in Cell B may indicate that there is no relation between the independent and dependent variable. On the one hand, it may indicate that the potency of the manipulation was not sufficiently strong. If the investigator has reason to believe that the manipulation could be strengthened, it might be worth testing the original hypothesis again. On the other hand, there must eventually be a point at which the investigator is willing to admit that his or her hypothesis was well tested but not supported.

No Effect on the Manipulation Check but an Effect on the Dependent Measure   In Cell C, the check on the manipulation reveals that the independent variable was not well manipulated, but the dependent measures do reflect the effect of the intervention. In this situation, the experiment demonstrated the effects of the independent variable, but ambiguity is introduced by checking the manipulation. If this were to happen, the investigator would probably regret having checked the effects of the manipulation (and understandably would tear out this chapter of this book).

The task of the investigator is to explain how the manipulation had an effect on the dependent measures but not on the check of the manipulation. The dependent measures, of course, are the more important measures and have priority in terms of scientific importance over the measure that checked the manipulation. Yet the haunting interpretation may be that the dependent measures changed for reasons other than the manipulation of the independent variable. There is no easy way to avoid the interpretation.

One reason that the dependent variable(s) may have reflected change when the available evidence suggests that the independent variable was not manipulated effectively pertains to the nature of statistical analysis. It is possible that the differences obtained on the dependent variable were the results of chance. The results may have been an instance in which the subjects' responses between groups were different, even though there is no real relation between the independent and dependent variables in the population of subjects who might be exposed to the conditions of the experiment. In short, the null hypothesis of the original experiment, that is, that groups exposed to the different conditions do not differ, may have been rejected incorrectly and a Type I error made. The probability of this error occurring, of course, is given by the level of significance used for the statistical tests (α).

Another reason that the manipulation check failed to show group differences may be that there were inadequacies with the measure itself. The most obvious question that arises is whether the measure assesses the construct reflected in the independent variable. Usually manipulation check assessment devices are based on face validity, that is, whether the items seem to reflect the investigator's interest. (*Face validity* is the psychologist's term to justify the basis for using specific items on a measure or a measure itself when in fact no good validation evidence has been obtained. Presumably, this is called "face" validity to emphasize how difficult it is for us to face our colleagues after having established the validity of an assessment device in such a shoddy fashion, especially when we know better.) It is quite possible for the manipulation check to reflect a construct other than the independent variable. It is of little consolation to raise this as a possibility after an investigation is completed. The manipulation check is part of the methodology for which the investigator can rightly be held responsible. Hence, prior to the experiment, it is important for the investigator to have some assurance that the manipulation check will reflect actual differences across conditions. Reflecting change on the measure should be accomplished prior to the full experiment as a minimal validation criterion of the assessment device.

Other assessment problems with manipulation checks may explain why differences were not found across experimental conditions. For example, the items to assess the manipulation may have been too obscure or unclear. The subjects may have heard the information about the intervention but not have realized its relevance for the assessment device. Alternatively, the variability of the responses to the measure may have been great, leading to the absence of statistically significant group differences. Moreover, the information might not be recalled for manipulation check (e.g., if fill-in items or essay questions were asked) but yet be easily recognized if questions were asked in another way, (e.g., multiple-choice questions). Whatever the reason, the failure of the manipulation check to agree with the changes in the dependent measure will interfere with interpretation of most results.

General Comments   Pointing out the ambiguities that can result from checking how successful the independent variable was manipulated could discourage use of such checking devices. This would be unfortunate because the investigator (and research more generally) has much to gain from knowing how effectively the independent variable has been manipulated. Such checks, as a supplement to information on the dependent measures, provide feedback about how well the hypothesis was tested. A failure to achieve statistically significant group differences on the dependent measures is instructive but does not convey specific details about the experimental manipulation. Changes in dependent measures reflect many events working together, including whether the intervention was implemented effectively, whether the measures were appropriate for the intervention, and whether procedural errors were sufficiently small to minimize variability. The absence of effects on dependent measures could be attributed to many factors, only one of which is the failure to implement the independent variable effectively. On the other hand, a manipulation check helps provide more specific information and hence can be very useful in interpreting a given study and guiding subsequent studies.

SPECIAL ISSUES AND CONSIDERATIONS

Assessment Issues

Multiple issues emerge in deciding how and when to use manipulation checks. One assessment issue relevant for deciding whether to check on the manipulation is the possible reactivity of assessment and the importance of reactivity for the particular experiment. By checking on the manipulation, an experimenter may arouse subjects' suspicions about the experiment and raise questions that ordinarily might not arise. The manipulation check may even sensitize subjects to the manipulation. For example, a self-report questionnaire to check on the manipulation may make the manipulation that occurred more salient to the subject. As an extreme case, the experimental manipulation might consist of altering the content of a subject's conversation during a standard interview as a function of events that happen to the subject in the waiting room prior to the interview. *Confederates,* persons who work for the investigator, may pose as waiting subjects but, in fact, engage in prearranged discussions that might influence the subject. The prearranged discussions would vary across subjects depending on the exact experimental conditions. To check on this manipulation, the investigator could ask subjects at the beginning of the interview questions about what they talked about in the waiting room, what their current mood is, and so on. The questions might suggest to the subjects that their interaction in the waiting room was part of the experiment and arouse suspicions and reactions that would not otherwise be evident if no manipulation check were used.

As a general point, reactivity of the manipulation check per se might not be important, depending on how the investigator conceives the manipulation and the process through which it affects the subject. For interventions involving subtle manipulations, the experimenter might not want to risk the possible influence of the manipulation check. Or, if the check is important, the investigator may wish to design unobtrusive measures that are less likely than direct self-report measures to arouse suspicions (see Chapter 12). For example, the experimenter might leave the subjects alone with another subject (a confederate) who asks, "Say, what is this experiment about anyway?" or "What did the experimenter say about what's going to happen?" Responses to a few such questions could be scored (e.g., from audiotapes, through a one-way mirror, or by the confederate) to address the question of whether the subjects perceived the purpose of the study or to assess other specific aspects of the manipulation.

Alternatively, the investigator may administer the manipulation check after the dependent measures are assessed. Even if the manipulation check is reactive, this could not influence the results because the dependent measures have already been completed. The disadvantage with this alternative is that the longer the delay between the manipulation and assessment of the manipulation's impact, the greater the chances that the check will not discriminate groups. During the delay, subjects may forget precisely what they heard in the instructions or original rationale. Also, it may be possible that the dependent measures, if completed first, could influence the results on the manipulation check. To avoid reactivity of the manipulation check, the investigator might assess the manipulation and its effects in pilot work prior to the investigation. In this way, self-report questionnaires can be used without the dependent measures being administered. In addition, the investigator will have a good basis for knowing in advance that the independent variable was effectively manipulated.

The decision whether to check on the effects of the manipulation also pertains to whether subject awareness of the independent variable is relevant. Effective manipulations do not necessarily operate through subject's awareness. For some manipulations, it may be entirely irrelevant whether subjects know or could recognize what has happened to them in the experiment. For example, in cases in which the manipulation involves administering different treatments to subjects, the check on the manipulation is likely to entail assessment of therapist behavior. Here, assessing subject involvement in the procedure per se is not of primary interest. Regardless of whether of subjects perceive themselves as receiving supportive therapy (as opposed to role-playing) may not be important as long as the manipulation check shows that the defining conditions of these treatments were followed. As discussed earlier, the type of manipulation determines the manner and focus of the manipulation check. This means that in some cases subject perceptions are relevant but in others of ancillary importance.

The Influence of Nonmanipulated Variables

In addition to checks on the independent variable, many occasions arise in which it also may be important to determine whether extraneous variables have changed during the course of the experiment. It is quite possible that the independent variable might change other features of subject behavior or of the situation and would thus be plausible rival hypotheses for the results. For example, if different treatments are to be compared, several variables might covary with treatment (e.g., warmth, congeniality, or competence of the therapist, the credibility of the treatment rationale, and the confidence that the subjects have in treatment). The number of such dimensions that could be assessed in any one study is vast. However, there is no need and little value in merely including a large number of dimensions along with the check on manipulation. Rather, dimensions should be included only if they are of direct interest or could account for or elaborate the results. Stated another way, dimensions are assessed to help the construct validity of the study, which can mean either ruling out the influence of other factors or establishing the basis or mechanism that accounts for the construct itself.

In treatment evaluation, it is often difficult to decide in advance what nonmanipulated variables should be observed. The objective is to assess variables that might enhance interpretation of the results. The variables are determined by substantive findings of the content area itself. If certain variables covaried with the manipulation and could explain the results (e.g., alliance of the therapist and patient, amount of advice by the therapist), it would be profitable to make some attempt to assess them.

Excluding Subjects in the Data Analyses

The discussion has presented the notion that an intervention is or is not effectively manipulated as determined by a check on the manipulation. It is unlikely that effectively manipulating an independent variable is an all-or-none matter. The manipulation will usually not succeed or fail completely but will probably affect subjects within a given condition differently. A certain proportion of subjects may be affected by the intervention. This proportion could be defined by specific answers to particular questions. For example, subjects who answer all questions about the experimental manipulation correctly may be considered those for whom the condition was successfully implemented. Whatever the criteria, there will usually be people for whom the experimental condition was effectively manipulated and others for whom it was not.

An important methodological and practical question is how to treat subjects who are differentially affected by the manipulation. This question pertains to the use of the subjects for the data analyses. On the one hand, it seems reasonable to include in the analyses only subjects who were truly affected by the manipulation. After all, only those subjects provide a real test of the hypothesis. On the other hand, merely using subjects who show the effects of the intervention on the manipulation check may lead to select groups of subjects that vary on several characteristics from the original groups that were formed through random assignment. Thus, using only the subjects across different groups who reflect the effects of the intervention on the manipulation check might lead to systematic subject variable differences across groups. Loss of subjects, in this case caused by the investigators excluding subjects from the analyses, can lead to subject-selection bias. Hence, eliminating subjects who do not show the effect of manipulation is usually inappropriate.

As an illustration of this problem, intervention studies are often conducted in the schools to prevent child maladjustment, substance abuse, teen pregnancy, and other threats to development. Interventions are implemented on a large scale, usually across several classrooms and schools. Treatment integrity is difficult to sustain and large differences are evident in the fidelity with which classroom teachers implement the interventions. Invariably, some teachers carry out the procedures extremely well, others less well, and others not at all (Botvin, Baker, Filazzola, & Botvin, 1990; Hawkins & Lam, 1987). At the end of such a study, investigators often exclude classrooms (teachers and subjects) in which the intervention was not carried out at all or not carried out well. It seems reasonable to exclude teachers (and their classes) in the intervention group who did not conduct the intervention or who did not meet minimal criteria for delivery of the intervention. The investigator is interested in evaluating the effect of the intervention when implemented or implemented well relative to no intervention. Thus, often the investigator selects intervention classes in which the program was well delivered. These teachers and classes are compared to nonintervention classrooms that did not receive the program.

The method of handling the intervention condition (all teachers and children in that large group) raises a significant problem. Selecting a subgroup of teachers who carried out the intervention adequately violates the original random composition of intervention and nonintervention groups or conditions in the study. Data analyses of the selected intervention group and nonintervention group now raises threats to internal validity (namely, selection x history, selection x maturation, and other selection variables) as a plausible explanation of the results. Group differences might be due to the special subset of teachers who were retained in the intervention group—these teachers are special. It is not the integrity of the intervention that is being evaluated as much as it is the specialness of the teachers who adhered to the procedures.

The most appropriate analysis of results is to include all subjects who were run in the various experimental conditions and ignore that only some of them may have shown the effect of the intervention on the manipulation check. An analysis that includes all subjects provides a more conservative test of the intervention effects. The original hypothesis of the study is the general one—that administration of different conditions will lead to differences in performance. This is best evaluated by looking at subjects who received the different conditions. To look only at subjects who meet requirements on the manipulation check is to test a different hypothesis; namely, that individuals who are the most responsive to their respective conditions will show changes on the dependent measures.

Another reason for not discarding subjects in the analyses is that the manipulation may have accomplished the intended results without showing any effect on the manipulation check (see Cell C of Figure 7.1). It is important to stress that the dependent measures are the major measures of the effect of treatment. Hence, data on the dependent measures should not be excluded on the sole basis that the manipulation check has not demonstrated an effect.

There is value in doing post hoc, unplanned, and explanatory analyses of the segments of data as a supplement to the major analysis of all of the data. These analyses could include only subjects who showed the appropriate intervention effects on the manipulation check to see whether the scores on the dependent measures were suggestive of a more potent effect. It may not necessarily be the case that subjects who score in a particular way on the manipulation check do better or worse on the dependent measures with respect to the investigator's hypotheses. Presumably, another supplementary analysis might be completed by separating subjects who showed a predicted directional change in behavior (if pre- and posttest assessment data are available) and comparing the scores of these individuals on the manipulation check. Similarly, correlations might be computed within groups (i.e., within an intervention group) between the dose of treatment (amount, quality) and treatment outcome (degree of change). These analyses must be interpreted cautiously because "receiving a high or good dose of the intervention" is not a randomly distributed variable. The factors that accounted for who received the good dose (e.g., a great therapist, teacher, trainer) could explain the dose effect, but these factors could be tested (e.g., is dose related to other confounding variables such as IQ, social class, or plausible variables that were assessed). Such analyses can be very instructive for the investigator and a guide for further work.

The fact that the intervention did not produce effects in a number of subjects is not something to be expected and resolved by supplementary analyses. Rather, it is the investigator's responsibility to ensure before the investigation that the intervention is manipulated in a potent fashion. Thus, it is useful to begin an investigation armed with information (pilot work, a few cases) that have established an effective or likely-to-be effective and potent intervention and procedures that can be used to monitor and ensure treatment integrity.

ESTABLISHING POTENT MANIPULATIONS

Establishing the efficacy of an experimental manipulation probably is best accomplished before an investigation, especially if an investigator is embarking in an area of research in which he or she has not had direct experience. The initial study should be based on preliminary information that the manipulation can be implemented and implemented effectively. Preliminary or pilot work to learn how to manipulate the independent variable successfully can be invaluable for the subsequent results of a research program. Pilot work usually consists of exploring the intended manipulations by running a set of subjects who may or may not receive all the conditions and measures that will be used in the subsequent experiment. In pilot work, the subjects can contribute directly to the investigator's conception and implementation of the manipulation. For example, the subject can receive the manipulation and complete the manipulation check. At this point, the subject can be fully informed about the purpose of the investigation and provide recommendations about aspects of the procedure that appeared to the subject to facilitate or detract from the investigator's overall objective. Detailed questions can be asked and the ensuing discussion can reveal ways in which the manipulations can be bolstered. An increasingly common practice is the use of focus groups, that is, meetings with individuals who are knowledgeable in light of their special role (e.g., consumers, parents, teachers) to identify what is likely to have impact in a particular area. Focus groups are a way to obtain opinions, often informally, about a question of interest. In relation to research, meeting with groups of individuals before designing a manipulation (e.g., remedial program) or after running a program can be useful for generating concrete ideas to improve the intervention.

Another reason for developing the manipulation in pilot work is that some of the problems of checking the manipulation can be eliminated. As discussed earlier, checking on the manipulation in an experiment may sensitize subjects to the manipulation and presumably influence performance on the dependent measures. Pilot work can check the success of the manipulation with, for example, self-report questionnaires. There is no need to obtain measures of performance on the dependent variable if preliminary work is to be used merely to establish that the experimental conditions are administered effectively. Once the manipulation has been shown to be effectively manipulated in pilot work, the investigator may wish to omit the manipulation check in the experiment to avoid the possibility of sensitization effects. Of course, a pilot demonstration does not guarantee that the experiment will achieve the same success in manipulating the independent variable because subjects differ in each application.

However, a pilot demonstration can greatly increase the confidence that one has about the adequacy of the experimental test.

To this point, the discussion presupposes a clear criterion for deciding when the manipulation has achieved sufficient potency. The main criterion is that the experimental manipulation produces change on the dependent measures. When such changes are demonstrated, the ambiguity about whether the intervention was effectively manipulated diminishes. Except for potent changes on the dependent measures, it is unclear to this point what the investigator should aim for as he or she is developing the intervention. In most studies, the criterion to determine whether the independent variable was effectively manipulated is statistical significance. If experimental conditions reflect statistically significant differences (in the expected direction) on the manipulation check, the investigator usually infers that the intervention was effectively manipulated. Statistical significance may provide a weak criterion for determining whether the intervention was well manipulated.

Pilot work can be very useful in advance of an investigation to develop distinct experimental conditions consistent with the desired manipulation. An investigation usually reflects a considerable amount of effort and resources, so it is important to ensure that the independent variable is successfully manipulated and the experimental conditions are as distinct as possible. If the manipulation is weakly implemented and doubt can be cast on the effectiveness with which the hypothesis is being tested, the interpretation of the final results may leave much to be desired.

SUMMARY AND CONCLUSIONS

The adequacy with which an independent variable is manipulated is a matter of degree. If the independent variable has its intended or predicted effects on the dependent measure, this is usually sufficient evidence that the intervention was adequately manipulated. It is desirable to have additional information to assess whether the independent variable was adequately manipulated. A check on the manipulation can be obtained by determining whether the subjects were affected by the particular changes in conditions or whether the procedures to which they were exposed were executed properly. This check, distinct from performance on the dependent variables, provides some assurance about the adequacy of the experimental test.

The manner in which this check is accomplished depends on the type of manipulation. When the manipulation consists of different kinds of information or instructions provided to the subjects, self-report questionnaires often are used to assess whether subjects noticed, heard, believed, or remembered the information presented. When the manipulation consists of varying the type of tasks subjects perform, self-report questionnaires or direct observation of subject performance may be used. When the manipulation consists of different treatment conditions to which the subjects are exposed, it may be checked by examining the behavior of the experimenters or therapists directly. Providing checks on the adequacy with which the independent variable was manipulated is particularly useful in situations in which there are no differences between groups on the dependent measures, in clinical treatment in which there is no therapeutic change or the amount of change is insufficient, and in situations in which there may be a problem in keeping experimental conditions distinct.

Occasionally, interpretive problems may arise if discrepancies exist between the information provided by check on the manipulation and the dependent variables. However, as a general rule, assessing the adequacy with which the independent variable is manipulated can be extremely useful for interpreting the results of a particular experiment and for proceeding to subsequent experiments. Interpretive problems that can arise in experiments can be attenuated in advance by conducting pilot work to explore different ways to manipulate the conditions of interest. Assessment of the experimental manipulation can ensure that the independent variable receives the most potent empirical test.

In passing, it is important to reiterate that checking on the manipulation was discussed in this chapter in relation to experimental, not observational studies. As described in the next chapter, checking on the manipulation in observational studies (e.g., a case-control study) is rather different and is based on how the sample is selected. In both experimental and observational studies, the general task of the investigator is similar, namely, to ensure that there was an intervention (or manipulation), that the intervention differentiated groups, and that the intervention was provided in ways consistent with the investigator's hypotheses.

FOR FURTHER READING

Hoffart, A. (1994). Use of treatment manuals in comparative outcome research: A schema-based model. *Journal of Cognitive Psychotherapy, 8,* 41–54.

Waltz, J., Addis, M., Koerner, K., & Jacobson, J.S. (1993). Testing the integrity of a psychotherapy protocol: Assessment of adherence and competence. *Journal of Consulting and Clinical Psychology, 61,* 620–630.

Wilson, G.T. (1996). Manual-based treatments: The clinical application of research findings. *Behaviour Research and Therapy, 34,* 295–314.

Yeaton, W.H., & Sechrest, L. (1981). Critical dimensions in the choice and maintenance of successful treatments: Strength, integrity, and effectiveness. *Journal of Consulting and Clinical Psychology, 49,* 156–167.

Chapter 8

Observational Research

Case-Control and Cohort Designs

Previous chapters focused primarily on designs in which some condition is manipulated experimentally by the investigator and on the control and comparison conditions that the designs often include. An exception was discussed in relation to factorial designs in which subject variables (e.g., sex, age, ethnicity) may be included as one of the independent variables not "manipulated" by the investigator. In much of clinical research, subject characteristics and other variables are not manipulated directly by the investigator. Rather, the variables are "manipulated by nature" and the investigator evaluates the impact of the variables by selecting for study persons who have the characteristic of interest. Such studies are sometimes referred to as *observational research* (distinguished from *experimental research*) to convey that the role of the investigator is to observe (assess) different characteristics and their associations, rather than to intervene experimentally. Although observational research can identify many patterns of association and can describe the nature of various characteristics (e.g., disorders), its goal also includes understanding causal relations in much the same way as experimental research.

Designs in which intact groups are studied concurrently or over time are not presented very often in teaching research design in psychology. There is a strong experimental tradition (i.e., manipulation of conditions) within the field in which "correlational" research has secondary status. This has changed considerably for a number of reasons. First, key questions of interest for many domains within clinical psychology and indeed many disciplines (e.g., astronomy, economics, anthropology) do not permit experimental manipulation. For example, in clinical psychology, we are interested in understanding the effects of being exposed to special conditions or experiences (e.g., trauma, war, parents who are depressed) and having special status or characteristics (e.g., firstborn children, criminals, octogenarians, Nobel laureates). Within the mental health professions, a great deal of research focuses on studying persons with various types of clinical disorders (e.g., diagnosis of depression, anxiety, schizophrenia), which, of course, are not manipulated by the investigator. In each area, research is designed to address a host of questions such as What are the past, present, and future characteristics of such individuals? What factors predict who will show the outcome of interest? What are the causes of the outcome? Obviously, one cannot assign individuals to experience one condition versus another (e.g., receiving harsh vs. more mellow child-rearing; receiving vs. not receiving a Nobel prize). However, individuals with the varying characteristics can be identified and studied.

Second, the influence of other disciplines on clinical research has helped to broaden design strategies that are used within psychology. In particular, epidemiology and public health have had tremendous impact on clinical psychology, psychiatry, and related disciplines (e.g., health psychology, psychiatric epidemiology).[1] Within epidemiology studying special groups of interest (e.g., cigarette smokers vs. nonsmokers) represents the primary research strategy and design variations and special data-analytic strategies have been well developed (Hulley & Cummings, 1988; Schlesselman, 1982). Strong inferences can be drawn from such designs, including causal inferences, even though conditions are not manipulated experimentally. For example, the vast majority of studies on the factors leading to various diseases (e.g., acquired immunodeficiency syndrome [AIDS], heart disease, and various forms of cancer) have come from observational, rather than experimental studies. From the research, we have learned about multiple influences on diseases (morbidity) and death (mortality), the relative weight of various influences, and whether some factors play a causal role. The designs can be very powerful indeed.

Third, models in science have evolved in ways that also accord greater value to observational designs. Experimental research, as powerful as it is, is often restricted to the manipulation of one or two variables at a time. Isolation of variables is a key advantage of experimentation to understand how variables operate. However, in many areas of science (e.g., physiology, meteorology, economics), including psychology, we know that there are multiple variables that may influence a phenomenon of interest and that these variables may be related in dynamic, interactive, and reciprocal ways. Observational studies can take into account multiple variables, study them over time, and examine the role of the influence of variables on each other. This chapter presents major design strategies that are used with intact groups in which the investigator cannot manipulate directly the independent variables of interest.

CASE-CONTROL DESIGNS

Case-control designs refer to strategies in which the investigator studies the characteristic of interest by forming groups of individuals who vary on that characteristic and studying current or past features of the groups. The key characteristic is in identifying groups who vary in the outcome (criterion) of interest, that is, have the "problem" or characteristic that the investigator wishes to elaborate. Case-control designs are used extensively in epidemiology and public health in which "case" typically means someone who has the disease (e.g., particular type of cancer) or the characteristic of interest to the investigator. In the most basic, two-group version, the investigator compares subject who show the characteristic (cases) with individuals who do not (controls). The independent variable is the characteristic or criterion that served as the basis for selection. That characteristic may reflect a particular experience (e.g., being abused, exposure to a particular parenting style) or status (e.g., being firstborn, widowed, divorced). The investigator compares the two groups on the measures of interest and then interprets the differences to reflect a critical facet of the problem. Two major variations of the designs are worth distinguishing, depending on the time perspective in which the groups are studied.

Cross-Sectional Design

In a *cross-sectional case-control design*, the most commonly used version in clinical psychology, subjects (cases and controls) are selected and assessed in relation to current characteristics. This is distinguished from studies that are designed to evaluate events or experiences that happened in the past (retrospective studies) or that will happen in the future (prospective studies). The goal of a cross-sectional case-control study is to examine factors that are associated with a particular characteristic of interest. The study can describe and explore characteristics of interest (e.g., what are peer and family relations like for young women who have poor vs. good body image) or test theoretical propositions or conceptual models (e.g., first- and secondborn children might be compared to test a hypothesis about different patterns of attachment in their current adult relations).

Cross-sectional designs are useful for identifying correlates and associated features and these findings may be quite informative and significant. For example, the investigator may wish to test whether depressed mothers interact differently with their children (e.g., infants, toddlers) compared to nondepressed mothers. Mothers are identified and assessed on a measure of depression and classified as depressed (cases) or not (controls); they are then brought into the laboratory or observed at home to assess how they interact with their children. Several studies with this focus have shown that depressed mothers, compared with nondepressed controls, display decreased attention, affection, and vocal behavior, are less expressive (flatter affect), and show more anger, negativism, and hostility in their interactions (Hammen, 1991). This work has very important implications regarding early child development, patterns of emotional attachment of parents to children, and the likely risk that children may have for later dysfunction.

Cross-sectional designs are commonly used and have generated provocative findings, theories, and further research. For example, from such studies we have learned that individuals who are depressed are likely to show a set of negative cognitions (e.g., helplessness, hopelessness) compared to nondepressed controls; children whose parents survived the holocaust experience significantly greater psychological dysfunction than do matched controls whose parents had no such experience; children who are depressed compared to those who are not have significant impairment in peer relations and school functioning; and girls who mature early (in relation to their peers) are more likely to have low self-esteem than those who mature later, to mention a random (well not entirely random) list of fascinating findings. Such findings generate theory and concrete hypotheses to analyze further the reasons for these relations and the conditions under which they do and do not operate.

In the usual case, the investigator begins with hypotheses about how various groups will differ, perhaps based on a theoretical perspective. The subjects are identified and assessed on multiple characteristics beyond those used to delineate their status as cases or controls. Because all measures are obtained at the same point in time, the results are correlational, that is, one cannot know from the study whether the outcome preceded or was caused by a particular characteristic. (There are exceptions in which a characteristic such as sex or race may be assumed to antedate an outcome of interest such as onset of a disorder.) Cross-sectional designs may have important *implications* for causal hypotheses insofar as the findings support the theory underlying the study. In many cases, cross-sectional designs are used to form the basis of further research in which one can identify antecedents leading to the outcome of interest.

Retrospective Design

In a *retrospective case-control design*, the goal is to draw inferences about an antecedent condition that has resulted in or is associated with the outcome. This design represents an explicit effort to identify the time line between possible causes or antecedents (risk factors) and a subsequent outcome of interest. Subjects are identified who already show the outcome of interest (cases) and compared with those who do not show the outcome (controls). Assessments are administered to find out information about the past of the individuals in each group.

For example, a retrospective case-control design was used to examine the relation of attachment patterns to suicidal behavior among adolescents (Adam, Sheldon-Keller, & West, 1996). Attachment refers to a system in which the infant maintains close proximity to the caregiver, particularly under conditions in which there may be danger or distress (Bowlby, 1969). Several different patterns of attachment have been delineated. The most adaptive is considered to be a se-cure attachment in which the infant is confident that the caregiver will respond to the threat and the infant may adapt quickly after the threat has passed. In con-trast, insecurely attached infants are uncertain of caregiver availability and adopt strategies to maintain proximity to caregivers.

In this study, maladaptive early attachment patterns were hypothesized to characterize suicidal adolescents. Adolescents (13–19 years old) from multiple inpatient and outpatient treatment services were identified. They completed sev-eral measures within a 2-week period. The measures included an interview that evaluated whether they had significant suicidal ideation in their past (i.e., none, moderate, or greater than moderate; assessment based on frequency, intens-ity, or duration). From the interview, case (suicidal) and control (nonsuicidal patient) groups were formed. Among many other measures was an interview to assess early attachment relationships, that is, how individuals represented (con-ceived of) their relations with their parents. The main results indicated that sui-cidal patients, compared with controls, showed disturbed early attachment patterns (e.g., lack of resolution of attachment-related trauma such as parent death or abuse and greater preoccupation with the parents in an angry or pas-sive fashion). The study is important in raising the prospect that attachment pat-terns early in life play a role in delineating suicidal and nonsuicidal patients. Subsequent work can now test additional hypotheses about paths, mechanisms, and moderators that might explain or elaborate the connection between attach-ment and suicidality.

The retrospective nature of the study also raises cautions, of which the au-thors were aware. Attachment (A), suicidality (B), or other variables (C) have re-lations whose temporal ordering is not resolved by the design. The conceptual view underlying the study is that a type-attachment pattern is an antecedent to suicidality (i.e., A $\rightarrow$ B), but from the standpoint of the design of the study, it is possible that the results could be explained as B $\rightarrow$ A. That is, when youths be-come suicidal, perhaps they view all relations quite differently and thus recast their parents somewhat differently. Alternatively, other variables not included in the study (C) may lead both to suicidality and reevaluation of relations with sig-nificant others (i.e., C $\rightarrow$ A and B). The point is that one cannot know the rela-tion of these influences from the design of the study. Other possibilities exist, namely, that suicidal and nonsuicidal adolescents have identical attachment patterns but recall their pasts quite differently. With all the interpretations, is there any value to the findings? Absolutely! Knowing that attachment is related, knowing that there are specific identifiable patterns (not just "attachment problems" generically), and knowing that the patterns could not be accounted for by other subject and demographic variables (e.g., age, socioeconomic status) advances an area of research considerably.

Obviously a key issue in retrospective designs pertains to the assessment. As a general rule, retrospective reports permit the investigator to identify correlates. For instance, one correlates may be recall of a past event. There are significant problems that usually preclude establishing the recalled event as a risk factor (antecedent) for the outcome of interest. First, selective recall, inaccurate recall, or recall biased by the outcome (e.g., dysfunction) interfere with drawing valid conclusions about the past event, its occurrence, or differential occurrence for groups that vary in a later outcome. In the case of historical records, the quality, reliability, and completeness of the data also raise potential interpretive problems. It is important to acknowledge that there are different methods of retrospective assessment (e.g., self-report, archival records), types of events that are assessed (e.g., parenting practices, death of a relative), time frames (e.g., recall of events or experiences within the past week vs. past 25 years), and means of soliciting or prompting the recalled material (Brewin, Andrews, & Gotlib, 1993; Kessler, Mroczek, & Belli, in press). These are not all subject to the same sorts or degrees of bias. As a general rule, retrospective reports of psychological states (e.g., family conflict, mental health, difficulties of childhood) and duration, level, and dates of particular events are rather poor; recall of discrete events (e.g., changes in residences) and more stable characteristics (e.g., reading skills) tends to be more reliable but is still not highly related to assessment of the same characteristics obtained at the time (Henry, Moffitt, Caspi, Langley, & Silva, 1994).

Considerations in Using Case-Control Designs

There are special strengths of case-control designs. First, the designs are well suited to studying conditions that are relatively infrequent. In clinical psychology, groups with particular disorders, personality characteristics, or exposure to particular experiences would be difficult or impossible to obtain from sampling a population randomly or from following a community population over time until individuals showed the characteristic of interest (e.g., depression). A case-control study identifies individuals with and without the characteristic and asks How are they alike and different? Second, the designs are feasible and efficient in terms of costs and resources. Because they do not involve following samples prospectively, there is not a long delay in answering questions from the research. Third, loss of subjects, a constant concern in longitudinal studies, is not a problem in the usual case-control design. Subjects are assessed at a single point in time, usually in one assessment period. Fourth, case-control studies can go well beyond merely showing that two (or more) variables are correlated. The magnitude and type of relations (e.g., direct and indirect relations) can be studied and different patterns of relations within a sample can be delineated. Identifying subtypes within a sample, for example, occurs when the variables of interest correlate differently for one type of case (e.g., males vs. females) rather than another. These differences are considered as moderator variables and can lead to hypotheses about different types of onset and clinical course.

There are also weaknesses of the designs. First, the designs do not usually provide evidence for causal relations because which variable or factor came first is not clear. This is obvious in the cross-sectional study. The retrospective study too is usually limited unless there can be some certainty that the antecedent occurred prior to the outcome. Even though case-control designs are not well suited to demonstrating causal relations, they are often very good at generating hypotheses about them.

Second, there are sampling biases that may influence the relation between the characteristics of interest. Selection of cases and controls may inadvertently draw on samples in which the relation is quite different from the relation in the general population. For example, if one is interested in studying women who are abused by their spouses, one can identify cases at a women's shelter and compare them to a control group (e.g., in the community or from another clinic but who have not been abused). The goal may be to identify whether abused women, compared to controls, have fewer social supports (friends and relatives on whom they can rely). Although the women in the case group may in fact be abused, they may not represent the larger population of abused women who do not go to shelters. In fact, absence of a support system (and other characteristics such as level of stress) may influence who comes to shelters; thus, this group is unique. That is, the lack of social support may actually relate to who comes to shelters. Consequently, the correlation between abuse and social support may be spurious because support influenced the referral process, that is, who comes to a shelter. Stated more generally, how cases are identified can greatly influence the relations that are demonstrated within the data. If a special sample is identified because they have self-selected by volunteering to come to a clinic facility or have been directed to do so (e.g., court ordered), the relations that are demonstrated may have little generality to the larger population of interest. For this reason epidemiological research, in which these designs are commonly used, relies heavily on random sampling from the general population to identify cases and controls.

On balance, the design strategy is quite valuable. Apart from elaborating concurrent and past characteristics associated with a given problem, characteristic, or facet of functioning, the designs can identify relations among multiple influences. Among multiple variables that might be studied, the magnitude of the relations and variation in the relations as a function of other variables such as sex, age, or race may be very important.

COHORT DESIGNS

Cohort designs refer to strategies in which the investigator studies an intact group or groups over time, that is, prospectively. *Cohort* is the term that means a group of individuals who are followed over time. The design is also referred to as a *prospective, longitudinal study.* Two key differences help distinguish case-control and cohort designs. First, cohort designs follow samples over time to identify factors leading to an outcome of interest. Second, the group is assessed before the outcome (e.g., depression) has occurred. In case-control designs, the groups (cases and controls) are selected on the basis of an outcome that has already occurred.

The special strength of cohort designs lies in establishing the relations between antecedent events and outcomes. Because cases are followed over time, one can be assured of the time line between events, that is, that the antecedent occurred before the outcome of interest. The time frame of a prospective study may be a matter of weeks, months, or years, depending on the goals of the study. In such a study, the antecedent condition is assessed (e.g., birth defects, early attachment, sibling relations), and one is assured that the outcome has not occurred (e.g., school competence, anxiety disorder). That is, the temporal order of antecedent and outcome is clear. Hence, a necessary condition for demonstrating a causal relation is met within the design. Of course, demonstrating that an antecedent condition preceded an outcome, by itself, does not establish a causal relation. There are many variations of the design; two are considered here.

Single-Group Cohort Design

Typically, a cohort design begins by identifying a group of subjects and following the group over time. We refer to this as a *single-group cohort design* to note that all subjects who meet a particular criterion are selected (e.g., all cases born in a given year, all cases in a particular community or hospital). The group is selected to study the emergence of a later outcome (e.g., a disorder, successful employment, drug addiction). The basic requirements include assessment minimally at two different points in time and a substantial sample that, during that span of time, changes status on the outcome of interest. For example, all cases referred to a clinic may be identified and assessed. They are then followed prospectively (e.g., during the next 3 years) to identify who shows a relapse (return of symptoms) and who does not. Although the subjects were identified and selected as a single group, following cases over time has as its goal identification of those who have different outcomes, that is, delineation of subgroups at the point of outcome assessment.

When one considers a longitudinal, prospective study, this immediately conjures up an image of a study of several years or decades. In fact, most uses of this design have a much shorter time frame (e.g., 1–2 years). The characteristics and strength of the design still applies. For example, a cohort design was used to study the impact of a hurricane on children (Hurricane Andrew in Florida in 1992; La Greca, Silverman, Vernberg, & Prinstein, 1996). This hurricane was one of the worst national disasters in the United States. It left 175,000 families homeless, without adequate food or supplies, and exceeded costs of any other national disaster (more than $15.5 billion). The investigators examined the extent to which the hurricane led to persistent symptoms of posttraumatic stress during the ensuing months. Symptoms include reexperiencing the disaster (intrusive thoughts and dreams), difficulty sleeping and concentrating, and detachment and avoidance of disaster-related activities. In current psychiatric classification, these symptoms characterize posttraumatic stress disorder (PTSD), impairment that results from the experience of trauma or disaster (e.g., exposure to war, rape, or other extremely stressful event).

School children (third to fifth grade, N = 442) exposed to the hurricane were identified and assessed over time on three occasions: 3, 7, and 10 months after the hurricane. Among the goals was to predict which children showed PTSD symptoms at the final assessment and what factors predicted this effect from the earlier assessments. The results indicated that PTSD symptoms decreased for the sample over time. At the final (10-month) assessment, 12 percent of the children continued to show severe symptom levels. The most salient predictors of who would show severe PTSD symptoms were the extent to which the initial disaster was perceived by the youths to be life threatening and their severity of loss and disruption during and after the disaster (e.g., loss of property, disruption of housing, routines). Greater threat and disruption were associated with more severe PTSD symptoms. Less social support from family and friends, the occurrence of other life events, and high efforts to cope with the trauma (e.g., blame and anger) also predicted persistence of symptoms. These results help understand factors that lead to persistence of symptoms of trauma and also provide clues of what might be addressed to intervene early (e.g., stabilization of disruption) and in an ongoing way (e.g., beyond the immediate catastrophe) among youths at greatest risk. The design nicely illustrates selecting a single group, following the group over time, delineating different outcomes (e.g., remission vs. continuation of symptoms), and identifying antecedent factors that are associated with varied outcomes.

Several prospective, longitudinal studies have contributed to our understanding the emergence of clinical dysfunction and antecedent–outcome relations. Especially noteworthy are *birth-cohort studies,* in which a group of subjects is identified at birth and followed for an extended period, often spanning 10, 20, or 30 years (Esser, Schmidt, & Woerner, 1990; Farrington, 1991; Silva, 1990; Werner & Smith, 1982). Multiple measures are administered at several points during the course of childhood, adolescence, and adulthood. Antecedent events at different points in development can be used to predict outcomes of interest (e.g., criminality, psychopathology).

For example, a birth-cohort study has been ongoing for some time in New Zealand to understand the development of psychopathology and adjustment (Silva, 1990). The study began by sampling all children that could be identified

(N = 1037) who were born in the city of Dunedin (approximate population, 120,000) within a 1-year period (1972–1973). From the ages of 3 to 15, subjects were assessed every 2 years then reassessed at ages 18 and 21. At each assessment period, participants came to the research setting (within 2 months of their birthday) and completed a full day of assessments (physical exam, mental health interview, etc.) with measures changing with age of the subjects. Many findings have emanated from this project. For example, a recent report evaluated whether temperamental style of the children at age 3 predicted psychiatric disorders at age 21 (Caspi, Moffitt, Newman, & Silva, 1996). On the basis of the observations of the children at age 3, behavioral characteristics were rated by examiners who classified children as inhibited, undercontrolled, well-adjusted, confident, and reserved.

Consider only two groups for the moment: inhibited (very socially inhibited and reticent) and undercontrolled (irritable, impulsive, difficulty in sitting still, uncontrolled in their behavior). At age 21, 92 percent were interviewed to obtain information about their mental health. Official crime records and informant reports were also obtained. Among the many findings, inhibited and undercontrolled children were the most likely groups to show psychiatric disorders at age 21. Inhibited children were particularly at increased risk for mood disorders. Undercontrolled children were more likely to show antisocial personality disorder and to have more violent offenses in adulthood. Both inhibited and undercontrolled children were more likely than other groups to attempt suicide and (for boys) to report alcohol-related problems. Overall, the study shows that early child behavior predicted psychopathology in adulthood. Although the richness of the findings cannot be fully represented here, the few results mentioned convey the benefits of a birth-cohort study. Apart from looking at antecedents and later outcomes, interim assessments along the way can help elaborate the steps from one age to another as a particular outcome unfolds. In the process, one can generate theory regarding how disorders emerge (causes, risk factors), what factors decrease the likelihood that the outcome will emerge (protective factors), and what might be done to intervene early before the outcome emerges (prevention).

The effort, cost, and obstacles (e.g., retaining investigators, cases, and grant support) make birth-cohort studies relatively rare. From the standpoint of this chapter, the critical point to note is that cohort studies do not necessarily mean *birth*-cohort studies. The defining advantage of the cohort study is being able to identify the time line between antecedents and outcomes; 1 year to a few years is the usual time frame for such studies within psychological research.

Multigroup Cohort Design

The two-group cohort design is a prospective study in which two (or more) groups are identified at the initial assessment (Time 1) and followed over time to examine outcomes of interest. One group is identified because they have an experience, condition, or characteristic of interest; the other group does not. So far, this description is exactly like a case-control design. However, one of the two groups in the case-control design shows the *outcome* of interest (e.g., is depressed) and the other does not (e.g., not depressed). A two-cohort design begins by selecting two groups that vary in exposure to some condition of interest or risk factor (e.g., prisoners of war or not) and follows the subjects to see what the outcomes will be. As noted before, the distinguishing feature of a cohort design is that cases are *followed prospectively* to see what happens (i.e., the outcomes that emerge).

For example, a two-cohort design was used to determine whether a head injury in childhood increases the chances of later psychiatric disorder (Rutter, 1981; Rutter, Chadwick, & Shaffer, 1983). The hypothesis was that brain damage is one factor that can lead to later psychiatric disorders. Youths who received head injuries (e.g., accident) were identified and assessed over time for a 2-year period. The obvious control group would be a sample of youths without a head injury, matched on various subject variables (e.g., sex, age, ethnicity) and demographic variables (e.g., social class) that are known to influence patterns of psychiatric disorders. However, a noninjury group may not provide the best comparison or test of the hypothesis because the hypothesis focuses on *head* injury. Perhaps experiencing *any* injury increases later psychiatric impairment. An injury that leads to hospitalization, for example, for a child (or anyone) may be traumatic and the trauma (whether to the head or toes) and entry into a hospital could increase later impairment. In this study, the second group consisted of youths who were hospitalized for orthopedic injury (e.g., broken bones from accidents). Thus, both groups experienced injury, but head injury was the unique feature of the index group expected to predict later psychiatric disorder. The results indicated that, as predicted, youths with head injury had much greater rates of psychiatric disorder at the follow-up 2 years later compared to rates for youths with orthopedic injury. The study might have ended here and still have been considered to support the original hypothesis. However, more was accomplished to strengthen the inferences that could be drawn.

First, one interpretation of the results was that children who get head injuries are not a random sample of youths in the population. Perhaps they already had more psychological and psychiatric problems to begin with (i.e., before the head injury). In fact, emotional and behavioral problems among children are correlated with more risky and impulsive behavior and physical clumsiness, which could increase the risk of head injury. Showing that a head injury group, when compared to another group, has higher a rate of psychiatric disorder would not establish the temporal order of head injury and later psychiatric disorder. The goal of this study was to show not only that injury was related to later psychiatric impairment but also to establish that injury preceded such impairment. Collection of retrospective data during the study helped address this goal. Immediately after the injury, families of both groups completed assessments that evaluated preinjury emotional and behavioral problems. Preinjury problems did not differ between groups nor predict later child psychiatric impairment. Thus it is unlikely that preexisting psychological problems could explain the relation of head injury and later psychiatric disorder.

Second, if brain damage were the key factor, one hypothesis would be that severity of the injury and subsequent incidence of psychiatric disorder would be related. As mentioned previously, observational studies often look for a dose–response relation within the index or case group to see whether there is a gradient in the association between the amount of one variable and the rate of the outcome. The presence of a dose–response relation is one more bit of evidence suggesting that the construct of interest is key in explaining the outcome. In this study, severity of brain injury was considered to provide a further test of the hypothesis. As a measure of severity of brain injury, the authors used number of days of postinjury amnesia (not remembering the incident). Youths with more days of amnesia (≥ 8 days) compared with those who experienced a few days of amnesia (≤ 7 days) showed much higher rates of later psychiatric impairment, which further suggests that the construct (head injury) is likely to explain the relation. Overall, noteworthy features of this study were the use of a comparison group that helped evaluate the specific role of head injury, the use of assessment (albeit retrospective) to address one threat to construct validity (that group differences were due to preinjury emotional and behavioral problems), and data analyses (dose–response relation) to suggest further that head injury was the likely variable accounting for the follow-up results. The careful selection of controls, assessment, and data analyses acted in concert to reduce the plausibility that factors other than head injury were responsible for the findings.

A two-group cohort design was also used to understand wife assault among men who engaged in violence against their wives (Aldarondo & Sugarman, 1996). Men identified as engaging in violence against their wives were interviewed annually for a 3-year period. The goal was to identify factors that predicted who continued to assault their wives and who ceased assaultive behaviors. A control group of nonviolent men who had never engaged in violence was also included. Key factors that differentiated groups pertained to reported childhood experiences of the violent men. Violent men, whether they continued or ceased their violence, reported more exposure to violence when they were teenagers, both in terms of witnessing their fathers assault their mothers and in receiving abuse themselves, as compared to the experiences of nonviolent men. Among the violent men, those who persisted rather than desisted experienced greater marital discord during the course of the study, were younger, and had experienced greater exposure to violence when they were young, compared to those who discontinued their violence. Interestingly, among the predictors of continuation of wife assault, marital discord made the greatest contribution. Also, although witnessing violence and experiencing abuse when these men were young contributed to continuation of violence, witnessing was more potent in its effect on wife assault. This is an interesting example of a cohort design because individuals with an identified problem were evaluated to see what factors predicted continuation and discontinuation.

Accelerated, Multicohort Longitudinal Design

An *accelerated multicohort longitudinal design* is a prospective, longitudinal study in which multiple groups (two or more cohorts) are studied in a special way. The key feature of the design is the inclusion of cohorts who vary in age when they enter the study. The design is referred to as *accelerated* because the period of interest (e.g., development over the course of 10 years) is studied in a way requires that less time than if a single group were followed over time. This is accomplished by including several groups, each of which covers only a portion of the total time frame of interest. The groups overlap in ways that permit the investigator to discuss the entire development period (Stanger & Verhulst, 1995).

Consider an example to convey how this is accomplished. Suppose one were interested in studying how patterns of cognitions, emotions, and behavior emerge over the course of childhood, say from ages 5–14, a period which might be of keen interest in light of school entry, school transitions, and entry into adolescence. An obvious study would be to identify one group of youths (a cohort) and to follow them from first assessment (age 5) until the final assessment when they become 14. That would be a single-group cohort design, as discussed previously. Another way would be to study the question with an accelerated multicohort longitudinal design. The study could begin with three groups who are sampled in the same way (e.g., selection criteria) but who vary in age. For this example, let us say that a group of 5-, 8-, and 11-year-olds are identified. Each group is assessed at the point of entry and then followed and assessed for the next 3 years. Assume that assessments are conducted annually during the month of each child's birthday.

Figure 8.1 diagrams the study with three groups to show that each group is assessed for a period of 4 years beginning at the point of entering the study. There is a cross-sectional component of this design, which consists of comparing all youths at the time they first enter the study and are at different ages. Also, we are interested in comparing the 5-year-old group when they become 8 years old with the data from the 8-year-olds when they entered the study to see whether the two groups are similar on the measures. That is, there are two 8-year-old groups at some point in the design so that one can see whether the data are similar from different cohorts that are the same age. The longitudinal component is to examine development during the period of 5–14 years of age. By seeing how each cohort develops and the relations over time within a group, one hopes to be able to chart development across the entire period from ages 5 through 14, even though no one group was studied for the entire duration. The example conveys only one way of selecting groups. The number of groups, the assessment intervals, and the overlap among the groups during the course of development can vary.

There are two significant issues that an accelerated longitudinal design is intended to address. First, the design can identify whether the characteristics of a particular cohort are due to historical influences or special features of the period

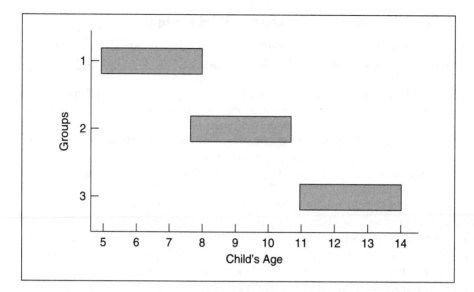

FIGURE 8.1 An accelerated multicohort longitudinal design in which separate groups are selected and assessed. The groups are selected so that their ages span the entire period time frame of interest (ages 5–14 in this hypothetical example) but no one group is followed for the entire duration. Time 1 (first assessment) is when the youths are 5, 8, and 11 years of age, respectively.

in history in which the cohort is assessed. Consider this potential artifact. In a single-group cohort design, a group is followed for an extended period. It is quite possible that the information generated by the group is special in light of the period in time in which the study was completed. For example, if one is interested in studying the relation of factors that occur during the course of adolescence to outcomes in young adulthood, a longitudinal design can begin by identifying adolescents and assessing them repeatedly at various intervals until they become adults. The data may reveal patterns among the measures (e.g., correlations among key characteristics), changes over time, and factors that predict particular unique outcomes. There is the possibility that the results might be attributable in part to the *period* in which the individuals have been studied; that is, this cohort may show special results because of being youths who grew up during a period with or without the availability of some factors that might influence the variables that are studied. For example, changes in the availability of television, computers, cigarettes, or having two parents rather than one parent in the home are influences that could affect a given cohort and many outcomes of interest (e.g., violence, addictions, marital happiness of that cohort).

The results of some studies raise the likelihood of cohort effects due to the historical period in which the cohort was studied. For example, adolescents in the 1980s who used small amounts of alcohol appear to show *better* psychological and social adjustment than their peers who were abstinent (Newcomb & Bentler, 1989). Some use of alcohol had become normative, and those who engaged in that use were not an extreme group. It is likely that the finding has to do in part with the historical period that was sampled. When grandparents and parents of these teenagers were young, alcohol may not have been readily available (e.g., time of prohibition) and, even if available, alcohol was probably restricted more to a very special group of teenagers. In other words, alcohol use and its correlates probably vary at the time in which the sample is studied. More generally, culture is always changing (e.g., unemployment, crime rates, wars, values) and these historical events can influence the pattern than any particular cohort shows. Thus, in a single-group cohort design, it is possible that the group shows a pattern that is influenced in critical ways by events occurring during this period (i.e., history as a threat to *external* validity). The results (relations among variables, developmental paths) may differ for another cohort studied at a different period or point in time.

An accelerated multicohort design allows one to better separate historical period effects from developmental change. That is, because each cohort within the study has a slightly different history, one can make comparisons to address whether there are period influences. In Figure 8.1, the investigator can compare the data of the 5-year-olds when they turn 8 years of age with the data of 8-year-olds. These groups ought to provide similar information, namely, how 8-year-olds rate on the measures of interest. Major differences at this point raise the prospect of some other broad historical influence that is at work. In any case, one advantage of an accelerated longitudinal design is the ability to evaluate whether the findings for the cohort are restricted to possible historical influences that are unique to that group.

Second and more obvious, the accelerated longitudinal design addresses the most difficult part of longitudinal designs, namely, that they take an extended period to complete. The period can be reduced by using multiple cohorts to represent different and overlapping periods of that time frame. In the example in Figure 8.1, the goal was to study development covering a period of 10 years. Using an accelerated design, each of the three groups in the example was assessed for a 4-year period, although the 10 years of interest was examined. In making the study shorter, some problems of longitudinal research (attrition, expense of following and finding cases) are likely to be reduced.

Considerations in Using Cohort Designs

There are several strengths of cohort designs. First, the time line between proposed antecedents (risk factors, causes) and the outcome of interest can be firmly established. This is not a minor point and is the primary basis for distinguishing the design variations (case control vs. cohort designs) we have discussed. Second, careful assessments can be made of the independent variables (antecedents, predictors) of interest. Because the outcome of interest has not yet occurred, one can be assured that the outcome did not bias the measures. Measurements at Time 1 (and other occasions) will not be influenced by the outcome because it will not be determined until much later (at Time 2). Third and related, because the designs are prospective and assessments are made on multiple occasions, the investigator can plan and administer measures that will thoroughly assess the predictors (e.g., multiple measures, multiple methods of assessment) at the different points in time.

Fourth, among the many strengths of a prospective, longitudinal study is the ability to examine the full set of possibilities among those who do and do not experience antecedent condition and those who do and do not show the outcome. For example, consider the hypothesis that watching aggression on television (TV) in early childhood is associated with later aggressive behavior in adolescence. Assume that we will conduct this study with a two-group cohort design and assess all children in community who are ages 5–7 years old. We follow the children for 10 years and evaluate their aggressive behavior (fighting at school). For simplicity, let us classify exposure to aggression on TV and later aggressive behavior in a dichotomous fashion, even though we know that each is a matter of degree (dimensional). Thus let us say that at Time 1 (childhood) we identify children who are exposed to high levels of TV aggression or are not exposed to high levels (two groups). This makes the study a two-group cohort design. At Time 2 (adolescence), we identify the outcome as high in aggression at school or not high in aggression (two outcomes). We can divide the cohort into four subgroups according to these combinations:

A. Those who *experienced the antecedent* in childhood (exposed to high levels of TV aggression), and *the outcome* (high in aggression in adolescence)
B. Those who *experienced the antecedent* (low level of TV exposure), but *did not show the outcome*
C. Those who *did not experience the antecedent*, but *did show the outcome*
D. Those who *experienced neither the antecedent* nor *the outcome*

Figure 8.2 diagrams the above four groups (A,B,C,D) and labels the cells in which they appear. The four cells convey one strength of a prospective design. The design permits one to evaluate whether exposure to TV aggression has higher rates of later aggression but has many other interesting possibilities. For example, in Cells A and B, are all children exposed to TV aggression. Some of these children became aggressive later (Cell A) but others did not (Cell B). Comparing these individuals on a host of antecedent conditions may suggest why individuals who are exposed to TV aggression do not develop aggression later. This can be very useful in generating hypotheses about why these individuals did not become aggressive in adolescence. Also, we can look at children who were not exposed to any TV violence. Some of these children became aggressive (Cell C) but others did not (Cell D). What factors are involved in developing aggression in adolescence among youth who have not been exposed to TV violence? Measures obtained before the outcome and that are available in the

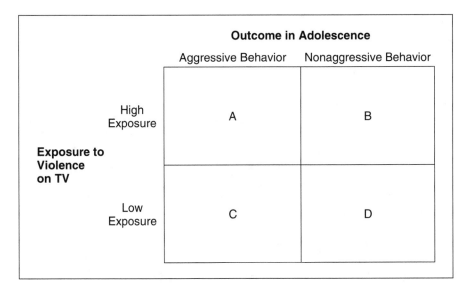

FIGURE 8.2   A hypothetical two-group cohort design in which youths are identified during childhood and assessed on a number of factors. On the basis of this initial assessment, youths are classified as exposed to TV aggression or not exposed to TV aggression. The youths are then followed prospectively. Typically in such research, assessment continues on multiple occasions (e.g., every year or few years); in this example, we are considering only Time 2 assessment (a later point in the youths' adolescence). In adolescence we assess all cases and classify them at that point on whether they are exhibiting aggressive behavior. The four groups resulting from the design are delineated in the cells.

study may shed light on these questions. I have not elaborated all the comparisons of interest. Yet, the larger point can be made, namely, that one advantage of a prospective study is evaluation of the rates of onset of an outcome in the cohort of interest and exploration of factors that increase or decrease the likelihood of the outcome on the basis of comparisons of subgroups who vary on the presence (or degree) of the antecedent condition and the presence (or degree) of the outcome.

For example, more than 800 children born on the island of Kauai in Hawaii in 1955 were included in a single-group cohort study (Werner & Smith, 1982, 1992). Many domains were assessed in infancy (e.g., prenatal events, temperament), childhood (e.g., social development, school and educational achievement, stress), adolescence (e.g., stress, academic performance, criminal behavior), and adulthood (e.g., mental health problems, military records, criminal behavior). By their early thirties, 505 cases remained in the sample. Consider a small portion of the findings. One set of findings focused on all youth who had been exposed early in life to factors associated with later delinquency. These factors included parental conflict, alcohol abuse by a parent, and below-normal intellectual functioning. If one considers all such youth at risk, two groups could be delineated at the outcome, namely, those who in fact became delinquent and those who did not. This would be equivalent to Cells A and B in Figure 8.2, that is, individuals who were exposed to the risk factors but who varied in their outcome. A comparison of these groups was completed to identify other factors that might differentiate the groups. The at-risk group that did *not* become delinquent showed a number of characteristics that seemed to protect them from deleterious influences. For instance, they were more likely to be firstborn, to be perceived by their mothers as affectionate, to show higher self-esteem and locus of control, and to have alternative caretakers (other than parents) in the family and a supportive same-sex model who played an important role in their development. (*Protective factor* is the term commonly used to refer to characteristics, events, or experiences that decrease the likelihood of an undesirable outcome in a high-risk group.) The prospective nature of the design, the multiple assessments for an extended period, and the different outcomes for subgroups within the design permit very interesting and important analyses.

With the wonderful benefits of prospective cohort designs, why are they not dominant in clinical research? There are also weaknesses of prospective longitudinal designs. First, the design can take a considerable time to complete, depending on the time frame. The cost in money and personnel and the delay in the results (i.e., understanding the antecedents) can be enormous. Depending on the time frame, the designs may require an extended period (e.g., decades) to address questions for which immediate or indeed urgent answers are needed. Second, if the study is conducted for an extended period (e.g., 2 years or longer), many cases can be lost over time (attrition). The potential for selection biases in the remaining sample and obstacles in estimating rates of the outcome are two problems that can emerge. Third, if the base rate of the outcome of interest is low (e.g., few individuals who will become depressed, will divorce, will enter a convent), large numbers of subjects are needed in the original cohort because in the end, the tests will evaluate characteristics of those who show the outcome versus those who do not. If only 10 percent are likely to show the outcome, a very large number of subjects are needed at the beginning to have sufficient power to conduct the analyses of interest.

General Comments

We have not exhausted all the variations of case-control and cohort designs (Hulley & Cummings, 1988). The variations that we have discussed are those most frequently used within psychology. More important, the designs convey the scope of questions that can be addressed. The challenge of the designs is isolating the construct of interest and the direction of influence among predictors and outcomes. In the next section, these issues are discussed to convey considerations that help ensure that strong inferences can be drawn.

CRITICAL ISSUES IN DESIGNING AND INTERPRETING OBSERVATIONAL STUDIES

There are special issues that case-control and cohort studies raise to which the investigator ought to be particularly sensitive at the design stage. The issues pertain primarily to the construct validity of the findings, that is, the extent to which the results can be attributed to the construct that the investigator wishes to study. Table 8.1 outlines several interrelated issues pertaining to construct validity.

Specifying the Construct

The first issue for the investigator is to specify the construct to study. As basic as this sounds, this can have tremendous implications for interpretation of the findings. Constructs that serve as the impetus for observational studies can vary in their level of specificity. Broad and global variables such as age, sex, social class, and race are less preferred as the basis of an investigation than are more specific variables with which the broad variables may be associated (e.g., patterns of interacting with friends, child-rearing practices, social support patterns).

TABLE 8.1. Critical Issues in Designing and Evaluating Case-Control and Cohort Studies

Specifying the Construct
What is the construct of interest?

Selecting Groups
From what population, setting, context will the sample be drawn?
What are the operational criteria to separate or delineate groups (e.g., the specific measures or selection criteria)?
To what extent is the assessment procedure (e.g., criteria, measure) known to reliably separate or select persons with and without the characteristic?
Why is this particular control group the one most suitable for the study? For what influences or constructs is it intended to control?

Possible Confounds
Are the groups with and without the characteristic of interest similar on subject and demographic variables (e.g., age, sex, race, socioeconomic status)?
Does the comparison group (without the characteristic) share all the characteristics but the one of interest? If not, how are the other characteristics to be evaluated, partialled out, or addressed in the design (e.g., additional control group[s] or data analyses)?
Could the construct as described (e.g., depression) be interpreted to reflect a broader construct (e.g., having a disturbance, being a patient)?

Direction and Type Influences
Do the results permit conclusions about the time line, that is, that one characteristic of the sample (e.g., exposure to an event, some experience) antedates the other?
Do the results permit conclusions about the role that one (or more) variable (i.e., risk factor, causal factor, mediator) plays in the outcome?

A more specific construct helps move from description of a relation (e.g., that males and females differ) toward explanation (e.g., processes that may explain the differences).

To illustrate the point, consider for a moment that we are interested in studying the impact of socioeconomic status (SES) on health. SES is a broad variable that encompasses (is related to) a plethora of other variables. SES has been studied extensively and from this research we have learned that low social class (as measured by income, educational and occupational status) predicts a very large number of untoward mental and physical health outcomes (e.g., earlier death, greater history of illness, and higher rates of mental illness) (Adler et al., 1994). This research has been extremely important. A limitation of the work is that we know very little about the reasons for these effects; that is, the construct is broad and encompasses so many other variables that we now need more specific studies to identify possible bases for the findings.

Some work of this kind has been completed. For example, cohort studies have shown that low SES relates to later psychopathology in children (Dodge, Pettit, & Bates, 1994; Lipman, Offord, & Boyle, 1994). Several factors correlated with SES, including low parent educational attainment, family dysfunction, harsh child-rearing practices, limited parental warmth, single-parent families, peer group instability (e.g., moving to different child care facilities), lack of cognitive stimulation, and exposure to aggressive behavior (e.g., in the home), have been analyzed. Each predicts later psychiatric dysfunction in children and partially accounts for the relation between low SES and clinical dysfunction. Even after these factors are taken into account, SES contributes to the prediction indicating that other factors are operative. Fine-grained analyses have indicated that some of these factors are more highly related to the outcomes than others. For example, harsh discipline practices on the part of the parents is one of the stronger contributors to later aggressive child behavior (Dodge et al., 1994; Patterson, Reid, & Dishion, 1992). Armed with this finding, we can better theorize about how discipline might be involved in developing aggressive behavior.

As a general guideline, broad constructs (e.g., minority group status) may be a useful beginning of research. However, in general, greater specification of the construct of interest is strongly encouraged within psychological research. Although it may be useful to test whether women and men may differ on some variable of interest in a cross-sectional case-control study, it would be even better to specify a process variable (e.g., patterns of interacting with others) that may explain that difference. On a continuum of description to explanation, research that can move toward explanation is usually more informative. In brief, one should specify the construct of interest and, when possible, hypothesize and test why the differences would occur.

Selecting Groups

Special Features of the Sample   As noted in Table 8.1, movement from the general construct to how the groups will actually be selected is critical. The first task is identifying the population from which cases will be drawn. Among the options are samples from the community, clinic, or other social agency. Cases who are drawn from a clinic or social agency may have special characteristics that make them unrepresentative of the larger community sample. These special characteristics may distort the direction or magnitude of the relation between the variables of interest from what would be present in the community sample. This is a particularly important point to underscore in psychology studies using case-control designs. In epidemiological studies, more effort is made to complete large-scale investigations with randomly selected cases. In psychology's use of the designs, samples are often selected from special settings (e.g., clinics, agencies, schools) in which some feature about the recruitment process may influence the associations that are studied.

For example, if one is interested in studying agoraphobia (fear of open places) and in comparing cases with controls, the population from which one samples may be critical. Agoraphobics who come to a clinic for treatment may be very special insofar as they have come to a clinic, by whatever means, and that variable alone may contribute to or interact with the results. Agoraphobics referred for treatment may be more severely impaired (or less severely impaired because they could leave their homes to begin with) or more (or less) likely to have other disorders than agoraphobics in the community who never sought treatment. It is not necessarily the case that one sample is better than another—it depends on the question of the investigator. However, it is important to think about the population in a case-control or cohort study because features of that population may not only limit the external validity of the results but also the construct validity, that is, what the reasons are for group differences.

Operationalizing the criteria to delineate groups also raises important issues. What are the criteria used to delineate cases from controls? There are many separate issues. In the earlier discussion of single- and multiple-operationism, we noted that different measures may yield different groups. Thus, a self-report measure or clinical rating scale may be used to define individuals as cases in a case-control study. To what extent are the procedures, methods, and measures used to delineate groups valid and in keeping with prior findings? If possible within the design, it is desirable to have more than one operational definition that can be used to delineate groups.

In studies of intact groups, investigators may neglect attention to reliability of the operational criteria. Regardless of what measure or operational criterion is invoked to classify subjects as cases or controls, we want to be sure we have a reliable measure. If the measure or criterion used to delineate the groups is unreliable, some of the individuals counted as depressed really may end up in the control group and some of the individuals not identified as depressed may end up in the case or index group. Thus, there would be a *diffusion* of the variable (internal validity threat) because both cases (individuals with the characteristic) and controls (individuals without the characteristic) would inadvertently be in each group instead of being restricted to their respective groups. The unreliability of measures is often surprising. Among the dramatic examples, there is keen interest in research in identifying racial and ethnic differences. One of the dilemmas for research is that there is tremendous unreliability in classifying these groups (e.g., Caucasian, African American, Hispanic American) because there are no standard criteria and no firm biological classification system. When investigators or subjects themselves identify race, the classification can be very unreliable (Betancourt & Lopéz, 1993; Beutler et al., 1996; Wright, 1994). In considering the major or broad classifications of racial differences, the unreliability within a study and across multiple studies will yield very inconsistent findings.

For many variables, reliability of classification is not likely to be a problem (e.g., subject sex, country of origin). In cases in which there may be unreliability of the measure, sometimes a large sample is assessed and only the extremes of the distribution are considered. For example, on a personality trait, one might assess a large group and for purposes of the study select persons who are high ($\geq$ 67th percentile) and compare them to those who are low ($\leq$ 33rd percentile). The rationale is that the middle group is likely to be more unreliably identified because a few points in one direction or the other could move them above or below the median. Selecting extreme groups can be very useful, depending on the goals of the study, but deleting a large segment of the sample (in our example, the middle third) can greatly distort the relations among the measures. The statistics that result (correlations, multiple correlations, beta weights, odds ratios) will be quite different from results that came from using the entire sample. The desirable practice here depends on the question. Sometimes one is interested in talking about and studying only a very special subgroup (e.g., extremely inhibited children); therefore, focusing on a very special group is quite fine.

Selecting Suitable Controls   In case-control and two-group cohort studies emphasis is given to defining the case group, that is, persons who have the characteristic or problem of interest. The control or comparison group warrants very careful consideration because it is often this group that limits the study and the kinds of statements the investigator can make. Typically, the investigator is interested in evaluating a special group (e.g., depressed patients, children with a specific disease, persons exposed to a special experience) and wishes to make specific statements about this group on a set of dependent measures. The difficulty arises when the special group is compared to a "normal" (community sample) control group (persons who do not have the disorder, dysfunction, or special experience). The results invariably show that the special group is different from the "normal" group. Although the interpretation may focus on the special group, the "normal" comparison group is often insufficient to permit specific inferences to be drawn about the special group.

For example, in a cross-sectional case-control study, the investigators proposed that antisocial youths would show a particular type of personality organization according to object–relations theory (Matthys, Walterbos, Njio, & van Engeland, 1989). Children diagnosed as having conduct disorder were compared with control children from an elementary school. The children wrote various descriptions about other children, adults, and themselves. These descriptions were scored to evaluate personality traits, organization of writing, affective statements, and other characteristics. The results indicated several differences in object–self relations between children with conduct disorder and the control group.

The construct of interest from the independent variable was conduct disorder and how children with this disorder respond on important measures of personality style. However, the comparison group of "normal" children raises interpretive ambiguity. Perhaps any patient group would show the demonstrated pattern. By design, the study does not speak specifically to conduct disorder. Cases and control groups differ on several variables (e.g., child age, proportion of cases living in single-parent homes), which might plausibly explain the results. Also, youths with conduct disorder were residents of an inpatient setting, but controls lived in their own homes. (The latter group differences can be ignored for the moment to convey a more subtle point.) The selection of a patient sample versus a community sample does not necessarily permit conclusions about the specific dysfunction of the patient sample. The primary conclusion one might draw is that patients and nonpatients differ. To draw more specific statements would require an additional group. A patient group without conduct disorder, added to the design, would permit evaluation of whether object–relations and personality organization are specific to conduct disorder. Children with anxiety disorder or attention deficit disorder (but no conduct disorder) would be a great addition to the design and permit a discussion at the end of the study about the hypotheses and constructs of interest to the investigators.

In general, case-control studies require special efforts to isolate the construct of interest. Special attention is required in assessing the construct by making implausible other interpretations that might explain group differences. The selection of groups that vary in the construct of interest and, to the extent possible, *only* in the construct of interest, is a critical beginning. Emphasis in developing a study is on identifying the case group, but more attention must be given to deciding and finally selecting controls to which cases will be compared.

An excellent example of careful consideration of control conditions is shown in a study that evaluated characteristics of homeless adults (Toro et al., 1995). Many studies have reported that homeless adults are more deviant than nonhomeless adults in multiple domains (e.g., psychopathology, substance abuse, criminal behavior, and health problems). A difficulty is that the bulk of the literature has focused on comparing the homeless to the general population (very much like the comparison in the study on children with conduct problems). However, if one is interested in characterizing homelessness and its special contribution to psychopathology, it would be important to control for other influences that are likely to be part of and related to but still distinguishable from homelessness. For example, level of poverty ought to be controlled because it would represent a rival interpretation of many prior findings; that is, being poor, regardless of being homeless, is likely to be associated with a variety of untoward outcomes (Adler et al., 1994). In this study, homeless adults were compared with individuals who were equally poor but not homeless (and, less relevant to the present point, a third group of individuals who had been, but were not currently, homeless) (Toro et al., 1995). The results indicated that homeless persons showed higher levels of stress, more substance abuse, victimization from domestic violence, and were more likely to have a history of child abuse compared to poor but nonhomeless controls. However, differences did not emerge in relation to severe mental illness, physical health symptoms, social support, and social networks. The findings are important in suggesting that when poverty is controlled, a number of differences previously considered to be associated with homelessness may not emerge. The importance of the study is that it draws attention to the controls that are used in a case-control study.

In many instances, the use of community ("normal") controls is the appropriate comparison, depending on the questions the investigator is asking and the specificity of the conclusions he or she wishes to reach about the case sample. Even so, other considerations emerge in relation to the use of "normal" controls in case-control studies. In a study of a particular disorder, cases may be readily identified through an interview or standard questionnaire. Controls may be identified from a community sample and defined as individuals who do not meet criteria for the diagnosis of interest or indeed for any diagnosis. Excluding individuals from the group of controls on the basis of diagnostic information is fine, but so-called "normal" persons may have a significant amount of clinical dysfunction; in fact they may often meet criteria for psychiatric disorders (e.g., 20 percent lifetime rate of a mental disorder) (Robins et al., 1984). Thus, sampling individuals from the community to be controls will inevitably include some individuals with clinical dysfunction. This may or may not be important to consider in the screening criteria used for controls. Again, it is important for the investigator to consider quite precisely what purpose the control group is to serve and to make sure, to the extent possible, that the selection criteria invoked address the specific issues the investigator has in mind.

Possible Confounds

A critical issue is that there may be variables that are possibly confounded with the selection criterion for delineating groups. For example, one might compare teenage mothers and female teenagers who do not have children. Any group differences on a set of dependent measures might be due to the differences in being a mother. Obviously, other variables may also be different for these groups (e.g., SES, academic achievement) and are potential confounds that could explain the results. Some effort has to be made within the study to address these other variables and their role in differentiating groups. If confounding variables are not evaluated, conclusions will be reached that the primary variables were the basis of the findings.

There are several ways in which confounds can be addressed—some from the standpoint of the design and some from the standpoint of the data analyses. From the standpoint of the design, groups (e.g., in a case-control study) can be matched on variables that could confound the group differences. For example, if one is comparing teen mothers with nonmothers, it is reasonable to match on SES and educational achievement because these variables are known to be related. A dilemma of matching is that if one equalizes groups on these potential confounding variables, this does not permit one to analyze their influence. That is, it might be that the variables that predict which teenagers become pregnant are SES and poor educational attainment. By matching on these variables, one will not be able to evaluate their impact in differentiating groups. Matching on a set of variables has to be decided on the basis of the purpose of the study, that is, whether one wishes to hold one variable constant so that others can be evaluated or whether one wishes to identify the range of predictors that delineate groups.

Data-analytic strategies play a major role in evaluating potential confounds. The goal of data analyses usually is to identify whether the variable of interest makes a contribution to the outcome independent of the confounding variable(s). Analysis of the role of the confounding variable may also be of interest to assess whether it contributes to the outcome on its own or only because of its association with the primary variable of interest. For example, if one is interested in comparing parents who physically abuse their children with parents who do not, it is possible that other variables will also distinguish the groups (e.g., education, SES). At the end of the study, although the investigator wishes to talk about abuse, powerful confounding variables may be the actual bases for the differences. Statistical adjustments for possible confounding variables can be made (e.g., partial correlations, analyses of covariance) to consider confounding variables individually or as a group. Also, regression analyses can be completed (e.g., hierarchical regression) to test individual predictors (primary variable, confounding variables) in relation to the outcome.

Statistical analyses (e.g., path analyses, structural equation modeling) are tools to evaluate the relations. It is useful to precede statistical analyses with a conceptual model of the relation among variables that are being assessed. Conceptual models can specify the relations of constructs to each other (e.g., education, SES, abuse practices) and in relation to the outcome. Among the options, the models can test whether education and SES make separate contributions to the outcome, whether their influence is direct or indirect (e.g., through some other variable), and the relative contribution (strength of the relations among different variables). Testing a model to evaluate multiple variables is an excellent way to handle potentially confounding variables because "confound" is a relative concept, that is, the main variable and potential confound in *my* study (e.g., SES and diet, respectively) may be the confound and main variable, respectively, in *your* study. If the issue is to understand multiple influences on an outcome and how they work together, use of models to explain the interrelations among influences is an excellent design strategy.

Time Line and Causal Inferences

A critical issue in case-control research pertains to the time line and type of inferences that are drawn. One hazard the investigator must consider is to keep the conclusions in line with what the design can demonstrate. The most common problem is to imply a causal relation when the design does not permit comments about the time line. Consider, as an example, a cross-sectional case-control study. The outcome of interest (grouping variable) may be an anxiety disorder in children (present or not) and the other characteristic (hypothesized antecedent) may be family stress. Children and their parents are assessed on a single occasion and complete various measures of child anxiety and family stress. The results may indicate that children who show the outcome (anxiety disorder cases), compared to those who do not (no-disorder controls), come from families that are more highly stressed. Clearly, the study demonstrates a correlation between two variables. The theory underlying the study may pose a directional relation in which family stress occurs before child dysfunction and through some process makes the child vulnerable so that new stressors manifest themselves in anxiety. Actually, the results are consistent with hypotheses in either direction: stress as an antecedent to anxiety or anxiety as an antecedent to stress. In the absence of other evidence, this study does not establish stress as a risk factor for anxiety.

Statistical analyses commonly used in this type of research (e.g., discriminant analysis, logistic regression, structural equation modeling) may inadvertently contribute to the view that one variable precedes the other. The language of many data-analytic strategies identifies some variables as *predictors* or independent variables (e.g., family stress) and others as *outcomes* or dependent variables (e.g., presence or absence of anxiety disorder). The analyses make no assumption of a time line for the variables that are entered; the distinction between antecedent (independent) and outcome (dependent), from the standpoint of the steps (discriminant function) of the analyses, is arbitrary. Clearly, the statistics are not at fault, but it is easy to misinterpret the results. The language used in reporting results often exacerbates the misunderstanding. In this example, a typical conclusion might be that family stress *predicted* child anxiety disorder [discriminant function] or that family stress *increased the risk of* child anxiety disorder [logistic regression]. Such communications could be mistaken to suggest that family stress came first in the family stress–child anxiety sequence and even perhaps had a causal role in anxiety.

Although the example is hypothetical, the problem is not. Within clinical psychology there are many instances in which concurrent correlates from cross-sectional case-control studies are taken to imply that one condition is an antecedent to another. For example, one interpretation of unipolar depression is that the disorder emerges as a result of negative cognitions about oneself, the world, and the future (negative triad) (Beck, Rush, Shaw, & Emery, 1979). When studied in cross-sectional designs, the results show that, in fact, the cognitions and depression often go together. These findings are taken as support for the conceptual model of a temporal ordering of cognitions preceding and indeed leading to depression. Yet, prospective, longitudinal studies suggest that the negative triad may emerge with, rather than precede, depression (Barnett & Gotlib, 1988; Lewinsohn, Steinmetz, Larson, & Franklin, 1981). This does not detract from the findings relating cognitions to depression, but it does show that it is important to note that by changing the placement of one letter in a word we can move from *casual* thinking to *causal* thinking.

Misleading inferences about the time line are often drawn from retrospective studies. For example, several studies have focused on the extent to which the experience of sexual abuse in childhood places individuals at risk for untoward mental health outcomes in adulthood (Wyatt & Powell, 1988). Retrospective case-control designs are used for identifying adults who have been abused and comparing them to controls who have not. Retrospective assessment (e.g., interviews, questionnaires) is used to identify the onset, nature, type, duration, and other characteristics of sexual abuse (the antecedents) by asking adults to recall earlier experiences. Findings have been fairly consistent in showing that adults who report early sexual abuse, compared to matched clinic or community controls who do not, have higher rates or greater degrees of depression, sleep disorder, sexual dysfunction, and substance use and abuse (Briere & Runtz, 1988; Stein, Golding, Siegel, Burnam, & Sorenson, 1988). The conclusion explicitly drawn in such studies is that early sexual abuse is a risk factor for many untoward consequences.

Although the conclusions might be correct (sexual abuse leads to or is associated with later problems), consider plausible rival interpretations. First, it is possible that clinical dysfunction *preceded* sexual abuse. Individuals with dysfunction very early in life might have a higher base rate of being abused. However, persons may not recall the time sequence in that way. Second, persons with greater current dysfunction may be more likely to report abuse when it did not happen or to attribute their problems to the experience of abuse when it did. People with little or no dysfunction may be less likely to report the same type of events that more dysfunctional persons might recall as abusive. Third, those who have been abused but who *cannot recall* the experience (due to forgetting, dissociation, repression) may be less likely to show symptoms. These persons would not be selected for inclusion as index cases because they have little or no dysfunction and/or have abuse in their past but do not recall that abuse. These are only some of many possibilities that must be considered in interpreting the results of retrospective studies based on self- or other types of reports. This is a good example of a situation in which the retrospective study is extremely valuable in generating causal hypotheses, but a prospective study is likely to be needed to provide the critical test.

General Comments

Case-control designs and their variations permit evaluation of many variations of human characteristics and experiences that cannot be readily studied experimentally. The designs are not inherently weak because they are observational rather than experimental. However, the investigator's thinking and methodological sophistication must be particularly acute with observational designs. Ingenuity of the investigator in selecting cases and controls and in data-analytic strategies that might be used to partial out influences are particularly important in observational designs. Many basic design classes and statistics classes in psychology do not begin to address the options that can be helpful in this regard (Aiken et al., 1990). Observational designs, like their experimental sisters, share the common ingredient at the planning stage. The task of the investigator is to decide before the study precisely what he or she wishes to conclude. The precision of the statements one wishes to make determines key features of sampling, group formation, design, and data analyses.

This chapter has focused on observational designs because of their frequent use in clinical research. The designs were treated at length to give attention to the many issues that can emerge in their execution and interpretation. It is important to note that observational and experimental research can be combined in a single study. One might hypothesize that two groups of individuals (e.g., new criminal offenders vs. career criminals) will respond differently to an experimental manipulation (e.g., an affect task that is designed to induce empathy). The study is both observational (cases, controls) and experimental (manipulation provided to one half as cases and the other half as controls) and forms a 2 x 2 factorial design. Factorial designs are a convenient way to combine different types of variables and, in this context, to combine different types of designs. I mention the designs again to avoid the impression that research is *either* experimental or observational.

SUMMARY AND CONCLUSIONS

In observational studies, the investigator evaluates the variables of interest by selecting groups rather than experimentally manipulating the variable of interest. The goals of the research are to demonstrate associations among variables but these associations may move beyond correlations to causal relations. The studies can be descriptive and exploratory by trying to assess the scope of characteristics that may be associated with a particular problem or theoretically driven by trying to test models that explain the characteristics and how different influences relate to each other and to the outcome.

Case-control studies were identified and include investigations in which groups that vary in the outcome or characteristic of interest are delineated. Typically, two groups are compared (e.g., depressed and nondepressed patients) to evaluate a range of characteristics that may be evident currently (*cross-sectional case-control study*) or may have occurred in the past (*retrospective case-control study*). These designs are extremely valuable in understanding characteristics associated with a particular outcome, in unraveling the patterns of multiple influences and their relation, and in delineating subtypes by showing distinctions among individuals who have experienced the outcome (e.g., types of depression among the depressed group). A limitation of these designs is that they do not permit strong influences to be drawn about what led to the outcome of interest.

Cohort studies are quite useful in delineating the time line, that is, that some conditions are antecedent to and in fact predict occurrence of the outcome. In a *single-group cohort design,* a group that has not yet experienced the outcome of interest is assessed on multiple occasions and followed over time. At a later assessment, subgroups are delineated as those who do or do not show the outcome of interest. Analyses can then identify which antecedents predicted the outcome. Although a cohort study may begin with a single group, sometimes two or more groups are studied (*multigroup cohort design*) to evaluate their outcomes. In this case, individuals may be selected because they show a characteristic but will be followed to examine yet another outcome. In some cases, multiple cohorts of different ages may begin the study and then be followed over time (*accelerated multicohort longitudinal design*). The goal is to chart a particular developmental course for an extended period but draw on different groups to sample portions of that period.

Case-control and cohort designs provide very powerful strategies that have been developed in other disciplines (epidemiology and public health) but are used increasingly in clinical psychology and related disciplines. The designs require special attention to ensure construct validity of the results, that is, that the conclusions can be attributed to the constructs the investigator has in mind rather than to other influences. Critical issues is designing and interpreting observational studies were discussed, such as the importance of specifying the construct that will guide the study, selecting case and control groups, addressing possible confounds in the design and data analyses, and drawing causal inferences.

NOTE

[1]Epidemiology refers to the study and the distribution of diseases and related conditions and the factors that influence the distribution. Research focuses on associations between characteristics and diseases and the nature of these associations (e.g., risk factors, cause). The study of clinical disorders from an epidemiological perspective, an area sometimes referred to as psychiatric epidemiology, is directly relevant to many topics of interest in clinical psychology (Verhulst & Koot, 1992).

FOR FURTHER READING

Hulley, S.B., & Cummings, S.R. (Eds.). (1988). *Designing clinical research: An epidemiological approach.* Baltimore: Williams & Wilkins.

Magnusson, D., Bergman, L.R., Gudinger, G., & Torestad, B. (1991). *Problems and methods in longitudinal research.* New York: Cambridge University Press.

Schlesselman, J.J. (1982). *Case-control studies: Design, conduct, and analysis.* New York: Oxford University Press.

Verhulst, F.C., & Koot, H.M. (1992*). Child psychiatric epidemiology: Concepts, methods, and findings.* Newbury Park, CA: Sage.

Chapter 9

The Case Study and Single-Case Research Designs

CHAPTER OUTLINE

Traditionally, psychology has focused on experimentation with groups of individuals and has reached conclusions about important variables on the basis of group differences. "Laws" of behavior based on group analyses provide general statements that apply to many individuals on average. Yet, research design refers broadly to an approach toward evaluating phenomena and establishing valid inferences; nothing inherent in the approach requires groups. Evaluation and valid inferences can be readily accomplished with the individual subject or single case. Illustrations can be provided from virtually every branch of psychology in which the individual subject has provided important information, as reflected in diverse topics such as memory, animal behavior, cognitive development in children, language, and psychopathology (Bolgar, 1965; Dukes, 1965). There is a long tradition within clinical and experimental research advocating the use of systematic research methods to study the individual (Chassan, 1967; Shapiro, 1966; Skinner, 1957). Beyond psychology, other disciplines (e.g., psychiatry, education, rehabilitation, anthropology, and business) have used the study of cases to advance knowledge (Yin, 1994).

In psychological research, the designs have been referred to by different terms, such as *intrasubject replication designs, N = 1 research*, and *intensive designs*.[1] The unique feature of these designs is their capacity to conduct true experiments with the single case, that is, one subject. The designs also can (and often have) evaluate the effects of interventions with large groups. As we shall see, the logic of the designs pertain to how data are collected and how the intervention is presented rather than the number of cases that are studied.

This chapter discusses case studies and single-case experimental designs and their characteristics. The case study as a method of evaluating the individual has a long history in clinical work and is an important backdrop for experimental methods with the individual case. Single-case designs and the methods they share permit careful evaluation of individual cases in research and practice. The specific requirements and procedures of single-case experiments are presented to convey the logic of the designs and how they address threats to validity. Apart from describing and illustrating single-case experimental designs, the chapter also identifies ways of adapting these designs in quasi-experiments for their use clinically.

THE CASE STUDY IN CLINICAL PSYCHOLOGY

The case study has played a more central role in clinical psychology than in other areas of psychology because psychological principles and techniques are often applied to the problems of the individual. In the usual application, the *case study* has referred to uncontrolled observations of the individual client (e.g., in the context of therapy). Information that is based on anecdotal information, on qualitative data not collected in a systematic or replicable fashion, and without the usual control procedures to address threats to validity is reported. These characteristics of the case stand in sharp contrast to empirical research in which there is an effort to control circumstances that permit inferences to be drawn and to utilize assessment methods and controls that permit the observations to be replicable. The bifurcation between traditional case studies and controlled research is unnecessary because methods of evaluation are available to study the individual case experimentally. As a backdrop for presenting single-case research designs, it is useful to consider the more traditional applications of the case-study method. Case studies, even without serving as formal research, have made important contributions.

The Value of the Case Study

The lack of controlled conditions and failure to use measures that are objective (e.g., replicable, reliable, valid) have limited the traditional case study as a research tool. Yet the naturalistic and uncontrolled characteristics also have made the case study a unique source of information that complements and contributes to theory, research, and practice. First, case study has served as a *source of ideas and hypotheses* about human performance and development. For example, case studies from quite different conceptual views, such as psychoanalysis and behavior therapy (e.g., case of Little Hans [Freud, 1933]; case of Little Albert [Watson & Rayner, 1920]), were remarkably influential in suggesting how fears might develop and in advancing theories of human behavior that would support these views.

Second, case studies have frequently been the *source for developing therapy techniques.* Some remarkably influential cases within psychoanalysis and behavior therapy can be cited. For example, in the 1880s, the treatment of a young woman (Anna O.) with several hysterical symptoms marked the inception of the "talking cure" and cathartic method in psychotherapy (Breuer & Freud, 1957). Within behavior therapy, development of treatment for a fearful boy (Peter) followed by evaluation of a large number of different treatments to eliminate fears among children exerted great influence in suggesting several different interventions (Jones, 1924a, 1924b). Many of the interventions are still used in some form in clinical practice.

Third, case studies permit the *study of rare phenomena.* Many problems seen in treatment or that are of interest are so infrequent as to make evaluation in group research impossible. An individual client with a unique problem or situation can be studied intensively with the hope of uncovering material that may shed light on the development of the problem and its effective treatment. For example, the study of multiple personality, in which an individual manifests two or more different patterns of personality, emotions, thoughts, and behaviors, has been elaborated greatly by the use of case study. A prominent illustration is the well-publicized report of the "three faces of Eve" (Thigpen & Cleckley, 1954, 1957). The intensive study of Eve revealed quite different personalities, mannerisms, gait, psychological test performance, and other characteristics of general demeanor. The analysis at the level of the case provided unique information not accessible from large-scale group studies.

Fourth, the case study is valuable in *providing a counterinstance* for notions that are considered to be universally applicable. For example, in the development of behavior therapy, case studies in which overt symptomatic behaviors were successfully treated were often cited. In traditional forms of treatment such as psychoanalysis, treatment of overt symptoms was discouraged because of the notion that neglect of motivational and intrapsychic processes presumed to underlie dysfunction would be ill advised if not ineffective. However, repeated demonstrations that overt symptoms could be effectively treated without the emergence of substitute symptoms cast doubt on the original caveat (Kazdin, 1982b). Although a case study can cast doubt on a general proposition, it does not itself allow affirmative claims of a very general nature to be made. By showing a counterinstance, the case study does provide a qualifier about the generality of the statement. With repeated cases, each showing a similar pattern, the applicability of the original general proposition is increasingly challenged.

Finally, case studies have *persuasive and motivational value*. From a methodological standpoint, case studies provide a weak basis for drawing inferences. However, this point is often academic. Even though case studies may not provide strong causal knowledge on methodological grounds, they often provide dramatic and persuasive demonstrations and make concrete and poignant what might otherwise serve as an abstract principle. Seeing is believing even though philosophy and psychology teach us that perception is a shaky basis of knowledge and that believing influences seeing. One case may be especially convincing because of the way anecdotal information is compiled to convey a particular point. The absence of objective measures or details that might be inconsistent often convey unqualified support for a particular belief.

Another reason that individual cases are often so dramatic is that they are usually selected systematically to illustrate a particular point. Presumably, cases selected randomly from all those available would not illustrate the dramatic type of change that typically is evident in a particular case provided by an author. This point can be readily illustrated by analogy to advertisements for fad diets or exercise devices. Typically, such advertisements show "before and after" photographs of someone who has completed the recommended program. The fad-diet subject is used to illustrate the "miraculous" effects of the diet program—perhaps someone who has lost 50 pounds after being on the program for only 10 minutes. Even if the illustrated case were accurately presented, it is likely to be so highly selected as not to represent the reaction of most individuals to the program. Nevertheless, the selection of extreme cases does not merely illustrate a point; it often compels us to believe in causal relations that reason and data would refute.

As noted earlier, case studies often have been the basis for developing both specific therapeutic techniques and hypotheses about the nature of clinical disorders. Successful applications of a treatment technique at the case-study level can be very persuasive to the therapist–investigator, but the persuasive appeal is a mixed blessing. Often a case study is so convincing that writers fail to maintain scientific restraint before careful evaluation of the specific findings. On the other hand, rigorous endorsement of a position usually stimulates research by others who test and critically evaluate the claims made previously solely on the basis of anecdotal information. Thus, the very persuasiveness of a case study may lend heuristic value. Because case studies provide dramatic and concrete examples, they often stimulate investigation of a phenomenon. Empirical research can test the claims made previously on the basis of case studies.

Limitations of the Case Study

The case study has special value that stands on its own. Yet as a basis for establishing knowledge, it has limitations. First, an important limitation is that *many alternative explanations usually are available* to account for the current status of the individual other than those provided by the clinician. Indeed, virtually all basic threats to internal validity can be applied to the traditional case. The basic information provided in case studies often can be seriously challenged. Postdictive or retrospective accounts try to reconstruct early events and show how they invariably led to contemporary functioning. Although such accounts frequently are persuasive, they are scientifically questionable. Many events in the individual's past might have accounted for contemporary functioning other than those highlighted by the clinician or client. More important, there is no way to test a hypothesis with the usual case report to assess the causal events in the past.

Second, case reports rely heavily on *anecdotal information* in which clinical judgment and interpretation play a major role. Many inferences are based on reports of the clients; these reports are the data on which interpretations are made. The client's reconstructions of the past and remembered events from the past (particularly those laden with emotion) are likely to be distorted and highly selective. To this is added the interpretation and judgment of the therapist. Unwitting but normal human biases operate to weave a coherent picture of the client's predicament and the change of events leading to the current situation. As with the client reports, the reports may have little bearing on what actually happened to the client in the past. Unless subjective accounts are independently corroborated, they could be completely unreliable. Many case reports give the appearance of literary stories rather than scientific investigations, not merely because of the style of writing but also because of the type of information made available.

Third, a major concern about the information derived from a case study is the *generalizability to other individuals or situations*. Scientific research attempts to establish general laws of behavior that hold without respect to the identity of any individual. It is possible that an individual case will reflect marked or unique characteristics and not provide widely generalizable findings. The absence of standardized or replicable procedures to evaluate the case makes replication of the study often difficult. Hence, knowledge about several potentially similar cases is difficult to achieve.

Sometimes several cases may be studied as a basis for drawing general conclusions beyond the individual. Although each case is studied individually, the information may be aggregated in an attempt to reveal relations that have broad generality. For example, the development of psychiatric diagnosis, which is concerned with the identification of psychological disorders, was greatly advanced by Kraepelin (1855–1926), a German psychiatrist. He identified specific "disease" entities or psychological disorders by systematically collecting thousands of case studies on hospitalized psychiatric patients. He described the history of each patient, the onset of the disorder, and its outcome. From this extensive clinical material, he elaborated various types of "mental illness" and provided a general model for contemporary approaches to psychiatric diagnosis (Zilboorg & Henry, 1941).

When individual cases are aggregated, the resulting information may be more convincing than information obtained from a single case. Conclusions drawn from several individuals seem to rule out the possibility of idiosyncratic findings characteristic of one case. Yet the extent to which information from many combined cases can be informative depends on several factors, such as the manner in which the observations were made (e.g., anecdotal reports vs. standardized measures), the number of cases, the clarity of the relationship, and the possibility that the individuals studied were selected in a biased fashion. Generally, the accumulation of cases provides a much better basis for inference than does an individual case, but it still falls short of the success in demonstrating relationships that can be achieved in experimental research.

In clinical psychology and other mental health disciplines, the accumulation of multiple cases is common among persons involved in clinical practice. The absence of objective measurement has made difficult the codification and utilization of this experience as part of the knowledge base. Even so, aggregated experience among professionals involved in practice occasionally reveals consistencies in beliefs about factors that contribute to treatment and therapeutic change (Kazdin, Siegel, & Bass, 1990). Consensus on the basis of experience does not substitute for demonstrated findings. However, the information provides important leads for research to pursue.

The case study serves an important function in clinical psychology and has provided leads for theory, research, and practice. Yet, from a methodological standpoint, the traditional anecdotal case study raises several problems because of the lack of experimental control techniques to determine what actually accounted for the client's performance or functioning. For this reason, the case study sometimes is viewed more basically as uncontrolled evaluations in which the role of specific variables on performance cannot be isolated unambiguously. This broader meaning extends the definition of a case study beyond the study of individual subjects to evaluations in which one or several individuals are studied in an uncontrolled way. In sharp contrast, single-case designs permit the clinical researcher to draw valid inferences about factors that influence performance. The designs focus on individuals or groups of individuals who are studied over time. Both true and quasi-single-case experiments provide methods that improve on the case study for research and clinical ends.

SINGLE-CASE EXPERIMENTAL DESIGNS: BASIC CHARACTERISTICS

The underlying rationale of single-case experimental designs is similar to that of the more familiar group designs. All experiments compare the effects of different conditions (independent variables) on performance. In traditional group experimentation, the comparison is made between groups of subjects who are treated differently. By random assignment to conditions, some subjects are designated to receive a particular intervention and others are not. The effect of the intervention is evaluated by comparing the performance of the different groups. In single-case research, inferences are usually made about the effects of the intervention by comparing different conditions presented to the same subject over time. Experimentation with the single case has special requirements that must be met if inferences are to be drawn about the effects of the intervention.

Continuous Assessment

The most fundamental design requirement of single-case experimentation is the reliance on repeated observations of performance over time. The client's performance is observed on several occasions, usually before the intervention is applied and continuously during the period in which the intervention is in effect. Typically, observations are conducted on a daily basis or on multiple occasions each week. These observations allow the investigator to examine the pattern and stability of performance. The pretreatment information over an extended period provides a picture of what performance is like without the intervention. When the intervention is implemented, the observations are continued so that the investigator can examine whether behavior changes coincide with the intervention.

The role of continuous assessment in single-case research can be illustrated by examining a basic difference in between-group and single-case research. In between-group research, treatment is evaluated by giving the intervention to some persons (treatment group) but not to others (no treatment group). One or two observations (e.g., pre- and posttreatment assessment) are obtained for several different persons. In single-case research, the effects of the intervention are examined by observing the influence of treatment and no treatment on the performance of the same person(s). Instead of one or two observations of several persons, several observations are obtained for one or a few persons. Continuous assessment provides the several observations over time to allow the comparisons of interest within the individual subject.

Baseline Assessment

Usually, each single-case experimental design begins with observing behavior for several days before the intervention is implemented. This initial period of observation, referred to as the *baseline phase*, provides information about the level of behavior before the intervention begins. The baseline phase serves two functions. First, data collected during the baseline phase describe the existing level of performance. The *descriptive function* of baseline data provides information about the extent of the client's problem. Second, the data are the basis for predicting the level of performance for the immediate future if the intervention is not provided. Even though the descriptive function of the baseline phase is important for indicating the extent of the client's problem, from the standpoint of single-case designs, the *predictive function* is central.

To evaluate the impact of an intervention in single-case research, it is important to have an idea of what performance will be like in the future without the intervention. A description of present performance does not necessarily provide a statement of what performance will be like in the future. Performance might change even without treatment. The only way to be certain of future performance without the intervention would be to continue baseline observations without implementing the intervention. However, the purpose is to implement and evaluate the intervention to see whether the client improves in some way. Baseline data are gathered to help predict performance in the immediate future before treatment is implemented. Baseline performance is observed for several days to provide a sufficient basis for making a prediction of future performance. The prediction is achieved by projecting or extrapolating into the future a continuation of baseline performance.

A hypothetical example can illustrate how observations during the baseline phase are used to predict future performance and how this prediction is pivotal to drawing inferences about the effects of the intervention. Figure 9.1 illustrates a hypothetical case in which observations were collected on a hypochondriacal patient's frequency of complaining. Observations during the baseline (pretreatment) phase were obtained for 10 days. The hypothetical baseline data suggest a reasonably consistent pattern of complaints each day in the hospital. The base-

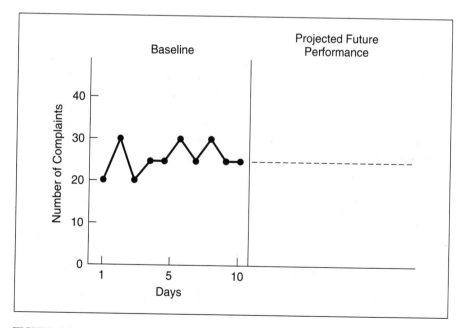

FIGURE 9.1 Hypothetical example of baseline observations of frequency of complaining. Data in baseline (*solid* line) are used to predict the likely rate of performance in the future (*dashed* line).

line level predicts the likely level of performance in the immediate future if conditions continue as they are. The projected (dashed) line suggests the approximate level of future performance and helps to evaluate whether the intervention led to change. Presumably, if treatment is effective, performance will differ or depart from the projected level of baseline. For example, if a program is designed to reduce a hypochondriac's complaints and is successful in doing so, the level of complaints should decrease well below the projected level of baseline. In any case, continuous assessment in the beginning of single-case experimental designs consists of observation of baseline or pretreatment performance. As individual single-case designs are described later in the chapter, the importance of initial baseline assessment should become especially clear.

Stability of Performance

Because baseline performance is used to predict how the client will behave in the future, it is important that the data are stable. A *stable rate* of performance is characterized by the absence of a trend (slope) in the data and relatively little variability in performance. The notions of trend and variability raise separate issues even though they both relate to stability.

Trend in the Data A *trend* or slope refers to the tendency for performance to decrease or increase systematically or consistently over time. One of three simple data patterns might be evident during baseline observations. First, baseline data may show no trend or slope. In this case, performance is best represented by a horizontal line indicating that it is not increasing or decreasing over time. As a hypothetical example, observations may be obtained on the disruptive and inappropriate classroom behaviors of a hyperactive child. The upper panel of Figure 9.2 shows baseline performance with no trend. The absence of trend in baseline provides a relatively clear basis for evaluating subsequent intervention effects. Improvements in performance are likely to be reflected in a trend that departs from the horizontal line of baseline performance.

If behavior does show a trend during the baseline phase, behavior would be increasing or decreasing over time. The trend during the baseline phase may or may not present problems for evaluating intervention effects, depending on the direction of the trend in relation to the desired change in behavior. Performance may be changing in the direction *opposite* from that which treatment is designed to achieve. For example, a hyperactive child may show an *increase* in disruptive and inappropriate behavior during baseline observations. The middle panel of Figure 9.2 shows how baseline data might appear—during the period of observations, the client's behavior becomes worse (i.e., more disruptive). Because the intervention will attempt to alter behavior in the opposite direction, this initial trend is not likely to interfere with evaluating intervention effects.

In contrast, the baseline trend may be in the *same direction* that the intervention is likely to produce. Essentially, the baseline phase may show improvement in behavior. For example, the behavior of a hyperactive child may

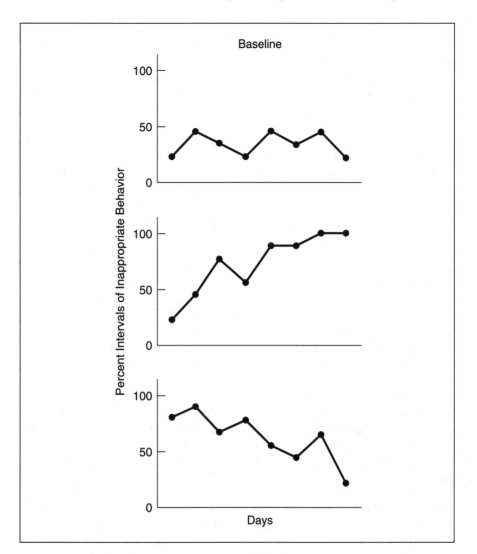

FIGURE 9.2   Hypothetical data for disruptive behavior of a hyperactive child. The *upper* panel shows a stable rate of performance with no systematic trend over time. The *middle* panel shows a systematic trend with behavior becoming worse over time. The *lower* panel shows a systematic trend with behavior becoming better over time. This latter pattern of data (in the *lower* panel) is the most likely one to interfere with evaluation of interventions because the change is in the same direction as change anticipated with treatment.

improve as disruptive and inappropriate behavior decrease during the course of the baseline phase, as shown in the lower panel of Figure 9.2. Because the intervention will attempt to improve performance, it may be difficult to evaluate the effect of the subsequent intervention. The projected level of performance for baseline is toward improvement. A very strong intervention effect of treatment would be needed to show clearly that treatment surpassed the projected level from baseline.

If improvement occurs during the baseline phase, one might raise the question of why any intervention should be provided. Even when behavior is improving during the baseline phase, it may not be improving quickly enough. For example, an autistic child may show a gradual decrease in head banging during baseline observations, but the reduction may be so gradual that serious self-injury might be inflicted unless the behavior is treated quickly. Hence, even though behavior is changing in the desired direction, additional changes may be needed.

Occasionally, a trend may exist in the data and still not interfere with evaluating treatments. Also, when trends to exist, several design options and data-evaluation procedures can help clarify the effects of the intervention. For present purposes, it is important to convey that the one feature of a stable baseline is little or no trend and that the absence of trend provides a clear basis for evaluating intervention effects. Presumably, when the intervention is implemented, a trend toward improvement in behavior will be evident. This is readily detected with an initial baseline that does not already show a trend toward improvement.

Variability in the Data   *Stability* of the data refers to the fluctuation or variability in the subject's performance over time. Excessive variability in the data during baseline or other phases can interfere with drawing conclusions about treatment. As a general rule, the greater the variability in the data, the more difficult it is to draw conclusions about the effects of the intervention. Excessive variability is relative; whether the variability is excessive and interferes with drawing conclusions about the intervention depends on many factors, such as the initial level of behavior during the baseline phase and the magnitude of behavior change when the intervention is implemented. In the extreme case, baseline performance may fluctuate daily from extremely high to extremely low levels (e.g., 0 to 100 percent). Such a pattern of performance is illustrated in Figure 9.3 (upper panel), in which hypothetical baseline data are provided. With such extreme fluctuations in performance, it is difficult to predict any particular level of future performance.

Alternatively, baseline data may show relatively little variability. A typical example is represented in the hypothetical data in the lower panel of Figure 9.3. Performance fluctuates but the extent of the fluctuation is small compared with the upper panel. With relatively slight fluctuations, the projected pattern of future performance is relatively clear; hence, intervention effects will be less difficult to evaluate. Ideally, baseline data will show little variability.

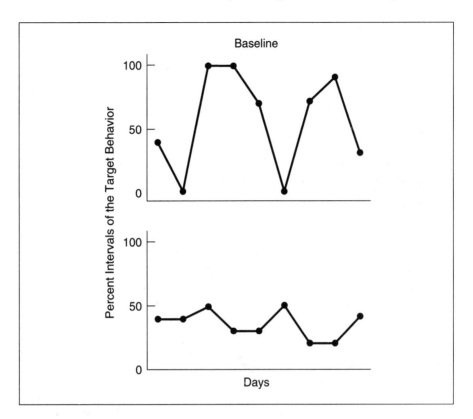

FIGURE 9.3   Baseline data showing relatively large variability (*upper* panel) and relatively small variability (*lower* panel). Intervention effects are more readily evaluated with little variability in the data.

MAJOR EXPERIMENTAL DESIGN STRATEGIES

Single-case designs vary in the ways that the effects of an intervention are demonstrated, the requirements for experimental evaluation, and the types of questions that are addressed. The designs provide a range of options for careful evaluation of the individual case and hence contribute in an important way to the science and practice of clinical work. The major designs are presented and illustrated here. For more detailed discussions of designs, see Barlow and Hersen (1984), Kazdin (1982a), and Krishef (1991). It is worth noting that in this chapter illustrations of the designs will be made with behavior-modification applications. Although the designs are not restricted to a particular type of treatment, behavioral interventions have commonly been evaluated with these designs and provide a rich pool of examples.

ABAB Design

The discussion to this point has highlighted the basic requirements of single-case designs. In particular, assessing performance continuously over time and obtaining stable rates of performance are pivotal to the logic of the designs. Precisely how these features are essential for demonstrating intervention effects can be conveyed by discussing ABAB designs, which are the most basic experimental designs in single-case research. ABAB designs consist of a family of experimental arrangements in which observations of performance are made over time for a given client (or group of clients). During the course of the investigation, changes are made in the experimental conditions to which the client is exposed.

Description   The ABAB design examines the effects of an intervention by alternating the baseline condition (A phase), when no intervention is in effect, with the intervention condition (B phase). The A and B phases are repeated to complete the four phases. The effects of the intervention are clear if performance improves during the first intervention phase, reverts to or approaches original baseline levels of performance when treatment is withdrawn, and improves when treatment is reinstated in the second intervention phase.

The design begins by observing behavior under baseline (no treatment) conditions. When a stable rate of behavior is evident and is not accelerating or decelerating, treatment is implemented. Treatment may consist of a particular intervention conducted by a therapist, parent, spouse, or any other person and is carried out in individual outpatient therapy sessions and at home. Assume that the intervention is associated with some change in the observed behavior. When this change is stable, the intervention is temporarily withdrawn. The baseline condition or absence of treatment is reinstated. The return-to-baseline condition sometimes is referred to as a *reversal phase* because the behavior is expected to reverse, that is, return to or closely to the level of the original baseline. After behavior reverts to baseline levels, the intervention is reinstated.

The design depends on continuous assessment of behavior; thus, within each phase, several data points show the level of behavior. The logic of the design is based on comparing the level of behavior and the trends in the data across different phases. In each phase the data are used to describe current performance and to predict what performance will be like in the future if no changes are made in how the client is treated. When treatment is implemented, performance is expected to change. The change in performance moves the level of behavior from what it was at the baseline level and what it was predicted or extrapolated to be if baseline conditions were continued. Similarly, the new level of behavior during treatment predicts what behavior would be like if treatment were continued. When treatment is withdrawn, behavior should revert to baseline levels. If this pattern is obtained, the predicted level of treatment phase is violated. If the level of behavior changes as treatment is implemented or withdrawn, it suggests that treatment is responsible for the change. Other effects resulting from history or maturation would be expected to result in a continuation of the trend of a previous phase.

The ABAB design and its use can be illustrated with a relatively simple treatment application to eliminate thumbsucking in a 9-year-old boy (Ross, 1975). The thumbsucking was associated with malocclusion of the front teeth, which could not be treated until sucking was eliminated. Thumbsucking was altered at home by the boy's mother. The parents recorded sucking at predetermined times during the day (while the boy watched television) and at night and early morning (while the boy was asleep). Treatment consisted of simply turning off the television set for 5 minutes if the boy was caught sucking his thumb during the day. His siblings were told to help keep him from thumbsucking so that their television time would also not be lost. The program was implemented and withdrawn in accord with requirements of the ABAB design.

The effects of the program are extremely clear (Figure 9.4). When treatment was in effect, thumbsucking was almost eliminated. Sucking returned and approached baseline levels when treatment was withdrawn but was virtually eliminated when treatment was reinstated. Interestingly, observations at night and in the early morning while the boy slept showed a similar pattern even though the program was not introduced for nighttime thumbsucking. The daytime program was continued for 6 months beyond the sixteenth week, reportedly with similar effects.

Considerations The most commonly used version of the ABAB design has been discussed as a four-phase design that alternates a single treatment with

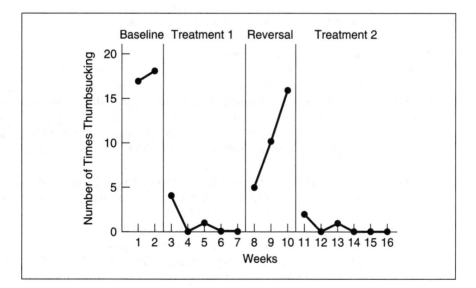

FIGURE 9.4 Thumbsucking frequency during television viewing (21 observations per week).

Source: Adapted from Ross, J.A. (1975). Parents modify thumbsucking: A case study. *Journal of Behavior Therapy and Experimental Psychiatry, 6,* 248–249, with permission from Elsevier Science and the author.

baseline phases. However, designs that include more than one treatment and more than four phases are available. For example, suppose that the treatment (B_1) does not change behavior after the baseline phase. The therapist–investigator would not continue the phase but would try another treatment (B_2), which would constitute a new phase and would probably be implemented later in the design. The design could be represented as an $AB_1 B_2 AB_2$ design. The ability to improvise treatment as part of the design is a key feature that makes variations compatible with and quite useful for clinical application (Kazdin, 1993).

The central requirement of the design is having stable levels of behavior. Evaluating data in an ABAB design and drawing a conclusion about the causal role of treatment are difficult when treatment effects merely seem to continue a pattern of behavior or trend already evident in the data from the baseline phase. Hence, most investigators recommend waiting until behavior is stable (i.e., no trend) and is relatively consistent over time or shows a trend only in the direction opposite of the change anticipated with treatment. Statistical techniques have been developed to take into account baseline trends that might interfere with drawing conclusions about interventions (Kazdin, 1984; Krishef, 1991).

Another key feature of the design is demonstration of a causal relation by showing that behavior reverts to or approaches the original baseline level after the intervention is withdrawn or altered (during the second A phase). This requirement introduces problems that restrict use of the design in clinical work. One problem is that withdrawing treatment does not always show a change in behavior. Indeed, it is the prime hope of both therapists and clients that once treatment is terminated, its therapeutic effects will continue. Clinically, continued performance of the appropriate behavior is important; yet, from the standpoint of an ABAB design, it could be disappointing. If behavior is not made to revert to baseline levels after showing an initial change, a causal relation cannot be drawn between the intervention and behavior. Some events other than treatment might account for change because the behavior is not under the control of the administration or termination of treatment.

Even if behavior did revert to baseline levels when treatment was suspended temporarily, such a change would be clinically undesirable. Essentially, returning the client to baseline levels of performance amounts to making behavior worse, but treatment can be withdrawn for only a brief period, such as 1 day or a few days. In most circumstances, the idea of making a client worse when treatment may be having an effect is ethically unacceptable. There may be important exceptions if, for example, the required treatment has undesirable side effects and suspension of treatments occurs to test whether the intervention is still needed. Aside from ethical problems, there are also practical problems. It is often difficult to ensure that the client, therapist, or relatives responsible for conducting treatment will actually stop treatment when some success has been achieved.

As a general rule, problems related to reversing behavior make the ABAB design and its variations undesirable in clinical situations. Yet the power of the design in demonstrating control of an intervention over behavior is very compelling. If behavior can, in effect, be "turned on and off" as a function of the intervention, this is a potent demonstration of a causal relation. Few threats to internal validity remain plausible in explaining the pattern of results. Yet, the investigator's desire for clear demonstrations of experimental control conflicts with the clinician's (and client's) desire for protracted therapeutic change. Hence, this design is not advocated strongly for clinical work in which the roles of investigator and clinician should merge.

Multiple-Baseline Design

Description   The *multiple-baseline design* demonstrates the effect of an intervention by showing that behavior change accompanies introduction of the intervention at different points in time. Once the intervention is presented, it need not be withdrawn or altered to reverse behavior to or near baseline levels. Thus, the clinical utility of the design is not limited by the problems of reverting behavior to pretreatment levels.

There are different versions of the multiple-baseline design. In each version, data are collected continuously and concurrently across two or more baselines. The intervention is applied to the different baselines at different points in time. The versions differ according to whether the baselines are *different responses* (symptoms, behaviors, areas of functioning) for a given individual, the same response of *different individuals*, or the same response for an individual across *different situations*. For example, in the multiple-baseline design across responses, a single individual or group of individuals is observed. Data are collected on two or more behaviors, each of which eventually is to be altered. The behaviors are observed daily or on several occasions each week. After each baseline shows a stable pattern, the intervention is applied to one response. Baseline conditions remain in effect for the other responses. The initial response to which treatment is applied is expected to change while other responses remain at pretreatment levels. When the treated behavior stabilizes, the intervention is applied to the second response. Treatment continues for the first two responses while baseline continues for all other responses. Eventually, each response is exposed to treatment but at a different point in time. A causal relation between the intervention and behavior is clearly demonstrated if each response changes only when the intervention is introduced and not before.

For example, an imagery-based flooding procedure was used to treat a 6½-year-old boy named Joseph, who suffered a posttraumatic stress disorder (Saigh, 1986). This disorder is a reaction to a highly stressful event or experience and has a number of symptoms, such as persistently reexperiencing the event (e.g., thoughts, dreams), avoidance of stimuli associated with the trauma, numbing of responsiveness, outbursts of anger, difficulty in sleeping, and exaggerated startle responses. Joseph experienced the disorder after exposure to a bomb blast in a war zone in which he lived. His reaction included trauma-related nightmares, recollections of the trauma, depression, and avoidance behavior. To treat Joseph, five scenes that evoked anxiety (e.g., seeing injured people and debris, approaching specific shopping areas) were developed. To measure discomfort to the scenes, Joseph rated his level of anxiety as each scene was described. During the sessions he was trained to relax, after which scenes were presented for extended periods (longer than 20 minutes). During this exposure period, he was asked to imagine the exact details of the scenes. The five scenes were incorporated into treatment in a multiple-baseline design. Exposure to scenes occurred in sequence or at different points in time. In each session, discomfort was rated in response to all five scenes.

The results, presented in Figure 9.5, showed that Joseph's discomfort consistently decreased after only 10 sessions (1 session of baseline assessment, 10 sessions of treatment). The reduction of anxiety for each scene was associated

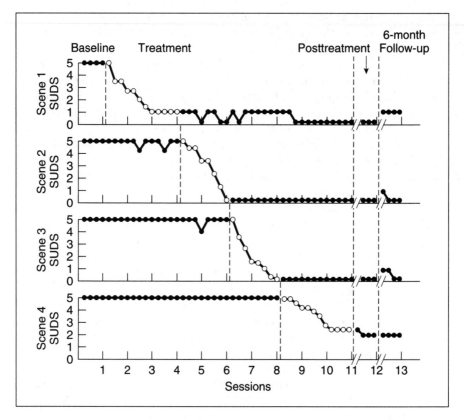

FIGURE 9.5   Joseph's Ratings of Discomfort referred to as Subjective Units of Disturbance (SUDS) in which 5 = maximum discomfort and 0 = no discomfort. Assessment was conducted to measure discomfort for each scene during treatment session. Treatment (*open* circles) reflects the period in which imagery-based exposure (flooding) focused on the specific scene.

Source: Saigh, P.A. (1986). In vitro flooding in the treatment of a 6-year-old boy's posttraumatic stress disorder. *Behaviour Research and Therapy, 24,* 685–688. Reprinted with permission from Elsevier Science and the author.

with implementation of the intervention. Assessment immediately after treatment and 6 months later indicated that he was no longer discomforted by the situations. The results from other measures also reflected change. Before and after treatment, Joseph was assessed in the market place in which the bomb blast had occurred. His performance had improved after treatment as reflected by his remaining in the area longer and thereby showing less avoidance. Other measures, including assessment of anxiety, depression, and classroom performance at school, also indicated improvement after treatment. Thus, the effects of treatment appeared to affect several important areas of functioning.

The multiple-baseline design can be extended across individuals. Baseline data can be collected for a behavior across different individuals (e.g., siblings in a family, children in a classroom, patients on a ward) by introducing the intervention at different points in time to each individual. Similarly, baseline data can be collected across different situations (e.g., at home, at work) for a given individual, with the intervention implemented at different points in time for each situation. In each version, the impact of the intervention is demonstrated if behavior changes when (and only when) the intervention is introduced.

Considerations   The multiple-baseline design demonstrates the effect of the intervention without a return-to-baseline conditions and a temporary loss of some of the gains achieved. Two major considerations that affect the clarity of the demonstration are the number and the independence of the baselines. The number of baselines adequate for a clear demonstration is difficult to specify. Two baselines are a minimum, but another one or two can measurably strengthen the demonstration. The clarity of the demonstration across a given set of baselines is a function of factors such as the duration of baselines, the presence of trends or extensive variability of behavior during the baseline phase, the rapidity of behavior change after treatment is implemented, and the magnitude of behavior change. Depending on the factors, even a few baselines may provide a sufficiently convincing demonstration.

The number of baselines needed to demonstrate clear effects may depend on the problem of interdependence of the baselines. The design depends on being able to show that the behavior changes when and only when the treatment is implemented. Ideally, behaviors still exposed to the baseline condition will not change until the intervention is applied. If they do change, it suggests that the intervention may not have been responsible for change. Rather, extraneous factors (e.g., history, testing) may have led to the change. Occasionally, the effects produced by an intervention may be general rather than specific; that is, a change in one behavior is associated with changes in other behaviors but generalized effects across different baselines appear to be exceptions rather than the rule. When generalized effects are present, features from other single-case designs (e.g., a brief reversal phase) can be added in separate experimental phases to demonstrate a causal relation between treatment and behavior change.

Multiple-baseline designs are often user friendly in clinical applications because the intervention is applied in a gradual or sequential fashion across different responses of the individual (or different individuals or different situations). If the intervention is effective, it can be extended to all other responses for which change is desired. In addition, if the intervention is not effective or not effective enough to achieve important changes, it can be altered or improved before it is extended.

Changing-Criterion Design

Description   The changing-criterion design demonstrates the effect of an intervention by showing that behavior changes incrementally to match a performance criterion. A causal relation between an intervention and behavior is demonstrated if behavior matches a constantly changing criterion for performance during the course of treatment. The design begins with a baseline phase after which the intervention is introduced. When the intervention is introduced, a specific level of performance is chosen as a criterion for the client. The daily criterion may be used as a basis for providing response consequences or as an incentive of some sort. The criterion can be negotiated with the client. When the performance meets or surpasses the criterion level on a given day (e.g., certain number of cigarettes smoked, number of calories consumed), the response consequence (e.g., monetary reward) is provided.

A particular criterion usually is invoked continuously for at least a few days. When performance consistently meets the criterion, the criterion is made more stringent (e.g., fewer cigarettes or calories consumed daily). Consequences are provided only for meeting the new criterion on a given day, and the criterion is changed again if the performance meets the criterion consistently. The criterion is repeatedly changed throughout the intervention phase until the terminal goal of the program is achieved. The effect of the intervention is demonstrated if behavior matches a criterion as the criterion is changed. If behavior changes with the criterion, it is likely that the intervention and criterion change, rather than extraneous influences, accounted for behavior change. By implementing a given criterion for at least a few days (or even longer), the behavior shows a steplike effect that is not likely to result from a general incremental change occurring as a function of extraneous events.

In one situation, a changing-criterion design was used to evaluate a program to decrease caffeine consumption in three adults (Foxx & Rubinoff, 1979). Caffeine consumed in large quantities has been associated with a variety of symptoms ranging in severity from general irritability and gastrointestinal disturbances to cardiovascular disorders and cancer. The intervention consisted of having participants, at the beginning of the program, deposit $20, which was returned in small portions if caffeine consumption fell below the criterion set for a given day. Participants signed a contract that specified how they would earn or lose the money. Each person recorded daily caffeine consumption on the basis of a list of beverages that provided their caffeine equivalence (in milligrams).

The effects of the program for one subject, a female schoolteacher, are illustrated in Figure 9.6. During the baseline phase, the teacher's daily average caffeine consumption was 1000 mg (equal to approximately 8 cups of brewed coffee). When the intervention began, she was required to reduce her daily consumption by about 100 mg less than baseline. When performance was consistently below the criterion (solid line), the criterion was reduced further by approximately 100 mg. Change in the criterion continued during separate subphases. In each subphase, money was earned only if caffeine consumption fell at or below the criterion. The figure shows that performance consistently fell below the criterion. Assessment 10 months after the program had ended indicated that the teacher had maintained her low rate of caffeine consumption.

Considerations   The design depends on repeatedly changing the performance criterion and examining behavior relative to the new criterion. The design is especially well suited to terminal responses that are arrived at or approximated gradually. For most therapeutic problems, individuals must acquire the skills, overcome problematic situations, or gain comfort gradually so that the require-

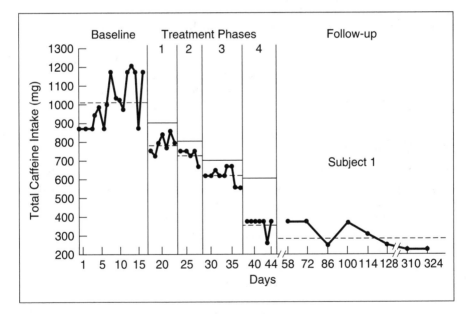

FIGURE 9.6   Subject's daily caffeine intake in milligrams during baseline, treatment, and follow-up. The criterion level for each treatment phase was 102 milligrams of caffeine less than that of the previous treatment phase. *Solid horizontal* lines indicate the criterion level for each phase. *Broken horizontal* lines indicate the mean for each condition.

Source: Foxx, R.M., & Rubinoff, A. (1979). Behavioral treatment of caffeinism: Reducing excessive coffee drinking, *Journal of Applied Behavior Analysis, 12,* 335–344. Reprinted with permission of the authors.

ment may be met. If behavior change occurs in large steps and does not follow the criterion, the specific effect of the intervention in altering behavior will not be clear. Thus, the design tends to be limited to demonstrating gradual rather than rapid changes because of the requirement of the changing criterion.

In general, the changing-criterion design is less powerful than other single-case designs because the effects of extraneous events could account for a general increase or decrease in behavior. The design depends on showing a unidirectional change in behavior (increase or decrease) over time. However, extraneous events rather than the intervention could result in unidirectional changes. The demonstration is unambiguous only if performance matches the criterion very closely and the criterion is changed several times. The design is strengthened by making bidirectional changes in the criterion during the intervention phase. Rather than making the criterion uniformly increasingly stringent, it can be made more stringent at some points and less stringent at others to weaken the plausibility that extraneous events account for the results. Nevertheless, reversing behavior, even if only to a small degree and for a brief period, may be countertherapeutic.

As with the multiple-baseline design, the changing-criterion design can be quite compatible with the demands of the clinical situation. Many therapeutic regimens focus on gradual development of behavior or skills (e.g., improving marital communication, participation of activities) or reduction of problematic function (e.g., overcoming anxiety). Shaping these behaviors or gradually exposing individuals to anxiety-provoking situations may proceed in ways that can reflect increasing the performance criteria as changes are evident. Thus, progress can be monitored and evaluated in a changing-criterion design.

General Comments

Single-case research encompasses many different designs, only a few of which are illustrated in this chapter. The designs are true experiments in the sense that causal relations can be demonstrated and threats to validity, particularly internal validity, can be ruled out. The designs offer a distinct advantage for treatment research. To begin with, single-case methodology provides the means to investigate treatments empirically with individual clients. Traditionally, study of the individual client has been restricted to anecdotal reports about the course of change. Therapist impressions and uncontrolled implementation of treatment eliminate the possibility of drawing unchallenged causal inferences. In contrast, single-case designs allow careful evaluation of treatment by addressing threats to internal validity that are the bases for drawing causal inferences. Actually, several different questions can be addressed. The methodology permits evaluating the effects of an overall treatment package, withdrawing components of treatment over time to determine an essential treatment ingredient, adding components of treatment to enhance behavior change, and comparing different treatments, and the relationship between treatment processes and outcomes (see Jones, 1993).

Another advantage of single-case designs is that they permit investigation of problems that are not likely to be studied in between-group research. There are many clinical problems that are relatively rare; thus, recruiting subjects for a large-scale treatment evaluation project would be extraordinarily difficult. Single-case designs allow careful investigation of an individual client. Thus, information that otherwise might not be available can be obtained from experimentation using a single-case design.

For example, psychological treatment of transsexual behavior is relatively rare, and careful evaluation of such treatment is not likely to emerge from randomized controlled treatment trials with groups of cases. A very interesting case was reported and evaluated using a single-case design (Barlow, Reynolds, & Agras, 1973). The case was a 17-year-old male who desired to be a female. His behaviors and attitudes reflected his transsexual interest—attraction to other males; a history of cross-dressing; interest in traditionally feminine role behaviors such as knitting, crocheting, embroidering; sexual fantasies in which he imagined himself as a woman; and effeminate mannerisms in sitting, standing, and walking. Extensive treatment based on modeling, rehearsal, and feedback was used to alter a variety of effeminate mannerisms, speaking patterns, social skills, sexual fantasies, and sexual arousal. The effects of training were demonstrated in a combined ABAB and multiple-baseline design. This report is unique in experimentally demonstrating successful psychotherapeutic treatment of a transsexual. It is unlikely that this demonstration could have been accomplished with several transsexuals in a between-group design if for no other reason than the difficulty in recruiting such clients in sufficient numbers who would be interested in treatment other than direct physical change through surgery.

Although single-case designs provide an important contribution to treatment evaluation, they have distinct limitations. For example, the designs are weak in revealing subject characteristics that may interact with a specific treatment. Focusing on one subject or client does not allow systematically comparing treatments across multiple subjects who differ in various characteristics, at least within the same experiment. Examination of subject variables is more readily accomplished by group research, specifically factorial designs, in which multiple subjects necessarily are required.

Related to the study of subject variables, the results of single-case investigation provide no hint of the generality of findings (external validity) to other subjects. Quite possibly, the effects of treatment demonstrated with the individual case will not generalize to other individuals. Within the single-case investigation, the investigator cannot determine how many clients would reveal the same pattern of change. However, it is important to note that the lack of generality of single-case findings is not a limitation of current research. Findings obtained in single-case experiments have had no less generality, and possibly greater generality, than findings from between-group research. Part of the reason for the generality of findings from single-case research is that treatment applications with the single case have sought extremely potent effects. Consequently, it has been argued that interventions with such effects for the single case are likely to generalize more broadly than are interventions that may meet the relatively weaker criterion of statistical significance (Baer, 1977).

DATA EVALUATION IN SINGLE-CASE RESEARCH

In areas of clinical research in which single-case designs are used, data typically are evaluated without reliance on statistical tests. Statistical tests are available for single-case designs even though they involve techniques that are somewhat less familiar (e.g., time-series analyses, randomization tests) than the usual methods taught in graduate training (Kazdin, 1984). It is not the availability of statistical tests for the single case that is the issue. Investigators working with single-case designs as a matter of choice often prefer nonstatistical evaluation of the data. Given the training of most students and professionals in psychology, nonstatistical evaluation seemingly represents an inappropriate form of analysis. An obvious concern is that by not using statistical techniques, subjective judgment may enter into deciding which findings are significant or veridical and which are not. The concern is reasonable because, regardless of how arbitrary statistical evaluation or decision making seems, the criteria appear quite explicit (e.g., $p <$ .05) and consistent across investigators.[2] Before entering into objections and concerns, it is useful to consider the rationale and use of nonstatistical evaluation. At the very least, the approach sensitizes us to critical properties of the data we collect; at best, it provides another viable approach for determining the reliability, significance, and importance of a particular result.

Nonstatistical evaluation usually refers to examining the data and determining whether the intervention had an effect by visual inspection. Visual inspection is commonly used in single-case research in which continuous data are available for one or several subjects. With single-case designs, the investigator has the advantage of seeing the data for a single subject for consecutive periods without the intervention, followed by data with the intervention in effect. If the intervention abruptly changes the pattern of data, an inference about the effect of the intervention is clearer than merely looking at pre- and postintervention differences across two observations. Assessment of the individual's performance on several occasions makes examination of the data through visual inspection less arbitrary than the method might appear at first glance.

Criteria for Visual Inspection

Evaluation of data nonstatistically has the same goal as statistical analysis, namely, to identify whether the effects are consistent, reliable, and unlikely to have resulted from chance fluctuations between conditions. Although visual inspection is based on subjective judgment, this is not tantamount to noting that decisions are by fiat or vary with each person making the judgment. In many uses of single-case designs in which visual inspection is invoked, the applied or clinical goals are to achieve marked intervention effects. In cases in which intervention effects are very strong, one need not carefully scrutinize or enumerate the criteria that underlie the judgment that the effects are veridical.

Several situations arise in applied research in which intervention effects are likely to be so dramatic that visual inspection is easily invoked. For example, whenever the behavior of interest is not present in the client's behavior during the baseline phase (e.g., social interaction, exercise, reading) but occurs during the intervention phase, a judgment about the effects of the intervention is easily made. If the behavior never occurs during baseline, there is unparalleled stability in the data. Both the mean and standard deviation equal zero. Even a minor occurrence of the target behavior during the intervention phase would be easily detected. Similarly, when the behavior of interest occurs frequently during the baseline phase (e.g., reports of hallucinations, aggressive acts, cigarette smoking) and stops completely during the intervention phase, the magnitude of change usually permits clear judgments by visual inspection. In cases in which behavior is at the opposite extreme of the assessment range before and during treatment, the ease of invoking visual inspection can be readily understood. Of course, in most situations, the data do not show a change from one extreme of the assessment scale to the other, and the guidelines for making judgments by visual inspection need to be considered more deliberately.

Visual inspection depends on many characteristics of the data, especially data that pertain to the magnitude of the changes across phases and the rate of these changes. The two characteristics related to magnitude are changes in *mean* and *level*. The two characteristics related to rate are changes in *trend* and *latency of the change*. It is important to examine each characteristic separately even though they act in concert.

Changes in *means* across phases refer to shifts in the average rate of performance. Consistent changes in means across phases can serve as a basis for deciding whether the data pattern meets the requirements of the design. An example showing changes in means across phases can serve as a basis for deciding whether the data pattern meets the requirements of the design. A hypothetical example showing changes in means across the intervention phase is illustrated in an ABAB design in Figure 9.7. As evident in the figure, performance on the average (horizontal dashed line in each phase) changed in response to the different baseline and intervention phases. Visual inspection of this pattern suggests that the intervention led to consistent changes.

Changes in *level* are a little less familiar but very important in allowing a decision through visual inspection about whether the intervention produced reliable effects. Changes in level refer to the shift or discontinuity of performance from the end of one phase to the beginning of the next phase. A change in level is independent of the change in mean. When one asks about what happened immediately after the intervention was implemented or withdrawn, the implicit concern is the level of performance. Figure 9.8 shows change in level across phases in ABAB design. The figure shows that whenever the phase was altered, behavior assumed a new rate; that is, it shifted up or down rather quickly. A change in level in Figure 9.8 would also be accompanied by a change in mean

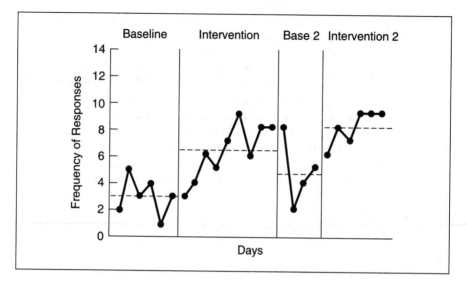

FIGURE 9.7   Hypothetical example of performance in an ABAB design with means in each phase represented with *dashed* lines.

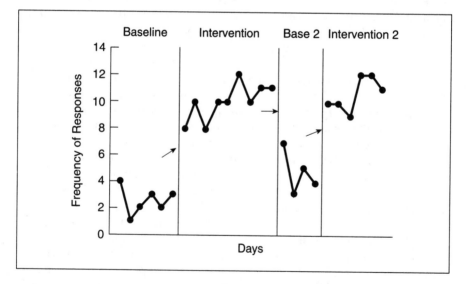

FIGURE 9.8   Hypothetical example of performance in an ABAB design. The *arrows* point to the changes in level or discontinuities associated with a change from one phase to another.

across the phases. However, level and mean changes do not necessarily go together. It is possible that a rapid change in level occurs but that the mean remains the same across phase or that the mean changes but no abrupt shift in level has occurred.

Changes in *trend* are of obvious importance in applying visual inspection. Trend or slope refer to the tendency for the data to show systematic increases or decreases over time. The alteration of phases within the design may show that the direction of behavior changes as the intervention is applied or withdrawn. Figure 9.9 illustrates a hypothetical example in which trends have changed during the course of an ABAB design. The initial baseline trend is reversed by the intervention, reinstated when the intervention is withdrawn, and again reversed in the final phase. A change in trend would still be an important criterion even if there were no trend in the baseline phase. A change from no trend (horizontal line) during the baseline phase to a trend (increase or decrease in behavior) during the intervention phase would also constitute a change in trend.

Finally, the *latency of the change* that occurs when phases are altered is an important characteristic of the data for invoking visual inspection. Latency refers to the period between the onset or termination of one condition (e.g., intervention, return to baseline) and changes in performance. The more closely in time that the change occurs after the experimental conditions have been altered, the clearer the intervention effect. A hypothetical example is provided in

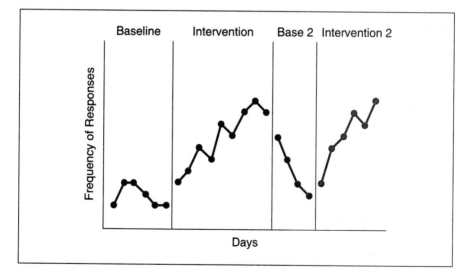

FIGURE 9.9 Hypothetical example of performance in an ABAB design with changes in trend across phases. Baseline shows a relatively stable or possibly decreasing trend. When the intervention is introduced, an accelerating trend is evident. This trend is reversed when the intervention is withdrawn (Base 2) and is reinstated when the intervention is reintroduced.

Figure 9.10, which shows only the first two phases of separate ABAB designs. In the top panel, implementation of the intervention after baseline was associated with a rapid change in performance. The change would also be evident from changes in mean and trend. In the bottom panel, the intervention did not immediately lead to change. The time between the onset of the intervention and behavior change was longer than that in the top panel, and it is slightly less clear that the intervention may have led to the change.

As a general rule, the shorter the period between the onset of the intervention and behavior change, the easier to infer that the intervention led to change. The rationale is that as the time between the intervention and behavior increases, the more likely that intervening influences may have accounted for behavior change. Of course, the importance of the latency of the change after the onset of the intervention depends on the type of intervention and behavior studied. For example, one would not expect rapid changes in applying diet and exercise to treat obesity. Weight reduction usually reflects gradual changes after treatment begins. Similarly, some medications do not produce rapid effects. Change depends on the buildup of therapeutic doses.

Changes in means, levels, and trends and variations in the latency of change across phases frequently accompany each other. Yet they are separate characteristics of the data and can occur alone or in combination. Visual inspection is conducted by judging the extent to which changes in these characteristics are evident across phases and whether the changes are consistent with the requirements of the particular design. When changes in mean, level, and trend, and latency of change go together, visual inspection is relatively easy to invoke. In such cases, the data across phases may not overlap. Nonoverlapping data refer to the pattern in which the values of the data points during the baseline phase do not approach any of the values of the data points attained during the intervention phase.

It is important to note that invoking the criteria for visual inspection requires judgments about the pattern of data in the entire design, not merely about changes across one or two phases. Unambiguous effects require that the criteria be met throughout the design. To the extent that the criteria are not consistently met, conclusions about the reliability of intervention effects become tentative. For example, changes in an ABAB design may show nonoverlapping data points for the first AB phases but no clear differences across the second AB phases. The absence of a consistent pattern of data that meets the criteria limits the conclusions that can be drawn.

Problems and Considerations

Visual inspection has been quite useful in identifying reliable intervention effects both in experimental and clinical research. When intervention effects are potent, the need for statistical analysis is obviated. Intervention effects can be extremely clear from graphic displays of the data because persons can judge for them-

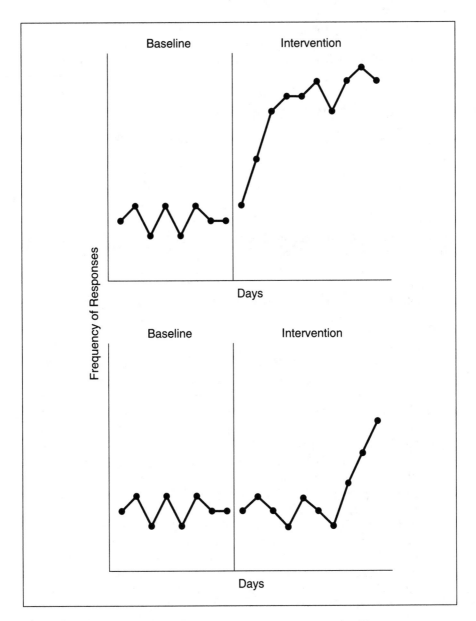

FIGURE 9.10 Hypothetical examples of first AB phases as part of larger ABAB designs. *Upper* panel shows that when the intervention was introduced, behavior changed rapidly. *Lower* panel shows that when the intervention was introduced, behavior change was delayed. The changes in both upper and lower panels are reasonably clear. Yet as a general rule, as the latency between the onset of the intervention and behavior change increases, questions are more likely to arise about whether the intervention or extraneous factors accounted for change.

selves whether the criteria have been met; many methods of displaying the data graphically can facilitate the evaluation (Kazdin, 1982a; Krishef, 1991).

The use of visual inspection as the primary basis for evaluating data in single-case designs has raised major concerns. Perhaps the major issue pertains to the lack of concrete decision rules for determining whether a particular demonstration shows or fails to show a reliable effect. The process of visual inspection would seem to permit, if not actively encourage, subjectivity and inconsistency in the evaluation of intervention effects. Studies of how individuals invoke the criteria for visual inspection have shown that judges, even when experts in the field, often disagree about particular data patterns and whether the effects were reliable (e.g., DeProspero & Cohen, 1979; Gottman & Glass, 1978; Matyas & Greenwood, 1990). The disagreement among judges using visual inspection has been an argument to favor statistical analysis of the data as a supplement to or replacement of visual inspection. The attractive feature of statistical analysis is that once the statistic is decided, the result that is achieved is usually consistent across investigators. And the final result (statistical significance) is not altered by the judgment of the investigator.

Another criticism levied against visual inspection is that it regards as significant only effects that are very marked. Many interventions might prove to be consistent in the effects they produce but the effects are relatively weak. Such effects might not be detected by visual inspection and would be overlooked. Overlooking weak but reliable effects can have unfortunate consequences. First, weak but reliable effects may have theoretical significance in relation to understanding personality, dysfunction, or treatment. Second, the possibility exists that interventions, when first developed, may have weak effects. It would be unfortunate if these interventions were prematurely discarded before they could be developed further. Interventions with reliable but weak effects might eventually achieve potent effects if investigators developed the interventions further. On the other hand, the stringent criteria may encourage investigators to develop interventions to the point that they produce marked changes before claims about their demonstrated efficacy can be made.

A final problem with visual inspection is that it requires a particular pattern of data in baseline and subsequent phases so that the results can be interpreted. Visual-inspection criteria are more readily invoked when data show little or no trend or trend in directions opposite from the trend expected in the following phase and slight variability. However, trends and variability in the data may not always meet the idealized data requirements. In such cases, visual inspection may be difficult to invoke. Other criteria, such as statistical analyses, may be of use in these situations.

General Comments

The data evaluation procedures highlighted here and the single-case designs with which they are associated are infrequently taught in undergraduate or graduate training. These methods are of special relevance in clinical psychology and other areas in which research findings are applied and in which clinically significant (important) change is a goal. The level of change required by visual-inspection criteria is usually much greater to infer a reliable (i.e., veridical) effect than that demonstrated by statistical significance testing.

Objections to nonstatistical data evaluation methods are strong because the methods, by their very nature, appear not merely to permit subjectivity but to court it directly. Yet, visual inspection can be reliably invoked and has generated a body of research with outcomes that are at least as reliable and replicable as those obtained through statistical evaluation. Regardless of whether the criteria are adopted in a given study, the criteria of visual inspection are worth noting. Changes in mean, level, slope, and latency of change sensitize us to critical properties of the data. In the evaluation of continuous data and in clinical and research situations in which performance is scrutinized over time, these properties can greatly influence decision making, treatment planning, and evaluation.

QUASI-EXPERIMENTS WITH THE SINGLE CASE

In our discussion of single cases, we have covered two methodological extremes. We began by mentioning uncontrolled case studies, which usually consist of narrative reports, undocumented interventions, subjectively filtered descriptions, and absence of experimental control. As a method of study, uncontrolled cases are wanting because they typically are subject to a vast range of validity threats. At the other extreme, we have discussed true single-case experimental designs. Such designs as the ABAB, multiple-baseline, and other designs provide arrangements that readily rule out threats to internal validity and permit causal conclusions about the effects of various interventions. Between the extremes of the uncontrolled case study and true single-case experiments are *quasi-single-case experiments*. These consist of explicit efforts to incorporate several features of true experiments. In clinical work, the conditions of true single-case experiments sometimes cannot be met. Several variations exist to evaluate interventions and to meet clinical exigencies of the case.

Characteristics

The essential features of true single-case experiments are (1) control of the intervention (e.g., withdrawing and presenting intervention, baseline conditions, or both), (2) assessing performance continuously over time and under different conditions, and (3) looking for stable patterns to make and test predictions about performance. These features of the true experiments are weapons that directly combat threats to validity, particularly internal validity. Case studies can be arranged to deploy various combinations of these weapons to greatly increase the extent to which threats to validity are ruled out or made implausible (Kazdin, 1981). There are several characteristics we seek to add to the uncontrolled case to improve their yield.

Type of Data   Case studies may vary in the type of data or information that is used as a basis for claiming that change has occurred. At one extreme is anecdotal and qualitative information, which includes reports by the client or therapist that therapeutic change has been achieved. At the other extreme, case studies can include systematic and qualitative information, such as self-report inventories, ratings by other persons, and direct measures of overt behavior. Objective measures have their own problems (e.g., reactivity, response biases) but still provide a stronger basis for determining whether change has occurred. If more standardized information is available, the therapist has a better basis for claiming that change has been achieved. The data do not allow one to infer the basis for the change. Objective assessment and the resulting data are prerequisites because they provide information that change has in fact occurred.

Assessment Occasions   Another dimension that can distinguish case studies is the number and timing of the assessment occasions. The occasions in which systematic information is collected have extremely important implications for drawing inferences about the effects of the intervention. Major options consist of collecting information on a one- or two-shot basis (e.g., posttreatment only or pre- and posttreatment) or continuously over time (e.g., every day or a few times per week for an extended period). When information is collected on one or two occasions, threats to internal validity associated with assessment (e.g., testing, instrumentation, statistical regression) can be especially difficult to rule out. With continuous assessment over time, these threats are much less plausible, especially if continuous assessment begins before treatment and continues during the course of treatment. Continuous assessment allows one to examine the pattern of the data and whether the pattern appears to have been altered at the point at which the intervention was introduced. If a case study includes continuous assessment on several occasions over time, some threats to internal validity related to assessment can be ruled out.

Past and Future Projections of Performance   The extent to which claims can be made about performance in the past and likely performance in the future can distinguish cases. Past and future projections refer to the course of a particular behavior or problem. For some behaviors or problems, an extended history may be evident, which indicates no change. If performance changes when treatment is applied, the likelihood that treatment caused the change is increased. Problems that have a short history or that tend to occur for brief periods or in episodes may change without the treatment. Problems with an extended history of stable performance are likely to continue unless some special event (e.g., treatment) alters its course. Thus, the history of the problem may dictate the likelihood that extraneous events, rather than treatment, could plausibly account for the change.

Projections of what performance would be like in the future might be obtained from knowledge of the nature of the problem. For example, the problem may be one that would not improve without intervention (e.g., terminal illness).

Knowing the likely outcome increases the inferences that can be drawn about the impact of an intervention to alter this course. The patient's improvement attests to the efficacy of the treatment as the critical variable because change in the problem controverts the expected prediction.

Projections of future performance may derive from continuous assessment over time. If a particular problem is very stable, as indicated by continuous assessment before treatment, the likely prediction is that it will remain at that level in the future. If an intervention is applied and performance departs from the predicted level, this suggests that the intervention rather than other factors (e.g., history, maturation, repeated testing) may have been responsible for the change.

Type of Effect   Cases also differ in terms of the type of effects or changes that are evident as treatment is applied. The immediacy and magnitude of change contribute to the inferences that can be drawn about the role of treatment. Usually, the more immediate the therapeutic change after the onset of treatment, the stronger the argument that the treatment was responsible for change. An immediate change with the onset of treatment may make it more plausible that the treatment, rather than other events (e.g., history, maturation), led to change. On the other hand, gradual changes or changes that begin long after treatment has been applied are more difficult to interpret because of the intervening experiences between the onset of treatment and the therapeutic change.

The magnitude of the change is also important. When marked changes in performance are achieved, this suggests that only a special event, probably the treatment, could be responsible. Of course, the magnitude and immediacy of change, when combined, increase the confidence one can place in according treatment a causal role. Rapid and dramatic changes provide a strong basis for attributing the effects to treatment. Gradual and relatively small changes might more easily be discounted by random fluctuations of performance, normal cycles of behavior, or developmental changes.

Number and Heterogeneity of Subjects   The number of subjects included in a case report can influence the confidence that can be placed in any inferences drawn about treatment. Demonstrations with several cases, rather than with one case, provide a stronger basis for inferring the effects of treatment. Essentially, each case can be viewed as a replication of the original effect that seemed to result from treatment. The more cases that improve with treatment, the more unlikely that any particular extraneous event was responsible for change. Extraneous events probably varied among the cases, and the common experience, namely, treatment, may be the most plausible reason for the therapeutic changes.

The heterogeneity of the cases or diversity of the types of persons may also contribute to inferences about the cause of therapeutic change. If change is demonstrated among several clients who differ in subject and demographic variables (e.g., age, gender, race, social class, clinical problems), the inferences that can be made about treatment are stronger than if the diversity does not exist.

With a heterogeneous set of clients, the likelihood that a particular threat to internal validity (e.g., history, maturation) could explain the results is reduced.

Design Variations

When applied to clinical cases, the previously mentioned characteristics can greatly increase the strength of inferences that can be drawn relative to uncontrolled case studies. Depending on how the different characteristics are addressed within a particular demonstration, it is quite possible that the inferences closely approximate those that could be obtained from a true single-case experiment. Not all dimensions are under the control of the clinician–investigator (e.g., immediacy and strength of treatment effects). On the other hand, critical features on which conclusions depend, such as the use of replicable measures and assessment on multiple occasions, can be controlled in the clinical situation and greatly enhance the demonstration.

It is useful to consider a few of the many types of quasi-experiments using the single-case design that vary on the characteristics mentioned previously. These designs convey how the quality of the inferences that are drawn can vary and what the investigator can do in clinical applications or research to strengthen the demonstration. Table 9.1 illustrates a few types of uncontrolled case studies that differ on some of the dimensions mentioned. Also presented is the extent to which each type of case rules out specific threats to internal validity. The collection of data was included for each type of case because the absence of objective or quantifiable data usually precludes drawing conclusions about whether change occurred.

Case Study Type 1: Pre- and Postassessment   A case study in which a client is treated may utilize pre- and posttreatment assessment. The inferences that can be drawn from a case with such assessment are not necessarily strengthened by the assessment procedures alone. Whether specific threats to internal validity are ruled out depends on characteristics of the case with respect to the other dimensions. Table 9.1 illustrates a case with pre- and postassessment but without other characteristics that would help rule out threats to internal validity.

If changes occur in the case from pre- to posttreatment assessment, one cannot draw valid inferences about whether the treatment led to change. It is quite possible that events occurring in time (history), processes of change within the individual (maturation), repeated exposure to assessment (testing), changes in the scoring criteria (instrumentation), or reversion of the score to the mean (regression), rather than treatment, led to change. The case in Table 9.1 included objective assessment; thus there is a firmer basis for claiming that changes were made than if only anecdotal reports were provided. However, threats to internal validity were not ruled out, so the basis for change remains a matter of surmise.

TABLE 9.1. Selected Types of Hypothetical Cases and the Threats to Internal Validity They Address

Type of Case Study	Type I	Type II	Type III
Characteristics of case present (+) or absent (–)			
Objective data	+	+	+
Continuous assessment	+	+	+
Stability of problem	+	+	+
Immediate and marked effects	+	+	+
Multiple cases	+	+	+
Major threats to internal validity ruled out (+) or not ruled out (–)			
History	–	?	+
Maturation	–	?	+
Testing	–	+	+
Instrumentation	–	+	+
Statistical regression	–	+	+

Note: In the table, a plus sign (+) indicates that the threat to internal validity is probably controlled, a minus sign (–) indicates that the threat remains a problem, and a question mark (?) indicates that the threat may remain uncontrolled. In preparation of the table, selected threats were omitted because they arise primarily in the comparison of different groups in experiments. They are not usually a problem for a case study, which does not rely on group comparisons.

Case Study Type 2: Repeated Assessment and Marked Changes If the case study includes assessment on several occasions before and after treatment and the changes associated with the intervention are relatively marked, the inferences that can be drawn about treatment are vastly improved. Table 9.1 illustrates the characteristics of such a case, along with the extent to which specific threats to internal validity are addressed. The fact that continuous assessment is included is important in ruling out the specific threats to internal validity related to assessment. First, the changes that coincide with treatment are not likely to result from exposure to repeated testing or changes in the instrument. When continuous assessment is utilized, changes due to testing or instrumentation would have been evident before treatment began. Similarly, regression to the mean from one data point to another, a special problem with assessment conducted at only two points in time, is eliminated. Repeated observation over time shows a pattern in the data. Extreme scores may be a problem for any particular assessment occasion in relation to the immediately prior occasion. However, these changes cannot account for the pattern of performance for an extended period.

Aside from continuous assessment, this example includes relatively marked treatment effects, that is, changes that are relatively immediate and large. These types of changes produced in treatment help reduce the possibility that history and maturation explain the results. Maturation in particular may be relatively implausible because maturational changes are not likely to be abrupt and large. Nevertheless, a question mark was placed in the table because maturation cannot be ruled out completely. In this case example, information on the stability of the problem in the past and future was not included. Hence, it is not known whether the clinical problem might ordinarily change on its own and whether maturational influences are plausible. Some problems that are episodic in nature (e.g., depression) conceivably could show marked changes that have little to do with treatment. With immediate and large changes in behavior, history and maturation may also be ruled out, although these factors are likely to depend on other dimensions in the table that specifically were omitted from this case.

Case Study Type 3: Multiple Cases, Continuous Assessment, and Stability Information   Several cases (rather than only one) in which each includes continuous assessment may be studied. The cases may be treated one at a time and accumulated into a final summary statement of treatment effects or treated as a single group at the same time. In this example, assessment information is available on repeated occasions before and during treatment. Also, the stability of the problem is known in this example. Stability refers to the dimension of past–future projections and denotes that other research suggests that the problem does not usually change over time. When the problem is known to be highly stable or to follow a particular course without treatment, the investigator has an implicit prediction of the effects of no treatment. The results can be compared with this predicted level of performance.

As is evident in Table 9.1, several threats to internal validity are addressed by a case report meeting the specified characteristics. History and maturation are not likely to interfere with drawing conclusions about the causal role of treatment because several different cases are included. All cases are not likely to have a single historical event or maturational process in common that could account for the results. Knowledge about the stability of the problem in the future also helps to rule out the influence of history and maturation. If the problem is known to be stable over time, this means that ordinary historical events and maturational processes do not by themselves provide a strong enough influence. Because of the use of multiple subjects and the knowledge about the stability of the problem, history and maturation probably are implausible explanations of therapeutic change.

The threats to internal validity related to testing are handled mainly by continuous assessment over time. Repeated testing, changes in the instrument, and reversion of scores toward the mean may influence performance from one occasion to another. Yet problems associated with testing are not likely to influence the pattern of data for a large number of occasions. Also, information about the stability of the problem helps to further make changes due to testing implausible. The fact that the problem is known to be stable means that it probably would not change merely as a function of repeated assessment.

In general, the case study of the type illustrated in this example provides a strong basis for drawing valid inferences about the impact of treatment. The manner in which the multiple-case report is designed does not constitute an experiment, as usually conceived, because each case represents an uncontrolled demonstration. However, characteristics of this type of case study can rule out specific threats to internal validity in a manner approaching that of true experiments.

Case Illustrations

A few additional illustrations convey more concretely the continuum of confidence one might place in the notion that the intervention was responsible for change. Each illustration qualifies as a quasi-experiment because it captures features of true experiments and varies in the extent to which specific threats can be made implausible. In the first illustration, treatment was applied to decrease the weight of an obese 55-year-old woman (180 lb., 5'5") (Martin & Sachs, 1973). The woman had been advised to lose weight, a recommendation of some urgency in light of her recent heart attack. The woman was treated as an outpatient. The treatment consisted of developing a contract or agreement between the woman and her therapist. The contract involved adherence to a variety of rules and recommendations that would alter the woman's eating habits. Several rules were developed pertaining to rewards for resisting tempting foods, self-recording what was eaten after meals and snacks, weighing frequently each day, chewing foods slowly, and so forth. The patient had been weighed before treatment, and therapy began with weekly assessment for a period of 4.5 weeks.

The results of the program, which appear in Figure 9.11, indicate that the woman's initial weight of 180 pounds was followed by a gradual decline in weight over the next few weeks before treatment was terminated. For present purposes, what can be said about the impact of treatment? Actually, statements about the effects of the treatment in accounting for the changes would be tentative at best. The stability of the woman's pretreatment weight is unclear. The first data point indicated that the woman was 180 pounds before treatment. Perhaps her weight would have declined over the next few weeks even without a special weight-reduction program. The absence of clear information regarding the stability of the woman's weight before treatment makes evaluation of her subsequent loss rather difficult. The fact that the decline is gradual and modest (albeit understandable given the expected course of weight reduction) introduces further ambiguity. The weight loss is clear, but it would be difficult to argue strongly that the intervention rather than historical events, maturational processes, or repeated assessment led to the same results.

The next illustration provides a slightly more persuasive demonstration that treatment may have led to the results. This case included a 49-year-old woman with a long standing history of obsessional thoughts related to shame and worry about toilet odors and flatulence (Ladouceur et al., 1993). The woman had a history of intestinal problems and anxiety disorders. The goal of treatment was to

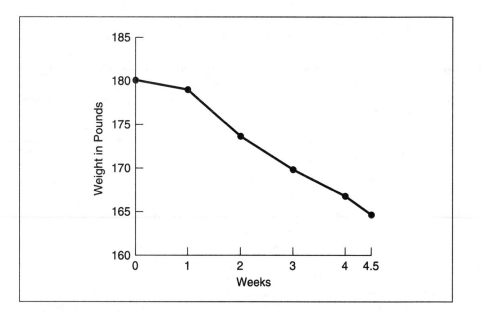

FIGURE 9.11   Weight in pounds per week. The line represents the connecting of the weights, respectively, on the days 0, 7, 14, 21, 28, and 31 of the weight loss program.

Source: Martin, J.E., & Sachs, D.A. (1973). The effects of a self-control weight loss program on an obese woman. *Journal of Behavior Therapy and Experimental Psychiatry, 4,* 155–159. Reprinted with permission from Elsevier Science and the authors.

reduce intrusive thoughts, which usually took the form of internal statements (e.g., "I'm going to fart" and "I'm going to have diarrhea") that occurred several (12–21) times a day. A program was designed to decrease these thoughts and the anxiety with which they were associated by repeated exposure to the thoughts via a taperecording she made (on which she repeated the statements); she listened to the tape through a cassette recorder she used in everyday life. Also, she was instructed to identify cognitions that could prevent or neutralize the intrusive thoughts. Before treatment, her initial rate of intrusive thoughts was self-monitored. After several days, the program was introduced, and her thoughts continued to be self-monitored. The results of the program appear in Figure 9.12, which shows the woman's daily rate of intrusive thoughts across baseline and intervention phases.

The results suggest that the intervention may have been responsible for change. The inference is aided by continuous assessment over time before and during the intervention phase. The number of intrusive thoughts fluctuated during the baseline phase, but still were relatively stable (i.e., no clear trend). The baseline pattern suggests that no change was likely to occur with continued observations alone. When the intervention was introduced, intrusive thoughts de-

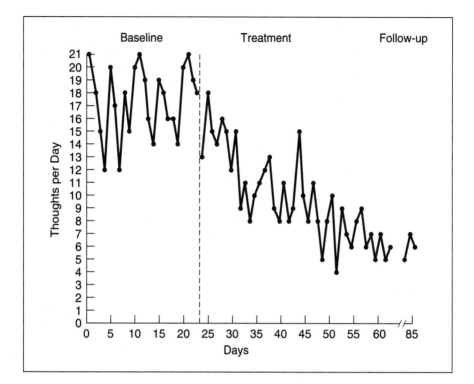

FIGURE 9.12   Intrusive thoughts per day over the course of baseline, treatment, and follow-up (3 weeks after treatment ended).

Source: Ladouceur, R., Freeston, M.H., Gagnon, F., Thibodeau, N., & Dumont, J. (1993). Idiographic considerations in the behavioral treatment of obsessional thoughts. *Journal of Behavior Therapy and Experimental Psychiatry, 24,* 301–310. Reprinted with permission from Elsevier Science and the authors.

clined and continued to show a decline, which was maintained at a follow-up assessment 3 weeks after treatment ended. The data pattern suggests that intervention was probably responsible for the change.

A few features of the demonstration may detract from the confidence one might place in according treatment a causal role. The gradual decline evident in Figure 9.12 might also have resulted from influences other than the treatment, such as increased attention to the problem (historical event) or boredom with continuing the assessment procedure (maturation). Also, the fact that the patient was responsible for collecting the observations raises concern about whether accuracy of scoring changed over time (instrumentation), rather than the actual rate of intrusive thoughts. Yet the data can be taken as presented without undue methodological skepticism. As such, the intervention appears to have led to change, but the quasi-experimental nature of the design and the pattern of results make it difficult to rule out threats to internal validity with great confidence.

In the next illustration, the effects of the intervention appear even more clearly. In this report, a female adult with agoraphobia and panic attacks participated in outpatient treatment to overcome her fear of leaving home and her self-imposed restriction to her home (O'Donohue, Plaud, & Hecker, 1992). The patient kept a record of the type and duration of all activities in which she engaged. At the beginning of treatment, activities that might be reinforcing were also identified. The intervention consisted of instructing the woman to engage in rewarding activities (e.g., time with her pet, reading, entertaining visitors) only when outside the home. Examples included walking down the street, socializing with neighbors, and watching television at a neighbor's home.

The effects of the procedure in increasing time away from home are illustrated in Figure 9.13. The baseline period indicated a consistent pattern of no time spent outside the home. When the intervention began, time outside the home sharply increased and remained high at both the 2-month and the 18-

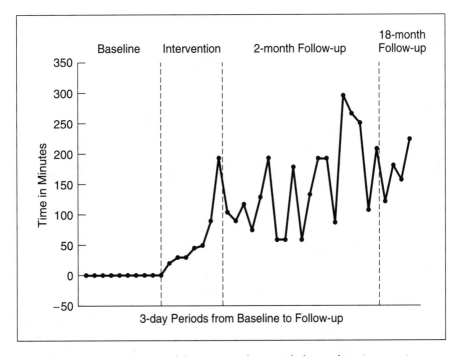

FIGURE 9.13 Total time an adult patient with agoraphobia and panic spent in activities outside the home over baseline, intervention, and two follow-up assessment periods.

Source: O'Donohue, W., Plaud, J.J., & Hecker, J.E. (1992). The possible function of positive reinforcement in home-bound agoraphobia: A case study. *Journal of Behavior Therapy and Experimental Psychiatry, 23*, 303–312. Reprinted with permission from Elsevier Science and the authors.

month follow-ups. Corroboration of the changes was made by acquaintances and relatives, who reported on specific activities in which the patient had engaged. The stable and very clear baseline and the marked changes with onset of the intervention suggest that history, maturation, or other threats could not readily account for the results. Within the limits of quasi-experimental designs, the results are relatively clear.

Among the previous examples, the likelihood that the intervention accounted for change was increasingly plausible in light of characteristics of the report. In this final illustration, the effects of the intervention are extremely clear. The purpose of this report was to investigate a new method of treating bedwetting (enuresis) among children (Azrin, Hontos, & Besalel-Azrin, 1979). Forty-four children, ranging in age from 3–15 years, were included. Their families collected data on the number of nighttime bedwetting accidents for 7 days before treatment. After the baseline phase, the training procedure was implemented—the child was required to practice getting up from bed at night, remaking the bed if he or she had wet, and changing clothes. Other procedures, such as waking the child early at night in the beginning of training and developing increased bladder capacity by reinforcing increases in urine volume were also used. The parents and children practiced some procedures during the training session, but the intervention was essentially carried out at home when the child wet his or her bed.

The effects of training are illustrated in Figure 9.14, which shows bedwetting during the pretraining (baseline) and training periods. The demonstration is a quasi-experimental design because several of the conditions discussed previously were included to help rule out threats to internal validity. The data suggest that the problem was relatively stable for the group as a whole during the baseline period. Also, the changes in performance at the onset of treatment were immediate and marked. Finally, the group was probably not very homogeneous because the subjects' ages encompassed young children through teenagers. In light of these characteristics of the demonstration, it is not very plausible that the changes could be accounted for by history, maturation, repeated assessment, changes in the assessment procedures, or statistical regression.

The use of features of single-case designs as aids in clinical situations addresses a broader point. Threats to internal validity in any given research and clinical situation warrant close scrutiny. When recognized in advance, plausible threats can be circumvented or addressed in many ways. In clinical work, adopting many features of true single-case experimental designs can greatly strengthen the conclusions that can be drawn. In any given case, the arrangement of approximations or quasi-experiments can reduce the plausibility of threats to validity in ways that are as clear as methods used in true experiments. The use of design features from single-case experiments are not mere methodological niceties. When integrated with clinical work, they can greatly improve the quality of patient care and evaluation of treatment progress (Kazdin, 1993). Such work no doubt entails complexities not addressed here such as developing measures to assess special characteristics and using standard measures in new ways

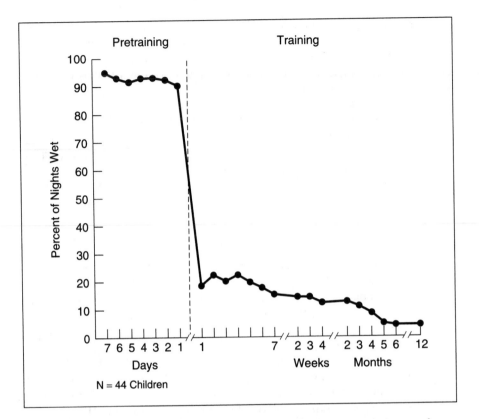

FIGURE 9.14   Bedwetting by 44 enuretic children. Each data point designates the percentage of nights on which bedwetting occurred. The data prior to the *dotted* line are for a 7-day period prior to training. The data are presented daily for the first week, weekly for the first month, and monthly for the first 6 months and for month 12.

Source: Azrin, N.H., Hontos, P.T., & Besalel-Azrin, V. (1979). Elimination of enuresis without a conditioning apparatus: An extension by office instruction of the child and parents. *Behavior Therapy, 10,* 14–19. Reprinted with permission from the Association for Advancement of Behavior Therapy and the authors.

(e.g., continuous assessment of psychopathology, depression, with standardized scales). However imperfect or quasi-experimental evaluations may prove, they offer distinct advantages to anecdotal cases with which they often compete.

SUMMARY AND CONCLUSIONS

The study of the individual has played an important role in clinical psychology. Historically, *case studies* have led to important insights about the development of human personality, treatment, diagnosis of dysfunction, and other areas. As a method of study, uncontrolled and anecdotal case reports are limited. Results from a case study usually can be reinterpreted in so many ways that specific conclusions cannot be made without great ambiguity.

Single-case designs allow experimentation with the individual subject or client. The designs are true experiments in the sense that they address threats to experimental validity and demonstration of causal relations. The designs allow examination of several questions traditionally of interest in treatment evaluation: evaluating an overall treatment package, analyzing the components of treatment, building more effective treatments by adding components, and comparing different treatments. Three major design strategies, ABAB, multiple-baseline, and changing-criterion designs, were highlighted. The designs vary in the questions that can be addressed, the way in which treatment effects are demonstrated, and the requirements for experimental evaluation. Also, the designs vary in their suitability in light of practical or clinical considerations.

Single-case designs help draw inferences through *nonstatistical evaluation* or *visual inspection* of the data. This is greatly facilitated by the collection of continuous data over time and across phases of the designs. Nonstatistical criteria for judging whether independent variables have produced reliable effects include *changes in mean* and *level, trend,* and in the *latency of changes* across phases. Judgments are required to invoke these criteria in situations that are not always clear.

In clinical settings, the conditions for true single-case experiments cannot always be met. Nevertheless, selected features of the designs can be used to form *quasi-single-case experiments.* The use of key features, such as assessment over time and consideration of some of the criteria for data evaluation, can strengthen the inferences that can be draw about intervention effects.

NOTES

[1]Although several terms have been proposed, each of these is partially misleading. For example, *single-case* and $N = 1$ designs imply that only one subject is included in an investigation. This implication is misleading because it hides the fact that large numbers of subjects or entire communities and cities have been included in some single-case designs. The term *intrasubject* is a useful term because it implies that the methodology focuses on performance of the same person over time, but it is also partially misleading because some designs depend on looking at the effects of interventions across (i.e., between) subjects. The term *intensive designs* has not grown out of the tradition of single-case research and is used infrequently. Also, the term *intensive* has the unfortunate connotation that the investigator is working intensively to study the subject, which probably is true but is beside the point. The term *single-case designs* has been adopted here to draw attention to the unique feature of the designs, that is, the capacity to conduct empirical research with individual subjects and because this term enjoys the widest use. (Of course, in emphasizing *single* cases, it is important to bear in mind that these designs can also be used for *married* cases.)

[2]Statistical evaluation and statistical tests are laced with subjectivity; hence, one has to be rather careful in invoking this particular argument in relation to use of nonstatistical evaluation methods. Many statistical tests (e.g., factor analysis, regression, cluster analyses, time-series analysis, path analyses) include a number of decision points about various so-

lutions, parameter estimates, and levels or criteria to continue or include variables in the analysis or model. These decisions are rarely made explicit in the data analyses. In many instances "default" criteria in the data-analytic programs do not convey that a critical choice has been made and that the basis of the choice can be readily challenged because there is no necessary objective reason that one choice is the better than another. Statistical evaluation and these issues are addressed in a later chapter.

FOR FURTHER READINGS

Jones, E.E. (Editor). (1993). Special section: Single-case research in psychotherapy. *Journal of Consulting and Clinical Psychology, 61,* 371–430.

Kazdin, A.E. (1982). *Single-case research designs: Methods for clinical and applied settings.* New York: Oxford University Press.

Kazdin, A.E. (1993). Evaluation in clinical practice: Clinically sensitive and systematic methods of treatment delivery. *Behavior Therapy, 24,* 11–45.

Krishef, C.H. (1991). *Fundamental approaches to single-subject design and analysis.* Malabar, FL: Kreiger.

Stake, R. (1995). *The art of case study research.* Thousand Oaks, CA: Sage.

Yin, R.K. (1994). *Case study research: Design and methods* (2nd ed.). Thousand Oaks, CA: Sage.

Chapter 10

Qualitative Research Methods

CHAPTER OUTLINE

Key Characteristics
>   Background
>   Definition and Core Features
>   Contrast of Qualitative and Quantitative Research

Methods and Analyses
>   Data for Qualitative Analysis
>   Quality Control: Checks on the Methods and Results
>   Utility and Generality of the Results
>   Illustration

Contributions of Qualitative Research

Summary and Conclusions

When we discuss or consider empirical research, there is a specific methodological paradigm we have in mind. That paradigm or approach is within the positivist tradition and includes the whole package of concepts and practices (e.g., theory, hypothesis testing, operational definitions, careful control of the subject matter, isolation of the variables of interest, quantification of constructs, and statistical analyses). Such is the approach of this book, an approach in which one tries to devise investigations to rule out threats to validity, to test specific hypotheses, to identify the impact of variables on some outcome of interest, and to analyze the data statistically. Even the single-case designs of the previous chapter fall into this tradition because of the nature of assessment, specification and careful control of key variables of interest, and methods of data evaluation. For present purposes, it is useful to refer to the dominant research paradigm in the field with the above characteristics as *quantitative research*. When people speak of scientific or empirical research, they are usually referring to quantitative research; however, among most scientists, the term quantitative research is not even used because the specific methodological paradigm described above is viewed as the *only* approach.

Another approach to research that is referred to as *qualitative research* also reflects an empirical approach to the subject matter. The tradition of qualitative research is by no means new but is increasing in emphasis within the social sciences and indeed has been referred to as a "quiet methodological revolution" (Denzin & Lincoln, 1994, p. ix). Qualitative research is a broad term that encompasses multiple approaches, disciplines, and definitions. In advance of highlighting the approach, a useful albeit oversimplified way of distinguishing this approach is by noting that the method of data collection and analysis in qualitative research is based on words, whereas quantitative research deals with numbers (i.e., measurement of constructs reduced to numerical data and analyses of these data with statistical techniques). This chapter highlights qualitative research and conveys and illustrates its special contributions to knowledge and to quantitative research more generally.

Qualitative research is discussed here for three reasons. First, the research is a legitimate methodological approach in its own right and, as already noted, is receiving increased attention. Qualitative research seeks knowledge in ways that are systematic, replicable, and cumulative. The approach is very relevant to many topics within psychology, particularly perhaps within clinical psychology. Hence, researchers trained in the current quantitative tradition ought to be familiar with key tenets of the approach, its goals, uses, and relation to quantitative research. Second, as a different approach toward obtaining knowledge, qualitative research yields data and information not likely to emerge from quantitative studies. Qualitative research looks at phenomena in ways that are intended to reveal many facets of human experience that the quantitative tradition has been designed to circumvent—the human experience, subjective views, and how people represent (perceive, feel), and hence react to their situations in context. Third, delineating the unique features of qualitative research also helps one understand the strengths, contributions, and limitations of quantitative research. In much the same way that learning a foreign language brings to light features of one's native language, both in making the tacit explicit and by providing an appreciation of differences in native and foreign tongues, discussion of qualitative research has parallel benefits.

KEY CHARACTERISTICS

Background

Many influences and traditions within philosophy and various scientific disciplines underlie qualitative research (Hamilton, 1994; Vidich & Lyman, 1994). A few key influences place qualitative research in context so it does not in any way appear as a recent fringe moment by scientists who like case studies. Three broad influences place into context the emergence of qualitative research. First, there is a tradition within philosophy that focuses on description, meaning, intentions, purpose, and context (Hamilton, 1994).[1] Approaches within phenomenology in particular (e.g., Husserl, Merleau-Ponti) provide an important starting point in light of the emphasis on description of the human experience, the role of the perceiver in understanding (constructing) the world, and constructs such as intentionality, purpose, and meaning. The development of science and scientific methods has been marked by explicit efforts to shy away from facets of subjectivity and related internal states (e.g., how one perceives, thinks, and experiences the world). These facets are studied (e.g., cognitive processes), but an effort is made to move away from the individual and contexts in which such facets are experienced. For example, within the quantitative tradition, efforts to operationalize facets of experience (e.g., fear, loneliness, love, thoughts) are reflected in various inventories, scales, and questionnaires. The same facets of experience, within the qualitative tradition, are studied to reflect the richness, depth, and meaning within the contexts and complex situations in which they emerge.

Second, within the social sciences, particularly sociology and anthropology, there has been a tradition of research in which the investigator participates in and elaborates the subject matter in great detail as a way of bringing key facets to light. Familiar examples within these disciplines can be seen from many descriptions of primitive societies, gangs, or life in the slums (Vidich & Lyman, 1994). The work is qualitative in the sense that it encompasses in-depth knowledge of the people in context, participation with these cultures, rich description and narration of activities, and interpretation to place the belief, culture, and practices in context. The work is usually regarded as informative, even by quantitative researchers, and perhaps useful for generating ideas, but it is not usually considered science. Thus, much of the work is in the tradition of qualitative research, but it may not meet standards involved for this line of research.

Third, there has been a dissatisfaction with and reaction to quantitative research as currently conceived and practiced. The focus on groups of individuals (e.g., mean differences between groups), the view of participants as objects of study and the investigator as an objective observer, simplification of the research situation to isolate variables, and reducing experience to quantitative results are central points of concern. This dissatisfaction does not receive very much attention among professionals within the quantitative tradition, as reflected in journal publications, graduate training, and professional meetings. Yet, to the qualitative researcher, the goal of understanding requires elaborating rather than simplifying the phenomena of interest; instead of using controlled contexts (e.g., in the laboratory) and key variables, the goal is to investigate phenomena in context and as experienced by the individual. For understanding behavior, key concepts such as meaning and purpose, usually avoided in quantitative studies of human functioning, are central topics within qualitative research. The broad variables including context in which variables operate (perceptions, goals, and interactions) are the central foci of qualitative research.

Definition and Core Features

Qualitative research is an approach to the subject matter of human experience and focuses on narrative accounts, description, interpretation, context, and meaning. The goal is to describe, interpret, and understand the phenomena of interest. Through description and interpretation, our understanding of the phenomena can be deepened. The process of achieving this goal is to study in depth the experience of the participants (i.e., those who are studied), to convey how their experience is felt or perceived, and to explain the meaning it has for those whose experience is being presented.

Table 10.1 lists general characteristics of qualitative research, although there are several variations of the approach. As a general rule, qualitative research relies heavily on description and interpretation of the experience or action that is studied. The purpose is to describe the experience (e.g., thoughts, feelings, and actions of a person in a particular context; interactions in which people engage) but to do so in a way that captures the richness of the experience and the meaning it has for the participants. We say that qualitative analysis increases our understanding because the level of analysis is detailed and in-depth and, ideally, brings to light new ways of speaking about the phenomena that the investigator, reader, and participants, may have not fully understood prior to the analysis. In

TABLE 10.1.   Key Characteristics of Qualitative Research

- Qualitative research is conducted through an intense and/or prolonged contact with a "field" or life situation. These situations are typically "banal" or normal ones, reflective of the everyday life of individuals, groups, societies, and organizations.
- The researcher's role is to gain a "holistic" (systemic, encompassing, integrated) overview of the context under study: its logic, its arrangements, its explicit and implicit rules.
- The researcher attempts to capture data on the perceptions of local actors "from the inside," through a process of deep attentiveness, of empathic understanding and of suspending preconceptions about the topics under discussion.
- Reading through these materials, the researcher may isolate certain themes and expressions that can be reviewed with informants, but that should be maintained in their original forms throughout the study.
- A main task is to explicate the ways people in particular settings come to understand, account for, take action, and otherwise manage their day-to-day situations.
- Many interpretations of this material are possible, but some are more compelling for theoretical reasons or on grounds of internal consistency.
- Relatively little standardized instrumentation is used at the outset. The researcher is essentially the main "measurement device" in the study.
- Most analysis is done with words. The words can be assembled, subclustered, broken into semiotic segments. They can be organized to permit the researcher to contrast, compare, analyze, and bestow patterns on them.

Source: Miles & Huberman (1994). *Qualitative data analysis.* Thousand Oaks, CA: Sage. Reprinted with permission.

more colloquial words, we know *about* many of life's experiences (e.g., being infatuated, being in love, breaking up of relationship, experiencing stress). A qualitative analysis is designed to bring these experiences to light and to make the tacit explicit in ways that provide a deeper and more empathic understanding.

Because the above discussion may appear too fuzzy, permit me a brief time-out and quasi-digression. A reader who has been trained in the scientific method (i.e., the quantitative tradition) ought to experience a little discomfort (or a panic attack) at this point. Perhaps qualitative research sounds loose, laced with subjectivity, and riddled with precisely the problems (e.g., subjective interpretation of the investigator) that current scientific methods were designed to redress. Moreover, qualitative research may sound like writing or reading a good book or hearing a good case study, each of which may be a richly detailed account of some facet of human experience. Qualitative research very much relies on the traditions captured by literature, namely, descriptive accounts that elaborate experience. Yet, qualitative research is designed to provide a systematic approach to description and understanding and to provide replicable, reliable, and valid accounts, although these terms have somewhat different meanings. That is, there is an effort to be systematic in qualitative research that moves applications out of the realm of pure literature per se. (Mind you, there is nothing wrong with literature and some of my friends even read books once in a while.) Yet, qualitative analysis goes beyond this by providing systematic (but not usually quantitative) methods of data collection, analyses, replications, and efforts to address biases that can influence the data (Miles & Huberman, 1994). This makes qualitative research a systematic method for obtaining knowledge and hence different from other efforts (e.g., within the arts) that also may capture experience.

Contrast of Qualitative and Quantitative Research

Both qualitative and quantitative research seek to understand natural phenomena, to provide new knowledge, to permit the experience to be replicated by others, and to do so in systematic ways. Several key differences in how the subject matter is approached helps to convey the special characteristics of qualitative research. Table 10.2 provides salient dimensions of how one approaches research and the differences in quantitative and qualitative approaches.

Clearly, the key difference is in the major goals of quantitative and qualitative research because from these goals the different methods and foci naturally result. Qualitative research seeks to understand action and experience and hence must view broad sweeps of functioning (affect, cognition, behavior) in context. Apart from studying the complexity of experience in its full bloom (i.e., as it happens in uncontrolled everyday situations), the qualitative approach views the investigator quite differently from the ways in which he or she is viewed in the quantitative approach. The model in quantitative research is that of an objective scientist looking through a telescope; the goal is to have the investigator be the objective instrument (indeed, it is even better if the material observed through the telescope can be recorded in ways that minimize the

TABLE 10.2. Select Characteristics That Distinguish Quantitative and Qualitative Research

Characteristic	Quantitative Research	Qualitative Research
Goals	Test theory and hypotheses; identify causal relations, seek group differences or patterns	Describe and interpret experience; provide new insights, describe and explain with few or no initial hypotheses
How to study	Isolate variables, control potential artifacts and extraneous influences; rule out rival hypotheses	Consider variables as they appear in context with all of the natural influences; complexity is embraced to elaborate the gestalt as well as any key influences in context
Subjects	Study (or try to study) a large number of subjects for statistical power	Study one or a few cases (individual, culture, organization) extensively
Role of the subject	The subjects are the object of study, the people who provide the data; the subjects do not reflect on the data or help the experimenter make sense out of the results	The participants are not objects; the experimenter and subjects become one in the sense that the experience described and understood cannot be removed from the one who describes (experimenter); the subjects are often consulted to ask whether the description and interpretation capture the experience
Role of investigator	Minimize the investigator's role; the perspective, views, and feelings of the investigator are reflected in the hypotheses or focus of the study, but not in the methods, presentation of the findings, nor interpretation of the data; the investigator is detached to the extent possible	The investigator is part of the interpretation in light of his or her perspective; the perspective is made explicit, but it can never be removed; empathy of the investigator is encouraged as a key to deeper understanding; the investigator is *engaged* rather than *detached* and can understand better to the extent that meaning of the situation is experienced
Data	Scores on measures that operationalize the constructs; standardized measures are used whenever possible; the data refer to information that has been reduced to numbers	Narrative descriptions, full text, lengthy interviews, accounts, examples; the story, details the subject matter in the context of how it unfolds, happens, and is experienced; the words are the data and are not reduced to numbers

TABLE 10.2.   *(Continued)*

Characteristic	*Quantitative Research*	*Qualitative Research*
Data evaluation	Statistical analyses to find patterns, averages, to control influences further, to identify the impact of variables on each other and on an outcome	Literary, verbal, non-reductionist, go from description to interpretation to identify themes to bring new qualities to light
Criteria for knowledge	Procedures and findings can be replicated	Descriptions are coherent and viewed by others (colleagues, participants) as internally consistent capturing the experience
A major contribution	A new theory, hypothesis, or relation that will increase our understanding of the phenomenon is brought to light	Our understanding of the experience is elaborated and brought to light in depth and in ways and that extend our understanding

Note: As a general rule, personally I strongly object to tables that contrast approaches with two columns because the structure implies qualitative (i.e., categorical) differences, emphasizes extremes, and fails to consider the inevitable fuzziness of many of the distinctions. The value of the table is to draw sharp lines to introduce the approach, but it is not difficult to identify a study in one tradition (i.e., quantitative or qualitative) and show how many of its features are captured by the columns of the table designed to characterize the other tradition.

influence or active role of the investigator). Quantitative research methods in psychology and social sciences more generally have been modeled after the hard sciences (e.g., biology, physics, astronomy), and keeping the investigator separate from the subject matter is axiomatic. In qualitative research, the investigator is not someone who collects data, but someone who integrates the information in a way that affects the data, that is, gives it meaning and substance. Elimination of a frame of reference or perspective of the investigator may not be possible, but if possible, not necessarily desirable. In fact, to really understand the phenomenon, many qualitative investigators become deeply involved in the subject matter; understanding is optimal when one experiences the phenomenon directly. Thus, studies that have provided the greatest insights of other cultures often stem from persons who entered and lived in the culture for an extended period.

METHODS AND ANALYSES

Data for Qualitative Analysis

The basic information (data) used for a qualitative study can be obtained in many different ways. Among the salient methods and sources are interviews, direct observations, statements of personal experience, documents (e.g., personal journals, letters, biographical stories passed across generations), photographs, audio- or videotapes, and films. Each method has its own recommended approaches and options for data collection (Denzin & Lincoln, 1994). At first, these methods may not look different from measures and ways of collecting data in quantitative research. For example, direct observation and interviewing are also used in quantitative clinical research. In qualitative research, direct observation is more naturalistic, that is, it occurs in naturalistic contexts in the ways subjects would normally participate and interact. The investigator is drawn into the world of the subjects (i.e., the family, playground, school), and predetermined categories (to code behavior) are not usually used (Adler & Adler, 1994). In contrast, within the quantitative approach, much of the direct observation consists of standardized assessments in which the world of the subjects is brought into the laboratory (e.g., observation of marital interaction on standardized tasks) or the world of the investigator is brought to natural settings (e.g., observations conducted in the home with efforts to standardize the situations that govern family interactions). In both instances, the investigator knows the codes to operationalize constructs of interest. Beginning a study with codes to assess functioning and the constructs of interest are typical of (and essential to) quantitative research. Usually the qualitative researcher wishes to take the phenomena as presented and to derive the constructs and codes from them.

Information obtained from these sources is initially taken as descriptive material that becomes the basis for analysis. The analysis takes many different forms because there are multiple orientations and approaches to the information. A key approach is to interpret the meaning to better understand the subject matter (e.g., an individual, group, culture) in context. However, this can be accomplished by looking for recurring themes or key concepts that emerge in peoples' descriptions of their experiences, identifying processes or a progression that seems to show the flow of experience, linking variables that emerge concurrently or over time, and, in general, looking for consistencies and patterns in the material. Computer software designed to facilitate making these connections and interpretating qualitative data by displaying the information and pointing to possible patterns is available (Miles & Weitzman, 1994). Occasionally, the approach to cull meaning and to examine connections among variables utilizes methods of quantitative analyses. For example, in some qualitative studies, the descriptive material is coded into categories and analyzed statistically to examine the occurrence of themes and their interrelations. In other cases, a goal of the interpretation is to develop theory from the material. Indeed, one advantage of the approach is to discover and to generate new conceptualizations of phenomena in the process of bringing special features to light.

Quality Control: Checks on the Methods and Results

The goal of qualitative research is to provide information that has some validity, that is, yields an analysis that has some truth or confirmability. In qualitative research, coherence of the interpretation, agreement among others (and, when possible, the participants themselves) about the interpretation, and consensus that understanding of the experience or phenomenon is enhanced as a result of the analysis are salient among the criteria to evaluate the findings. Does the analysis capture the experience and extend our understanding (e.g., of the experience of living with acquired immunodeficiency syndrome [AIDS], of growing older, of being a child, of living in a particular culture, of serving as a prisoner of war)?

The perspective and approach of the qualitative investigator necessarily influences and shades the interpretations that are generated. Indeed, this is also true in quantitative research. The objectivity of many components of quantitative research is illusory—the formulation of the research question, what is viewed as "noise" versus the variable of interest, the entire business of what is statistically significant (e.g., the criterion of $p < .05$), other facets of statistical analyses (e.g., linear models) are part of the part of the subjectivity, even though they are rarely made explicit. Yet, plainly, qualitative research raises even greater issues of subjectivity on the part of the investigator.

Understandably, in qualitative research, there is the concern that the views of the investigator may play a particularly significant and unchecked role in the interpretation. Although the perspective of the investigator is important, as consumers of research we do not accumulate findings that are only pertinent to or generalizable to the particular investigator. Procedures are included to check on the extent to which a particular case or focus may be representative, whether the researcher's views, made explicit at the outset, are likely to account for a particular slant in the interpretation, and whether others who view the data or similar cases converge on a common understanding and interpretation.

Multiple strategies are used to help ensure that the data are not mere reflections of the investigator's perspective. First, investigators are encouraged to make explicit their own views, including how their expectations may or may not have been met, what was consistent and discrepant from any preconceived views, and what orientation or approach they may be taking to the subject matter (e.g., observing it from a particular perspective or a theoretical orientation, discipline, or frame of reference). Noting this perspective, orientation, and expectation permits others in the scientific community to evaluate the interpretations in light of potentially important influences.

Second, there is an iterative process in which investigators are encouraged to consult other investigators to identify the extent to which the raw material (e.g., lengthy narratives, audio- or videotaped materials) are likely to reflect key tenets the investigator has identified. Are the interpretations cohesive and do they capture the experience? These are questions posed to others who evaluate the qualitative material. The participants are also part of this verification process, when possible. During the process of collecting the information or after the information is collected, participants are encouraged to review the categories, broader concepts, sequence of experiences that have been proposed, and to make comments. The comments are brought into the process to elaborate, refine, or alter what has been proposed by the investigator. Thus, the fact that the investigators are people who have their own perspectives, experiences, and shaded glasses does not in any way doom the resulting data to an idiosyncratic perspective. There is a consensual process involving both other investigators and participants.

Other investigators evaluate the process of reaching the interpretation by examining the procedures, raw data, analytic strategies, and the conclusions (Miles & Huberman, 1994). The investigator is encouraged to make raw data available to others during the investigation to permit a check on how the information (e.g., transcripts) reflects themes that have been identified. Thus, an internal replicability is part of the evaluation, that is, scrutiny by others. All of this is facilitated by procedures and computer software that help to display, code, systematize, and retrieve the data and to test the emergence of broader constructs and categories that form the basis of the investigator's interpretation.

Researchers have been concerned with making explicit criteria for ensuring that the findings from a qualitative analysis are reliable and valid, although the meaning of these terms departs somewhat from how the terms are used in assessment. Reliability pertains both to the methods of studying the data (e.g., how themes and categories are identified, how interpretations are made) and to the coherence or internal consistency of the interpretations. Validity refers to the extent to which there is a finding that makes sense, captures experience, is confirmed and confirmable by others.

Many different terms have been introduced to specify how to check the data of qualitative research, only some of which can be highlighted here (Miles & Huberman, 1994). *Trustworthiness* of the data has been proposed as an important criterion and includes multiple components, namely, credibility, transferability, dependability, and confirmability (Lincoln & Guba, 1985). *Credibility* pertains to whether the methods and subjects are appropriate to the goals and are likely to represent the sample of interest. *Transferability* pertains to whether the data are limited to a particular context (are context bound) and is evaluated by looking at any special characteristics (unrepresentativeness) of the sample. Transferability is similar to generality of findings and hence to external validity, as discussed in quantitative research. *Dependability* pertains to the reliability of the conclusions and data evaluation leading to the conclusions. Finally, *confirmability* refers to the extent to which an independent reviewer could conduct a formal audit and reevaluation of the procedures and generate the same findings.

Another concept that is sometimes used to add validity to the findings is *triangulation,* which refers to the extent converging data from separate sources exist to support the conclusions. Triangulation may rely on separate bits of data, different methods of qualitative analyses, qualitative and quantitative analyses of the same data, different theoretical frameworks, or different investigators. When different ways of examining the problem or phenomenon converge in the information they yield, this is triangulation, and it strengthens (better establishes) the validity of the finding. Essentially, in more familiar terms, triangulation reflects a multimethod approach to qualitative methods. However, the methods are designed to cover more than multiple assessment methods; many different aspects of the study including the range of participants (investigators, subjects) and types of analyses are used to derive conclusions. In general, as with quantitative research, there are methods within qualitative research to address alternative interpretations, bias and artifact, replicability, and generality of results.

Utility and Generality of the Results

If the findings are dependent on the special context and experience of the participants and the investigator, how can any finding be replicable or provide any general understanding? In the terms of a quantitative tradition, can there be external validity to any qualitative finding in light of the tenet that person–context–investigator form a very special gestalt? There are separate answers. In one way, experiences are always different because people (participants, experimenters) bring to bear unique histories and perspectives. In another way, there are thematic similarities. For example, falling in love, getting married, experiencing the death of a child or parent, recovering from trauma, and living with a disability are never identical experiences for individuals. Yet, understanding and elaborating the experiences of one or two individuals may bring to light intricacies and nuances as well as common reactions. Although the qualitative researcher seeks to elaborate experience of the individual (e.g., person, culture), the interpretive facet moves to broader themes with greater universality. We know that intense appreciation of the individual experience rings with great universality. Individuals who experience trauma (e.g., diagnosis of a terminal illness, disaster) often join and profit from support groups with others who have shared this experience. The constant emergence of these support groups and their documented benefits, such as increased longevity among terminally ill patients (Spiegel, Bloom, Kraemer, & Gottheil, 1989), suggests that individual, unique experiences have universal features that can be elaborated and appreciated by others. Similarly, appreciation of literature may derive from the very special experiences of the protagonist and from appreciation of experiences that are rather universal (e.g., love, impulsiveness, grief, despair, ambition).

Although many experiences that are elaborated are likely to have universal facets, many qualitative researchers would say that universality and generalization to all people are not the criteria for evaluating the contribution of qualitative research. If a particular account is restricted to a context (individual in a situation), that is not a flaw or limitation. The goal of the approach is to elaborate meaning, understanding, and experience, and there will be many facets that are specific to particular contexts. This, too, is much like quantitative research in which general findings are sought, but there are many laboratory paradigms for studying something that is not likely to have very much generality beyond that particular paradigm. We do not value findings only in terms of their generality.

The value and contribution of qualitative research can be highlighted informally by showing the relation of the general to the specific in a qualitative-like description. There are, for example, lessons to be learned from the biblical rendition of Job. From the perspective of the description, it is unlikely that another person would experience the set of life events that Job experienced or have the special background, beliefs, and perceptions of these events as Job experienced them. The specificity of the case does not in any way detract from its contribution. The value of the description stems from deepening our understanding of faith and that has considerable generality beyond the specific case. The description of Job is not qualitative research in psychology, but is noted here merely to convey that placing a microscope on experience has value in deepening our understanding.

Qualitative researchers vary in their views of the generality and importance of generality of the results. Qualitative analysis is influenced by the investigator, participants, and context, each of which can further be divided into multiple influences. Consequently, it is possible (and, in principle, likely) that analyses of similar cases will not be the same in any future replication attempt because the key influences change. However, analyses are assumed to have some generality and specificity in the sense that the experience, although unique, special, and nonreplicable, may resonate with the experiences of others. Also, some qualitative studies include multiple cases, so the issue of common themes in understanding experience are evaluated directly. Although general themes may emerge, it is important to reiterate that qualitative research is not intended to derive or discover the sole experience that characterizes all people.

Illustration

Qualitative analyses are available in psychological research journals, but they are still relatively rare. To illustrate the approach is an example from a quantitative research program that has focused on the treatment of children who are oppositional, aggressive, and antisocial (Webster-Stratton, 1996). A series of quantitative studies (randomized controlled trials) showed that training parents to interact differently with their children, on the basis of the application of various reinforcement and punishment practices, effectively reduces child behavior problems.

To better understand the experience of therapy, the parents' perceptions, and the reactions to the training program, separate qualitative studies were completed (Spitzer, Webster-Stratton, & Hollinsworth, 1991; Webster-Stratton & Spitzer, 1996). From a sample of 77 families (children ages 3–8 years), random selection was made of recorded material from participants in treatment. The materials included intake assessment interviews for all families, videotaped sessions among parents who received group treatment, and audiotaped material from those who received self-administered treatment but then consulted individually with a therapist. Material was transcribed and each family was studied separately over time. The transcripts were examined in small units to try to identify concepts raised by the parents, using the words of the parents as they described their responses to the program. Tentative codes were identified and used to reflect broader categories, akin to a conceptually based factor analysis in which one looks for groupings of codes (items) into larger constructs (factors).

From analyses of the transcripts, the investigators identified experiences of the families and cognitive, social, and behavioral changes from intake through the end of the treatment program to approximately 1 year after the program. The experience of the parents was represented by five phases, which seemed to characterize the parents over time. These phases were: (1) acknowledging the family's problem, (2) alternating between despair and hope in achieving change, (3) recognizing that hopes and expectations for the child needed to be tempered, (4) tailoring the concepts and procedures of treatment to the needs of their child, and (5) coping effectively. Within each phase, subcategories and subthemes were identified. For example, the final phase, coping effectively, included themes such as parents' recognition that the child had chronic problems or would require ongoing special attention at home, improved acceptance and understanding of the child's perspective, acceptance of their own limitations as parents, the need for the parents to take time for themselves to gain a more positive perspective, and the benefits of a support group for the parents.

Several checks were made within the approach of qualitative analysis to ensure validity to the results and whether we can have confidence both in how the investigators reached their conclusions and in the conclusions themselves. The criteria related to trustworthiness of the data (credibility, transferability, dependability, and confirmability) were examined. The credibility was established by focusing on the sample of interest for the inquiry. Was the sample really the group of relevant persons to study? Yes, this study focused on the parents of problem children who are candidates for and in fact received treatment, so this criterion is satisfied. Transferability or whether the project was limited to a highly specific context was addressed. Was this sample special in some way that would may the findings unrelated to any other sample? The investigators noted that the sample represented different socioeconomic strata and the children had diverse behavioral problems, so a very narrow context was not evident in the sample. Dependability or reliability of the conclusions was also examined. Can one trust the data procedures, consistency of invoking definitions, and related matters? Yes, coding and recoding the data and evaluating actual agreement (reliability) among coders helped address these questions (using quantitative methods of checking agreement). Finally, confirmability (an effort to independently check on the conclusions) was examined. One investigator reviewed and audited the procedures in a step-by-step fashion to provide a check on the other.

What do we know from this qualitative analysis that we did not know from a series of quantitative controlled trials? A great deal (even though the richness of the transcripts, phases, and themes cannot be completely reproduced here)— the transcripts describe individual experience of the families and some common themes that emerge during treatment. Among the benefits of the analyses is that there are phases that can be meaningfully described to capture the experience, that there is a waxing and waning of expectations, enthusiasm, despair, and realistic appraisals of child-rearing processes and likely outcomes, that parental morale is likely to play a pivotal role in treatment, and that in treatment there are points at which certain types of obstacles are likely to emerge.

Also, these investigators noted that research on parenting practices among children with oppositional and aggressive behavior emphasized how inept the parents are in disciplining their children and how they unwittingly exacerbate their children's problems as a result. On the other side, qualitative analyses have revealed that parents with such children often feel they are "held hostage" and inadvertently sacrifice their relations with their partner as the problem child dominates the focus of the family and the spouses become more distant and alienated (Webster-Stratton & Spitzer, 1996). Parents in this position often come to feel helpless. The qualitative analyses revealed the progression from efforts to cope, to intense feelings of inadequacy, and finally to helplessness. The authors related the qualitative results to learned helplessness and self-efficacy as a way of conceptualizing parenting experiences. Drawing these connections can help understand parenting experiences, facets of the home environment that may contribute to family relations and interactions more generally, and what feelings, expectations, and sources of hope and despair are likely to emerge during the course of treatment. This information raises many prospects for conceptualizing and understanding the clinical problem and for intervening to address the panoply of parent-and-child issues.

Parent training is one of the more effective treatments for children with conduct problems, as attested to in scores of quantitative studies (e.g., randomized controlled trials) (Kazdin, 1997). Even so, many families drop out of treatment, others do not respond to treatment, and the impact on the family in the short and long run are far from understood. These qualitative analyses raise a host of new constructs and themes that could be studied further (in qualitative and quantitative research). Many of the feelings and experiences (e.g., despair, helplessness) themselves could become outcomes of interest for special attention or intervention, as needed among individual families. From the quantitative studies, we would be much less likely to reflect on the experience of the families and how that may influence clinical outcomes and indeed quality of life for the entire family. Documenting the experiences of the families in ways not covered by quantitative research is valuable in its own right insofar as it addresses a significant lacunae in our knowledge. At the same time, the hypotheses and constructs generated from the analyses could lead to important lines of research that highlight processes for further study and ways of improving clinical outcomes.

CONTRIBUTIONS OF QUALITATIVE RESEARCH

The purpose of this discussion was to highlight characteristics of qualitative research. The methodology is separate from current quantitative, empirical research, and therefore has its own textbooks that elaborate phases of investigation (from developing the focus and idea through the methods to code and evaluate the findings) (see For Further Readings). As we began this chapter, anyone trained in the rigors of quantitative research might initially squirm when seeing the seemingly fuzzy concepts (meaning, subjectivity, experience) and approaches embraced by qualitative analyses. The extent to which the reader is still squirming represents a failure on my part to present the case. Perhaps I have unwittingly conveyed that qualitative analysis basically is an uncontrolled, anecdotal case study of yesteryear—like those intriguing cases of Freud, which began much of psychotherapy research. Although qualitative analyses often include case studies (e.g., of individuals, but also of cultures, societies), the analyses are not anecdotal case studies. If they are not case studies, perhaps they are somewhat like other efforts to capture and to understand experience, as reflected in the arts (theater, literature, film making). Talent abounds in the arts and many products place a microscope on individual or general human experience. The contribution of the arts stands on its own, but the arts, too, ought to be distinguished from qualitative research.

The contribution of qualitative research is its systematic approach to the subject matter. There are formal procedures and guidelines for:

- Collecting information;
- Guarding against or minimizing bias and artifact;
- Making interpretations;
- Checking on these interpretations and on the investigator;
- Ensuring the internal consistency and confirmability of the findings;
- Seeking triangulation of methods and approaches to see what conclusions are similar when the methods of study are varied; and
- Encouraging replication, both within a particular data set (by other investigators) and with additional data (e.g., multiple cases).

The purpose of qualitative research is to understand, elaborate meaning, and to uncover the experience of the participants. Anecdotal case studies and various forms of art may accomplish this, but building the knowledge base, developing and testing theory, and accruing knowledge in a cumulative way are the domain of qualitative research. There is not much more we can ask of an empirical approach to psychological phenomena than formal procedures and explicit guidelines on data collection and evaluation.[2]

Qualitative research can make a special contribution to clinical psychology and to dominant research methods in general. First, qualitative research makes a unique contribution to knowledge and understanding by elaborating the nature of experience and its meaning. Needless to say, the information and level of analysis does not replace, compete with, or address the yield from quantitative research on such factors, for example, as incidence, prevalence, risk factors associated with a problem, or differences between groups (e.g., depressed vs. not depressed) on a variety of other measures (family history, cognitive processes, etc.). Yet, the information from quantitative studies, however important, omits the richness of individual experience and what it is like to be depressed or to live with someone who is. Also, the quantitative research tradition by necessity has to omit many variables to study some. The qualitative approach emphasizes many variables in their multiplicity and context and brings to bear another level of analysis by elaboration and consideration of the details.

This initial contribution of qualitative research, stated another way, is the ability to bring phenomena to life. Many investigators who conduct programmatic quantitative research have sought avenues to convey the qualitative details of the subject matter well beyond the confines of the usual journal publications. For example, one investigator who studied adolescents and families provided a separate source of detailed narrative material focusing on individual cases in contexts and how adolescents and parents interact on a daily basis over key issues (Hauser, Powers, & Noam, 1991). Another researcher provided a film of autistic children who participated in a special treatment program (Lovaas, 1988). The treatment had been evaluated in the usual quantitative tradition, which could not convey the impact of the intervention on the daily lives of children and their families in context for each family (Lovaas, 1987). Yet, another researcher provided a detailed personal account about the experience, treatment, and recovery of depression (Endler, 1990). The account provides the rich details about how depression affects and is affected by life. These accounts convey keen interest in providing the rich details of experience. The contribution of qualitative research is providing guidelines and options for systematically developing, presenting, and interpreting such data.

Second, qualitative research can have enormous impact by bringing experience into sharp focus. A qualitative analysis can make a phenomenon vivid and include the complexity of experience that can move others to action. For example, quantitative research has conveyed the worldwide epidemic of human immunodeficiency virus (HIV) and AIDS. Qualitative research can describe in detail (and thus make the experience of HIV and AIDS vivid and poignant) what it is like on a daily and indeed moment-to-moment basis to learn of the diagnosis, to interact with one's partner and relatives, and to face death. This type of analysis can very much move others and have remarkable impact.

Third, qualitative research can elaborate causal relations and paths during the course of their development. Quantitative approaches have made enormous gains in identifying multiple factors and their contribution to a particular outcome. The findings are valid at the level of group analyses. It is important to know the general variables that are likely to yield a particular outcome and to view them in the contexts in which they may or may not operate. The causal sequence and path leading to an outcome for *individuals* is not really addressed in quantitative research. Literature can provide intriguing accounts and generate many hypotheses about the individual, but a more systematic approach to elaborating the richness of individual experience is needed. Qualitative analyses provide a systematic way of looking at causal paths, unfolding of events, and dynamic and reciprocal influences of events for individuals (Miles & Huberman, 1994).

Finally, qualitative research can contribute directly to quantitative research. Much of qualitative research is discovery oriented because it details human action and experience in ways that can generate theory and hypotheses. We already know that in-depth study of individuals (e.g., Kraeplin's work on diagnosis noted in the previous chapter) has had a major contribution on topics within clinical psychology. Knowing a phenomenon in depth permits one to generate hypotheses about what the key constructs are for understanding that phenomenon and what its likely causal paths and influences are. Becoming deeply involved with the subject matter without restricting oneself to a very small set of constructs as measured in narrow way is an excellent strategy for beginning quantitative research. Apart from its own contributions to knowledge, qualitative research can also influence quantitative research directly by suggesting what to study, what the key influences are, and how they may interact to influence a particular outcome.

Although qualitative and quantitative research derive from and pursue somewhat separate traditions, they can be combined in various ways. For example, one can use the rich detail and extensive records of qualitative analysis for testing and for generating hypotheses. Coding the content and looking for themes and sequences not only describe interactions but also pose and test the extent to which some events or explanations are plausible. The constructs and categories that emerge from qualitative analyses can be used to develop new measures, that is, new ways of operationalizing concepts for empirical quantitative research. Indeed, measures would probably be much better in capturing constructs of interest if they began from in-depth appreciation of the construct and how individuals experience life. When we develop a measure, there is often a concern with the psychometric properties, that is, reliability and validity. Qualitative analysis in this context alerts us to other issues, namely, the extent to which experience is suitably captured by the items. Occasionally the term *face validity* is used. This term reflects an informal way of saying whether the items of a scale seem to be relevant. Qualitative methods provide ways of codifying experience, generating items (e.g., from themes and emergent content), and checking to see whether others (e.g., participants) view the items as relevant and as reflective of the experience. Clearly, the approach could help develop better measures of constructs related to experience in everyday life. These measures then could be subjected to the usual methods of scale development and evaluation, but would begin with content well grounded in experiences and contexts to which the investigator may wish to generalize.

SUMMARY AND CONCLUSIONS

Qualitative research is designed to describe, interpret, and understand human experience and to elaborate the meaning that this experience has to the participants. The data are primarily words and are derived from in-depth analysis of cases. The cases can be one or a few individuals or a group, but also a culture, tribe, organization, or other unit of in-depth analysis, depending on the discipline (e.g., sociology, anthropology, education). A key feature of the approach is a detailed description without presupposing specific measures, categories, or a narrow range of constructs.

The approach differs in many ways from the dominant research paradigm (referred to as *quantitative research*) in how the study is completed, the roles of the participants and investigator, what the data are, how the data are examined, and the conclusions. Although extensive data (e.g., narratives, case descriptions, video- or audiotapes) are collected, they are not reduced in a quantitative way. Rather, interpretations, overarching constructs, and theory are generated from the data to better explain and understand how the participants experienced the phenomenon of interest. Although there are major differences in qualitative and quantitative research, there are also fundamental similarities that make them both empirical research. Among the key similarities are interest in reliability and validity of the methods of procuring the data, efforts to address sources of bias that can impede the conclusions that are drawn, replication of both how the study was done and the conclusions that were reached, and the accumulation of knowledge verifiable by others. Qualitative research can contribute to psychology by elaborating the nature of experience and its meaning, by bringing everyday experiences into sharp focus, by elaborating causal relations and paths during the course of development, and by guiding directly the focus of quantitative studies.

NOTES

[1]For a fuller discussion of the multiple histories underlying contemporary qualitative research, see Denzin and Lincoln (1994), a source book on qualitative research detailing the traditions from which qualitative research has emerged.

[2]A number of scientific journals, such as *Qualitative Health Research, Qualitative Studies in Education,* and *Culture, Medicine, and Psychiatry*, are devoted to qualitative research.

FOR FURTHER READING

Denzin, N.H, & Lincoln, Y.S. (Eds.) (1994). *Handbook of qualitative research*. Thousand Oaks, CA: Sage.

Krahn, G.L., Hohn, M.F., & Kime, C. (1995). Incorporating qualitative approaches into clinical child psychology research. *Journal of Clinical Child Psychology, 24,* 204–213.

Miles, M.B., & Huberman, A.M. (1994). *Qualitative data analysis* (2nd ed.). Thousand Oaks, CA: Sage.

Stiles, W.B. (1993). Quality control in qualitative research. *Clinical Psychology Review, 13,* 593–618.

Webster-Stratton, C., & Spitzer, A. (1996). Parenting of a young child with conduct problems: New insights using qualitative methods. In T.H. Ollendick & R.J. Prinz (Eds.), *Advances in clinical child psychology* (Vol. 18, pp. 1–62). New York: Plenum Press.

Chapter 11

Assessment Methods and Strategies

The previous chapters have taken excursions to various approaches to research. Let us return to research methods and approaches within the quantitative tradition. Prior discussions within this tradition have emphasized experimental design, without comment on assessment. Needless to say, any interpretation of a given study depends heavily on the measures that are used, the specific constructs they assess, and the confidence one can place on precisely what these measures mean. When we consider identifying measures for research, attention usually is drawn to the dependent measures or outcomes that will evaluate the hypotheses. Clearly, this is important but is only part of what we as researchers are interested in. The assessment of independent variables (e.g., comparing groups of depressed vs. nondepressed persons), mediators and processes (e.g., alliance in therapy, cognitions or motivational states, arousal), and dependent variables (e.g., treatment outcome) raises critical and indeed similar assessment issues.

The research plan emphasizes hypotheses, key constructs of the study, the underlying model or conceptual view that relates the constructs to each other, identification and selection of the sample, and plans for data analyses. Selecting measures is often relegated to looking at the existing literature and seeing what other investigators have used. Measures that have been used frequently and appear to show the effects of interventions or group comparisons by other investigators are selected. On the one hand, using a common or consistent set of measures drawn from the literature has the advantage of being able to compare results across studies. On the other hand, much research is conducted in a tradition of weak or narrow assessment. There is often a complacency in selecting measurement strategies and specific measures within these strategies. Precedence is a de facto criterion for measurement selection, but is not a strong criterion.

The measures of a study can materially influence the conclusions that are drawn. In relation to statistical conclusion validity, whether the results of a study reflect change or group differences can be affected directly by the reliability of the measure, that is, how much error there is in the assessment. The error or variability may reduce the power to detect differences because of the impact on effect sizes. Also, limitations in the range of scores permitted in a measure (e.g., ceiling or floor effects) may occasionally restrict obtaining group differences that would exist if the measure had not been restricted.

Perhaps even more of an assessment issue in relation to experimental validity is external validity or generality of the findings. We have discussed external validity as the extent to which the results can be generalized to other persons, settings, and situations. No less critical is the extent to which the results can be generalized beyond the specific measures used in the study. When hearing the results of a study, it is almost always meaningful, cogent, and important to ask, How was X (e.g., dependent variable) measured? (It is important to name the dependent variable—my experience is that people look quizzical if you actually say "X.")

There are important exceptions in which the measure is viewed as the sole critical index of the construct of interest and there is relatively little or no ambiguity about the measure and the construct it reflects. For example, death is often used as a dependent measure in research on diseases and their treatment (e.g., treatment of heart disease and cancer). The measure (mortality) usually does not raise epistemological questions (How do you know they were really dead?) or methodological challenges (Does "not breathing" *really* get at the central features of the construct? What was the test–retest reliability of the measure?).

Of course, definitional questions arise when discussing life and death in the context of personal, social, and ethical issues (e.g., abortion, termination of life-support systems). In most psychological measurement, multiple indices can be used to assess the construct of interest and they are not interchangeable or identical in what they actually measure.

Historically, science began with a somewhat naive view of operational definitions and the way they represent constructs. That view, not entirely a straw-man argument, is that operational definitions are signs of the construct and that many different signs are interchangeable as ways of representing the construct. More concretely, in the Introduction and Discussion sections of research papers, we can focus on the constructs of interest. The method of measurement is incidental and relegated to the bowels of the Method section. Yet, operational definitions of the same construct can yield quite different findings, and the measures we use are part of the findings in fundamental ways—points to which we shall return.

In this chapter, we address fundamental issues of assessment, particularly issues pertaining to the selection of measures for research. For ease of presentation reference is made to the assessment methods used to test the hypotheses, that is, the dependent measures because studies, by definition, use dependent measures that reflect psychological assessment. Not all studies use psychological measures to operationalize independent variables (e.g., experimental manipulations rather than scores on a measure to define groups), assess the impact of the experimental manipulation, or evaluate processes or mechanisms that explain the relation between the independent and dependent variables. However, the assessment points apply to constructs and measures in general. The chapter discusses the selection of measures for research, types of measures that are available, and strategies to guide use of the measures.

SELECTING MEASURES FOR RESEARCH

The selection of measures for research is made on the basis of several considerations related to the construct validity of the measure, psychometric properties, and sensitivity of the measure to the changes predicted by the hypotheses.

Construct Validity

As a general rule, we are not really interested in measures. An exception is when we are developing or evaluating a measure. In the usual case, we are interested in constructs or the concepts that these measures reflect. As obvious as this sounds, it is critical to bear in mind because measures are often selected without sufficient attention to the extent to which they measure the construct or facet of the construct of interest to the investigator. For example, there are very many measures of stress or social support, two constructs often studied in clinical research. But the measures are not interchangeable, do not invariably examine the same aspects of stress or social support, and may be quite different in their utility and relevance depending on the facets of the constructs they emphasize.

The initial criterion for selecting a measure is evidence that the measure assesses the construct of interest. In assessment, the term *construct validity* is used to refer generally to the extent to which the measure assesses the domain, trait, or characteristic of interest (Cronbach & Meehl, 1955). Construct validity is used throughout this text to refer to a type of experimental validity that relates to the interpretation of the basis for the effect of the experimental manipulation. In the context of assessment, the interpretation of the measure is at issue, namely, to what extent is the construct underlying the measure the basis for interpretation of the measure. Construct validity does not reduce to a correlation between measures or the measure and some other criterion. Rather, it refers more broadly to the pattern of findings and to many other types of validity. In a given study, the investigator may be interested in measuring adjustment, emotional distress, or some other construct. There should be some initial assurance that the measure actually reflects the construct.

It is easy to be enticed by many available measures into the assumption that they assess a particular construct. Measures usually have names that reflect the construct the investigator *intended* the scale to measure (and often carry the name of the investigator). Unfamiliar (and fictitious) examples readily convey the sorts of measures that are available (e.g., the Lipshitz Depression Inventory, the Stop-Following-Me Scale of Paranoia, or the You-Bet-Your-Life Measure of Risk Taking). The names of various measures may be based on supporting evidence that a particular characteristic or construct in fact is assessed (i.e., construct validity) or merely reflect what the originator of the measure had in mind without the requisite evidence.

In a related fashion, many questionnaires and inventories have been evaluated by factor analysis, a statistical procedure designed to identify sets of correlated items that cluster together. Names of the factors also suggest what is actually measured. Essentially, the factors may be presented as minimeasures, that is, scales to assess different constructs or different facets of a single construct. Here, too, one must be cautious because the connection between the name of the factor and what the items have been shown to measure (construct validity) is not always clear. Also, whether a scale, factor, or subscale with a given name is what the investigator means by the construct underlying the investigation is not automatic. For example, one might develop a measure of love, but there are different types of love and different relations in which the types are manifest. Is this measure of love the type the investigator has in mind, is it distinguished from other types of love, or from positive affect in general (technically known as "warm fuzzies") that is not necessarily love? These are construct validity questions and are not minor issues. Needless to say, there should be some evidence that the measure selected for research in fact assesses the construct of interest. If there is no evidence available, steps should be taken within the study to provide information on validity and other psychometric properties.

Psychometric Characteristics

There are many steps for establishing or deciding whether a measure adequately assesses the construct of interest. These steps, broadly conceived, refers to how the measure "behaves" in relation to a variety of circumstances. These can be discussed as the characteristics or rather psychometric characteristics of the scale or measure. *Psychometric characteristics* refer here to evidence of reliability and validity on behalf of a measure. Reliability and validity have diverse definitions. *Reliability* generally refers to consistency of the measure. This encompasses consistency within the measure (i.e., how the items relate to each other), consistency in performance on the measure over time (test–retest), and consistency between different parts or alternate forms of the same measure. *Validity* refers to the content and whether the measure assesses the domain of interest. This encompasses the relation of performance on the measure to performance on other measures at the same time or in the future and to other criteria (e.g., school achievement, occupational status, psychiatric diagnosis). Any single definition is hazardous because reliability and validity are broad concepts, each with several subtypes. Also, over the years the different types of reliability and validity and their meanings have varied (Angoff, 1988; DeVellis, 1991). The net effect is that there has been remarkable unreliability in use of the terms reliability and validity. Table 11.1 presents major types of reliability and validity that are commonly referred to and are of clear relevance in evaluating measures for possible use in research.

The concepts of reliability and validity sensitize the investigator to a range of considerations. In any given situation, a specific type of reliability and validity may or may not be relevant. For example, high test–retest reliability during a period of a few months might be expected for a measure designed to assess a stable characteristic (e.g., a trait such as extroversion) but not for a more transient characteristic (e.g., a state such as irritated mood). Apart from characteristics of the construct, evaluation of the measure depends on its demonstrated psychometric characteristics. Measures known to reflect the construct of interest and to do so in a reliable and valid fashion bolster the confidence to which the investigator is entitled when one interprets the results of the study. In selecting a measure, it is important for the investigator to examine the available literature to identify the extent to which the measure has in its behalf relevant data on reliability and validity in ways that approximate the use in the present study. Within the measurement literature resources are available to help this search (e.g., Murphy, Conoley, & Impara, 1994; Schutte & Malouff, 1995).

Sensitivity of the Measure

The measure ought to be sensitive enough to reflect the type and magnitude of change or group differences that the investigator is expecting. Sensitivity in this context refers to the capacity to reflect systematic variation given the experimental conditions or groups that are to be compared or evaluated. The sensi-

TABLE 11.1. Common Types of Reliability and Validity

Type	Definition and/or Concept
Reliability	
Test–retest reliability	The stability of test scores over time; the correlation of scores from one administration of the test with scores on the same instrument after a particular time interval has elapsed.
Alternate-form reliability	The correlation between different forms of the same measure when the items of the two forms are considered to represent the same population of items.
Internal consistency	The degree of consistency or homogeneity of the items within a scale. Different reliability measures are used toward this end such as split-half reliability, Kuder-Richardson 20 Formula, and coefficient alpha.
Interrater (interscorer) reliability	The extent to which different assessors, raters, or observers agree on the scores they provide when assessing, coding, or classifying subjects' performance. Different measures are used to evaluate agreement such as percent agreement, Pearson product–moment correlations, and kappa.
Validity	
Construct validity	A broad concept that refers to the extent to which the measure reflects the construct (concept, domain) of interest. Other types of validity and other evidence that elaborates the correlates of the measure are relevant to construct validity. Construct validity focuses on the relation of a measure to other measures and domains of functioning of which the concept underlying the measure may be a part.
Content validity	Evidence that the content of the items reflect the construct or domain of interest; the relation of the items to the concept underlying the measure.
Concurrent validity	The correlation of a measure with performance on another measure or criterion at the same point in time.
Predictive validity	The correlation of a measure at one point in time with performance on another measure or criterion at some point in the future.
Criterion validity	Correlation of a measure with some other criterion. This can encompass concurrent or predictive validity. In addition, the notion is occasionally used in relation to a specific and often dichotomous criterion when performance on the measure is evaluated in relation to disorders (e.g., depressed vs. nondepressed patients) or status (e.g., prisoners vs. nonprisoners).
Face validity	The extent to which a measure appears to assess the construct of interest. This is not a formal type of validation or part of the psychometric development or evaluation of a measure.

TABLE 11.1.   *(Continued)*

Type	Definition and/or Concept
Convergent validity	The extent to which two measures assess similar or related constructs. The validity of a given measure is suggested if the measures correlate with other measures with which it is expected to correlate. The correlation between the measures is expected based on the overlap or relation of the constructs. A form of concurrent validity that takes on special meaning in relation to discriminant validity.
Discriminant validity	The correlation between measures that are expected *not* to relate to each other or to assess dissimilar and unrelated constructs. The validity of a given measure is suggested if the measures show little or no correlation with measures with which they are not expected to correlate. The absence of correlation is expected based on separate and conceptually distinct constructs.

Note: The types of reliability and validity presented here refer to commonly used terms in test construction and validation. The terms are used in various ways by authors. The purpose here is to highlight critical concepts for evaluating measures. For further discussion, the reader is referred to Angoff (1988).

tivity required to reflect differences or change depends on the manner in which the independent variable is manipulated and on precisely what the variable is. For example, if a study compared the effects of relaxation training versus no training to reduce anxiety among persons visiting a dentist, a rather large difference (effect size) might be expected between the two conditions. But, if the comparison were between two treatments (e.g., brief versus extended relaxation training), the differences might be more subtle. Whether an effect is obtained in either case might be a function of the sensitivity of the dependent measure. A less sensitive measure would be needed to reflect change in the first comparison (relaxation vs. no relaxation) than in the case of the second comparison (very brief vs. more extended relaxation training).

Whether and how much a dependent measure is sensitive to change are difficult to specify before the study. A few general desirable characteristics of the dependent measure can be identified. To begin with, the dependent measure should permit a relatively large range of responses so that varying increments and decrements in performance can be detected. If subjects score at the extremes of the distribution at pretest, this allows the investigator to detect only varying degrees of change in the opposite direction at postassessment. If it is necessary to be able to detect change in only one direction, as might be the case in studies designed to compare two treatments that are both known to be effective, the measure need not allow for bidirectional changes. However, there should be some assurance before the intervention that ceiling or floor effects will not be a limitation that could interfere with detecting differences among various experimental and control conditions.

Psychometric data and a wide range for scores to vary are important, but it is also useful for the investigator to study the items. Often scales are used without really looking at the items carefully to see whether it is reasonable to expect scores on the items to reflect change for a given group or differences between groups. Also, scrutiny of the items may lead to hypotheses about some portions of the scale (e.g., subscales, factors) that might be more sensitive to group differences than others and that may provide a more direct or specific test of the hypotheses. As the investigator ponders the contents of a scale, he or she may begin to think of alternative or additional measures to better test or elaborate the hypotheses.

An important, heavily relied on guideline in research is whether a given dependent variable has reflected change or group differences in prior studies. Investigators examine published research in a particular area of study to see what measures have reflected change with what sorts of interventions. There is an advantage in looking to previous research because it is a filter for many measures that probably would not reflect change for the type of intervention or group comparison to be investigated. Measures that have reflected change in previous experiments have proved themselves to be sensitive to some manipulations. As mentioned already, an advantage of using previously reported measures is that investigators can more readily compare their findings with those obtained in previous research. The use of similar measures across studies allows investigators to evaluate whether groups were similar to begin with and whether the independent variable affected the dependent measure(s) in the same way (direction) and to the same extent (magnitude). There may be disadvantages in using measures from previous investigations. Specifically, looking to other investigations for sources of dependent measures may lead to overreliance on a few measures, which can lead to stagnation in the development of new and perhaps more useful measures. Also, a given construct can be assessed in many ways. By assessing the construct in new and different ways, our understanding of the construct can be enhanced.

Overall, the sensitivity of a measure in an investigation should be assured prior to conducting the study. If a body of literature already shows the sensitivity of the measure to the intervention, manipulation, or group comparisons of interest, preliminary work in this issue can be avoided. If such evidence is not available, preliminary work before the full investigation might evaluate whether different manipulations reflect change on the measure. A small pilot study (e.g., 20 cases, 10 in each of two groups) can provide preliminary information about whether the measure yields differences. It is important to know whether the measure could reflect the predicted relation between independent and dependent variables. If no relation were demonstrated between the independent and dependent variables at the end of the investigation, it would be reassuring to know that the cause was not the insensitivity of the dependent measure. An alternative to pilot work is to include the measure with several others on an exploratory basis and explicitly acknowledge in the investigation that one purpose is to explore the relation of a new measure with those already available in the literature.

General Comments

The discussion has focused on desirable features of individual measures. It is important to place the comments into context. As a rule, any individual measure is inherently limited in terms of how it assesses the construct of interest and the potential limitations in generality of findings across measures. A key strategy for selecting measures is to use multiple measures of the constructs of interest in any study. The use of multiple measures does not necessarily compensate for weaknesses of individual measures (e.g., very low reliability) but addresses broader points we shall discuss later. In addition, it is possible to combine measures of the same construct, even though they have quite different metrics, methods, or characteristics (e.g., through the use of latent variable or principal-components analyses). The advantages of using combined multiple measures are also addressed later.

USING AVAILABLE MEASURES OR DEVISING NEW MEASURES

Selecting measures requires considerable thought based on the criteria outlined at the outset and the range of modalities and measures available. Often this issue is not one of merely selecting measures but of modifying or developing measures to address the goals of the research.

Using a Standardized Measure

In most cases, the investigator will use available measures whose psychometric characteristics are known. Many measures are available in an area of research, and there is usually tacit agreement that certain types of measures, modalities of assessment, and specific instruments are important or central. For example, in studying adult depression, it is very likely that an investigator will include a self-report measure (Beck Depression Inventory) and clinician rating scale (Hamilton Rating Scale for Depression). These modalities and these specific instruments have enjoyed widespread use, a feature that does not necessarily mean that the measures are flawless or free from ambiguity. These scales are considered to be the most well researched within this area, and performance on the scales (e.g., scores that relate to degree of depressive symptoms and correlates among these different levels of symptoms) is quite meaningful among investigators. The frequent use of the measures has fostered continued use; thus, researchers embarking on a new study (e.g., evaluating treatment for depression) usually include one or both in the broader assessment battery.

Another reason for using standardized measures is the amount of work that may have gone into the measures by other researchers. The work facilitates interpretation of the measure. For example, to assess intellectual functioning or psychopathology among adults, one might rely on the Wechsler Adult Intelligence Scale—Revised (WAIS) and the Minnesota Multiphasic Personality Inventory (MMPI-2), respectively. Extensive research on each of these measures facilitates their interpretation. Also, use of such well-studied measures lends credence that the study assessed the construct of interest.

Varying the Use or Contents of an Existing Measure

A standardized measure of functioning, personality, behavior, or some other domain may be available, although some facet of the investigator's interest may make the measure not quite appropriate. The measure may have been developed, established, and validated in a context different from that of the proposed study. For example, one might wish to assess geriatric patients but the measure of interest may have been developed, evaluated, or standardized with young adults. Alternatively, the investigator may wish to assess a particular ethnic group whose language, culture, and experiences differ from samples with whom the measure was developed. The reason for selecting the measure is that the method or content seems highly suitable for the investigator's purposes. Yet, the measure may not have been used in the new way or validated in the new context.

Nevertheless, the investigator may elect to use the measure. In so doing, it is essential to include within the study an effort to evaluate psychometric properties. The task is to provide evidence that the measure behaves in a way that parallels the standard use of the measure. Evidence regarding reliability is very useful, but greater concerns are likely to be voiced in relation to validity of the measure in its new use. Evidence might include correlating scores on the measure in its new use with scores on other measures in the study or using the measure to delineate subgroups and showing that the findings resemble those obtained in studies when the original measure was used as intended. It may not be sufficient to show that the new use of the measure leads to predictable differences on the dependent measure, although this may vary as a function of the complexity of the predicted relations and the plausibility of alternative interpretations of the results on the measure. In the general case, it is advisable within the study or as part of pilot work to provide additional evidence that the construct of interest is still measured with the new use of the measure and that the measure still enjoys adequate psychometric properties relevant to the study.

Use of existing measures in new ways is often preferable to creating entirely new measures because the available research on the existing measure is still relevant for interpretation of the measure. Data on the original factor structure, correlations with other measures, and psychometric characteristics provide some information that may be relevant to the new application. If an entirely new measure were created, no background information would be available. On the other hand, use of standardized measures in new ways may be viewed and labeled by colleagues who review the research as "inappropriate" or beyond the intention of the founding fathers and mothers who devised the measure. This view is not extreme; there becomes a point at which applicability of the measure to new samples, populations, and circumstances is strained. For many colleagues that point consists of any extension beyond the specific purposes for which the measure has been developed and standardized. Reasonable people differ on this point; but reasonable investigators provide validity data to allay the cogent concern that the novel use is inappropriate or difficult to interpret.

Investigators often make slight variations in a standardized measure such as deleting a few items, rewording items, or adding new items. The purpose is to make the measure more well suited to the new population or application. For example, questions asking about suicide attempt or violent acts may be omitted in a study of a community sample because the base rates of these behaviors might be low and the items would be potentially upsetting and provocative in that context. The same measure in a clinic setting would include the items if the goal is to identify the full range of symptoms and the expectation is that such items may be required. Omission of one or two items is a minimal alteration of the scale; the items usually can be interpreted as if the scale were the original, and by prorating missing items, changes can be made in subscale or total scores.

There are few data available on the extent to which investigators make minor alterations in measures and the impact of these changes on the findings. A recent analysis of research using the Hamilton Rating Scale for Depression found that at least 10 distinct versions of the scale are in use, depending on variations in wording and number of the items (Grundy et al., 1994). Moreover, each variation of the measure did not have suitable reliability or validity on its behalf nor the strength of data that characterized the original version of the scale. It is likely that many researchers have lost track of the original scale because, as Grundy and colleagues noted, citations to the scale in a given study often are mistaken; that is, they refer to a different version from the one used in the study. In short, standardized tests are likely to be altered; it is important to provide data to show that the altered version is as meaningful and valid as the original version. As a more general rule, when one tinkers with the content or format of a measure, the requirements are similar. As a minimum, some evidence is needed within the study to show the measure continues to assess the construct of interest and behaves psychometrically in a defensible fashion. To the extent that the measure is altered and that the new use departs from the one for which the measure was standardized, stronger and more extensive validity data are likely to be demanded by the research community.

As an illustration, in the work of our research group, we have been interested in measuring hopelessness in children. Among the issues that makes hopelessness interesting is the relation to depression and to suicidal attempt and ideation in adults. Hopelessness (negative expectations toward the future) has been reliably assessed in adults with a scale devised for that purpose (Beck, Weissman, Lester, & Trexler, 1974). In developing the scale for children, the items from the adult scale were altered to simplify the content and to be more relevant to children's lives. Clearly, such changes are not minor modifications of a scale but lead to qualitative differences in focus and content. Hence, it is not very reasonable to assume that the original validational evidence would apply. Two studies were conducted to provide reliability and validity data. Internal consistency data and analyses of items paralleled the results obtained with the adult scale. In addition, the construct of hopelessness in children generated results similar to those obtained with adults. For example, hopelessness was found to be related to suicide ideation and attempt and to be positively correlated with depression and negatively correlated with self-esteem (Kazdin, Rodgers, & Colbus, 1986; Kazdin, French, Unis, Esveldt-Dawson, & Sherick, 1983).

The initial findings on the Hopelessness Scale for Children were promising but quite preliminary. In developing a new measure or revising an existing one, one or two studies are limited for different reasons. In the case of our research, the children were within a restricted age range (6–13 years) and were all inpatients from a psychiatric hospital. Also, a limited range of constructs and other measures were examined as the basis for evaluating validity. In short, the two studies provide some, albeit very incomplete, evidence regarding the new scale and how it behaves. The task in developing a measure is not necessarily to complete the full set of validational steps. Once an investigator provides preliminary evidence and places the measure within the public domain, others may complete further studies that evaluate a broader set of psychometric issues (Kashani, Dandoy, & Reid, 1991; Spirito et al., 1988b).

Developing a New Measure

Sometimes measures of the construct of interest are not available. The investigator may wish to develop a new measure to address the questions that guide the study. Instrument development can be a program of research in itself and occupy a career. In most cases, investigators are not interested in developing or evaluating a measure with that in mind. Rather, the goal is to address a set of substantive questions and to conduct studies that measures the construct in a new way.

Developing a new measure is a weighty topic in its own right in light of advances in measurement theory and scale construction (DeVellis, 1991; Reckase, 1996). Minimally, in developing a new measure, the investigator has several obligations to the research community. Specifically, some evidence is required, either in pilot work reported in the write-up of the study or as part of the study itself, that attests in some way to the construct validity of the measure. The steps extend beyond face validity, that is, that the content of the items is reasonable or obvious. Various types of reliability and validity, as presented in Table 11.1, might be relevant. Particularly crucial would be evidence that supports the assertion that the measure assesses the construct of interest. Such evidence might be reflected in one or more of the following:

1. Differences between groups on the measure (e.g., older vs. younger, clinically referred vs. nonreferred cases) in ways that are consistent with the construct allegedly assessed (criterion validity)
2. A pattern of correlations showing that the new measure behaves as predicted, that is, evidence that the direction and magnitude of the correlations are consistent (e.g., low, moderate, high) with what would be predicted from the relation of the constructs encompassed by the new and standardized measures (concurrent, predictive, or concurrent validity)
3. Evidence that the new measure is not highly correlated with standardized measure of another more established construct, which might suggest that the new construct

is fairly well encompassed by or redundant with the other (more established) construct (discriminant validity)

4. Evidence that, over time, performance on the measure does or does not change depending on the nature of the construct (e.g., mood vs. character trait) (test–retest reliability)

With the use of a new measure, evidence on one or more types of validity is a minimum required to argue that the construct of interest is encompassed by the measure. As noted in the discussion of altering a standardized measure, it is usually insufficient to add the measure to the study and to show that it reflects changes that are predicted. Within the study, separate and independent types of evidence are needed about the measure apart from or in addition to how the measure reflects change as a dependent measure. However, the persuasiveness of any particular demonstration on behalf of a new measures depends on a host of factors (e.g., complexity of any predictions and clarity of the findings).

For example, we have been interested in why families drop out of therapy prematurely, that is, early and against advice of the therapist (Kazdin, 1996b). Rates of attrition in child therapy are high in general (40–60 percent), and some factors that predict dropping out are well studied (e.g., low socioeconomic status of the family, parent stress, single-parent families, younger age of the mothers). We felt that for many families treatment itself raises barriers or obstacles that influence who drops out. We developed a scale, called the Barriers to Participation in Treatment Scale, on the basis of our experiences with parents and the obstacles they report in coming to treatment (Kazdin, Holland, & Crowley, 1997; Kazdin, Holland, Crowley, & Breton, in press). The scale consists of 58 items that reflect stressors and obstacles that compete with treatment, treatment demands, perceived relevance of treatment, and relationship of the parent and therapist. The scale is completed by the parent or therapist; both versions are designed to capture parents' experience in coming to treatment. The results of initial studies showed that scores on the measures predicted dropping out of treatment and other measures of participation in treatment (e.g., canceling appointments, not showing up) and that scores on the measure were not explained by other more easily assessed variables that also contribute to dropping out (e.g., lower socioeconomic status, stress, etc.). What do we know from these initial studies? Probably only that the measure is worth pursuing. The results are consistent with the construct and provide preliminary support. All sorts of questions remain about the scale, content, and correlates. Developing a new scale begins the path of validation completely anew, and initial studies are only a very first step.

General Comments

The strength, specificity, and very likely the value or utility of the conclusions from a study depend on interpretation of what was measured and the meaning of performance on the measures. If extensive evidence is available for the construct validity of the measure, which is often the case for standardized measures, the burden of interpretation is reduced. The burden is never eliminated because psychological measures by their very nature raise manifold issues about construct validity, external validity, and potential bias. Intelligence tests, for example, tend to be the most well studied psychological instruments, but the tests are surrounded in controversy related to their interpretation and use. If extensive evidence is not available for the measure, if a standardized measure is altered in some way, either through application to novel circumstances or by item tinkering, or if a new measure is developed, validity data are essential to include within the study.

MODALITIES OF ASSESSMENT: AN OVERVIEW

The diverse measures available in clinical research and the range of characteristics they assess are difficult to enumerate. Measures used in clinical psychology vary along a number of dimensions. Table 11.2 presents salient characteristics that vary among measures and that have implications for selecting measures. In a given study it is usually important to select more than one measure of the construct of interest and to select measures that vary in their methodological characteristics. In this way the investigator can be assured that the finding is not restricted to the construct as measured in a particular way. Characteristics in Table 11.2 help to identify different types of measures that may be selected and major selection options.

The characteristic that may distinguish measures most sharply (not encompassed by Table 11.2) is the modality or type of measure. Although the different types of measures and the requirements for devising useful measures within each modality are beyond the scope of this chapter, much can be gained by highlighting major modalities of assessment and the kinds of uses and problems they provide for clinical research.

Global Ratings

Characteristics *Global ratings* refer to efforts to quantify impressions of somewhat general characteristics. They are referred to as global because they reflect overall impressions or summary statements of the construct of interest. Typically, ratings are made by the therapist or by significant others who are in contact with the clients. A major justification for use of these ratings is that certain individuals other than the client may be in a position by virtue of expertise (e.g., therapist, ward staff member of a psychiatric hospital) or familiarity with the client (e.g., spouse, parent) to provide a well-based appraisal. However, there are also global self-ratings. Who completes the ratings is not critical in defining global ratings.

The judgments may vary in complexity in terms of precisely what is rated. Very often global ratings are made in areas such as overall adjustment, improvement in therapy, social adequacy, ability to handle stress, and similar broad concepts. These ratings are usually made by having raters complete one

TABLE 11.2.   Dimensions/Characteristics of Psychological Measures

Characteristic	Definition and/or Concept
Global–Specific	Measures vary in the extent to which they assess narrowly defined vs. broad characteristics of functioning. Measures of overall feelings, stress, and quality of life are more toward the global side; measures of narrowly defined domains and experience are more specific.
Publicly Observable Information–Private Event	Measures may examine characteristics or actions that can be observed by others (e.g., cigarette smoking, social interaction) or assess private experience (e.g., headaches, thoughts, urges, and obsessions).
Stable–Transient Characteristics	Measures may assess traitlike characteristics or long-standing aspects of functioning or short-lived or episodic characteristics (e.g., mood immediately after being subjected to a frustrating experience in an experiment).
Direct–Indirect	Direct measures are those whose purpose can be seen by the client. Indirect measures are those that obscure from the client exactly what is being measured.
Breadth of Domains Sampled	Measures vary whether they assess a single characteristic (e.g., introversion, anxiety, risk-taking ability, or need for social approval), or reveal many different characteristics of personality or psychopathology (e.g., several personality traits or different types of symptoms within a single measure).
Format	Measures vary in the methods through which subjects can provide their replies such as true–false, multiple-choice, forced-choice, fill-in, and rating scale formats of self-report scales and inventories and extended narrative reports subsequently coded as in projective techniques.

or a few items rated on a multiple-point continuum by which the degree of the rated dimension can be assessed. For example, a typical item might be:

To what extent has the client improved in therapy? (*check one*)

1	2	3	4	5	6	7
no improvement			moderate improvement		very large improvement	

or

How much do the client's symptoms interfere with everyday functioning?

1	2	3	4	5	6	7
not at all			moderately		very much	

The preceding samples not only illustrate the format for global ratings but also the generality of the dimension frequently rated. Usually ratings ask for an appraisal of a multifaceted or complex area of functioning.

Global ratings are often used because they provide a very flexible assessment format for an investigator. Virtually any construct of interest to the investigator (e.g., symptomatology, overall functioning, comfort in social situations) can be included. The flexibility also means that a general characteristic can be used to rate individuals who may differ greatly in their individual problems. By rating clients on a global dimension that encompasses diverse problems (e.g., degree of improvement, extent to which symptoms interfere with ordinary functioning), a similar measure can be used for persons whose characteristics vary greatly at a more molecular level. Another reason that global ratings have been popular is that they provide a summary evaluation of a client's status. The problems clients experience may include many facets. It is important to determine with specificity how the different facets have changed. It is often useful to have an overall statement that distills the effects of treatment into a relatively simple statement or question (e.g., Are you better off now than you were when you came for treatment?).

Global ratings also provide a convenient format for soliciting judgments of experts, peers, or other informants. Presumably, an expert in the nature of clinical dysfunction is uniquely skilled to evaluate the status of the client, the severity of the client's disorder, and the degree to which change, deterioration, or improvement has occurred. Similarly, individuals in the natural environment who interact with the client (e.g., peers, spouses, employers) also are in a unique position to evaluate performance. In this context, global ratings of client change often have been incorporated into treatment evaluation. For example, the Global Assessment of Functioning Scale, used to assess overall functioning on a mental health–illness continuum, consists of a single item rated from 1–100 (American Psychiatric Association, 1994). Broad descriptive guides are provided at 10-point increments (e.g., 1–10, some danger of hurting self- or others; 51–60, moderate symptoms or moderate difficulty in social, occupational, or school functioning; 91–100, superior functioning in a wide range of activities). Multiple constructs and domains are interspersed on the continuum (e.g., symptoms, interpersonal relations, work and school functioning). The rating scale is global in the sense that one summary item is designed to represent how one is doing in life.

Issues and Limitations   One major problem with global ratings is evaluating precisely what they measure. The phrasing of global ratings *suggests* what the item is designed to measure (e.g., symptoms). However, there is no assurance that in fact this is what is actually measured. Few or, more often, no concrete criteria are specified to the assessor who completes the ratings. By definition, the ratings are rather general, and all sorts of variables may enter into the rater's criteria for evaluating the client.

Because the criteria are not well specified, it is possible that the global ratings may change over time independent of whether the client has changed, as reflected on another more specific measure. For example, therapists may view clients as improving over time simply because of changes in the criteria used in making their overall ratings of improvement. Thus, a client's greater ease, candor, or warmth within the therapy session may influence a therapist's rating of client improvement at the end of therapy regardless of whether clinical change in the problem area (e.g., obsessions or compulsive rituals) has occurred. Changes in the measurement procedures or criteria over time were referred to earlier as instrumentation, a threat to the internal validity. Instrumentation can account for changes over time as a function of assessment (procedures, definitions, or criteria) rather than change in client behavior. Global ratings are especially subject to the instrumentation threat because the criteria that go into making ratings are general and varying definitions are fostered by the generality of the items or questions.

Another problem with global ratings, certainly related to the problem of what they measure, is their potential lack of sensitivity. Essentially, global ratings ask a general question for a given dimension, for example, How severe are the client's symptoms? How much improvement has there been? How anxious is the client? By posing general questions, the measures lose some of the sensitivity that could be obtained from assessing very specific characteristics of the relevant dimensions of interest. Global ratings greatly oversimplify the nature of functioning and therapeutic change. By utilizing a global measure, the richness of detail is lost, and loss of detail may or may not be important, depending on other measures.

The strengths and limitations of global ratings can be illustrated by a survey completed by *Consumer Reports* (1995) that asked adults to report on the extent to which they were satisfied with psychotherapy. Approximately 3000 individuals who had seen a mental health professional completed questions reflecting their treatment. Global questions asked about how much they were helped, whether the problem for which they sought treatment improved, and the degree to which they were satisfied with their treatment. The results showed that people were generally very satisfied with their treatment and that they were helped. Different treatments did not make a difference in the results. Overall, the results could be interpreted as a glowing report of psychotherapy for a host of problems that people bring to treatment. Indeed, some have interpreted the data to be a very strong endorsement of treatment effectiveness (Seligman, 1995), but this is by no means the majority view (Jacobson & Christensen, 1996). The relation between scores on a few nonvalidated items and actual changes in therapy is tenuous at best. Evidence is required about the measure before any conclusions can be made. This is not mere skepticism for its own sake. We have developed the steps for validating measures precisely to protect against drawing simple conclusions without basis. For example, the global items in the above survey might, when validated, reduce to measures of a completely different construct (e.g., how much one liked one's therapist, whether symptoms improved spontaneously). Global ratings, as any other measure, are meaningful, but that meaning requires evidence.

Global ratings raise significant problems, two of which are particularly salient. First, the generality of the items fosters conclusions that are also likely to be general. That is, there is little precision in what is being asked. The format of a global rating usually does not permit sufficient variation (i.e., a wide range of scores from multiple items known to measure the construct) to identify differences (e.g., treatments) if they exist. Consider as an alternative for a large-scale evaluation of therapy, use of a well-developed self-report scale (e.g., MMPI-2) with multiple scales and subscales that have been thoroughly validated. If all treatments showed no differences on such a measure, that would be more interpretable than the global ratings because we know that the scale *can* differentiate populations, clinical problems, and status of individuals who vary in their psychological conditions.

Second, global ratings like those in *Consumer Reports* are often homemade. There are no data that attest to the construct validity of the individual scales. Indeed, a frequent problem with surveys is that they rely on face validity; that is, they seem reasonable to persons who invent them, to those who answer them, and to those who read the results about them. Yet, there are rarely data that show the measures are valid, that is, actually reflect the constructs of interest, or indeed reliable (e.g., show high test–retest reliability). Also, surveys may well be influenced by assessment conditions (e.g., reactivity) and artifact (e.g., socially desirable responding, fabrication). When 99 percent of people say they are dissatisfied or satisfied with their spouse, we want to know a lot about assessment, such as whether the spouse was present when the question was answered, how the results will be used, what domain of satisfaction is being assessed, and maybe most important, how the global rating relates to standardized measures of martial satisfaction that have traversed the psychometric hurdles that permit interpretation.

In a larger battery in which specific constructs are assessed, one may want to include a global rating scale to answer a set of global questions. After one has addressed changes or group differences on the main constructs of interests, we may want to know answers to questions such as Do the clients feel better? Do they see life differently? Do they relate better to significant others? These are global questions, but the global questions of life are not trivial. In using measures to address them, it is important to ensure that other measures are also included to better evaluate the critical constructs that the investigator may wish to talk about in explaining the findings. Also, it is useful to evaluate the global ratings within the study (e.g., to correlate them with other measures and to regress other variables onto them) to facilitate interpretation of what they measure and mean.

Self-Report Inventories, Questionnaires, and Scales

Characteristics   Self-report inventories, questionnaires, and scales are the most commonly used type of measures within clinical research. These measures require clients to report on aspects of their own personality, emotions, cognitions, or behavior. Unlike global ratings, such measures typically include multiple items that are designed to sample specific domains of functioning (e.g., depression, quality of life, psychopathy) and often have extensive supportive data on the construct validity of these domains.

The widespread use of self-report measures can be traced to several factors. First, an obvious factor that makes self-report measures absolutely central is the fact that many states, feelings, and psychological problems are defined by what clients say or feel. Persons may feel helpless, self-critical, generally unhappy, or have a low self-esteem; self-report is a direct assessment of these feelings, thoughts, and perceptions. Second, self-report measures permit assessment of several domains of functioning that are not readily available with other assessment techniques. The client is in a unique position to report his or her own thoughts, feelings, wishes, and dreams, and overt acts and his or her states and behaviors across a wide range of different situations and hence can provide a comprehensive portrait of everyday performance. Third, the ease of administration has made such measures especially useful for purposes of screening. Screening refers to the initial assessment phase in which the investigator must select a small sample of cases from a larger population. Often a simple assessment device (e.g., self-report scale) is used as a means to divide the sample. Individuals who meet particular criterion levels on the self-report measures or questionnaires can be selected and studied more intensively through other techniques.

There are many different types of self-report measures—so many that it is difficult to consider them as part of a single category. For many self-report measures, extensive research exists. For example, one of the most widely investigated measures in clinical psychology is the Minnesota Multiphasic Personality Inventory, an objective self-report test that has been the topic of over 12,000 books and articles and has now spanned research for a period of almost 6 decades. The revised version (MMPI-2) includes 567 true–false items and multiple scales that assess different facets of personality and psychopathology (Butcher, Graham, Williams, & Ben-Porath, 1990; Graham, 1990). The measure is often used in its entirety, but several of its subscales have been used and validated by themselves (e.g., measures for alcoholism, depression, anxiety). The overall scale has been used with diverse populations (e.g., psychiatric patients, prisoners) and for multiple purposes (e.g., screening of prospective employees, treatment planning, evaluation of therapy outcome). Apart from a single measure, there is an extraordinary large range of measures designed to assess an overwhelming number of characteristics, traits, states, moods, feelings, impulses, strivings, and trepidations. Self-report measures can assess diverse aspects of a given characteristic or multiple characteristics by having the client respond to many different items. The number of measures available and the number of personality characteristics that can be assessed make self-report measures very convenient and widely used.

Issues and Limitations   There are two general categories of problems that characterize many self-report measures: the biases on the part of the participant and lack of evidence that the measure assesses the construct of interest. First, self-report measures are a candidate for distortion on the part of the subjects. Distortion refers to the alteration of participants' responses in some way in light of their own motives or self-interest. At the extreme, participants can dissimulate to such a degree that the answers they report are simply untrue. Occasionally, inventories have special scales (e.g., Lie scales) to assess the extent to which the subject is not telling the truth, is being inconsistent, or is endorsing response alternatives that are extremely unlikely. Blatant dissimulation aside, subjects are likely to alter slightly the image of themselves that they present and to interpret very loosely the meaning of the items so that they appear to place themselves in the best possible light. The tendency to do this is referred to as *social desirability* and has been shown to be extremely pervasive on self-report measures. Long ago we learned that inventories designed to measure psychiatric symptoms and personality traits often correlate very highly with measures of social desirability (e.g., Edwards, 1957). Thus, individuals who complete self-report items are likely to endorse the socially condoned behaviors rather than the socially inappropriate behaviors. The pervasiveness of social desirability as a response style has led investigators to posit a specific personality trait referred to as the *need for social approval* (Crowne & Marlowe, 1964). Individuals who are high in their need for social approval on a self-report measure behave in experimental situations in a way that maximizes approval from others. Thus, the bias on self-report inventories has behavioral correlates beyond the testing situation.

There are other biases that may operate depending on the format of the self-report measure. Showing a tendency to acquiesce or agree with items (e.g., in true–false format) regardless of their content, to check extreme values on rating scales, to give cautious or qualified answers, and to be inconsistent across items are some of the biases that may emerge. In treatment evaluation, another source of bias that has been discussed but not well studied pertains to changes in severity of symptoms that have little to do with genuine improvements. Before therapy, clients may exaggerate their complaints because the exaggerations may ensure that they receive treatment or increase the speed with which treatment is provided. After therapy, clients may respond to the same measures in a more socially desirable fashion in the sense that they provide the therapist and clinic with evidence of improvement, presumably the reward of providing treatment. The changes in self-report responses before and after therapy due to exaggeration and underplaying of problems has been referred to as the *hello–good-bye effect* (Meltzoff & Kornreich, 1970). This effect is difficult to estimate because of the actual changes in treatment or because of influences such as statistical regression, that is, improvements that may result simply from having extreme scores at the initial assessment.

The problems of distorting answers on self-report inventories (e.g., socially desirable responding) stem from the fact that the subjects are aware that they are being assessed and act differently than they ordinarily would respond without this awareness. Because participants are aware of the assessment procedure, they can bring to bear their own motives and self-interest in responding. The extent to which distortion may occur is a function of many factors, including whether subjects can detect the purpose of the measure and whether their motives are consistent with those of the investigator. Presumably, the conditions for responding on self-report measures can be arranged in such a fashion as to minimize distortion, although how low the minimal level will be is open to question. Having clients complete tests under conditions of anonymity, ensuring confidentiality, providing incentives for candor, or conveying to the client that his or her best interests are served by honest self-evaluation are designed expressly for this purpose.

The pervasive use of self-report inventories and questionnaires derives in part from their ease of use. However, the use of such measures would have ended or diminished greatly if they had been shown to provide meaningless information. In fact, self-report inventories have been extensively validated and shown in many instances to relate to non-self-report criteria. Even in cases in which we might expect maximum bias or distortion, meaningful validation data are provided. For example, if we ask parents to complete a measure that assesses the likelihood that they physically abuse their children (Milner, 1989) or ask adolescents to report the extent to which they engage in delinquent behavior (Elliott, Dunford, & Huizinga, 1987), we would expect socially desirable responding and denial as a rule. In fact, quite reliable and valid data that elaborate the nature, characteristics, and predictive benefits of self-report of the respective constructs have been generated. Thus, the use of self-report is not merely a matter of convenience in selecting measures. The primary concern is the pervasive use of self-report measures and in any given study the sole reliance on self-report as a method of assessing the construct or domain of interest.

Projective Techniques

Characteristics   *Projective techniques* refer to a specific class of measures that attempt to reveal underlying intrapsychic characteristics, motives, processes, styles, themes, and sources of personality conflict. These characteristics are measured indirectly. Clients are provided with an ambiguous task to which they are free to respond with minimal situational cues or constraints. The ambiguity of the cues and minimization of stimulus material allow the client to freely project onto the situation important processes within his or her own personality.

There are many projective techniques that differ according to the responses required of the subject, the type of stimuli presented, the manner in which content or style of responding is interpreted, the purposes of the test, and other factors. Among the most commonly used are the Rorschach Test and the Thematic Apperception Test, which serve as a useful frame of reference. These tests present stimuli to the subject that consist of inkblot designs or unclear drawings, respectively. The participant is required to interpret what he or she sees. The stimuli are ambiguous so that they can be interpreted in an indefinite number of ways. The purpose of making the stimuli ambiguous is to examine the material or content the subject produces. Given the ambiguous stimuli, this material is considered to be a product of the individual's personality and reflect unconscious processes, underlying themes and motives, and conflicts.

Responses to projective techniques are considered to be traceable to content themes and perceptual processes that unify and organize personality. Content domains such as how the individual handles sexual or aggressive impulses, relates to authority, or expresses need for achievement stylistic or coping methods such as expressing affect and managing needs, are inferred. The many different interpretations provided by the subject usually are condensed to reflect a small number of themes or processes. Performance on projective tests has been viewed as a way to provide insights on the inner workings and organization of personality. Indeed, in conveying this point, some projective techniques (e.g., Rorschach) are considered to reflect a method to evaluate perceptual and associative processes rather than a test per se (Weiner, 1995). The measures provide broad themes, styles of coping, attitudes, and other general facets of personality. The level of analyses has contributed to the widespread use of the measures in clinical settings (Watkins et al., 1995). Among the advantages considered to accrue to projective techniques such as the Rorschach is the reduced vulnerability to response sets and biases that might be evident on self-report inventories. Although subjects may adopt particular strategies as they make their responses, the specific areas that are to be measured and the scoring of answers are clearly less transparent to the subject than would be the case in self-report inventories.

Issues and Limitations   Projective techniques have received considerable attention in personality assessment. Their use and popularity have waxed and waned during the past 30 years due in part to their association with a particular theoretical approach toward the nature of personality. Several projective techniques have adhered to intrapsychic models, primarily psychoanalytic models that explain human functioning in terms of underlying personality characteristics and psychodynamic processes.

Research on projective techniques has enjoyed a resurgence of interest in personality assessment (Craik, 1986). Developments and current topics in central interest in psychoanalytic theory (e.g., object relations) and methods of scoring diverse scales have been reflected in accelerated research on projective techniques (Erdberg, 1990; Stricker & Healey, 1990). Nevertheless, use of the measures is generally restricted within pockets of clinical psychology. The measures are not routinely incorporated into studies related to topics such as the diagnosis, assessment, and treatment of clinical dysfunction, treatment process research, and studies of special populations. Studies utilizing projective techniques address these diverse topics. However, when compared to other types of measures, such as self-report inventories, projective techniques are less frequently employed.

Many projective techniques traditionally have relied heavily on interpretations and inferences of the examining psychologist. Scoring methods of many projective methods are somewhat cumbersome and complex (Groth-Marnat, 1997), and some of the major scoring methods have been subject to criticism (Exner, 1995; Nezworski & Wood, 1995). These interpretations often have been shown to be inconsistent across examiners, which has led researchers to question the basis for making judgments about personality.

Many changes within the field of clinical psychology have reduced the attention accorded projective techniques in research and in graduate training. Salient influences include the emergence of cognitive psychology and interest in assessment of cognitive processes (e.g., beliefs, attributions, expectations), the development of personality assessment in terms of broad traits (e.g., Big 5 personality characteristics) rather than psychodynamic process, and the move within psychopathology research to describe symptoms rather than draw inferences of what they may putatively reflect (e.g., American Psychiatric Association, 1994). The latter influences have with them strong traditions of empirical research and test validation in ways that are part of more mainstream clinical research.

In light of the complexity of scoring, many projective measures are not likely to be adopted casually to expand an assessment battery. Thus, if the investigator would like to assess aggression, symptoms, or stress and wishes to choose multiple methods to operationalize the construct, projective tests are not the usual choice. Investigators are more likely to select measures that are more convenient to administer and score. Notwithstanding these considerations, projective techniques have occupied a very special place in clinical assessment. The full range of clinical topics including "normal" functioning of personality, characteristics of different diagnostic groups, personality and human performance, and other areas can be evaluated from the standpoint of intrapsychic processes. Elaboration of the content areas of the field and development of new tests and scoring methods have made projective assessment an area of work in its own right.

Direct Observations of Behavior

Characteristics   Several measures assess behavior of interest by looking at what the client actually does. The overt behaviors may be sampled from how the client performs in everyday situations or in situations that are designed explicitly to reveal specific responses. Thus, the resulting responses are considered to provide actual samples of the relevant behaviors rather than more indirect indices such as global ratings, self-report, and projective tests.

The potential utility of direct assessment of overt behavior can be illustrated in the context of therapy. Many problems that arise in therapy consist of overt behavioral problems, such as interpersonal (e.g., marital) communication, sexual dysfunction, inadequate social or dating skills, enuresis, tics, stuttering, failure to approach situations because they evoke anxiety, and verbalizations of hallucinations and delusions. The fact that these problems include behavioral components does not in any way deny that other modalities of assessment are important or relevant. Yet, as a modality of assessment, direct observations operationalize problems in terms of ordinary types of performance.

An important feature of direct observations is that measures can be constructed to suit the behaviors of individual clients. Such assessment procedures are constructed by carefully defining the behaviors that are to be observed and scoring the behaviors as the client functions in everyday situations. In many cases, direct observations are made in the situations in which the client's behavior is to be altered (e.g., at home, at school, at work, in psychiatric hospitals, in the community). Sampling behavior under conditions of the natural environment or conditions resembling that environment is designed to assess the behavior of interest directly to diminish concerns about external validity of the findings, that is, whether the results generalize to everyday life.

Observation in the natural environment is not always feasible because many behaviors are private, have low base rates, or raise logistic nightmares (e.g., sexual activity, fire setting, gambling, binge eating at midnight). Observations are often more convenient and permit more detailed evaluation when they are conducted in the laboratory under contrived or simulated conditions. For example, it is possible to observe marital communication in the home among families seeking treatment for marital discord. Yet, the communication is more readily assessed under standardized conditions in the laboratory in which multiple tasks can be presented to the couple and the interactions can be easily recorded (e.g., videotaped and later coded to assess a variety of verbal and nonverbal behaviors).

There are many examples of behavioral measures in naturalistic and contrived (e.g., laboratory) situations. As an example, parent and child behaviors have been observed directly in the home to elaborate interaction patterns that contribute to and maintain child aggressive behavior (Patterson, 1982). Observations of parent–child interaction (Family Interaction Coding System) includes 29 different behaviors that are coded in brief time intervals (e.g., 30 seconds) over a period of an hour and for a period of several days. Prosocial and deviant child behaviors (e.g., complying with requests, attacking someone, yelling) and parent behaviors (e.g., providing approval, playing with the child, humiliating the child) are included. Observations are conducted in the home when family members are together and under conditions that are standardized to the extent possible (e.g., no television watching, no outgoing phone calls). The observational system has led to significant advances in understanding parent–child interaction and the development of aggressive behavior (Patterson et al., 1992).

Parent and child interaction has also been observed in the laboratory, which is usually more feasible from the perspective of the family. Videotaping is readily accomplished in the laboratory and permits review of the interactions, repeated evaluation of the material to provide new measures (e.g., ratings of affect, which go beyond counts of the behaviors themselves). Certainly, videotaping can take place in naturalistic situations such as the home and at school, although this in fact is much less practical for most researchers than assessment in the laboratory.

Issues and Limitations   Because the behaviors of interest are observed directly, the measures are seemingly straightforward indices of the problems. Yet, even direct samples of behavior are not necessarily representative samples of what behaviors are like during periods when samples are not obtained. It is possible that the sampled behaviors or period of time when assessment is conducted do not accurately portray the client's performance at other times. If the periods of observation samples (e.g., 1 hour of observation per day) are to represent all the potentially available observation periods (e.g., all waking hours), assessment methods need to ensure that there are no differences that occur across the available periods of assessment. This can be accomplished by randomly selecting periods throughout the day for observation. Although this is not feasible for most behaviors because of practical considerations, it would seem to resolve the problem of obtaining a direct and representative sample of behavior. More important perhaps than randomness of the period in which behavior is assessed are the conditions in which assessments are conducted. Individuals are aware of assessment and indeed in the usual situation must be so because of ethical obligations of the investigator. Performance may change when individuals are aware they are being studied.

As noted earlier, many direct observations are made in contrived situations in the laboratory. Yet, performance in contrived situations may differ considerably from what would be reflected in everyday life. Marital interaction and communication in a laboratory may reflect dysfunction but still not resemble very closely the nature of the interactions in everyday life in the privacy of one's own home. Participants may be aware of the special assessment arrangement and respond differently as a result (e.g., show less intense conflict and no physical abuse). Simulated situations are not inherently limited. However, direct observations cannot be assumed to be valid, that is, to relate to performance in other settings better than other types of measures (e.g., self-report inventories) can. Validational evidence is needed to draw conclusions about the generality of the measures to the extent that the conditions of measurement differ from those of behaviors in everyday life.

On balance, direct observations provide a unique focus that extends the method of evaluation beyond the more familiar and commonly used self-report scales and inventories. Also, for many facets of functioning studied in clinical psychology (e.g., attachment patterns, agoraphobia, panic attacks, child-rearing practices), overt behavior plays a major role. Evaluation of samples of behaviors can provide central information.

Psychophysiological Measures

Characteristics   Psychophysiological measures refer to assessment techniques designed to examine biological substrates of affect, cognition, and behavior or the links between biological processes and psychological constructs. The number of available psychophysiological measures is vast and includes measures of different types of functions (e.g., arousal of the autonomic system) and systems (e.g., cardiovascular, gastrointestinal, neurological). In clinical research, psychophysiological measures have been used rather extensively to assess arousal (e.g., in response to anxiety-provoking stimuli) and response to stimuli (e.g., fear-related factors) that are not consciously identified or recognized by the individual through self-report.

An important use of psychophysiological measures is to focus on biological underpinnings, mechanisms, and processes related to psychological functioning. Currently, neuroimaging is of keen interest with use of techniques such as positron emission tomography (PET) and magnetic resonance imaging (MRI). For example, fast magnetic resonance imaging (fMRI) permits one to identify areas of the brain that are activated when individuals are given a task to perform. The nature of the task can call on different psychological abilities (e.g., memory, problem solving). From activity that is evident from the imaging techniques one can hypothesize neurological processes involved. Also, differences among patient groups (e.g., individuals with various diagnoses) are studied with fMRI and other imaging techniques to focus attention on possible biological underpinnings or correlates of dysfunction (Peterson, 1995). Obviously, imaging techniques require quite special equipment, facilities, and training and hence are not standard fare in assessment batteries in most programs of clinical research.

A major area within psychology that has given great attention to psychophysiological response assessment is biofeedback. Biofeedback explicitly attempts to alter performance of psychophysiological functioning. Several measures have been used to look at the effects of feedback on cardiovascular responses (e.g., heart rate, blood pressure), electromyographic responses (muscle tension), electroencephalographic responses (e.g., alpha activity, seizure-related neurological activity), skin temperature, gastrointestinal responses (e.g., activity of the colon, sphincter reflexes), and others. Biofeedback involves use of psychophysiological assessment devices and is unique in that sense.

Depending on the target focus, physiological functioning may be viewed as a direct, or as the most direct, measure of the problem of interest. For example, in the area of sexual arousal, sexual stimuli can be presented in the actual situation, on slides or on audiotape to determine whether the stimuli arouse the clients. Arousal to the stimuli can be assessed directly by looking at blood volume changes in the penis or lining of the vagina. Such assessment does not replace or obviate the need for a self-report assessment of arousal but points to the possibility of direct assessment of the physiological aspects of arousal.

Psychophysiological measures have also figured prominently in the area of anxiety management and its treatment (Marks, 1987). Treatment studies have relied heavily on heart or pulse rates as measures of anxiety. Traditionally, physiological arousal has played a central role in conceptualizing emotional states such as anxiety. As a result, research has attempted to assess the level of physiological functioning as individuals experience specific emotional states. Obviously, when physiological measures can be uniquely associated with experienced states, such measures present very important advances in psychological assessment. One reason is that physiological measures are less subject to some artifacts that seem to plague many other measures. For example, response patterns such as socially desirable responding and acquiescence do not seem relevant when monitoring such measures as heart rate, blood pressure, and respiration rate. Also, voluntary alteration of responses to psychophysiological measures in light of demands of the experiment situation are likely to be less than the alteration likely to occur on self-report or behavioral test measures. For these reasons, psychophysiological measures often have been regarded as direct measures to circumvent many sources of artifact and bias present in other modalities of assessment. Nevertheless, psychophysiological measures have their own sources of problems, artifact, and bias.

Issues and Limitations   A view traditionally adhered to in psychophysiology, but long since challenged, was that many psychological states can be identified with specific and straightforward physiological measures. There was a hoped-for simplicity in which the measure could relate directly and simply to some underlying state. As measures become more fine-grained and complex and dynamic biological processes can be assessed, there may be greater movement in this direction. However, the view tended to oversimplify the nature of psychophysiological responses. Response systems can be measured physiologically but they are not isomorphic with psychological states and there are remarkable individual differences in the patterns of responding among subjects. For a set of measures within a given system (e.g., heart rate, blood pressure, and blood volume as measures of the cardiovascular system) and across systems (e.g., measures of cardiovascular functioning, respiration, skin resistance), responses to specific events may not be interrelated in a consistent fashion for different subjects. This state of affairs has led to much less emphasis on measuring general constructs such as anxiety or emotional states and more emphasis on viewing assessment alternatives as reflecting more specific psychophysiological functions. Specific research is needed to validate measures of physiological measurement to ensure that they are in fact related to the construct of interest. Indeed, interpretation of many psychophysiological measures, that is, what processes they *really* reflect, is a significant issue for many measures (Tomarken, 1995). The ambiguity in many cases stems from the fact that multiple systems and processes can affect performance on the measure; inferring one specific type of process as mediated by a specific system alone is not always clear.

There are considerations in using psychophysiological measures that are much more mundane than concerns about precisely what is being measured. Psychophysiological recording often requires rather expensive equipment, particularly if multiple response systems are monitored simultaneously. Also, someone in the laboratory usually is needed to maintain, repair, and calibrate the equipment. The expense is prohibitive for many research programs. For other measures that are not so difficult to obtain (e.g., blood samples, salivary cortisol), procedures to maintain the samples and to ensure their proper analyses are obviously critical.

Artifacts unique to particular assessment methods can influence responsiveness on measures. Movements of the subject, changes in respiration, electrical interference from adjacent equipment, and demands of the situation may enter into the responses of subjects who are connected to various devices. Whether the potential sources of artifact occur is in part a function of the particular measures used and the nature of the recording system. For example, inadvertent or intentional changes in respiration on the part of the participant can affect heart-rate data and can introduce artifacts. Such influences can be readily controlled or addressed by monitoring systems that might mediate changes in the response of interest or by ruling out the possibility of involvement in a specific system by removing its influence (as in the case of animals given curare so that skeletal responses cannot alter heart rate).

Psychophysiological measures provide unique information and level of analysis in relation to the available assessment modalities. The measures are developing in two directions. First, higher resolution and finer-grained methods of assessing brain processes and functions no doubt will continue to emerge and use of these methods requires continued advances in hardware and software. The significance of these assessment developments pertain to closer examination of mechanisms, processes, and substrates of more complex and dynamic biological functions. Second, more physiological measures that permit wider use beyond well-equipped laboratories are likely to be available. More portable, less expensive, and user-friendly measures also have increased (e.g., caps that can be worn to assess electroencephalographic activity or sleep patterns, automated blood pressure cuffs). Thus, many measures have become more practical and less expensive and can be more easily integrated into assessment batteries.

General Comments

This overview of major modalities of assessment is not intended to be complete in terms of the number of modalities available or the variations within each modality. Major options were highlighted that may be differentially relevant for an investigation depending on the purpose and constructs of interest on the part of the investigator. Selection of a given modality of assessment might be dictated by theoretical predictions, the nature of the client's complaint, and interpretation of the therapist as to the primary modality of the problem. Practical decisions might also dictate the methods of assessment finally selected.

The discussion has focused on assessment modalities free from the content areas of clinical psychology. Often the measures are dictated by the content area and the interests they inherently reflect. For example, within clinical psychology a great deal of research focuses on neuropsychological assessment. The area considers the diagnosis and evaluation of neurological and cognitive functioning as, for example, associated with brain injury, psychological dysfunction, medical illness, and aging. A variety of specific measures and tasks are routinely included to assess intellectual skills, sensation, memory, speech perception, tactile discrimination, and other domains (Goldstein, 1990). Many measures are regarded as standard to address the range of questions that neuropsychological assessment requires. For other areas of research in clinical psychology, one might identify measures and modalities in frequent use. The issue for this discussion was options for selecting dependent variables more generally.

In most studies it may be difficult to discern precisely why one modality of assessment was selected rather than another. Yet the description of the purpose of the research should directly state why a particular modality has been selected. Within that modality it is desirable to justify further why a particular measure was selected. In most cases in which such a justification is not explicit, there may be extensive evidence attesting to the utility, reliability, and validity of the assessment technique. In other cases, many options might be available and the decision appears arbitrary. Specific hypotheses about the constructs that constitute the dependent measures may dictate not only the modality of assessment (e.g., psychophysiological measures) but also the particular measure within the modality (e.g., heart rate rather than skin conductance). For a given research or clinical purpose, one modality may be more well suited than another because it reflects the construct and level of analysis of interest (e.g., projective techniques for unconscious processes; behavioral measures for samples of everyday interactions). However, one type of measure is not inherently superior to another. The investigator's purpose or concern about a particular source of bias or artifact may dictate which modality of assessment and measurement devices within a given modality will be appropriate.

The use of different assessment modalities in light of purposes of the study is nicely illustrated in an investigation of adult heterosexual males who varied in their attitudes toward gay individuals (Adams, Wright, & Lohr, 1996). The study compared homophobic and nonhomophobic males and the extent to which they were sexually aroused by various stimuli. Homophobia was defined as negative emotional responses (e.g., fear, anger, anxiety, discomfort, and aversion) in the context of interacting with gay individuals. Males who identified themselves as exclusively heterosexual were divided (median split) into two groups (homophobic and nonhomophobic) on the basis of a measure used to operationalize homophobia. All subjects were then exposed individually to videotaped segments of erotic material depicting explicit heterosexual activity, female homosexual activity, and male homosexual activity (presented in counterbalanced order across subjects). Sexual arousal in response to these videos was measured with two modalities. Self-report ratings of arousal included subjects' reports of their arousal (how "turned on" they were) and ratings of the degree of penile erection (1–10 point scale). The psychophysiological measure was a penile plethysmograph, a strain gauge (mercury in rubber ring) that assessed penile circumference. This is a frequently used and validated measure of degree of male sexual arousal.

Among the findings, homophobic and nonhomophobic males did not differ in subjective ratings—both groups reported arousal to heterosexual and female homosexual videos and these ratings were higher than those given for the male homosexual videos. On the psychophysiological measure, both groups were aroused by and did *not* differ from each other in their arousal to heterosexual and female homosexual videos. However, homophobic males were significantly more aroused to male homosexual videos than were the nonhomophobic males. (The level of arousal among homophobic males was lower for male homosexual videos than for the other types of videos.) In light of the different patterns across measures, the authors concluded that homophobic males are sexually aroused by homosexual stimuli, although they may not recognize it. The different patterns of responding across modalities raise intriguing hypotheses about potential discrepancies between response systems and aspects of homophobia.

In the above study, separate assessment modalities were central to the goals of the study, namely, to see whether awareness of arousal (self-report) and physiological arousal might show a different pattern. Multimeasures and measures from different modalities are valuable as a general strategy in research, regardless of whether one is making predictions about discrepancies among measures. Each modality of assessment includes different sources of bias and potential limitations. No single measure overcomes all the problems that arise in assessment. Indeed, the measures are complementary. Selecting several different measures, each with different sorts of problems, increases confidence that the response dimension of interest in fact is being assessed. Using separate measures can help distinguish responses that may be due to methodological idiosyncrasies of a given assessment device from systematic changes in the construct or domain of interest.

MEASUREMENT STRATEGIES AND ISSUES

Use of Multiple Measures

As a general rule, multiple measures ought to be used in a given study to assess the (or each) construct of interest. This makes the study more complex in many ways (e.g., time consuming for the participant, data scoring for the investigator, potential inconsistencies in the results). The recommendation is based on three considerations.

Nature of Clinical Problems   Most constructs of interest (e.g., personality characteristic, clinical problem) are multifaceted, that is, they have several different components. No single measure is likely to capture the different components adequately. Consider the construct of depression. Some components of depression are based on self-report. Individuals *report* that they feel sad, worthless, and no longer are interested in activities that were previously pleasurable. In addition, there are *overt behavioral components*, such as reduced social interaction, changes in eating (more or less eating), and reduced activity. Similarly, *psychophysiological components* include changes in sleep electroencephalogram activity. *Unconscious processes* may reflect sad affect and negatively valenced interpretations of ambiguous stimuli presented with projective techniques. The different facets of depression may overlap but they are not likely to be so highly related that one is redundant with another. Any evaluation of depression in, say, a test of treatment would be incomplete if change were merely demonstrated in one modality. Unless problems are highly circumscribed (e.g., enuresis, isolated fears, and specific habit disorders) or the goal is to address a single facet of a problem, multiple measures are recommended.

Specificity of Performance The prior rationale for using multiple measure focused on the *response* or behavior, that is, that there are many different components that may be of interest. Another side also argues for multiple measure. Performance may vary greatly as a function of changes in the *stimulus conditions or situations* in which the behavior is observed. Multiple measures assess how an individual responds under different stimulus conditions. The measures (e.g., format, items, domains, or context in which the construct is presented) consist of different stimulus configurations in which the construct is assessed; performance is likely to vary across these configurations.

Traditionally, personality has often been characterized as a set of traits. These traits reflect dispositions to respond in ways that are consistent over time and across situations. Trait views emphasize characteristics of performance within the individual. Broad dispositions (e.g., aggressiveness) might lead one to expect performance consistently over time and across diverse situations. Indeed, there are remarkable consistencies in performance over time. Performance also varies markedly across situations for a given individual. In other words, there is a specificity of performance—individuals high in a particular trait may behave quite differently as the situation or stimulus conditions change.

Recall the classic studies of Hartshorne and May (1928; Hartshorne, May, & Shuttleworth, 1930) who examined the moral conduct of children in a variety of different settings. Children were given the opportunity to be dishonest about their performance and to steal on various tasks at home, at school, and in athletic contests. One might expect to find rather high correlations among the measures of dishonesty, suggesting that individuals have general dispositions to be honest or dishonest and are consistent across diverse situations. If fact, there were small positive correlations across situations, indicating consistency to some degree. Yet, the correlations were lower than expected and raised the question about the existence of a general trait of honesty. The major finding was that honesty varied considerably across situations. Thus, how children performed tended to be situation specific. The greater the differences among the situations, the lower the relation between cheating across these situations.

Personality research has indicated that understanding and predicting performance are greatly enhanced by knowing both the disposition or trait within an individual as well as the stimulus conditions and situational determinants in which the individual is placed (Magnusson, 1981). From the standpoint of assessment, this means that a person's performance is likely to vary across measures of a given construct. Thus, the investigator should be prepared for the possibility that changes in dependent measures may be confined to peculiar aspects of a given problem or a particular aspect only in certain situations. Placing faith on demonstrating behavior change in one situation or for one facet of performance may be unwise. Also, multiple measures provide a broader picture of the facets of performance of the construct (e.g., anxiety) to which the results might apply.

Trait and Method Variance Multiple measures of a construct are needed to ensure that the results are not restricted to the construct as assessed by a particular method and measure. Performance on a given measure (e.g., score, level of the characteristic) is a function of both one's standing on the characteristic (e.g., level of self-esteem) and the precise method in which assessment is conducted (e.g., self-report questionnaire, one questionnaire vs. another). In other words, the measure itself contributes to the findings and conclusions.

The contribution of the method of assessment to the score for a given dependent measure can be seen by looking at some of the characteristics of measurement devices in general. When a new measure is developed, it is important to establish that the measure correlates with other measures of the same construct (assuming other measures are available) and that the measure does not correlate with measures of seemingly unrelated constructs (Campbell & Fiske, 1959). The notion of *convergent validity*, mentioned earlier, was used to denote that independent methods of assessing a given construct agree with each other, that is, correlate relatively highly. For example, if two measures that supposedly assess empathy correlate highly, this would be evidence of convergent validity. The fact that the measures converge suggests that they assess the same construct. The notion of *discriminant validity* was introduced to denote that a newly proposed measure should be distinguished from measures of other constructs; that is, little or no correlation. If a newly proposed measure of empathy were found *not* to correlate highly with measures of other constructs that are conceptually distinct from empathy (e.g., intelligence, social desirability, anxiety), this would be evidence of discriminant validity. If high correlations were found between the newly proposed measure and a more established measure of another construct, this would suggest that the measures really were assessing similar characteristics, no matter what the two assessment devices were called. The new measure would be suspect to the extent that the results can be explained by a more well-validated measure whose construct validity (for some other construct) has been established.

The way in which convergent and discriminant validity can be examined is to conduct a study designed to evaluate the interrelations among various measures. Whether one measure *converges* with other measures of the same construct can be assessed by administering two or more measures designed to assess the *same construct* and seeing whether they correlate highly. The way to see whether a measure *diverges* from others with which it should not correlate is achieved by including measures of *different or unrelated constructs* and seeing whether they do not correlate or correlate only to a very small degree. To obtain this set of correlations requires administering a number of measures to the same individuals. Some measures would be designed to assess the same construct or personality dimensions; some would assess different constructs or dimensions.

The correlations obtained to determine convergent and discriminant validity cannot be viewed uncritically. It is quite possible that correlations between two measures will be influenced not only by the *construct* that is being assessed but also by the *method of assessment*. For example, if two paper-and-pencil measures of empathy were administered, they might correlate rather highly. Is this evidence of convergent validity? Actually, it may be that the high correlation is due to the similarity in the method of assessment (two self-report scales) rather than or in addition to the construct being assessed. In addition, it is possible that a high correlation will be obtained between measures because of a common source of bias or artifact. For example, participants may respond in a socially desirable fashion across both measures, and this will be misinterpreted as convergent validity for the construct that the investigator originally had in mind.

To evaluate the contribution to the assessment method it is important to include with the assessment of multiple constructs or dimensions some measures that rely upon different modalities or methods. A *multitrait–multimethod matrix* refers to the set of correlations obtained from administering several measures to the same participants when these measures include more than one trait (construct) and method (Campbell & Fiske, 1959). The purpose of the matrix is to evaluate convergent and discriminant validity and to examine the extent to which the correlations between measures is due to the similarities in the way the responses are assessed (method variance) rather than in what constructs supposedly are measured (trait variance).

Consider as an example a study that assessed depression and aggression (two constructs) among inpatient children (N = 120, ages 5–13) (Kazdin, Esveldt-Dawson, Unis, & Rancurello, 1983). Children, mothers, and fathers completed a questionnaire and an interview designed to assess depression and then a parallel questionnaire and interview designed to assess aggression. Consider this a study with two constructs (depression, aggression) and three methods of assessment (raters). All measures focused on the depression and aggression of the child. Figure 11.1 presents the correlation matrix in the form that permits examination of convergent and discriminant validity and the role of the rater (method variance) in the correlations. Several numbers are in diagonals (not enclosed in triangle). These are correlations indicating when the rater is different but the construct and measure are the same. They are used to support convergent validity. For example, child and mother scores for the Children's Depression Inventory was $r = .10$. Child and father scores for this measure was $r = .40$. These correlations and others in the diagonals indicate that child and parent ratings correlate in the low to moderate range both for depression and aggression.

Of greater interest are the correlations enclosed in the triangles. The solid triangles include measures completed by the same rater. In general, the correlations within a given solid triangle correlate relatively highly. This means that measures completed by the same rater or informant share an important source of variance even if the constructs they rate are different. Indeed, correlations by the same rater who rates different constructs (depression, aggression) tend to be higher than correlations of the same construct (depression) by different raters.

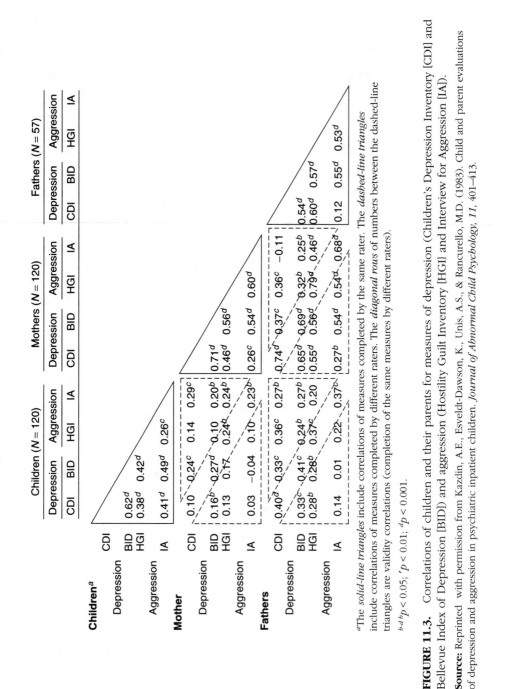

FIGURE 11.3. Correlations of children and their parents for measures of depression (Children's Depression Inventory [CDI] and Bellevue Index of Depression [BID]) and aggression (Hostility Guilt Inventory [HGI] and Interview for Aggression [IA]).

Source: Reprinted with permission from Kazdin, A.E., Esveldt-Dawson, K., Unis, A.S., & Rancurello, M.D. (1983). Child and parent evaluations of depression and aggression in psychiatric inpatient children. *Journal of Abnormal Child Psychology, 11,* 401–413.

[a]The *solid-line triangles* include correlations of measures completed by the same rater. The *dashed-line triangles* include correlations of measures completed by different raters. The *diagonal rows* of numbers between the dashed-line triangles are validity correlations (completion of the same measures by different raters).

[b-d]$p < 0.05$; [c]$p < 0.01$; [d]$p < 0.001$.

For example, child ratings of depression and aggression on two interviews (Bellevue Index of Depression and Interview of Aggression) were correlated at $r = .49$ (same rater and measures but different constructs). This is higher than ratings of depression between mother and child, which were correlated at $r = .10$ and $.27$ (same construct different raters), respectively.

The example permits separation of construct (trait variance) from rater (method variance). The study and many others like it show the strong contribution of rater variance. That is, measures of different traits within raters often are more likely to correspond than measures of the same traits between different raters. This finding has been consistent across different informants including children, parents, teachers, peers, and hospital staff as sources of information. Stated more succinctly, there is a strong method (rater) component that often pervades the ratings even though children can be reliable distinguished in terms of their depression and aggression (Kazdin, 1994).[1]

Assessment in experiments can profit from knowledge that both substantive and methodological characteristics of assessment devices contribute to a subject's score. If information is desired about a construct, it is important to use more than a single measure. Any single measure includes unique components of assessment that can be attributed to methodological factors. Evidence for a particular hypothesis obtained on more than one measure increases the confidence that the construct of interest has been assessed. The confidence is bolstered further to the extent that the methods of assessing the construct differ.

Interrelations of Different Measures

Although the use of multiple measures is advocated as a general strategy for evaluating a construct, this strategy is not without problems. The main issue stemming from use of multiple measures is that the results may be inconsistent across measures. Some dependent measures may reflect changes or differences in the predicted direction and others may not. Indeed, some measures may even show changes or differences in the opposite direction. When results vary across measures designed to assess the same construct, this makes interpretation difficult or at least more complex.

For example, the longitudinal study of physical abuse, sexual abuse, and neglect has shown that youths who experience abuse in childhood (≤ 11 years old), compared to nonabused children, show greater violence and criminal behavior 20 years later (Widom & Shepard, 1996). Interestingly, the results varied by how the key predictors and outcomes were assessed. Early physical abuse in children was identified in two ways (official records, self-report in adulthood) and violence was also assessed in two ways (records of arrest and reports of violent activity). Early physical abuse, as measured by official records, predicted later arrest for violence in young adulthood. However, self-reported physical abuse did not predict later arrests. Interestingly, self-report measures of early abuse predicted self-report of violent activity. The results suggest that common method components (i.e., predictors and outcome measures that share the same methods) are related. Measures predicted less well or not at all when methods varied. A strength of the study is assessing predictors and outcomes using multiple measures and methods.

The failure of multiple measures to agree in a study is a problem only because of traditional assumptions about the nature of personality and human behavior and the manner in which independent variables operate. Actually, there are many reasons to expect multiple measures not to agree. Four explanations of lack of correspondence among measures pertain to the contribution of method variance in assessing behavior, the multifaceted nature of behavior, the magnitude of a client's standing on the characteristic, and the course of changes across different facets of behavior.

Contribution of Method Variance   An overriding assumption of traditional assessment has been that there are different measures of a given construct and that these measures should correlate highly. The notions of convergent and discriminant validity embody this assumption. The notion of convergent validity fosters the view that measures of a given personality or behavioral characteristic have a common component that is highly correlated. The view encourages researchers to conceptualize constructs as unidimensional, that is, as single and relatively simple constructs that measure roughly the same thing but in many different ways. Hence, investigators should search for correlations among measures of a given trait.

The lack of correspondence among measures can be handled by the view that different measures of the same characteristic or trait should not necessarily go together or correlate highly in a given investigation. Specifically, if the methods of assessment differ (e.g., true–false vs. multiple-choice self-report measures, self-report vs. behavioral measures), the lack of high correlations between the measures might be due to the contribution of method variance. With this explanation, method variance becomes the culprit that interferes with interpretation of experimental results. Indeed, method variance may account for the correlations or lack of correlations between measures. The potential problem with this interpretation is that it implies that lack of correspondence between measures is merely a methodological artifact stemming from the assessment devices. Systematic error variance associated with the measurement devices is used to explain lack of correspondence between measures that would seemingly otherwise be related. However, we have learned that performance may differ as a function of different stimulus, situational, and assessment conditions. The imperfect agreement among measures is not an artifact or limitation of the measure but an expected feature.

Multifaceted Nature of Personality and Behavior   The view that characteristics of personality or behavior are multifaceted has challenged the notions of convergent validation to some extent. As discussed earlier, if one views a given characteristic as multidimensional, the insistence on correspondence between dependent measures of that characteristic is reduced. Personality characteristics may have several different components that overlap but are not inter-changeable, redundant, or isomorphic. For example, several measures are available to assess depression. However, depression is not a unidimensional characteristic or simply sadness. Manifold characteristics can be identified involving affect (e.g., sadness), cognition (e.g., beliefs that things are hopeless), and behavior (e.g., diminished activity). Within a given domain, several finer distinctions can be made. Thus, within the cognitive domain of depression, measures are available to assess negative beliefs about oneself, hopelessness, helplessness, and others. Given the multidimensional nature of personality, behavior, and clinical dysfunction, as illustrated by depression, lack of correspondence between measures is to be expected.

On a priori grounds, the different components of a given characteristic might be expected to diverge. For convenience and parsimony, psychologists have adhered to general construct labels such as anxiety, personality, and extroversion. Although proposing such constructs helps simplify findings across different areas of research or different measurement devices, it does not follow that all components of one of these constructs occur together in a given individual (co-occur) or change together even if they are present (covary). There may be largely independent components that individuals refer to under a general construct label. Lack of correspondence among dependent measures related to a particular construct or target problem may not be a problem from the standpoint of interpreting research. Although some lack of correspondence could be attributable to different methods of assessment, measuring different aspects of the problem could also account for the low correlations.

Magnitude of the Characteristic   Another way to interpret the lack of correspondence among dependent measures relates to the magnitude of the characteristic, trait, disposition, or clinical problem. It may be that different measures designed to assess the same characteristic of personality or behavior covary as a function of the client's standing on the characteristic. For example, in the case of anxiety, clients may be measured on self-report, overt behavioral, and psychophysiological measures. The different measures may or may not correspond, depending on the magnitude of the client's anxiety. Clients who are overwhelmed by anxiety may score at a very high level on each measure. At the other extreme, individuals who show absolutely no anxiety may score the equivalent of zero or "none" on each measure. The extreme groups (very high vs. no anxiety) may show a consistent or a more consistent pattern across measures.

Most people are not at the extreme and hence are likely to show varied patterns on measures of the construct across several measures. For example, individuals in the group with only slight or moderate anxiety might report anxiety on self-report measures. Such mild levels of reported anxiety may not be associated with any specific overt behaviors or autonomic arousal. Verbal reports may be more capable of reflecting gradations of reactions relative to measures of overt behavior or psychophysiological states. Thus, some anxiety is evident on portions of the assessment battery.

Lack of correspondence among measures might be expected on the basis of varying levels of intensity of the characteristic for which clients are selected. Consistency may be expected and found for extreme groups (low or high) on the construct when different measures are used, but most individuals in the middle may show greater variability among measures. In this formulation, seeming inconsistencies among measures occur because of characteristics of the sample and the organization of behavior for individuals with different levels of the characteristic of interest.

Course of Behavior Change   The lack of correspondence between measures can be explained by considering how different facets of affect, behavior, and cognition may change over time. Quite possibly, different facets of behavior change at different rates or at different points in time. Hence, studies showing a lack of correspondence between measures from, say, pretreatment to posttreatment assessment, may reflect only that different aspects of performance change at different rates.

Changes over time among multiple measures of a given client characteristic, state, or behavior might or might not go together. When changes across measures do correspond, this is referred to as *synchrony* (Rachman & Hodgson 1974). When changes do not go together, this is referred to as *desynchrony*. In the case of desynchrony, different measures of change might vary independently or even inversely. For example, in the context of adult psychotherapy, evidence suggests that the changes clients make traverse phases; that is, not all domains that are to change will change at the same time. Clients change first in their subjective well-being, then change in symptoms, and finally change in life functioning and in more enduring characteristics (Howard et al., 1993). If measures of these three domains were administered at a given point in time to reflect improvements, the measures would not correspond. This does not reflect inconsistencies in the usual way or have to do with method variance among measures; it has to do with how different systems (e.g., feelings, behavior) and different domains change.

Overall, the lack of correspondence between measures of change (desynchrony) may occur because some aspects of personality or behavior change before others. The lack of correspondence may be a function of looking at the measures at one point only (e.g., immediately after treatment). The different facets of behavior may become synchronous as time progresses and separate response systems come into line with each other. Essentially, therapy may more readily alter some systems than others and alter some systems more rapidly than others. Indeed, analyses of behavioral and self-report measures in among outcome studies have shown increases in the correspondence among measures over time (Hodgson & Rachman, 1974). In general, the notions of synchrony and desynchrony allow correspondence or lack of correspondence among diverse measures and highlight the importance of evaluating the relations among measures over time.

SUMMARY AND CONCLUSIONS

Selection of measures for research is based on several considerations such as construct validity, psychometric properties, and sensitivity of the measures to reflect change or differences. Standard or currently available measures are usually used in a given study because these considerations have evidence in their behalf. Occasionally, investigators alter standardized measures to apply them to populations or to contexts in which the measures have not been used or intended. The measure may be used as originally developed or be modified slightly by rewording or omitting items. Investigators may develop an entirely new measure because a standard measure is not available or because alteration of an existing measure would on prima facie grounds render it of limited value. If a measure is used in a new way, altered in any way, or if a new measure is developed, it is essential to include validity data within the study or as pilot work to that study to support construct validity.

Several modalities were highlighted as a means of encompassing the broad range of measurement strategies used in clinical research. Commonly used measures fall within several modalities: global ratings; self-report inventories, questionnaires, and scales; projective techniques; direct observations; and psychophysiological measures. Within each modality an extraordinarily large number of specific measures exist. The modality of assessment and the specific measure within the modality should be carefully thought out and explicitly justified prior to the investigation.

In general, it is useful to rely on multiple measures rather than on a single measure because clinical problems tend to be multifaceted and no single measure can be expected to address all the components. Performance may vary as a function of the assessment modalities and devices used, and an individual's standing on a particular dimension or construct is partially determined by the method of assessment. It is useful to demonstrate that changes in the construct of interest (e.g., anxiety) are not restricted to one method of assessment. Essentially, demonstrations relying on multiple assessment techniques strengthen the confidence that can be placed in the relationship between independent and dependent variables.

The agreement (correspondence, convergence) and lack of agreement among measures of the same construct raises many methodological issues. The evaluation of trait and method variance was discussed in the context of a *multitrait–multimethod matrix*. The purpose of the matrix was to evaluate the *convergent* and *discriminant validity* of a measure and also the contribution of method variance. It is possible that two measures are related to each other in part because they share similarities in the method of assessment (e.g., two self-report inventories). The use of multiple measures to assess a construct and measures that involve different methods of assessment is recommended.

An important issue in using multiple measures pertains to the lack of correspondence among measures. Thus, an investigation using multiple measures may demonstrate that the independent variable affects some measures in one way but has no effect or an opposite effect on other measures. Hence, what might have been a clear conclusion with a single measure seems obfuscated by the use of several different measures. Yet, the relation between different measures itself is an important aspect of understanding human functioning and the way in which it is affected by independent variables.

NOTE

[1] There are many different ways to analyze the results of multitrait–multimethod matrices to identify the extent to which trait and method variance contribute to the results (Kenny & Kashy, 1992; Schmidt, Coyle, Saari, 1977).

FOR FURTHER READING

Butcher, J.N. (Ed.) (1995). Methodological issues in psychological assessment research. *Psychological Assessment, 7* (3) (special issue).

DeVellis, R.F. (1991). *Scale development: Theory and applications.* Newbury Park, CA: Sage.

Groth-Marnat, G. (Ed.) (1997). *Handbook of psychological assessment* (3rd ed.). New York: Wiley.

Lowman, R.L. (Ed.) (1996). What every psychologist should know about assessment. *Psychological Assessment, 8*, 339–368 (special section).

Murphy, L.L., Conoley, J.C., & Impara, J.C. (Eds.) (1994). *Tests in print IV* (Vols. 1 and 2). Lincoln, NE: Buros Institute of the University of Nebraska. Buros Institute of Mental Measurements: University of Nebraska Press.

Nunnally, J.C., & Bernstein, I.H. (1994). *Psychometric theory* (3rd ed.). New York: McGraw-Hill.

Schutte, N.S. & Malouff, J.M. (Eds.) (1995). *Sourcebook of adult assessment strategies.* New York: Plenum.

Chapter 12

Special Topics in Assessment

CHAPTER OUTLINE

Reactivity of Assessment
> Problems of Reactive Assessment
> Potential Solutions

Unobtrusive (Nonreactive) Measures
> Measurement Techniques
> General Comments

Evaluating Interventions
> Client-Related Criteria
> Efficiency and Cost-Related Criteria
> Consumer-Related Criteria
> General Comments

Follow-Up Assessment
> Attrition
> Decisions and Options
> General Comments

Summary and Conclusions

A variety of assessment issues emerge in clinical psychological research. They can vary considerably as a function of the content area. In this chapter, several issues are addressed pertaining to the types of measures that are used and options for new measures to supplement commonly used assessment modalities. In addition, evaluation of intervention and follow-up raise special assessment issues, which are also discussed. In each area, methodological issues, potential solutions, and assessment strategies are presented.

REACTIVITY OF ASSESSMENT

Measures most frequently used in research are presented to participants who are well aware that their performance is being assessed. Such measures are said to be *obtrusive,* which denotes that participants are aware of the assessment procedures. Obviously, participants know some facet of their personality or behavior is being assessed when they complete a self-report questionnaire, projective test, or are placed into a somewhat contrived situation in which their behavior is observed directly. Participants are aware that their performance is being assessed regardless of whether they know the specific purposes or foci of the measures.

Awareness raises the prospect that performance on the measure is altered or influenced by this awareness. If performance is altered by awareness of the measure, the assessment is said to be *reactive*. It is not necessarily the case that subjects' awareness (obtrusiveness) influences their performance (reactivity). Among other influences, knowledge of the purposes of the measures, motivation of the subjects, and subject roles, contribute to reactivity. Reactivity raises several methodological issues that can influence selection of assessment devices in a given study.

Problems of Reactive Assessment

Several interrelated problems, such as the contribution of reactivity as a method factor in assessment, the external validity of the results, the motivation of the participants to present a particular image, and the influence of the individual who administers the assessment device, are likely to result from reliance on reactive measures.

Reactivity as a Method Factor   The previous chapter discussed the possible contribution of method variance when two measures are similar in method of assessment (e.g., two self-report measures) or in format within a given modality of assessment (e.g., two true–false measures). The similarity in method factors may increase the correlation between the two measures. Aside from similarity in the assessment device, reactivity is another method factor that may contribute to the subjects' scores. Participants may show a general set of responding such as placing themselves in a socially desirable light. To the extent that this response set influences each measure because each is reactive, the correlation among different measures may be higher. The correlation between the measure might be lower if one measure were reactive and the other were not.

Essentially, reactivity may be viewed as a method factor that contributes to an individual's responses on an assessment device. In general, interpretation of psychological measures can be greatly enhanced by using multiple measures that vary in reactivity. If similar results are obtained across such measures, the investigator has greater assurance that conclusions are not restricted to some aspect of the assessment method.

External Validity   The problem of reactivity of assessment can be elaborated by discussing external validity more directly. Two different external validity issues can be raised. The first is whether the results of an experiment using obtrusive assessment differ from results obtained if assessment were unobtrusive. Because almost all psychological research relies on subjects who know that their performance is being assessed, this question is extremely important. The influence of obtrusive assessment on external validity is difficult to address directly because investigators usually cannot administer a given assessment device (e.g., questionnaire) under conditions in which some participants are aware of assessment and others are not. Obtrusive and unobtrusive assessment usually require entirely different measures (e.g., self-report vs. observations reported by peers).

It is possible to see whether measures of the same construct that differ in potential reactivity reflect the same effect of the independent variable. For example, behavior could be directly observed in a contrived situation in the laboratory and in the natural environment in which a contrived situation is designed to appear as part of everyday experience. These would constitute obtrusive and unobtrusive assessment techniques, respectively. If performance is similar between the two measures and conclusions are similar, one can assume that the conclusions are not restricted to potentially reactive measures.

Whether results of an experiment extend to unobtrusive measures is especially important in therapy research, in which the goal of treatment is to change ordinary behavior of the clients in everyday life under conditions in which the clients do not believe they are being specially monitored. Obtrusive and reactive assessment in a laboratory or clinic setting does not really provide the vital information needed about performance in everyday life unless evidence is available that the laboratory- or clinic-based measures in fact correlate highly with everyday experience assessed unobtrusively.

Another external validity issue pertains to pretest sensitization, which has been discussed earlier. Administering assessment devices prior to an intervention may sensitize subjects to the intervention, and the results therefore may not apply to individuals who do not receive a pretest. Whether a pretest limits generality of a particular finding is easily addressed either by studying the independent variable in separate investigations that include or omit the pretest or by using a Solomon four-group design, as elaborated earlier. The problem of reactive pretest as a threat to external validity could be avoided entirely if the pretest relied on an unobtrusive measure.

Motivation of the Participants

One reason that reactivity is viewed as a potential problem pertains to how subject awareness might influence performance. If participants are aware that their behavior is being assessed, they can often alter their responses accordingly to achieve their own purposes. Obtrusive assessment allows for the possibility that participants will respond in a particular way to present a certain kind of image (e.g., place themselves in a socially desirable light). Although we tend to think of self-report questionnaires as vulnerable to such biases, protective techniques and direct samples of behavior can also show such effects (Crowne & Marlowe, 1964).

The issue is not the modality of assessment per se but whether the assessment is reactive. Some methods of assessment (e.g., self-report questionnaires) may be more susceptible to distortion than others (e.g., psychophysiological measures). Yet the reactivity of each different method allows for some distortion. The individual may respond in a way other than he or she would if the measures were unobtrusive.

Influence of the Assessor   The responses of participants in an experiment can be influenced by various characteristics of the individuals who administer the assessment devices (assessors). For example, results obtained from questionnaires or interviews may be influenced by variables such as age, sex, race, social class, and even the religion of the assessor or interviewer (Masling, 1960; Rosenthal, 1969). The personal or demographic attributes of an assessor usually are not of interest in clinical investigations in which an assortment of assessment devices are administered; nevertheless, these attributes can influence the response pattern on the dependent measures.

Investigators often console themselves by the fact that a given experiment may hold potential sources of artifact constant. Thus, if a single assessor administers the assessment devices across all subjects, assessor characteristics could not differentially influence the data. However, in principle, statistical interactions may result from complex relation between the independent variable and characteristics of the assessor. The influence of the assessor may operate differentially across experimental conditions or types of subjects in the experiment. Using two or more assessors may help evaluate the influence of the assessor, but it does not eliminate the possible contribution of the assessor on subject performance. The assessor may be a source of influence primarily because the subject is aware that assessment is conducted and is exposed to someone in the role of an assessor. Assessor characteristics could not as readily exert their direct influence if assessment did not expose the subject to someone in the position of an assessor. That is, this source of bias can be reduced or eliminated through unobtrusive assessment.

Potential Solutions

Several solutions can minimize or eliminate entirely the influence of subject awareness on performance. The solutions vary as a function of the specific method of assessment. With self-report questionnaires and rating scales, the instructions given to the participants often are designed to increase their candor and to decrease the influence of reactivity. One tactic is to tell the participants that their answers to the test items are anonymous and that their individual performance cannot be identified. Of course, in most investigations these claims are accurate, although the participants may not believe them. In other situations, instructions may be provided to minimize the likelihood that participants will answer the items in a particular way. Subjects are more likely to respond candidly and less likely to place themselves in a socially desirable light if they believe they cannot be identified.

Another strategy to minimize the influence of subject awareness on performance is to add *filler* or *buffer items* on a given measure. The filler items are provided to alter the appearance of the focus or to make the measure appear less provocative or intrusive. In the process, the true purpose of the measure, that is, the construct of interest, is obscured. For example, a self-report measure of various psychiatric symptoms, criminal activity, or sexual practices might be infused with items about interests, hobbies, and physical health. The participants are aware of the assessment procedures but the filler items may obscure or diffuse the focus that would heighten reactive responding. The filler items may soften the impact of the measure and the reactions that might otherwise be prompted. Of course, the success of such items to obscure or attenuate the emphasis is a matter of degree; adding a few buffer items (e.g., do you frequently get colds, have you ever collected coins) to a newly developed Jack-the-Ripper Tendency Scale may not help very much.

Another solution is to vary what participants are told about the task and how it should be performed. For example, the purpose of the test may be hidden or participants may be told that their test responses have no real bearing on their future and will not be used for or against them. Alternatively, participants may be told to respond to the items very quickly. The purpose of "speed instructions" is to have subjects give little attention to what actually is measured and hence not deliberate about the content or purpose of the items. These instructional ploys may or may not be plausible, depending on the circumstances of testing and the exact facets of personality or behavior that are assessed.

The use of computers in psychological assessment may have implications for reducing the reactivity of assessment. Computers can serve several roles in psychological assessment, including administration of the measure, scoring, and interpretation of the items (Ager, 1991; Butcher, 1987). In relation to administration, computers permit participants to answer questions directly by responding to items presented on a monitor or screen. The questions are presented and answers are recorded automatically without a human examiner. Computerized assessment compared with a measure administered by an examiner often yields more information about sensitive topics (e.g., alcohol consumption, sexual problems) (Erdman, Klein, & Greist, 1985). In addition, respondents often report favorable attitudes toward computerized test administration.

Computers also permit more sophisticated presentation of items than the usual printed self-report inventory. On the basis of responses that the client provides, the computer can branch into only the necessary remaining items to obtain the score on a given scale or subscale. Also, other measures not readily available when a questionnaire is administered in the usual way can often be derived. Answers on a keyboard or touch-screen monitor of the computer may permit assessment of latency to respond, changing one's answers, and pressure (finger to the keyboard or touch-screen monitor). In any case, it is possible that the use of computers to administer all or portions of the assessment may decrease participants' reactive responding to some topics.

When reactive procedures are used because of the unavailability of alternative assessment devices, one strategy that might be adopted is to encourage participants to respond as honestly as possible. Although this may be naive when participants have a particular interest in their performance in light of some goal (e.g., job procurement, discharge from a hospital), the overall approach may be sound. In many cases, such as evaluation of progress in therapy, it is usually in the best interests of the client to respond as candidly and accurately as possible. In such cases, the message may be worth elaborating to the respondents during assessment to obtain samples of performance that are as representative of daily performance as the measures allow.

Assessment occasionally consists of direct observation of behavior during an extended period. With such measures, different solutions have been sought to decrease the influence of reactivity. For example, when behavior is directly observed in a naturalistic situation such as the home or at school, there may be a novelty effect and the early data may not represent performance. Usually a few days are needed for individuals to habituate to the observers. It is assumed that after a period of time, obtrusive assessment will become less reactive over time and exert little or no influence.

Whether performance under obtrusive and unobtrusive assessment conditions is similar requires empirical evaluation. Even under ideal conditions of administration, the fact that participants are aware that their behavior is to be assessed might affect generality of the results. Possibly the results of an experiment have little bearing on behavior outside the reactive assessment procedures.

UNOBTRUSIVE (NONREACTIVE) MEASURES

The obtrusiveness of measures used in most psychological research does not make the results necessarily inaccurate or unreliable. The only limitation might be that the performance of the participants under conditions in which they are aware of assessment may not resemble performance under conditions in which they are unaware of assessment. The conclusions that can be drawn in a given study can be greatly bolstered by showing that the results are similar across both obtrusive and unobtrusive measures.

Measurement Techniques

Although the importance of unobtrusive measures may be readily apparent, incorporating such measures into research may seem extremely difficult. Nonreactive assessment requires measuring behavior without arousing suspicions that assessment is being conducted. It is useful to mention the major types of unobtrusive measures and illustrate their relevance for clinical and social psychological research (Webb et al., 1981). The major techniques of unobtrusive measurement are listed in Table 12.1. The techniques include simple observation, observation in contrived situations, archival records, and physical traces. Within the social sciences, numerous examples that illustrate how these methods have been used are available.

TABLE 12.1.   Major Methods of Unobtrusive Measurement

Type of Measure	Definition	Examples
Simple observation	Observing behavior in a naturalistic situation in which the assessor does not intervene or intrude. The assessor is passive and does nothing to alter the normal behavior or to convey that behavior is being observed.	Observing nonverbal gestures or body distance as a study of social behavior; recording the clothing individuals wear to reflect mood states.
Observations in contrived situations	Simple observation of behavior in naturalistic situations in which the experimenter or assessor intervenes or does something to prompt certain kinds of performance. The assessor plays an active role without violating the reactivity of the situation.	Using confederates who seem to be in need of assistance to test for altruism; testing for honesty in a situation that allows cheating.
Archival records	Records kept for reasons other than psychological research such as institutional, demographic, social, or personal records.	Records of birth, marriage; institutional data such as discharge records or patient history; documents.
Physical traces	Physical evidence, changes, or remnants in the environment that may stem from accumulation or wear resulting from performance.	Wear on pages to discover magazine or book passages read; deposits of trash to study littering; graffiti to study sexual themes.

Simple Observation   Directly observing behavior as it occurs in naturalistic settings, unbeknownst to the subject, is the most obvious unobtrusive measure. Simple observations in naturalistic settings sample behavior unaffected or less affected by the situational constraints of the laboratory and methodological characteristics of the more commonly used assessment procedures. The fact that the observations are outside the awareness of the subjects eliminates reactivity. The actual behaviors that are observed may also be relatively subtle and may be behaviors that subjects would not suspect reflect the construct of interest.

An interesting example of simple observation derived from the study of people touching each other. One function of touching other individuals (e.g., having a hand on another person's back, putting an arm around someone's shoulder, holding someone's arm while talking to them) is to convey status or power (Henley, 1977). Higher-status or more powerful individuals may be more likely to touch others than to be touched by others. If touching is a sign of power or an unwitting effort to display power, individuals with higher status or who wish to convey that status (e.g., persons who have higher socioeconomic status, are older, male) would be expected to touch others (i.e., their respective counterparts) more than be touched. In fact, unobtrusive observations of touching in public situations supported the prediction. Individuals who were male, older, and rated as higher in socioeconomic status more frequently touched others (females, younger individuals, persons of lower socioeconomic status, respectively) than were touched by them. By itself the findings do not establish that touching necessarily assesses status or power. Yet the observational data have supplemented questionnaire research that has related touching others to dominance, status, and being placed in a position of power (Henley, 1977). Thus, direct observation adds credence to other assessment methods for evaluating social behavior.

Simple observation is very useful because of the almost unlimited situations in everyday life that are open to scrutiny and direct tests of hypotheses. Of course, the method has potential problems. One problem that may arise that would defeat the value of unobtrusive observation in naturalistic situations is detecting the presence of the observer qua observer. As an unobtrusive measure, the observer must not influence the situation. Usually this amounts to disguising the role of the observer if an observer is required in the situation. If performance can be sampled without observers, perhaps by hidden cameras, even less opportunity might be present to alter the nonreactivity of the situation.

Another problem with simple observation is ensuring that the behaviors of interest occur with sufficient frequency to be useful for research purposes (e.g., differentiation of groups, data analyses). Merely watching participants in the situations of interest does not guarantee that the response of interest will occur. The response of interest may be so infrequent as to make assessment prohibitively expensive, inefficient, or of little use.

A final problem with simple observation pertains to the standardization of the assessment situation. The environmental conditions in which the response occurs may change markedly over time. Extraneous factors (e.g., presence of other individuals) may influence behavior and introduce response variability in the measure. The net effect of this variability might be to obscure the effects of the independent variable. Simple and naturalistic observation can be influenced by uncontrolled factors that make it difficult to assess performance in a relatively uniform fashion.

Observation in Contrived Situations   Observations in contrived situations resolve some problems of simple observation. Contrived situations maximize the likelihood that the response of interest will occur. Hence, the problem of infrequent responses or conditions that do not precipitate the response is resolved. Also, arranging the naturalistic situation allows standardizing extraneous factors; thus, the data are less subject to uncontrolled influences. The important requirement of observations in contrived situations, of course, is to control the situation while maintaining the unobtrusive conditions of assessment. This may be accomplished by utilizing an observer, experimenter, or confederate to work with the observer to help stage the conditions that are designed to evoke certain kinds of behaviors.

A prime example of contrived situations for the purposes of assessment are television programs (*Candid Camera, Totally Hidden Video*) that place people into situations varying in degrees of frustration. The situations are well planned so that as each new unwitting subject enters into the situation (e.g., a cafeteria), the stimulus conditions presented to him or her are held relatively constant (e.g., someone sitting next to the subject wearing a feathered hat that keeps hitting the subject in the face while he or she is eating at the counter). The subject's behavior is recorded on film, which is the basis for the television program. The reactions of the participants when they are informed that they are really being filmed for the show often reveal the success in hiding the contrived nature of the situation. Of course, even though the conditions are relatively natural, subjects may occasionally see through them.

Archival Records   Records of all sorts provide a wealth of information about people and have been sampled in psychology to test many hypotheses. The unique feature of records is that they usually can be examined without fear that the experimenter's hypothesis or actions of the observers will influence the raw data themselves. A classic study in clinical psychology that used archival records examined whether schizophrenic patients had a history of social isolation prior to their hospitalization (Barthel & Holmes, 1968). One characteristic of schizophrenic patients is social withdrawal and isolation. This study examined the history of hospitalized patients through an archival record, namely, high-school yearbooks. The number of social activities in which each patient participated was counted from each patient's senior-year yearbook. Social activities included participation in clubs, organizations, special-interest groups, student government, and others. As predicted, schizophrenic patients engaged in significantly fewer activities than did control subjects (individuals in the yearbooks who were pictured next to them). The results supported the notion that schizophrenic patients are socially isolated prior to hospitalization and convey the creative use of archival records.

Archival records have their own sources of measurement problems. One problem is the possible changes in criteria for recording certain kinds of information. For example, records of crime rates may vary over time as a function of changes in the definition of crime or sociological variables that may alter the incidence of reporting certain crimes (e.g., rape). The changes in the criteria for recording information (an example of instrumentation) may lead to interpretive problems regarding the true rates of the problem and changes over time.

A related problem is the selectivity in the information that becomes archival. For example, historical records of births are likely to omit many individuals. Before extensive methods of recording births and population statistics came into use, many births were likely to have gone unrecorded. Births unlikely to be recorded may have varied as a function of socioeconomic status, age, and marital status of the mother, geographical location, and race. Thus, there may be a selective deposit of the information that becomes archival for subsequent research.

Physical Traces   Physical traces consist of selective wear (erosion) or the deposit (accretion) of materials. Either the wear or deposit of materials may be considered to reflect specific forms of behavior. An excellent example of a physical trace measure has been used to evaluate the long-term impact of lead exposure in school-age children. Lead is a heavy metal to which individuals can be exposed through multiple sources including water, air (e.g., from leaded automobile fuel exhaust), paint, and other sources. Lead leaves a physical trace by collecting in one's bones and teeth. Ethics and research review committees tend to be a little testy when an investigator proposes removal of bones from children as part of research. A creative alternative was to collect baby teeth that were normally extruded (Needleman & Bellinger, 1984). Teeth were collected from thousands of children to assess lead deposits. Groups of children exposed to high and low lead levels were formed from this assessment and compared in their academic and classroom performance over a period of several years. The results indicated that relatively low doses of lead exposure are associated with hyperactivity, distractibility, lower IQ, and overall reduced school functioning in children (Needleman et al., 1990). Moreover, follow-up 11 years later showed that the impairments had been maintained.

A potential problem with physical trace measures is that changes over time may occur as a function of the ability of certain traces to be left. For example, research on wall inscriptions (graffiti) in public bathrooms has shown differences in the frequency of inscriptions between males and females and cross-cultural differences in erotic themes (Webb et al., 1981). If one wished to study graffiti over time, as a physical trace, this might be difficult. Many institutions have "seen the writing on the wall" and have used surface materials that are less readily inscribed or cover marks before they accumulate. Thus, the material on which traces are made may change over time.

The selective deposit of physical traces is another potential problem. Physical trace measures may be subject to some of the same limitations of archival data. It is possible for the traces to be selective and not represent the behavior of all the participants of interest. Also, physical traces may be influenced by a number of variables that determine what marks are left to evaluate and hence what data will be seen. For example, fingerprints are the best example of a physical trace measure. However, they are not always available as signs of someone's presence at the scene of a crime. Individuals not interested in leaving such traces are well aware of the necessary procedures to ensure that their presence and their fingerprints go unrecorded.

A final problem with physical traces is that they may become reactive. Once the trace becomes known as a measure of interest, potential subjects may become aware of this and may respond accordingly. For example, social scientists and news reporters occasionally have a keen interest in the trash of celebrities and politicians to measure their private affairs (e.g., correspondence) and potential vices (e.g., weekly consumption of alcohol). Publicity about these practices probably has limited the types of items that are publicly discarded for trash pickup. Secretive, cautious, and perhaps wise celebrities may use other means of disposal (e.g., paper shredder, trash compactor).

General Comments

Unobtrusive measures provide a rich source of information. One advantage of such measures is that they can supplement more commonly used techniques and thereby add strength to the external validity of experimental findings. For example, unobtrusive measures of therapy outcome (e.g., hospital visits, days of work missed) would provide tremendously important information about treatment efficacy and would uniquely supplement the data obtained from the more frequently relied on self-report questionnaires and inventories. If findings are obtained across diverse measures with different methodological features (e.g., obtrusive and unobtrusive measures), this suggests the robustness of the relation between the independent and the dependent variables.

Another advantage of unobtrusive measures is their persuasive appeal. Such measures are often drawn from everyday life (e.g., arrest rates, doctor visits, truancy). Research that reports such measures is often much more persuasive to consumers of research (e.g., policy makers) because the measure (rather than the construct) is of interest in its own right. For example, showing that psychotherapy reduces scores on the best self-report inventories and questionnaires is not likely to be viewed by outsiders as nearly as important as showing that visits to medical doctors or attendance at work are favorably affected. Thus, adoption and dissemination of findings may be improved by supplementing more commonly used psychological measures with unobtrusive measures in which society has interest.

Unobtrusive measures have their own problems. Apart from the issues mentioned already, each measure must be interpreted with some caution. Unlike more commonly used measures, unobtrusive measures usually undergo little validation research, so there are few assurances that they measure what the investigator wishes to measure. In addition, whether the unobtrusive measure will be sufficiently sensitive to reflect the relation of interest is difficult to determine in advance. In general, there is less collective experience with a given unobtrusive measure than with standardized measures such as questionnaires and inventories. The diverse types of reliability and validity are not readily known for most unobtrusive measures.

Unobtrusive measures need to be corroborated with other measures in the usual way that assessment devices are validated. This can be done both by empirical research that examines the relation among different measures and by theoretical formulations that place a particular measure into a context that makes testable predictions. Increasingly greater confidence can be placed in the measure as additional predictions are corroborated. This logic, of course, applies to any psychological measure, regardless of whether it is unobtrusive.

Unobtrusive measures can raise very special ethical issues. Research obligations to participants require that they provide informed consent regarding assessment and intervention facets of the experiment. Unobtrusively observing performance in everyday life and using information to which subjects have not consented violate the letter and spirit of consent (see Chapter 16). On the other hand, unobtrusive measures may vary widely in the ethical issues they raise. For example, archival measures and physical traces may not raise concern because they address past performance and thus could not threaten or jeopardize in any way the identity of the participants. The very nature of unobtrusive assessment means that the investigator must be sensitive to possible ethical concerns in the use of specific strategies.

EVALUATING INTERVENTIONS

A major area of assessment in clinical psychology pertains to the evaluation of interventions as reflected in treatment, prevention, educational, and enrichment programs. Evaluating interventions raises unique issues and opportunities for assessment. Intervention studies are often costly in time and money; they may span years for recruitment of cases and assessment of follow-up. Repetition of the experiment (replication) is not very feasible. Hence, one wishes to maximize the information obtained from the initial (possibly only) test of the specific hypothesis.

Evaluation of client functioning is obviously important as part of intervention research. However, the applied nature of such research raises opportunities to consider measures and outcome criteria that extend beyond the usual scores on various self-report inventories, direct observations, and other modalities. The measures that are used and the ways in which existing measures are evaluated can greatly expand the yield from research. Several options are highlighted here to encourage the development and use of measures other than client change and symptomatic or social functioning. Psychotherapy outcome is used to illustrate several points about assessment strategies, but the comments apply more generally to intervention research.

Client-Related Criteria

In treatment research, conclusions about treatment or the relative effectiveness of different treatments are drawn on the basis of comparing average (mean) scores of clients among various treatment or control conditions. Statistical analyses are the basis for concluding that groups differ. From group differences, conclusions are drawn that one treatment is more or less effective than another or, in the case of no differences, is equally effective. Group differences in mean performance on a measure provide an important, but extremely limited criterion for evaluating treatment. Other criteria that reflect improvement are also very important measures of change.

Importance of the Change   For clinical research, a major criterion for evaluating treatment should be whether the change is clinically significant, that is, whether the improvement enhances the client's everyday functioning. Recent research has begun to address clinical significance as a criterion for evaluating treatment. Assessing the clinical significance of change can be examined by defining a level or range of functioning that is adaptive or that constitutes a normative range. The importance of the change is evaluated by determining whether clients change to such an extent that their posttreatment functioning falls within the normative range. (Chapter 14 elaborates the evaluation of clinical significance and various criteria that are used.)

In general the magnitude of therapeutic change warrants greater attention in treatment evaluation. The importance of therapeutic change may be even more useful in evaluating a given technique or the relative strength of different techniques than the usual statistical comparison of mean differences. In Chapter 6 the notion of normative data was introduced in the discussion of "patched-up" control groups. Treatment studies might profit by adding such a group to determine whether change on a particular assessment device has placed the client appreciably closer to normative levels of functioning, as shown by peers whose behaviors have not been brought to treatment.

Proportion of Clients Who Improve   A problem with a statistical evaluation of group differences is that it averages the amount of change across all clients within a given treatment group. Conceivably, one treatment might make some clients worse but still produce a better overall average change than another treatment. One particular therapy technique may be recommended on the basis of the proportion of clients who are likely to improve. Selecting a treatment that produces improvements in the largest proportion of clients maximizes the probability that a given client will be favorably affected by treatment. In contrast, selecting a treatment that produces the greatest average change may not improve the highest proportion of clients.

For example, in one study, cognitive–behavioral therapy and medication (alprazolam) were compared for the treatment of panic disorder among adults (ages 18–65 years) (Klosko et al., 1990). At the end of treatment, the therapy and medication groups generally were not different from each other on mean (average) amount of change. Yet the proportion of clients who reported zero panic attacks in a 2-week period after treatment provided a clear pattern. The percentage of clients who completed the study and who were free from panic attacks was 87 percent for the cognitive–behavioral therapy group and 50 percent for the group receiving medication. Both treatments produced better results than waiting-list and attention–placebo controls (33 percent and 36 percent free from attacks, respectively). In terms of the proportion of clients favorably affected by treatment, the therapy procedure was apparently more effective than medication.

The proportion of clients who improve may not in itself be an important criterion in cases in which the actual amount of improvement is very small and of little clinical significance. The magnitude of behavior change needs to be considered in conjunction with the proportion of clients who improve. The primary interest is to evaluate which among various treatments produces the greatest proportion of clients who have achieved a clinically significant change.

Breadth of Changes   The efficacy of treatment may be appropriately judged on the basis of how well it alters the problem for which the client sought treatment. Another criterion that might differentiate treatments is the breadth of changes that are produced. Both case reports and experimental research have shown that treatment effects often extend beyond the target focus of therapy. For example, in the context of adult psychotherapy, improvements in psychological symptoms and physical health (e.g., diverse symptoms including pain, headaches, numbness, pains, heart pounding, nausea) are moderately correlated (e.g., $r = .53$ for residual change scores in psychological and physical health) (Luborsky, Crits-Christoph, Mintz, & Auerbach, 1988). It is conceivable that two treatments might be shown to be equally effective in altering psychological symptoms but vary in the impact they have on physical health.

Included in the breadth of changes are ancillary effects or side effects of treatment. Two treatments may be equally effective in altering the target problem but differ in important side effects. Side effects are more commonly discussed in the context of medications and medical treatments (e.g., chemotherapy) in which they may determine how well patients adhere to treatment or indeed whether the patients participate in any treatment. In the context of psychological interventions, side effects are less well studied. Dropping out of treatment is one area that has been studied. For example, independent of their efficacy, various inpatient and outpatient treatments occasionally differ in rates of attrition (Davis, 1973; Rush et al., 1977). Thus, side effects may include whether clients complete treatment and be important supplementary information for evaluating a given treatment.

Other side effects are occasionally shown. For example, parent training is an intervention used to treat noncompliant, aggressive, and antisocial children. Apart from outcome data on child improvements, studies occasionally show improvements in siblings, reductions in parent psychopathology, and improved family interaction (Kazdin, 1997). Another treatment that might be used for these children might be equally effective in reducing symptoms of the referred children but might not show the breadth of changes in other domains of family life. Generally, the breadth and nature of side effects are important criteria for evaluating a given treatment and for comparing the utility of different treatments (Dewan & Koss, 1989). Beneficial and deleterious side effects of treatment have been sufficiently documented to warrant their systematic evaluation.

Durability of Improvements   An obviously important criterion for evaluating treatment is the durability of therapeutic change. In clinical research there is a paucity of follow-up data for virtually all treatments, so the long-term effects of treatments are a matter of surmise. Follow-up data are important in part because the conclusions about the effects of different treatments may vary greatly, depending on when the assessments are conducted (Kolvin et al., 1981; Meyers et al., 1996; Newman et al., 1997). Thus, even if two techniques are equally effective immediately after treatment, the course of change during follow-up may differ considerably. Because fundamental conclusions about treatment outcome can vary from posttreatment to follow-up and from follow-up assessments of different durations, durability of outcome is an important criterion.

Efficiency and Cost-Related Criteria

The above criteria refer to treatment efficacy and the ways in which efficacy can be assessed. The client-related criteria usually involve commonly used modalities of assessment (e.g., self-report, interviews). Other criteria exist related to the efficiency and cost of treatment and can supplement measures of efficacy.

Duration of Treatment The length of time required to achieve a given level of effectiveness is an important criterion for evaluating treatment, particularly in light of current economic pressures (e.g., insurance coverage, managed care) for brief treatment. A technique that reaches a specified level of improvement in a shorter period of time is preferred in general. Hence, showing that two or more treatments do not differ on client-related criteria does not attest to all relevant differences among treatments. Duration of treatment in relation to the changes that are achieved adds important information about treatment.

There appears to be a dose–response relation in psychotherapy (Howard, Kopta, Krause, & Orlinsky, 1986). Approximately 50 percent of adult patients show marked improvement after about 8 treatment sessions; 75 percent show marked improvement after 26 sessions. Even if shorter-term therapy (e.g., 10 sessions) were slightly less effective than longer-term therapy (e.g., 30 sessions), the shorter-term therapy might be preferred by clients, therapists, and agents acting on behalf of insurance companies.

Duration warrants much greater attention in research, apart from the cost-containment issues that have made duration salient. A variety of minimal interventions (e.g., single or few sessions of contact with a therapist, telephone contact only, use of self-help manuals with brief instructions) for alcohol abuse, sexual dysfunction, and cigarette smoking have yielded rather surprising results (Ryder, 1988). In some cases, minimal interventions had as great and as enduring as an effect as more protracted, intensive, and traditional models of treatment and have surpassed the effects of various control conditions. In any case, duration is an important measure to evaluate treatment and has far-reaching implications for disseminability of the intervention.

Disseminability of Treatment Treatments vary in the ease with which they may be widely disseminated to those in need, that is, the public at large. Disseminability encompasses the efficiency of treatment, as reflected in how many persons in need can be served and in the ease of extending treatment beyond the confines in which it was developed. For example, a familiar distinction in treatment is delivery of group and individual therapy. If individual and group treatments were equally effective, group treatment might be preferred because of its efficiency in terms of number of clients per therapist and treatment session. Yet there is more to efficiency in administration than individual versus group treatment.

Some techniques may be widely disseminated because they can be implemented by clients themselves or because they might be able to be presented through mass media (e.g., television). For example, many self-help manuals, also referred to as bibliotherapy, are designed to treat diverse problems such as overeating, cigarette smoking, sexual dysfunction, anxiety, social skills, and conduct problems (Rosen, 1987). Often extravagant claims are made about the effectiveness of do-it-yourself treatments for which empirical evidence is absent. Yet, many treatments have evidence in their behalf. Indeed, a recent meta-analysis concluded that self- and therapist-administered treatments were equally effective when compared to controls and retained their benefits at follow-up (Marrs, 1995). Even if bibliotherapy were less effective, the self-administered treatment may be preferred because it is more easily disseminated to the public on a larger scale than is therapist-administered outpatient treatment. It is likely that extremely severe cases (e.g., of depression, substance abuse) may not respond to self-help manuals, but many less severe cases may be responsive.

Self-help is a matter of degree, and sometimes the therapist can be used to supplement the self-help materials that are used by the clients. For example, the therapist–trainer can guide or lead a group in which self-help manuals and materials serve as the main source of information and intervention (Webster-Stratton, 1996). The role of the therapist in supplementing self-help groups may require much less training than that required for traditional therapy. Hence, treatment may be more disseminable because less professional training is needed to develop therapists. Self-help is not new in developing treatment and as a basis for disseminating treatment widely. Self-help groups led by nonprofessionals have been used for some time in the treatment of alcohol and drug abuse and weight control (e.g., Alcoholics Anonymous, Synanon, and Take Off Pounds Sensibly, respectively).

The use of media such as television, computers, and the internet provide opportunities to disseminate treatment widely. Access to the internet through television and personal computers could reach a large number of individuals for a host of concerns (e.g., child-rearing, coping with stress), problems of living (e.g., divorce, bereavement) and clinical dysfunction (e.g., anxiety disorders, depression). Computerized psychotherapy has been available in some form for decades and continues to develop in treatment outcome studies (Marks, in press). At present, few applications are available in clinical practice, but no doubt this will accelerate with advances in software and software accessibility.

In discussing the ease of disseminating treatment, it is important to mention medication. An advantage of medication is that treatments often can be widely disseminated. For example, when a new drug for depression emerges from clinical trials and is approved for use, it is widely prescribed and quickly reaches millions of clients. Effective psychotherapy, if equally effective or indeed even more effective, is clearly less readily disseminated to others. Of course, disseminability of treatment is only one criterion for evaluating an intervention. The difficulty is that medication, although widely disseminable, raises other issues (e.g., adherence to treatment, side effects, restriction of other behaviors (when combined with other medications or alcohol). The ease of dissemination may be compensated by other issues related to use and effects.

There are no simple measures to assess the ease of disseminating a treatment. Several variables, such as the cost of professional training, complexity of the procedures, and need for ancillary equipment or apparatus, may determine disseminability. The latter criteria should be assessed carefully when contemplating the widespread use of a particular treatment.

Costs   Disseminability of treatment is related to cost; in general, less costly treatments are more widely disseminable. However, cost is important to consider as a criterion for evaluating treatment. Obviously, a less costly treatment is preferred to a more costly treatment if both are effective. There are different ways of evaluating cost.

One cost question for evaluating both large-scale social interventions and individual treatment is the benefit that derives from the costs. *Cost-benefit analyses* are designed to evaluate the monetary costs of an intervention with the benefits that are obtained. The benefits must be measured in monetary terms also. This requirement makes cost-benefit analysis difficult to apply to many psychological interventions in which the beneficial effects might extend well beyond monetary gains (Yates, 1995). For example, providing programs to help parents rear their children may have monetary benefits (e.g., preventing some children from entering treatment, from being adjudicated, from dropping out of school). Another gain may be to increase harmony in the homes of many families, an effect that cannot be readily evaluated in monetary terms. Many returns of treatment can be examined in terms of social benefits, such as those derived from clients' returning to work, missing fewer days of work, having fewer car accidents, staying out of hospitals or prison, and from other measures, that can be translated into monetary terms. Changes on psychological measure are also important to consider from the standpoint of treatment costs.

Cost-effectiveness analysis does not require placing a monetary value on the benefits and can be more readily used for evaluating treatment. *Cost-effectiveness* analysis examines the costs of treatment relative to a particular outcome. The value for therapy evaluation is that it permits comparison of different treatment techniques if the treatment benefits are designed to be the same (e.g., reduction of drinking, increase in family harmony). Such information would be very useful and address important questions independent of narrow debates about statistical differences that distinguish treatments. For example, one study compared two variations of parent training for parents of kindergarten children with behavior problems (Cunningham et al., 1995). One variation consisted of individual treatment provided at a clinical service; the other consisted of group-based treatment conducted in the community (at community centers or schools). Both treatments were better than a wait-list control condition, and on a number of measures the community-based treatment was more effective. Even if the treatments were equally effective, the monetary costs (e.g., start-up costs, travel time of families, costs of the therapist–trainer in providing treatment) of individual treatment were approximately six times greater per family than was the group treatment. Clearly, this is a significant criterion for evaluating the different ways of administering treatment.

Although monetary costs can represent an important criterion for evaluating treatment, psychological costs may also be relevant, although obviously difficult to quantify. For example, treatments may vary on the amount of stress they induce (e.g., flooding vs. graduated exposure for anxiety). The psychological and physical costs of completing treatment might be relevant to assess in evaluating therapy, particularly for techniques that are likely to be aversive to clients. The psychological costs of treatment may be too great to entice participants no matter what the data show about treatment efficacy.

As yet, within psychology, the costs, cost-benefit, and cost-effectiveness measures are infrequently used. Estimating cost is not entirely straightforward because of the range of costs that can be included and the difficulty in translating benefits into monetary terms. Even so, efforts to describe costs of different treatments represent a worthwhile addition to intervention research because decision making for use of treatments at the level for individual services (e.g., clinics and hospitals) and public policy are driven heavily by costs and related disseminability data and, lamentably, often even more by these data than by outcome results related to efficacy.

Consumer-Related Criteria

Acceptability of Treatment   Different treatments for a given problem may not be equally acceptable to prospective clients. Efficiency and cost considerations may contribute to the acceptability of a treatment but there are also other factors. Procedures may be more or less objectionable in their own right, independent of their efficacy. Indeed, many procedures that are readily acceptable to clients often have little or no demonstrated efficacy. For example, commonly advertised procedures to control diet or cigarette smoking are highly sought by clients despite the lack of demonstrated efficacy. On the other hand, there are instances in which several treatment options are available and do have evidence in their behalf. The treatment of depression is one such problem; various forms of psychotherapy and medication are viable options. Although sparse research is available on the topic, some evidence suggests that forms of psychotherapy (e.g., cognitive therapy, behavior therapy) are viewed as more acceptable than is medication for depression (Banken & Wilson, 1992). This is consistent with the greater rates of attrition occasionally (but not uniformly) noted with use of medication rather than attrition rates for therapy conditions in treatment studies for depression (Rush et al., 1977). The point is that in addition to efficacy, it is important to evaluate how acceptable or palatable treatments are to clients. Treatments that are acceptable are more likely to be sought and adhered to once clients have entered into treatment. The wider audience that such highly acceptable treatments attract makes techniques more disseminable.

Techniques might be selected by clients not only for their likely effects but also because of the manner in which these effects are obtained. Thus, stress-inducing techniques (e.g., aversion therapy, flooding) may not be as acceptable as viable alternatives (e.g., incentive systems, cognitive–behavioral therapy). Different treatments also may vary in their objectives. These objectives may be more or less acceptable to clients. For example, some treatments for alcoholism aim for complete abstinence; others aim for controlled (social) drinking. The different goals may make treatments differentially preferred by prospective clients. In making treatment decisions, it would be useful to have clients evaluate acceptability of the procedures (Kazdin, 1986b; Kazdin, French, & Sherick, 1981; Tarnowski & Simonian, 1992). Such information can greatly supplement data on effectiveness and also provide guidelines regarding how to make effective treatments more acceptable.

General Comments

Evaluation of therapy techniques and interventions in general should extend beyond traditional measures of change on a narrowly defined set of outcome criteria. Psychological measures of different modalities are essential and need not be replaced. However, by themselves, they do not address the range of important outcome questions that might be raised both from substantive and decision-making perspectives. The value of various treatments and whether they should be used for the individual client or for large-scale application depends on much more than the average amount of change produced among clients. Multiple criteria are required to address the diverse interests that various parties have in a treatment and its effects. Interests vary among those who receive (e.g., clients), deliver (e.g., therapists), evaluate (e.g., researchers), and financially support (e.g., health insurance) the treatment. Hence, the criteria used for evaluation necessarily depend on many different considerations.

FOLLOW-UP ASSESSMENT

Assessment immediately after treatment or other intervention is referred to as posttreatment assessment; any point beyond that, ranging from weeks to years, typically is referred to as follow-up assessment. Follow-up raises important issues for intervention research. Among the issues are whether the gains are maintained, whether the gains continue to surpass gains achieved without formal intervention (e.g., no-treatment groups sometimes catch up to the treatment group by the follow-up assessment), and whether any conclusions can be reached, given the attrition that may ensue during the follow-up interval. Significant methodological and assessment issues emerge in follow-up and they deserve comment.

Attrition

Ideally, intervention research provides long-term follow-up data (e.g., several years after the intervention), although this is infrequent. For example, in psychotherapy research, most studies do not report follow-up, but among those that do, the follow-up interval usually is a matter of months rather than years (Durlak, Wells, Cotten, & Johnson, 1995; Kazdin, Bass et al., 1990; Shapiro & Shapiro, 1983). There are many methodological problems involved in obtaining and interpreting follow-up data. These problems seem to be greater as the interval between posttreatment and follow-up assessment increases.

Certainly the main problem is attrition. Usually, the longer the follow-up period, the greater the loss of subjects. Obviously, over time it is increasingly difficult to locate or to induce participants to respond. Subjects change addresses, change their names (usually through marriage), enter institutions, die, and do other things that show that the original treatment investigation in which they participated is not the most important event in their lives. Even if subjects can be located, they do not always wish to comply with requests for follow-up data. This, of course, may depend on their view of the treatment and the actual requirements of follow-up. The methods of obtaining follow-up information differ greatly in the extent to which they may inconvenience subjects.

Loss of subjects is a problem because the follow-up data may not represent the true level of functioning that would be achieved if the complete sample were reassessed. The subjects remaining at follow-up may represent a highly select sample and vary from other subjects within the same treatment group in ways that are directly related to the treatment outcome. For example, subjects who are located one year after treatment, compared to those not located at follow-up, may vary in subject and demographic variables, mobility (moving from city to city), severity of the target problem or related problems, and other factors. There can never be certainty that the obtained group represents the group that could not be located, but one can estimate whether various patterns in the data of those missing might alter the conclusions. As a general rule, it is difficult to interpret the follow-up data when attrition takes a significant toll.

Loss of subjects may lead to even greater ambiguity if there is a differential loss among groups in a study comparing several different treatments. Treatments may be responsible for differential loss of subjects. Some treatments may be more acceptable than others or lead to more positive changes at posttreatment or follow-up. Participants may vary in their cooperativeness with attempts to obtain follow-up data as a function of their impressions and benefits of treatment. Hence, there may be a differential responsiveness to solicitations for follow-up among groups. If two treatments differ significantly in their loss of subjects at follow-up, the resulting follow-up data may be difficult to interpret. The fact that different numbers of subjects responded may signify something important about the different treatments. However, the psychological status of the treated clients across groups cannot be meaningfully compared.

Decisions and Options

Several assessment decisions need to be made about the nature of follow-up, such as strategies regarding the modalities of assessment, setting of follow-up assessment, the informants, and method of contacting the clients. The different modalities of assessment (e.g., questionnaires, interviews, direct observations) and their strengths and liabilities were highlighted in the previous chapter. The settings in which follow-up assessment is conducted usually refers to reassessment at the clinic (or laboratory setting) or at the homes of the participants. If the follow-up assessments are conducted in the laboratory or clinic, the clients can be seen and evaluated by trained assessors or can be observed directly for their behavior in the interview situation. A wider range of assessment options (e.g., videotaping, physiological measurement) and better standardization of assessment procedures characterize the laboratory setting. Any advantages of having clients come in for an assessment are likely to be offset by a greater loss of subjects. Asking participants to come in makes follow-up more difficult and costly for the subjects. Subjects are likely to be more willing to chat on the phone for a few minutes at their convenience.

Follow-up assessments are rarely conducted at the homes of the participants in treatment studies. Practical problems of conducting the visits (obtaining permission, costs to assessors who go to the home) make such procedures difficult. Prospective longitudinal studies of children and adolescents more commonly include visits to the home and include well-developed procedures to maintain contact with families and to ensure that the assessments are acceptable to the participants. In many ways, the ideal is to observe behavior of the clients in their natural environment to see whether the changes in treatment have transferred and are maintained in everyday life. If the experimenter or clients cannot provide the information, individuals in contact with the clients may be able to do so.

Decisions need to be made about the informants to be used at follow-up, that is, the persons who will provide information about the status of the client. Obviously, the client is in a unique position to provide information about the benefits of treatment. For many clinical dysfunctions, clients are the primary (occasionally the sole) source of information, especially when private events and subjective states (e.g., headaches, obsessive thoughts, feelings of despair, urges) are evaluated. Concomitant behaviors might be assessed by observers, but self-report is viewed as the most direct assessment of such states. Even outside the context of private events, the perspective of the client is usually central. Consequently, most follow-up assessments utilize the clients themselves as the source of information.

Someone in contact with the client, such as peers, spouse, roommates, employers, teachers, friends, colleagues, or others, can be contacted to be informants. Sometimes clients are asked to identify a relative or close friend who could be contacted by mail for information about the how the client is doing. There are obvious ethical issues and practical problems in soliciting and utilizing informants. It is important to ensure that the informant not jeopardize the status or standing of the client (e.g., having an employer rate problems of the client's substance abuse of which the employer was unaware). Informed consent with the client is obviously a requisite for any use of informants. In addition, the investigator ought to have confidence that the informants have access to the relevant information.

Obviously, the most reliable way to obtain follow-up information is to find a way to utilize an experimenter or assessor as the informant. Assessors can be used to measure overt behavior either at the laboratory or clinic setting or home. On the other hand, practical problems usually prohibit sending someone to measure behavior to each individual client. Telephone follow-up assessment is a compromise that uses the assessor to evaluate behavior of the client directly in a contrived phone situation. Sending an assessor to the client or using a contrived situation introduces reactivity into the situation. Thus, the results obtained might be a partial function of changing the natural situation, a disadvantage that the use of other informants may not have.

Finally, a decision needs to be made regarding how to contact the client. One option is to ask clients at follow-up to return to the setting at which the study was completed and to complete various measures. Face-to-face (live) follow-up assessment is desirable because the assessment conditions are similar, if not identical, to those in which prior assessments (pre- and posttreatment) were conducted. Thus, conditions of assessment are held constant. Also, face-to-face assessment permits the use of a broad range of measurement strategies (e.g., self-report, direct observation, psychophysiological measures). More extensive assessment (i.e., more constructs, more measures) is available because once clients are in the setting, a large block of time may be available. Although more assessment is not invariably better assessment, the options provided by face-to-face contact are noteworthy. Yet, face-to-face assessment is not feasible in situations in which there are multiple informants (e.g., spouses, peers, employers) to evaluate client functioning.

Another option is to mail the measures to the clients or to those who are to complete the follow-up assessment. Persons are asked to complete the measures and to return them, perhaps in a self-addressed, stamped envelope. This assessment option has the advantage that one can usually reach a large number of participants and diverse informants. Also, completing measures at home (for the clients or relatives) is more convenient than coming to the clinic or research setting. Hence, a higher rate of compliance (lower attrition) may be more likely. However, mailing measures has its own liabilities. The investigator is restricted in the range of measures that can be used, namely, to self- or other-report measures that can be completed with little verbal instructions. Also, measures sent by mail, if completed at all, are likely to be completed under diverse testing conditions. Some participants will complete the measures after work, while watching television, while sipping beer, or while listening and nodding half-attentively to a roommate or spouse. The uncontrolled and diverse testing conditions raise the likelihood of introducing additional variability in the measure. A related consideration has to do with the quality of the data. Assessment by mail can lead to missing data from participants who complete and return the measures. Individual items invariably are omitted, completed inaccurately, or are otherwise indecipherable. These problems are less likely in face-to-face assessment because an examiner can query at the moment or remind the person to answer a given item or measure.

Another option is to contact the clients or significant others by telephone. The person is called and the measure is presented item by item over the phone. The caller can be experimentally naive (blind) to the conditions in which the subject participated. The caller can complete the measure as the call progresses by reflecting the verbal answers to the questionnaire or inventory. For later checking, the call can be taperecorded, pending subject permission. The convenience of telephone follow-up assessment is obvious. Clients can respond to items without the effort of either visiting the clinic or taking the additional time to read and complete measures on their own. From the standpoint of the investigator, more subjects are likely to comply with telephone assessment than with other options. Also, fewer missing or incomplete data from clients who do complete the assessment are likely because the caller can ensure the integrity of the measure. Given the ease of administration, it is encouraging to note that evidence suggests that telephone contact can yield equivalent results to those of face-to-face interviewing in the assessment of clinical dysfunction (Wells, Burnam, Leake, & Robins, 1988).

General Comments

Too few follow-up data are collected in intervention studies. The options discussed vary in convenience, cost, and likely success in procuring the data. A number of options can be combined, and at least one option ought to be feasible to obtain follow-up. A very small follow-up assessment battery can be selected from the data obtained at pre- and posttreatment assessment. Usually pre- and posttreatment assessment batteries are quite comprehensive and cover multiple domains, methods of assessment, and measures. From the data obtained at these assessment periods, one can identify statistically which measures, subscales, or items provide the best estimate of other more extensive measures in the battery. The follow-up assessment can be more abbreviated if the full battery is not possible. The specific measures that are used can be dictated by the data and by convenience so that any burden to the subject and costs to the project are minimal.

SUMMARY AND CONCLUSIONS

Subjects are usually aware that some facet of their performance is assessed (obtrusive assessment). The methodological issue with obtrusive measures is that performance may be altered in some way as a result of that awareness (reactive assessment). The possibility exists that the results may be restricted to circumstances in which subjects know that their performance is assessed and that the measures have contributed to the pattern of performance. To ensure that conclusions are not restricted to reactive conditions of assessment, *unobtrusive* or *nonreactive measures* can be used. Because subjects are unaware that behavior is assessed, the resulting data can be considered free from reactive influences and can be used to corroborate or extend more commonly used assessment methods. Unobtrusive measures may be conducted in different ways, such as *simple observation, observation in contrived situations, archival records,* and *physical traces.* Each of these methods has been used creatively in clinical research to extend greatly the conclusions that can be drawn.

Several outcome criteria for evaluating interventions beyond those commonly used in current research were discussed. The criteria were illustrated in the context of psychotherapy research and include evaluating the clinical importance of behavior change; the proportion of clients who achieve clinically important change; the breadth and durability of change; the duration, disseminability, and costs of treatment; and the acceptability of treatment to the clients. These criteria greatly extend the research questions that can be asked about treatment.

The durability of treatment is generally accepted in clinical research as an important outcome criterion. However, follow-up data are infrequently collected to evaluate long-term intervention effects. Many methods of follow-up assessment involving various modalities of assessment, settings in which assessment is completed, sources of information, and different methods of contacting the clients are available. The assessment options are so rich that follow-up assessment in some form can be readily incorporated into intervention trials.

FOR FURTHER READING

Lambert, M.J., Christensen, E.R., & DeJulio, S.S. (Eds.) (1983). *The assessment of psychotherapy outcome.* New York: Wiley.

Meier, S.T., & Wick, M.T. (1991). Computer-based unobtrusive measurement: Potential supplements to reactive self-reports. *Professional Psychology: Research and Practice, 22,* 410–412.

Webb, E.J., Campbell, D.T., Schwartz, R.D., Sechrest, L., & Grove, J.B. (1981). *Nonreactive measures in the social sciences* (2nd ed.). Boston: Houghton Mifflin.

Chapter 13

Sources of Artifact and Bias

CHAPTER OUTLINE

Sources of Bias
> Rationales, Scripts, and Procedures
> Experimenter Expectancy Effects
> Experimenter Characteristics
> Situational and Contextual Cues
> Subject Roles
> Data Recording and Analysis

Subject-Selection Biases
> The Sample: Who Is Selected for the Study?
> Attrition: Who Remains in the Study?

Summary and Conclusions

Artifacts and biases in experimental research refer to extraneous influences that may threaten the validity of an experiment. Each type of experimental validity can be affected by extraneous influences. However, artifacts and biases generally raise concerns with the interpretation of the experiment and outcomes that might be incorrectly attributed to the intervention. Thus, interpretative issues are central to construct validity. An artifact or extraneous influence includes all variables that the experimenter is not interested in examining. The factors that can give rise to conclusions in an experiment are virtually unlimited. Which ones are artifacts and biases depend on the focus of the investigation. For example, one investigator may wish to study the effects of therapist beliefs on treatment efficacy and view beliefs as the independent variable. Another experimenter may be interested in the efficacy of different treatments and regard therapist beliefs as a potential source of artifact. Thus, a given source of influence may be viewed at times as an artifact and at other times as an independent variable.

Influences commonly identified as artifacts evolve through three stages (McGuire, 1969). The first stage is *ignorance*. During this stage, investigators are unaware that an extraneous variable is operative in an experiment and may account for the results. When such a source of artifact is posed, it may be denied. The second stage is *coping*. In this stage, the existence and possible importance of the artifact are recognized. Investigators increasingly recognize the potential influence of the artifact in their experiments and implement control procedures to assess, minimize, or eliminate its impact. The third and final stage is *exploiting* the source of artifact in its own right; rather than trying to minimize or eliminate the effect, research attempts to examine the source of influence as an independent variable. The influence is maximized in experiments, and variations are examined to establish the way in which it operates. At this stage, substantive knowledge accrues and the variable is more widely understood as a source of influence.

This chapter examines several sources of influence often regarded as artifacts in psychological research. Conceptualization of many of these influences has evolved, and they are recognized as important independent variables in their own right. From a methodological standpoint, however, it is important to consider methods of coping with these influences in research and hence to look at different influences as potential contaminants of experimental results. Several types of influence are discussed that may interfere with drawing conclusions about a given independent variable. These include biases stemming from those who conduct research, demand characteristics, subject roles, and subject selection.

SOURCES OF BIAS

Sources of artifact and bias can enter into the research process at many different places. Considered below are several influences from the procedural stage or how the study is run to how the data are treated. In delineating some sources of bias, it is useful to make a distinction between the individual(s) who designs the investigation (referred to as the investigator) and the individual(s) who actually executes it (referred to as the experimenter) (Barber, 1976). Distinguishing an investigator and experimenter may oversimplify the different roles because the same person may serve as investigator and experimenter. Alternatively, there may be multiple investigators and experimenters, or, in automated and mechanized experiments, no real experimenter in the usual sense. However, the different roles or functions of an investigator and experimenter help delineate a number of problems that may contribute to the results of an experiment.

Rationales, Scripts, and Procedures

Nature of the Problem   Potential sources of bias in an experiment include the instructions and experimental material or procedures to which subjects are exposed. The source of bias varies depending on precisely what the experimenter and subject are supposed to do. A major source of bias may result from imprecision in the script or protocol that the experimenter should follow in the experiment. The script refers to the specific activities, tasks, and instructions that the experimenter should administer. Depending on the investigation, this may entail delivering a rationale, providing a brief interview, answering questions, assisting the subject, and performing a task or implementing the experimental manipulation. The experimenter's script must be well specified by the investigator. Failure to specify in detail the rationale, script, and activities of the experimenter has been referred to as the *loose protocol effect* (Barber, 1976).

Several problems may result from failing to specify how the experimenter should behave. First, the lack of specificity of the procedures means that the investigator does not know what actually was done with the subjects and hence cannot convey the procedures to other investigators. The study cannot be repeated by the original investigator or by others because of the lack of important details.

A second problem from not specifying the script is inconsistency among different experimenters when two or more experimenters are used to run the experiment. The procedures may vary systematically from experimenter to experimenter in terms of what is said to the subject, the general atmosphere that is provided, and other features. This variation in experimenter behavior is more likely when details of implementing the procedures are not well specified. For example, in one study, interviewers obtained different sorts of data when the procedures they conducted were not well structured and when they had latitude in devising the questions for the subjects (Feldman, Hyman, & Hart, 1951). On the other hand, very similar data were obtained when the procedures were structured and the questions were specified in advance. Interactions that can be, or by design are, somewhat unstructured or free-flowing (e.g., interviews, psychotherapy sessions), unlike many laboratory arrangements, might maximize the influence of the experimenter (interviewer, therapist) because of the nature of the interaction.

Inconsistencies among experimenters may readily obscure the effects of an independent variable. When the experimenters perform differently, this introduces "noise" into the data. Within-group variability (error variance) is increased, which can reduce the obtained effect size and power of an experiment and threaten the statistical conclusion validity. The effect of the independent variable may need to be extremely potent to overcome this variability. For this reason, it is advisable to standardize the performance of the experimenters so that the experimenters perform alike and so that a given experimenter performs consistently over time.

Standardizing the rationales, procedures, and experimenter's script is a matter of degree. In clinical research it may not be possible or desirable to codify all statements and types of comments made by the experimenter. For example, a therapist may adhere to procedures that are well spelled out. As mentioned previously, treatment manuals are commonly used in research to specify in varying degrees of explicitness what procedures are to be followed during the course of the intervention. Yet the very process of therapy calls for statements on the part of the therapist, and they cannot be completely specified in advance. In the context of therapy, specifying the procedures requires delineating the aspects of treatment considered to be important for change. Of course, not all statements and interactions between the therapist and client can be specified. Additional comments and extended dialogues may arise as distressed clients report events in their lives during the course of treatment. In many areas of research other than therapy, the interactions between an experimenter and subject can be completely specified, and the experimenter may not have to deviate from a carefully detailed script except for an occasional unpredicted question from the subject.

Even if the investigator specified the procedures in careful detail, another problem that can arise is the failure of experimenters to adhere to the procedures. There is no guarantee that the experimenter will carry them out as specified. The experimenter may alter the procedures to suit his or her own personality or may neglect specific aspects that appear irrelevant, awkward, or redundant. Over time, experimenters may become increasingly divergent in how they run subjects; hence, they may deviate from the original procedures. Therefore, the task of the investigator is not only to specify the experimenter's script in detail but to ensure that the script is executed as specified.

Recommendations   To ensure that the experimental procedures are conducted in a consistent fashion, the procedures should be explicit and standardized for the experimenters. For laboratory research and in varying degrees in applied research, many aspects of the procedures can be automated or taped in advance. Taperecordings of instructions to the subjects, videotapes of visual material, and the use of computers for instructions and tasks to be presented to the subject can ensure standardization. When these options are unavailable or seem undesirable by virtue of the goals of the intervention, the statements to be made by the experimenters may be spelled out verbatim. Detailed specification of the rationale or instructions guarantees a certain amount of consistency. Experimenters may vary some of the words used and introduce their own statements, but these variations do not necessarily compete with the overall consistency of the script.

One source of variation among experimenters is how they respond to sensitive questions on the part of the subject (e.g., "Am I just a guinea pig?" "Is this the control group?"). Depending on the experiment, it may be useful to try to anticipate the range of questions that may arise and to provide guidelines or particular statements for answering them. Of course, variations in handling an occasional question may reflect inconsistencies among experimenters but are not likely to be as serious as basic differences in how subjects are routinely run.

Another recommendation is to train experimenters together. During training, experimenters can practice conducting the experiment on each other or the investigator as subjects to see how the procedures are to be performed. By having experimenters practice and receive feedback together, relatively homogeneous behavior during the actual experiment is more readily assured. Homogeneity in performance can be sustained by conducting training sessions periodically with all experimenters as a group while the experiment is actually being run. One procedure to examine and sustain consistency of performance among experimenters is to include in the study "subjects" who are working for the investigator. These subjects, referred to earlier as confederates, enter the study as if they were completing the experiment. However, their task is to discuss with the investigator what was done, how it was done, and so on after they participate in the experiment. In my own work, occasionally I have utilized as confederates persons who know the procedures well because of their prior work as experimenters. Perhaps the most useful facet of the procedure is to tell experimenters at the beginning of the project that individuals will be coming through the experiment as subjects. The confederates are unannounced, of course, and interspersed with other subjects. Probably, the most interesting aspect of this procedure is that it may increase vigilance of the experimenters as they ponder who is working as a confederate; thus, they may remain especially careful in adhering to the experimental script.

Another procedure to evaluate the consistency in performance among experimenters is to interview the subjects after the experiment. Subjects can be interviewed by someone not involved with the experimental manipulation to reduce the bias conveyed to subjects to respond in a particular way during the interview. An alternative is a questionnaire (administered to the subject after the experiment) that asks questions about the experimenter's behavior and the manner in which the procedures were executed. A problem with a questionnaire is that the answers are based on the subjects' perceptions and hence may not reflect accurately what the experimenter did. Also, questionnaire responses based on an individual subject's perceptions may not be sensitive enough to reveal inconsistencies in how subjects were treated by different experimenters. On the other hand, if subjects' responses differ systematically among different experimenters, this may provide important clues about the procedures. If there is some reason why the experimenter's behavior needs to be very closely monitored, video- or audiotapes can be made of all experimenter–subject interactions. This might be completed as part of the experiment, for instance, in studying process variables in psychotherapy research. Yet, even if the interaction is not of interest, occasional, perhaps even unobtrusive, recordings of an experimental session may be desirable.

Experimenters ought to be encouraged to report sessions in which they have deviated from the script. Experimenters should not be expected to perform consistently beyond a certain point or to be entirely free from error. For example, subjects may be run in a condition other than the one to which they were assigned, receive a portion of some other condition, or through some unusual event receive a diffuse or interrupted version of their condition. Ideally, the investigator establishes a climate in which high standards of performance are expected, yet errors are readily acknowledged and reported to serve the goals of the research, namely, to provide a meticulous test of the hypotheses. Encouraging experimenters to report instances in which they inadvertently deviated from the script or were forced to deviate by virtue of the subject's behavior will help the investigator monitor the sorts of inconsistencies that transpire. Gross deviations from the procedures may require excluding subjects from data analysis.

Although it is important to specify the script of the experimenters, this requirement must be placed in context. A considerable amount of research, usually laboratory-based research, includes straightforward procedures on the part of the experimenter and deviation from the script may not be very serious. Experimenters frequently provide simple instructions, play taperecordings, show slides, administer questionnaires, and explain the tasks and benefits of treatment. Presumably, loose protocols are less likely than in more complex social interaction or intervention studies involving more intricate manipulations.

In some studies, however, it may be important not to standardize heavily what experimenters do. For example, the research questions may be based on providing general guidelines that convey how the conditions are to be distinct. Experimenters may be allowed to act within these boundaries. This approach occasionally is taken in therapy outcome research. Therapists are instructed to follow guidelines characteristic of one technique and to avoid the guidelines that characterize the other treatment technique (Sloane et al., 1975). Of course, unless the general guidelines are well specified and can be expressed as a set of operations in the experiment, the investigator may still have no firm idea of what experimenters actually are doing.

Experimenter Expectancy Effects

Nature of the Problem   One source of potential bias in experimental research that received considerable attention in the mid-1960s is experimenter *expectancy effects*. These effects refer to the influence of the experimenter's belief and desires about the results on how the subject performs. The effects are considered to be unintentional because the experimenter may not do anything on purpose to influence subjects' responses. Rather, through tone of voice, posture, facial expressions and other cues, the experimenter may influence how the subject responds. Leading experimenters to expect certain results was shown to influence how the subjects actually performed; expectancy effects were demonstrated with human and infrahuman subjects (Rosenthal, 1966, 1976). The research on unintentional expectancy effects has been critically reviewed by noting such problems as inappropriate statistical analyses and selective omission of data in many of the studies. Nevertheless, some evidence has shown that experimenters expectancies influence what the subjects do (Barber, 1976). In addition, characteristics of experimenters and how they behave (e.g., those who act more professional, competent, and relaxed) systematically relate to the magnitude of the expectancy effects (Rosenthal, 1976).

In treatment research, the problem of expectancy effects might be particularly acute in situations in which the experimenter may have a strong investment in the outcome and is completely responsible for running subjects in the various treatment and control conditions. This is rarely the experimental arrangement used in treatment studies. Yet, if an investigator has special interest or commitment to one condition in the study and this commitment is conveyed to the experimenter, it is conceivable that group differences might be explained by expectations conveyed to the subjects. The use of multiple experimenters (e.g., therapists) and manualization of treatment are designed to reduce the uncontrolled influences, such as expectancies, or at least limit the ways in which they can be conveyed to influence subject performance.

Expectancies can threaten the construct validity of the experiment. Features of the experimenter considered to be irrelevant to the experimental manipulation (e.g., expectancies, enthusiasm, suggestions for improvement) may vary systematically with the conditions. Expectancies alone or in combination with the manipulation may be responsible for the pattern of results. Whether expectancies of the experimenter represent a plausible account of the results is difficult to say.

Recommendations   Current evidence suggests that the experimenter's expectancies can influence results although the pervasiveness of the influence among different areas of research is not known. How experimenter expectancies exert their influence is also unclear. It is important to know the different ways in which experimenter expectancies operate because this will suggest the type of control procedures needed. For example, expectancies operating through loose protocols or systematic errors in calculating data would lead the investigator to control certain features, but expectancies operating through subtle verbal or nonverbal cues would lead the investigator to control entirely different procedures.

Currently, the most conservative practice would be to keep experimenters naive (blind) with respect to the purpose of the experiment and to evaluate the extent to which this is accomplished.[1] In medical research, in which this practice is commonly employed, keeping experimenters blind usually refers to not informing experimenters which conditions or treatments subjects receive. For example, different drugs might be administered in coded capsule form. Although experimenters may be involved in the administration of the capsules, they are not informed who receives the active drug (or which active drug) and who receives a placebo; moreover, they have no way of telling from the capsules themselves.

In psychological research, keeping the experimenters naive usually refers to withholding the hypotheses of the experiment. However, the experimenters who administer the different treatments cannot always be kept blind in the sense of not knowing who receives treatment or who receives one variation of treatment rather than another. Thus, even though experimenters are not told about the hypotheses, they are likely to guess what the study is about and to make plausible estimates about conditions that are likely to effect greater change. In treatment research, for example, therapists are likely to develop hypotheses about what treatments should produce more change than others and what treatments actually are control procedures for the investigation. The hypotheses that are developed may be quite similar across experimenters because of some of the obvious differences among treatments. Of course, whether the investigators' hypotheses are accurately guessed may depend on the complexity of the hypotheses (e.g., whether complex interactions among variables are predicted), the similarities among different conditions, and whether the individual experimenter has access to all relevant information delineating treatments.

Even if experimenters are naive to begin with, the effects of the interventions may develop expectancies and hypotheses that are fairly accurate. In treatment research, for example, not telling experimenters or clinicians what drug conditions are administered does not always really keep them blind. Studies have repeatedly shown that experimenters and clinicians kept blind can readily guess correctly who received active medication versus placebo, who received which medication (Margraf et al., 1991; Weiss et al., 1971), and who received psychotherapy, medication, or placebo (Carroll, Rounsaville, & Nich, 1994). In the latter study, seeing through the blind also influenced clinical ratings of patients treated for cocaine dependence. Evaluators who accurately guessed who received a placebo rated those subjects as more severe in their symptoms during the treatment phase compared to subjects they had accurately guessed to have received medication. In short, clinical ratings of treatment outcome varied as a function of whether the evaluator had accurately guessed the condition to which patients were assigned. More objective measures (e.g., days of drug use, money spent on drugs) were not so influenced by whether the clinical evaluator had correctly guessed the treatment condition.

In psychology experiments, it may be difficult to keep experimenters naive. In laboratory studies, it is possible that crucial aspects of the interventions might be administered by taperecorder or by experimenters who differ from those who are in charge of assessing the subject's performance. In this way, the experimenters who administer the conditions may not be naive but those who obtain the data from the subject are. In clinical studies in which treatment is provided and multiple sessions are involved, it is more difficult to keep experimenters blind.

Obviously, it is especially important to keep individuals in charge of data collection blind. Whether this is successfully accomplished can be determined empirically. A relatively simple procedure has been proposed to assess whether experimenters or observers (e.g., assessors in contact with the subject) are blind (Beatty, 1972). Specifically, observers are asked to guess which specific treatments subjects have received. If the observers guess among the available alternatives, the investigator can compare the frequency of correct identifications obtained with identifications expected by chance. If observers correctly identify a larger proportion than that expected by chance, this suggests that they were not naive. If the observer can distinguish conditions, the bias and expectancies during assessment might have influenced the results.

The above method of estimating whether experimenters can identify the conditions to which subjects are exposed does not solve the problem of keeping experimenters naive. However, it provides information that can greatly enhance the interpretation of the findings. At present, researchers routinely say that the experimenters are blind merely because they were not explicitly told what the hypotheses were. Yet, whether experimenters are blind can be evaluated empirically. This may mean assessing the expectancies about the outcome of different conditions or correctly identifying the conditions to which subjects are exposed, depending on the role of the experimenter. In either case, information about the actual expectations of the experimenters would be very useful.

Experimenter Characteristics

Nature of the Problem   Several different characteristics of the experimenters may influence subject behavior. Subject and demographic variables of the experimenters may interact with the independent variable or characteristic of the subjects to produce the results. Characteristics of the experimenter, such as age, gender, race, ethnic identity, level of anxiety, friendliness, and prestige, have been found to affect responses given by the subjects on self-report and projective tests, measures of intelligence, and various laboratory tasks (Barber, 1976; Masling, 1960).

Under most circumstances, the influence of experimenter characteristics may restrict only the external validity of the findings. Conceivably, the relationship between the independent and dependent variables may hold up only with experimenters who have specific characteristics. In most experiments this is not likely to be a problem. Two or more experimenters may be used and run subjects across all conditions. The results can be analyzed to determine whether experimenters affected subjects differently. If no differences are obtained, this suggests that the results are not restricted to a particular characteristic of the experimenter. Of course, it is possible that all experimenters share a characteristic (e.g., are college students) that contributes to the results. However, this becomes less plausible as the number of experimenters and the heterogeneity of experimenters increase and as the amount of interaction between the experimenter and subject in the experiment decreases.

Characteristics of the experimenter could threaten the construct validity of the results. This is possible when one experimenter administers one experimental condition and another experimenter administers another condition. When experimenters are perfectly confounded with conditions, the characteristics of the experimenters rather than the independent variable may account for the pattern of results. Confounding of experimenters with conditions occasionally arises and raises the prospect that experimenter characteristics accounted for or contributed to group differences.

The characteristics of experimenters as a source of influence are not well studied in psychology in general. In clinical psychology, an important exception is research in psychotherapy, in which characteristics of persons who administer the interventions (therapists) are often studied (Beutler, Machado, & Neufeldt, 1994). A variety of therapist characteristics can play an important role in treatment outcome such as level of empathic understanding, amount of experience, and degree of openness, and directiveness, to mention a few. Thus, in the case of treatment delivery, therapist characteristics can make an important difference.

Recommendations   The range of experimenter attributes that may influence the results, and the pervasiveness of this influence across experimental paradigms and areas of research are not known. Many tests of experimenter characteristics have been reported in interview, testing, or therapy situations in which the amount of interaction between subjects and experimenter is relatively great and where the subjects may be placed in a situation where they might be evaluated. The literature would not seem to justify the potentially great experimental effort of routinely sampling a broad range of experimenter characteristics in an investigation. Experimenter characteristics are not easily balanced across conditions or groups in an experiment because so many different characteristics (e.g., sex, ethnicity, race, age) might easily be identified.

It would be useful if investigators more carefully specified the characteristics of experimenters in their reports of research. This would allow other investigators to examine these characteristics in subsequent research and to evaluate whether the characteristics are important for a particular area of inquiry. Also, many investigators could analyze their data for experimenter characteristics (e.g., therapist sex, experience) that might provide additional information about the generality of the results. If particular characteristics cannot be examined, data can and should be analyzed for differences among experimenters. Within a given investigation, there may be too few experimenters to permit careful evaluation of experimenter effects. However, if experimenters were described better in published reports and data associated with different types of experimenters were available, meta-analyses would be able to elucidate the nature of these effects within a given area of research.

Situational and Contextual Cues

Nature of the Problem   Demand characteristics, discussed in the context of construct validity, refer to cues in the experimental situation that may influence how subjects respond. Their significance derives from the possibility that these cues rather than or in conjunction with the experimental manipulation account for the pattern of results. The range of cues that may contribute to subject behavior is difficult to specify. Any facet of experimenter behavior, the setting, experimental materials, and context of the research that are irrelevant conceptually to the variables of interest and that might foster certain types of performance could contribute to demand characteristics.

All experiments include multiple characteristics that are unique to the study. These cues do not necessarily contribute to demand characteristics. Cues that are plausibly related to the pattern of results (e.g. differences between groups) and are confounded with the groups can be considered as demand characteristics. Demand characteristics may be a plausible rival interpretation of results attributed to a particular independent variable. For example, in a study described earlier, the extraneous cues of sensory-deprivation research were shown to lead to effects resembling effects attributed to diminished sensory input, even when sensory input was not reduced in the group in which demand characteristics were maximized (Orne & Scheibe, 1964). The research design allowed a rather clear separation of the extraneous cues and the independent variable (reduced sensory input).

In many areas of research, the independent variable may include cues that lead subjects to behave in ways that cannot be so easily separated from the portion of the variable that is considered crucial. The cues that may give subjects hints on how to perform may be part of the manipulation itself. In such cases, it is not particularly meaningful to say that demand characteristics accounted for the results. For example, in psychotherapy research, the intervention usually carries with it a strong expectation for the desired change on the part of the subject. Many cues associated with treatment (e.g., a convincing therapist, a coherent treatment rationale, office decor suggesting a qualified and competent professional) may lead subjects to expect change. These cues are not always alterable. Subjects can be given an instructional set that attempts to negate the implicit expectancy. It is not clear that we would want to alter these expectancies because they are central to treatment; that is, in some sense, they are not extraneous.

Recommendations   In an investigation, there may be special cues associated with the experimental condition or cues may vary greatly between different conditions. Special equipment or arrangements (e.g., unusual activities) that vary across conditions are examples. If it is plausible or perhaps conceivable that different cues across experimental conditions could affect the dependent measures in systematic ways, the role of demand characteristics may be worth evaluating.

Three procedures have been suggested to evaluate the influence of demand characteristics (Orne, 1969). These techniques assess whether the cues of the experimental situation itself would lead to performance in the direction associated with the independent variable. If the cues of the situation do not lead subjects to perform in the way that they would when exposed to the experimental manipulation, this suggests that demand characteristics do not account for the results.

One method of estimating whether demand characteristics account for the results is to assess whether subjects are aware of the purpose of the experiment and the performance that is expected of them. This is referred to as a *post-experimental inquiry* and is accomplished by asking the subjects after the experiment what their perceptions were about the purpose of the experiment, what the experimenter expected from them, and how subjects were supposed to respond. Presumably, if subjects are aware of the purpose of the experiment and the performance expected of them, they can more readily comply with the demands of performance. Hence, their responses may be more a function of the information about the experiment than the manipulation itself.

The postexperimental inquiry of subjects may convey useful information but has unique restrictions. The inquiry may generate its own set of demands so subjects will not tell all they know or feign their motivation for responding. Also, subjects may not have perceived the demand characteristics but still responded to them in the experiment. The cues of the experiment that dictate performance may be subtle and depend on behaviors of the experimenter or on seemingly irrelevant procedures. The subject may not necessarily integrate all the cues and be able to verbalize their net effect. Even if the subjects respond in a way that indicates awareness of the purpose of the experiment, it is possible that the inquiry itself, rather than the experiment, stimulated the awareness. The questions may stimulate insights that were not present while the subjects were responding to the manipulation.

Another technique for evaluating the demand characteristics of an experiment is *preinquiry* (Orne, 1969). With this technique, subjects are not actually run through the procedures in the usual way. Rather, they are asked to imagine themselves in the situation to which subjects would be exposed. These subjects may see the equipment that will be used, hear the rationale or instructions that will be provided, and receive all the information that will be presented to the subject short of actually going through the procedures. Essentially, the procedures are explained but not administered. After exposing the subject to the explanations of the procedures and the materials to be used in an experiment, the subjects are asked to complete the assessment devices as if they actually had been exposed to the intervention. The task is to respond as subjects would who have experienced the procedures.

The preinquiry assesses the extent to which the cues of the experimental setting and the specific experimental condition can generate certain kinds of responses. Differences among experimental conditions suggest the direction in which demand influences may operate. Preinquiry research can inform the investigator before conducting further investigations whether demand characteristics operate in the direction of expected results derived from actually running the subjects. Preinquiry data also may be useful when compared with data from actually conducting the investigation and running subjects through the procedures. If the preinquiry data and experimental data are dissimilar, this suggests that the cues of the experimental situation itself are not likely to explain the findings obtained from actually being exposed to treatment. If the preinquiry data and experimental data are similar, this makes the influence of demand characteristics a potential explanation of the results and something to be considered or controlled in subsequent research.

A third method of examining demand characteristics is to use *simulators*. Subjects who serve as simulators are asked to act as if they received the experimental condition or intervention even though they actually do not. These simulators are then run through the assessment procedures of the investigation by an experimenter who is blind as to who is a simulator and who is a real subject (i.e., a subject run through the procedures). Simulators are instructed to guess what real subjects who are exposed to the intervention might do and then to deceive a blind experimenter. If simulators can act as real subjects on the assessment devices, this means that demand characteristics could account for the results. As noted with the preinquiry data, correspondence in the data does not mean that demand characteristics are responsible for the results. If the data do not correspond, it suggests that simulators apparently were unable to derive the demand characteristics of the actual conditions or to act consistently with these characteristics in the expected direction.

If data from postinquiry, preinquiry, or simulators and from real subjects who completed the experiment are similar, the data are consistent with a demand-characteristics interpretation. The consistency does not mean that demand characteristics account for the results. Both demand characteristics and the actual effects of the independent variable may operate in the same direction. The consistency raises issues for construct validity and interpretation of the basis for the findings. If the data from evaluation of demand characteristics and real subjects do not correspond, this suggests that the cues of the situation do not lead to the same kinds of effects as actually running the subjects. Yet, even here there is some ambiguity. Being exposed to an explanation of treatment (as in preinquiry or simulator techniques) is not the same as actually undergoing treatment and could generate different demand characteristics. Thus, differences between these subjects do not completely rule out demand characteristics.

Efforts to evaluate the role of demand characteristics are to be actively encouraged if demand is a plausible and conceptually interesting or important threat to construct validity. If demand characteristics generate results different from those generated by subjects who completed the experimental conditions, interpretation of the findings can be clarified. If demand characteristics can threaten construct validity, it is useful to design experiments so that merely exposing subjects to the cues (irrelevancies) of the experiment is not plausible as an explanation of the results. This can be accomplished by controlling or holding fairly constant all cues or designing experiments so the predicted results are counterintuitive, that is, go in a direction opposite from what experimental demands would suggest.

Subject Roles

Nature of the Problem Demand characteristics draw attention to the cues of the experiment that may influence subject behavior. Subjects are assumed to respond to these cues in such a way as to give the experimenter what he or she wants in the way of results. Yet exposure of subjects to a particular set of cues does not invariably result in certain responses. The discussion of demand characteristics glosses over the fact that subjects may interpret cues differently and respond as a function of their own perceptions and purposes rather than the purposes of the investigator (Kihlstrom, 1995).

Subjects may adopt different ways of responding to the experimental cues of the experiment. The different ways of responding are referred to generally as *subject roles* and reflect how the subject intends to respond to the task or problem of the experiment. Several different roles have been distinguished, including the good, negativistic, faithful, and apprehensive subject roles (see Greenberg & Folger, 1988; Weber & Cook, 1972). The roles are described in

Table 13.1. The adoption and impact of different subject roles have been difficult to evaluate in part because the different roles can lead to similar predictions in how subjects will behave. Also, subjects often need information (e.g., knowledge of the experimenter's hypothesis) to enact a particular role. Studies rarely provide evidence that this condition is met (Greenberg & Folger, 1988).

The apprehensive subject role may be the most applicable across areas of research within clinical psychology. Subjects frequently attempt to place themselves in a desirable light. Adoption of the apprehensive role might be expected given the stereotypes and suspicions that subjects have about research. Research may foster the apprehensive role if subjects assume the focus is designed to assess psychological adjustment and psychopathology. Indeed, telling subjects that the experiment is related to clinical psychology and determining responses that are "normal" elevates the apprehensiveness of the subject and further evoke apprehensive role behavior.

Subject roles can threaten the validity of an experiment in different ways. If roles are likely to vary systematically with conditions, the construct validity of

---

TABLE 13.1.   Roles That Subjects May Adopt When Participating in an Experiment

Good Subject

This role refers to the attempt of subjects to provide responses in the experiment that will corroborate the investigator's hypotheses. This role may reflect a subject's concern that his or her responses provide information that is useful to science. To adopt this role, the subject must identify the hypotheses and then act in a fashion that would be consistent with these hypotheses.

Negativistic Subject

This role refers to the attempt to refute or inform the investigator's hypotheses. The negativistic subject is assumed to provide evidence for some alternative, perhaps opposing hypothesis, or to provide information that will be of no use. This role may result from the subject's concern over being controlled, predictable, or in a position where he or she is somehow forced to respond.

Faithful Subject

This role refers to the attempt of subjects to follow carefully the experimental instructions and to avoid acting on the basis of any suspicions that they might have about the actual purpose of the investigation. This role may be performed passively if subjects apathetically follow the instructions of the experiment or actively if subjects are highly motivated to help science and take special care in not letting their suspicions or preconceptions enter into their responses.

Apprehensive Subject

This role is adopted when subjects are concerned that their performance will be used to evaluate their abilities, personal characteristics (e.g., adjustment), or opportunities (e.g., employment). Subjects often are motivated to present themselves favorably to psychologists, who presumably are regarded as experts in evaluating one's psychological adjustment and other characteristics. When subjects respond in a socially desirable fashion and hence place themselves in a desirable light, such responding may reflect the apprehensive subject role.

the study may be threatened. If a particular condition fosters diverse roles, variability of performance among the subjects may be increased and threaten statistical conclusion validity. External validity might be threatened if the results only apply to subjects who adopt a particular role.

Recommendations   Several different procedures might be implemented to minimize the influence of subject roles in an experiment. Perhaps the greatest attention should be paid to the apprehensive subject role because evidence suggests this is the most pervasive role that subjects select. If subjects are apprehensive that their behavior is to be evaluated, attempts might be made to reduce these concerns. The procedures may assure the subjects that their performance will not be used to infer psychological adjustment or mental health. It may be useful to convey that there are no right or wrong answers or correct responses to the task and that their responses will be valuable and important no matter what they are. In practice, this is difficult to do in situations in which questions included in the measures (e.g., about presence of deviant behaviors) arouse apprehensiveness about being evaluated.

Any inducements for performance normally included as part of the experiment, such as money or course credits, might be given prior to the subject's performance. Subjects otherwise might believe that the rewards for participating in some way depend on how well they do or the impression they convey. Despite disclaimers at the beginning of an experimental session, subjects often seem to associate the rewards for participating in the session with how well they perform.

Apprehensiveness may be minimized by conveying to subjects that their responses are anonymous and confidential. Presumably, subjects who believe that their responses cannot be identified are less motivated to convey a specific image. In addition, feedback from the experimenter about how well subjects are doing should be minimized. The feedback, unless part of the independent variable, conveys the responses that are highly valued and provides guidelines on how subjects are to perform if they wish to appear in a favorable light.

Subject roles might be minimized by ensuring that the subjects do not perceive the hypotheses of the experiment. When subjects know what the hypotheses are (e.g., by speaking to a confederate or receiving the hypotheses as part of the procedures), their responses may be altered (Weber & Cook, 1972). Subjects are less readily able to respond in a manner consistent with the role they may have adopted if they are unaware of the specific hypotheses.

Subjects might always be said to have some role or specific reaction to the experiment. They have perceptions about the experiment and expectations about what is likely or not likely to happen. These perceptions and expectations can readily influence how they perform (Kihlstrom, 1995). Exceptions are when subjects do not realize they are participating in research because of the type of study (e.g., in naturalistic or field settings) and when the assessment is unobtrusive (e.g., archival records). In studies in which subjects are aware of their participation, the experimenter may wish to foster a set that encourages candid and honest responding. The task is to convey to subjects that their participation, honesty, and candor, rather than the direction of the results, are critical. This is a set that may be fostered to the subjects directly from experimenter to subjects. The set may be equally important to convey from investigator to experimenter, namely, that accurate information, rather than support for a specific hypothesis, is critical.

Data Recording and Analysis

Nature of the Problems   Several different kinds of problems pertain to the data obtained in an experiment. These problems include making errors in recording or computing the data, analyzing select portions of the data, and fabricating or "fudging" the data. Errors in recording or calculating the data include inaccurately perceiving what the subject has done, arithmetic mistakes, errors in transposing data from one format to another (e.g., questionnaires to data sheets or computer files), and similar sources of distortion. These errors are not necessarily intentional or systematic.

Evaluation of recording and arithmetic errors across several studies has yielded a rate of approximately one percent. This refers to the percentage of data points incorrectly recorded or scored. Errors tend to be in the direction of the investigator's or experimenter's hypotheses (Barber, 1976; Rosenthal, 1984). Errors in scoring or calculating data obviously are important because they may lead the investigator to make unwarranted conclusions. Systematic errors in the data may alter the affirmative conclusions; unsystematic or random errors in the data may negate or obscure group differences because the errors add variability to the data.

The heavy reliance on computers might seem to aid in reducing computational errors. To be sure, there are obvious advantages in the use of computers in scoring and checking data and computing or transforming scores based on operations that previously would be completed by calculator or by hand. However, computers do not necessarily reduce data errors. Coding subjects incorrectly in reference to the experimental condition they received, or to sex, age, and other characteristics can be done easily by one or two numbers or entries in a data base. The fact that computers play a critical role in data entry and in scoring of measures does not reduce the importance of checking the data. Computers can facilitate verification of the data because of the relative ease of entering the data independently on separate occasions and checking to ensure the numbers are correct. It is likely that many investigators check their data, particularly data that depart from the expected findings. In fact, if data are not routinely checked, investigators are likely to assume that data supporting a hypothesis are accurate and are more likely to check data that are discrepant with a hypothesis. The biases resulting from selective checking are obvious and are likely to apply to published studies that have yielded data consistent with their predictions.

Biases in the data analyses may refer to a host of problems. Many problems stem from biased selection on the part of the investigator of data that should be analyzed or reported. An investigator may select data from the experiment that appear most promising and subject them to extensive analyses. Alternatively, all data may be analyzed but only select portions reported. The implication for these types of selective uses of the data is that the predicted results were achieved. The conclusions will be misleading because they fail to include all data and all analyses that were completed.

The problem may be relatively common when many different dependent measures are used and only a small number are reported. The reader of the published account of the investigation may not know that a particular percentage of the analyses would be expected to be statistically significant on the basis of chance. The percentage of statistically significant differences expected on the basis of chance often is much higher than the frequently cited 5 percent (for analyses conducted at the .05 level of confidence). The percentage of chance differences may increase depending on the nature of the tests, independence of the sets of data included in the tests, and other factors, which are discussed in Chapter 14. Without knowing how many analyses are expected to be significant, the results might be attributed to nonchance differences.

A related issue pertains to the specific statistical tests and the implications their selection may have for the conclusions. Often the investigator has many choices of different methods of analyzing the data. The different analyses may lead to different conclusions. The different analyses do not refer to choosing between alternative statistical tests (e.g., analysis of variance or multiple regression), although the point also applies in this situation. Within a given type of analysis, changes in seemingly minor decisions can generate a different set of significant results and lead to different conclusions. The problem is exacerbated by the use of a fixed threshold calling effects statistically significant (i.e., $p < .05$) at one point but not at another (e.g., $p < .06$). As such, seemingly minor decisions, such as adoption or alteration of default criteria or the treatment of missing data within the analysis, can alter the findings regarded as statistically significant.

Default criteria refer to decisions that are made in software programs regarding assumptions of the data analysis, underlying statistical model, or criteria for proceeding or stopping within the analysis. For example, in using factor analysis to identify the internal structure of the scale, selecting among alternative multiple comparison tests to compare means, deciding criteria for entry and removal of variables from discriminant analysis to predict group status, using multivariate versus univariate tests, and conducting cluster analyses to identify typologies, can produce very different results from the same data set, depending on decisions made within the analysis. A bias can occur if the results are analyzed in several different ways and then selectively reported on the basis of the pattern of statistically significant findings.[2]

The selective reporting of data and data analyses raises a broader issue. Many experiments are completed but yield findings that are not statistically significant. The results of such experiments usually are not reported but merely allocated to a file drawer. The *file-drawer problem* (Rosenthal, 1979), as this is sometimes called, refers to the possibility that the published studies represent a biased sample of all studies that have been completed for a given hypothesis. Studies that are published may be the ones that obtained statistical significance, that is, the 5 percent at the $p < .05$ level. There may be many more studies, the other 95 percent, that did not attain significance. Methods can be used to estimate how many studies with no-difference findings would be needed to place reasonable doubt on a finding that has attained significance (Rosenthal, 1984). Thus, the bias can be addressed. For present purposes, the broader point is critical; namely, findings must be viewed in a broader context of other findings and other studies that attempt to replicate the research.

Certainly, the most misleading type of bias in data analysis is reporting fraudulent data. If the investigators have sole access to the data, systematic fudging on a large scale may be difficult to detect. Instances of making up data instead of running the investigation or changing aspects of the results are difficult to detect, but many dramatic instances across diverse areas of scientific research have been documented (Bell, 1992; Miller & Hersen, 1992; National Academy of Sciences, 1989). Efforts to monitor research and to underscore the responsibilities of the researcher to the broader scientific community are responses to such instances. We discuss this matter further in the context of ethical issues that guide research (Chapter 16).

Recommendations   The recommendations for handling various biases that may enter into the data vary greatly depending on the precise source of error. Misrecording and miscalculating data are relatively easily controlled, although these errors may be difficult to eliminate entirely in very large data bases. Obviously, individuals who record data should be kept uninformed of the experimental conditions so that the possibility of directional (biased) errors in favor of the hypotheses is removed. Scoring and entry of the data can include a variety of steps that may vary as a function of the nature of the data, such as whether the dependent measures (e.g., questionnaires) are scored by hand or by computer, whether data are entered directly from scored forms or are first entered on data sheets, and others. Whenever possible, it is preferable to have subjects enter their responses directly on a computer (keyboard, touch screen). If the data are self-reported and direct entry is not possible, the score sheets ought to be scanned and entered directly onto the computer data base by use of this procedure. The use of computers in these ways is not only efficient in moving from data to data analyses but also omits a number of steps that can lead to errors.

However, the use of computers in these ways is still the exception rather than the rule. The scoring of data and transposition to data sheets or computer should be checked at each stage. The beginning step is ensuring that the subject has completed all the measures (e.g., all items, all assessments) and that the marks or subject responses can be unambiguously scored. Interim steps vary but are determined by places in which error could reasonably enter the process. Checking data is a process that one can integrate into routine activities of the research team. It is helpful to convey to all research assistants that errors can be expected, but that all errors need to be found and corrected.

Eventually, the data are usually entered on computer files for analyses. Here editing of the data can be completed to check accuracy for the number of subjects in each condition, on each assessment occasion, and for each measure, whether the range of scores for a given measure represents a legitimate (i.e., possible) score, whether there are outliers, and so on. Compulsive checking may be time consuming, but it involves a relatively small cost considering the amount of time that goes into the planning and implementation of the experiment. If all data cannot be checked, certainly a generous proportion from all conditions should be randomly sampled to provide an idea of whether errors occurred and what their influence on the results might be.

It is more difficult to address the problems of selectively reporting data or data analyses. Presumably, instructing investigators about the need to plan analyses in advance, conveying their responsibilities in the reporting of data and their analyses, and noting the consequences of selectively reporting data may help. Yet the problems extend beyond the individual investigator. Publication practices continue to emphasize investigations that find statistically significant differences. The message is clearly conveyed to most investigators to find significance rather than to report whatever results come from their experiments. When significance is obtained for some dependent variables but not others, journal editors occasionally require authors to delete portions of their results that did not obtain significance. (This may be one of the reasons I was asked to delete the entire Results section when I wrote my dissertation.) The pressure for journal space may lead editors and authors to delete details and qualifications about the results (e.g., different patterns across different analyses). The intent is to save journal space, but the effect is that the conclusions the readers may draw from the published report are greatly altered.

The problem of fudging is also difficult to control directly. The threat of expulsion from the scientific community, the strong demands for accurate reporting in science, and improved efforts to educate scientists during training are intended to hold data fabrication in check, topics to which we return in Chapter 16. Cases of fudging may be difficult to detect if data are kept secret. Conveying the purposes and goals of research and modeling responsible practices in the training of researchers, requiring investigators to make raw data available, and encouraging investigators to replicate each other's work are possible solutions. Probably one of the best checks is to replicate work that has been reported. This not only addresses the veridical nature of the findings but serves many other functions in the accumulation of scientific knowledge (see Chapter 15).

SUBJECT-SELECTION BIASES

Subject-selection biases refers to influences attributable to types of subjects who participate in experiments. Different selection biases may operate at different points in the experiment beginning with the type of person who is recruited for participation and ending with those who finally complete the experiment. Two major sources of selection biases are the use of special samples and the loss of subjects during an experiment.

The Sample: Who Is Selected for the Study?

Nature of the Problem   A pervasive concern about psychological research is the restricted range of subject populations that are sampled. A frequent criticism of psychological research is that experiments on humans rely very heavily on college students, particularly students enrolled in psychology courses. Typically, students are enticed into participation in an experiment by receiving credit toward an undergraduate psychology course, monetary incentives, or by being solicited as volunteers by experimenters who circulate among psychology classes. An issue of concern is whether the findings obtained with college students will generalize to other samples. As mentioned in the discussion of external validity, the issue may be significant in areas of clinical research. For example, psychotherapy research has occasionally utilized student samples whose subject and demographic characteristics and types and severity of dysfunction depart from those of persons who are referred for treatment. The generality of findings of such samples to persons who are referred for treatment might plausibly be challenged because subject, demographic, and problem-related characteristics (severity, chronicity, comorbidity) are likely to influence the effect of treatment and who responds to treatment.

Apart from college students, occasionally there is concern about the using of *samples of convenience*. This refers to the selection and use of subjects merely because they are available. Obviously, a sample of subjects must be available to be included in a study. However, occasionally subjects are included without a clear rationale why they were selected. Sometimes subjects are selected because they are present in a convenient situation (e.g., waiting room, hospital ward) or are available for a quite different purpose (e.g., participation in another experiment that requires a special population). An investigator may use an available sample to test a particular idea or to evaluate a measure he or she has just developed.

The most common use of samples of convenience is in situations in which a sample is recruited for and is well suited to one purpose. As the study is begun, the original investigators or other investigators realize that the data set can be used to test other hypotheses, even though the original sample may not be the sample that would have been identified originally if the other, new purposes had been the central part of the study. When samples of convenience are used, the onus is on the investigator to evaluate whether unique features of the sample may contribute to the results. The use of a highly specialized population that is selected merely because it is convenient raises concern. The specialized population and the factors that make them particularly convenient may have implications for generalizing the results.

A more pervasive way that could lead to selection biases has to do with *volunteer status*. In most research, all subjects are volunteers in a sense. Informed consent procedures require subjects to agree to participate voluntarily rather than to participate under duress of any kind. One can define volunteer status in a more restricted sense. From a large group of available subjects (e.g., college students, samples of convenience, community members), participants may be solicited through newspapers, notes posted on kiosks on college campuses, and public radio or television announcements. Some individuals agree to serve (volunteers) and participate in the study; others do not (nonvolunteers). The subjects determine whether they will participate. The possibility that those who volunteer to participate may differ in important ways from those who do not can restrict the generality of experimental findings.

Obviously, an important question is whether volunteer subjects differ in any important ways from nonvolunteer subjects. Considerable research has been conducted comparing individuals who volunteer to participate with nonvolunteers whose responses can also be assessed within the experiment (e.g., routine administration of test batteries, pursuing contact with nonvolunteers to induce their participation). Several variables have been related to volunteering for experiments. Major variables and their relation to volunteering are listed in Table 13.2. The literature is equivocal in many areas and, no doubt, the impact of volunteer status may vary greatly among areas of research and type of experiment. For most purposes, it is important to note that sufficient evidence is

TABLE 13.2. Relationship between Subject, Demographic, and Personality Variables and Volunteering for Experiments

Variable	Volunteers Relative to Nonvolunteers
Education	Better educated
Socioeconomic status	Higher occupational status
Intelligence	Higher in intelligence
Need for approval	Higher in the need for social approval
Sociability	More social
Arousal seeking	More sources of stimulation
Conventionality	Less conventional in their behavior
Sex	Female
Authoritarianism	Less authoritarian
Religious affiliation	Jewish more likely than Protestant and Protestant more likely than Catholic
Conformity	Less conforming
Town of origin	From a smaller town
Religiosity	More interested in religion
Altruism	More altruistic
Self-disclosure	More self-disclosing by providing information about their beliefs, aspirations, and preferences
Adjustment	More maladjusted when volunteering for unusual situations
Age	Younger

Note: The variables are ordered according to the confidence that has been placed in the relation indicated on the basis of available evidence (Rosenthal & Rosnow, 1975). The material presented here is a guideline; volunteer status and its correlates can vary as a function of the type of task and experiment.

available indicating that individuals who volunteer for psychological experiments differ on a number of dimensions from nonvolunteers. Thus, findings obtained with volunteer subjects may be limited in their generality across certain subject characteristics.

It is important not to cast aside too quickly the potential significance of volunteer status as an influence on findings of research and on clinical research specifically. It is quite possible that persons who volunteer differ in ways that are systematically related to the hypotheses of interest and hence lead to conclusions that might not represent the population. For example, in a study of social relations and behavior among school-age children, data were obtained on how peers and teachers rated the children (Noll et al., 1997). Parent consent was sought to have children included in the ratings by peers and by the teacher. Data were obtained for children whose parents provided consent and for children whose parents did not. (The authors and school personnel felt that excluding children from peer-rating lists might present its own stigma and therefore all children ought to be included as part of routine assessment.) The results showed systematic differences among children as a function of whether their parents provided consent. Volunteer children (i.e., those with consent) were more sociable, less aggressive, and more athletically competent than nonvolunteer children. Clearly, volunteer status made a considerable difference.

When volunteers and nonvolunteers differ in the ways the previously cited study illustrates, there is the question of whether the results from the sample of volunteers can be generalized to nonvolunteers. Stated another way, within the sample of volunteers in the study, any relations that are demonstrated (e.g., correlations, interactions with other variables, or the absence of correlations and interactions) might be quite different from what the larger population would show. The people who do not volunteer are not randomly drawn from the distribution of scores on the dependent variables of interest. By representing a particular part of the distribution (e.g., a more extreme group, a more varied group), the quantitative findings within the study and the inferences drawn from them are likely to be quite different from those that would be reached if the entire population were included.

In clinical research, a cautionary note is important to raise whenever one studies clinically referred samples (e.g., at an outpatient or inpatient treatment service, crisis center). Individuals who are referred often have other significant factors (e.g., impairment, concerned relatives, insurance coverage) that separate them from the larger population of individuals with similar problems but who are not referred. This is not necessarily a problem; we are quite interested in groups who come to clinics, hospitals, and medical health services. Yet it is important to be careful about the conclusions that are drawn from special samples who volunteer to participate or are volunteered, recommended, or referred by others to participate.

Recommendations   Perhaps the most obvious recommendation that might be made is to increase the range of persons from among whom volunteers are sought. Certainly, as behavioral scientists, psychologists should be able to devise techniques to encourage individuals to volunteer when solicitations are made. More intense efforts at recruiting presumably would bring into experiments individuals who would not usually volunteer. Also, better understanding of the determinants of subject participation may be helpful. Many variables influence the rate of volunteering, such as aversiveness of the task, the magnitude of incentives for participation, and apparent importance of the subject's participation to the experimenter. Structuring the situation so that the research actively fosters greater participation and simultaneously serves a need or interest of the subjects is likely to increase the rate of volunteering.

The differences between volunteers and nonvolunteers do not necessarily restrict the generality of the results obtained with volunteer subjects. It is likely that some findings are not influenced by whether subjects were volunteers and that other findings are influenced in varying degrees. In cases in which findings are influenced by the volunteer status of the subjects, the research conclusions may merely vary in terms of the magnitude of performance on the dependent variables. For other findings, the volunteers may behave in a fashion diametrically opposed to that of nonvolunteer subjects. Experiments are needed to assess the impact of volunteer status on external validity across a variety of independent and dependent variables and experimental arrangements and tasks. This research would be of great benefit if guided by conceptual models about key processes that might mediate volunteer status so that our understanding about the basis of these effects could advance.

There are situations in clinical work in which volunteer status can be readily studied. For example, occasionally in treatment and institutional programs some persons within the same program vary in the extent to which they volunteer to participate (e.g., self-referred for treatment, court referred). The difficulty in evaluating volunteer status is that it often covaries with other characteristics (e.g., clinical problems, demographic variables). In laboratory research, volunteers might be examined and compared with persons who initially did not volunteer. Further attempts to recruit these subjects would provide an opportunity to evaluate the impact of volunteer status on the measures of interest. In clinical studies, it is sometimes helpful to consult findings from population studies. For example, epidemiological studies of clinical disorders are based on sampling from the population at large and include more representative samples than does a sample obtained from a clinical service (Regier et al., 1984). One can compare characteristics of a clinic sample with characteristics of community-based samples to identify differences in subject and demographic variables as well as other characteristics possibly related to the clinical focus of the study (e.g. comorbidity). Such comparisons can help, albeit informally, to examine the extent to which a clinic sample departs from the population or from a sample in which an effort was made to represent the population.

In general, the plausibility and relevance of volunteer status in contributing to the results must be considered in relation to the specific area of research. The concern emerges in circumstances in which the investigator draws sweeping conclusions about the effect of a manipulation without acknowledging that how subjects were recruited might have contributed to generality of the findings. In advance of information about the generality of findings with volunteer subjects, it is essential to specify how subjects are recruited and any factors that may operate to select some subjects over others. In treatment research, selection factors often refer to screening requirements used to select clients who are reasonably homogeneous (e.g., with respect to psychiatric diagnosis). In experimental research, variables related to subject selection, such as year or major in college, circumstances of solicitation, and others, might warrant specification because they may relate to who volunteers to participate and who does not. If recruitment and subject-selection practices relate to the results, the failure of findings to be replicated among separate studies may be accounted for by these variables.

Attrition: Who Remains in the Study?

Nature of the Problem   Whether subjects volunteer for research constitutes a potential selection bias that operates prior to the experiment. Yet there is a continuation of the selection process during the experiment. If there is repeated assessment of the subject over time, as in the case of follow-up assessment, the selection process continues. The loss of subjects during the course of an investigation can affect virtually all facets of experimental validity by altering random composition of the groups and group equivalence (internal validity), limiting the generality of findings to a special group (e.g., subjects who are persistent) (external validity), by raising the prospect that the intervention combined with special subject characteristics account for conclusions the investigator would like to attribute to the intervention (external and construct validity), and by reducing sample size and power (statistical conclusion validity).

In laboratory research with one or two sessions to complete the experiment, loss of subjects is not likely to be a major problem. In clinical research, in the context of treatment, prevention, and longitudinal studies, loss of subjects is common. In psychotherapy research, attrition has been the subject of considerable study and hence offers examples of some of the major problems. First and most obvious, subjects who drop out of a treatment outcome study are likely to differ from those who remain in the study. Dropouts may differ on a range of variables (e.g., type, severity, or chronicity of dysfunction, family history, past treatment experiences) that could interact with the intervention (Kazdin, 1996b). Conclusions about the effect of treatment may be restricted to a highly select group, depending on the proportion of subjects lost.

Second, the number of subjects who drop out may vary significantly between or among groups. For example, in a study showing that cognitive therapy was more effective than medication (imipramine) in treating depression, the medication condition led to more dropouts before posttreatment assessment (Rush et al., 1977). Differential attrition between conditions groups itself is an interesting outcome but also raises questions about the comparisons at posttreatment. Were the two treatments differentially effective on measures of depression or were group differences due to differential selection? The questions are not easily resolved.

Third, it is possible that the type of person who drops out varies among conditions or groups within the study. That is, the people who drop out from one condition may differ systematically from those who drop out from another condition. For example, if five subjects drop out of a psychotherapy condition and five other subjects in the study drop out of a medication condition, it is not necessarily the case that these persons are "the same." There may be systematic differences in the conditions leading to attrition in ways that affect different types of people. Perhaps, psychotherapy subjects who did not wish to chat about their past and never considered their therapists to be like a father or mother (transference) tired of psychotherapy and left; medication subjects who were discomforted by a dry mouth and heart palpitations (side effects) may have quit their treatment. The subjects remaining in each group and included in statistical comparisons may be different kinds of subjects in terms of subject, demographic, and personality characteristics; this cannot be easily tested given the small sample sizes and absence of available information on a vast range of possible differences in these characteristics. Usually, the number of attrition cases is too small to compare groups in a statistically sensitive way. Indeed, investigators may show no statistically significant differences between dropouts from two or more groups. This could provide illusory comfort that attrition did not lead to any selection biases that would favor one group.

Finally, it is possible that so many cases drop out that valid conclusions about treatment cannot be made. For example, in one large-scale investigation, youths (N = 450) received one of three treatment or control conditions designed to reduce antisocial behavior (Feldman et al., 1983). The design evaluated several factors (therapist experience, type of treatment, type of group) in a factorial design ($2 \times 3 \times 3$ or 18 groups). A one-year follow-up was conducted. Almost 90 percent of the cases (396/450) who completed treatment were lost one year later. The small sample ($n = 54$) divided among the set of experimental conditions precluded evaluation of the effects of treatment. The loss of a large number of studies in intervention research is not rare. Indeed, between 40–60 percent of children, adolescents, and adults drop out of treatment studies (Kazdin, 1996b; Wierzbicki & Pekarik, 1993). In such cases, selection biases are readily plausible. Moreover, the large number of lost cases has dire consequences for sample sizes and, hence, statistical conclusion validity. Studies of treatment in clinical research usually begin with samples that are relatively small (Kazdin & Bass, 1989; Rossi, 1990). Attrition further weakens the sensitivity of statistical tests.

The problem of subjects dropping out or terminating their participation may be exacerbated greatly by investigators. Investigators may use subjects who drop out in such a way as to obfuscate further the conclusions that might be drawn by reassigning subjects to conditions in the investigation on the basis of whether they have dropped out. For example, occasionally investigators use persons who drop out as no-treatment control subjects to evaluate the treatment condition (Beneke & Harris, 1972). The obvious rationale is that because these subjects were in the original subject pool and did not receive treatment, they ought to provide a suitable control. Yet, the random assignment of conditions is violated if subjects who drop out are reassigned to some other condition. Even if dropouts are shown not to differ from nondropouts at pretreatment assessment on subject and demographic variables, the extent to which the dropouts and nondropouts are *likely* to improve may be quite different. Threats to internal validity (selection x history, selection x maturation) may be plausible as rival hypotheses in explaining group differences or the absence of differences.

Recommendations   There are several options available to address the problem of attrition. Special orientation (pretreatment) interviews, various mailings during the course of treatment, reminders and methods of scheduling appointments, and monetary incentives have been effective (Baekeland & Lundwall, 1975; Flick, 1988). For example, one technique to decrease attrition in treatment research is to request clients to provide a deposit that will be refunded after treatment. Clients are told that the deposit will be refunded if they attend all or a specified percentage of sessions. Requesting and holding a deposit has been found to reduce attrition, and larger deposits (e.g., $20) have been more effective in this regard than smaller ones (e.g., $5) (Hagen, Foreyt, & Durham, 1976). The use of a deposit has its own problems. For one, it may actually be a form of coercion or may be viewed by clients, investigators, or research evaluation committees as a form of coercion. On the other hand, it may be reasonable to ask clients at the beginning of treatment to make a commitment to participate.

Another strategy for minimizing attrition is to identify variables correlated with attrition and utilize the information to decide who participates in subsequent research. For example, in a study of antisocial children seen for outpatient treatment, several variables (e.g., family socioeconomic disadvantage, level of parent stress, number of child symptoms) reliably predicted who remained in and who dropped out of treatment (Kazdin, Mazurick, & Bass, 1993; Kazdin, Stolar, & Marciano, 1995). From this type of information, one might identify cut-off scores or a profile of families at risk for attrition and use this as the basis for selecting clients for research. Such a strategy raises other compromises. With more stringent selection, a larger number of subjects will need to be recruited and screened. Also, there may be greater restrictions on the generality of the results with more exclusions.

An additional strategy is to try to understand the reasons why people drop out (e.g., Kazdin, Holland, & Crowley, 1997) and to devise specific procedures to combat attrition (Prinz & Miller, 1994). For example, in the latter study, personal issues and problems of the parents were proposed as the basis for children dropping out of therapy. Providing parents with opportunities to discuss personal problems and issues significantly lowered dropout rates. Thus, much can be done on the part of investigators to retain cases in treatment.

Attrition is likely to occur in studies that extend beyond more than one or a few sessions. In studies covering several months or years, researchers understand at the outset that attrition will occur. Several statistical approaches to attrition have been developed and provide useful strategies to complement active efforts to minimize attrition. Statistical approaches utilize existing data (e.g., the last available data point) from cases who drop out and utilize other data in the study to estimate what the lost data might reflect. These methods allow researchers to identify the likely bias that attrition will introduce into the data and the conclusions that would be warranted if the lost subjects had improved, remained the same, or became worse (Flick, 1988; Howard, Krause, & Orlinsky, 1986; Little & Rubin, 1987).

SUMMARY AND CONCLUSIONS

Sources of artifact and bias in an experiment are a function of what the investigator is interested in studying. Extraneous factors that may account for the results may be viewed as artifacts and threaten each type of experimental validity. The *loose protocol effect* refers to sources of artifact and bias that emerge when the investigator does not carefully specify the rationale, script, and activities of the experimenter. Departures from the intended procedures may influence the results by systematically biasing one condition or by introducing variability, such as obscuring group differences.

Experimenter expectancy effects refer to unintentional influences that stem from beliefs of the experimenter about what ought to happen; that is, what would support the hypotheses. Situational and contextual influences refer to cues of the experiment that can influence the results. *Demand characteristics* were described as extraneous cues that prompt subjects to behave within the experiment. The results may reflect responses to these cues rather than the different experimental manipulations the investigator intended to evaluate. *Subject roles* refer to ways that subjects may respond to the experiment and can introduce biases in the results. Evidence suggests that subjects are most likely to be concerned with evaluation of their performance in an experiment and hence adopt the apprehensive-subject role. Adoption of subject roles can be minimized by attempting to reduce subject concern about being evaluated, dissociating any inducements for participation in the experiment with the results or responses that the subject produces, informing subjects that their responses are confidential and anonymous, and keeping subjects blind about the specific hypotheses to be tested.

Subject-selection biases encompass different types of considerations. First, the use or overuse of specific populations (e.g., college students), samples selected merely because they are available (*samples of convenience*), and persons who are asked to *volunteer* often raise major concerns of generality of the results (external validity). Second, selection biases may emerge over the course of the investigation. The advantage of random assignment at the beginning of the investigation is to distribute "nuisance" variables (i.e., potential sources of bias) across groups. Attrition eliminates this advantage; whether it interferes with the results of any particular investigation is not always clear. Yet, loss of subjects over time raises special problems. Differential attrition in terms of number or types of cases may lead to bias that can threaten each type of experimental validity.

NOTES

[1]The term *blind* is used to denote procedures in which the investigator, experimenter, and others (e.g., staff, assessors) are kept naive with respect to the hypotheses and alternative experimental or control conditions of the study. The term continues to be used in research. Because of confusion of the term with loss of vision and the potential pejorative reference to that condition, other terms (e.g., experimentally naive, masked conditions) are often preferred. Nevertheless, the term has a well-established meaning, continues to have wide usage in research, and consequently is retained here.

[2]Default criteria within statistical analyses are often given little or no attention. However, in many cases the criteria have enormous implications for the substantive or conceptual model underlying the study and the investigator's thinking. A common example is in the use of factor analysis. Routinely, analyses that are based on principal components, orthogonal factor structure, and varimax rotation are conducted. In any given study, all these components might be challenged—not from a statistical standpoint but from a conceptual point. For example, orthogonal factors suggest that the factors or subscales of a measure are really independent (uncorrelated) in the mind of the investigator, but with thought the investigator may not really believe that. The issue is not which factor solution ought to be used but the prior question—how the factor solution relates to the investigator's model.

FOR FURTHER READING

Greenberg, J. & Folger, R. (1988). *Controversial issues in social research methods.* New York: Springer-Verlag.

Kihlstrom, J. (1995). *From the subject's point of view: The experiment as conversation and collaboration between investigator and subject.* Keynote address presented at the meeting of the American Psychological Society, New York.

Kruglanski, A. W. (1975). The human subject in the psychology experiment: Fact and artifact. In L. Berkowitz (Ed.), *Advances in experimental social psychology* (Vol. 8, pp. 101–147). Orlando, FL: Academic Press.

Rosenthal, R., & Rosnow, R.L. (1969). *Artifact in behavioral research.* New York: Academic Press.

Rosenthal, R., & Rosnow, R.L. (1975). *The volunteer subject.* New York: Wiley.

White, L., Tursky, B., & Schwartz, G.E. (Eds.). (1985). *Placebo: Theory, research, and mechanisms.* New York: Guilford.

Chapter 14

Statistical Methods of Data Evaluation

CHAPTER OUTLINE

Significance Tests and the Null Hypothesis
    Overview
    Significance Level (alpha)
    Power
    Ways of Augmenting Power

Special Topics in Data Analysis
    Analyses Involving Multiple Comparisons
    Multiple Outcomes: Multivariate and Univariate Analyses
    Data Analyses and Designing the Study

Objections to Statistical Significance Testing
    Interpretation of Statistical Tests
    Null Hypothesis Testing
    Replication and Cumulative Knowledge

Alternatives or Supplements to Tests of Significance
    Magnitude and Strength of Effect
    Confidence Intervals
    Meta-Analysis
    General Comments

Clinical Significance: Evaluating Intervention Effects
    Comparison Methods
    Subjective Evaluation
    Social Impact Measures
    General Comments

Summary and Conclusions

Assume that we have designed and run the study, gathered data on multiple measures, executed all elegant controls possible, and now are ready, in the privacy of our own laboratories, to find out what the effects were. At last, we are ready to examine the data statistically. Statistical evaluation refers to the use of quantitative techniques to describe the data or to draw inferences about the effects; that is, whether they are likely to be due to chance or to a veridical effect. Facets of the statistical evaluation that influence the conclusions that can be drawn pertain to statistical conclusion validity. The quantitative evaluation of the study depends on more than merely running a few tests. Current research in psychology and other sciences is based primarily on testing the null hypothesis and the search for statistically significant effects. Most journal articles utilize this approach (reflected in familiar phrases in "Results" sections noting that the findings are or are not "statistically significant.") Mastering research methodology requires understanding central features of statistical evaluation insofar as they influence designing experiments and drawing valid inferences. Consequently, this chapter covers key concepts and practices related to statistical evaluation of the data.

Since the emergence of statistical evaluation, there has been dissatisfaction with the approach to null-hypothesis testing. The dissatisfaction continues today with recommendations to eliminate tests of statistical significance or at the very least to supplement them with other indices (Kirk, 1996; Schmidt, 1996b; Shrout, 1997). The dissatisfaction is important to understand because there are myths about what significance testing means. Moreover, the practice of significance testing may even detract from the accumulation of knowledge. Thus, to understand conventional approaches to data evaluation, it is central to discuss the limits of these approaches. More than that, there are alternative methods of statistical data evaluation that continue to be suggested to move us away from tests of significance. This chapter conveys key issues and practices of conventional statistical evaluation, problems with testing for statistical significance, and strategies to supplement or replace conventional tests of the null hypothesis. In addition to null-hypothesis testing and the search for statistical significance, statistical techniques are used in clinical psychology to evaluate the clinical significance or importance of effects or changes. Methods of evaluating the clinical significance of results are also discussed.

SIGNIFICANCE TESTS AND THE NULL HYPOTHESIS

Overview

Once upon a time there was no statistical testing and no statistical evaluation. Actually, this statement probably reflects my poor scholarship. No doubt one of the first uses of statistical tests, like so many other firsts, can be traced to the ancient Greeks and specifically most likely to Aristotle. The first statistical evaluation emerged when Aristotle's mother played the money game with him and, with two closed hands said, "Ari, which hand holds *more* drachma? If you guess correctly, you can keep money in that hand." Ari replied, "Trick question Mom, although one hand has three coins and the other has one coin, the two numbers are not really different "statistically speaking." Aristotle's mom, no slouch herself (e.g., after all, she spoke fluent ancient Greek), quickly replied, "If they are not different, then let me give you what is in this hand!" at which point she handed him the one coin. (Aristotle learned early that one can accept the null hypothesis—no difference—when it is really not wise to do so.) In any case, invoking statistical significance as a criterion for decision making was a major contribution to science, for which we thank Aristotle. Showing that even when there is no statistical difference, there may be a real and important difference is also a major a contribution, for which we thank his mother.

Moving forward a bit in time and to nonfictional history, it is useful to stop in the 1920s and 1930s. During this period, statisticians devised practices that dominate current statistical methods of evaluation in psychology, and indeed in the sciences in general (Fisher, 1925; Neyman & Pearson, 1928). The practices include the actual statistical tests as well as key concepts such as posing a null hypothesis (no difference between groups) and using tests of significance to determine whether the difference obtained in the sample is of a sufficient magnitude to reject this hypothesis. A goal was to provide an objective or at least agreed-on criterion (e.g., significance levels) that can be used to decide whether the results in a particular study are likely to be due to chance, that is, normal fluctuation and sampling differences, and the differences that such fluctuations are likely to yield. From this approach, all sorts of worries emanated, such as power, effect size, chance, and other problems that are presumably so horrible that we have to disguise their real names (Type I and Type II errors).

The broad characteristics of significance testing are sufficiently clear to most individuals and they need not be elaborated. Essentially, in most research, statistical evaluation examines whether groups differing on a particular independent variable (e.g., different conditions) can be distinguished statistically on the dependent measure(s). Statistical evaluation consists of applying a test to assess whether the difference obtained on the dependent measure is likely to have occurred by chance. Typically, a level of confidence (such as .05 or .01) is selected as the criterion for determining whether the results are *statistically significant*.[1] A statistically significant difference indicates that the probability level is equal to or below the level of confidence selected, for example, $p \leq .05$. This means that if the experiment were completed 100 times, a difference of the magnitude found on the dependent variable would be likely to occur only five times on a purely chance basis. If the probability obtained in the study is lower than .05, most researchers would reject the null hypothesis and concede that group differences reflect a genuine relation between the independent and dependent variables.

To state that a relation in an experiment is statistically significant does not mean that there is necessarily a genuine effect (i.e., that a relationship exists between the variables studied). Even a statistically significant difference could be the result of a chance event because of sampling of subjects and other factors. Chance is the one rival hypothesis that can never be completely ruled out. Nevertheless, by tradition, researchers have agreed that when the probability yielded by a statistical test is as low as .05 or .01, there is a sufficiently conservative level of confidence to permit one to conclude that a relation between the independent and dependent variables exists.

Essentially, statistical evaluation provides a criterion to separate *probably veridical* from *possibly chance* effects. Although subjectivity and bias can enter into the process of statistical evaluation, for example, in terms of the tests that are applied and the criteria for statistical significance, the goal of statistics is to provide a relatively bias-free and consistent method of interpreting results. The prevalent use of statistics does not imply that agreement on their value is universal. Diverse facets of statistical evaluation have been challenged, including (1) the arbitrary criterion that a particular confidence level such as $p < .05$ represents, (2) the all-or-none decision making reached on the basis of that criterion, (3) the absence of information regarding the strength or practical value of the relationship between the independent and dependent variable regardless of whether statistical significance is attained, and (4) the likelihood that the null hypothesis on which tests are based is never really true (Chow, 1988; Kupfersmid, 1988; Meehl, 1978). Despite these concerns, hypothesis testing and statistical evaluation to detect relations among variables continue to dominate research.

Statistical evaluation provides consistent criteria for determining whether an effect is to be considered veridical. This advantage is critically important. We lose sight of this advantage as researchers because we are sequestered from nonresearch-based influences and advocacy in which the cannons of research are largely neglected. Claims for effective treatment, for example, for losing weight or reducing cigarette smoking, as advocated in trade books, magazine articles, and new exercise devices (e.g., to tighten one's stomach muscles ["abs"]) are rarely based on experimental methods and statistical evaluation. Testimonials by proponents of the techniques or those who have participated in the programs are the bases for evaluation. It would be valuable in these cases to apply experimental methods and to evaluate the results statistically.

There is another side. Statistical significance is required in part because it is not otherwise clear in many (indeed most) situations whether effects are beyond the changes, differences, or variations that would be evident by chance or without an intervention. Yet, clearly there are some situations in which statistical evaluation is not needed. We discussed marked changes in the chapter on case studies and single designs in which nonstatistical data evaluation criteria are invoked, in part to help detect only those changes that are marked. In general, whether for group or single-case research, very dramatic changes might be so stark that there is no question that something important, reliable, and veridical took place, the type of changes referred to as "slam bang" effects (Gilbert, Light, & Mosteller, 1975). Clarity of the finding may have to do with both the extent of impact and the confidence one can place in the outcome measures. For example, most of us would be persuaded about a special treatment if three individuals who were terminally ill continued to live after the treatment, but three others who did not receive the treatment died. The characteristics of this demonstration—the clarity of the dependent measure, the predicted outcome without treatment, and the vast differences in the outcomes—make this persuasive, even though, as always, we want replication. Yet, most situations from which we wish to draw inferences do not show such slam-bang effects; hence, it is important to use some criterion to decide whether the results, differences, or changes within or between groups are likely to be due to chance or random fluctuations in samples. Statistical significance is designed to serve this purpose.

Endorsement of statistical evaluation does not mean that statistics provide the "answer" or the "real truth." Statistical evaluation is subject to all sorts of abuses, ambiguities, misinterpretation, and subjectivity. Different methods of analyzing the same data can lead to different conclusions, even with seemingly minor variations in decision points and default criteria in the analyses.[2] Yet an advantage is that ambiguities can often be made explicit, studied, and understood. The explicitness of statistical procedures helps us raise questions and understand the limits of the conclusions.

Statistical evaluation is strongly emphasized in psychology; indeed, statistical significance often is regarded as the definitive test of whether the variables under investigation are important or worth pursuing. Yet statistical significance is a function of many different features of an experiment, only one of which is whether there is a relation between the independent and dependent variables. Testing for statistical significance depends on multiple, interrelated concepts. The researcher ought to know the concepts, how they interrelate, and how to control them. In the section that follows we consider key concepts, what they mean, and what the investigator can do to maximize the likelihood of demonstrating an effect, when in fact there is a difference.

Significance Level (alpha)

Significance level (alpha) is well known as a criterion for decision making in statistical data evaluation. Tradition has led us to use an alpha of $p < .05$ and .01 for decision making.[3] Will the results of the experiment be statistically significant? Among the determinants of the answer is the number of subjects per group in the study. It can be assumed that groups will never (well, hardly ever) have identical means on the outcome measures, simply because of normal fluctuations and sampling differences. Even if the observed difference is not statistically significant, the investigator can be assured that the same magnitude of difference between groups might be statistically significant or much closer to statistical significance if two or three times as many subjects were used.

Statistical significance is a direct function of sample size. That is, the larger the sample size, the smaller the group differences needed for statistical significance for a given level of confidence. Stated another way, a given difference between two groups will gradually approach statistical significance as the size of the samples within each group is increased. Indeed, statistical significance is virtually assured if a large number of subjects is used. (The importance of the sample size in relation to statistical significance is particularly evident with correlations. With a sample of 40,000 subjects, a correlation of $r = .01$ is significant at the .05 level.) When psychological studies began in the military, large-scale testing was completed that encompassed thousands of subjects. Invariably, investigators reported that statistical significance was virtually guaranteed no matter what variables were studied (Bakan, 1966; Nunnally, 1960). Large sample sizes make small, trivial, and chance differences more likely to lead to the conclusion that the results are statistically significant.

Power

The Problem Power (the extent to which an investigation can detect a difference when a difference exists) was discussed in an earlier chapter. It is important to revisit the issue because weak power is the Achilles' heel of psychological research. That is, if we are going to use tests of statistical significance to evaluate results, it is critical to ensure that there is a good chance (adequate power) to show a difference when the difference in fact exists. The level of power that is "adequate" is not justified or derived mathematically. As with the level of confidence (alpha), the decision is based on convention about the margin of protection one should have against accepting the null hypothesis when in fact it is false (beta). Cohen (1988) recommended adoption of the convention that beta = .20 and hence power (1 − beta) = .80 when alpha = .05. This translates to the likelihood of 4 in 5 in detecting an effect when a difference exists in the population. Although power greater than .80 is used as a criterion here, higher levels (.90, .95) are often encouraged as the acceptable criterion (Freiman et al., 1978; Friedman, Furberg, & DeMets, 1985).

Reviews within many different specialty areas of psychology and other fields as well have shown that most studies have insufficient power to detect differences (Cohen, 1992; Rossi, 1990; Sedlmeier & Gigerenzer, 1989). Moreover, repeated exhortations about the problem and consistently clear recommendations to rectify the problem have had little or no impact on research. (The value of this work in relation to clinical psychology has been in showing that insight and awareness into a problem often are not very potent interventions for changing the problem.) Nevertheless, it is important to convey the issues.

Weak or insufficient power is not a minor nuisance or merely a worry for misinterpreting a particular study. Broad areas of research can be characterized by weak power and the conclusions that these areas have generated might be attributed to this characteristic. For example, noted earlier was the finding in psychotherapy outcome research that treatments usually do not differ from each other. A conclusion that treatments are no different (i.e., support for the null hypothesis) is often interpreted to indicate that treatments are equally effective. Yet, for much of psychotherapy research, weak power is a rival interpretation because of the small sample sizes (10–20 cases per group) (Kazdin & Bass, 1989).

Relation to Alpha, Effect Size, and Sample Size Four different concepts of statistical inference have been discussed at varying points—the criterion for statistical significance (alpha), effect size (ES), sample size, and power. These concepts are interrelated in the sense that when three of these are specified, the remaining one can be determined. Their interrelations are critical in that they permit one to consider all sorts of options in an experiment, such as the level of power (given a specific level of alpha, ES, and a fixed N), what ES is needed (if alpha, power, and sample size are predetermined), and so on. The most frequent use of this information is to decide how many subjects to include in a study. Thus, to identify our sample size, we need to make decisions to fix the other three parameters, alpha, power, and ES. At this point, let us adopt alpha of .05 to adhere slavishly to tradition. As for level of power, we also might follow convention and accept power of .80. Now we must estimate ES. How can we possibly do this? The ES formula requires us to know the difference between the groups on the dependent variables of interest and the standard deviation (ES = $(m_1 - m_2)/s$).

Actually, in many areas of research, ES has been studied. The secondary analysis procedure, referred to as *meta-analysis*, has been used extensively for evaluating many areas of research (Cook et al., 1992). Meta-analyses provide estimates of ES for research in a given area. The ES is used as a common metric to combine studies using different dependent variables. We can consult such analyses to identify likely ESs for the study we propose to undertake. For example, if we are about to conduct a psychotherapy study comparing treatment with no treatment, we can estimate the ES from the many meta-analyses of psychotherapy (Brown, 1987; Roth & Fonagy, 1996; Weisz & Weiss, 1993). Effect size for such comparisons tends to be about .70. Alternatively, if we are comparing two or more treatments to each other, we know that ESs are likely to be smaller (e.g., in the range of .40–.60). The point is that ES estimates can be obtained from published research including individual studies or more conveniently from meta-analyses. Effect sizes vary across measures; thus, there is no one ES. Even so, estimating the likely ES for the main dependent measures is wise to do before the study.

When individual studies or meta-analyses are unavailable, ES can be estimated on rational grounds. The investigator may believe that there is no precedent for the type of work he or she is to conduct. (Indeed, we tend to believe this already about our research.) The investigator may have to guess whether the ES is likely to be small, medium, or large. Cohen (1988) provided us with admittedly arbitrary but quite useful guidelines in this regard by noting small, medium, and large ESs correspond to .20, .50, and .80 respectively. It is helpful to select a conservative estimate. If the investigator is new to an area of research (e.g., first or second study), it is likely that the strength of the experimental manipulation and many sources of variability may be unfamiliar and difficult to control. In such cases, it is likely that the investigator is slightly overoptimistic about the ESs he or she expects to achieve and may underestimate the sources of variability that attenuate group differences.

In any case, assume that by one of the above methods we consider the likely ES to be about .50. We have alpha = .05, power = .80, and ES estimated at .50. At this point, we can check power tables in various books (Cohen, 1988; Kraemer & Thiemann, 1987). As an illustration, Table 14.1 reprints portions of a power table for comparing two means, using an alpha of .05. The column marked *n* is the number of cases per group; across the top of the table is *d* (ES),

TABLE 14.1. Sample Power Table: Power, Sample Size, and Effect Size for a *t* Test

Power of *t* test of $m_1 = m_2$ at .05

					d						
n	.10	.20	.30	.40	.50	.60	.70	.80	1.00	1.20	1.40
10	06	07	10	13	18	24	31	39	56	71	84
15	06	08	12	18	26	35	45	56	75	88	96
20	06	09	15	23	33	45	58	69	87	96	99
25	06	11	18	28	41	55	68	79	93	99	
30	07	12	21	33	47	63	76	86	97		
31	07	12	21	34	49	64	77	87	97		
32	07	12	22	35	50	65	78	88	98		
33	07	13	22	36	51	67	80	89	98		
34	07	13	23	37	53	68	81	90	98		
35	07	13	23	38	54	70	82	91	98		
36	07	13	24	39	55	71	83	92	99		
37	07	14	25	39	56	72	84	92	99		
38	07	14	25	40	57	73	85	93	99		
39	07	14	26	41	58	74	86	94	99		
40	07	14	26	42	60	75	87	94	99		
42	07	15	27	44	62	77	89	95	99		
44	07	15	28	46	64	79	90	96			
46	08	16	30	48	66	81	91	97			
48	08	16	31	49	68	83	92	97			
50	08	17	32	50	70	84	93	98			
52	08	17	34	51	71	86	94	98			
54	08	18	34	53	73	87	95	98			
56	08	18	35	55	74	88	96	99			
58	08	19	36	57	76	89	96	99			
60	08	19	37	58	77	90	97	99			
64	09	20	39	61	80	92	98	99			
68	09	21	41	64	82	93	98				
72	09	22	43	66	85	94	99				
76	09	23	45	69	86	95	99				
80	10	24	47	71	88	96	99				
84	10	25	49	73	90	97	99				
88	10	26	51	75	91	98					
92	10	27	52	77	92	98					
96	11	28	54	79	93	99					
100	11	29	56	80	94	99					
120	12	34	64	87	97						
140	13	38	71	92	99						
160	14	43	76	95	99						
180	16	47	81	97							
200	17	51	85	98							
250	20	61	92	99							
300	23	69	96								
350	26	75	98								
400	29	81	99								
450	32	85	99								
500	35	88									

Note: $p < .05$ The column *n* is the number of subjects needed within each of the two groups; the column across the top marked *d* is effect size; the numbers within the body of the table are power. The example we are discussing in the text is one that asks: What sample size do we need if we have an effect size of .50, alpha = .05, and power of .80? Obviously, the table can be used another way by saying, if I start with a certain number of subjects (e.g., 50), what will be the power for a given effect size, and so on. Only a portion of the table is provided here. (The decimals are omitted from the power figures.)

Source: Adapted from Cohen, J. (1988). *Statistical power analysis in the behavioral sciences* (2nd ed.), pp. 36–37. Hillsdale, NJ: Erlbaum. Reprinted with permission.

with each column representing a different ES. The entries within the body of the table itself reflect power. For instance, let us enter the table in the column with ES = .50 to get an idea of how the table works. As we go down the column, we are looking for .80, which is the power we would like for our study. The table is marked to show .80 and the horizontal line moving to the left shows the *n* we need. When alpha = .05, ES = .50, and desired power is .80, we need 64 subjects per group (i.e., N = 128).

Most studies do not have a sample size this large, so maybe we can loosen up a bit. In fact, after seeing the N we need, we might say, "Who cares about power anyway?" If we lighten up and reduce power to .50, we need a sample size of only 32 per group (N = 64). Relaxing power in this way is very risky. In my own research, I care a lot about power. I am not going to do many studies in my lifetime, so I am not too keen on handicapping myself with weak power for studies that I do conduct. Designing a powerful test is really important to get the most sensitive test feasible. If one adheres to the tradition of statistical significance testing, power and its related concepts are absolutely critical and cannot be neglected.

When we consider power in advance of a study, we are likely to learn that to detect a reasonable (medium) ES we need a much larger N than we planned or perhaps even than we can obtain. This fact is excellent to identify before one conducts the study. We may then decide to vary alpha (e.g., $p < .10$) or reduce power slightly (e.g., power = .75) or to select experimental conditions (or variations of the manipulation) that are likely to yield a larger ES. Such informed deliberations and decisions are praised when they are completed *prior to* an investigation. The use of power tables helps one to experiment intelligently with possible options regarding alpha, power, ES, and N.

The frustrations of persons advocating attention to power stem in part from the ease of using power tables. The information is readily available. Estimating power, sample size, ES, or alpha when the other three concepts are fixed requires little time (2 minutes for the unseasoned researcher, 1 minute for the seasoned researcher). (The 1 minute is divided as follows: 40 seconds for turning to the correct table in one of the books, 10 seconds for getting the correct columns, 10 seconds to react and make such statements as, "You've got to be kidding.") The task has become easier because computer software that allows one to enter any parameter (N, ES, alpha, power) and to see any or all other parameters is readily available (e.g., Gorman, Primavera, & Allison, 1995; Statistical Solutions, 1995). From these or other programs, one can readily identify needed sample size with a keyboard click or two. This places a lot of power at the investigator's fingertips.

One further point about sample size and power is worth noting. Power pertains to the statistical comparisons the investigator will make, including subanalyses that may divide groups into various subgroups. For example, the investigator may have N = 100 subjects in two groups. The main comparison of interest may contrast group 1 (*n* = 50) with group 2 (*n* = 50). The investigator may plan several analyses that further divide the sample, for example, by sex (males vs. females), age (younger vs. older), intelligence (median IQ split), or some other variable. Such comparisons divide the groups into smaller units (or subgroups). Instead of groups with $n = 50$, the subgroups are much smaller and power is commensurately reduced. The lesson is simple. Ensure adequate power for the comparisons of primary interest.

Variability in the Data   Power is a function of alpha, N, and ES. However, there is more to power than the formula for its computation. Noted already was the notion that excessive variability within an experiment can threaten statistical conclusion validity. Variability is inherent in the nature of subject performance in any investigation. However, the investigator can inadvertently increase variability in ways that will reduce the obtained ES. Obviously, if the mean difference between groups equals 8 on some measure, ES will increase or decrease depending on the size of the standard deviation by which that difference is divided. The standard deviation can be larger as a function of the heterogeneity of the subjects (e.g., in age, background, sex, socioeconomic class, etc.). The effects of the intervention or experimental manipulation are likely to be less consistent across subjects whose differences (heterogeneity) are relatively great. The heterogeneity of the subjects is reflected in a larger within-group variability. This variability, referred to as error variance, is directly related to ES and statistical significance. For a given difference between groups on the dependent measure, the larger the error variance, the less likely the results will be statistically significant. As discussed in Chapter 3, error variance can be increased by sloppiness and lack of care in how the experiment is conducted, by using heterogeneous and diverse subjects who vary on characteristics related to the outcome, and by using measures that have poor reliability. Procedures and practices that reduce or minimize extraneous variability increase the obtained effect size and power.

Ways of Augmenting Power

Varying Alpha Levels within an Investigation   To increase power, the obvious alternatives are to increase sample size and to minimize error variability. Because alpha levels are related to power, their use and variation warrant attention. Alpha at $p < .05$ or .01 is rather fixed within the field and represents constraints over which the investigator would seemingly have little control. Yet, there are separate circumstances in which we may wish to reconsider the alpha level. The investigator may decide to relax the alpha level (reduce the probability of Type II error) on the basis of substantive or design issues that are decided before data collection.

Several circumstances may lead the investigator to anticipate specific constraints that will attenuate the likely ES. First, the criterion for selecting groups in a case-control study might be known to be imperfect or somewhat tenuous. Thus, some persons in one group (e.g., nondepressed controls) might, through imperfect classification, belong in the other group (e.g., depressed persons). Comparison of groups will be obscured by variability and imperfect classification. Second, the measures in the area of research may not be very well established. The unreliability of the measure may introduce into the situation variability that will affect the sensitivity of the experimental test. The predicted relation may have been evident with more sensitive and reliable measures.

Third, the specific comparison of interest may be expected to generate a very small difference between groups. If we expect small differences, the usual advice is to increase sample size so that power will be high for this small effect. When college student samples can be run and a large subject pool is available, that alternative is quite useful. In clinical settings, increasing sample size is not always that easy; sometimes it is not possible because there are relatively few subjects available with the characteristics of interest (e.g., children with a particular chronic disease, cohabiting adults of the same gender raising children, professors with social skills). Obtaining large numbers of cases might require sampling across a wide geographical area or continuing the study for a protracted period; in fact, it might preclude conducting the research. Altering alpha might be reasonable as a way of evaluating predicted differences between groups.

Fourth, we might alter alpha on the basis of consideration of the consequences of our decisions. Consequences here refer to patient care (benefit, suffering), cost, policy issues (e.g., ease of dissemination, providing the greatest care to the greatest number), and other considerations in which the weight of accepting or rejecting the null hypothesis has greatly different implications and value. For example, if we are studying whether a particular procedure has side effects, we might want to alter alpha to $p < .20$. In such a study, we may wish to err (Type II) on the side of stating the side effects exist if there is any reasonable suggestion that they do exist.

In a given experiment, alpha is one of many decision points. Even though the acceptable level of alpha is deeply ingrained by tradition, the investigator ought to consider thoughtful departures because of circumstances of the particular experiment. There are also circumstances in which the investigator may plan to use different levels of alpha within an experiment. For example, suppose we are studying three conditions in a psychotherapy study: (1) treatment A, (2) treatment A with an added ingredient to enhance outcome, and (3) a no-treatment control group. We sample 75 persons who meet various criteria (e.g., diagnosis, age, physical health) and assign them randomly to conditions, with the restriction that an equal number will appear in each group. What shall we use for the alpha level? We could use an alpha of .05 and let the matter rest. Alternatively, we might before the study consider the comparisons of interest and their likely ESs. The difference between treatments versus no treatment is likely to be large. The usual alpha level ($p < .05$) to detect a difference might be reasonable in this situation. In contrast, the difference between treatment A with and without a special ingredient is likely to be smaller. A sample of 75 subjects with 25 cases per group in our hypothetical study is larger than the samples of most studies in psychotherapy research but is still likely to be too small to show statistically significant differences (Kazdin & Bass, 1989). It might be reasonable to use a more lenient alpha level (e.g., $p < .20$) for comparisons of the two treatments.

In general, in a given instance it may be useful to reconsider alpha level before a study or for some of the tests or comparisons within the study. If on a priori grounds special conditions within the design can be expected to attenuate sensitivity of an effect, a more lenient alpha may be justified. Both theoretical and applied concerns might lead to reconsidering alpha. Altering alpha level might be guided by evaluating the nature of the consequences of different decisions; that is, concluding that there is or is not a reliable difference between conditions.

Tinkering with alpha levels has to be considered very carefully. Obviously, relaxing alpha levels after the fact or when the results just miss conventional significance levels is inappropriate and violates the model on which significance testing is based. It is tempting to relax alpha levels in this way because few believe that a finding has been supported at $p < .05$ but is unsupported at a p level above that (e.g., $p < .06$ or $.10$). However, within the conventional model of significance testing, some generally agreed-on criterion has to be selected. Whatever that criterion is, there will always be instances that just miss and in which the investigator, but not many others of the scientific community, would say that the effect is close enough to be regarded as reliable.

Use of Pretests   Noted previously were experimental designs that used pretests. From a design standpoint, the advantages of using pretests were manifold and included issues related to the information they provide (e.g., about magnitude of change, number of persons who change, etc.). The statistical advantages of a pretest are the most universal basis for using such designs. The advantage of the pretest is that with various analyses, the error term in evaluating ES is reduced. With repeated assessment of the subjects (pre- and posttest), the within-group (subject) variance can be taken into account to reduce the error term.

Consider the impact on the ES formula. When there is a pretest measure or another measure that is related to performance at posttreatment (e.g., covariate), the ES error term is altered. The formula is represented by $ES = (m_1 - m_2)/s\sqrt{1-r^2}$ where r equals the correlation between the pretest (or other variable) and posttest. As the correlation between the pre- and posttest increases, the error term (denominator) is reduced; hence, the power of the analysis increases. Several statistical analyses that take advantage of the use of a pretest, such as analyses of covariance, repeated measures analyses of variance, and gain scores, can be used (Lipsey, 1990).

Use of Directional Tests   Another issue related to power is the controversial matter of one- versus two-tailed tests. In significance testing, alpha is used to decide whether a difference between groups is reliable. Consider a two-group study and a t test to evaluate group differences. The null hypothesis is that the groups do not differ; that is, the ES equals 0. A two-tailed test evaluates the obtained difference in light of departures from 0 in either direction; that is, whether one group is better or worse than another. The alpha of .05 refers to both "tails" (ends of the normal distribution), which are used as the critical region for rejection.

In much research, the investigator may have a view about the direction of the differences. He or she may not wish to test if the ES is different from zero but rather whether the treatment is better than the control condition or whether treatment A is better than treatment B. The hypothesis to reject is not bidirectional (better or worse) but unidirectional (better). As such, the investigator may wish to use a one-tailed test. A lower *t* value is required for the rejection of the null hypothesis if a one-tailed directional test is provided.

Most hypotheses in research are directional in the sense that investigators have an idea and interest in differences in a particular direction. For this reason, some authors have suggested that most significance testing should be based on one-tailed tests (Mohr, 1990). However, there is resistance to this, and the reader should be alerted. There is often an implicit assumption that investigators who use one-tailed tests may have done so because the results would otherwise not be statistically significant. Often it is unclear to the reader of the research report that the use of one-tailed tests was decided before seeing the results. The implicit assumption does not give the benefit of doubt to the investigator. At the same time, relatively few studies in clinical psychology and related areas utilize one-tailed tests. One rarely sees such tests or sees them only in situations in which the results would be significant regardless of whether the tests were completed as one- or two-tailed tests.

In general, investigators are encouraged to be conservative in their analyses of the data and in drawing conclusions about relations that are reliable or statistically significant. The discussion of multiple comparisons (in the next section) conveys this tradition rather well. Yet, directional hypotheses and use of one-tailed tests warrant consideration. Critical to their use is clarification of the basis of the prediction so that consumers of research can identify whether the tests are reasonable. Also, because one-tailed tests are occasionally viewed suspiciously, the investigator might wish to note tests that would or would not have been significant with two-tailed tests. Comments on both type of tests within a study do not reflect concerns of the statistician who might lobby for a rational evaluation of using one or the other form of tests (but not both). Yet, comments about the conclusions drawn from statistical tests raise broader issues. Among these issues is the importance of informing colleagues about the dependence of conclusions on assumptions and methods of analyses.

SPECIAL TOPICS IN DATA ANALYSIS

Analyses Involving Multiple Comparisons

Controlling Alpha Levels   In an experiment, the investigator is likely to include multiple groups and to compare some or all groups with each other. For example, the study may include four groups—three treatment groups and one control group. The investigator may conduct an overall test (analysis of variance) to see whether there are differences among the groups. If the differences are statistically significant, several individual comparisons may be made to identify which groups differ from each other. Alternatively, the investigator may forego the overall test. Several two-group (pair-wise) comparisons may be completed as each treatment is compared to each other treatment and to the control group. Alpha might be set at $p \leq .05$ to protect against the risk of a Type I error. This alpha refers to the risk for a given comparison, sometimes referred to as a *per comparison error rate*. However, there are multiple comparisons. With multiple tests, the overall error rate or risk of a Type I error can be much higher. This increase is sometimes referred to as *probability pyramiding* to note that the accumulation of the actual probability of a Type I error increases with the number of tests. How much higher the p level increases depends directly on the number of different comparisons. In fact, with a number of comparisons, each held at the per comparison rate of .05, the probability of concluding that some significant effect has been obtained can be very high. In our hypothetical example with four groups, the investigator may make all possible comparisons of the groups (six total pair-wise comparisons). Although the pair-wise error rate is .05, the risk of a Type I error for the experiment is higher because of the number of tests. The overall rate is referred to as the *experiment-wise error rate*. We must control for the probability of a Type I error for the all the comparisons or for the experiment-wise error rate. That is, the alpha selected must account for the number of pair-wise comparisons.

There are several multiple comparison tests that are available to address the problem of experiment-wise error rate and to control the increased Type I risk (Hochberg & Tamhane, 1987). Many more familiar multiple-comparison tests are known by the name of the persons primarily responsible for their development (e.g., various tests by Tukey, Duncan, Scheffé). A relatively simple alternative is referred to as the Bonferroni procedure, which consists of a way to adjust alpha in light of the number of comparisons that are made. Consider how the test operates. In a set of comparisons, the upper boundary of the probability of rejecting the null hypothesis is the number of comparisons (k) times alpha (α) (e.g., $p = .05$). Obviously, if there are 10 comparisons to be made, the overall error rate is $k\alpha$, or .50. As a protection against a Type I error, $p = .50$ would clearly be unacceptable. To control the overall error rate, alpha can be adjusted for the number of comparisons.

The Bonferroni adjustment is based on dividing alpha ($p = .05$) by the number of comparisons. In our four-group study, there are six possible pair-wise comparisons. If we set alpha at .05, we know the risk is actually much higher because of the number of comparisons. To make an adjustment, we divide alpha by the number of tests. In our example, we divide .05/6 which yields $p = .0083$. For each individual pair-wise comparison we complete (treatment 1 vs. treatment 2, treatment 1 vs. control group, etc.), we use $p \leq .0083$ as the criterion for significance. If we use this criterion, the overall experiment-wise error rate is controlled at $p = .05$.

The Bonferroni adjustment controls the overall (experiment-wise) error rate, for example, at $p \leq .05$. The error rates for the individual comparisons (per comparison) need not be equal (e.g., all at $p \le .0083$ in the prior example). If the investigator wishes greater power for some tests rather than others, individual comparisons can vary in their per comparison alpha level as long as the overall per comparison alpha levels do not exceed the experiment-wise error rate of .05 when summed for all comparisons.

The adjustment of alpha, as noted here, arises when several pair-wise comparisons are made on a given measure. A similar concern, for elevated alpha emerges when there are multiple outcome measures and multiple tests comparing the same groups for each measure. For example, if two groups of patients (anxious vs. nonanxious patients) are compared on several different measures, the chance of finding a significant difference when there is none in the population is higher than $p = .05$ for a given comparison. Here too, the Bonferroni adjustment can be used for the number of comparisons in which k refers still to the number of comparisons or tests. As before, for each pair-wise test, the adjusted level is used to decide whether the effects are statistically significant.

Considerations   There is general agreement that multiple comparisons require some adjustment to control for Type I error. Failure to consider the multiplicity of the comparisons has direct implications for statistical conclusion validity, in this case, often concluding that there are significant differences when, by the usual criteria for alpha, none exists. Beyond these general points and at the point investigators need to make data-analytic decisions, agreement diminishes. For example, which multiple-comparison tests are appropriate and whether a given test is too conservative or stringent are two areas in which reasonable statisticians can disagree. Use of an adjustment such as the Bonferroni procedure is fairly common. Although the adjusted alpha is reasonable, the consequence can be sobering in a given study. In practice, the number of significant effects decreases when an adjusted level is used. Stated differently, as the alpha for individual pair-wise comparisons becomes more stringent, power decreases, and the probability of a Type II error increases.

Within the current practices of significance testing, control of Type I error rather than Type II error and power is given the highest priority. Hence, investigators are encouraged (by tradition, research advisors, reviewers, editors) to keep alpha at .05 or .01 almost at all costs. The difficulty for this orientation in research is that we already know that power in most psychological studies is likely to be weak. When adjustments are made to control overall alpha levels, power of a study decreases even further. That is, apart from a relatively small sample size, the investigator is burdened by correcting for the number of statistical tests. Understandably, investigators are reluctant to adjust for the large number of tests that are often completed.

There are alternatives for the investigator who believes central findings are supported by the statistical comparisons but sees them disappear when alpha is adjusted to control the experiment-wise error rate. First, the investigator can present the results for both adjusted and nonadjusted alpha levels. The results can note the tests that remain significant under both circumstances and the tests that are significant when left unadjusted. This is not a completely satisfactory solution, but it addresses the ambivalence and tension both in the author and field at large, namely, to identify what the effects are, to retain power at a reasonable level, but not to get carried away with an extraordinarily large number of tests, only a few of which are statistically significant.

Second, the investigator can select an experiment-wise alpha that is slightly more lenient than $p < .05$, such as $p < .10$ prior to making the adjustment. The Bonferroni adjustment will divide this alpha by the number of comparisons. The per comparison alpha is still below .05, depending on the number of comparisons. Adopting an experiment-wise rate of .10 is usually of less concern to other researchers than adopting this rate for individual comparisons (per comparison rate).

Third, the investigator may not be interested in all possible comparisons, but rather in only a preplanned subset that relates specifically to one or two primary hypotheses. Adjusting alpha for this smaller number of comparisons means that the per comparison rate (of alpha) is not as stringent. Indeed, for a few planned comparisons, not adjusting for the number of tests is usually viewed as satisfactory. Here the difference is in conveying at the outset of the study what the hypotheses are and what specific tests will be used to evaluate them. Direct, planned, and a priori comparisons are usually favored. If any additional, supplementary, or exploratory analyses are conducted, they might be more conservatively tested (e.g., with adjusted p levels).

The alternatives do not exhaust the range of possibilities. Among the options is the use of less conservative variations of the Bonferroni adjustment (Simes, 1986) or a variety of other procedures to control Type I error (Hochberg & Tamhane, 1987). Also, one can deemphasize all tests of significance in the data analysis. Measures of the strength of the relation such as ES can be used and are not subject to the same concerns as statistical tests. (This alternative is elaborated later because of the broader implications in relation to current research practices.) The central point is not to argue for one specific solution but to underscore the importance of addressing the issue in the data analyses. Any data-analytic issue that can be anticipated also requires consideration at the design stage. Identifying the major comparisons of interest in the study, the statistical tests that will be used, and the number of tests may have implications for sample size and power. All such matters directly affect the conclusions to which the investigator is entitled and hence are critical to consider before the first subject is run.

Multiple Outcomes: Multivariate and Univariate Analyses

In most clinical research, multiple measures are used to evaluate the impact of an intervention. For example, in a therapy outcome study, several measures may be obtained to assess different perspectives (e.g., clients, relatives, therapists) about the client's functioning in several domains (e.g., depression, self-esteem, adjustment at home and at work) and to rely on different assessment formats (e.g., interviews, questionnaires, direct observations). When there are multiple measures, the interrelations of the measures raise issues relevant to the data analyses.

Performance on several outcome measures may be conceptually related because they reflect a domain the investigator views as a unit or empirically related because the measures correlate highly with each other. For instance, if we have 10 dependent measures, we could analyze these separately with *t* or F tests. We could avoid the problem of an inflated Type I error with the adjustment (e.g., Bonferroni) noted previously. Another issue pertains to the fact that the measures may be interrelated. Univariate tests, that is, separate tests for each measure, do not take into account the possible redundancy of the measures and their relation to each other. It is possible, for example, that two outcome measures show significant effects due to treatment. The investigator may discuss how robust the effects are across two measures, when in fact the high correlation between the measures argues for one construct rather than two. It is also possible that neither measure shows a significant effect but, when viewed as a conceptual whole, in fact does show an effect. The measures individually may not provide as robust or indeed as reliable an effect as they do when combined.

When there are multiple outcome measures, we can consider the data to be multivariate. It may be desirable to conduct multivariate analyses (e.g., such as multivariate analyses of variance). Multivariate analyses include several measures in a single data analysis, whereas univariate analyses examine one measure at a time. We do not use multivariate analyses because we have several dependent measures. Rather, the primary basis is the investigator's interest in understanding the relations among the dependent measures. The multivariate analyses consider these relations by providing a linear combination of the measures and evaluating whether that combination provides evidence for significant differences. For example, the study may include three measures of anxiety. One multivariate analysis might be completed by combining these measures. If the overall multivariate analysis indicates a significant effect, this suggests that some combination of variables has shown the effect of the intervention or independent variable of interest.

After finding the overall effect of the multivariate analysis, one might conduct univariate tests (individual F tests on each measure) to identify the specific differences on each dependent variable. As before, the alpha would need to be adjusted to avoid elevated Type I error. However, univariate tests may or may not show significant effects following an overall multivariate analysis. The multivariate analysis takes into account the relation of the measures to each other and evaluates the combination of measures. Univariate analyses ignore this facet of the structure of the data and may not lead to similar conclusions.

Considerations   It may be quite appropriate to analyze the multiple outcome measures with multivariate analysis or with several univariate tests (Haase &

Ellis, 1987; Huberty & Morris, 1989). Multivariate analyses are particularly appropriate if the investigator views the measures as conceptually interrelated and is interested in various groupings of the measures separate from or in addition to the individual measures themselves. For example, there may be several measures of patient adjustment and family functioning. Within the study, the investigator may group all the measures of patient adjustment and conduct a multivariate analysis to identify a combination for the overall conceptual domain and do the same for the measures of family functioning. Separate analyses may also be conduced for the individual scales within each conceptual domain if they, too, are of interest. For example, drug use has been studied among adolescents to understand its onset, course, and relation to later adult adjustment (Newcomb & Bentler, 1988). Drug use was conceived as a latent variable (construct with multiple indices) and included three measures, namely, the use of alcohol (beer, wine, liquor), cannabis (marijuana and hashish), and hard drugs (e.g., cocaine, barbiturates, LSD, and others). The data analyses focused on drug use (e.g., all the measures together) because they were conceived as a general tendency toward substance use. The three individual measures were also evaluated separately because some substances (hard drugs) were expected (and were shown) to have particularly deleterious long-term outcomes. However, both levels of analyses—the combined variable and the individual variables—led to meaningful and important findings.

Multivariate analyses evaluate the composite variables based on their interrelations. This is a unique feature and is not addressed by performing several separate univariate tests. Separate univariate tests might be appropriate under a variety of conditions if the investigator does not view the measures as conceptually related, if the measures in fact are uncorrelated, or if the primary or exclusive interest is the individual measures themselves rather than how they combine or relate to each other. Investigators occasionally use the multivariate analysis as an overall test. After the multivariate analysis is significant, they proceed with several univariate tests. Usually, these tests are conducted with a per comparison alpha of .05; hence, the overall risk of Type I error is greatly increased. Findings of statistical significance in this situation is a problem because the multivariate test was assumed to control for a Type I error at the level of alpha (p = .05). The individual univariate tests, if conducted, still require consideration of the number of tests and the experiment-wise error rate.

Data Analyses and Designing the Study

Significance testing is the mainstay of contemporary research. Issues related to alpha, power, anticipated ES, and error rates stemming from multiple tests, to mention a few, are critical to ponder as the study is being planned. These are not esoteric issues nor merely quantitative nuances. Rather, they squarely affect the conclusions the investigator wishes to draw and the strength and quality of the design. More concretely, as the purpose of the study and design are being formulated, it is useful to write each hypothesis and next to each one to outline the tentative data-analytic strategies that will be used. In light of the specific tests and analyses, one can ask:

- Do I have sufficient power given the likely ES?
- Can I vary alpha, sample size, or reduce variability in some ways (e.g., homogeneity of the sample, how the study is run) to augment power?
- Can I increase the strength or potency of the independent variable or magnify the effect that will occur by using different groups in the design or by contrasting conditions (experimental and control) that are likely to produce stronger effect sizes?
- Do I need each group in this study or can I deploy all the subjects to fewer groups (thereby increasing power)?
- Will there be other tests related to this hypothesis that will divide the groups further (e.g., contrasting males vs. females) and thereby reduce power?

Addressing, and to the extent possible, resolving these questions at the design stage are very helpful. After the experiment is completed, no doubt other questions and data-analytic issues will emerge; hence, not all the results and plans for their evaluation can be anticipated. At the same time, the plan for the major analyses ought to be worked out at the design stage so that changes can be made in the design to enhance the facets of statistical conclusion validity.

OBJECTIONS TO STATISTICAL SIGNIFICANCE TESTING

Because statistical significance testing continues to dominate contemporary research, mastery of the issues and methods discussed previously is critically important for persons planning a career in research. At the same time, there is another side; namely, that as currently practiced and interpreted, statistical significance testing is misleading and counterproductive. Recommendations include that we either abandon the practice entirely or supplement significance testing with other information (for recent reviews, see Kirk, 1996; Schmidt, 1996b). This view is not new, nor is it a radical minority view held by extremists whose dissertations, like mine, turned them against conventional alpha levels.

A brief historical comment is in order. When statistical tests and null-hypothesis testing first emerged (Fisher, 1925; Neyman & Pearson, 1928), objections that challenged the logic and utility of such an approach followed (Berkson, 1938). From that time until the present, there has been a continuous "crescendo of challenges" (Kirk, 1996, p. 747). For example, among the stronger statements, Meehl (1978, p. 817) noted that significance testing to evaluate the null hypothesis "is a terrible mistake, is basically unsound, poor scientific strategy and one of the worst things that ever happened in the history of psychology." (Of course, as a clinical psychologist, this statement is hard to interpret, but it sounds negative to me.) Meehl has been articulate in stating the case but is by no means alone in the concern. The objections to significance testing pertain to what they do and do not accomplish and how they are misinterpreted. The objections are mentioned briefly as a way of moving toward an alternative recommendation for statistical evaluation of research.

Interpretation of Statistical Tests

One objection (or rather, set of objections) pertains to how tests of significance are interpreted. First, a *p* value (e.g., .05) is often interpreted to reflect the likelihood that the null hypothesis (no difference) is not true and therefore that the alternative hypothesis is true. The *p* value is not a measure of the veracity of a hypothesis nor the degree to which it may be true. The null hypothesis might be true no matter what the results show; also, even if the null hypothesis were not true, this does not necessarily argue specifically for the alternative hypothesis.

Second, a nonsignificant difference may be mistakenly interpreted to reflect *no relation* between the independent and dependent variables. If the null hypothesis is not rejected, it must be accepted. Accepting the null hypothesis is usually interpreted as no effect; that is, the differences between groups is probably just due to chance. In fact, researchers tend to believe that findings at *p* < .05 or lower are real effects and reflect a relation but that above this level (*p* > .05) group differences do not exist or are just chance (Rosenthal & Gaito, 1963). There is no rational basis for this belief. In their now classic quote, Rosnow and Rosenthal (1989, p. 1277) noted that, "Surely, God loves the .06 nearly as much as the .05." Whether the null hypothesis is rejected is based on power and on a veridical effect. When the null hypothesis is accepted, there could still be an effect (i.e., group differences) and even a fairly potent effect (ES). Not significantly different is not tantamount to no difference or no effect of the independent variable.

Third, a higher level *p* value (e.g., *p* < .0001 rather than *p* < .05) is often interpreted to mean that the effect is more potent, stronger, more important, or more likely to be replicated in a subsequent study. The use of the term "highly significant effect" in many articles belies implicit misconceptions about what a statistically significant result means. *The p level does not tell us the magnitude or strength of the difference.* In fact, it is quite possible that a statistically significant difference in one experiment (at *p* < .0001) reflects a *weaker* effect than a nonsignificant finding (*p* < .20) in another study. The reason is that *p* level is related to strength of the relation (e.g., ES) *and* sample size, not strength of the relation alone. In one study, a smaller ES might lead to a statistically significant difference, purely as a function of power. For the same reason (power), a stronger ES in another study may not yield a statistically significant difference.

The trouble with statistical tests is that in their current use they require us to make a binary decisions (accept, reject) for the null hypothesis. If we do not accept the null hypothesis, then we must reject it and turn to the alternate hypothesis. What we would rather have is some idea of the likelihood that the scientific hypothesis *is* true (i.e., treatment A is better than treatment B) and forget the null hypothesis altogether.

Null Hypothesis Testing

Hypothesis testing is based on controlling alpha (Type I error), as reflected in the concern for setting *p* at ≤ .05 or .01. That is, we do not want to reject the null hypothesis (no difference) when in fact it is true. The problem with this is that there is no control of Type II error; it is allowed to vary widely and wildly. If alpha (Type I error) is set at $p = .05$, what does this mean for beta (Type II error)? Usually, Type II is about .50 or .80. All discussion of power pertains to Type II errors (power $= 1 - \beta$). Thus, when power is weak (e.g., .50), beta is high (.50). Weak power means we are very likely to accept the null hypothesis when it is false.

As noted earlier, a concern with significance testing is that the null hypothesis is always false. That is, the means for two groups will always be different (e.g., at some decimal) and asking whether groups are different "is foolish" (Tukey, 1991, p. 100). If the null hypothesis is false, we cannot commit a Type I error (i.e., we cannot reject the null hypothesis when it is false). Yet, it is very likely that we will commit a Type II error because the chances of showing a difference given weak power of experiments is so high. Weak power is exacerbated when we perform adjustments on the analyses (e.g., Bonferroni) that make alpha more stringent for individual comparisons. Whether a particular study rejects that effect is a function of power, as we have noted. When groups are truly different, we care less about the actual p value and more about whether the differences are large, small, or in-between. Also, when we consider multiple independent variables (e.g., prediction studies), we want to know their relative impact in relation to some criterion or outcome. Statistical significant testing alone does not provide such information.

Replication and Cumulative Knowledge

Significance testing may impede replication and the accumulation of knowledge. There are all sorts of contradictory findings and failures to replicate. To be sure, many might come from the fact that a given finding may depend on moderating influences (e.g., age, sex, social class of the population) and variations in the samples among the different studies. In relation to the present discussion, we are confronted with a more dramatic point, namely, that identical findings can yield contradictory results when statistical significance testing is the basis for drawing influences.

Consider for a moment that we have completed a study and have obtained an effect size of .70. This magnitude of effect is about the level of ES demonstrated when psychotherapy is compared with no treatment. An ES of this magnitude indicates a fairly strong relation and is considered a moderate-to-large ES. Would an ES of this magnitude also be reflected in statistically significant group differences? The answer depends on the sample size. Consider two hypothetical studies, both with an ES of .70. In Study I, we have a two-group study with 10 cases in each group (N = 20). In Study II, we have two groups with 30 cases in each group (N = 60). We complete each study and are ready to analyze the data. In each study, we have two groups, so we decide to evaluate group differences using a t test. The test formula can be expressed in many ways. The relation between statistical significance and ES for our two-group study can be seen in the following formula:

$$t = \text{ES} \times \frac{1}{\sqrt{1/n_1 + 1/n_2}}$$

where ES $= (m_1 - m_2)/s$.

In Study I, in which ES $= .70$ and there are 10 cases in each of the two groups, the above formula yields $t = 1.56$ with degrees of freedom (df) of 18 (or $n_1 + n_2 - 2$). If we consult a table for the Student's t distribution, we note that a t of 2.10 is required for $p = .05$. Our t does *not* meet the $p \leq .05$ level; therefore, we conclude no difference between group 1 and group 2. When ES $= .70$ and there are 30 cases in each of the two groups, the above formula yields $t = 2.71$, with a df of 58. If we consult Student's t distribution, we note that the t we obtained is higher than the t of 2.00 we required for this df at $p < .05$. Thus, we conclude that groups 1 and 2 *are* different. Obviously, we have two studies with identical effects but diametrically opposed conclusions about group differences. This is chaos and not how we want our science to proceed.

In this example, identical results yielded different conclusions. The implications on a broad scale are enormous. When we express skepticism in noting that a finding was found in one study but not replicated in another, this is based on the fact that in one study the results were statistically different and in another study they were not. In the accumulation of knowledge, we cannot really separate those failures to replicate effects that in fact reflect similar results (ESs) from those that represent genuine differences in the findings.

ALTERNATIVES OR SUPPLEMENTS TO TESTS OF SIGNIFICANCE

It is easy to criticize statistical significance testing; the arguments have been well articulated for the past 60 years and real examples can be cited to show the foolishness of our ways. Generating alternatives has not been a problem and three common suggestions are noted here.

Magnitude and Strength of Effect

In place of (or in addition to) statistical significance testing, it would be helpful to report some measure of the magnitude or strength of the relation between the independent and dependent variable or the magnitude of the differences between groups. In clinical research, the notion of the strength of the relation is obviously important. For example, if we wish to compare parents who abuse their children with parents who do not, we do not merely wish to demonstrate statistically significant differences on several measures (e.g., parent stress, family functioning). In addition, we wish to know the strength of association and magnitude of the relation between parental abuse status and other variables. If all the variables we study differentiate abusive from nonabusive parents, we would like to know the strength of these connections and the relative contribution of each.

Magnitude of effect or strength of the relation can be expressed in many different ways—omega^2 (ω^2), eta (η), epsilon^2 (ε^2), and Pearson product–moment correlation (r, r^2) and in multiple regression (R and R^2) (Haase, Ellis, & Ladany, 1989; Kirk, 1996; Rosenthal, 1984; Rosenthal & Rosnow, 1991). One measure we have already discussed is ES, which illustrates nicely the informational yield provided beyond statistical significance. Effect size permits one to provide a point estimate of what the strength of the relation is between variables. The utility of this estimate is in conveying the relation, not in deciding whether the relation is or is not statistically significant. Also, ES is familiar in light of its frequent use in meta-analyses. Moreover, with ES, the magnitude of effect is provided in a common metric that allows comparison (and combination) of different experiments using different outcome measures.

An effect size of .20, .50, or .80 can be interpreted in terms of standard deviation units. In a study comparing an intervention and control group, an ES of .70 is readily interpretable in relation to the differences in the distributions between the treatment and the no-treatment group. That is, ES can be translated into more concrete terms. Figure 14.1 shows two distributions, one for the treatment group and one for the control group. The means of the group (vertical lines) reflect an effect size of .70; that is, the mean of the intervention group is 7/10 of a standard deviation higher than the control group. One can go to a table of the normal distribution and convert this information into how persons in the intervention group fared relative to control subjects in standard deviation units. Given the effect size of .70, the average subject treated is better off than 76 percent of the persons who did not receive treatment. This percentage was

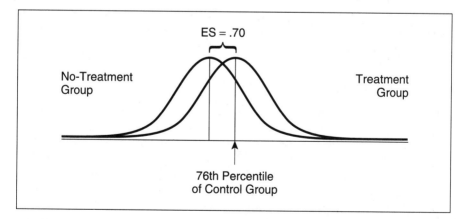

FIGURE 14.1 Representation of an effect size of .70 between an intervention and control group. Each group is reflected in its own distribution (normal curve). If the groups in fact are not different, the two distributions would be superimposed on one another and look like one distribution (same mean, same standard deviation). With an effect size of .70, the mean of the intervention group is .70 standard deviation units above the mean of the control group. The two distributions are discrepant.

TABLE 14.2. Simple Conversions to Move from Tests of Statistical Significance to Magnitude of the Relation or Effect Size

$$ES = \frac{2t}{\sqrt{df}}$$

$$r = \sqrt{\frac{t}{t^2 + df}}$$

$$r = \sqrt{\chi^2 (1) / N}$$

$$ES = \frac{2r}{\sqrt{1 - r^2}}$$

obtained by identifying what percentage of the population is below +.70 standard deviation units on the normal distribution.

Another familiar measure for evaluating the strength of the relationship is r. The correlation reflects the relation between the independent variable and dependent variable. The correlation squared (r^2) is used to reflect shared variance in these variables. Correlation is provided in many studies. Studies using multiple regression often report R or R^2 to convey how much variance is accounted for by predictors and outcomes. Both effect size and r are easily computed from formulae provided in introductory statistics books. Also, the estimates can be computed directly from familiar statistical tests of significance for comparing two groups. Note the easy conversions in Table 14.2. The equations convey that once one has t or χ^2, one can provide further information on ES and r. Thus, in terms of reporting results, one can derive with relative ease more (and perhaps more important) information than statistical significance.

Confidence Intervals

Effect size (or some other measure of magnitude of effect) provides a point estimate, that is, a specific value that estimates the population value. To supplement this estimate, confidence intervals are also recommended (Kirk, 1996; Schmidt, 1996b). A confidence interval provides a range of values and reflects the likelihood that the ES in the population falls within a particular range. Common values used for confidence intervals are 95 percent or 99 percent, which parallels statistical criteria for alpha of .05 and .01. The formula for computing confidence intervals (CIs) is:

$$CIs = m \pm z_\alpha s_m$$

where m = the mean score; z_α = the z score value (two-tailed) under the normal curve, depending on the confidence level (e.g., z = 1.96 and 2.58 for p = .05 and

p = .01, respectively), and s_m is the standard error of measurement.[4] The standard error is *not* the standard deviation of the sample but rather the standard deviation divided by the square root of $N (s_m = s/\sqrt{N})$. To provide the lower- and upper-bound estimates of the confidence interval for the 95 percent interval, the z – 1.96 and + 1.96, respectively, is multiplied by the s_m.

Confidence intervals provide a range of values within which the true differences between groups are likely to lie. Even though the interval is a range, it also includes the information that one obtains from a statistical test of significance, because z values used for significance testing (e.g., z score of 1.96 for p = .05) are used to form the upper and lower confidence intervals. Effect size provides a point estimate of the differences of groups in standard deviation units; confidence intervals provide the same metric above and below that mean. In addition, the data can be easily presented in terms of the original measurement unit (e.g., total scores, IQ points) so they are more readily interpretable. Thus, the $m_1 - m_2$ portion of the ES formula is the difference in the original measurement unit of the scale (not standard deviation units); confidence intervals can also be presented in this original metric. Thus, one could state, for example, that in a psychotherapy study treatment A was better than treatment B with an ES = .70, with $CI_{95\%}$: .35, 1.05. This means that we can be 95 percent confident that the ES we obtained falls within the range of .35 to 1.05. Alternatively, the same data may be presented as a mean difference (i.e., difference scores between group 1 and 2 on some symptom scale) as 15 points with (for example) a $CI_{95\%}$: 10, 20 points on that symptom measure. Both are equivalent. The ES in standard deviation units is readily interpretable in terms of strength of effect (e.g., as in Cohen's recommendations for small, medium, and large effects); the mean difference presented on the original metric of scores on a measure, with the confidence intervals, communicates to those familiar with the measure exactly how great the difference is.

Meta-Analysis

For individual studies, ESs and confidence intervals provide useful statistics that have been proposed to replace or supplement statistical tests. The advantage extends beyond the individual study. Meta-analyses is an extension of the use of ES for evaluating multiple studies. As mentioned before, meta-analysis is a methodology or secondary analyses in which multiple studies are evaluated and combined. Meta-analyses have many purposes, one of which is to permit a quantitative evaluation (review) of a literature. In relation to the present discussion, meta-analysis is useful as a method to contribute to the knowledge base more generally. The method permits combining several studies but in the process accomplishes much more than merely providing a review of the studies. We have learned that one has to interpret any single study quite cautiously. Sampling alone might mean that the results are not representative of the true population value (or difference). Also, characteristics of a single study (sample, geography, way in which the intervention was manipulated, specific measures used) raise threats to external validity, that is, the extent to which the results might be generalizable.

Meta-analyses combine many different ESs and many different studies; hence, they can provide a better estimate of the population parameters. Moreover, questions can be asked of the literature that an individual study cannot easily provide. For example, in meta-analyses of psychotherapy research, investigators have examined whether treatment is more effective (ESs are larger in treatment vs. no-treatment comparisons) as a function of experience of the therapist, age of the subjects, types of problems for which subjects are referred for treatment, and methodological quality of the study (Brown, 1987; Shadish & Ragsdale, 1996; Weisz & Weiss, 1993). These questions were not asked in the original investigations. However, across many studies, each study can be coded on new variables of interest. Effect sizes become the dependent variable for the new questions that are asked of research. Thus, meta-analysis goes beyond describing a given literature and can be used to address questions and test explanations of the literature that were not raised in the original investigations (Cook et al., 1992).

The use of ES as a part of individual investigations facilitates the integration of studies in systematic ways through meta-analyses. The meta-analyses, apart from their ability to review a literature in a quantitative way, permit us to have better estimates of true effects (population ES) and the range within which these lie (confidence intervals of the ESs). This is much more valuable than tests that seek statistical significance. We want to know the impact of our interventions and differences that specific variables yield (e.g., in case-control studies). Estimates of the magnitude of effect or strength of relations through some other measure (e.g., ES, r) give us the information we seek. Combining measures across studies, as illustrated by meta-analyses, not only allows us to provide better estimates of ES but also permits us to use the literature to address new questions.

General Comments

It is not clear whether statistical significance testing is here to stay. At this point, we know that there has been a continuous literature lamenting the use of significance tests and recommending alternatives. Indeed, R.A. Fisher, who is credited with (or, given fickle history, blamed for) beginning significance testing, recommended that researchers supplement their significance tests with measures of the strength of the association between independent and dependent variables. Indeed, we would like to know more than whether a null hypothesis can be rejected; in fact, we may not really care about the null hypothesis, in light of comments (noted previously) that the null hypothesis is never really true. Also, we want to know about *our* hypotheses, that is, the size or magnitude of the effects we study and whether they are important (very strong). Some efforts are underway to consider refocusing psychological research to move away from significance testing in favor of methods highlighted here. For example, the American Psychological Association is currently considering the issue of significance testing, its use, and its potential alternatives for research (Schmidt, 1996a, 1996b). It is important for researchers to be familiar with the tradition of statistical significance testing, but as well to (at the very least) supplement research with additional statistics that convey magnitude of effect.

CLINICAL SIGNIFICANCE: EVALUATING INTERVENTION EFFECTS

One problem with statistical evaluation, especially in clinically relevant research, is that it detracts from the question of the applied importance of the outcome or effect. This issue is central to intervention research or efforts to change performance or functioning for an applied end, as reflected in treatment, prevention, education, and rehabilitation. In such research, the usual data-analytic methods are still invoked (e.g., statistical significance). The added criterion is to evaluate whether the differences are clinically significant, that is, make a difference. *Clinical significance* refers to the practical value or importance of the effect of an intervention, that is, whether it makes any *real* difference to the clients or to others in their functioning and everyday life.

It is important to distinguish statistical significance and strength of an effect from clinical significance. Statistical significance has to do with the probability-based criterion for judging whether an effect is reliable but has little to do with the practical importance of the effect. Strength of effect (ES, correlation) is related to the magnitude of the experimental effect, the amount variance shared, and other such measures. Strength of the relationship can be strong or weak depending on all sorts of influences (e.g., within-group variability). A statistically significant effect and a large ES may not have anything to do with clinical significance if the dependent measure is unrelated to everyday performance (e.g., a reaction time). Also, there can be a very large ES, for example, if everyone in the intervention group for the treatment of obesity loses 2 pounds and everyone in the control group gains 2 pounds. Yet, at the end of the study, all participants may still be very obese. Effect size does not convey whether anyone's weight and health status have actually improved. In other words, statistical significance, ES (or other magnitude of effect measures), and clinical significance provide different information about the data even though they are all quantitative methods of evaluating the results.

Evaluation of the clinical or applied importance of the change usually is used as a supplement to statistical methods of determining whether group differences or changes over time are reliable. Once reliable changes are evident, further efforts are made to quantify whether treatment has moved the client appreciably closer to adequate functioning, that is, whether the change is important. In some cases, one may be able to tell readily whether the change moves the client close to adaptive functioning. For example, self-injurious behavior (e.g., head banging) may be at a high rate in an autistic child, perhaps 100 self-hits per hour during an observation period. Reduction to 50 hits per hour is dramatic but probably would not be regarded as clinically important. Without a further reduction or complete elimination, the client may still experience serious damage. Virtual, if not complete, elimination of self-injurious behavior would be required to effect a clinically important change.

In many cases, the presence or absence of a behavior at the end of treatment is not necessarily the criterion for deciding whether an important change was achieved. The degree of change and the impact of that change is relevant for deciding clinical significance. For example, in the treatment of obesity, a mean loss of 50 pounds for subjects might seem like a clinically important change. Yet, whether the change has impact (e.g., on health, daily functioning) may depend on the initial weight of the subjects who participated (e.g., mean weight 500 or 600 lb. vs. mean weight of 200 lb.). Thus, merely examining the absolute level of change is not always enough to determine whether the difference or change really makes a difference. Several methods of evaluating the clinical significance of treatment effects have been elaborated. Each method is based on quantitative evaluation to make the decision about the importance of the change. Three broad strategies can be delineated—comparison methods, subjective evaluation, and social impact (Jacobson & Truax, 1991; Kazdin, 1977; Wolf, 1978).

Comparison Methods

At the end of treatment the client can be compared to some other standard to determine whether the change is clinically significant. Different methods have been used on the basis of normative or ipsative comparisons. *Normative* comparisons refer to comparing the person's performance with the performance of others; *ipsative* comparisons refer to comparing the individual with himself or herself. Consider the most commonly used methods for comparison.

Normative Samples   The question addressed by this method is to what extent do patients or clients, after completing treatment (or some other intervention), fall within the normative range of performance? Prior to treatment, the clients presumably would depart considerably from their well-functioning peers on the measures and in the domain that led to their selection (e.g., anxiety, depression, social withdrawal). Demonstrating after treatment that these same persons were indistinguishable from or within the range of a normative, well-functioning sample on the measures of interest would be a reasonable definition of a clinically important change (Kazdin, 1977; Kendall & Grove, 1988). To invoke this criterion, a comparison is made between treated patients and peers who are functioning well or who are without significant problems in everyday life. This requires that the measures used in the study have normative data in their behalf based on community (nonpatient) samples.

As a rather typical example, one of our own studies evaluated treatments for aggressive and antisocial children ages 7–13 (Kazdin et al., 1992). The effectiveness of three conditions was examined including problem-solving skills training (PSST), parent management training (PMT), and PSST + PMT. Two outcome measures are plotted for the three groups at pretreatment, posttreatment, and a 1-year follow-up (Figure 14.2). The measures were the parent- and teacher-completed versions of the Child Behavior Checklist (Achenbach, 1991), which assess a wide range of emotional and behavioral problems. Extensive normative data (of nonreferred, community children) are available for boys and girls within the age group. These data have indicated that the 90th percentile score on overall (total) symptoms is the score that best distinguishes clinic from community samples of children. In the treatment results plotted in Figure 14.2, scores at this percentile from community youths were used to define the upper limit of the normal range of emotional and behavioral problems. Clinically significant change was defined as whether children's scores fell *below* this cutoff, that is, within the normative range.

Figure 14.2 shows that children's scores were well above this range before treatment on the parent (left panel) and teacher (right panel) measures. Each group approached or fell within the normal range at posttreatment, although the combined treatment was superior in this regard. The results in Figure 14.2 provide group means (average performance of each group). One can also compute how many individuals fall within the normative range at the end of treatment. In this example, for the parent-based measure, results at posttreatment indicated that 33 percent, 39 percent, and 64 percent of youths from PSST, PMT, and combined treatment, respectively, fell within the normal range. These percentages are different (statistically significant) and suggest the superiority of the combined treatment on the percentage of youths returned to normative levels of functioning. The results underscore the importance of evaluating clinical significance. In this study, even with statistically significant changes within groups and differences between groups, the data convey that most youths who received treatment continued to fall outside the normative range of their nonclinically referred peers.

Dysfunctional Samples　Another method to define clinical significance uses a dysfunctional sample for comparison. The idea is that, in a treatment study, all subjects might be considered to reflect a dysfunctional sample (assuming that recruitment and screening were intended to identify such a sample). At the end of treatment, if a clinically important change is made, scores of the clients ought to depart *markedly* from the original scores of the dysfunctional cases. How much of a change is "markedly"? There is, of course, no logical justification for the answer. A departure of 2 standard deviations from the mean of the dysfunctional sample is one criterion proposed to delineate that magnitude of change as clinically significant (Jacobson & Revensdorf, 1988). Thus, at posttreatment, individuals whose scores depart at least 2 standard deviations from the mean of the dysfunctional group (untreated cases with demonstrated dysfunction) would be regarded as having changed in an important way.

At first, this criterion seems similar to the one used for ordinary statistical significance, namely, a comparison of two groups with the same problem; one group is treated, the other is not. However, the criterion for clinical significance

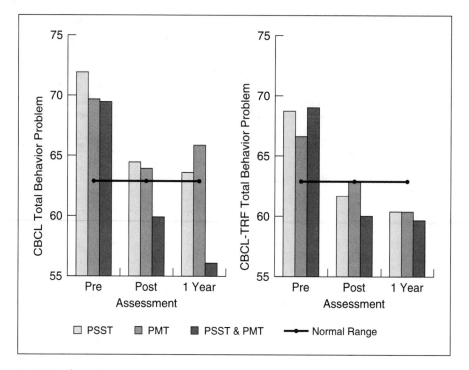

FIGURE 14.2   Mean scores (T scores) for Problem-Solving Skills Training (PSST), Parent Management Training (PMT), and both combined (PSST + PMT) for the total behavior problem scales of the parent-completed Child Behavior Checklist (CBCL, *left* panel) and the teacher-completed Child Behavior Checklist–Teacher Report Form (CBCL-TRF *right* panel). The horizontal line reflects the *upper* limit of the nonclinical (normal) range of children of the same age and sex. Scores *below* this line fall within the normal range.

Source: Kazdin, A.E., Siegel, T., & Bass, D. (1992). Cognitive problem-solving skills training and parent management training in the treatment of antisocial behavior in children. *Journal of Consulting and Clinical Psychology, 60,* 733–747. Reprinted with permission.

is invoked in relation to the performance of individual clients. Clinically significant change is evaluated in relation to whether a given client has made a change of 2 standard deviations and the percentage of individuals who do so within a given experimental condition. To be considered clinically significant, the changes must reflect a departure from the deviant sample in the direction of a decrease of symptoms or increase in prosocial functioning. Why a criterion of 2 standard deviations? First, if the individual is 2 standard deviations away from the mean of the original group, this suggests that he or she is not represented by the mean and distribution from which that sample was drawn; indeed, 2 standard deviations above the mean reflects the 98th percentile. Second, 2 standard deviations approximates the criterion used for statistical significance when groups are compared (e.g., 1.96 standard deviations for a two-tailed *t* test that compares groups for the *p* < .05 level of significance).

For example, a study for the treatment of depression among adults compared two variations of problem-solving strategies (Nezu & Perri, 1989). To evaluate the clinical significance of change the investigators examined the proportion of cases in each group whose score on measures of depression fell 2 or more standard deviations below (i.e., less depressed) the mean of the untreated sample. For example, on one measure (the Beck Depression Inventory), 85.7 percent of the subjects who received the full problem-solving condition achieved this level of change. In contrast, 50 percent of the subjects who received the abbreviated problem-solving condition achieved this level of change. The more effective treatment led to a clinically significant change for most subjects, clearly, one treatment was better than the other in this regard. The comparisons add important information about the impact of treatment.

For many measures used to evaluate treatment or other interventions, normative data that could serve as a criterion for evaluating clinical significance either do not exist or are insufficient (may not quite apply to the group that is studied). That is, we cannot really tell at the end of treatment whether subjects fall within a normative range. In these instances, it is useful to evaluate the extent to which individuals have made a change that moves them away from the mean of a dysfunctional sample. Normative data are not required for this evaluation. If normative data are available, one can evaluate the clinical significance of change by assessing whether the client's behavior returns to normative levels, departs from dysfunctional levels, and is closer to the normative level (e.g., mean) than to the dysfunctional level.

No Longer Meeting Diagnostic Criteria Another way clinical significance is evaluated is to examine whether the diagnostic status of the individual has changed with treatment. In many treatment studies, individuals are recruited and screened on the basis of whether they meet criteria for a psychiatric diagnosis. Those with a diagnosis are included in the study and assigned to various treatment and control conditions. A measure of clinical significance is to determine whether the individual, at the end of treatment, continues to meet criteria for the original (or other) diagnoses. Presumably, if treatment has achieved a sufficient change, the individual no longer meets criteria for the diagnosis. Sometimes this is referred to as showing that the individual has *recovered.* For example, in one study, adolescents who met standard psychiatric diagnostic criteria for clinical depression were assigned to one of three groups: adolescent treatment, adolescent and parent treatment, or a wait-list condition (Lewinsohn, Clarke, Hops, & Andrews, 1990). At the end of treatment, 57 percent and 52 percent of the cases in the two treatment groups, respectively, and 95 percent of the cases in the control group continued to meet diagnostic criteria for depression. Clearly, treatment was effective in an important way.

There is something appealing about showing that, after treatment, the individual no longer meets diagnostic criteria for the disorder that was treated. It suggests that the condition (problem, disorder) is gone or "cured." Indeed, one dramatic effect of current treatment of human immunodeficiency virus (HIV) is that the combination of drugs seems to eliminate the virus so that it is no longer detectable; hence, the individual no longer shows the diagnosis (Balter, 1996). Yet, in psychiatry and psychology, not meeting criteria for the diagnosis of a disorder (e.g., depression) can be achieved by showing a change in only one or two symptoms. Also, we know that with some diagnoses (e.g., depression, conduct disorder), falling below the threshold for meeting the diagnostic criteria does not mean the individual is problem free. Individuals who do not quite meet the criteria for the diagnosis but are close can still have current and enduring problems (Gotlib, Lewinsohn, & Seeley, 1995; Offord et al., 1992). Above and below the precise cutoff point for defining disorder is not the point at which clinical dysfunction, impairment, or a poor prognosis begins and ends. Showing that an individual no longer meets criteria for a diagnosis is informative insofar as the diagnostic criteria have become a meaningful way to communicate about dysfunction and rates of dysfunction.

Problems and Considerations   The comparison methods raise several issues. An initial question is Who should serve as the normative group when that group is used as the basis for deciding clinical significance? For example, to whom should mentally retarded, chronic psychiatric patients, or prisoners be compared in evaluating treatment or rehabilitation programs? Developing normative levels of performance might be an unrealistic ideal in treatment if the level is based on individuals functioning well in the community. Also, how does one define a normative population? We know, for example, that a normative sample, that is, individuals in the community not involved in treatment, and "normals" recruited for research can have high rates (e.g., 20–50 percent) of current or lifetime psychopathology and clinical dysfunction (Halbreich et al., 1989; Kruesi, Lenane, Hibbs, & Major, 1990; Robins et al., 1984). Thus, there is a lot of dysfunction in the group that would serve as the basis for comparison. Also, rates of dysfunction and symptom patterns vary as a function of social class, ethnicity, and culture. Presumably forming a normative group ought to take such moderators into account.

Even if a normative group can be identified, exactly what range of their behaviors would be defined as within the normative level? Among individuals whose behaviors are not identified as problematic there will be a range of acceptable behaviors. Defining what the upper and lower limits of that range (e.g., ± 1 standard deviation) is somewhat arbitrary unless data show that scores above or below a particular cutoff have different short- or long-term consequences on other measures of interest (e.g., hospitalization, showing another disorder).

For many measures of interest, bringing individuals into the normative range is a questionable goal. Consider, for example, reading skills of elementary school children. A clinically significant change might be to move children with reading dysfunction so that they fall within the normal range. However, perhaps the normal range itself should not be viewed as an unquestioned goal. The reading of most children might be accelerated from current normative levels. Thus, normative data itself need to be considered. More extreme would be bringing youth who abuse drugs and alcohol to the level of their peers. For some groups, the peer group itself might be engaging in a level of deviant behavior that is potentially maladaptive.

Finally, it is quite possible that performance falls within the normative range or departs markedly from a deviant group but does not reflect how the individual is functioning in everyday life. Paper-and-pencil measures, questionnaires, interviews, and other frequently used measures may not reflect adaptive functioning for a given individual. Even for measures with high levels of established validity, performance of a given individual does not mean that he or she is happy, doing well, or adjusting in different spheres of life.

Subjective Evaluation

The subjective evaluation method refers to determining the importance of behavior change in the client by assessing the opinions of individuals who are likely to have contact with the client or in a position of expertise (Wolf, 1978). The question addressed by this method of evaluation is whether changes have led to differences in how clients and other people see the change. The views of others are relevant because people in everyday life often have a critical role in identifying, defining, and responding to persons they regard as dysfunctional or deviant. Subjective evaluations permit assessment of the extent to which the effects of an intervention regardless of whether statistically significant on primary outcome measures can be readily noticed by others.

Consider the case of Steven, a college student who wished treatment to eliminate two muscle tics (uncontrolled movements) (Wright & Miltenberger, 1987). The tics involved head movements and excessive eyebrow raising. Individual treatment sessions were conducted in which Steven was trained to monitor and identify when the tics occurred and to be more aware of their occurrence in general. In addition, he self-monitored tics throughout the day. Assessment sessions were conducted in which Steven read at the clinic or college library and observers recorded the tics. Self-monitoring and awareness training procedures were evaluated in a multiple-baseline design in which each tic declined in frequency as treatment was applied.

A central question is whether the reduction was very important or made a difference either to Steven or to others. At the end of treatment, Steven's responses to a questionnaire indicated that he no longer was distressed by the tics and that he felt they were no longer very noticeable to others. In addition, four observers rated randomly selected videotapes of Steven without knowing which tapes came from before or after treatment. Observers rated the tics from the posttreatment tapes as not at all distracting, normal to very normal in appearance, and small to very small in magnitude. In contrast, they had rated tics on the pretreatment tapes as much more severe on these dimensions. Observers were then informed which were the posttreatment tapes and asked to report how satisfied they would be if they had achieved the same results as Steven had. All observers reported they would have been satisfied with the treatment results. The evaluations from Steven and independent observers help attest to the importance of the changes; that is, they made a difference to the client and to others.

Subjective evaluation is obviously important. If treatment is working and has an important impact, the effects ought to make a perceptible difference to clients themselves and to those with whom they interact. The opinions of others in contact with the client are important as a criterion in their own right because they often serve as a basis for seeking treatment in the first place and also reflect the evaluations the client will encounter after leaving treatment. Subjective evaluation is relevant as a criterion.

Problems and Considerations   Global rating scales are usually the basis for obtaining subjective evaluations. Such scales are regarded with suspicion because they are more readily susceptible to biases on the part of raters than are questionnaires and interviews or direct observations in which the items are more concrete and anchored to clearer descriptors. Because the evaluations are global rather than concrete, they are likely to be highly variable (e.g., have different meanings and interpretations) among those who respond. Also, subjective evaluations, whether completed by the clients or by others in contact with the clients, are likely to be fairly nonspecific in the ability to differentiate among different treatments.

The fact that the client or persons associated with a client notice a difference in behavior as a function of the client's treatment does not mean that the client has changed or has changed very much. Persons in contact with the client may perceive a small change and report this in their ratings. But this does not necessarily mean that treatment has alleviated the problem for which treatment was sought or has brought the client within normative levels of behaving.

In general, one must treat subjective evaluations cautiously; it is possible that subjective evaluations will reflect change when other measures of change do not. Subjective evaluations are extremely limited and of unclear value as the sole or primary outcome measure for most clinical dysfunctions. However, as supplementary data, subjective ratings can provide a piece of information regarding how the problem and degree of change is viewed. It really *does* make a difference how people feel and think and whether treatment makes people experience life as better than it was prior to treatment. (Also, we would like the effects not to result simply from statistical regression.) Subjective evaluation is designed to supplement other measures and to address these broader issues.

Social Impact Measures

Another type of measure that helps to evaluate the clinical or applied importance of treatment outcomes is to see whether measures of social impact have been altered. *Social impact measures* refer to outcomes assessed in everyday life that are important to society at large. Rates of arrest, truancy, driving while intoxicated, illness, hospitalization, and death are prime examples of social impact measures. Such measures are often regarded by consumers of treatment (i.e., persons who request or pay for treatment) as the "bottom line." To the public at large and to persons who influence policy, these measures are often more meaningful and interpretable than the usual psychological measures. At the end of treatment, psychologists may become excited to show that changes were reflected in highly significant effects on psychological measures (e.g., MMPI-2, Beck Depression Inventory). However, what does this really mean? To the public, the effects are clearer if we can say that fewer work days were missed, fewer visits were made to the doctor for health problems, or fewer suicides were completed as a result of treatment.

Social impact measures have often been used in clinical and applied studies. For example, prevention programs often focus on infants or young children from socioeconomically disadvantaged homes who are at risk for later mental and physical health problems (Lally, Mangione, & Honig, 1988; Schweinhart & Weikart, 1988). Follow-up 10–20 years after the children have received the program has shown higher rates of school attendance, of high-school graduation, of subsequent employment, and lower rates of arrest and reliance on welfare among persons who received the intervention, compared to nonintervention controls. These measures and outcomes are clearly significant to society.

Cost is also a measure of social impact. Although it is not usually a measure of interest as a psychological construct, showing that an intervention has impact on the cost of care is very important. Indeed, cost may determine utilization of a given treatment and its endorsement at the level of policy. Hence, cost is not an ancillary measure to consumers of research.

Problems and Considerations   Measures of social impact are by definition very important and provide a bridge from our research to persons we seek to help. In too much of our research, we are speaking to ourselves, even in areas (e.g., psychotherapy, assessment of psychopathology) in which the topic has very direct implications for the public at large. Consequently, as a measure of intervention effects, the addition of social impact measures to the battery is encouraged.

Social impact measures have a number of liabilities that prompt interpretive caution. Measures (e.g., grades, crime rates, fatalities) are often relatively insensitive as measures of intervention effects. They are gross measures and subject to a variety of influences other than those associated with the intervention and investigation. Stated more precisely, error in the measures can be relatively high. Random error may come from variations in how consistently the measures are recorded, as in the case of many archival records (e.g., attendance in school, records in city hall). We take for granted that most psychological measures have a standardized method of administration. Social impact measures are more likely to be recorded and scored somewhat haphazardly over time, which introduces noise (error variability) into the results. Changes in funding (usually budget cuts), policy, procedures, and persons responsible for recording all may operate in a systematic way to influence the reliability and validity of the data. Also, error may be introduced by systematic changes in how the measure is scored (instrumentation) over time.

Interpretative and assessment obstacles can plague social impact measures. For example, crime rate is of interest for both psychological and social interventions. First, what does the crime rate really assess, as evaluated in official reports (Uniform Crime Reports)? Crime is usually recorded in a hierarchical fashion, which means that whenever a given crime occurs, only the worst crime is counted (DiLulio, 1997). For example, on a given day, a criminal may rape someone, steal a getaway car, and assault the person from whom the car was taken. This is counted as one crime; the worst crime is counted (rape, in this case). Similarly, if two cars are stolen on the same night and two people are beaten up in the process but the incidents were done by the same criminal, this is counted as one crime. In general, the most serious crime is counted, only that crime is counted in a given episode, and it is counted only once. Therefore, the crime rate does not necessarily reflect the number of crimes completed or number of victims. Showing a change in crime rate might be important, but the meaning of the measure is not obvious to most of us.

Another issue is instrumentation. Continuing with a crime rate example, most crimes (approximately 65 percent) are not reported. Annual household surveys are conducted by the Bureau of Justice Statistics to assess crimes regardless of whether the crimes were reported to the police. The difficulty is that the survey (begun in 1973) has changed over time; hence, there are major changes (increases) in crime rates as a function of changes in the instrument (DiLulio, 1997). Changes in rates again may reflect intervention effects, social changes, or instrumentation in varying degrees and combinations. Apart from any misleading statistics in actual rate of crime, changes in criteria for recording crimes adds variability over time. Showing an intervention effect superimposed on that variability may be difficult, even when there is a veridical effect.

Social impact measures are often seized on by nonresearchers as reflecting the bottom line to evaluate the value and effectiveness of a program. If the intervention has not shown social impact, this is often considered by the media or by nonresearchers as evidence that the intervention makes no difference, is not important, and perhaps has failed. Yet, social impact measures need to be thoughtfully evaluated and interpreted. The absence of change on such a measure, given the very nature of many of these measures, may not be an adequate, reasonable, or interpretable index of the program's effect. The danger of social impact measure comes from their two most salient characteristics, namely, their high believability and their often poor psychometric properties (e.g., alternative types of reliability and validity). Notwithstanding these caveats, social impact data can be quite useful to see whether the improvements identified on specific psychological measures are reflected directly on measures of primary interest to consumers of treatment and to society at large. When such measures show a change, they convey important evidence that the impact of the intervention was socially important.

General Comments

There is no single way to measure clinical or applied significance of intervention effects. In a given project, measures such as truancy, crime, or school drop-out rates may be included as a matter of course because they were the impetus for designing and evaluating the intervention. Measures other than those highlighted previously might also be devised to evaluate clinical significance. It is not difficult to conceive of other ways to operationalize clinical significance. For example, in therapy research, measures of symptoms are usually used to evaluate clinical significance. Yet, one might assess other constructs, such as quality of life or impairment. Changes on measures of these constructs, if statistically significant or large in their ES, might be reasonable operational efforts to define clinical significance because the measures themselves are intended to reflect real-life experience.

For all the measures of clinical significance, some words of caution are in order. Measures of clinical significance are defined mainly by researchers, with the exception of social impact measures. That is, the measures are operational definitions of what we consider reasonable bases for saying that there was clinically important impact. Yet, few firm data can be assembled to show that the definition we elect is one that in fact makes a difference in some other way (beyond our measure) to the client in everyday life. For example, we may show that on a measure of symptoms the client completing therapy is now within the normative range or has made a large change (2 standard deviations). Is the individual functioning better in some palpable way in everyday life? We really do not know because measures of clinical significance have not been validated against each other or other indices of functioning (e.g., work performance, relationships).

A difficulty in interpreting measures of clinical significance is that given levels of performance have not been studied in ways for us to know what they mean. By way of contrast, consider measures within health. There are relatively well-accepted standards for normative and healthy levels of weight, hypertension, and cholesterol, although these change with advances in research. Even so, we know there are risks for mortality and morbidity associated with different levels of weight, and we know that some levels are clearly much better than others in relation to these outcomes. The picture is less clear for measures of psychopathology, adjustment, and personality because the correlates and long-term prognosis associated with a particular score are not well understood. This means that it is more difficult to defend a particular outcome (e.g., change in 2 standard deviations) as a criterion that really makes a difference, that is, is clinically significant.

Notwithstanding these considerations, the reader is encouraged to include one or more measures of clinical significance in any intervention study (Walker et al., 1996). The purpose of the addition is to move beyond mere statistical significance and also to help foster dissemination of the findings. The results are likely to have impact on society at large to the extent they are interpretable by nonresearchers. Consequently, use of measures of clinical significance advances clinical work by ensuring that patients are helped to an important extent and also addresses a broader research agenda by encouraging dissemination of findings.

SUMMARY AND CONCLUSIONS

Statistical significance testing is the dominant method to analyze the results of research. In the vast majority of instances, statistical tests are completed to test the null hypothesis (no difference) and to determine whether the differences between or among groups are statistically significant. Statistical tests use probability levels to make this judgment and are based primarily on the concern for protecting a Type I error, that is, rejecting the null hypothesis when that hypothesis actually is true. Because statistical significance remains the primary criterion in evaluating results of research, it is incumbent on the researcher to understand how to design studies that have a reasonable test of demonstrating differences when they exist.

Issues critical to statistical evaluation were discussed, including significance levels, power, sample size, multiple-comparison tests, significance and magnitude of effects, and multivariate data. Statistical power has received the greatest discussion in research because it shows most clearly the interrelation of alpha, sample size, and effect size. Evaluations of research have shown repeatedly that the majority of studies are designed in such a way as to have weak power. The obvious solution to increasing power is to increase sample size, although usually this is not very feasible, in part because adding very many rather than a few subjects is often required. Alternative strategies were discussed, including relaxing alpha in selected circumstances, using statistical tests that augment power, minimizing error variability in all facets of the experiment to the extent possible, and considering conditions (e.g., experimental manipulations, what groups to include in the design) that will maximize the obtained effect size.

Since statistical significance testing emerged, there has been ongoing dissatisfaction about its utility for research. Among the many concerns are the ways in which statistical significance is misinterpreted by researchers (e.g., it does not measure strength of an effect or the likelihood of replication), is misleading (e.g., the null hypothesis is never true and does not have to be tested), gives us arbitrary cutoff points to make binary decisions (accept or reject the null hypothesis), and, most important, does not provide the critical information we would like (e.g., direct tests of *our* hypotheses and information about the strengths of our interventions). Among the recommendations, there has been some consensus that measures of the strength or magnitude of the relation ought to be provided in presenting the quantitative results. Effect size and Pearson product–moment correlation were discussed, but there are many such measures. A point estimate of the likely effect (e.g., effect size) and a range of values about that effect (confidence intervals) would provide more useful information for interpreting our studies.

Clinical significance has been defined in many ways. Three general strategies that have been used were discussed: *comparison methods, subjective evaluation,* and *social impact measures.* The comparison methods usually demonstrate clinically significant change by showing that performance of the clients after treatment falls within the range of a normative comparison sample or departs markedly from the level of functioning that characterizes the sample who continue to evince the problem for which treatment was applied. The subjective evaluation method consists of having clients themselves or individuals in contact with the clients provide qualitative evaluations of performance. The social impact method consists of evaluating interventions on measures of direct interest to consumers and society at large. These three methods address in different ways the importance and magnitude of behavior change for the client's functioning and provide criteria not available in other forms of data evaluation.

NOTES

[1] It is worth complaining for a moment about the poor choice of the word "significant" in statistical evaluation. In everyday parlance "significance" is close to the meanings of "importance," "consequential," and "meaningful." Naturally, we, as investigators, move with regrettable ease in noting that a statistically significant effect is important. In fact, a statistically significant effect may not be important in any sense that affects anyone or anything. Some other term would be desirable. To be constructive and to suggest an alternative, my own preference would be to call some findings "fishy"; that is, we are a little suspicious of them. This adds more suspense to the terminology than the now rather droll "statistical significance." Here is one way to use the word. When no significant difference is obtained, we should call that a *fishy effect*, rather than significant effect. The groups probably are really different (as discussed later in the chapter), and there is something fishy if that difference has not been demonstrated in the study. Similarly, a *nonfishy effect* could be the substitute term for denoting a statistically significant effect. Obviously, if there is a statistically reliable difference, this is nonfishy—something we are not suspicious of and regard as genuine. Thus, a finding that met $p < .05$ would be called a nonfishy effect. Fishy and nonfishy not only suggest that something is or is not suspicious but also gives due credit to R.A. Fish(er).

[2] As mentioned previously, many statistical tests (e.g., factor analysis, regression, cluster analyses, time-series analysis, path analyses) include a number of decision points about various solutions, parameter estimates, cutoffs for including or deleting variables in the analysis or model, and so on. These decisions often are not made by the investigator but are accepted by the default criteria in the data-analytic programs. Descriptions of the material in statistical manuals that accompany the software describe how to run the program and are not intended to present the many criteria that can enter into the decisions.

[3] An interesting and very readable discussion of how these p levels came be adopted and hence why they ought to be viewed quite tentatively is available elsewhere (Cowles & Davis, 1982). The article conveys that conventional levels of .05 and .01 are rather arbitrary. (Early in my career—actually when analyzing the results of my dissertation— I began to abandon $p < .05$ and adopted $p < .33$ as the level for significance. Through a rather amazing coincidence, most hypotheses in my dissertation were supported at

$p < .33$. The bulk of my dissertation orals was spent by my committee's quibbling with my attorney about my right to adopt this level for alpha and how the Constitution of the United States is rather hazy on this point.)

[4]It is worth conveying the meaning of the standard error of the mean, noted here as s_m. This refers to the estimate of the *standard deviation of a sampling distribution of means*. That is, the mean of a study is an estimate of the mean in the population. If one were to run the study many different times—indeed an infinite number of times, each drawing a random sample of subjects for the population—each study would yield a mean. These means form a sampling distribution of means; that is, each mean is a data point. The overall mean or the mean of these means would provide the real (population) mean μ. But not all the means that were sampled would be the same; they would vary a bit. The standard error of the mean is the standard deviation of the sampling distribution of the means and reflects how much sample means may be expected to depart from the population mean. In a single study, the standard error of the mean helps us to estimate, with some level of confidence, the likelihood that the population mean will fall within the range we present. If the standard error of the mean is small, then when multiplied by $\pm$ the z score (1.96), the range will be relatively small, and we can be reasonably assured that the population mean is within the range.

FOR FURTHER READING

Cohen, J. (1990). Things I have learned (so far). *American Psychologist, 45*, 1304–1312.

Cohen, J. (1992). A power primer. *Psychological Bulletin, 112*, 155–159.

Cohen, J. (1994). The earth is round ($p < .05$). *American Psychologist, 49*, 997–1003.

Frick, R.W. (1996). The appropriate use of null hypothesis testing. *Psychological Methods, 1*, 379–390.

Jacobson, N.S., & Truax, P. (1991). Clinical significance: A statistical approach to defining meaningful change in psychotherapy research. *Journal of Consulting and Clinical Psychology, 59*, 12–19.

Mohr, L.B. (1990). *Understanding significance testing*. Newbury Park, CA: Sage.

Rossi, J.S. (1990). Statistical power of psychological research: What have we gained in 20 years. *Journal of Consulting and Clinical Psychology, 58*, 646–656.

Schmidt, F.L. (1992). What do data really mean? Research findings, meta-analysis, and cumulative knowledge in psychology. *American Psychologist, 47*, 1173–1181.

Schmidt, F.L. (1996). Statistical significance testing and cumulative knowledge in psychology: Implications for training of researchers. *Psychological Methods, 1*, 115–129.

Shrout, P.E. (Editor). (1997). Special series: Should significance testing be banned? Introduction to a special section exploring the pros and cons. *Psychological Science, 8*, 1–20.

Chapter 15

Selected Topics in the Interpretation of Data

Interpretation of the findings in an investigation depends on the methods of data evaluation. Quantitative methods based on hypothesis and significance testing dominate current research. Within this framework, several issues regarding the interpretation of research findings can be identified. In this chapter, we consider topics related to interpretation of findings that affect both individual investigations and the accumulation of studies. The topics are data patterns and types of experimental effects, negative findings, and replication.

DATA PATTERNS AND TYPE OF EFFECTS

The type of effects that a given investigation yields refers to the impact of the experimental conditions. It is useful to discuss factorial designs briefly to convey common patterns in data analyses. As discussed in Chapter 5 on group research designs, in a factorial design two or more independent variables are studied simultaneously. In the simplest version, two variables (or factors) are studied, each of which has two different levels or conditions. This version of the factorial design is called a 2 x 2 design. (If one variable had three levels, it would be a 2 x 3 design.)

There are different reasons for singling out factorial designs for discussion. First, factorial designs are common in the literature; the efficiency of factorial designs and the questions they can address make them popular. Second, the designs permit evaluation of intervention effects of varying complexity. Specifically, with a factorial design one can look at the effects of a single independent variable (main effect) or in combination (interaction) with other independent variables. Third, factorial designs draw attention to broader issues regarding data interpretation. The effect of a given variable may depend on (i.e., be moderated by) other variables. This might be evident in a given experiment when a statistically significant interaction is obtained. However, an experiment may show no main effect of the independent variable because of a hidden interaction. The result may be due to an interaction of which the investigator is unaware and inclusion of the condition or level of the condition within the experiment for which there is no effect for that independent variable.

Main Effects and Interactions

Statistical evaluation of the results of a factorial experiment may yield significant main effects, interactions, or both. The main effect is equivalent to an overall effect of an independent variable. For example, an investigation might consist of a 2 x 2 design in which the variables Sex of Subject (males vs. females) and Type of Instructions (instructions to subjects leading them to expect therapeutic improvement vs. no instructions) are combined. The effects of these variables might be evaluated on changes in treatment for a particular clinical problem. The study would consist of four groups (2 x 2) representing all combinations of the different levels of each of the variables. Figure 15.1 illustrates how the study might be diagrammed with the four groups.

Statistical analyses (two-way analysis of variance) of the outcome measure might reveal no, one, or two main effects. Consider the hypothetical results when a main effect of the variable Sex of Subject is statistically significant. This would mean that males and females showed different amounts of therapeutic change. The statistical difference that accounts for the main effect is the mean level of performance across all males and all females in the experiment ignoring the specific instructions that they received. If a main effect of the variable Type of Instructions were obtained, it would mean that what subjects were told made a difference in their performance independent of their sex. The final possibility for the design is an interaction. The interaction refers to the pattern of results in which the effect of one variable depends on the specific conditions of the other variables. In an experiment, an interaction may be statistically significant regardless of whether there are any significant main effects.

Many different patterns of data might be evident when an interaction is statistically significant. In the example, Sex of Subject and Type of Instructions

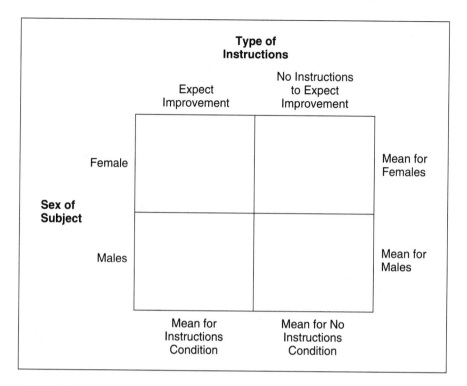

FIGURE 15.1   A 2 x 2 factorial design evaluating the separate (main effects) and combined (interaction) influences on a dependent measure.

might interact. In general, the interaction would mean that the impact of instructions depended on the sex of the subject. Yet the precise effect and specific statement that would characterize this interaction depend on the nature of the data. Figure 15.2 shows some of the different patterns of the interactions that could results from the hypothetical study. The interaction (top portion of the figure) suggests that males were not affected by the instruction conditions. In contrast, females showed greater treatment effects in the instruction condition than in the no-instruction condition. The middle portion of the figure shows a different type of interaction. Males responded differently across the two instruction conditions, but females did not. In the bottom portion of the figure, a more complex interaction is illustrated; males and females were affected by instructions but in the opposite fashion. Males showed greater therapeutic change when they received instructions; females showed greater change when they did not.[1]

In designing an experiment, the minimal prediction involved in a factorial design is a significant main effect for one or both of the independent variables. Simply stated, this means that the investigator predicts that conditions for the variables or factors will differ statistically. A factorial design is efficient because it allows the experimenter to study more than one main effect, that is, more than

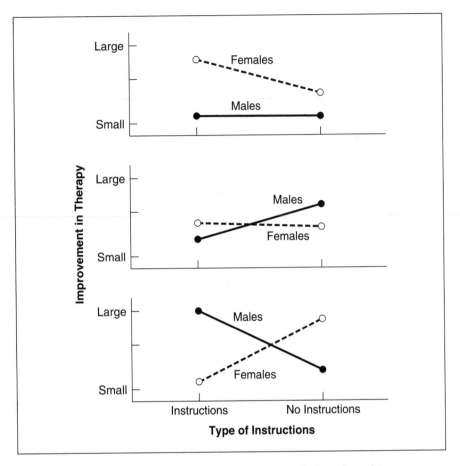

FIGURE 15.2   Samples of the different patterns that might be reflected in a statistically significant interaction.

one variable in a single experiment, and for that reason alone the design is highly valued.

If at all possible, it is especially useful to predict and search for interactions among variables. Predictions about the interactions of independent variables often reflect greater understanding of how the independent variables operate than do predictions about main effects. Interactions refer to the specific conditions under which effects of a given independent variable are obtained and are much more specific than global statements about main effects. In the above example, it might be useful to find that instructions leading subjects to expect therapeutic improvement leads to greater therapeutic change than not providing instructions (main effect of Type of Instructions). Yet, a more sophisticated understanding of instructions would be evident if the precise conditions under which the instructional effects were obtained were known. Research examining variables in combination with instructions might show that the effects of instructions vary as a function of sex, therapists, or other factors. As the interactions are enumerated by the research, the boundary conditions for the effects of instructions are drawn and a more complete understanding is available than would be from the demonstration of a straightforward main effect. Of course, merely littering the knowledge base with interactions is not the goal of research. Rather, we wish to have a deeper understanding of mechanisms and processes that explain how variables work and why their effects vary under different conditions. Consequently, findings are viewed in the context of how they draw from and contribute to theory and understanding of process. Interactions can provide important leads by identifying what factors are important and by prompting considerations of how the factors might operate.

Aside from the understanding afforded by identifying interactions, these effects often are the most intriguing. Consider an example of an experiment that looked at factors that contribute to how clients view their therapists (Bloom et al., 1977). In this study, the main task of the subject was to rate how qualified, dynamic, and generally believable the therapist was. The investigators proposed that people have stereotypes about therapists based on many different characteristics of the therapy situation. One characteristic may be decor of the therapist's office. Therefore the investigators varied office decor, which was one factor in the design with two different levels: a traditional professional office and a "humanistic" office.

The traditional professional office was a room with a therapist's chair behind a desk, a file cabinet, and various books. Diplomas were on the wall to help convey the traditional office decor. In the humanistic professional office, using the same room, the desk was placed in a corner so it did not separate the therapist's and client's chairs. Indeed, the chairs were placed relatively close together. In lieu of diplomas, posters were displayed around the room with slogans such as "Love makes the world go round." Throw pillows and a beanbag chair were also in the room. In short, office decor was varied to create different atmospheres. The authors also considered the possibility that the decor might lead to different reactions, depending on the sex of the subject and the sex of the therapist. Thus, the design then included three factors, each with two levels: Sex of Subject (male, female), Sex of Therapist (male, female), and Office Decor (traditional, humanistic). The subjects came to the room individually and read a description of the therapist who supposedly occupied the office. The descriptions were the same for all subjects and for each decor but varied in whether the therapist was said to be a male or female. Subjects never actually met the therapist but filled out a questionnaire about the kind of therapist that was likely to occupy the office.

The major results yielded an interaction of the variables Sex of Therapist and Office Decor. Female therapists were rated as more credible when seen to occupy a traditional professional office than a humanistic office. The opposite was found for males, who were seen as more credible in the humanistic than in the traditional office. One explanation offered for this interesting finding pertains to the stereotypic reactions that individuals might have toward therapists. The investigators suggested that traditional offices might trigger reactions about whether the occupant was well trained, scientific, and authoritarian. Traditionally, these characteristics might also be stereotypically applied more frequently to males than to females. In contrast, a humanistic office might convey cues that the occupant is sensitive, warm, and caring. These characteristics may be more stereotypic of females.

Credibility was greatest in situations in which office cues and gender cues were complementary. Complementary characteristics might convey to subjects the best of both worlds, namely, that the therapist is professional and well trained, but also warm and sensitive. Of course, the precise explanation of the findings remains to be tested further. The interaction demonstrates an intriguing result that only could be evaluated by combining separate factors in a single experiment.

General Comments

Although the search for interactions is advocated here, this point can be debated. Whether one looks for main effects or interactions in research depends mainly on the state of knowledge in a given area of research, the purpose of the research, and one's view of the world. In a relatively new or unexplored area of research, investigators usually attempt to discover variables that have any effect (main effects). Only later, after initial work, do the interactions take on more significance as the qualifying conditions are unraveled.

Research would be much simpler if variables were restricted to main effects. Results of experiments could be accepted or rejected more easily if a given variable were always shown to have either an effect or no effect. Because variables often do interact with each other, it is difficult to interpret the results of a single experiment. If a variable has no effect, it is always possible that it would have an effect if some other condition of the experiment were altered. That is, the variable may produce no effect for certain subjects, experimenters, or other specific conditions but later produce great effects when any of the other conditions is altered. Often in research we question the external validity (generality) of the findings obtained in a study. Equally, we can question the generality of the findings when an effect is not obtained, that is, whether the variable would have no impact if tested under other conditions.

In one sense, variables studied by psychologists can always be considered to interact with other variables rather than to operate as individual main effects. Even if no interactions emerge in the analyses of the results, conditions other than those included in the design or data analyses may influence the pattern of results. The conditions of the experiment that are held constant may reflect a narrow set of circumstances under which the variable produces a statistically significant effect. The effect might not be produced as these conditions change. Obviously, the effect of variable X on variable Y may depend on age of the subjects (e.g., infants vs. adults) or species (e.g., primates vs. nonprimates). Few, if any, results obtained by psychologists would be replicated across all possible variations in conditions that could be studied; that is, there are implicit interactions among the conditions studied.

The examples to convey interactions and data patterns have been limited to 2 x 2 factorial designs and analyses of variance. In passing it is important to mention that more than two variables can be studied at one time and in the process more complex interactions can be evaluated (e.g., 2 x 2 x 2 designs and interaction of all three factors [variables] in the design). As the number of variables increases, the interaction terms become more difficult to describe, explain, and detect. Consequently, if any interactions are examined, research focuses primarily on the more simple interaction terms.

Analyses of variance are not the only means to evaluate interaction effects. Regression analyses are also used to evaluate interactions. For example, to predict a particular outcome (e.g., severity of depression or presence or absence of the diagnosis of depression), regression techniques (e.g., multiple regression for the continuous outcome or discriminant analysis for the categorical outcome), can be used to evaluate the impact of separate variables (predictors) alone (as a main effect) or in combination (interactions). If sex and negative cognitions were two predictors, they can be entered alone and in combination to predict the outcome. Of course, as in any data evaluation, the key is in the hypotheses of the investigator rather than in what the statistical analysis can produce.

Comments on interactions underscore the fact that the impact of one variable can depend on the level of another variable. Interactions are important for interpreting the results within a study and the results across multiple studies. In particular, discrepant results among studies raise the prospect that some condition varied among the studies and that condition moderated the relation between the independent and dependent variable. Research that can identify these moderators is often a significant contribution to the literature.

NEGATIVE RESULTS OR NO-DIFFERENCE FINDINGS

In most investigations, the presence of an effect is decided if the null hypothesis is rejected. The null hypothesis states that the experimental conditions will not differ, that is, that the independent variable will have no effect. Typically, rejection of this hypothesis is regarded as a positive or favorable result; failure to reject this hypothesis is regarded as a negative result. Advances in research usually are conceived as a result of rejecting the null hypothesis. As researchers know all too well, many investigations do not yield statistically significant findings or any other evidence that the independent variable influenced the subjects. The term *negative results* has come to mean that there were no statistically significant differences between groups that received different conditions or that the result did not come out the way the investigator had hoped or anticipated. Usually, the term is restricted to the finding that groups did not differ, leading to acceptance of the null hypothesis.

The presence of a statistically significant difference between groups (i.e., a positive result) often is a criterion—indeed, a major criterion—for deciding whether a study has merit and warrants publication. The search for group differences so that the results of a study will be publishable may encourage sacrifice of methodological criteria, the possibility of inadvertent bias, or outright dissimulation (Barber, 1976). Poor methodology and sources of experimental bias are more likely to be overlooked when a predicted or plausible finding of significant differences is obtained. The implicit view is that group differences demonstrate that, whatever the failings of the experiment, they were not sufficient to cancel the effects of the independent variable. In contrast, negative results often imply that the independent variable was weak or that the study was poorly designed or conducted.

The value of a study can be assessed as a function of its conceptualization and methodological adequacy rather than whether differences are found. The conceptualization and design of an investigation bear no necessary relation to the outcome of an experiment. Many sloppy, ill-conceived, and horribly uncontrolled studies can lead to systematic group differences (to paraphrase a statement by my dissertation committee when summarizing the lessons from my dissertation). As investigators, we wish to proceed with the best or strongest available design and greatest methodological care so that the results of the study, whatever their pattern, will be interpretable. Assuming that the question addressed in the investigation is important to begin with, methodological adequacy of the design, rather than pattern of the results, ought to be the main criterion for evaluating the study. This point has been advanced for some time (Greenwald, 1975; Kupfersmid, 1988; Lykken, 1968), although it has yet to be adopted. The difficulty in judging the value of any study is that neither the importance of a finding nor methodological adequacy is invariably agreed on by those who do the judging. Rejection of the null hypothesis and statistical significance are overly relied on because they present relatively simple bases for evaluating research.

Ambiguity of Negative Results

The absence of group differences in an experiment is usually not met with enthusiasm by the investigator or by the reviewers and editor who may be considering the manuscript for possible publication. This reaction derives from the ambiguity usually associated with negative results. The reason for or basis of "no-difference" findings usually cannot be identified in the experiment. The most straightforward reason for accepting the null hypothesis is that there is in fact no relation between the independent and dependent variables. There are, however, many other explanations for a no-difference finding.

One possibility is that the experimental manipulation was not carried out as intended. No differences between conditions would be expected because of a diffusion of treatment or excessive variability in how the manipulation was implemented. For example, in one treatment study of antisocial youth (Feldman et al., 1983), various treatments (behavior modification, traditional group social work, activity control group) did not differ in their impact. Yet, the treatments were not implemented faithfully and control subjects inadvertently received some of the treatment. The absence of group differences is understandable. In many studies, implementation is not assessed in a way that would permit this type of evaluation.

The absence of group differences may also result from the levels of the independent variable selected for the study. Group differences might result from comparing other levels of the same variable. For example, the relation between the amount of treatment and therapeutic change might be readily influenced by the levels of "amount" that are used. In general, more therapy sessions are associated with greater patient improvements (Howard et al., 1986). However, the relation between treatment duration and outcome is not linear. As shown in Figure 15.3, approximately 40 to 55 percent of the patients improved by session 8 (solid line) and 60 to 75 percent improved by session 26. Assume we did not know of

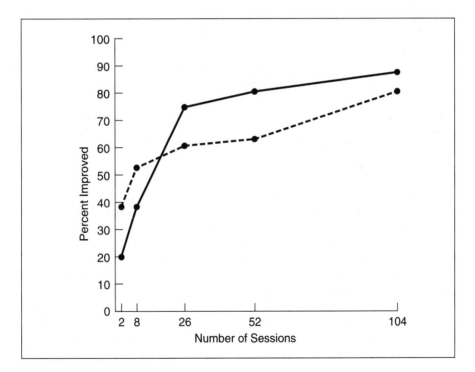

FIGURE 15.3   The relation between the number of sessions of psychotherapy for adult patients and the percent of patients improved. The *solid* line reflects ratings at the end of treatment completed by researchers based on chart review. The *broken* line reflects patient self-report ratings during the course of treatment.

Source: Howard, K.I., Kopta, S.M., Krause, M.S., & Orlinsky, D.E. (1986). The dose–effect relationship in psychotherapy. *American Psychologist, 41,* 159–164. Reprinted with permission of American Psychological Association.

this relation and conducted a study to evaluate treatment duration. We may compare a group that receives 20 sessions with another group that receives 30 sessions. The difference between these groups may be too small to produce a statistically significant difference. On the other hand, if the levels of the independent variable were more discrepant and at different stages of treatment (e.g., 10 vs. 30 sessions), group differences might be more likely. The example is provided to illustrate the potential problem of not selecting sufficiently discrepant levels of the independent variable to reflect change or inadvertently selecting levels from a range where the discrepancy may not be as relevant to outcome.

In cases in which the relation of the independent variable to the dependent variable is not linear, selecting groups that are very discrepant (e.g., very high vs. very low) may not lead to sharp differences on the dependent measure. For example, the effects of parental control (e.g., inconsistent discipline) on problem behaviors (e.g., aggression, antisocial behavior) of adolescents is curvilinear. High and low levels of control are associated with much greater adolescent problem behaviors than are moderate amounts of control (Stice, Barrera, & Chassin, 1993). Not armed with this information, an investigator might design a study in which high and low parent groups were selected. The results might not show differences in behavioral problems among adolescents, because high versus low, in this case, are not the most discrepant conditions. An advantage to selecting multiple levels of an independent (beyond high vs. low) is in part the ability to evaluate whether there is a linear relation, that is, whether differences between groups are evident at only some places along the dimension of the independent variable.

Any factor in the experiment that operates to increase within-subject variability also may increase the likelihood of a no-difference finding. As we discussed in relation to statistical conclusion validity and power, the magnitude of an effect can be measured in terms of effect size (the difference between means divided by the standard deviation). A given difference between means is lower in the effect size that is generated as the standard deviation (denominator) increases. The sensitivity of the experiment in detecting a difference can be reduced by allowing uncontrolled sources of variation or "noise" into the experiment. Allowing factors such as the adequacy of training of different experimenters and methods of delivering instructions to vary can increase the variance within-treatment groups and reduce the likelihood of finding group differences. Indeed, negative results have sometimes been used implicitly to infer that the investigator may be incompetent for not controlling the situation well enough to obtain group differences (Greenwald, 1975). The methodological adequacy of a study can be readily distinguished from the pattern of the results, but the distinction may be lost when the manuscript is read and the results show startling group differences.

Several areas of an experiment that do not necessarily reflect procedural sloppiness are related to the sensitivity of the experimental test and the likelihood that group differences will be found. The assessment device(s) may show sufficiently variable performance that only the most robust relations would emerge as statistically significant. In addition, the dependent measures may not be the most appropriate for detecting a relation of interest. Measures are often selected because of what they are called rather than for what they have been shown to measure empirically or because they are readily available, inexpensive, and expedient.

Several statistical considerations directly influence the sensitivity of the experiment. For example, sample size is related directly to whether the differences between groups on the dependent measure will be statistically significant. Whether group sizes are equal, whether the assumptions of the analyses are met, and similar factors dictate the sensitivity of the experimental test. As a general rule, experiments are too weak to detect differences unless the actual effect of the intervention is relatively large, a point elaborated in our discussions of power. Since most treatment effects are not likely to be very large, experimenters can expect to have negative results because of the lack of power of their statistical tests.

When Negative Results Are Interpretable

The absence of group differences is routinely dismissed as ambiguous and is often given much less attention than it should receive. There are several situations in which negative results are very informative and interpretable. First, in the context of a program of research, negative results can be very informative. A program of research refers to a series of studies conducted by an investigator or group of investigators. The studies usually bear great similarity to each other along dimensions such as the independent variables, subjects, and measures. Presumably several studies would have produced some group differences (otherwise it would be a masochistic rather than programmatic series of studies). The demonstration of group differences in some studies means that the experimental procedures are at least sensitive to some interventions. Thus, one can usually rule out the problem that the experiments are conducted poorly or that the methodology is too insensitive to detect group differences, even though these explanations may be true of one experiment. However, if the program of research has established itself in terms of demonstrating group differences across repeated studies, research showing no differences for a related variable can be viewed with greater confidence than would be the case in an isolated study.

Second, negative results are also informative when the results are replicated (repeated) across several different investigators. A problem in the psychological literature, and perhaps in other areas, is that once a relation is reported, it is extremely difficult to qualify or refute the relation with subsequent research. If negative results accumulate across several studies, however, they strongly suggest that the original study resulted either from very special circumstances or possibly through various artifacts. Failures to replicate do not invariably influence how the field interprets or views the status of the original finding. A classic example is the well-known study of Little Albert, an 11-month-old boy in which a loud noise (and a startle reaction) was paired with an object (white rat) that had not generated a reaction. After several pairings, presentation of the rat alone led to the startle response (Watson & Rayner, 1920). This study has been extremely influential and is cited often in texts, even though several failures to replicate are well documented (Kazdin, 1978b). The replication failures did not challenge the finding that fears could be easily conditioned in children.

Third, negative results are informative when the study shows the conditions under which the results are and are not obtained. The way in which this is easily achieved is through a factorial design that permits assessment of an interaction. An interaction between the different factors indicates that the effect of one variable depends on the level of another variable. An interaction may be reflected in the finding that there are no differences between groups for some levels of the variables but statistically significant differences between groups for a different level of the variables; that is, negative results may occur in only some of the experimental conditions. For example, one study examined whether early aggressive behavior (elementary school) predicted later delinquency in adolescence (Tremblay et al., 1992). The results indicated that early aggressive behavior predicted later delinquency for boys but not for girls. A no-difference finding (early aggressive and nonaggressive girls show similar outcomes) was informative because of the demonstration that the presence or absence of one variable (early aggression) depended on another condition (e.g., sex). This type of demonstration can advance research considerably by raising hypotheses about different mechanisms involved to explain these effects.

A related way in which a no-difference finding is informative is in relation to the pattern of results across multiple measures. A no-difference finding may be evident on some measures but not others. For example, one study focused on antecedents of externalizing behavior (aggression, overactivity, delinquency) and internalizing behavior (withdrawal, anxiety, depression) among children (Dodge et al., 1994). Several variables (e.g., harsh discipline practices, lack of maternal support, exposure to aggressive behavior in the home, lack of cognitive stimulation) were shown to predict later externalizing behavior but not internalizing child behavior. That is, the no-effect finding was obtained for one domain of functioning but not for another. As a general rule, when an investigator can show within a single study that a particular relation does and does not hold depending on another variable or set of circumstances (another independent variable) or does not hold across measures (e.g., dependent variables), the study is likely to be particularly informative. Such studies often provide a fine-grained analysis of the phenomenon and can generate theory and other hypotheses to explain the varied effects.

When Negative Results Are Important

Noting that negative results are interpretable suggests that a no-difference finding is salvageable. Actually, in a variety of circumstances, finding no differences may be extremely important. Many questions of interest in clinical and applied research are important in relation to demonstrating no difference. Does consumption of a particular fruit laced with pesticide increase risk for cancer? Is a less painful, expensive, or invasive treatment as effective as treatment given "as usual"? Do children who spend time in day care differ in psychological dysfunction from children who spend their time at home with a parent? A no-difference finding between the appropriate comparison groups in well-conducted studies for these questions would be quite informative and socially important.

As an example of a valuable no-difference finding, consider the treatment of breast cancer. Research has shown that for many women a radical mastectomy (complete removal of the breast) is no more effective in terms of long-term mortality than a lumpectomy (a more circumscribed operation in which the tumor and a small amount of surrounding tissue is removed) (Fisher et al., 1985, 1996). This no-difference finding in terms of outcome is critically important because the two treatments are very different in their cost (for the surgery, complications, hospitalization, and for subsequent plastic surgery for breast implants) and psychological impact (on subsequent depression and body image).

No-difference findings may also be important because of the potential questions they raise. For example, programs that are extremely costly and mandated for treatment for special populations may be shown to have little or no impact in the outcomes they produce (Weisz et al., 1990). Such findings are critically important to ensure that further resources are not deployed in a fashion that has no effect and to stimulate innovative and more promising intervention efforts. Indeed, such findings underscore the importance of demonstrating no-difference effects when they are present to ensure that resources are not deployed for ineffective programs.

In the general case, negative results may be important on the basis of substantive and methodological considerations. The substantive considerations refer to the significance of the experimental or clinical questions that guide the investigation. As in the above examples, the question may be one in which no differences between two groups, conditions, or interventions are actively sought. The methodological considerations refer to the care with which the study is planned, implemented, and evaluated. In particular, given documented weaknesses of research, the power of the study to demonstrate differences (if they exist) is pivotal. Power analyses, of the type discussed earlier, can be completed before and after a study is conducted to provide the investigator and reader with a statement of the sensitivity of the test in light of actual effect sizes obtained. No-difference findings in a well-conceived and controlled study with adequate power (e.g., > .80) ought to be taken as seriously as any other finding.

REPLICATION

Evaluation of the results of an experiment, regardless of whether a significant difference is demonstrated, entails more than scrutiny of the experiment. The reliability of a finding across studies greatly enhances evaluation of any particular investigation. Replication is a pivotal topic that relates to evaluation of findings and accumulation of knowledge.

Types of Replication

Replication refers to repetition of an experiment. Many different types of replication have been distinguished on the basis of the extent to which the replication follows characteristics of the original investigation and the dimensions along which the replication effort may vary (e.g., types of subjects, tasks, means of operationalizing independent or dependent variables) (Carlsmith, Ellsworth, & Aronson, 1976; Rosenthal, 1991). Direct or exact replication and systematic or approximate replication provide a useful way to convey critical points. *Direct replication* refers to an attempt to repeat an experiment exactly as it was conducted originally. Ideally, the conditions and procedures across the replication and original experiment are identical. *Systematic replication* refers to repetition of the experiment by systematically allowing various features to vary. The conditions and procedures of the replication are deliberately designed to approximate only those of the original experiment. It is useful to consider direct and systematic replication as opposite ends of a continuum.

A replication at the direct end of the spectrum would follow the original procedures as closely as possible. This is easiest for the researcher who conducted the original investigation because he or she has complete access to all the methods, the population from which the original sample was drawn, and the nuances of the laboratory procedures (e.g., tasks for experimenters and subjects, all instructions, data-handling procedures) that optimize similarity with the original study. An exact replication is not possible, even by the original investigator, because repetition of the experiment involves new subjects tested at a different point in time and by different experimenters, all factors that could lead to different results. Thus, all replications necessarily allow some original factors to vary; the issue is the extent to which the replication study departs from the original investigation.

Direct replication by someone other than the original investigator is often difficult to conduct. Many of the procedures are not sufficiently described in written reports and articles of an investigation. Journals routinely limit the space available in which authors may present their studies. Hence, further materials about how the study was conducted usually must be obtained from the original investigator. Ideally, an individual interested in a close replication of the original experiment would obtain and use as many of the original experimental materials as possible.

A replication at the systematic end of the spectrum would vary the experiment deliberately along one or more dimensions. For example, a systematic replication might assess whether the relation between the independent and dependent variable holds when subjects are older or younger than subjects in the original experiment, when subject (patient) diagnoses differ, or when the therapists are inexperienced rather than experienced. Of course, a systematic replication tends to vary only one or a few of the dimensions along which the study might differ from the original experiment. If the results of a replication differ from the original experiment, it is desirable to have a limited number of differences between these experiments so the possible reason for the discrepancy of results can be more easily identified. If there are multiple differences between the original and replication experiments, discrepancies in results might be due to a host of factors not easily discerned without extensive further experimentation.

Importance of Replication

The importance of replication in scientific research cannot be overemphasized. Unfortunately, the importance is not commensurate with the number of replications that seem to be attempted or at least reported.[2] Reviews of journal publications many years ago found that 0–1 percent of studies are replications in some form (Bozarth & Roberts, 1972; Greenwald, 1975) although, of course, these surveys need to be replicated. Replication of findings are more common in the physical and biological sciences (e.g., identifying subatomic particles, showing that a particular chemical inhibits a virus). The paucity of replication studies in psychology is ironic because the range of influences that might operate in psychology experiments (e.g., primacy and recency effects, subject and experimenter expectations) is at least as great and very likely greater than influences that can operate to distort findings in experiments within the physical sciences.

Within the social sciences, there are few professional rewards for replication attempts, particularly direct replication attempts. Direct replications may be met with indifference because the outcome may be considered uninformative or ambiguous. If the results of the original study are successfully replicated, the replication project may be given little attention because it does not add new information to the literature. If the replication study does not yield the same results, the onus is implicitly on the second investigator to explain and demonstrate why there was a difference across the investigations.

The major reason that replications are not usually viewed with great excitement is that, by definition, replications are partly repetitions of experiments that already have been done. Repetition of the experiment seems undramatic and lacking in originality. (Indeed, at cocktail parties with psychologists, one would not want to boast about the fact that his or her research is devoted to replication of work done by other investigators.) Yet, a replication experiment should not be viewed as mere repetition of previous work. Rather, replications can be better conceptualized as tests of robustness and generality of the original finding or as more careful evaluations of the original hypotheses. This is not merely a terminological change but rather, I believe, a more accurate characterization of the contribution of replications.

Replication studies are direct tests of robustness and the generality of the original experimental findings. They ask whether the relation holds across changes in the conditions of the experiment. If the results of a replication do not support the original research, they do not necessarily impugn the original finding. Rather, they may suggest that the relation holds only for a narrow set of conditions or relates to a specific circumscribed set of factors, perhaps some unspecified in the original report. The original finding may be veridical and not the result of experimental biases or artifacts, but still be insufficiently robust to have wide generality.

Replications as tests of generality are particularly important in clinical psychology in which research and application are so intertwined. Tests of generality partially address the applied value of many findings and have implications for decisions about treatment. Both researchers and clinicians wish to know how widely the results of a given treatment can be applied or, indeed, whether the results can be applied beyond a very narrow set of experimental conditions. We are rarely surprised when an experienced investigator reports results that treatment is effective and indeed even has dramatic effects (e.g., for delinquency [Henggeler et al., 1986] and anxiety disorders [Kendall, 1994]). When these studies are replicated by the same investigator in different settings and with a different sample (Henggeler et al., 1992; Kendall et al., 1997) or replicated by a different team of investigators with variations in the treatment (Barrett, Dadds, & Rapee, 1996), we can have increased faith in the original findings and in the generality of the results.

Direct and systematic replications add to knowledge in different ways. Replications that closely approximate the conditions of the original experiment increase one's confidence that the original finding is reliable and not likely to have resulted from chance or a particular artifact. Replications that deviate from the original conditions suggest that the findings hold across a wider range of conditions. Essentially, the greater the divergence of the replication from the conditions of the original experiment, the greater the generality of the relation that was demonstrated.

Several replication attempts may reveal findings that show the original relation to be evident across a wide range of laboratory and even field conditions. On the other hand, several unsuccessful replication attempts may reveal findings that show the original relation not to be present anywhere else. The original finding then may be viewed as trivial in the sense that it is narrowly restricted to a very specific set of circumstances. Alternatively, the original finding may have resulted from uncontrolled factors or biases not evident in the original report or simply from chance (Type I error).

Obviously, replication attempts do not invariably produce the same results as the original experiment. Examples may be plentiful but they are difficult to find because replication studies and so-called negative results are infrequently published. One example of a failure to replicate was evident in a single-case experiment. In a study completed several years ago, self-instruction training was used to alter the behavior of three children who were highly disruptive in class in a Head Start program (Bornstein & Quevillon, 1976). Training was conducted for 2 hours outside the classroom. The children and a trainer worked on tasks to develop problem-solving skills. The skills were intended to alter the children's on-task behavior in the classroom. The children were instructed to administer instructions to themselves—first aloud, then in a whisper, and finally without sound (covertly). Self-instruction training was administered and evaluated in a multiple-baseline design across children. The results indicated marked increases in on-task behavior in the classroom for each child. Moreover, the markedly improved classroom performance was maintained several weeks after treatment.

Several investigators have tried to repeat this demonstration with little or no success (Bryant & Budd, 1982; Friedling & O'Leary, 1979). One direct replication effort closely followed the procedures implemented in the original study using children who were disruptive in class in a Head Start program (Billings & Wasik, 1985). Yet, the children's classroom performance was not improved by the procedures, and the original effects were not replicated. Clearly, this raises questions about the original findings and the conditions under which they apply. Some of the ambiguities have prompted different types of studies to understand when and how self-instruction training can alter child behavior. The failures to replicate the original findings lend emphasis to the importance of routine replication studies.

The nature of publication practices undoubtedly fosters biases about the information disseminated in the literature. The journal review process favors positive effects (i.e., group differences) and systematically excludes similar studies (replications) that find no differences. Thus, when there is a chance finding (Type I error), it is more likely to enter the literature. Failures to replicate are less likely to be published. The paucity of replication research may obscure the number of findings that can be confidently embraced as robust. The notion of the file-drawer problem, mentioned previously, refers to the prospect that many nonpublished papers may not have shown the finding and are thus relegated to the investigator's file drawer. Studies that are published are more likely to be the chance findings (5 in 100 for $p = .05$) if the studies were conducted many times and the null hypothesis is false. Computations can be completed to estimate how many unpublished findings without significant effects (i.e., the file drawer) would be required for the finding in the literature to be challenged (Rosenthal, 1984; Rosenthal, 1991). For example, hundreds of studies attest to the effects of psychotherapy (Durlak et al., 1995; Smith, Glass, & Miller, 1980; Weisz & Weiss, 1993). It would take several thousand studies with no effects to contest this basic finding. Consequently, it is not very plausible that the effects in the studies is due to chance or biased reporting. As a general rule, as more studies support a particular finding, the less likely that unpublished findings would negate the overall relationship that has been found.

From the standpoint of a prospective investigator, replication work is important to consider as a research strategy, particularly at the inception of one's work in an area in which it is important to ensure that the phenomenon can be reproduced. After a phenomenon has been reproduced, it can be analyzed and elaborated in subsequent research. Although replication research is advocated in this text as an important focus, it would be naive to neglect the point noted earlier—that simple replication may conflict with professional rewards. The rewards are for original experimentation, for something that has not yet been done. (In some areas, any well-controlled research would meet this criterion.) Yet, replications are not necessarily mere repetitions of studies; often they provide much more careful evaluations of the hypothesis studied in the original experiment. Typically, these evaluations have implications for the interpretation (construct validity) of the original experiment. The very basis for conducting a replication may be that there is an alternative explanation for the results, one that the original investigator did not rule out. A replication may repeat the original experiment with additional control conditions and provide a methodological and theoretical advance.

The value of replication efforts can depend on a number of factors. Replications early in the development of an area of research are particularly important as the bedrock of the theory and empirical phenomena are established. Replications conducted by persons other than the original investigator and with variations in some of the methods and procedures (e.g., subjects, settings, and tasks) are also particularly important. An excellent strategy is to include in one's investigation a partial replication of previous research; for example, an investigator could include conditions that closely resemble those in a previous experiment. In addition, conditions can be included that conceptually extend the experiment and the experimental conditions. Essentially, this strategy includes an attempt to combine direct and systematic replication strategies in a single experiment. The results of such research not only allows one to comment on the reliability of the phenomenon, but also allows generality of the findings, all within the same experiment. Also, the researcher may be able to predict an interaction indicating the conditions across which the original findings may hold.

General Comments

Replication and negative results, two topics treated separately, are related in important ways. In the usual situation, we say that a finding is replicated if the original (first) study and the next study both show a significant effect. We say that a finding is not replicated when the first study finds a significant effect but one or more subsequent studies do not. However, as illustrated in the chapter on statistical evaluation of the data, statistical significance is a poor measure of the results of the experiment. Identical findings, as measured by effect size, may lead to rejection of the null hypothesis in one situation but acceptance in another study, purely as a function of power. Thus, seeming failures to replicate occasionally may be artifacts of the methods used to analyze the data.

Although the importance of replication has been advocated for decades, the impact on research practices in psychology have been limited—the same story that was noted for power. What is relatively new to address the problem is the use of meta-analyses to evaluate and to integrate related studies, which may vary in the degree to which they replicate each other. By combining multiple studies, the meta-analysis can give an estimate of the true effects in the population and confidence limits about that effect. Also, one can analyze whether characteristics of the study (e.g., methodological features) make a difference in relation to the strength of the effects that were obtained. The ability to combine multiple studies and to analyze characteristics of the studies that may influence (moderate) the effect have served some of the key purposes of replication research.

SUMMARY AND CONCLUSIONS

Three areas were discussed related to interpretation of research findings: data patterns and types of experimental effects, negative results, and replication. Factorial designs were used to illustrate the difference between *main effects* and *interactions*. The designs alert us to the fact that the impact of a given variable must be viewed in relation to other variables. The notion that variables may interact with each other has important implications for the types of research we conduct and for interpretation of research more generally. The presence or absence of a finding or relation may be due to or restricted by other conditions because of these interactions.

Another topic critical to interpretation of data is the notion of *negative results*, a concept that has come to mean that no statistically significant differences were found in the experiment. The concept has received attention because the putative importance of a given study and its publishability often depend on whether statistically significant results are obtained. Unfortunately, such an emphasis has detracted considerably from other considerations, that is, whether the conclusions can be accepted because of the theoretical or empirical importance of the question and quality of the research design, independent of statistical significance. Hence, methodologically weak studies with statistically significant results are more likely to be published, and methodologically sound studies or studies at least as sound as those published without statistically significant effects often go unpublished.

Related to the topic of negative results is the notion of *replication* or full repetition of a previously conducted study. Replications can vary in similarity to the original experiment. *Direct* replications attempt to mimic the original experiment; *systematic* replications purposely attempt to vary the conditions of the original experiment. Replication research may lead to negative results, which can bring into question the basis for the results of the original experiment or the generality of the original findings. Replication research is exceedingly important because it is the most reliable test of whether the original finding is veridical. The logic of statistical analyses suggests that statistical significance will be occasionally achieved even when there are no group differences in the population, that is, findings significant by chance alone. Because these findings are likely to be published because of the bias for positive findings, there could be a great many findings that would not stand up under any replication conditions. Thus, to distinguish findings that have a sound basis requires replication research.

Replications need not merely repeat a previous experiment. They can address nuances of the original experiment or pose entirely new questions, such as the conditions under which the original relation is or is not likely to hold.

NOTES

[1]The purpose in highlighting the notions of main effects and interactions at this point is to raise more general issues about evaluating results. Thus, a simple example and variations of results of the factorial design were selected. Interactions are complex subjects in their own right and are treated extensively elsewhere (see Rosenthal & Rosnow, 1991; Rosnow & Rosenthal, 1989).

[2]The sweeping statement about the dearth of replication studies has important exceptions (Neuliep, 1991). In some areas of psychology (e.g., experimental psychology), replication studies are included in a single publication in which multiple investigations are combined. In laboratory investigations with college students who attend a single session or in which animal subjects are used, replication tends to be more common, in part as a function of the brevity of the experiment and ease of recruiting subjects. In contrast, in clinical, counseling, and educational psychology, and in other areas, recruiting and running subjects may be more difficult and protracted. The concern here is not with practical impediments to replication but a broader ethos in which replication and its critical role in science are uniformly appreciated.

FOR FURTHER READING

Fagley, N.S. (1985). Applied statistical power analysis and the interpretation of nonsignificant results by research consumers. *Journal of Counseling Psychology, 32,* 391–396.

Jaccard, J., Turrisi, R., & Wan, C.K. (1990). *Interaction effects in multiple regression.* Newbury Park: Sage.

Neuliep, J.W. (Ed.) (1991). *Replication research in the social sciences.* Newbury Park, CA: Sage.

Prentice, D.A., & Miller, D.T. (1992). When small effects are impressive. *Psychological Bulletin, 112,* 160–164.

Rosnow, R.L., & Rosenthal, R. (1989). Definition and interpretation of interaction effects. *Psychological Bulletin, 105,* 143–146.

Chapter 16

Ethical Issues and Guidelines for Research

Psychological research raises a number of ethical issues and dilemmas. To begin with, experiments require manipulation of variables, which often may subject participants to experiences that are undesirable or even potentially harmful, such as stress, failure, and frustration. Whether participants in research should be subjected to such experiences is in part an ethical decision. Second, implementing many experimental manipulations may require withholding information from the subject. The experimental question may address how subjects respond without being forewarned about exactly what will happen or the overall purpose. Withholding information also raises important ethical issues. Third, experimentation requires assessment or observation of the subject. Many dependent measures of interest pertain to areas that subjects may consider private, such as views about themselves, beliefs about important social or political issues, and signs of adjustment or maladjustment. Descriptive information from the sample (e.g., family income) also may raise concerns that the information might be publicly disclosed and have untoward implications (e.g., for collection of social assistance, payment of income taxes, child support). Clearly, issues pertaining to invasion of privacy and violation of confidentiality are raised by assessment. Fourth, the methodological requirements of psychological experiments, which are particularly acute in intervention research, also raise ethical issues. For example, assigning clients randomly to one of several treatment or control conditions entails an ethical decision favoring experimental design rather than the seeming appropriateness of one condition over another for the client's problem. Whether treatment should ever be withheld also reflects an ethical decision made by an investigator.

Aside from substantive and methodological issues, the relationship between the investigator or experimenter and the subject raises ethical concerns. Differences in the power and status of the experimenter and subject allows for potential abuses of the rights of the individual participant. Research participants, particularly in clinical research, often are disadvantaged or dependent by virtue of their age, physical or mental condition, captive status, educational level, or political and economic position. For example, by virtue of their status, children and adolescents, the aged, college students, psychiatric patients, prisoners, and military recruits have much less power than the investigator. The power differential increases vulnerability to abuse for these individuals. The subjects may be more readily induced into research, and they may have, or at least feel they have, relatively little freedom to refuse or discontinue participation.

The status of the investigator is sustained by several factors. The investigator structures the situation in which the subject participates and is seen as an expert who is justified in determining the conditions for performance. The legitimacy, prestige, and importance of scientific research place subjects in an inferior position. Although subjects can withdraw from the research, doing so may not be viewed as a realistic option because of the status differential. Subjects may see themselves as lacking both the capacity and the right to question both the investigator and what is being done in the study. Subjects are at a disadvantage in terms of the information at their disposal about the experiment, the risks that are taken, and the limited means for counteracting objectionable aspects of the treatment.

In current research, subjects are usually informed of the goals of the study and of any risks and benefits that might accrue. Written consent is obtained to confirm that subjects understand the study and their rights not to participate and to withdraw. Both legal codes (e.g., for universities receiving any federal funds) and ethical codes (from professional organizations) guide the process of disclosing information to and obtaining consent from the subjects.[1] The codes and practices that follow from these codes ensure that the rights of the individual subject are protected and are given the highest priority in research.

This chapter raises a number of ethical issues and highlights contemporary guidelines for ethical research practices and professional obligations in the conduct and reporting of research. The focus of this chapter is on issues primarily in the context of research with human participants. Ethical and practical issues pertaining to infrahuman species are no less significant, but most research in clinical, counseling, school, and related areas is with human participants. Similarly, many ethical issues related to the practice of psychology (e.g., in the context of delivering therapy or consulting) are not addressed in light of the focus on research.

CRITICAL ISSUES IN RESEARCH

Although many ethical issues can be identified, a few seem particularly salient: using deception in experiments, informing participants about the deception after the experiment is completed, invading the subject's privacy, and obtaining informed consent.

Deception

Deception may take many different forms and often refers to quite different operations. At one extreme, deception can refer to entirely misrepresenting the nature of an experiment. At the other extreme, deception can refer to being ambiguous about the experiment or not specifying all or many important details. The extent to which active (e.g., misrepresentation) or passive (e.g., failure to mention specific details) forms of deception are objectionable in part depends on the situations in which they are used and the effects they are likely to have on the participants. Misleading the participant may not be objectionable in many experimental arrangements. For example, when participants perform a memory task involving lists of words or syllables, they may be told initially that the purpose is to measure the way in which individuals memorize words. In fact, the purpose may be to assess the accuracy of recall as a function of the way in which the words are presented. In this situation, there seems to be little potential harm to the participants or to their evaluations of themselves. Alternatively, participants may be placed under psychological stress or led to raise important questions about themselves. For example, participants may be told they have latent adjustment or sexual problems or are odd in the way they think. The goal may be to evaluate such induced states on some other area of functioning.

The ethical dilemma lies in deciding whether deception is justified in a given experiment and whether its possible risks to the participant outweigh its potential benefits in the knowledge the study is designed to yield. Both the risks to the participant and the potential benefits usually are a matter of surmise, so the decision is not straightforward. The dilemma is particularly difficult because the risks to the individual subject are weighed against the benefits to society. In most psychological experiments, the benefits of the research are not likely to accrue to the participant directly. Weighing potential benefits to society against potential risks to the individual subject is difficult, to say the least. The safest way to proceed is to minimize or eliminate risk to the subject by not using active forms of deception.

The potential harm that deception may cause for the individual subject certainly is a major ethical objection to its use. Moreover, aside from its direct harmful consequences, the act of deception has been objected to because it violates a value of honesty between individuals, in this case between the investigator and subject. Investigators engage in behaviors as part of deception that would not be condoned outside of the experimental setting because these behaviors violate the basic rights of individuals. Thus, deception fosters a type of behavior that is objected to on its own grounds independent of its other consequences. Alternatively, it may not be the deceptive behaviors in which investigators may engage as much as the context in which these behaviors occur. Many forms of deception occur in everyday life; individuals occasionally also object to these deceptions (e.g., surprise parties). The problem with forms of deception and surprises in an experiment is that the professional context of an experiment may lead people to expect full disclosure, candor, and respect for individual rights.

Actually, deception in research rarely involves efforts to mislead subjects. The central issue for research is the extent to which subjects should be aware of the purpose and procedures of the experiment. Ideally, investigators would fully disclose all available information about what will take place. Complete disclosure would entail conveying to subjects the nature of all procedures, even procedures to which the subjects in a particular condition will not be exposed, and revealing the investigator's view and expectations about what the results might yield.

However, in most psychological experiments with human subjects, full disclosure of available information may not be realistic. If the subject knows about the purpose, hypotheses and procedures, this information could influence or alter the results. To begin with, full knowledge about the experiment could raise all the problems associated with demand characteristics and subject roles, as discussed earlier. These influences are much more likely to occur when subjects are aware of the purpose of the experiment. More generally, the conclusions reached in an experiment may differ drastically when subjects are completely aware of the facets of the experiment from when they are unaware.

The effects of disclosing the purpose and hypotheses to the subjects was demonstrated in the 1970s when the issue of disclosure began to be mandated. In a seminal study, college students participated in a verbal conditioning experiment in which their selection of pronouns in a sentence-construction task was reinforced by the experimenter who said, "Good" or "Okay" (Resnick & Schwartz, 1973). Some subjects (informed group) were told that the purpose was to increase their use of *I* and *we* pronouns to determine whether telling subjects the purpose of the experiment affected the results. These subjects were told the true purpose (i.e., to evaluate the effects of full disclosure). Other subjects (uninformed group) were told that the experiment was designed to study verbal communication. They were not informed of the real purpose of the experiment. Subjects in both groups constructed sentences and received approval when *I* or *we* pronouns were used in the sentences. As expected, the uninformed subjects increased in their use of the target pronouns that were reinforced over their base rates in a practice (nonreinforced) period, a finding shown many times in the literature on verbal conditioning. In contrast, the informed subjects decreased their use of target pronouns relative to their initial practice rates. Thus, disclosing information about the purposes of the experiment altered the findings.

The results suggest that informing subjects about the purposes and expected results of an experiment might dictate the specific relation that is obtained between the independent and dependent variable. Of course, one might view the results in another way, namely, that not telling subjects about the experiment also dictates a specific relation, one that is not more or less "real" or informative than results obtained under informed circumstances. Yet, a major goal of psychology is to study behavior and to extrapolate findings to circumstances in which individuals normally behave. That is, most theories we develop about human functioning are not intended to account for phenomena only evident in the laboratory. Thus, investigators wish to understand how subjects respond to events when subjects are not forewarned about their anticipated effects and the purpose of exposure to these events. Although investigators, in principle, would like to avoid deception, its use in some form may be necessary to understand certain behavioral processes.

In general, guidelines for informing subjects are dictated by law and by ethical principles that govern research and informed consent. Such guidelines do not require elaborating all views, hypothesis, expectations, and related possibilities to the subjects. Thus, some information invariably is withheld. Of special concern in relation to deception are active efforts to mislead subjects. Such efforts are quite rare in clinical, counseling, and educational research. Research proposals that include efforts to mislead subjects must establish that deception is essential to achieve the research goals and that special procedures to protect subjects are provided to reduce any lingering effects of the experience.

To establish that deception is necessary, at least three criteria must be met. First, the investigator who designs the experiment must make the case to others that deception is justified because of the importance of the information that is to be revealed by the experiment. Yet an investigator may not be the best judge because of his or her investment in the research. Hence, review committees involving individuals from different fields of inquiry ordinarily examine whether the proposed procedures are justifiable. The committees, formally developed in most universities and institutions in which research is conducted, follow guidelines for evaluating research and for protecting subjects (discussed later in the chapter). Second, if there is deception in the planned experiment, there must be assurances that less deceptive or nondeceptive methods of investigation could not be used to obtain the information. This is also difficult to assess because whether similar methods would produce the information proposed in an experiment that uses deception is entirely empirical. Researchers genuinely disagree about the extent to which deception is essential. Third, aversiveness to deception itself bears strongly on the justification of the study. The aversiveness refers to the procedures and degree of deception and the potential for and magnitude of harmful effects. Deceptions vary markedly in degree, although ethical discussions usually focus on cases in which subjects are grossly misled about their own abilities or personal characteristics.

Research begins with the view that individual rights are to be protected. Investigators are to disclose to the extent possible details of the design, purposes, risks, benefits, and costs (e.g., monetary or other). The purpose is to permit the subject to make an informed decision regarding participation. If deception is to be used, either by withholding critical information or by misrepresenting the study, the onus is on the investigator to show cause at the research proposal stage that doing this is essential for the necessary benefits of the research. Unless the case for using deception can be made to review committees that evaluate such proposals, the work may not be permitted.

In many cases, if deception seems necessary, the investigator's creativity and methodological and statistical skills can provide a path to avoid deception. It is useful to begin with the premise that there may be no need to deceive subjects. Alternative experimental procedures may address whether deception is necessary. For example, the investigator may present to different groups varying degrees of information to see whether the information affects the findings. Alternatively, perhaps the methods used to evaluate demand characteristics (e.g., preinquiry or use of simulators) can be explored to evaluate whether subjects would be likely to perform differently under different conditions of disclosure. The absence of differences between groups studied in this way are consistent with the view that deception may not be critical to the research findings and methods of study in the area of work. The alternatives are not perfect in providing unambiguous answers that might be obtained with deception. These options begin to develop the empirical basis for deciding whether deception would in some way tarnish the empirical relations of interest to the investigator.

Debriefing

If there is any deception in the experiment or if crucial information is withheld, the experimenter should describe the true nature of the experiment after the subject has been run. Providing a description of the experiment and its purposes is referred to as *debriefing*. The purpose of debriefing is to counteract or minimize any negative effects that the experiment may have had. By debriefing, the experimenter hopes the subjects will not leave the experiment with greater anxiety, discomfort, or lowered self-esteem than when they arrived. Apart from overcoming possible deleterious effects of deception, debriefing is often considered to convey educative objectives, such as communicating the potential value of research and acknowledging the subjects' contribution to research (Kidder & Judd, 1986). These features focus on conveying the benefits of subject participation in research and are of value in their own right.

Debriefing is usually discussed in the context of overcoming the deleterious effects of deception. The manner in which debriefing is conducted and the information conveyed to the subject vary enormously among experiments. Typically, subjects meet with the experimenter immediately after completing the experimental tasks. The experimenter may inform the subject what the experiment was really about and explain the reasons that the stated purpose did not convey this information. The importance of debriefing varies with the type of experiment and the nature of the deception. For instance, as part of an experiment, subjects may have been told that they have tendencies toward mental illness or an early grave. In such situations, subjects obviously ought to be told during debriefing that the information was not accurate and that they are "normal." Presumably such information will be a great relief to the subjects. On the other hand, subjects may be distressed that they were exposed to such deception or that they were gullible enough to believe it.

Debriefing has been assumed to be a procedure that resolves the potentially harmful effects of deception. Yet debriefing has its own problems and may not achieve its intended purposes. Subjects may believe that the debriefing session is merely a continuation of the experiment and the deception by the experimenter. Suspiciousness on the part of the subject has a reasonable basis. Although quite rare, there are historical examples in which subjects were told that the experiment was over, and they were debriefed, but in truth the debriefing itself involved deception and the subject continued unwittingly to serve in the experiment (Festinger & Carlsmith, 1959). Also, in introductory psychology courses, college students invariably read about or view films of classic experiments in which clear deception was invoked, even though such experiments would not be allowed by current standards.

Even if subjects are not suspicious about debriefing, questions can be raised about whether the effects of the manipulation can be nullified with a postexperimental explanation. The effectiveness of debriefing is likely to depend on several considerations, such as the characteristics of the subject, the nature of the deception, and the time interval between deception and debriefing. Yet, debriefing subjects by providing full information about the deception does not necessarily erase the false impressions (e.g., about subject skills) established during the experiment (Ross, Lepper, & Hubbard, 1975; Walster, Berscheid, Abrahams, & Aronson, 1967). The fact that the effects of deception may linger after debriefing provides us with further caveats. If deception is to be considered, it must be clearly justified because of the risks to individual rights and integrity.

Debriefing requires considerable thought in research, particularly when subjects are deliberately misguided about the experiment. Debriefing must convey to the subject what the experiment was about, what the purpose was, and how reactions of the subject were typical. It may be necessary to individualize debriefing to meet questions of the individual subjects. The timing of debriefing may also be important. Sometimes experimenters wait until all subjects have been run in the experiment and then contact subjects with a printed handout or class announcement. The reason for waiting is that information provided early in the experiment might filter to other subjects before they are run. However, delayed debriefing may not be as effective as immediate debriefing. If subjects are potentially harmed by the deception, the experimenter's obligation is to debrief as soon and as effectively as possible.

An investigator using deception should demonstrate that the debriefing procedures will effectively eliminate incorrect beliefs induced in the experiment. Whether subjects are debriefed should refer more to the outcome of providing certain kinds of information rather than the experience to which subjects are exposed. The effectiveness of a particular debriefing technique could be demonstrated in the experiment itself or as part of pilot work prior to the investigation.

Invasion of Privacy

Invasion of privacy represents a broad concept that encompasses practices extending well beyond research. Generally, invasion of privacy refers to seeking personal information that intrudes on what individuals view as private. Information may be sought on topics such as religious preferences, sexual beliefs and behaviors, income, and political views. Individuals vary considerably on the areas they regard as sensitive and private. For example, one survey reported that married women provided detailed answers to questions about birth-control practices, a topic that might have been viewed as very sensitive a few decades ago (Clark, 1967). The respondents were very cooperative in providing answers until they were asked to reveal their family's income, at which point they refused to answer. This question apparently invaded what subjects thought was private information, presumably because it was not part of the topic they had agreed to discuss. Surveys assess attitudes on all sorts of personal topics. Beyond surveys, other sources, such as credit bureaus, investigative and sales agencies, and potential employers, solicit information from individuals.

The use of tests that measure psychopathology and personality also raises concerns over invasion of privacy. Test results can reflect directly on an individual's psychological status, adjustment, and beliefs and uncover personal characteristics that the subject might regard as private. Moreover, the information obtained through psychological testing might be potentially damaging if made public. The threat of personality testing to the invasion of privacy has been a topic of considerable concern. Indeed, Congressional hearings have addressed the use of psychological tests for selecting employees in the government. (For interested readers, the Congressional inquiry into psychological testing was presented in a condensed form with commentaries in the *American Psychologist*, 1965, 20(11).) Measures of psychopathology and personality had been used routinely to screen potential government employees. Many of the questions asked of prospective employees seemed to be of a personal nature and not clearly related to the tasks for which individuals were being selected.

In psychological research, the major issues regarding invasion of privacy pertain to how the information from subjects is obtained and used. Ordinarily, information provided in experiments must to be provided willingly. Obviously, there are many kinds of research in which consent of the individual is neither possible (e.g., in cases of severe psychiatric or neurological impairment) nor especially crucial (e.g., in the case of studying archival records for groups of unidentifiable subjects).

Two conditions designed to protect the subject's right to privacy in research are anonymity and confidentiality. *Anonymity* refers to ensuring that identify of subjects and their individual performance are not revealed. Subjects who agree to provide information must be assured that their responses are anonymous. Anonymity can be ensured at the point of obtaining the data, for example, when subjects are instructed not to identify themselves on an answer sheet and, after the information is obtained, by separating the names of participants from the measures or any associations with the scores. Typically, data are coded so that participants' names cannot be associated with a particular set of data. Only the investigator may have the information revealing the identity of the subject. In most research, confidentiality is maintained by obtaining the data under conditions of anonymity or converting the data through coding or data-reduction procedures to a format in which the individual's identity cannot be discerned. Research with clinic populations or in special settings may require specific safeguards regarding the protection of confidentiality (e.g., clinic records) because many persons may have special interest in the information obtained as part of the research (e.g., employers, relatives, school administrators) and the nature of the information (e.g., measures of adjustment, psychopathology) may be potentially damaging if misinterpreted or misused.

Invasion of privacy extends beyond the process of obtaining information. Once the information is obtained, participants must be assured that their performance is confidential. *Confidentiality* means that the information will not be disclosed to a third party without the awareness and consent of the participant. Conceivably, situations in which confidentiality is violated might arise, such as having information that might conceal a clear and imminent danger to an individual or society. For example, clinical psychologists are involved with research on the evaluation, treatment, and prevention of acquired immunodeficiency syndrome (AIDS). Confidentiality about who is participating in the research and about test results for infection are obviously important. The information, if inadvertently made available, can stigmatize research participants and subject them to discrimination in several areas of everyday life (e.g., employment, housing).

Invasion of privacy enters into many different areas in clinical research. For example, privacy is an important issue in writing the results of research investigations and treatment applications. Clinical research reports in which an individual case is involved often are prepared for publication. In these instances, efforts to maintain confidentiality require the investigator to disguise the ancillary information about the client in such as way that his or her identity could not be recognized. Typically, pseudonyms are used when a case is described in published form. Yet for many case reports, a change in the name may not protect the subject's confidentiality. Cases are often selected for presentation *because* they raise special issues, circumstances, and challenges. If there is any risk that preparation of a research report could reveal the identity of a subject, the subject must to be informed of this in advance and provide appropriate consent.

Another area in clinical research in which invasion of privacy is possible is the use of informants for data collection. Occasionally, treatment research with a client or group of clients may solicit the aid of friends, spouses, neighbors, teachers, or employers. The purpose is to ask these individuals to provide data about the client. The information is used to evaluate the effects of treatment or the severity of the client's problem, although the client may not be aware of the assessment. Seeking information about the client may violate the client's right to privacy and confidentiality. The client may not want his or her problem widely advertised, and any attempts at unobtrusive assessment may violate this wish. For example, asking employers to assess whether the client's alcoholic consumption interferes with work performance may apprise the employer of a problem of which he or she was unaware.

Invasion of privacy is often discussed at the level of the individual subject. However, much larger units are relevant and of deep concern in clinical research. Privacy of communities and cultural and ethnic groups also emerge. For example, a clinically relevant study was designed to survey alcohol use in an Inupiat community in Barrow, Alaska (Foulks, 1987; Manson, 1989). Impetus of the study was to examine cases of alcohol abuse and to evaluate community detention programs for acute alcohol detoxification. A representative sample of persons (N = 88) older than age 15 was drawn from the community and interviewed regarding their attitudes, values, and behavior in relation to alcohol use. Other measures of functioning also assessed were church membership and social and work behavior. The results indicated that 41 percent of the sample considered themselves to be excessive drinkers; more than 50 percent said that alcohol use caused problems with their spouse and family; 62 percent said they regularly got into fights when drinking. These and similar types of descriptive statements indicated that alcohol use was a problem in this community.

Reports of the findings were viewed by the community as highly objectionable and invasive. The community's view was that alcohol use and associated problems resulted from a new way of life imposed on them rather than on implied deficits, biological or otherwise, or problems inherent to the people. The report was criticized as denigrating, culturally imperialistic, and insensitive to the values of Native American and Alaskan native culture (Foulks, 1989). Great oversimplification of the findings in the news media (e.g., a byline column titled "Alcohol Plagues Eskimos" in the *New York Times,* January 22, 1980) and emphasis of alcoholism and violence in various articles exacerbated the problem.

The consequences of this study might be used to illustrate many issues, only one of which is invasion of privacy (e.g., relations with the members of the population of interest at the design and reporting stages, dissemination of research findings, and contact with the media). In relation to invasion of privacy, individual community members could not be identified by the report. Nevertheless, community members, regardless of whether they had been subjects, viewed their privacy as violated and objected that they were misrepresented (Manson, 1989). Such examples convey that investigations do not merely describe relations and report findings of abstract scientific interest. The methods of obtaining information, the reporting of the information, and the way information is and could be used are part of the ethical considerations of research.

INFORMED CONSENT

Conditions and Elements

A pivotal ethical issue in research is informed consent. This issue is central because it encompasses many other topics including deception and invasion of privacy. An ethical imperative is that investigators obtain informed consent from the subjects so that they can take part in research. Of course, as is usually the case with imperatives, there are occasional exceptions (e.g., archival research when subjects are no longer living and cannot consent). Also, implementing the imperative raises special obstacles. In principle, consent can never be completely informed. All possible consequences of the experimental procedures, measures, and participation cannot be known and hence cannot be presented to inform the subject. The impact of the experimental manipulation or intervention, however seemingly innocuous, can also have quite different impact (e.g., direct and side effects) among the subjects. Because new knowledge is the desired outcome, the information of interest to both investigator and subject is not completely available.

Stating the logical status and limits of presenting information is important as a backdrop for the tasks of the investigator. Information cannot be complete. Yet the responsibility of the investigator is to provide available information and reasonable statements of repercussions so that the subject can make a rational decision. Informed consent consists of three major elements: competence, knowledge, and volition. *Competence* refers to the individual's ability to make a well-reasoned decision and to give consent meaningfully. *Knowledge* refers to understanding the nature of the experiment, the alternatives available, and the potential risks and benefits. *Volition* refers to the basis of agreeing to participate. Subjects must provide their consent free from constraint or duress. To ensure that participation is and remains voluntary, subjects may revoke their consent at any time.

In principle, ensuring competence could be a major issue. In practice, there are large segments of research in which this is not an issue. For example, in laboratory studies with college students given psychological tasks (e.g., listening to tapes of innocuous interactions, reading passages and remembering details), competence is not an issue. Subjects are considered capable of making rational decisions to participate on the basis of the information provided. In other cases, a characteristic of the sample may impede decision making (e.g., very young or very old subjects; individuals with clinical dysfunction that impedes cognitive functioning); thus, competence is an issue. The competence of others who act on behalf of the client (e.g., spouses, parents, other relatives) becomes the issue because these persons take over responsibility for decision making. Obviously, having others make critical decisions can raise its own problems if those who provide consent do not have interests of the subject at heart (be nice to your relatives). Such circumstances arise in considering invasive or risky medical or psychiatric procedures and do not pertain to the vast majority of research.

Knowledge about the experiment is essential. To provide adequate knowledge for informed consent, investigators are obligated to describe all facts, risks, and sources of discomfort that might influence a subject's decision to participate willingly. All conceivable risks need not be described; only those that might plausibly result from the procedure should be included. The information must be presented to the subject in an easily understandable fashion. In addition, subjects should be allowed to raise questions to clarify all issues that might be ambiguous.

Volition means that the subject agrees to participate without coercion. Participation in the experiment cannot be required to fulfill a class assignment, according to current requirements for consent. For subjects to provide consent, they must have a choice pertaining to their involvement in the investigation. The choice cannot be one in which participation in the experiment is substituted for some aversive or coercive alternative (e.g., completing two extra term papers), although in any given case, this may be difficult to discern. Whether the subject can freely choose to participate is sometimes evident from the consequences for not agreeing to participate or from withdrawing once consent has been provided. The absence of any penalty partially defines the extent to which the subject's consent was voluntary.

The differences in power and status between the investigator or experimenter and the subjects in the experimental setting can militate against voluntary consent. Subjects may not feel they can choose freely to participate or to withdraw because of their position in relation to the investigator. Because the research situation is structured by the investigator, the subject depends almost completely on the information provided to make choices about participation or continuation in the investigation. Thus, consent at any point in the research may not be completely informed because the subject may not have access to important information.

Operationally, informed consent is obtained in research when subjects sign a consent form. The form usually includes several ingredients, such as a description of the purpose of the study, the procedures to be followed, a statement of potential risks to the subjects, and any benefits for the subject or for society. Moreover, statements in the form usually indicate that the client was permitted to ask questions of the experimenter, that the client received answers to his or her satisfaction, that he or she does give permission to participate, that the information included will remain confidential, and that he or she is free to withdraw from the experiment at any time without penalty. The subject signs the form indicating that each condition has been met and that he or she agrees to participate.

Competence to provide consent is a central issue of concern and is heightened with populations who may be incapable or less than fully capable of providing consent (e.g., fetuses, young children, comatose patients, persons with intellectual impairment, institutionalized populations such as psychiatric patients and prisoners). Determining whether individuals are competent to provide consent presents many problems in its own right. For individuals regarded as incompetent, parents or guardians may give permission, but in medical research a parent or guardian may not consent to participation of an incompetent person in a treatment that promises no direct therapeutic benefit. Competent guardians may not sign away the rights of their incompetent wards.

Even when consent can be sought and obtained from the persons themselves, it is often unclear whether consent is adequate or meaningful. When consent guidelines and procedures had first been formulated, early research showed that following consent procedures as described here may not be sufficient to achieve the goals of actually informing the subjects. For example, in one study with voluntarily admitted psychiatric patients, 60 percent of the patients were unable to recall signing the admission form consenting to hospitalization when they were asked within 10 days after admission (Palmer & Wohl, 1972), and 33 percent of the patients did not recall or could not recall accurately the content of the form. Some patients even denied having signed it. Similarly, an evaluation of biomedical research in the Veterans Administration hospital system revealed that approximately 28 percent of patients interviewed were not aware that they were participating in a research investigation (Committee on Biomedical Research in the Veterans Administration, 1977). Moreover, at least 20 percent of the individual patients had very little or no idea of what the research was about, even though the patients had received carefully implemented informed consent procedures and had signed the appropriate forms. These investigations raise questions about the competence of the patients or the adequacy of the procedures to secure informed consent.

Providing knowledge about the treatment often is a problem in clinical research. The risks and potential benefits of treatment are not always well known, particularly for populations that have been refractory to conventional treatments. Last-resort or experimental techniques may be improvised. Hence, the necessary information for making a knowledgeable decision is unavailable. For example, in an extreme instance, psychosurgery was recommended to control the aggressive behavior of a psychiatric patient. Although the patient consented to the procedure, in a landmark decision, the court ruled that consent could not be "informed" because of the nature of the treatment and the lack of available information about its benefits and risks (*Kaimowitz v. Michigan Department of Mental Health*).

Whether institutionalized populations can truly volunteer for treatment or research also is a problem. Individuals may agree to participate because they feel compelled to do so. They may anticipate long-term gains from staff and administration whose opinions may be important for status or commodities within the institution or for release from the institution. The lure of release and the involuntarily confined status of many populations for whom treatment is provided may make voluntary consent impossible.

In research and treatment, informed consent has become the central issue for ensuring the protection of the individual subject. This does not mean that all facets of an experiment are routinely described to the subject prior to participation. However, it does mean that, prior to research, procedures that might affect the subject's willingness to participate are described and subjects are informed of their right to information about the experiment. Moreover, subjects are assured that they may terminate their participation at any time if they so desire.

Consent Forms

In advance of a study, a consent form is provided to convey information about the study that the subject needs to know to make an informed decision. Usually, institutional review boards and committees (e.g., at colleges, universities, hospitals, prisons) are charged with evaluating the research proposal, consent procedures, and consent form. Members who review the proposal are drawn from diverse disciplines. The research proposal is evaluated to examine the research design, specific procedures, the conditions to which the subject will be exposed, and risks and benefits. Evaluation of the research design deserves comment. The general plan of the research must be made clear to permit committee members to determine whether the questions underlying the investigation are reasonable and can be answered by the study. If the questions cannot be answered by the study, the subjects should not be placed at any risk or inconvenience.

Most psychological experiments do not involve risk situations and are designated as minimal risk. The subjects (e.g., college students), experimental tasks (e.g., memorizing lists of words, completing personality measures), and risks (e.g., mild boredom if the task continues too long) do not exceed the risks of normal living. Review of such studies is relatively straightforward because concerns about subject rights are not raised by the research paradigm. In some cases, review of the study or even informed consent procedures are omitted because the experiment is considered to be in a class of procedures that is innocuous. In clinical work, several features often extend the situation well beyond minimal risk by virtue of the population (e.g., patient samples), focus of assessment or intervention (e.g., suicidal intent, depression), and special ethical dilemmas (e.g., random assignment, delaying treatment), as discussed further below. Understandably, the review of proposals and consent procedures of such studies are more stringent. In many universities, separate review committees are available for different types of research. For example, psychological experiments with minimal risk are often reviewed by a social sciences review committee. In contrast, research with clinical populations are likely to be reviewed by a biomedical committee.

Critical to the consent procedure is the consent form that the subjects sign to indicate their willingness to participate. The overall purpose of the form is to convey information, to do so clearly and simply, and to ensure subjects are aware of what they are entering. Although specific details of the forms vary as a function of the type of research and level of risk, several components are common. Table 16.1 lists and highlights these components, each of which might be represented by a brief paragraph or two within the consent form.

Letter and Spirit of Consent

Concretely, the investigator is required to describe the procedures to the subject and to obtain signed consent. The signed consent form satisfies the research requirements and hence follows the "letter" of the rules that govern research and

TABLE 16.1.   Components of Informed Consent Forms

Section of the Form	Purpose and Contents
Overview	Presentation of the goals of the study, why this is conducted, who is responsible for the study and its execution.
Description of procedures	Clarification of the experimental conditions, assessment procedures, requirements of the subjects.
Risks and inconveniences	Statement of any physical and psychological risks and an estimate of their likelihood. Inconveniences and demands to be placed on the subjects (e.g., how many sessions, requests to do any thing, contact at home).
Benefits	A statement of what the subjects can reasonably hope to gain from participation, including psychological, physical, and monetary benefits.
Costs and economic considerations	Charges to the subjects (e.g., in treatment) and payment (e.g., for participation or completing various forms).
Confidentiality	Assurances that the information is confidential and will only be seen by people who need to do so for the purposes of research (e.g., scoring and data analyses), procedures to assure confidentiality (e.g., removal of names from forms, storage of data). Also, caveats are included here if it is possible that sensitive information (e.g., psychiatric information, criminal activity) can be subpoenaed.
Alternative treatments	In an intervention study, alternatives available to the client before or during participation are outlined.
Voluntary participation	A statement that the subject is willing to participate and can say no now or later without penalty of any kind.
Questions and further information	A statement that the subject is encouraged to ask questions at any time and can contact an individual (or individuals) (listed by name and phone number) who is available for such contacts.
Signature lines	A place for the subject as well as the experimenter to sign.

the investigator's responsibilities. In addition, there is a "spirit" of informed consent, which refers more nebulously to the overall intent of the procedures and the goal to ensure that clients genuinely understand what they are signing, what the study entails, and the risks, costs, and benefits. In most research (e.g., laboratory studies with college students) presentation of the consent information followed by the subject's signing of the form is sufficient for the letter and spirit of the consent procedures.

Research that is any way service related (e.g., treatment) or that involves personally or physically invasive procedures (e.g., obtaining private information that could be solicited by the courts, medical tests with remote albeit genuine risks) or persons who are or may not be competent to represent themselves fully (e.g., children, disadvantaged persons) raises special obstacles. Clients may be less likely to understand options, choices, and opportunities to change their minds about participation. In such cases, satisfying the letter of the informed consent requirements may not approach the spirit or intent of these requirements.

Interestingly, there are no formal research requirements that subjects actually understand what is presented to them. Thus, presentation of information and signing of consent forms might be accomplished without genuinely informed consent. For this reason, both the spirit and the letter of consent are important. The spirit of consent emphasizes the investigator's responsibility to maximize the clients' understanding of the investigation. Of course, all information is not known and hence cannot be presented. The spirit of consent refers to the researcher's best effort to convey the purpose, procedures, and risks of participation and generally to meet the consent conditions.

Presentation of the content by repeating significant facets of the study, paraphrasing the consent form, asking questions of the subject at critical points to assess understanding, and similar strategies may aid. The time allowed to explain the procedures and to obtain consent may need to be extended to foster the atmosphere required to inform the client. Obviously, protracted consent procedures, clinically oversensitive presentations, and ad nauseam requests for feedback on the part of the experimenter ("But do you really understand that you could have nightmares from meeting with such an ugly therapist? O.K. tell me what a nightmare is.") are likely to be inappropriate as a general strategy. This is why the spirit of consent is so important. The rules or letter of consent procedures specify the minimal conditions to be satisfied in discharging responsibilities to the subject. Beyond that, judgment, experience, and common sense are need to ensure the goals of consent and to balance research interests and subject rights.

Different ways of presenting details of the study, as part of the consent procedures, can be identified varying from perfunctory presentation of the consent form ("Here [consent form is handed to the subject], as soon as you sign this, we can begin"), lengthy deliberations of individual phrases and concepts (e.g., "You are probably wondering what "random" assignment really is and why we do this. Did you ever hear of R.A. Fisher—I didn't either . . . ."), and overly empathic and mushy understanding ("O.K., how do you feel about all of what I have said so far [about the task of memorizing nonsense syllables]? I'll bet this is a little threatening."). The sample and circumstances of the experiment obviously dictate the letter and spirit of consent and how these are to be achieved.

INTERVENTION RESEARCH ISSUES

Each issue above pertains to research generally. In studies of various interventions, such as psychotherapy, counseling, and education, additional ethical issues arise or nuances emerge that warrant consideration. Several issues emerge that may vary with the type of intervention (e.g., treatment vs. prevention), the population (e.g., young children, hospitalized adults), and setting (e.g., university, patient services).

Informing Clients about Treatment

An important issue is the information that is provided to the client about the intervention. Outside the rationale and procedures themselves, the investigator is required to convey the current status of the treatment, assuming that the client is able to understand the information. Whether treatment has been shown to be effective in previous applications would seem to be important and routine information. Many treatments are experimental and the subject normally can be provided with a statement to that effect.

Therapy research raises an interesting dilemma because honesty about the basis of treatment might dispel some of the therapeutic effects that ordinarily would result. In the process of mentioning the current status of treatment, the investigator might attenuate the placebo effects (e.g., expectancies for improvement, nonspecific treatment factors) that ordinarily might occur. Suspicions about treatment efficacy might be raised by full disclosure. In some treatment studies, the independent variable is the expectancy for success conveyed to the subjects. Hence, a treatment is claimed to be very effective or ineffective depending on the condition to which the subject is assigned. Disclosure of the current status of the technique would compete with this manipulation.

Information about treatment in an experiment may extend to treatments the subject will not receive. Conceivably, subjects could be told that there are different treatments, only one of which they will receive. Subjects might want to know whether some treatments are more effective than others and whether they have been assigned to a control group. In addition, subjects may show a clear preference for an alternative treatment and react adversely to one to which they are assigned. As alternative treatments become known, skepticism about a particular treatment may arise and therapeutic improvement may be affected.

At the beginning of the study, subjects ought to be told that there are various treatments offered and that assignment to treatment is random, assuming that these statements are true. Although subjects are rarely pleased to learn that their assignment to treatment will be random, the importance of randomness in assessing the impact of different treatments might be stressed. Only subjects who agree to the conditions of the investigation can be subjects and be assigned to conditions. This leads to selection of a special group and may have implications for the external validity of the results. These are constraints within most clinical research must work.

In passing, it is interesting to note that in research, the investigator is expected to convey to the subject what is known about treatment, including any limitations and risks. In contrast, in clinical practice the therapist is not required to clarify the status of the technique or knowledge base. The vast majority of psychotherapy techniques—more than 400 for the treatment of adults—have not been subject to empirical evaluation and do not have data attesting to their efficacy. In the same vein, most clinical practice includes combinations of treatment (eclectic treatment) that can be used as the practitioner sees fit in an individual case. The constituent interventions and the combination are rarely subjected to empirical research. One might argue that treatments without evidence on their behalf are "experimental" whether they are examined or used in research or clinical practice and that subjects (clients, patients) ought to provide consent in exposure to these treatments.

Withholding the Intervention

Intervention studies (e.g., treatment, prevention) often withhold the special procedure and assign some subjects to no-treatment or waiting-list control conditions. Although these conditions are essential to answer specific research questions, as discussed previously, their use raises obvious ethical questions. Assigning a client to one of these conditions withholds treatment from which a person may benefit. At the very least, treatment for the client is delayed. If the client's condition does not deteriorate, the delay increases the duration of misery that may have precipitated seeking treatment. At worst, the client's condition may deteriorate during the period that treatment is withheld.

An investigator is obligated to consider seriously whether a group that delays or completely withholds treatment is necessary for the questions addressed in the research. Because of the ethical problems, it may be more appropriate to reserve questions comparing treatment with no treatment to situations in which subjects are willing to wait and are unlikely to suffer deleterious consequences. Obviously, volunteer clients solicited from the community may be more appropriate for a study in which a waiting-list group is required than use of clients who seek treatment at a crisis intervention center. If clients have severe problems and warrant or demand immediate intervention, questions comparing treatment with no treatment are more difficult to justify and to implement.

In some cases, assigning subjects to a waiting-list control group will not really delay treatment. Waiting lists are common at many clinics. A delay before entering treatment may average a few or several months before clients are seen. All subjects who are to serve in the study and who agree to participate can be moved up on the list. Those who are randomly assigned to the intervention condition are treated immediately; those who are assigned to wait can be assessed and then await the usual delay period of the clinic before receiving treatment. Ethical issues are not eliminated by rearranging waiting-list status. Moving some clients up on the list may delay the treatment of others who are not in the study. Some problems of delaying treatment can be alleviated by informing clients at intake of the possibility that they will not be assigned to treatment for a particular (specified) interval. As noted before, the investigation uses only subjects who agree with this stipulation and randomly assigns them to the various treatment and control conditions.

Using Treatments of Questionable Efficacy

In outcome research, some treatments in a given study might be expected to be less effective than others. This expectation may derive from theoretical predictions, previous research, or from the nature of the design. For example, in a simple 2 x 2 factorial design, an investigator may study the effects of variables such as therapist experience (experienced vs. inexperienced therapists) and duration of treatment (1 session vs. 10 sessions). Subjects in one group resulting from this design will be exposed to inexperienced therapists for one treatment session, a condition likely to be less effective than the others. The use of treatments that have a low probability of being effective raises an ethical issue for the investigator.

The issue is much clearer in using groups that are designed to control for nonspecific treatment factors such as attending treatment sessions, meeting with a therapist, and believing that treatment may produce change. These groups are designed with the expressed idea that there are few if any components that will actively help the client. Providing a treatment designed to be weak or a control condition designed to be ineffective raises obvious ethical problems. First, the client's problem may not improve or may even become worse without an effective treatment. To withhold a treatment expected to be relatively effective renders these possibilities more salient. Second, clients may lose credulity in the process of psychological treatment in general. Clients expect to receive an effective treatment and to achieve change. If treatment is not reasonable in their judgment and does not produce change, clients may be generally discouraged from seeking help in the future. In general, the control conditions or treatments that may "fill out" the design warrant ethical evaluation by the investigator and review boards. This applies to any special control condition in which the likelihood of improvement is unexpected or minimal. Other contextual issues, such as who the clients are (e.g., patients seeking treatment, community volunteers) and provisions after the study is completed (e.g., free treatment and care), may affect evaluation of the issues.

General Comments

The ethical issues raised in intervention research depend on the precise research question and the control groups that form the basis of the design. Use of no-treatment or waiting-list control groups is essential in research that asks the basic question, Does this treatment work? The question usually requires assessing the extent of change without treatment.[2] Use of a nonspecific treatment control group is important in research that asks the question Why does this treatment work? Such research may require a group to look at the influence of nonspecific treatment factors alone.

The research questions that require ethically sensitive control conditions are fundamental to progress in understanding treatment. The questions themselves cannot be abandoned. However, the conditions under which these questions are examined can be varied to attenuate partially the objections that normally arise. For example, questions requiring control conditions that withhold treatment or provide nonspecific treatment control groups need not be conducted in settings in which clients are in need of treatment and have sought a treatment to ameliorate an immediately felt problem. On the other hand, when volunteer subjects are solicited and can be informed about the experimental nature of all treatment procedures, a wider range of experimental conditions is more readily justified. In short, if the setting has patient care and service delivery as the higher priority, the use of groups that withhold treatment or present nonspecific treatments that are expected to produce minimal change is generally unacceptable. When research, rather than service delivery, has the higher priority and clients can be informed of the implications of this priority, the use of such groups may be more readily justified.

Some ethical issues of treatment can be ameliorated by providing all subjects with the more (or most) effective treatment in the project after they have completed the treatment to which they were assigned. After treatment, clients who were in a no-treatment control group also should receive the benefits of treatment. Indeed, this is exactly what the waiting-list control group receives. In studies with several different treatments or a nonspecific control condition, clients who are not completely satisfied with their progress eventually might be given the most effective treatment. Thus, clients may benefit from the project in which they served by receiving the better (or best) treatment. From an experimental standpoint, this strategy is useful in further examining the extent of change in clients who continue in the superior treatment. Essentially, there is a partial replication of treatment effects in the design. From an ethical standpoint, providing all subjects with the most effective intervention may attenuate objections against assigning subjects to treatments varying in anticipated effectiveness. Of course, at some point in the research, long-term follow-up studies are needed in which one tests whether the seemingly effective intervention is better than no treatment for the long term. This might be done in a randomized controlled trial or by creative use of cohort designs in which groups who have not received treatment are followed.

ETHICAL GUIDELINES FOR RESEARCH PRACTICES

Many ethical problems that arise in research seem to be inherent in the research process itself. The use of human subjects often requires weighing alternatives that balance the individual rights of the subject against the search for scientific knowledge. Decisions about potential harm, deception, invasion of privacy, withholding of potential beneficial treatment practices, and similar issues have helped stimulate guidelines for research at both the professional and federal levels.

The American Psychological Association has provided a set of principles designed to guide research, practice, consultation, and other activities related to execution of the profession. The guidelines are revised periodically to make refinements, to address emergent issues, and to handle expanding roles of psychologists in daily life (e.g., litigation, consultation). Consider the most recent version of the guidelines (APA, 1992) and, in light of present purposes, the guidelines that pertain specifically to research with human subjects. The guidelines are formulated in such a way as to emphasize the investigator's responsibilities toward individuals who participate in research. The principles are listed in Table 16.2. As guidelines, the principles are necessarily ambiguous about concrete research practices. For example, the principles do not say that deception can or cannot be used. Indeed, the thrust of the principles is to point out the obligations of the investigator and to raise areas in which caution and deliberation are required. The guidelines point to the considerations included in making decisions about whether a given research project should be undertaken. Although it may be difficult to make decisions in a particular case, the overriding concern must be given to the protection of the subject. Indeed, the guidelines specify that as the pros and cons of the research are weighed, priority must be given to the subject's welfare. Whether a particular investigation adequately protects the rights of subjects usually is decided on the basis of an evaluation of the research by colleagues. As mentioned previously, universities and many other institutions in which research is conducted rely on review committees to evaluate the extent to which a proposed investigation provides safeguards for subjects and is consistent with the type of guidelines listed in Table 16.2.

The review process has been mandated by federal regulations for medical and psychological research. Beginning in the mid-1960s, the Surgeon General of the Public Health Service required institutions that received federal money for research to establish review committees to consider subjects' rights and to ensure that informed consent was procured for the proposed research. The guidelines for research have been revised and elaborated periodically.

Current federal regulations are designed to evaluate whether any risks to the subjects are outweighed by the potential benefits to them or by the likely benefits to society in light of the information obtained. In the early 1970s, Congress mandated a special commission to draft ethical guidelines for research with human subjects. The National Commission for the Protection of Human Subjects in Biomedical and Behavioral Research was established to examine research and applications in areas in which human rights have been or are likely to be violated. The Commission studied and made recommendations for practices in research with fetuses, prisoners, individuals considered for psychosurgery, and children, all of which raise special issues. These guidelines do not apply to the bulk of research in clinical psychology but are important to mention insofar as

TABLE 16.2. Ethical Principles in the Conduct of Research with Human Participants

Planning Research

(a) Psychologists design, conduct, and report research in accordance with recognized standards of scientific competence and ethical research.

(b) Psychologists plan their research so as to minimize the possibility that results will be misleading.

(c) In planning research, psychologists consider its ethical acceptability under the Ethics Code. If an ethical issue is unclear, psychologists seek to resolve the issue through consultation with institutional review boards, animal care and use committees, peer consultations, or other proper mechanisms.

(d) Psychologists take reasonable steps to implement appropriate protections for the rights and welfare of human participants, other persons affected by the research, and the welfare of animal subjects.

Responsibility

(a) Psychologists conduct research competently and with due concern for the dignity and welfare of the participants.

(b) Psychologists are responsible for the ethical conduct of research conducted by them or by others under their supervision or control.

(c) Researchers and assistants are permitted to perform only those tasks for which they are appropriately trained and prepared.

(d) As part of the process of development and implementation of research projects, psychologists consult those with expertise concerning any special population under investigation or most likely to be affected.

Compliance with Law and Standards

Psychologists plan and conduct research in a manner consistent with federal and state law and regulations, as well as professional standards governing the conduct of research, and particularly those standards governing research with human participants and animal subjects.

Institutional Approval

Psychologists obtain from host institutions or organizations appropriate approval prior to conducting research, and they provide accurate information about their research proposals. They conduct the research in accordance with the approved research protocol.

Research Responsibilities

Prior to conducting research (except research involving only anonymous surveys, naturalistic observations, or similar research), psychologists enter into an agreement with participants that clarifies the nature of the research and the responsibilities of each party.

Informed Consent to Research

(a) Psychologists use language that is reasonably understandable to research participants in obtaining their appropriate informed consent. Such informed consent is appropriately documented.

TABLE 16.2.   *Continued*

(b) Using language that is reasonably understandable to participants, psychologists inform participants of the nature of the research; they inform participants that they are free to participate or to decline to participate or to withdraw from the research; they explain the foreseeable consequences of declining or withdrawing; they inform participants of significant factors that may be expected to influence their willingness to participate (such as risks, discomfort, adverse effects, or limitations on confidentiality), and they explain other aspects about which the prospective participants inquire.

(c) When psychologists conduct research with individuals such as students or subordinates, psychologists take special care to protect the prospective participants from adverse consequences of declining or withdrawing from participation.

(d) When research participation is a course requirement or opportunity for extra credit, the prospective participant is given the choice of equitable alternative activities.

(e) For persons who are legally incapable of giving informed consent, psychologists nevertheless (1) provide an appropriate explanation, (2) obtain the participant's assent, and (3) obtain appropriate permission from a legally authorized person, if such substitute consent is permitted by law.

Dispensing with Informed Consent

Before determining that planned research (such as research involving only anonymous questionnaires, naturalistic observations, or certain kinds of archival research) does not require the informed consent of research participants, psychologists consider applicable regulations and institutional review board requirements, and they consult with colleagues as appropriate.

Informed Consent in Research Filming or Recording

Psychologists obtain informed consent from research participants prior to filming or recording them in any form, unless the research involves simply naturalistic observations in public places and it is not anticipated that the recording will be used in a manner that could cause personal identification or harm.

Offering Inducements for Research Participants

(a) In offering professional services as an inducement to obtain research participants, psychologists make clear the nature of the services, as well as the risks, obligations, and limitations.

(b) Psychologists do not offer excessive or inappropriate financial or other inducements to obtain research participants, particularly when it might tend to coerce participation.

Deception in Research

(a) Psychologists do not conduct a study involving deception unless they have determined that the use of deceptive techniques is justified by the study's prospective scientific, educational, or applied value and that equally effective alternative procedures that do not use deception are not feasible.

(b) Psychologists never deceive research participants about significant aspects that would affect their willingness to participate, such as physical risks, discomfort, or unpleasant emotional experiences.

continued

TABLE 16.2.   Ethical Principles in the Conduct of Research *Continued*

(c) Any other deception that is an integral feature of the design and conduct of an experiment must be explained to participants as early as is feasible, preferably at the conclusion of their participation, but no later than at the conclusion of the research.

Sharing and Utilizing Data

Psychologists inform research participants of their anticipated sharing or further use of personally identifiable research data and of the possibility of unanticipated future uses.

Minimizing Invasiveness

In conducting research, psychologists interfere with the participants or milieu from which data are collected only in a manner that is warranted by an appropriate research design and that is consistent with psychologists' roles as scientific investigators.

Providing Participants with Information about the Study

(a) Psychologists provide a prompt opportunity for participants to obtain appropriate information about the nature, results, and conclusions of the research, and psychologists attempt to correct any misconceptions that participants may have.

(b) If scientific or humane values justify delaying or withholding this information, psychologists take reasonable measures to reduce the risk of harm.

Honoring Commitments

Psychologists take reasonable measures to honor all commitments they have made to research participants.

Note: For a discussion of principles and guidelines, the original source should be consulted. See *Ethical principles of psychologists and code of conduct.* Washington, DC: American Psychological Association. Copyright © 1992 by the American Psychological Association. Reprinted with permission.

they reveal Congress' strong interest in ethical issues raised by research with human subjects.

To examine the risks and benefits and protection of the subjects welfare, research proposals in a university setting are reviewed by a committee that critically examines the procedures and possible risks to the subjects. The committee is referred to as an Institutional Review Board (IRB) in the federal codes to protect subjects (U.S. Department of Health and Human Services [USDHHS], 1983). The committee evaluates whether subjects are provided with the opportunity to give informed consent and made aware of their ability to withdraw consent and terminate participation at any time. Subjects must sign an informed consent form that explains the procedures and purpose in clear and easily understandable language and describes any risks and benefits. Risks are defined broadly to include the possibility of injury—physical, psychological, or social—as a consequence of participation in the experiment. Subjects must also be told that they are free to withhold information (e.g., of a personal nature) and to withdraw from the investigation at any time without penalty. Subjects must also be guaranteed that all information they provide will be anonymous and confidential and told how these conditions will be achieved.

Most investigations within psychology include procedures that may be without risk to the subject and hence do not provide problems for review committees to evaluate. Procedures that receive special scrutiny are projects involving a failure to disclose fully the purpose of the study, deception, the possibility of deleteriously affecting the subject's psychological or physical status, and research involving special populations in which competence to consent is in question (e.g., children). The committee must weigh the merits of the scientific investigation and the advance in knowledge the study may provide against possible potential discomfort to the subject.

Ethical responsibility for research cannot be placed solely on the formal review procedures. Ethical guidelines for research encourage investigators to seek advice of others and diverse perspectives to assess whether procedures that extend beyond minimal risk (e.g., covert observations, invasion of sensitive topics) are warranted. When weighing scientific merit and the likely benefits of the knowledge against subject rights, the investigator is advised to seek input from colleagues beyond that of formal review procedures (APA, 1992). In other words, the ultimate ethical responsibility for the integrity of the research falls to the investigator.

ETHICAL ISSUES AND SCIENTIFIC INTEGRITY

Ethics in research usually are discussed in relation to the subject and the subjects' rights, as illustrated by the issues raised by informed consent. Professional organizations have guidelines for ethical behavior of their members. The guidelines are intended to outline standards of integrity that pertain to diverse contexts beyond those associated with research and investigator–experimenter and subject interactions (APA, 1992). Although the full range of ethical standards are not entirely relevant to discussion of methodology and research design (e.g., contacts with clients in therapy), there are several research-related issues we have neglected. A set of ethical issues might be identified that is essential for maintaining the integrity of science. These issues encompass the obligations and responsibilities of the investigator in relation to one's colleagues, the profession, society, and science more generally.

Fraud in Science

Scientists are not immune to error, deception, and fraud in their work. Historical accounts of science provide a long line of examples in which scientists have made major errors in recording or interpreting their work, have tried to deceive others about their findings, and have altered or faked their data (Broad & Wade, 1982; Gould, 1981; Kohn, 1988; Miller & Hersen, 1992). The issues were mentioned briefly in the discussion of sources of artifact and bias in research. In the context of threats to validity, altering and making up data obviously bias research findings and their interpretation; in the context of ethical issues, they raise broader issues of great significance.

The distinction between error and fraud in research is major. *Errors* refer to honest mistakes that may occur in some facet of the study or its presentation. The processes entailed by collecting data, scoring measures, transcribing and entering data, and publishing raises multiple opportunities for error and for errors by many different persons. To err is human; to err frequently is careless. The investigator has the responsibility to minimize error by devising procedures to check, monitor, and detect errors and then to rectify them to the extent possible. When errors are detected (e.g., as in published reports), investigators are encouraged to acknowledge them. Often journal publications include isolated notes (errata) in which corrections can be written in the same outlet in which the original paper appeared.

Fraud in science refers to explicit efforts to deceive and misrepresent. Of all issues, fraud is the most flagrant because it undermines the foundations of the entire enterprise of scientific research (National Academy of Sciences, 1989). Although fraud is not new in science, recent attention has focused on deliberate efforts of researchers to mislead colleagues and the public. Dramatic instances in which critical procedures, treatments, or potential breakthroughs could not be replicated or were known by one's colleagues to reflect explicit attempts to misrepresent the actual findings have come to light. For example, findings on the cause of a type of leukemia were retracted because the investigator confessed to misrepresenting and fabricating the data (Waldholz, 1996). Such acts and their revelations greatly undermine public confidence in the research enterprise. It is not just public confidence; sometimes safety is involved. For example, a large-scale study (approximately 7000 patients from 13 countries) compared a new medication regimen (combination of medications), aspirin, and placebo for the prevention of recurrent strokes (Enserink, 1996). Aspirin, the generally accepted drug for the purpose, was greatly surpassed in effectiveness by the other medication condition. However, the data from one site were reported to be fabricated. Obviously, the extent to which results from such data had influenced clinical practice for stroke victims goes beyond undermining public confidence. Evaluations of scientific research have suggested that instances of fraud are likely to be rare (National Academy of Sciences, 1989). This does not mean that the status quo is acceptable. The impact and implications of any instance of fraud can be tremendous for the specific area of work (e.g., suggesting a new principle or treatment procedure) and for the scientific enterprise in general.

No single or simple cause of fraud is likely to be identifiable. Several influences can conspire to produce fraud, such as pressures of investigators to publish for recognition and career advancement, to produce critical breakthroughs, and to obtain funding for seemingly promising avenues of research. Protections to counter fraud include training in the central values of science, emphasis on the importance of the integrity of the investigator in advancing science generally, repeated opportunities in which an individual's work is subjected to review and evaluation by colleagues (e.g., as part of review processes before the study, when the report is submitted for publication), public access to data records, and efforts to replicate research.

An example conveys the thrust of some of the professional sanctions that loom over research. Early in 1997, a scientific breakthrough was reported, namely, the cloning of an adult mammal. A sheep (named Dolly) was cloned by embryologists in Scotland. Producing another living animal from one cell (Dolly's "mother") was considered to be a remarkable breakthrough because cloning was regarded as not possible given current knowledge and technology. When the finding was first reported, there was some faith in the reliability of the finding in part because of the reputation of the project's senior researcher whose years of work and high standards of integrity were known. In addition, the replicability of the demonstration became very important to ensure this breakthrough was not a hoax. A quote from one scientist on this point is instructive regarding this discovery. In referring to the research team that made the discovery, the scientist said, "I know and trust them, but if what they did isn't repeatable, they'll pay for it with their careers" (Waldholz, 1997, p. B1). As it turns out, by use of a different procedure and a monkey instead of a sheep, cloning was repeated by another research team in the United States a few weeks later. Yet, the quote is noteworthy in conveying the ethos guiding scientific findings and the consequences for findings that are not replicable or are fraudulent.

Apart from sanctions within the professions, there are also legal consequences for fraud. For example, the use of public funds in research and conduct of research within institutions brings to bear specific laws regarding fraud and oversight boards to monitor scientific integrity, to investigate allegations of fraud, and to pursue through the courts culpability and prosecution. The sanctions and consequences can be personally and professionally devastating. Indeed, being accused and later acquitted in one well-publicized case had very negative consequences from which it was difficult to recover. Notwithstanding the multiple factors to protect against fraud and various forms of sanction, the key remains the ethical commitment and responsibility of the individual investigator to the discipline by conducting studies, reporting data, and preparing reports in as honest and an objective fashion as possible and also to train those working under one's charge (e.g., students) in these standards and practices.

Allocation of Credit

Another issue related to obligations of the investigator pertains to allocation of credit. Several issues are encompassed, such as failure to acknowledge one's sources and reference to other material and the division of credit among collaborators in research and published projects of that research. Perhaps the most obvious and flagrant issue is that of *plagiarism* (the direct use and copying of material of someone else without providing credit or acknowledgment). The misconduct that plagiarism represents is generally brought to the attention of students early in their education. Special problems and opportunities emerge in science in the circulation of unpublished materials (e.g., manuscripts that are reviewed, convention presentations circulated in writing). A virtue of science is the public nature of the enterprise. Colleagues are encouraged to exchange ideas, to seek and to provide feedback, and to interact with colleagues to advance research ideas and objectives. The process generally works well without repeated claims of plagiarism or theft of ideas.

A more delicate and perhaps less concrete issue pertains to the credit accorded to those involved in research. Projects are usually collaborative. They involve multiple investigators and a team of persons who have responsibility of varying types and in varying degrees for completion of the study. The different components of research and responsibilities from idea to the final published report are numerous. Allocation of credit emerges in such contexts as deciding whom to list as authors on a research article, the order in which the names are to appear, the relation between junior and senior scientists or faculty and students, and how their different roles and contributions affect authorship.

Allocating credit is fraught with human frailties related to status, power, greed, ambition, insecurities, and personality style of the investigators, collaborators, and research assistants. (In fact, it is a little disappointing that Shakespeare did not develop a tragedy set in the context of scientific discovery, authorship, and publication.) Individual differences on these human characteristics inevitably lead to different perceptions about what is a contribution to the study and how much that contribution ought to count toward the final allocation of credit.[3] A key issue for participation as an author on a paper is evidence that there is a clear contribution to the study. There are no agreed-on guidelines about what constitutes a contribution. A contribution is likely to warrant authorship if a person working on the study completes one or more of the following (Fine & Kurdek, 1993):

- Develops the design
- Writes or prepares portions of the manuscript
- Integrates or brings together theoretical perspectives
- Develops novel conceptual views
- Designs or develops the measures
- Makes key decisions about the data analyses
- Interprets the results

Of course, some of these points are subject to interpretation. For example, "interprets the results," the last point, might range on a continuum from a pithy characterization ("We found nothing, nada!") to integration with cross-disciplinary, intergalactic, neuropsychosocial–meteorological models. Yet, the above roles of the researcher can be distinguished from other tasks such as entering data, running the data analyses under direct supervision, typing the manuscript, and preparing ancillary materials (e.g., references). The latter tasks might warrant acknowledgment in a footnote, but are not likely to be considered a professional contribution in the sense of the other activities listed above.

As we work in an area and complete a study, our evaluation of its contribution to the world occasionally is distorted. Because we believe the Nobel committee will want to know who generated the research, allocation and credit to others may take on unusual proportions. We long for simple rules and guidelines, and one provided by an advisor of mine ("If this study comes out, *I'm* first author; if it does not, *you're* first author.") at least has the advantages of explicitness and clarity. Although the issues of allocation of credit and participation in research can arise in any collaboration, attention has often been accorded to faculty–student collaborations because of special features that may impede allocation of credit and communication about that credit (e.g., different status, power, expertise) (Fine & Kurdek, 1993; Goodyear, Crego, & Johnson, 1992).

Investigators and the research team, whether faculty and student or multiple colleagues within the profession, are encouraged to discuss these matters explicitly at the inception of research. They should not merely address issues of authorship but also decide tasks to be completed, and the responsibility and credit in relation to all facets of the study. The degree to which these conversations seem awkward is directly related to their importance in allocating credit. At the same time, in some collaborative arrangements, it is difficult to approach a senior collaborator or advisor. Consequently, it is useful to place responsibility on senior investigators for initiating the topic of allocation of credit, to address the matter directly, and to encourage dialogue on the topic. We know from experience or understanding of human nature that senior investigators who take the responsibility and begin with open communication about such matters are the collaborators we may need be least concerned about in relation to allocation of credit.

Sharing of Materials and Data

A central feature of science is the ability to replicate the work of others. Indeed, replication is the primary guarantee of reliability of research findings. Replication is usually discussed in the context of repeating the procedures of a prior investigation. The obligations of an investigator are to provide colleagues with the materials to permit them to conduct replications. This might entail providing further descriptions of procedures and specific measures, responding to various questions that facilitate replication of the study, or making available special software to present materials to the subjects or to code, score, or analyze the data.

Often critical features of a study have required years to develop (e.g., treatment manuals) and have important financial implications (e.g., software, a new psychological test) that make investigators reluctant or occasionally unwilling to share materials. However, the obligation to share materials begins when the individual enters the role of scientific investigator and places his or her work in the scientific domain (e.g., presentation of a paper, publication of a scientific article). At that point, the investigator has entered an implied contract with the rest of the scientific community in which he or she will aid in continuation and evaluation of the research. As part of the contract, the scientific community is obligated to provide credit to whom it is due in relation to the original investigator and to restrict use of the materials to persons related to the research project.

The procedure generally appears to work well based on the exchange of a great deal of information informally among scientists. The information exchange is often prompted by a published report that helps to establish communication among scientists who begin a dialogue and exchange of materials. There are some formal protections to aid in making research information available. Funding agencies, both federal and private, often include materials, such as measures, detailed descriptions of procedures, and raw data, in the project proposal and final report. This information is available by request or as a matter of public record for further scrutiny and use.

One of the most frequently discussed issues pertains to the sharing of data. This, too, is related to replication. Can one obtain the same or similar findings when analyzing the original data that were published? A colleague may believe that the original data were not analyzed correctly or in the most appropriate fashion or that the data would lead to quite different conclusions if analyzed differently. Data are viewed as part of the public domain and are to be shared with others if requested.

There is often reluctance of investigators to share data. One reason is that a particular study may be drawn from a larger data base. Several other projects may be planned and the investigator may be unwilling to circulate the data until all the projects have been completed, analyzed, and reported. Here too, once an article has been published in a scientific journal, it is difficult to justify withholding the specific data set on which that article was based. That data set, even if not the entire data base, might be considered to be part of the information available to the scientific community.

Increasingly in research, data bases are made publicly available to other researchers to permit further analyses. For example in large, federally funded projects, the data may be made available to anyone who wishes to complete further studies. One prominent example was the Epidemiologic Catchment Area (ECA) study, which was a multisite investigation (five cities) of the prevalence of psychiatric disorders among community and institutionalized adults (N > 20,000, 18 years and older) in the United States (Eaton & Kessler, 1985; Regier et al., 1984). The study has led to hundreds of publications elaborating diverse facets of adult disorders. Data were made available to the scientific community more generally, and other studies continue to emerge from the original data.

Another example is the National Institute of Mental Health Treatment of Depression Collaborative Research Program. In this study interpersonal psychotherapy, cognitive therapy, and medication (imipramine) were compared for the treatment of adult depression (N = 250 cases assigned to treatment, 28 therapists) across multiple sites (three cities) (Elkin et al., 1985, 1989). Several articles have been reported and continue to appear from the original collaborative team. The data base has been made available to the scientific community, and other investigators are now analyzing the results. In both the ECA and the Depression study, publications continue to emerge because the data have been made available.

Placing data within the public domain has obvious advantages for science. A particular data set can represent a rich resource. The interests and creativity of an investigative team that obtained and analyzed the data may not exhaust the knowledge available from that data set. Other investigators with new hypotheses, varied conceptions of the research issues and underlying theory, and different training or orientations may extract new knowledge. Sharing data might be very useful as a general practice to optimize the knowledge that is gained from any study and to foster novel analyses among interested parties. Indeed, there is a remarkable untapped resource in data that have been collected but have not been fully mined. It would be quite useful if investigators could routinely provide in some computerized format of the original article, raw data and codes for the variables so the data could be analyzed by others. Inevitably, there would be problems (e.g., software incompatibility, incomplete reporting of the codes, and occasional studies [my dissertation] that would be better forgotten). Even so, large-scale studies that in many ways represent once in a lifetime data sets are prime candidates for data sharing in this fashion.

There may be ethical constraints for sharing all data because some review committees restrict use of data for the specific purposes outlined in the original proposal and by the investigator who provided that proposal. The purpose is to protect subjects whose consent does not extend to use of the information beyond the original project. Also, investigators are often wary to share data until they have completed their analyses, or they are protective in general because the ethos for sharing and making data available as a matter of course has yet to be required.

Guiding Principles and Responsibilities

The issues highlighted here are weighty, to say the least, and reflect areas in which ambiguity often remains. Obviously, in the case of fraud, the ethical and professional standards and sanctions are relatively clear. Guidelines for allocation of credit, sharing of data, and related matters are actively discussed and concrete rules cannot easily be provided. Guiding principles have been provided by the American Psychological Association to address these matters and to convey explicitly the ethical obligations of the investigator. Samples of selected principles to cover these obligations are presented in Table 16.3. The guidelines convey important facets of research obligations. In some ways they can be seen to fall beyond the scope of methodology and research design. However, they are pivotal to the use and interpretation of research and the accumulation of findings.

It is clear from the implications of research that science and scientists are central to society. In clinical work in particular, research may have critical implications that bring researchers into areas of social concern (e.g., day care, criminal behavior, child-rearing, treatment regimens, custody disputes). Apart

TABLE 16.3. Ethical Guidelines for Researchers

Reporting of Results

(a) Psychologists do not fabricate data or falsify results in their publications.

(b) If psychologists discover significant errors in their published data, they take reasonable steps to correct such errors in a correction, retraction, erratum, or other appropriate publication means.

Plagiarism

Psychologists do not present substantial portions or elements of another's work or data as their own, even if the other work or data source is cited occasionally.

Publication Credit

(a) Psychologists take responsibility and credit, including authorship credit, only for work they have actually performed or to which they have contributed.

(b) Principal authorship and other publication credits accurately reflect the relative scientific or professional contributions of the individuals involved, regardless of their relative status. Mere possession of an institutional position, such as Department Chair, does not justify authorship credit. Minor contributions to the research or to the writing for publications are appropriately acknowledged, such as in footnotes or in an introductory statement.

(c) A student is usually listed as principal author on any multiple-authored article that is substantially based on the student's dissertation or thesis.

Sharing Data

After research results are published, psychologists do not withhold the data on which their conclusions are based from other competent professionals who seek to verify the substantive claims through reanalysis and who intend to use such data only for that purpose, provided that the confidentiality of the participants can be protected and unless legal rights concerning proprietary data preclude their release.

Other

(a) *Duplicate Publication of Data:* Psychologists do not publish, as original data, data that have been previously published. This does not preclude republishing data when they are accompanied by proper acknowledgment.

(b) *Professional Reviewers:* Psychologists who review material submitted for publication, grant, or other research proposal review respect the confidentiality of and the proprietary rights in such information of those who submitted it.

Note: These guidelines constitute expectations regarding a much broader set of principles outlined elsewhere and which should be consulted directly. See *Ethical principles of psychologists and code of conduct.* Washington, DC: American Psychological Association. Copyright © 1992 by the American Psychological Association. Reprinted with permission.

from the specific line of work and social implications that the work may bear, the integrity of each researcher is critical. The guidelines convey that the integrity of the enterprise and obligations of the researcher to maintain ethical standards are essential.

Ethical issues of the researcher in relation to the scientific community are significant. In addressing these issues, it is important not to lose sight of the givens of science. To begin with, scientists are human. Thus, the full panoply of human characteristics, motives, and foibles are likely to be evident. This does not mean that the negative virtues are pervasive; it does mean that we should not be shocked to hear instances of less than desirable samples of humanness, for instance, when researchers argue ad hominem about their theoretical differences, when beliefs are held to tenaciously in the face of seemingly persuasive of counter evidence, when differential standards are applied to interpretation of some kinds of work (mine) rather than other kinds of work (yours), and so on. As humans, we are by our very nature limited. We are motivated viewers; we bring subjectivity to our experience and its interpretation. Not only is it true that "seeing is believing," but, more critically to our goals, "believing is seeing." Fraud, interests in primary credit, possessiveness of ideas, procedures, and data, occur and hence always warrant attention.

That scientists are human does not excuse lapses that compete with the very purposes of science. Indeed, humanness has invented science. Science consists, among other things, of methods, procedures, practices, and values aimed at increasing the objectivity and external scrutiny of our work. Strategies of research, methods, and evaluation procedures have been devised to reduce the role of subjectivity and to increase replicability. Some methods used to decrease subjectivity introduce their own sources of error and artifact. For example, statistics are used to provide a criterion to determine whether there is a reliable effect; yet chance, in a particular case, could explain the difference. Also, measures are used to permit evaluation of constructs and to provide more objective means of assessment than use of impressions and personal opinions of the investigator; reactivity of assessment and low validity of the measure are potential limits assessment often introduces. However, these sources of error can be placed within the scientific arena, investigated, and evaluated.

SUMMARY AND CONCLUSIONS

Psychological research raises many ethical issues that are intertwined with methodology. Experimental questions and design options, such as those considered throughout the text, do not always make explicit the need to protect the rights and welfare of the subject. Salient issues pertaining to the rights of subjects include deception and debriefing, invasion of privacy, and informed consent. *Deception* is a major concern when subjects are misguided about the purpose of the experiment and the misinformation may deleteriously affect their beliefs about themselves or others. Deception is infrequently used or indeed permitted in clinical research. If deception is used, subjects must be informed about the true purposes after they complete the experiment. Providing such information, referred to as *debriefing*, is designed to erase the effects of deception. However, the effects of deception are not invariably erased. Leaving aside the effects of debriefing, many investigators object to deception because of the relationship it fosters between experimenter and subject.

Invasion of privacy is often protected by ensuring that the responses subjects provide are completely anonymous and confidential. *Anonymity* refers to
ensuring that identify of subjects and their individual performance are not revealed. *Confidentiality* requires that the information will not be disclosed to others without the awareness of the subject. In most research situations, anonymity
and confidentiality are ensured by removing the identity of subjects when the
data are evaluated and conveying information publicly (in research reports) only
on the basis of group performance. In clinical work, however, threats to invasion of privacy may derive from reports of individual cases in which the individual's identity might be revealed. Also, reports from research may affect large
segments of society (e.g., ethnic or racial groups) even when the individual
identify of the subjects is not at issue.

Informed consent is a central issue that encompasses many ethical concerns
and means of protecting subjects in experimentation. Informed consent requires
that the subject willingly agrees to serve in an experiment and is fully aware of
the procedures, risks, and benefits when making the choice to participate.
Procuring and interpreting informed consent is not entirely straightforward because the subject must be competent to provide consent, know the relevant information to make a meaningful choice, and consent completely voluntarily.
Whether these criteria are met in a particular case often is a matter of debate.

Intervention research raises a number of special ethical issues, such as informing the client completely about treatment, withholding treatment, and using
treatments of questionable efficacy. Withholding treatment or using control procedures that may not be therapeutic are ethically objectionable and difficult to
justifying in situations in which clients are in need of immediate treatment.
Questions requiring control procedures may be conducted in situations in which
clients are not in immediate jeopardy and agree to the conditions of participation. Some ethical issues raised in treatment research can be addressed by providing all clients with the most effective treatment if they have not achieved
marked improvements after participation in a less effective condition.

The many ethical issues raised in research have prompted guidelines designed to protect the rights of individual subjects. The guidelines apprise investigators of their obligations and the priority of ensuring protection of the subject
at all times. The guidelines do not necessarily rule out practices that might be
objectionable (e.g., deception). However, the onus is on the investigator to
show that there are likely benefits of the research and that obtaining these benefits requires a departure from full disclosure of the study's purposes and procedures.

Not all ethical issues and obligations pertain to the relation of the investigator to research subjects. The investigator has obligations to the profession, scientific community, and public more generally. These obligations pertain to the
conduct of research. Three issues to convey concerns were discussed: fraud in
science, allocation of credit, and sharing of materials and data. Ethical guidelines
also are provided to convey these responsibilities.

NOTES

[1]Over time, the rights, status, and protection of the subjects in research have received increased attention. Some attention has been precipitated by abuses that occurred to individuals (e.g., in the military in the 1940s and 1950s) subjected to dangerous procedures as part of research (e.g., injection of cancer cells, exposure to radiation or harmful drugs such as LSD) and who did not know they were subjects or the risks to which they were exposed. Apart from developing procedures to protect subjects, efforts have been made to alter the ways in which we view persons who serve in research. The change in preferred terminology from *subjects* to *participants* (APA, 1994) reflects this thrust. (As noted earlier, in this text we have retained subjects as the primary term in part because it has been critical to distinguish among investigators, experimenters, and subjects, all of whom are participants in a study.)

[2]There are exceptions, and no-treatment control conditions may not be needed. As one case in point, when there is information that a particular outcome is inevitable (e.g., death) or the trajectory is very predictable (e.g., continued decline), a single treatment group without a control group may provide persuasive information that attests to the efficacy of treatment. Drawing inferences in such cases was discussed in the context of quasi-experimental single-case designs in Chapter 9. As a random example from outside of psychology, a recent study reported a new treatment with a small number of premature infants with severe respiratory distress (Leach et al., 1996). Eight of 13 infants who received the treatment were alive and doing well 4 months later; the remaining five had died. Without a no-treatment control condition, the results are still fairly clear because conventional treatments had failed and the infants would be expected to die. Most of us would be persuaded that there was an effect of treatment without a no-treatment comparison group.

[3]I recall the animosity I caused on three occasions in which I tried to persuade collaborators that my contribution—completing the Reference section—warranted sole or (my default position) first authorship. My position was invariably weakened by some undergraduate in charge of proofing the footnotes who was making a similar case. Of course, everyone knows that there are usually more references than footnotes, but I still lost out in each case.

FOR FURTHER READING

American Psychological Association (1992). *Ethical principles of psychologists and code of conduct.* Washington, DC: American Psychological Association.

Beauchamp, T., King, N., & Faden, R.R. (1986). *A history and theory of informed consent.* New York: Oxford University Press.

Fine, M.A., & Kurdek, L.A. (1993). Reflections on determining authorship credit and authorship order on faculty–student collaborations. *American Psychologist, 48,* 1141–1147.

Gould, S.J. (1981). *The mismeasure of man.* New York: W.W. Norton.

Keith-Spiegel, P. (Editor). (1994). Special section: The 1992 Ethics Code: Boon or bane? *Professional Psychology: Research and Practice, 25,* 315–387.

Miller, D.J., & Hersen, M. (Eds.) (1992). *Research fraud in the behavioral and biomedical sciences.* New York: Wiley and Sons.

National Academy of Sciences, Committee on the Conduct of Science (1989). *On being a scientist.* Washington, DC: National Academy Press.

Rosenthal, R. (1994). Science and ethics in conducting, analyzing, and reporting psychological research. *Psychological Science, 5*, 127–133.

Rosnow, R.L., Rotheram-Borus, M.J., Ceci, S.J., Blanck, P.D., & Koocher, G.P. (1993). The Institutional Review Board as a mirror of scientific and ethical standards. *American Psychologist, 48*, 821–826.

Chapter 17

Publication and Communication of Research Findings

The research process is comprised of the design, execution, analysis of the results, and preparation of the report (e.g., journal article). The final step seems straightforward and relatively easy, given the nature and scope of the other steps. In fact, one often refers to preparation of the article as merely "writing up the results." Yet the implied simplicity of the task belies the significance of the product in the research process. The article is not the final step in this process. Rather, it is an important beginning. The article is often a launching platform for the next study for the authors themselves and for others in the field who are interested in pursuing the findings. Thus, the report is central to the research process.

The article itself is not only a description of what was accomplished, it also conveys the extent to which the design, execution, and analyses were well conceived and appropriate for the conclusions that were drawn. Recognition of this facet of the report is the reason why we require proposals for research (e.g., for students pursuing a dissertation and investigators pursuing a grant). At the proposal stage, we can examine the thought processes, design, planned execution, and data analyses and make the necessary changes in advance. Even so, writing the full article at the completion of the study raises special issues, many of which could not be completely anticipated at the proposal stage. At that point, the authors evaluate critical issues, see the shortcomings of the design, and struggle with any clashes or ambiguities of the findings in light of the hypotheses.

In previous chapters, methodology has been discussed from the standpoint of specific strategies in planning, designing, and implementing research. At a broader level, methodology can be conceived as an approach toward thinking and problem solving. The approach considers specific types of obstacles to knowledge. These obstacles are codified in various ways under such rubrics as threats to validity, biases, and artifacts. The skill of the investigator in addressing these obstacles is often reflected in the quality of the design. The quality of a given investigation is invariably a matter of degree and is evaluated both in relation to the criteria for experimental validity and to the constraints placed on the research setting. In relation to manuscript preparation, the task is to convey the rationale for method and design decisions. This chapter discusses publication and communication of the results of research. The chapter emphasizes the facets of manuscript preparation and publication that pertain to methodology and research design. The task of the author is to translate methodological, design, and evaluation issues raised in previous chapters into a rational and readable manuscript. The publication process serves as a backdrop for many of the demands placed on the author in writing up the findings. This chapter focuses on preparing papers for journal publication, although the remarks may apply to other formats (e.g., conference presentations, chapters and books in which research is described).

PUBLICATION PROCESS: AN OVERVIEW

After an investigation or set of investigations is completed, the results are often published so that they can be disseminated to the scientific community and become part of the accumulated knowledge base. Publication and communication of results of research findings involve a process with many decision points and steps. For examples, decisions are required regarding whether to publish the paper, what to publish (e.g., when a large data base may need to be subdivided), where to publish (e.g., journal article, chapter, book), and when to publish (e.g., in an ongoing longitudinal study when interim segments of the data may be of interest). Also, authorship, responsibilities for completion and preparation of the paper, obligations to the scientific community in executing and reporting research, and making information and data available raise central issues. The many components of publication and communication are of keen interest because publications address both professional (e.g., development of the field) and personal issues (e.g., career advancement) and because these issues span diverse scientific disciplines. Within psychology and other scientific disciplines, professional journals serve as the primary publication outlet for research.

The publication process is usually conceived as beginning with preparation of a manuscript for journal submission. The process might be traced to a much earlier point. Indeed, decisions made at the design stage, including the focus of the study, the type of question, the strength of the planned design, and events throughout the investigation may govern or restrict the eventual publication choices. However, in discussing the publication process, we begin with the assumption of a completed study that contributes to the area of investigation in some substantive way and that adds important knowledge. Inherent in this assumption is that the study is sufficiently well designed to generate experimentally valid conclusions. However, this assumption does not invariably mean that a study will end in a published report of the findings. Not all studies that are begun are completed; of those completed, not all are prepared for publication; of those prepared for publication, not all submitted to journals for review and evaluation; and of those that are submitted, not all are accepted and published.[1]

After completion of the study, the author(s) prepare a written version of the paper in a very special format. In psychology, the format is specified by the American Psychological Association (1994), but their format is also used in many journals beyond the discipline of psychology. Once the manuscript is prepared, it is submitted to a journal the author has selected as a desirable and suitable publication outlet. Selection of the journal is often made on the basis of any of several criteria, such as the relevance of the journal in relation to the topic, the prestige value of the journal in an implicit hierarchy of journals in the field, the likelihood of acceptance, the breadth and number of readers or subscribers, the discipline and audience one wishes to address (e.g., psychology, psychiatry, medicine, social work, health, education), and others. Several hundred journal outlets are available in the behavioral and social sciences. Within the English language, journals in psychology have been described for purposes of aiding authors in the selection of appropriate outlets for their manuscripts (APA, 1990). The information includes the editorial policy, content area or domain, type of paper (e.g., investigations, literature reviews, case studies), and guidelines for manuscript preparation for each journal.

Once the manuscript is submitted, the journal editor usually sends the paper to two or more reviewers. The reviewers are usually selected because of their knowledge and special expertise in the area of the study or because of familiarity with selected features of the study (e.g., new methods of data analyses). Some reviewers are consulting editors who review often for the journal and presumably have a perspective of the type and quality of papers the journal typically publishes; other reviewers are ad hoc reviewers and are selected less regularly than consulting editors. Both consulting editors and ad hoc reviewers are often experts and active researchers in the specific area of the study and can well evaluate the contribution. Reviewers are asked to evaluate the substance and methods of the study. They evaluate specific details, including features we have discussed under the rubrics of threats to internal, external, construct, and statistical conclusion validity. The reviewers are instructed to evaluate the paper critically and to offer an opinions about its merit.

Once the paper is reviewed, the editor evaluates the manuscript and the comments of the reviewers. In some cases, the editor may provide his or her own independent review of the paper; in other cases, he or she may not review the paper but defers to the comments and recommendations of the reviewers. The editor writes the author and notes the editorial decision. Usually, one of three decisions is reached: the manuscript is accepted pending a number of revisions that address points of concern in the reviewers' comments; the manuscript is rejected and will not be considered further by the journal; or the manuscript is rejected but the author is invited to resubmit an extensively revised version of the paper for reconsideration.

The *accept* decision usually means that the overall study provides important information and was well done. However, the reviewers and the editor may have identified several points for further clarification and analysis. The author is asked to revise the paper to address these points. The revised paper would be accepted for publication. Occasionally, several revisions may be needed as the author and editor work toward achieving the final manuscript.

The *reject* decision means that the reviewers, editor, or both considered the paper to include flaws in conception, design, or execution or that the research problem, focus, and question did not address a very important issue. For journals with high rejection rates, papers are usually not rejected because they are flagrantly flawed in design. Rather, the importance of the study, the suitability of the methods for the questions, and specific methodological and design decisions conspire as the basis for the decision. In many cases, preparation of the manuscript in ways that emphasize the rationale for methodological practices selected by the investigator might readily lead to different reactions on the part of reviewers.

The *reject–resubmit decision* may be used if several issues emerged that raise questions about the research and the design. In a sense, the study may be viewed as basically sound and important but many significant questions preclude definitive evaluation. The author may be invited to prepare an extensively revised version that includes further procedural details, additional data analyses, clarification of many decision points pivotal to the findings and conclusions, and other changes. The revised manuscript may be entered into the review process anew to reach an accept or reject decision.

No individual study can address all concerns (or threats to validity). Consequently, the task of the reviewer is to assess what has been done and to judge whether the benefits and the knowledge yielded warrant publication in the journal. Concretely, reviewers examine general issues such as whether:

- the question(s) is important for the field
- the design and methodology are appropriate to the question
- the results are suitably analyzed
- the interpretations follow from the design and findings
- the knowledge yield contributes in an incremental way to the field

In noting these general areas, one cannot help but be struck by the judgments reviewers are asked to make. The judgments require both subjective and intellectual evaluations of the study. Science is an enterprise of people; hence, it cannot be divorced from subjectivity and judgment. In noting subjectivity in the manuscript review and evaluation process, there is a false implication of arbitrariness and fiat. Quality research often rises to the top and opinions of quality over time are not idiosyncratic.

Focus on the reviewers makes the author appear to play a passive role in the review process. However, it is just the opposite—the author has the advantage insofar as there is much that can be done in preparation of the manuscript to address the issues that will inevitably emerge. Whether these issues are addressed and how well they are addressed contribute greatly to the outcome.

Apart from the role of the reviewers and the author, characteristics of the journal are also critical contextual factors that influence the outcome. Individual journals can vary widely in their base rates of acceptance and the types of studies they are likely to accept. A particular article might be reviewed quite differently as a function of the journal. Indeed, it is not rare for the same reviewers to provide different recommendations for the same manuscript as a function of the journal for which they are reviewing.

Although beyond our purpose, the review process deserves passing comment. The entire process of manuscript submission, review, and publication has been heavily lamented, debated, and criticized. The imperfections and biases of peer review, the lack of agreement between reviewers of a particular paper, the influence of variables (e.g., prestige value of the author's institution, number of citations of one's prior work within the manuscript) on decisions of reviewers, and the control that reviewers and editors exert over authors have been and continue to be vigorously discussed (Bailar & Patterson, 1985; Cicchetti, 1991; Lindsay, 1988). Of special concern is the review process and the ways authors are treated, although there are many ways authors can prepare themselves for the journal review process.[2]

Understanding the review process can be aided by underscoring the one salient characteristic that authors, reviewers, and editors share, to wit, they are all human. This means that they (we) vary widely in skills, expertise, sensitivities, motives, and abilities to communicate. Consequently, the content, quality, and other features of manuscripts, comments of reviewers, and editorial decision letters vary in multivariate ways. As new investigators begin to enter into the journal publication process, they quickly develop a set of stories about irrational features of the process and unreasonable judgments against one of their own studies. Yet, the hurdles of the review process can be traversed with only minor assaults to one's self-esteem when one is armed with a perspective on how to design research and to communicate the design and findings to others.

METHODOLOGICALLY INFORMED MANUSCRIPT PREPARATION

Overview

In psychology, one's initial introduction to manuscript preparation often occurs at the undergraduate level in a course devoted to a topic within experimental psychology (learning, cognition, motivation) in which research design is also taught. The goal at this early stage of development is to encourage descriptive and objective scientific writing. Understandably, a particular view is fostered to distinguish the style of scientific writing from other forms in which opinion, subjectivity, and description are appropriately intertwined (e.g., a literary style in which the full range of experience, emotions, and views are central). The style of science writing is to be descriptive and to convey what was actually done so that the methods and procedures can be replicated. Concrete, specific, operational, tangible, objective, precise, and impersonal are some of the characteristics that capture the introduction to writing and scientific papers in the tradition of quantitative research. The effort to describe research in concrete and specific ways is critically important. However, the task of the author goes well beyond description.

Preparation of the report for publication involves three interrelated tasks, which I refer to as description, explanation, and contextualization. Failure to appreciate or to accomplish these tasks is a main source of frustration for authors as their papers traverse the process of manuscript review toward journal publication. *Description* is the most straightforward task and includes providing details of the study. Even though this is an obvious requirement of the report, basic details often are omitted in published articles (e.g., sex and race of the participants, means, standard deviation) (Shapiro & Shapiro, 1983; Weiss & Weisz, 1990). *Explanation* is slightly more complex insofar as this refers to presenting the rationale of several facets of the study. The justification, decision-making process, and the connections between the decisions and the goals of the study move well beyond description. There are numerous decision points in any study, most of which can be questioned. The author is obliged to make the case to explain why the specific options elected are well suited to the hypotheses or the goals of the study. Finally, *contextualization* moves one step further away from description of the details of the study and addresses how the study fits in the context of other studies and in the knowledge base more generally. This facet of article preparation reflects lofty notions such as scholarship and perspective because the author places the descriptive and explanatory material into a broader context.

The extent to which description, explanation, and contextualization are accomplished increases the likelihood that the report will be viewed as a publishable article and facilitates integration of the report into the knowledge base. Guidelines provided below emphasize these tasks in the preparation and evaluation of research reports. The guidelines focus on the logic of the study; the interrelations of the different sections; the rationale for specific procedures and analyses; and the strengths, limitations, and place in the knowledge base. Consider first the main sections of the manuscript that are prepared for journal publication and how these components can be addressed.

Main Sections of the Article

Title   Certainly the title is *not* a "main section" of the article, but it is not trivial, either. At least a passing comment is warranted. Usually one attempts to address the key variables, focus, and population with an economy of words. If the study focuses on diagnosis, assessment, treatment, or prevention, one of these words or variations might be included in the title. Similarly, if a specific disorder (e.g., depression), personality characteristic (e.g., repression–sensitization), treatment technique (e.g., structural family therapy), or sample (e.g., infants, elderly) is critical, the pertinent terms are likely to be integrated into the title.

Occasionally, one has a hint toward methodology in the title. Key terms, perhaps in the form of subtitles, are included to alert us to methodological points. Terms such as "a pilot study" or "preliminary report" may have many different meanings, for instance, that this is an initial or interim report of a larger research program. These words could also be gently preparing readers for methodological surprises that threaten experimental validity and thus may be telling the reader not to expect too much from the design. (My dissertation coined the subtitle "A pre-preliminary, tentative, exploratory pilot study."©) In some cases, terms such as "A Controlled Investigation," are added to the study, which moves expectation in the other direction, namely, that the present study is somehow well conducted and controlled and perhaps by implication stands in contrast to other studies in the field (or in the author's repertoire). Usually words noting that the investigation is controlled are not needed unless control is truly a new feature of research in the area. (Similarly, in the cases of review papers rather than empirical articles, the use of the subtitle "A Review" is usually unnecessary.)

Abstract   Two features of the Abstract make this section quite critical. First, the Abstract is likely to be read by many more people than is the article. The Abstract probably will be entered into various data bases and be accessible through computerized searches and the internet. Consequently, this is the only information that most readers will have about the study. Second, for reviewers of the manuscript and readers of the journal article, the Abstract is the first impression of what the author studied and found. Ambiguity, illogic, and fuzziness here are ominous. Thus, the Abstract is sometimes the only impression or first impression one may have about the study. What is said is critically important.

Obviously, the purpose of the Abstract is to provide a relatively brief statement of goals, methods, findings, and conclusions of the study. Critical methodological descriptors pertain to the participants and their characteristics, experimental and control groups or conditions, design, and major findings. Often space is quite limited; indeed a word limit (e.g., 100- or 120-word maximum) may be placed on the Abstract by the journals. It is useful to deploy the words to make substantive statements about the characteristics of the study and the findings rather than to provide general and minimally informative comments. Similarly, it is advisable to omit vacuous statements (e.g., "Implications of the results were discussed." or "Future directions for research were suggested.") and to replace them with comments about the findings or one or two specific implications and research directions (e.g., "The findings raise the prospect that there is a Tiny 2 rather than a Big 5 set of personality characteristics.").

Introduction   The Introduction is designed to convey the overall rationale and objectives. The task of the author is to convey in a crisp and concise fashion why this particular study is needed and the current questions, void, or deficiency the study is designed to address. The section should not review the literature in a study-by-study fashion but convey issues and evaluative comments that set the stage for the study that is to follow. It is in this section that the task of contextualization becomes critically important. Placing the study in the context of what is and is not known and the essential next step in research in the field requires mastery of the pertinent literatures, apart from reasonable communication skills. Saying that the study is important (without systematically establishing the context) or noting that no one else has studied this phenomenon (e.g., measure, sample) often are viewed as feeble attempts to short-circuit the contextualization of the study.

It may be relevant to consider limitations of previous work (e.g., threats to internal, external, construct, and statistical conclusion validity) and how the limitations can be overcome. These statements build the critical transition from an existing literature to the present study and the rationale for design improvements or additions in relation to the studies. Alternatively, the study may build along new dimensions to extend the theory, hypotheses, and constructs to a broader range of domains of performance, samples, settings, and so on. The rationale for the specific study must be very clearly established.

In general, the Introduction moves from the very general to the specific. The very general refers to the opening of the Introduction, which conveys the area, general topic, and significance of a problem. For example, in studies of diagnosis, assessment, treatment, or prevention of dysfunction, the Introduction invariably includes a paragraph to orient the reader about the seriousness of the topic, its prevalence or incidence, and the economic and social costs of the disorder. Although reviewers of the manuscript are likely to be specialists in the area of the study and hence know the context very well, many potential readers would profit from a statement that conveys the significance, interest, and value of the main focus of the study.

After the initial material, the Introduction moves to the issues that underlie the study. Here the context frames the specific hypotheses of the study and reflects theory and research that are the impetus for the investigation. Essentially, the author is making a case for conducting the study. Extended paragraphs that provide background but have no close connection to the hypotheses of the study are common weaknesses of rejected papers because the reviewers are forced to "wonder as they wander" through the circuitous path leading to the hypotheses.

The Introduction does not usually permit conveying all the information one wishes to present. In fact, the limit is usually two to four manuscript pages. A reasonable use of this space is to use brief paragraphs or implicit sections that describe the nature of the problem, the current status of the literature, the extensions to theory and research the study is designed to provide, and how the methods to be used are warranted. The Introduction must establish that the variables are of interest and that the study addresses a central issue. To the extent that the author conveys a grasp of the issues in the area and can identify the lacunae that the study is designed to fill greatly improves the quality of the report and the chances of its acceptance for journal publication.

Method This section of the paper encompasses several points related to who was studied, why, and how. The section not only describes critical procedures but also provides the rationale for methodological decisions. Initially, the subjects or clients are described. From a method and design standpoint, information beyond basic descriptors can be helpful. Why was this sample included? How is it appropriate to the substantive area and question of interest? In some cases, the sample is obviously relevant because the subjects have the characteristic or disorder of interest (e.g., parents accused of child abuse) or are in a setting of interest (e.g., nursing home residents). In other cases, samples are included merely because they are available. Such *samples of convenience* may include college students or a clinic population recruited for some purpose other than the study. The rationale for the sample should be provided to convey why *this* sample provides a good test of the hypotheses and whether any special features may be relevant to the conclusions. Subject selection, recruitment, screening, and other features warrant comment. The issue for the author and reviewer is whether features of the subject-selection process could restrict the conclusions in some unique fashion, or worse, whether in some way they represent a poor test given the purpose of the study.

The design is likely to include two or more groups that are treated in a particular fashion. From the standpoint of methodology and design, the precise purpose of each group and the procedures to which they are exposed should be clarified. Control groups should not merely be labeled (with the idea that the name is informative). The author should convey precisely what the group(s) is designed to control in terms of threats to validity. It is possible that some control procedures are not feasible under the circumstances of the study. Why and how the threats will be addressed should be clarified. Reviewers often criticize a study because certain control conditions were not included. After the paper is rejected by the journal, authors retort in an understandably frustrated way that the control procedure recommended by reviewers was not feasible, that the threats were not plausible, and so on. Generally, the responsibility lies with the author. The author is advised to identify the critical threats in the area and to convey how these are controlled in the design. Plausible threats that are uncontrolled deserve explicit comment to arrest the reasonable concerns of the reviewers.

Several measures are usually included in the study. Why the constructs were selected for study should be clarified in the Introduction. The specific measures and why they were selected to operationalize the constructs should be presented in the Method section. Information about the psychometric characteristics of the measures is often highlighted. This information relates directly to the credibility of the results. Apart from individual assessment devices, the rationale for including or omitting areas that might be regarded as crucial (e.g., multiple measures, informants, settings) deserve comment. The principle here is similar to that for other sections; namely, the rationale for the author's decisions ought to be explicit.

Occasionally, ambiguous statements may enter into descriptions of measures. For example, measures in previous research may be referred to as "reliable" or "valid" as part of the rationale for use in the present study. There are, of course, many different types of reliability and validity. It is important to identify characteristics of the measures found in prior research that are relevant to the present research. For example, high internal consistency (reliability) in a prior study may not be a strong argument for use of that measure in a longitudinal design in which the author hopes for test–retest reliability. Even previous data on test–retest reliability (e.g., more than 2 weeks) may not provide a sound basis for test–retest covering annual intervals. The information conveys the suitability of the measure for the study and the author's rationale for selecting the measure in light of alternative strategies.

Results   It is important to convey why specific analyses were selected and how a particular test or comparison addresses the hypotheses or purposes presented earlier in the paper. It is often the case that analyses are reported in a rote fashion in which, for example, the main effects are presented and then the interactions for each measure. The author presents the analyses in very much the same way as a computer printout. Similarly, if several dependent measures are available, a particular set of analyses is automatically run (e.g., omnibus tests of multivariate analyses of variance followed by univariate analyses of variance for individual measures). The tests may not relate to the hypotheses, predictions, or expectations outlined at the beginning of the paper (Wampold, Davis, & Good, 1990). Knowledge of statistics is critical for selecting the analysis to address the hypotheses of interest and conditions met by the data. In presentation of the Results, it is important to convey why specific tests were selected and how they serve the specific goals of the study. I personally find it useful to consider the results and data analysis in relation to the paragraph or statement of the specific purposes or hypotheses (e.g., usually the final paragraph of the Introduction). The results ought to speak directly to that narrative statement.

It is often useful to begin the Results section by presenting basic descriptors of the data (e.g., means, standard deviations for each group or condition) so the reader has access to the numbers themselves. The main body of Results is to test the hypotheses or to evaluate the predictions. Organization of the Results section (subheadings) or brief statements of hypotheses before presenting the analyses are often helpful to prompt the author to clarify how the statistical test relates to the substantive questions. Several additional or ancillary analyses may be presented to elaborate the primary hypotheses. For example, one might be able to reduce the plausibility that certain biases may have accounted for group differences on the basis of supplementary or ancillary data analyses. Ancillary analyses may be more exploratory and diffuse than are tests of primary hypotheses. Manifold variables can be selected for these analyses (e.g., sex, race, height differences), which are not necessarily conceptually interesting in relation to the goals of the study. The author may wish to present data and data analyses that were unexpected, were not of initial interest, and were not the focus of the study. The rationale for these excursions and the limitations of interpretation are worth noting. From the standpoint of the reviewer and reader, the results should make clear what the main hypotheses were, how the analyses provide appropriate and pointed tests, and what conclusions can be reached as a result. In light of our prior discussion of statistical evaluation, it would be advisable to move beyond tests of statistical significance and to include measures of magnitude of effects.

Discussion   The Discussion section consists of the conclusions and interpretations of the study; hence, it is the final resting place of all issues and concerns. Typically, the Discussion includes an overview of the major findings, integration or relation of them to theory and prior research, their limitations and ambiguities, their implications for interpretation, and future directions. The extent to which this can be accomplished in a brief space (e.g., in two to five manuscript pages) is to the author's advantage.

Description and interpretation of the findings invariably raise tension between what the author wishes to say about the findings and their meaning versus what can be said in light of how the study was designed and evaluated. It is in the Discussion that one can see the interplay of the Introduction, Methods, and Results sections. For example, the author might draw conclusions that are not appropriate given the method and findings. The Discussion conveys flaws, problems or questionable methodological decisions that were not previously evident within the design. They are flaws only in relation to the Introduction and Discussion. That is, the reader of the paper can now state that if these are the types of statement the author wishes to make, the present study (design, measures, sample) is not well suited. The slight mismatch of interpretative statements in the Discussion and the methodology is a common, albeit tacit, basis for not considering a study as well conceived and executed. A slightly different study may be required to support the specific statements the author makes in the Discussion; alternatively, the Discussion might be more circumscribed in the statements that are made. (For my dissertation, my committee noted that the Introduction and Discussion were sparkling and that it was a shame that I had not completed a study designed to address issues these sections raised.)

It is usually to the author's credit to examine potential sources of ambiguity because he or she is in an excellent position by familiarity with procedures and expertise to understand the area. A candid, nondefensive appraisal of the study is very helpful. Here too, contextualization may be helpful because limitations of a study are also related to the body of prior research, what other studies have and have not accomplished, and whether a finding is robust across different methods of investigation. Although it is to the author's credit to acknowledge limitations of the study, there are limits on the extent to which reviewers grant a pardon for true confessions. At some point, the flaw is sufficient to preclude publication, regardless of whether the flaw is acknowledged by the author. For example, the author of the study might note, "A significant limitation of the present study is the absence of a suitable control group. We are aware that this might limit the strength of the conclusions." Although awareness may have its own intrinsic value, reviewers of the study may not view the author's statement as sufficient to bolster the experimental validity of the findings.

At other points, acknowledging potential limitations conveys critical understanding of the issues and directs the field to future work. For example, in explaining the findings, the author may note that although the dependent measure is useful or valid, there are many specific facets of the construct of interest that it omits. Thus, the results may not extend to different facets of the construct as measured in different ways. This use of acknowledgment augments the contribution of the study and the likelihood of favorable evaluation by readers.

Finally, it is useful in the Discussion to contextualize the results to continue the story line that began in the Introduction; that is, with the present findings, to answer questions such as, What puzzle piece has been added to the knowledge base? What new questions or ambiguities are raised? What other substantive areas might be relevant for this line of research? What new studies are needed? From the standpoint of contextualization, the new studies referred to are not merely those that overcome methodological limitations of the present study, but are those that focus on the substantive issues of the next steps for research.

Questions to Guide Manuscript Preparation

The section-by-section discussion of the content of an article is designed to convey the flow or logic of the study and the interplay of description, explanation, and contextualization. The study ought to have a thematic line throughout, and all sections ought to reflect the theme in a logical way. The thematic line consists of the substantive issues guiding the hypotheses and decisions of the investigator (e.g., with regard to procedures and analyses) that are used to elaborate the hypotheses.

A more concrete and perhaps more helpful way of aiding preparation of the manuscript is to consider the task as that of answering many questions. There are questions for the authors to ask themselves or, on the other hand, questions reviewers and consumers of the research are likely to ask as they read the manuscript. These questions ought to be addressed suitably within the manuscript. Table 17.1 presents questions that warrant consideration. The questions are presented according to the different sections of a manuscript. The questions emphasize the descriptive information and the rationale for procedures, decisions, and practices in the design and execution of the study. The set of questions is useful as a way of checking to see that many important facets of the study were not overlooked. As a cautionary note, the questions alert one to the parts rather than the whole; the manuscript in its entirety or as a whole is evaluated to see how the substantive question and methodology interrelate and how decisions

TABLE 17.1.   Major Questions to Guide Journal Article Preparation

---

Abstract

What are the main purposes of the study?

Who was studied (sample, sample size, special characteristics)?

How were subjects selected?

To what conditions, if any, were participants exposed?

What type of design was used?

What are the main findings and conclusions?

Introduction

What is the background and context for the study?

What in current theory, research, or clinical work makes the study useful, important, or of interest?

What is different or special about the study in focus, methods, or design to address a need in the area?

Is the rationale clear regarding the constructs to be assessed?

What specifically are the purposes, predictions, or hypotheses?

Method

Participants

Who are the subjects and how many are there in this study?

Why was this sample selected in light of the research goals?

How was this sample obtained, recruited, and selected?

What are the subject and demographic characteristics of the sample (e.g., sex, age, ethnicity, race, socioeconomic status)?

What, if any, inclusion and exclusion criteria were invoked (i.e., selection rules to obtain participants)?

How many of eligible or recruited subjects actually were selected and participated in the study?

Was informed consent solicited? How and from whom, if special populations were used?

Design

What is the design (e.g., longitudinal, cross-sectional) and how does the design relate to the goals?

How were subjects assigned to groups or conditions?

How many groups were included in the design?

How are the groups similar and different in how they are treated in the study?

Why are these groups critical to address the questions of interest?

Procedures

Where was the study conducted (setting)?

What measures, materials, equipment, or apparatus were used?

What is the chronological sequence of events to which subjects were exposed?

What intervals elapsed between different aspects of the study (e.g., assessment, treatment, follow-up)?

TABLE 17.1.   Major Questions to Guide Journal Article Preparation *Continued*

If assessments involved novel measures created for this study, what data can be brought to bear regarding pertinent types of reliability and validity?

What procedural checks were completed to avert potential sources of bias in implementation of the manipulation and assessments?

What checks were made to ensure that the conditions were carried out as intended?

What other information does the reader need to know to understand how subjects were treated and what conditions were provided?

Results

What are the primary measures and data on which the hypotheses or predictions depend?

What analyses are to be used and how specifically do these address the original hypotheses and purposes?

Are the assumptions of the data analyses met?

If multiple tests are used, what means are provided to control error rates?

If more than one group is delineated (e.g., through experimental manipulation or subject selection), are they similar on variables that might otherwise explain the results (e.g., diagnosis, age)?

Are data missing due to incomplete measures (not filled out completely by the subjects) or due to loss of subjects? If so, how is this problem handled in the data analyses?

Are there ancillary analyses that might further inform the primary analyses or exploratory analyses to stimulate further work?

Discussion

What are the major findings of the study?

Specifically, how do these findings add to research and support, refute, or inform current theory?

What alternative interpretations, theoretical or methodological, can be placed on the data?

What limitations or qualifiers must be placed on the study because of methodological and design issues?

What research follows from the study to move the field forward?

Note: Concrete guidelines for the format of preparing articles are provided by the American Psychological Association (1994).

regarding subject selection, control conditions, measures, and data analyses relate in a fashion coherent to the guiding question.

General Comments

Preparation of an article often is viewed as a task of describing what was done. With this mind set, authors often are frustrated at the reactions of reviewers. In reading the reactions of reviewers, the authors usually recognize and acknowledge the value of providing more details (e.g., further information about the participants, or procedures). However, when the requests pertain to explanation and contextualization, authors are more likely to be baffled or defensive. This reaction may be reasonable because there is much less attention to these facets of preparing research reports in graduate training. Also, reviewers' comments and editorial decision letters may not be explicit about the need for explanation and contextualization. For example, some of the general reactions of reviewers may be comments such as, "Nothing in the manuscript is new," "I fail to see the importance of the study," or "This study has already been done in a much better way by others." (Thanks to my dissertation committee for letting me quote from their comments.) In fact, the characterizations may be true. Alternatively, the comments could also reflect the extent to which the author has failed to contextualize the study to obviate these kinds of reactions.

The lesson for preparing and evaluating research reports is clear. Describing a study does not automatically establish its contribution to the field, no matter how strongly the author feels that the study is a first. Also, the methodological options for studying a particular question are enormous in terms of possible samples, constructs and measures, and data-analytic methods included in the study. The reasons for electing the particular set of options the author has chosen deserve elaboration.

In some cases, authors select options because they were used in prior research. That warrant may be weak because objections levied at the present study may also be appropriate to the prior work. The author will feel unjustly criticized because of a general flaw in the literature. Yet, if a key methodological decision was based solely on the argument that "others have done this in the past," that is very weak as a rationale unless the purpose of the study was to address the value of the option as a goal. Also, it may be that new evidence that makes the past practice more questionable has emerged. Over time, standards and permissible methods may change.

In general, it is beneficial to the author and to the general scientific community to convey the thought processes underlying methodological and design decisions. This information will greatly influence the extent to which the research effort is appreciated and viewed as enhancing knowledge. The author is not advised to write a persuasive appeal about how important the study is and how this or that way was the best way to study the phenomenon. Yet, it is useful to convey that decisions were thoughtful and that they represent reasonable choices among the alternatives for answering the questions that guide the study. The contextual issues are no less important. As authors, we often expect the brilliance of the study to shine through, that is, to be self-evident. Any negative review or failure to grasp the brilliance is viewed by the author as a sign that the reviewer was wearing a sleep mask when he or she read the paper. Yet, the contribution of a study is a judgment call. From the perspective of the author, it is advantageous to state very clearly how and where the study fits into the literature, what the study adds, and what questions and research the study prompts.

SUMMARY AND CONCLUSIONS

Publication and communication of results of research represent a complex process involving many issues beyond methodology and research design. Diverse abilities are taxed, beginning with the author's skills in identifying and selecting critical substantive questions and culminating with skills in communicating the results. Methodology and design play major roles throughout the processes of planning, conducting, and communicating research results. In preparing the manuscript, the author invariably wishes to make a statement (conclusion). The strength of the conclusion is based on the extent to which the study addresses issues highlighted in prior chapters. It is important for the author to convey the focus and goals of the study clearly and concisely. The design decisions and the rationale for decisions, when presented clearly, greatly augment the manuscript.

NOTES

[1]In my own career, such as it is, there have been two separate occasions in which I have had a manuscript accepted for publication, entered into production, and noted officially as "in press." Before these manuscripts appeared in print, each journal went out of business and stopped publishing. A coincidence? Maybe. (But my acupuncturist, who specializes in shunned authors, feels otherwise. When you pin him down, he says that acceptance of one of my papers places a journal at risk for demise.)

[2]Excellent readings are available (Kafka, *The Trial*; Camus, *The Myth of Sisyphus*; Dante's *Inferno*). Also, within clinical psychology, various conceptual views (e.g., learned helplessness), clinical disorders (e.g., posttraumatic stress disorder), and intervention strategies (e.g., stress management, anger control training) are helpful in understanding and preparing oneself for negotiating the shoals of the review process.

FOR FURTHER READING

Agnew, N.M., & Pyke, S.W. (1987). *The science game* (4th ed.). Englewood Cliffs, NJ: Prentice-Hall.

American Psychological Association (1993*). Journals in psychology: A resource listing for authors* (4th ed.). Washington, DC: American Psychological Association.

American Psychological Association (1994). *Publication manual of the American Psychological Association* (4th ed.). Washington, DC: American Psychological Association.

Hyman, R. (1995). How to critique a published article. *Psychological Bulletin, 118*, 178–182.

Maher, B.A. (1978). A reader's, writer's, and reviewer's guide to assessing research reports in clinical psychology. *Journal of Consulting and Clinical Psychology, 46*, 835–838.

Maxwell, S.E., & Cole, D.A. (1995). Tips for writing (and reading) methodological articles. *Psychological Bulletin, 118*, 193–198.

Sternberg, R.J. (1992). *Psychological Bulletin*'s top 10 "hit parade." *Psychological Bulletin, 112*, 387–388. (The former editor invites comments of authors whose works have been the most frequently cited in that journal. The authors reflect on what has made their paper widely cited and offer advice in writing papers for publication.)

Chapter 18

Closing Comments

Methodology in Perspective

CHAPTER OUTLINE

Goals of Methodology

Substantive Contribution of Methodology

GOALS OF METHODOLOGY

We have covered several topics central to the design and execution of research. The goal of the book has been to describe diverse methodological practices and options, to convey the rationale for their use, and to relate methodological practices to the process of designing, executing, and evaluating a study. There are many aspects to which the investigator must attend to complete a methodologically sound study. In addition, an investigator is also asked to complete an important study and to communicate the findings in a way that is coherent. These are heavy demands, and methodological issues and concerns infuse each part of the process. In these final comments, it is worth returning to key issues and to discuss the relationship of methodology to substantive issues that guide research.

Methodology, somewhat like statistics, is often taught in a way that focuses on a cookbook approach. That is, there are special ingredients, and they can be combined in various ways:

- add one or two hypotheses
- select lots of subjects and mix thoroughly with random assignment
- add three or more assessment devices
- collect, score, and enter the data from the completed measures
- allow to cook for a few nanoseconds (depending on the chip in one's computer)
- generate F or *t* tests and maybe one or two regression analyses

- describe the study in a cryptic style (the write-up)
- allow to sit for 1–2 years (the review and publication process).

No doubt the art and science of methodology make cooking a reasonable metaphor, but not a terrifically helpful one. Clearly, there are ingredients that can characterize sound studies, but it is better to move away from the ingredients to understand the task and goals at a broader level.

There is much the investigator ought to understand because strategies are required at each stage of the investigation to ensure high quality research. *Before* the study is run, the investigator can ensure that threats to internal validity and other types of validity particularly relevant to the study (e.g., construct validity) are addressed, power is high so that differences can be detected, the experimental conditions are planned so that any effect that occurs is likely to be evident in this study (e.g., by the conditions or groups that are used), the constructs of interest are well represented (e.g., multiple measures), and the measures are sound in relation to the demands of the study (e.g., are reliable, valid, and sensitive to the predictions). *During* the study, the investigator can ensure that the conditions (e.g., intervention, manipulation) are administered carefully and consistently, experimenters retain their level of performance (across experimenters and over time for a given experimenter), subjects are treated in a way that is likely to generate minimally biased data, loss of subjects is likely to be minimal, and data are collected with great care to ensure they are complete. *After* the study and when the data are in, the investigator can complete data analyses to address various influences that can be ruled out or made implausible through careful statistical evaluation (e.g., to control for, partial out, examine the relations of various influences that might interfere with interpretation). These are only some of the strategies, but they convey that methodology is more than putting a few ingredients together (but, of course, so is cooking).

As discussed in prior chapters, methodology is a way of thinking and approaching substantive issues. Occasionally in prior chapters, I have used questions that investigators can ask themselves to help guide the consideration of specific methodological practices. The questions were designed to be very specific and hence optimally helpful, but providing specificity risks implying that a checklist feature exists—that is, "cover these questions and you're all set." Ultimately, of course, the task of the research is to address broad questions and to utilize all one knows about the substantive topic and methodology to address the questions well. Consider four questions to convey the task:

1. What is the best available and feasible way to test my theory, idea, or hypothesis?
2. If the study were completed as designed, what would be the salient threats to validity or sources of bias that could interfere with drawing valid inferences?
3. Before, during, and after the study is run, what can I do to reduce the plausibility of alternative interpretations of the findings?
4. Are the purposes (e.g., hypotheses), design, methods of data analysis, and discussion coherent; that is, are they addressing the same key issues, do they speak to the

same questions, and are they aligned so that what is said about results can indeed legitimately be stated?

These questions are the critical guideposts for research and underscore the task of the investigator. The prior chapters described practices to address these questions and explained the rationale for these practices. In the context of clinical psychology and other areas in which research is often conducted outside the laboratory, grasping the rationale for methodological practices is particularly crucial. Standard practices of random assignment, running many homogeneous subjects for a session or two, no attrition, equal sample size, and other luxuries of research are not always available. The importance of methodology is to alert one to the range of factors that compete with interpretation of the results and some of the practices that can be used. However, ingenuity in addressing the four questions is more important than any particular methodological practice. Indeed, even time-honored practices (e.g., random assignment, significance testing) that are standard fare in methodology and research design raise their own problems. This is not a call to abandon traditional methodology but an attempt to underscore that methodological practices are designed to address issues and that the issues are more critical than the practices.

SUBSTANTIVE CONTRIBUTION OF METHODOLOGY

A point that has not been conveyed in prior chapters provides a critical perspective on the contribution of methodology to the research enterprise. Practices related to the design of research, assessment, and data evaluation are not merely means toward an end, but in many ways they contribute to the end. More specifically, methodological practices contribute to the substantive conclusions we reach in our theories and about the phenomena we study. Because methodology is the lens through which we view phenomena empirically, it dictates directly what we see. Changes in the lens, such as advances in methodology and advances in theory and substantive findings also change what is revealed. For example, within the past 20 years, methodological and statistical advances such as meta-analyses and structural equation modeling have provided tools to evaluate questions that have been of interest for some time (e.g., effects of psychotherapy, causal sequences leading to different forms of psychopathology). The advances were not only new or different ways of answering the same questions of prior methods, but also ways of addressing, and hence raising, entirely new questions. This is illustrated by meta-analysis, which permits a quantitative, rather than a qualitative or narrative, review of a body of literature. When meta-analysis first emerged it was touted (appropriately) as a better way of accomplishing the task of reviewing the literature. Yet, meta-analysis is not merely a way of reviewing a literature in a quantitative fashion; it is also a way of asking questions about many different variables, alone and in combinations, from a body of research. New questions that cannot be easily (or in fact ever) addressed by an individual investigation can be asked about a topic (e.g., psychotherapy, education, social programs and interventions). This is accomplished in part by coding studies along new variables (e.g., therapist characteristics, type of methodology, conceptual views of the investigator) and seeing their impact on treatment. Consequently, with meta-analysis, new substantive conclusions emerged from the approach to methodology.

Substantive advances also emerge from new methods of assessment. A dramatic example is neuroimaging, which refers to diverse and constantly evolving methods of brain scanning. The advances resulting from neuroimaging are not merely a better way to assess brain activity. The method generates entirely new views about the nature of brain function, circuitry, and brain–behavior relations and permits evaluation of processes (e.g., during performance of various tasks) that could not be observed otherwise. In relation to more familiar psychological inventories, development of a new measure (e.g., of self-efficacy, helplessness, personality characteristics) permits investigation of construct that can elaborate our understanding of human functioning in new ways.

Methodology is always evolving. This text has focused on many standard practices and issues that are important to master as a foundation. Many traditional methodological practices have become traditional in part because they successfully address threats to validity and sources of bias. Adherence to traditional methodologies, although obviously useful, can also be constraining. For example, in clinical psychology there is a long tradition of using self-report inventories to measure all sorts of relations. Major advances have been made by using self-reports, and we depend on such reports to understand key topics in relation to the individual (e.g., self-esteem, feelings of helplessness and hopelessness) and society at large (e.g., rates of crime, substance use, utilization of health services). However, integrating these measures with new assessment modalities (e.g., social impact and unobtrusive measures) can give new perspectives and reveal new facets of the relations of interest.

As a better and more subtle example, most statistics used in psychology are based on linear models, that is, a particular view about how variables relate to each other. There is no reason to think that the world or the world of interest to us as investigators is linear; in fact, evidence suggests otherwise in many situations (Haynes, 1992; Kazdin & Kagan, 1994). Science is guided by a revered tenet of *parsimony,* which refers to selection of an interpretation among alternative interpretations that makes the fewest assumptions. That is, the simplest explanation possible to account for the data is the one to be preferred. However, parsimony does not promote simplicity for its own sake. If more complex models can better account for the evidence, the simpler model should be abandoned. Linear models, main effects, and bivariate relations often explain relations very well. Yet, one might also look for nonlinear models, interactions, and mutivariate relations to explain more complex ways that variables can relate to each other and to outcomes of interest. The goal is to explore new ways of looking at phenomena of interest, and in the process, identify new phenomena.

Conceptual paradigms that affect the way we see substantive topics also influence methodologies to study them. For example, overarching conceptual views are influencing the study of many topics (e.g., the weather, earthquakes, physiology). Conceptual approaches give increased attention to nonlinear, dynamic, and reciprocal relations among independent and dependent variables. More concretely, the tradition of research often considers single variables and unidirectional influences. For example, much of clinical research focuses on the effects of x on y (e.g., x may be maternal depression, attachment, parenting practices and y may be child development, school adjustment, adult relationships). That is fine, but there is much to be gained by considering the possibility of mutual, reciprocal, interactive, and dynamic influences of x and y. Dynamic models, chaos theory, fuzzy logic, and new ways of looking at causal relations reflect broad changes in thinking about phenomena, and they transcend many disciplines and require new methodologies not yet exploited in psychology (Barton, 1994; Hanson, 1995; Haynes, 1992; Robertson & Combs, 1995). Advances in computerization also permit new levels of analyses (e.g., integration of multiple variables and models that permit larger chunks of reality to enter into models, predictions, and empirical tests). The complex models permit evaluation of more intricate relations. The tradition of methodology has been to isolate variables so their influence can be studied free from confounds and other factors that could compete with drawing inferences. Some of this has been dictated by the lack of available methods to handle nonisolated variables, that is, the impact of x and y (as noted above), in the context and background of a, b, c, and d. Understanding how variables operate, rather than isolation per se, is the goal; new models and methods can bring us new ways of understanding.

The reader is encouraged to explore new methodologies. This can be accomplished in many ways. One way is to explore one's own data sets well beyond the goals of a particular study. Application of new data analyses or not-so-new analyses with different default assumptions (e.g., divide the sample with very different cutoff points to define groups, add other variables to make more complex subgroups such as individuals who show other characteristics in addition to being high vs. low on the main variable of interest) can help discover and generate hypotheses. (Remember when someone else does this with their data, it is called a *fishing expedition*, but when one does this with one's own data, it is referred to as the process of *hypothesis generation* and *discovery*.) The yield from a data set can go well beyond a test of the original hypotheses and can be used to develop conceptual models and hypotheses for the next study.

Another way to explore new methodologies is to enter into collaborative arrangements with investigators from other disciplines (e.g., public health, psychiatry, genetics, statistics). By definition, different disciplines have conceptual approaches that are likely to vary from those of psychology. Also, different disciplines often have quite different views about methods of data analyses that have implications for substantive views about reality. These methods can provide new perspectives on the substantive questions of interest and greatly enrich the yield from research.

At the highest level of mastery, methodology and substantive knowledge merge in the investigator. That is, knowledge of how to draw inferences combines in a seamless way with knowledge of what inferences are possible, likely, and worthwhile, given what is known or remains to be known about the phenomenon. The importance of methodology is not merely to design experiments well but also to sensitize one to different ways of viewing the world and to both generate and test hypotheses. A goal of this book was to provide initial stages in developing this level of mastery to foster a broader appreciation of the contribution of methodology to the substantive topics of our research.

Glossary

ABAB Design   A single-case experimental design in which the performance of a subject or group of subjects is evaluated over time across baseline (A) and intervention (B) conditions. A relation is demonstrated between the intervention and performance if performance changes in each phase in which intervention is presented and reverts to baseline or near baseline levels when it is withdrawn. Also called Reversal Design.

Accelerated, Multicohort Longitudinal Design   A prospective, longitudinal study in which multiple groups (two or more cohorts) are studied. Each group covers only a portion of the total time frame of interest. The groups overlap in ways that permit the investigator to discuss the entire developmental period in a special way.

Alpha (α)   The probability of rejecting a hypotheses (the null hypothesis) when the hypothesis is true. This is also referred to as a Type I error.

Alternate-Form Reliability   The correlation between different forms of the same measure when the items of the two forms are considered to represent the same population of items.

Analogue Research   Research that evaluates a particular condition or intervention under conditions that only resemble or approximate the situation to which one wishes to generalize.

Archival Records   Institutional, cultural, or other records that may be used as unobtrusive measures of performance.

Artifact   An extraneous influence in an experiment that may threaten validity, usually construct validity.

Attention–Placebo Control Group   A group in treatment research that is exposed to common factors associated with treatment such as attending treatment sessions, having contact with a therapist, hearing a logical rationale that describes the genesis of one's problem.

Attrition   Loss of subjects in an experiment. The loss of subjects can threaten all facets of experimental validity.

Baseline Assessment   Initial observations used in single-case designs that are obtained for multiple occasions (e.g., several days) prior to the intervention.

Baseline Phase   The initial phase of most single-case experimental designs in which performance is observed on some measure for several occasions (e.g., days) prior to implementing the experimental condition or intervention.

Behavioral Measures   Assessment that focuses on overt performance in laboratory or everyday settings. The performance attempts to sample directly the behavior of interest.

Beta (β)   The probability of accepting the null hypothesis when it is false. This is also referred to as a Type II error.

Blind   A term used to denote a procedure in which the experimenter and others associated with the investigation (e.g., staff, assessors) are kept naive with respect to the hypotheses and experimental conditions. Because of the confusion of the term with loss of vision and the pejorative reference to that condition, other terms (e.g., experimentally naive, masked conditions) are preferred.

Buffer Items   Items or content of a scale or measure that are intended to disguise or dilute the focus of interest evident in the measure. For example, items related to hobbies or physical health in a self-report scale on psychopathology might be added to serve as buffer or filler items.

Carryover Effect   In multiple-treatment designs, the impact of one treatment may linger or have impact on a subsequent treatment. This is equivalent to multiple-treatment interference.

Case-Control design   An observational research design in which the characteristic of interest is studied by selecting individuals to form groups who vary on that characteristic and studying current or past features of these groups. Minimally two groups are included, namely, those who show the characteristic of interest (cases) and those who do not (controls).

Case Study   An intensive, usually anecdotal, evaluation and report of an individual subject. Contrast with Single-Case Experimental Designs.

Ceiling Effect   This term refers to an upper limit in the range of scores of a measure. The limit of the score may not differentiate among groups that receive different conditions or may not permit demonstration of further movement or changes as a function of subsequent conditions in a multiple-treatment design. The term ceiling (or floor) effect is used depending on whether the upper or lower (floor) limit of the scale provides the restriction.

Changing-Criterion Design   A single-case experimental design that demonstrates the effect of an intervention by showing that performance changes in increments to match a performance criterion.

Clinical Significance   The extent to which the effect of an intervention makes an important difference to the clients or has practical or applied value.

Cohort   A group of subjects followed over time.

Cohort Designs   An observational research design in which the investigator studies an intact group or groups over time (i.e., prospectively). The design is also referred to as a prospective, longitudinal, study.

Comparison Methods   Methods of comparing clients with others, such as use of a normative sample as a means of evaluating the clinical significance of the changes achieved with an intervention.

Concurrent Validity   The correlation of a measure with performance on another measure or criterion at the same point in time.

Confederate   A person who works as an accomplice in the investigation; he or she appears to be another subject or part of the natural arrangement of the setting (e.g., someone in a waiting room).

Confirmability   A criterion invoked to evaluate data in qualitative research. The term refers to the extent to which an independent reviewer could conduct a formal audit and reevaluation of the procedures and generate the same findings.

Confound   A factor, other variable, or influence that covaries with the experimental condition or intervention.

Construct Validity   In the context of experimental design, this term refers to a type of experimental validity that pertains to the interpretation or basis of the effect that was demonstrated in an experiment. In the context of psychological assessment, the term refers to the extent to which a measure has been shown to assess the construct (e.g., intelligence) of interest.

Content Validity   Evidence that the content of the items of a measure reflects the construct or domain of interest; the relation of the items to the concept underlying the measure.

Continuous Assessment   A feature of single-case experimentation in which observations of performance are obtained repeatedly (e.g., daily) over time.

Convergent Validity   The correlation between measures that are expected to be related. The extent to which two measures assess the similar or related constructs. The validity of a given measure is suggested if the measure correlates with other measures with which it is expected to correlate. Contrast with Discriminant Validity.

Counterbalanced   A method of arranging conditions or tasks for the subjects so that a given condition or task is not confounded by the order in which it appears.

Credibility   A criterion invoked to evaluate data in qualitative research. The term reflects whether the methods and subjects are appropriate to the goals and are likely to represent the sample of interest.

Criterion Validity   Correlation of a measure with some other criterion. This can encompass concurrent or predictive validity. In addition, the notion is occasionally used in relation to a specific and often dichotomous criterion when performance on the measure is evaluated in relation to selected groups (e.g., depressed vs. nondepressed patients).

Crossover Design   A design in which two interventions are presented to each subject at different points in time. Halfway through the investigation, each subject is shifted to the other intervention or condition. The intervention is evaluated by comparing subject performance under the separate conditions.

Cross-Sectional Design   In clinical psychology, the most commonly used version of a case-control design in which subjects (cases and controls) are selected and assessed in relation to current characteristics. This design is to be distinguished from studies that are designed to evaluate events or experiences that happened in the past (retrospective studies) or the future (prospective studies).

Debriefing   Providing a description of the experiment and its purposes to the subject after the investigation when deception was used or information was withheld about the investigation. The purpose is to counteract or minimize any negative effects that the experiment may have had.

Deception   Presentation of misleading information or not disclosing fully procedures and details of the investigation.

Demand Characteristics   Cues of the situation that are associated with the experimental manipulation or intervention that may seem incidental but may contribute to or account for the results.

Dependability   A criterion invoked to evaluate data in qualitative research. The term pertains to the reliability of the conclusions and data evaluation leading to these conclusions.

Dependent Variable   The measure designed to reflect the impact of the independent variable, experimental manipulation, or intervention.

Diffusion or Imitation of Treatment   The inadvertent administration of treatment to a control group which diffuses or obscures the impact of the intervention. More generally, any unintended procedure that may reduce the extent to which experimental and control conditions are distinct.

Discriminant Validity   The correlation between measures that are expected not to relate to each other. The validity of a given measure is suggested if the measures shows little or no correlation with measures with which is it expected not to correlate because the measures assess dissimilar or unrelated constructs. Contrast with Convergent Validity.

Effect Size   A way of expressing the difference between alternative conditions (e.g., treatment vs. control) in terms of a common metric across measures and studies. The method is based on computing the difference between the means of interest on a particular measure and dividing the result by the standard deviation (e.g., pooled standard deviation of the conditions).

Effectiveness   The impact of treatment in the context of clinical settings and clinical work rather than in well-controlled laboratory conditions. In effectiveness studies, treatment is evaluated in clinical settings; clients are usually referred and therapists usually provide services without many of the rigorous controls of research. Effectiveness and efficacy studies can be considered to reflect a continuum of experimental control over several dimensions that may affect external validity of the results.

Efficacy   The impact of treatment in the context of a well-controlled study conducted under conditions that depart from exigencies of clinical settings. Usually in efficacy studies, there is careful control over the selection of cases, therapists, and the administration and monitoring of treatment. Distinguished from effectiveness or effectiveness studies.

Environmental Variables   Variables that consist of the environmental or situational conditions that are manipulated within an experiment. Varied conditions (e.g., treatments) or tasks provided to subjects are classified as environmental variables. Contrast with Subject Variables.

Experimenter Expectancies   Hypotheses, beliefs, and views on the part of the experimenter that may influence how the subjects perform. Expectancy effects are a threat to construct validity if they provide a plausible rival interpretation of the effects otherwise attributed to the intervention.

Experimenter   The person who conducts the experiment, runs subjects, or administers the conditions of research. See also Investigator.

Experiment-Wise Error Rate   The probability of a Type I error for the all comparisons in the experiment, given the number of tests. Contrast with Per Comparison Error Rate.

External Validity   The extent to which the results can be generalized or extended to persons, settings, times, measures, and characteristics other than those in the particular experimental arrangement.

Face Validity   The extent to which a measure appears to assess the construct of interest. This is not regarded as formal validation or part of the psychometric development or evaluation of a measure.

Factorial Designs   Group designs in which two or more variables are studied concurrently. For each variable, two or more levels are studied. The designs include the combinations of the variables (e.g., 2 x 2 design, which would encompass four groups) so that main effects of the separate variables and their combined effect (interaction) can be evaluated.

File-Drawer Problem   The possibility that the published studies represent a biased sample of all studies that have been completed for a given hypothesis. The published studies may reflect those that obtained statistical significance (i.e., 5 percent at the $p < .05$ level). There may be many more studies (the other 95 percent somewhere in a file drawer) that did not attain significance and were not published.

Follow-up Assessment   Evaluation of performance after posttreatment assessment.

Global Ratings   A type of measure that quantifies impressions of somewhat general characteristics. Such measures are referred to as global because they reflect overall impressions or summary statements of the construct of interest.

History   A threat to internal validity consisting of any event occurring in the experiment (other than the independent variable) or outside the experiment that may account for the results.

Independent Variable   The construct, experimental, manipulation, intervention, or factor whose impact will be evaluated in the investigation.

Informants   Persons in contact with the client, such as a spouse, peers, roommates, teachers, employers, friends, colleagues, and others who might be contacted to complete assessment or to provide information.

Informed Consent   Agreement to participate in research with full knowledge about the nature of treatment, the risks, benefits, expected outcomes, and alternatives. Three elements required for truly informed consent are competence, knowledge, and volition.

Instructional Variables   A specific type of environmental or situational manipulation in which the investigator varies what the subjects are told or are led to believe through verbal or written statements in the experiment.

Instrumentation   A threat to internal validity referring to changes in the measuring instrument or measurement procedures over time.

Interaction   The combined effect of two or more variables as demonstrated in a factorial design. Interactions signify that the effect of one variable (e.g., sex of the subject) depends on the level of another variable (e.g., age).

Internal Consistency   The degree of consistency or homogeneity of the items within a scale. Different reliability measures are used (e.g., split-half reliability, coefficient alpha, Kuder-Richardson 20 Formula).

Internal Validity   The extent to which the experimental manipulation or intervention, rather than extraneous influences, account for the results, changes, or group differences.

Interrater (Interscorer) Reliability   The extent to which different assessors, raters, or observers agree on the scores they provide when assessing, coding, or classifying subjects' performance.

Invasion of Privacy   Information of a personal nature that intrudes on what individuals or a group may view as private.

Investigator   The person who is responsible for designing and planning the experiment.

Ipsative   A comparison of the individual with himself or herself or comparison of scores from the same individual. Contrast with Normative.

Latin Square   The arrangement of experimental conditions in a multiple-treatment design in which each condition (task, treatment) occurs once in each ordinal position. Separate groups are used in the design, each of which receives a different sequence of the conditions.

Longitudinal Study   Research that seeks to understand the course of change or differences over time by following (assessing) a group or groups over time, often several years. Contrast with Cross-Sectional Study.

Loose Protocol Effect   A term referring to the failure of the investigator to specify critical details of the procedures, such as the rationale, script, or activities of the investigation, that guide the experimenter's behavior.

Main Effect   Equivalent to an overall effect of an independent variable. In a factorial design, main effects are the separate and independent effects of the variables in the design, and are distinguished from interactions. See Interaction.

Magnitude of Effect   A measure of the strength of the experimental effect or the magnitude of the contribution of the independent variable to performance on the dependent variable.

Matching   Grouping subjects together on the basis of their similarity on a particular characteristic or set of characteristics that is known or presumed to be related to the independent or dependent variables.

Maturation   Processes within the individual reflecting changes over time that may serve as a threat to internal validity.

Mediator   The process, mechanism, or means through which a variable produces a particular outcome; that is, beyond knowing that A may cause B, the mechanism elaborates precisely what happens (e.g., psychologically, biologically) to explain how B results.

Meta-Analysis   A quantitative method of evaluating a body of research in which effect size is used as the common metric. Studies are combined so that inferences can be drawn across studies and as a function of several of their characteristics (e.g., types of interventions).

Methodology   The diverse principles, procedures, and practices that govern research.

Mismatching   A procedure in which an effort is made to equalize groups that may be drawn from different samples. The danger is that the sample might be equal on a pretest measure of interest but regress toward different means at retesting. Changes due to statistical regression might be misinterpreted as an effect due to the experimental manipulation.

Moderator   A variable that influences the relationship of two variables of interest. The relationship between the variables (A and B) changes or is different as a functioning of some other variable (e.g., sex, age, ethnicity)

Multiple-Baseline Design   A single-case experimental design strategy in which the intervention is introduced across different behaviors, individuals, or situations at different points in time. A causal relation between the intervention and performance on the dependent measures is demonstrated if each behavior (individual or situation) changes when (and only when) the program is introduced.

Multiple Comparisons   The number of comparisons or statistical tests in an experiment.

Multiple Operationism   Defining a construct by several measures or in several ways. Typically, researchers are interested in a general construct (e.g., depression, anxiety) and seek relations among variables that are evident beyond any single operation or measure to define the construct.

Multiple-Treatment Designs   Designs in which two or more different conditions or treatments are presented to each subject. In most multiple-treatment designs in clinical research, separate groups are used so that different treatments can be presented in different orders.

Multiple-Treatment Interference   A potential threat to external validity when subjects are exposed to more than one condition or treatment within an experiment. The impact of a treatment or intervention may depend on the prior conditions to which subjects were exposed.

Multitrait–Multimethod Matrix   The set of correlations obtained from administering several measures to the same subject. These measures include two or more constructs (traits or characteristics), each of which is measured by two or more methods (e.g., self-report, direct observation). The purpose of the matrix is to evaluate convergent and discriminant validity.

Negative Results   A term commonly used to refer to a pattern of experimental results in which the differences or findings are not statistically significant.

No-Contact Control Group   A group that does not receive the experimental condition or intervention; subjects do not know they are participating in the research.

Nonequivalent Control Group   A group often used in quasi-experiments and selected to control for selected threats to internal validity. The group is referred to as nonequivalent because it is not formed through random assignment in the investigation.

Nonmanipulated Variables   Variables that are studied through selection of subjects or observation of characteristics imposed by nature. See Observational Research.

Nonspecific Treatment Control Group   See Attention–Placebo Control Group.

Nonstatistical Evaluation   A method of data evaluation based on visual inspection criteria. Characteristics of the data (e.g., changes in means, trends, and level, and the latency of change) are used to infer reliability of the impact of the experimental manipulation.

Normative   A comparison of the individual with others, especially with a group of individuals who are functioning adequately in everyday life. Contrast with Ipsative.

Normative Range   A range of performance among a nonreferred, community sample that is used as a point of reference for evaluating the clinical significance of change in intervention studies.

No-Treatment Control Group   A group that does not receive the experimental condition or intervention.

Novelty Effects   A potential threat to external validity when the effects of an intervention may depend in part on their innovativeness or novelty in the situation.

Null Hypothesis (H_o)   The hypothesis that specifies that there is no difference between conditions or groups in the experiment on the dependent measures of interest.

Observational Research   A type of research design in which the relations among variables are observed but not manipulated. Typically, the focus is on characteristics of different subjects or the relations among nonmanipulated variables.

Obtrusive Measures   Any measure or measurement condition in which subjects are aware that some facet of their performance is assessed. See Reactivity.

Operational Definition   Defining a concept by the specific operations or measures that are to be used in an experiment. The specific way in which the construct will be defined for inclusion in the investigation.

Order Effects   In multiple-treatment designs, the impact of a treatment may depend on whether it appears first (or in some other place) in the treatments that are presented to the subjects. If the position of the treatments influences the results, this is referred to as an order effect. Compare with Sequence Effects.

Patched-Up Control Group   A group that is not randomly composed from the pool of subjects in the study. The group is added to the design to help rule out specific rival hypotheses and decrease the plausibility of specific threats to internal validity.

Per Comparison Error Rate   The probability of a Type I error for a specific comparison or statistical test of differences when several comparisons are made. Contrast with Experiment-Wise Error Rate.

Physical Traces   Unobtrusive measures that consist of selective wear (erosion) or deposit (accretion) of materials.

Placebo   A substance that has no active pharmacological properties that would be expected to produce change.

Postexperimental Inquiry   A method of evaluating whether demand characteristics may account for the results by asking the subjects after the experiment about their perceptions of the purpose of the experiment, what the experimenter expected from them, and how they were supposed to respond.

Posttest-Only Control Group Design   An experimental design (with a minimum of two groups) in which no pretest is given. The effect of the experimental condition across groups is assessed on a postintervention measure only.

Power   The probability of rejecting the null hypothesis (that there are no differences) when in fact the hypothesis is false. Alternatively, detecting a difference between groups when in fact a difference truly exists.

Predictive Validity   The correlation of a measure at one point in time with performance on another measure or criterion at some point in the future.

Preinquiry   A method of evaluating whether demand characteristics may account for the results by conveying information to the subjects about the experiment without actually running them through the conditions. Subjects are also asked to complete the dependent measures to see whether their performance yields the expected results.

Pretest–Posttest Control Group Design   An experimental design with a minimum of two groups. Usually, one group receives the experimental condition and the other does not. The essential feature of the design is that subjects are tested before and after the intervention.

Pretest Sensitization   Effect of administering a pretest. Use of a pretest may alter the influence of the experimental condition that follows.

Probability Pyramiding   The error rate or risk of a Type I error that comes from conducting multiple comparisons (e.g., *t* tests) in an experiment.

Projective Techniques   Measures that assess facets of personality based on the presentation of ambiguous tasks or materials. Subjects respond with minimal situational cues or constraints.

Psychometric Characteristics   A general term that encompasses diverse types of reliability and validity evidence in behalf of a measure.

Psychophysiological Measures   Assessment techniques designed to quantify biological events as they relate to psychological states.

Qualitative Research   An approach to research that focuses on narrative accounts, description, interpretation, context, and meaning. The goal is to describe, interpret, and understand the phenomena of interest and to do so in the context in which experience occurs. Distinguished from the more familiar Quantitative Research.

Quantitative Research   The dominant paradigm for empirical research in psychology and the sciences more generally. The paradigm involves use of operational definitions, careful control of the subject matter, efforts to isolate variables of interest, quantification of constructs, and statistical analyses. Distinguished from Qualitative Research.

Quasi-Experimental Design   A design in which the conditions of true experiments are only approximated. Restrictions are placed on some facet of the design, such as the assignment of cases randomly to conditions, which affects the strength of the inferences that can be drawn.

Random Assignment   Allocating or assigning subjects to groups in such a way that the probability of each subject appearing in any of the groups is equal. This is usually accomplished by determining the group to which each subject is assigned by a table of random numbers.

Randomized Controlled Clinical Trial   A treatment outcome study in which clients with a particular problem are randomly assigned to various treatment and control conditions. This type of study is recognized to be the best and most definitive way of demonstrating that an intervention is effective.

Random Selection   Drawing subjects from a population in such a way that each member of the population has an equal probability of being drawn.

Reactivity   Performance that is altered as a function of subject awareness (e.g., of the measurement procedures, of participation in an experiment).

Regression Effect   See Statistical Regression.

Replication   Repetition of an experiment or repetition of the findings of an experiment.

Research Design   The plan or arrangement that is used to examine the question of interest; the manner in which conditions are planned so as to permit valid inferences.

Retrospective Design   A case-control design designed to draw inferences about some antecedent condition that has resulted in or is associated with the outcome. Subjects are identified who already show the outcome of interest (cases) and are compared with subjects who do not show the outcome (controls). Assessment focuses on some other characteristic in the past.

Reversal Phase   A phase or period in single-case designs in which the baseline (non-intervention) condition is reintroduced to see whether performance returns to or approximates the level of the original baseline.

Risk Factor   A characteristic that is an antecedent to and increases the likelihood of an outcome of interest. A correlate of an outcome of interest in which the time sequence is established.

Samples of Convenience   Subjects included in an investigation who appear to be selected merely because they are available regardless of whether they provide a suitable or optional test of the hypotheses or conditions of interest.

Sample Size   The number of cases included, which might refer to the overall number of subjects in the study (N) or the number of subjects within a group (n).

Sequence Effects   In multiple-treatment designs, several treatments may be presented to the subject. A series of treatments is provided (e.g., treatment A, B, then C for some subjects and B, C, then A for other subjects, and so on for other combinations). If the sequence yields different outcomes, this is referred to as sequence effects. See Order Effects.

Self-Report Inventories   Questionnaires and scales in which the subjects report on aspects of their own personality views or behaviors.

Significance Level   See Alpha.

Simulators   A method of estimating whether demand characteristics may operate by asking subjects to act as if they had received the treatment or intervention even though they actually do not receive treatment. Simulators are run through the assessment procedures of the investigation by an experimenter who is blind as to who is a simulator and who is a real subject.

Single-Case Experimental Designs   Research designs in which the effects of an intervention can be evaluated with the single case (i.e., one subject).

Single Operationism Defining a construct by a single measure or one operation. Contrast with Multiple Operationism.

Social Impact Measures Measures in outcome research that are important in everyday life or to society at large.

Solomon Four-Group Design An experimental design that is used to evaluate the effect of pretesting. The design can be considered as a combination of the pretest–posttest control group design and a posttest-only design in which pretest (provided vs. not provided) and the experimental intervention (treatment vs. no treatment) are combined.

Stable Rate Performance obtained from continuous observations over time, as in single-case designs, in which there is little or no trend (slope) or variability in the data.

Statistical Conclusion Validity The extent to which a relation between independent and dependent variables can be shown on the basis of quantitative and statistical considerations of the investigation.

Statistical Evaluation Applying statistical tests to assess whether the obtained results are reliable or whether differences in performance are likely to have occurred by chance.

Statistical Power See Power.

Statistical Regression The tendency of extreme scores on any measure to revert (or regress) toward the mean of a distribution when the measurement device is readministered. Regression is a function of the amount of error in the measure and the test–retest correlation.

Statistical Significance A criterion used to evaluate the extent to which the results of a study (e.g., differences between groups or changes within groups) are likely to be to be due to genuine rather than chance effects. A statistically significant difference indicates that the probability level is equal to or below the level of confidence selected (e.g., $p < .05$); that is, if the experiment were conducted repeatedly, the finding would occur $\frac{5}{100}$ on a chance basis.

Subject Roles Ways of responding that subjects may adopt in response to the cues of the experiment.

Subject Variables Variables that are based on features within the individual or circumstances to which they were exposed. These variables are usually not manipulated experimentally.

Subjective Evaluation A method of evaluating the clinical significance of an intervention outcome by assessing the opinions of clients themselves, individuals who are likely to have contact with the client, or persons in a position of expertise. The study question addressed by this method of evaluation is whether changes in treatment have led to differences in how the client is viewed by others.

Subject-Selection Biases Factors that operate in selection of subjects or selective loss or retention of subjects during the course of the experiment and that can affect experimental validity. Primary examples are selection, recruitment, or screening procedures that might restrict the generality (external validity) of the findings and loss of subjects that might alter group composition and lead to differences that would be mistaken for an intervention effect (internal validity).

Testing A threat to internal validity consisting of the effects of taking a test on repeated occasions. Performance may change as a function of repeated exposure to the measure rather than to the independent variable or experimental condition.

Test–Retest Reliability The stability of test scores over time; the correlation of scores from one administration of the test with scores on the same instrument after a particular time interval has elapsed.

Test Sensitization   Alteration of subject performance due to administration of a test before (pretest) or after (posttest) the experimental condition or intervention. The test may influence (e.g., augment) the effect of the experimental condition. Test sensitization is a potential threat to external validity if the effect of the experimental condition may not generalize to different testing conditions.

Threats to Construct Validity   Features associated with the experimental condition or intervention that interfere with drawing inferences about the basis for the difference between groups.

Threats to External Validity   Characteristics of the experiment that may limit the generality of the results.

Threats to Internal Validity   Factors or influences other than the independent variable that could explain the results.

Threats to Statistical Conclusion Validity   Considerations within the investigation that undermine the quantitative evaluation of the data.

Transferability   A criterion invoked to evaluate data in qualitative research. The term pertains to whether the data are limited to particular context (are context bound). Transferability is evaluated by looking at special characteristics (unrepresentativeness) of the sample.

Treatment Integrity   The fidelity with which treatment is rendered in an investigation.

Triangulation   The extent to which data from separate sources converge to support the conclusions; also used as a criterion to evaluate data in qualitative research.

True Experiment   A type of research in which the arrangement permits maximum control over the independent variables or conditions of interest. The investigator is able to assign subjects to different conditions on a random basis, to include various conditions (e.g., treatment and control conditions) as required by the design, and to control possible sources of bias that permit the comparison of interest within the experiment.

Trustworthiness   A criterion used to evaluate data in qualitative research. The multiple components of the criterion are credibility, transferability, dependability, and confirmability of the data.

Type I Error   See Alpha.

Type II Error   See Beta.

Unobtrusive Measures   Measures that are outside the awareness of the subject.

Visual Inspection   A method of data evaluation commonly used in single-case research and based on examining the pattern of change (means, level, trend, latency of change) across phases.

Waiting-List Control Group   A group that is designed to control for threats to internal validity. The experimental condition or intervention is not provided during the period that experimental subjects receive the intervention. After this period, subjects in this control group receive the intervention.

Yoked Control Group   A group or control condition designed to ensure that groups are equal with respect to potentially important but conceptually and procedurally irrelevant factors that might account for group differences. Yoking refers to equalizing the groups on a particular variable that might systematically vary across conditions.

References

Achenbach, T.M. (1991). *Integrative guide for the 1991 CBCL/4–18, YSR, and TRF profiles.* Burlington, VT: University of Vermont, Department of Psychiatry.

Adam, K.S., Sheldon-Keller, A.E., & West, M. (1996). Attachment organization and history of suicidal behavior in clinical adolescents. *Journal of Consulting and Clinical Psychology, 64,* 264–272.

Adams, H.E., Wright, L.W., Jr., & Lohr, B.A. (1996). Is homophobia associated with homosexual arousal? *Journal of Abnormal Psychology, 105,* 440–445.

Addis, M.E. (1997). Evaluating the treatment manual as a means of disseminating empirically validated psychotherapies. *Clinical Psychology: Science and Practice, 4,* 1–11.

Adler, N.E., Boyce, T., Chesney, M.A., Cohen, S., Folkman, S., Kahn, R.L., & Syme, S.L. (1994). Socioeconomic status and health: The challenge of the gradient. *American Psychologist, 49,* 15–24.

Adler, P.A., & Adler, P. (1994). Observational techniques. In N.H Denzin & Y.S. Lincoln (Eds.), *Handbook of qualitative research* (pp. 377–392). Thousand Oaks, CA: Sage.

Ager, A. (Ed.). (1991). *Microcomputers and clinical psychology: Issues, applications, and future developments.* New York: Wiley.

Aiken, L.S., West, S.G., Sechrest, L., & Reno, R.R. (1990). Graduate training in statistics, methodology, and measurement in psychology: A survey of PhD programs in North America. *American Psychologist, 45,* 721–734.

Aldarondo, E., & Sugarman, D.B. (1996). Risk marker analysis of the cessation and persistence of wife assault. *Journal of Consulting and Clinical Psychology, 64,* 1010–1019.

Alden, L. (1989). Short-term structured treatment for avoidant personality disorder. *Journal of Consulting and Clinical Psychology, 57,* 756–764.

American Psychiatric Association. (1994). *Diagnostic and statistical manual of mental disorders* (4th ed. revised). Washington, DC: American Psychiatric Association.

American Psychological Association (1990). *Journals in psychology: A resource listing for authors* (3rd ed.). Washington, DC: American Psychological Association.

American Psychological Association (1992). *Ethical principles of psychologists and code of conduct.* Washington, DC: American Psychological Association.

American Psychological Association (1994). *Publication manual of the American Psychological Association* (4th ed.). Washington, DC: American Psychological Association.

Angoff, W.H. (1988). Validity: An evolving concept. In H. Wainer & H.I. Braun (Eds.), *Test validity.* Hillsdale, NJ: Erlbaum.

Austin, N.K., Liberman., R.P., King, L.W., & DeRisi, W.J. (1976). A comparative evaluation of two day hospitals: Goal attainment scaling of behavior therapy vs. milieu therapy. *Journal of Nervous and Mental Disease, 163*, 253–262.

Azrin, N.H., Hontos, P.T., & Besalel-Azrin, V. (1979). Elimination of enuresis without a conditioning apparatus: An extension by office instruction of the child and parents. *Behavior Therapy, 10*, 14–19.

Azrin, N.H., Naster, B.J., & Jones, R. (1973). Reciprocity counseling: A rapid learning-based procedure for marital counseling. *Behaviour Research and Therapy, 11*, 365–382.

Baekeland, F., & Lundwall, L. (1975). Dropping out of treatment: A critical review. *Psychological Bulletin, 82*, 738–783.

Baer, D.M. (1977). Perhaps it would be better not to know everything. *Journal of Applied Behavior Analysis, 10*, 167–172.

Bailar, J.C. III., & Patterson, K. (1985). Journal of peer review: The need for a research agenda. *New England Journal of Medicine, 312*, 654–657.

Bakan, D. (1966). The test of significance in psychological research. *Psychological Bulletin, 66*, 423–437.

Balter, M. (1996). New hope in HIV disease. *Science, 274*, 1988.

Banken, D.M., & Wilson, G.L. (1992). Treatment acceptability of alternative therapies for depression: A comparative analysis. *Psychotherapy, 29*, 610–619.

Barber, J.G., Bradshaw, R., & Walsh, C. (1989). Reducing alcohol consumption through television advertising. *Journal of Consulting and Clinical Psychology, 57*, 613–618.

Barber, T.X. (1976). *Pitfalls in human research: Ten pivotal points.* Elmsford, NY: Pergamon.

Barkham, M., Rees, A., Stiles, W.B., Shapiro, D.A., Hardy, G.E., & Reynolds, S. (1996). Dose–effect relations in time-limited psychotherapy for depression. *Journal of Consulting and Clinical Psychology, 64*, 927–935.

Barlow, D.H., & Hersen, M. (1984). *Single-case experimental designs: Strategies for studying behavior change* (2nd ed.). Elmsford, NY: Pergamon.

Barlow, D.H., Reynolds, J., & Agras, W.S. (1973). Gender identity change in a transsexual. *Archives of General Psychiatry, 29*, 569–576.

Barnett, P.A., & Gotlib, I.H. (1988). Psychosocial functioning and depression: Distinguishing among antecedents, concomitants, and consequences. *Psychological Bulletin, 104*, 97–126.

Baron, R.M., & Kenny, D.A. (1986). The moderator–mediator variable distinction in social psychological research: Conceptual, strategic, and statistical considerations. *Journal of Personality and Social Psychology, 51*, 1173–1182.

Barrett, P.M., Dadds, M.R., & Rapee, R.M. (1996). Family treatment of childhood anxiety: A controlled trial. *Journal of Consulting and Clinical Psychology, 64*, 333–342.

Barthel, C.N., & Holmes. D.S. (1968). High school yearbooks: A nonreactive measure of social isolation in graduates who later became schizophrenic. *Journal of Abnormal Psychology, 73*, 313–316.

Barton, S. (1994). Chaos, self-organization, and psychology. *American Psychologist, 49*, 5–14.

Beatty, W.W. (1972). How blind is blind? A simple procedure for estimating observer naiveté. *Psychological Bulletin, 78*, 70–71.

Beck, A.T., Rush, A.J., Shaw, B.F., & Emery, G. (1979). *Cognitive therapy of depression.* New York: Guilford.

Beck, A.T., Weissman, A., Lester, D., & Trexler, L. (1974). The measurement of pessimism: The Hopelessness Scale. *Journal of Consulting and Clinical psychology. 42,* 861–865.

Bell, R. (1992). *Impure science: Fraud, compromise, and political influence in scientific research.* New York: Wiley.

Beneke, W.N., & Harris, M.B. (1972). Teaching self-control of study behavior. *Behaviour Research and Therapy, 10,* 35–41.

Berger, J.O., & Berry, D.A. (1988). Statistical analysis and the illusion of objectivity. *American Scientist, 76,* 159–165.

Berkson, J. (1938). Some difficulties of interpretation encountered in the application of the chi-square test. *Journal of the American Statistical Association, 33,* 526–542.

Betancourt, H., & Lopéz, S.R. (1993). The study of culture, ethnicity, and race in American Psychology. *American Psychologist, 48,* 629–637.

Beutler, L.E., Brown, M.T., Crothers, L., Booker, K., & Seabrook, M.K. (1996). The dilemma of factitious demographic distinctions in psychological research. *Journal of Consulting and Clinical Psychology, 64,* 892–902.

Beutler, L.E., Machado, P.P.P., & Neufeldt, S.A. (1994). Therapist variables. In A.E. Bergin & S.L. Garfield (Eds.), *Handbook of psychotherapy and behavior change* (4th ed., pp. 229–269). New York: Wiley.

Billings, D.C., & Wasik, B.H. (1985). Self-instructional training with preschoolers: An attempt to replicate. *Journal of Applied Behavior Analysis, 18,* 61–67.

Bloom, L.J., Weigel, R.G., & Trautt, G.M. (1977). "Therapeugenic" factors in psychotherapy: Effects of office decor and subject–therapist pairing on the perception of credibility. *Journal of Consulting and Clinical Psychology, 45,* 867–873.

Bolgar, H. (1965). The case study method. In B.B. Wolman (Ed.), *Handbook of clinical psychology* (pp. 28–38). New York: McGraw-Hill.

Bootzin, R.R. (1985). The role of expectancy in behavior change. In L. White, B. Tursky, G.E. Schwartz (Eds.), *Placebo: Theory, research, and mechanisms.* New York: Guilford.

Borduin, C.M., Mann, B.J., Cone, L.T., Henggeler, S.W., Fucci, B.R., Blaske, D.M., & Williams, R.A. (1995). Multisystemic treatment of serious juvenile offenders: Long-term prevention of criminality and violence. *Journal of Consulting and Clinical Psychology, 63,* 569–578.

Bornstein, P.H., & Quevillon, R.P. (1976). The effects of a self-instructional package on overactive preschool boys. *Journal of Applied Behavior Analysis, 9,* 179–188.

Botvin, G.J., Baker, E., Filazzola, A.D., & Botvin, E.M. (1990). A cognitive–behavioral approach to substance abuse prevention: One-year follow-up. *Addictive Behaviors, 15,* 47–63.

Bowlby, J. (1969). *Attachment and loss. Vol. I: Attachment.* London: Hogarth Press.

Bozarth, J.D., & Roberts, R. R. (1972). Signifying significant significance. *American Psychologist, 27,* 774–775.

Bracht, G.H., & Glass, G.V. (1968). The external validity of experiments. *American Educational Research Journal, 5,* 437–474.

Braver, M.C.W., & Braver, S.L. (1988). Statistical treatment of the Solomon Four-Group Design: A meta-analytic approach. *Psychological Bulletin, 104,* 150–154.

Breuer, J., & Freud, S. (1957). *Studies in hysteria.* New York: Basic Books.

Brewin, C.R., Andrews, B., & Gotlib, I.H. (1993). Psychopathology and early experience: A reappraisal of retrospective reports. *Psychological Bulletin, 113,* 82–98.

Briere, J., & Runtz, M. (1988). Post sexual abuse trauma. In G.E. Wyatt & G.J. Powell (Eds.) *Lasting effects of child abuse* (pp. 85–99). Newbury Park, CA: Sage.

Broad, W., & Wade, N. (1982). *Betrayers of truth*. New York: Simon & Schuster.

Brody, E.M., & Farber, B.A. (1989). Effects of psychotherapy on significant others. *Professional Psychology: Research and Practice, 20*, 116–122.

Brown, J. (1987). A review of meta-analyses conducted on psychotherapy outcome research. *Clinical Psychology Review, 7*, 1–23.

Brown, T.A., Antony, M.M., & Barlow, D.H. (1995). Diagnostic comorbidity in panic disorder: Effect on treatment outcome and course of comorbid diagnoses following treatment. *Journal of Consulting and Clinical Psychology, 63*, 408–418.

Brunswik, E. (1955). Representative design and probabilistic theory in a functional psychology. *Psychological Review, 62*, 193–217.

Bryant, L.E., & Budd, K.S. (1982). Self-instructional training to increase independent work performance in preschoolers. *Journal of Applied Behavior Analysis, 15*, 259–271.

Butcher, J.N. (1987). *Computerized psychological assessment: A practitioner's guide*. New York: Basic Books.

Butcher, J.N., Graham, J.R., Williams, C.L., & Ben-Porath, Y.S. (1990). *Development and use of the MMPI-2 content scales*. Minneapolis, MN: University of Minnesota Press.

Byrd, R.J. (1988). Positive therapeutic effects of intercessory prayer in a coronary care unit population. *Southern Medical Journal, 81*, 826–829.

Campbell, D.T., & Fiske, D. (1959). Convergent and discriminant validation by the multitrait–multimethod matrix. *Psychological Bulletin, 56*, 81–105.

Campbell, D.T., & Stanley, J.C. (1963). Experimental and quasi-experimental designs for research and teaching. In N.L. Gage (Ed.), *Handbook of research on teaching*. Chicago: Rand McNally.

Carlsmith, J.M., Ellsworth, P.C., & Aronson, E. (1976). *Methods of research in social psychology*. Reading, MA: Addison-Wesley.

Carroll, K.M., Rounsaville, B.J., & Nich, C. (1994). Blind man's bluff: Effectiveness and significance of psychotherapy and pharmacotherapy blinding procedures in a clinical trial. *Journal of Consulting and Clinical Psychology, 62*, 276–280.

Caspi, A., Moffitt, T.E., Newman, D.L., & Silva, P.A. (1996). Behavioral observations at age 3 predict adult psychiatric disorders. *Archives of General Psychiatry, 53*, 1033–1039.

Chassan, J.B. (1967). *Research design in clinical psychology and psychiatry*. New York: Appleton-Century-Crofts.

Chow, S.L. (1988). Significance test or effect size? *Psychological Bulletin, 103*, 105–110.

Christian, N.M. (1995). Call for bright yellow firetrucks has many firefighters seeing red. *Wall Street Journal*, June 26, p. B1.

Church, R.M. (1964). Systematic effect of random error in the yoked control design. *Psychological Bulletin, 62*, 122–131.

Cicchetti, D.V. (1991) The reliability of the peer review for manuscript and grant submissions: A cross-disciplinary investigation. *Behavioral and Brain Sciences, 14*, 119–186.

Clark, K.E. (1967). *Invasion of privacy in the investigation of human behavior*. Paper read at Eastern Psychological Association, Boston, MA.

Cohen, J. (1988). *Statistical power analysis in the behavioral sciences* (2nd ed.). Hillsdale, NJ: Erlbaum.

Cohen, J. (1992). A power primer. *Psychological Bulletin, 112*, 155–159.

Cohen, J. (1996). Likely HIV cofactor found. *Science, 272*, 809–810.

Committee on Biomedical Research in the Veterans Administration. (1977). *Biomedical research in the Veterans Administration*. Washington, DC: National Academy of Sciences.

Cook, T.D., & Campbell, D.T. (Eds.). (1979). *Quasi-experimentation: Design and analysis issues for field settings.* Chicago: Rand McNally.

Cook, T.D., Cooper, H., Cordray, D.S., Hartmann, H., Hedges, L.V., Light, R.J., Louis, T.A., & Mosteller, F. (1992). *Meta-analysis for explanation: A casebook.* New York: Russell Sage Foundation.

Cooney, N.L., Kadden, R.M., Litt, M.D., & Getter, H. (1991). Matching alcoholics to coping skills or interactional therapies: Two-year follow-up. *Journal of Consulting and Clinical Psychology, 59,* 598–601.

Considine, R.V., Considine, E.L., Williams, C.J., Hyde, T.M., & Caro, J.F. (1996). The hypothalamic leptin receptor in humans: Identification of incidental sequence polymorphisms and absence of the db-db mouse and fa-fa rat mutations. *Diabetes, 45,* 992–994.

Consumer Reports Editors. (1995). Mental health: Does therapy help? *Consumer Reports* (November) 734–739.

Cowles, M., & Davis, C. (1982). On the origins of the .05 level of statistical significance. *American Psychologist, 37,* 553–558.

Craik, K.H. (1986). Personality research methods: An historical perspective. *Journal of Personality, 54,* 18–51.

Cronbach, L.J. (1957). The two disciplines of scientific psychology. *American Psychologist, 12,* 671–684.

Cronbach, L.J. (1975). Beyond the two disciplines of scientific psychology. *American Psychologist, 30,* 116–127.

Cronbach, L.J., & Meehl, P.E. (1955). Construct validity in psychological tests. *Psychological Bulletin, 52,* 281–302.

Crowe, M.J., Marks, I.M., Agras, W.S., & Leitenberg, H. (1972). Time-limited desensitization, implosion and shaping for phobic patients: A crossover study. *Behaviour Research and Therapy, 10,* 319–328.

Crowne, D.P., & Marlowe, D. (1964). *The approval motive: Studies in evaluative dependence.* New York: Wiley.

Cunningham, C.E., Bremner, R., & Boyle, M. (1995). Large group community-based parenting programs for families of preschoolers at risk for disruptive behaviour disorders: Utilization, cost effectiveness, and outcome. *Journal of Child Psychology and Psychiatry, 36,* 1141–1159.

Davis, W.E. (1973). The irregular discharge as an unobtrusive measure of discontent among young psychiatric patients. *Journal of Abnormal Psychology, 81,* 17–21.

Denissenko, M.F., Pao, A., Tang, M., & Pfeifer, G.P. (1996). Preferential formation of benzo[a]pyrene adducts at lung cancer mutational hotspots in *P53. Science, 274,* 430–432.

Denzin, N.H, & Lincoln, Y.S. (Eds.) (1994). *Handbook of qualitative research.* Thousand Oaks, CA: Sage.

DeProspero, A., & Cohen, S. (1979). Inconsistent visual analysis of intrasubject data. *Journal of Applied Behavior Analysis, 12,* 573–579.

DeRubeis, R.J., Hollon, S.E., Evans, M.D., & Bemis, K.M. (1982). Can psychotherapies for depression be discriminated? A systematic investigation of cognitive therapy and interpersonal therapy. *Journal of Consulting and Clinical Psychology, 50,* 744–756.

DeVellis, R.F. (1991). *Scale development: Theory and applications.* Newbury Park, CA: Sage.

Dewan, M.J., & Koss, M. (1989). The clinical impact of the side effects of psychotropic drugs. In S. Fisher & R.P. Greenberg (Eds.), *The limits of biological treatments for psychological distress* (pp. 189–234). Hillsdale, NJ: Erlbaum.

Dies, R.R., & Greenberg, B. (1976). Effects of physical contact in an encounter group context. *Journal of Consulting and Clinical Psychology, 44,* 400–405.

DiLulio, J.J. (1997). What the crime statistics don't tell you. *Wall Street Journal,* January 8, p. A22.

Dishion, T.J., & Andrews, D.W. (1995). Preventing escalation in problem behaviors with high-risk young adolescents: Immediate and 1-year outcomes. *Journal of Consulting and Clinical Psychology, 63,* 538–548.

Dishion, T.J., Patterson, G.R., & Kavanagh, K.A. (1992). An experimental test of the coercion model: Linking theory, measurement, and intervention. In J. McCord & R.E. Tremblay (Eds.), *Preventing antisocial behavior* (pp. 253–282). New York: Guilford.

Dodge, K.A., Pettit, G.S., & Bates, J.E. (1994) Socialization mediators of the relation between socioeconomic status and child conduct problems. *Child Development, 65,* 649–655.

Dossey, L. (1993). *Healing worlds: The power of prayer and the practice of medicine.* New York: Harper Collins.

Dukes, W.F. (1965). N = 1. *Psychological Bulletin, 64,* 74–79.

Durlak, J.A., Wells, A.M., Cotten, J.K., & Johnson, S. (1995). Analysis of selected methodological issues in child psychotherapy research. *Journal of Clinical Child Psychology, 24,* 141–148.

Eaton, W.W., & Kessler, L. (Eds.). (1985). *Epidemiologic field methods in psychiatry: The NIMH Epidemiologic Catchment Area Program.* NY: Academic Press.

Edwards, A.L. (1957). *The social desirability variable in personality assessment and research.* New York: Dryden.

Elkin, I., Parloff, M.B, Hadley, S.W., & Autry, J.H. (1985). NIMH Treatment of Depression Collaborative Research Program: Background and research plan. *Archives of General Psychiatry, 42,* 305–316.

Elkin, I., Shea, M.T., Watkins, J.T., Imber, S.D., Sotsky, S.M., Collins, J.F., Glass, D.R., Pilkonis, P.A., Leber, W.R., Docherty, J.P., Fiester, S.J., & Parloff, M.B. (1989). NIMH Treatment of Depression Collaborative Research Program: General effectiveness of treatments. *Archives of General Psychiatry, 46,* 971–982.

Elliott, D.S., Dunford, F.W., & Huizinga, D. (1987). The identification and prediction of career offenders utilizing self-reported and official data. In J.D. Burchard & S.N. Burchard (Eds.), *Preventing delinquent behavior* (pp. 90–121). Newbury Park, CA: Sage.

Ellis, A. (1957). Outcome of employing three techniques of psychotherapy. *Journal of Clinical Psychology, 13,* 344–350.

Endler, N.S. (1990). *Holiday of darkness: A psychologist's personal journal out of his depression* (revised ed.). Toronto: Wall and Thompson.

Enserink, M. (1996). Fraud and ethics charges hit stroke drug trial. *Science, 274,* 2004.

Erdberg, P. (1990). Rorschach assessment. In G. Goldstein & M. Hersen (Eds.), *Handbook of psychological assessment* (2nd ed., pp. 387–399). Elmsford, NY: Pergamon.

Erdman, H.P., Klein, M.H., & Greist, J.H. (1985). Direct patient computer interviewing. *Journal of Consulting and Clinical Psychology, 53,* 760–773.

Esser, G., Schmidt, M.H., & Woerner, W. (1990). Epidemiology and course of psychiatric disorders in school-age children: Results of a longitudinal study. *Journal of Child Psychology and Psychiatry, 31,* 243–263.

Exner, J.E. (1995). Comment on "Narcissism in the comprehensive system for the Rorschach." *Clinical Psychology: Science and Practice, 2,* 200–206.

Eysenck, H.J. (1995). The outcome problem in psychotherapy: What have we learned? *Behaviour Research and Therapy, 32,* 477–495.

Farrington, D.P. (1991). Childhood aggression and adult violence: Early precursors and later life outcomes. In D.J. Pepler & K.H. Rubin (Eds.). *The development and treatment of childhood aggression* (pp. 5–29). Hillsdale, NJ: Erlbaum.

Farrington, D.P. (1992). The need for longitudinal–experimental research on offending and antisocial behavior. In J. McCord & R.E. Tremblay (Eds.), *Preventing antisocial behavior: Interventions from birth through adolescence* (pp. 353–376). New York: Guilford.

Feldman, J.J., Hyman, H., & Hart, C.W. (1951). A field study of interviewer effects on the quality of survey data. *Public Opinion Quarterly, 15,* 734–761.

Feldman, R.A., Caplinger, T.E., & Wodarski, J.S. (1983). *The St. Louis conundrum: The effective treatment of antisocial youths.* Englewood Cliffs, NJ: Prentice-Hall.

Festinger, L., & Carlsmith, J.M. (1959). Cognitive consequences of forced compliance. *Journal of Abnormal and Social Psychology, 58,* 203–210.

Fine, M.A., & Kurdek, L.A. (1993) Reflections on determining authorship credit and authorship order on faculty–student collaborations. *American Psychologist, 48,* 1141–1147.

Fisher, B., Bauer, M., Margolese, R., Poisson, R., Pilch, Y., Redmond, C., Fisher, E., Wolmark, N., Deutsch, M., Montague, E., Saffer, E., Wickerham, I., Lerner, H., Glass, A., Shibata, H., Deckers, P., Ketcham, R., Dishi, R., & Russell, I. (1985). Five-year results of a randomized clinical trial comparing total mastectomy and segmental mastectomy with or without radiation in the treatment of breast cancer. *New England Journal of Medicine, 312,* 665–673.

Fisher, E.R., Costantino, J., Fisher, B., Palekar, A.S., Paik, S.M., Suarez, C.M., & Wolmark, N. (1996). Pathologic findings from the National Surgical Adjuvant Breast Project (NSABP) protocol B-17: Five-year observations concerning lobular carcinoma in situ. *Cancer, 78,* 1403–1416.

Fisher, J.D., Silver, R.C., Chinsky, J.M., Goff, B., Klar, Y., & Zagieboylo, C. (1989). Psychological effects of participation in a large group awareness training. *Journal of Consulting and Clinical Psychology, 57,* 747–755.

Fisher, R.A. (1925). *Statistical methods for research workers.* London: Oliver & Boyd.

Fisher, R.A., & Yates, F. (1963). *Statistical tables for biological, agricultural and medical research.* Edinburgh: Oliver & Boyd.

Fisher, S., & Greenberg, R.P. (Eds.). (1989). *The limits of biological treatments for psychological distress: Comparisons with psychotherapy and placebo.* Hillsdale, NJ: Erlbaum.

Flick, S.N. (1988). Managing attrition in clinical research. *Clinical Psychology Review, 8,* 499–515.

Forgatch, M.S. (1991). The clinical science vortex: A developing theory of antisocial behavior. In D.J. Pepler & K.H. Rubin (Eds.), *The development and treatment of childhood aggression* (pp. 291–315). Hillsdale, NJ: Erlbaum.

Foulks, E.F. (1987). Social stratification and alcohol use in North Alaska. *Journal of Community Psychology, 15,* 349–356.

Foulks, E.F. (1989). Misalliances in the Barrow Alcohol Study. *American Indian and Native Alaska Mental Health Research, 2 (3),* 7–17.

Foxx, R.M., & Rubinoff, A. (1979). Behavioral treatment of caffeinism: Reducing excessive coffee drinking. *Journal of Applied Behavior Analysis, 12,* 335–344.

Frank, E., Johnson, S., & Kupfer, D.J. (1992). Psychological treatments in prevention of relapse. In S.A. Montgomery & F. Rouillon (Eds.), *Long-term treatment of depression* (pp. 197–228). Chichester: Wiley.

Frank, E., Kupfer, D.J., Perel, J.M., Cornes, C., Mallinger, A.G., Thase, ME, McEachran, A.B., & Grochocinski, V.J. (1993). Comparison of full-dose versus half-dose pharmacotherapy in the maintenance treatment of recurrent depression. *Journal of Affective Disorders, 27*, 139–145.

Frank, J.D., & Frank, J.B. (1991). *Persuasion and healing* (3rd ed.). Baltimore: Johns Hopkins University Press.

Frank, J.D., Nash, E.H., Stone, A.R., & Imber, S.D. (1963). Immediate and long-term symptomatic course of psychiatric outpatients. *American Journal of Psychiatry, 120*, 429–439.

Freiman, J.A., Chalmers, T.C., Smith, H., & Kuebler, R.R. (1978). The importance of beta, the Type II error, and sample size in the design and interpretation of the randomized control trial. *New England Journal of Medicine, 299*, 690–694.

Freud, S. (1933). Analysis of a phobia in a five-year-old boy. In *Collected papers of Sigmund Freud* (Vol. 3). London: Hogarth Press.

Friedling, C., & O'Leary, S. (1979). Effects of self-instructional training on second and third-grade hyperactive children: A failure to replicate. *Journal of Applied Behavior Analysis, 12*, 211–219.

Friedman, L.M., Furberg, C.D., & DeMets, D.L. (1985). *Fundamentals of clinical trials* (2nd ed.) Littleton, MA: PSG Publishing Company.

Galton, F. (1872). Statistical inquiries into the efficacy of prayer. *Fornightly Review, 12*, 125–135.

Gilbert, J.P., Light, R.J., & Mosteller, F. (1975). Assessing social interventions: An empirical base for policy. In C.A. Bennett & A.A. Lumsdaine (Eds.), *Evaluation and experiment: Some critical issues in assessing social programs* (pp. 39–193). New York: Academic Press.

Goodyear, R.K., Crego, C.A., & Johnson, M.W. (1992). Ethical issues in the supervision of student research: A study of critical incidents. *Professional Psychology: Research and Practice, 23*, 203–210.

Gorman, B.S., Primavera, L.H., & Allison, D.B. (1995). POWPAL: A program for estimating effect sizes, statistical power, and sample sizes. *Educational and Psychological Measurement, 55*, 773–776.

Gotlib, I.H., Lewinsohn, P.M., & Seeley, J.R. (1995). Symptoms versus a diagnosis of depression: Differences in psychosocial functioning. *Journal of Consulting and Clinical Psychology, 63*, 90–100.

Gottman, J.M., & Glass, G.V. (1978). Analysis of interrupted time-series experiments. In T.R. Kratochwill (Ed.), *Single-subject research: Strategies for evaluating change*. New York: Academic Press.

Gould, S.J. (1981). *The mismeasure of man*. New York: W.W. Norton.

Graham, J.R. (1990). *MMPI-2: Assessing personality and psychopathology*. New York: Oxford University Press.

Grant, D.A. (1948). The Latin square principle in the design and analysis of psychological experiments. *Psychological Bulletin, 45*, 427–442.

Greenberg, J., & Folger, R. (1988). *Controversial issues in social research methods*. New York: Springer-Verlag.

Greenwald, A.G. (1975). Consequences of prejudice against the null hypothesis. *Psychological Bulletin, 82*, 1–20.

Grenier, C. (1985). Treatment effectiveness in an adolescent chemical dependency treatment program: A quasi-experimental design. *International Journal of the Addictions, 20,* 381–391.

Gripp, R.F., & Magaro, P.A. (1971). A token economy program evaluation with untreated control ward comparisons. *Behaviour Research and Therapy, 9,* 137–149.

Groth-Marnat, G. (Ed.) (1997). *Handbook of psychological assessment* (3rd ed.). New York: Wiley.

Grundy, C.T., Lunnen, K.M., Lambert, M.J., Ashton, J.E., & Tovey, D.R. (1994). The Hamilton Rating Scale for Depression: One scale or many? *Clinical Psychology: Science and Practice, 1,* 197–205.

Haase, R.F., & Ellis, M.V. (1987). Multivariate analysis of variance. *Journal of Counseling Psychology, 34,* 404–413.

Haase, R.F., Ellis, M.V., & Ladany, N. (1989). Multiple criteria for evaluating the magnitude of experimental effects. *Journal of Counseling Psychology, 4,* 511–516.

Hackmann, A., & McLean, C. (1975). A comparison of flooding and thought stopping in the treatment of obsessional neurosis. *Behaviour Research and Therapy, 13,* 263–269.

Hagen, R.L., Foreyt, J.P., & Durham, T.W. (1976). The dropout problem: Reducing attrition in obesity research. *Behavior Therapy, 7,* 463–471.

Halbreich, U., Bakhai,Y., Bacon, I.B., Goldstein, S., Asnis, G.M., Endicott, J., & Lesser, J. (1989). The normalcy of self-proclaimed "normal volunteers." *American Journal of Psychiatry, 146,* 1052–1055.

Hamilton, D. (1994). Traditions, preferences, and postures in applied qualitative research. In N.H Denzin & Y.S. Lincoln (Eds.), *Handbook of qualitative research* (pp. 60–69). Thousand Oaks, CA: Sage.

Hammen, C. (1991). *Depression runs in families. The social context of risk and resilience in children of depressed mothers.* New York: Springer-Verlag.

Hanson, B.G. (1995). *General systems theory: Beginning with wholes.* Washington, DC: Taylor & Francis.

Hartshorne, H., & May, M.S. (1928). *Studies in nature of the character. I: Studies in deceit.* New York: Macmillan.

Hartshorne, H., May, M.A., & Shuttleworth, F.K. (1930). *Studies in the nature of character. III: Studies in the organization of character.* New York: Macmillan.

Hauser, S.T., Powers, S.I., & Noam, G.G. (1991). *Adolescents and their families: Paths of ego development.* New York: Free Press.

Hawkins, J.D., & Lam, T. (1987). Teacher practices, social development and delinquency. In J.D. Burchard & S.N. Burchard (Eds.), *Prevention of delinquent behavior* (pp. 241–274). Newbury Park, CA: Sage.

Haynes, S.N. (1992). *Models of causality in psychopathology: Toward dynamic, synthetic, and nonlinear models of behavior disorders.* Needham Heights, MA: Allyn & Bacon.

Heap, R.F., Boblitt, W.E., Moore, C.H., & Hord, J.E. (1970). Behavior-milieu therapy with chronic neuropsychiatric patients. *Journal of Abnormal Psychology, 76,* 349–354.

Henggeler, S.W., Melton, G.B., & Smith, L.A. (1992). Family preservation using multisystemic therapy: An effective alternative to incarcerating serious juvenile offenders. *Journal of Consulting and Clinical Psychology, 60,* 953–961.

Henggeler, S.W., Rodick, J.D., Borduin, C.M., Hanson, C.L., Watson, S.M., & Urey, J.R. (1986). Multisystemic treatment of juvenile offenders: Effects on adolescent behavior and family interaction. *Developmental Psychology, 22,* 132–141.

Henley, N.M. (1977). *Body politics: Power, sex, and nonverbal communication.* Englewood Cliffs, NJ: Prentice-Hall.

Henry, B., Moffitt, T.E., Caspi, A., Langley, J., & Silva, P.A. (1994). On the "rememberance of things past": A longitudinal evaluation of the retrospective method. *Psychological Assessment, 6,* 92–101.

Hewison, J., & Tizard, J. (1980). Parental involvement and reading attainment. *British Journal of Educational Psychology, 50,* 209–215.

Higgs, W.J. (1970). Effects of gross environmental change upon behavior of schizophrenics: A cautionary note. *Journal of Abnormal Psychology, 76,* 421–422.

Hoagwood, K., & Hibbs, E. (Ed.) (1995). Special section: Efficacy and effectiveness in studies of child and adolescent psychotherapy. *Journal of Consulting and Clinical Psychology, 63,* 683–725.

Hoagwood, K., Hibbs, E., Brent, & Jensen, P.J. (1995). Efficacy and effectiveness in studies of child and adolescent psychotherapy. *Journal of Consulting and Clinical Psychology, 63,* 683–687.

Hochberg, Y., & Tamhane, A.C. (1987). *Multiple comparison procedures.* New York: Wiley.

Hodgson, R., & Rachman, S.H. (1974). Desynchrony in measures of fear. *Behaviour Research and Therapy, 12,* 319–326.

Howard, K.I., Kopta, S.M., Krause, M.S., & Orlinsky, D.E. (1986). The dose–effect relationship in psychotherapy. *American Psychologist, 41,* 159–164.

Howard, K.I., Krause, M.S., & Orlinsky, D.E. (1986). The attrition dilemma: Toward a new strategy for psychotherapy research. *Journal of Consulting and Clinical Psychology, 54,* 106–110.

Howard, K.I., Lueger, R.J., Maling, M.S., & Martinovich, Z. (1993). A phase model of psychotherapy outcome: Causal mediation of change. *Journal of Consulting and Clinical Psychology, 61,* 678–685.

Hsu, L.M. (1989). Random sampling, randomization, and equivalence of contrasted groups in psychotherapy outcome research. *Journal of Consulting and Clinical Psychology, 57,* 131–137.

Huberty, C.J., & Morris, J.D. (1989). Multivariate analysis versus multiple univariate analyses. *Psychological Bulletin, 105,* 302–308.

Hulley, S.B., & Cummings, S.R. (Eds.) (1988). *Designing clinical research: An epidemiologic approach.* Baltimore: Williams & Wilkins.

Intagliata, J.C. (1978). Increasing the interpersonal problem-solving skills of an alcoholic population. *Journal of Consulting and Clinical Psychology, 46,* 489–498.

Jacobson, N.S., & Christensen, A. (1996). Studying the effectiveness of psychotherapy: How well can clinical trials do the job. *American Psychologist, 51,* 1031–1039.

Jacobson, N.S., & Revenstorf, D. (1988). Statistics for assessing the clinical significance of psychotherapy techniques: Issues, problems, and new developments. *Behavioral Assessment, 10,* 133–145.

Jacobson, N.S., & Truax, P. (1991). Clinical significance: A statistical approach to defining meaningful change in psychotherapy research. *Journal of Consulting and Clinical Psychology, 59,* 12–19.

Jones E.E. (Editor). (1993). Special section: Single-case research in psychotherapy. *Journal of Consulting and Clinical Psychology, 61,* 371–430.

Jones, M.C. (1924a). A laboratory study of fear: The case of Peter. *Pedagogical Seminary, 31,* 308–315.

Jones, M.C. (1924b). The elimination of children's fears. *Journal of Experimental Psychology, 7,* 382–390.

Kadden, R.M., Cooney, N.L., Getter, H., & Litt, M.D. (1989). Matching alcoholics to coping skills or interactional therapies: Posttreatment results. *Journal of Consulting and Clinical Psychology, 57,* 698–704.

Kaimowitz v. Michigan Department of Mental Health. (1973) 42 U.S.L. Week 2063 (Michigan Circuit Court, Wayne City, MI. July 10, 1973).

Kashani, J.H., Dandoy, A.C., & Reid, J.C. (1991). Hopelessness in children and adolescents: An overview. *Acta Paedopsychiatrica, 55,* 15–21.

Kazdin, A.E. (1977). Assessing the clinical or applied significance of behavior change through social validation. *Behavior Modification, 1,* 427–452.

Kazdin, A.E. (1978a). Evaluating the generality of findings in analogue therapy research. *Journal of Consulting and Clinical Psychology, 46,* 673–686.

Kazdin, A.E. (1978b). *History of behavior modification.* Baltimore: University Park Press.

Kazdin, A.E. (1981). Drawing valid inferences from case studies. *Journal of Consulting and Clinical Psychology, 49,* 183–192.

Kazdin, A.E. (1982a). *Single-case research designs: Methods for clinical and applied settings.* New York: Oxford University Press.

Kazdin, A.E. (1982b). Symptom substitution, generalization, and response covariation: Implications for psychotherapy outcome. *Psychological Bulletin, 91,* 349–365.

Kazdin, A.E. (1984). Statistical analyses for single-case experimental designs. In D.H. Barlow & M. Hersen (Eds.), *Single-case experimental designs: Strategies for studying behavior change* (2nd ed.). Elmsford, NY: Pergamon.

Kazdin, A.E. (1986). Acceptability of psychotherapy and hospitalization for disturbed children: Parent and child perspectives. *Journal of Clinical Child Psychology, 15,* 333–340.

Kazdin, A.E. (1988). *Child psychotherapy: Developing and identifying effective treatments.* Elmsford, NY: Pergamon.

Kazdin, A.E. (1989). Identifying depression in children: A comparison of alternative selection criteria. *Journal of Abnormal Child Psychology, 17,* 437–455.

Kazdin, A.E. (1993). Evaluation in clinical practice: Clinically sensitive and systematic methods of treatment delivery. *Behavior Therapy, 24,* 11–45.

Kazdin, A.E. (1994). Informant variability in the assessment of childhood depression. In W.M. Reynolds & H. Johnston (Eds.), *Handbook of depression in children and adolescents* (pp. 249–271). New York: Plenum.

Kazdin, A.E. (1995a). Child, parent, and family dysfunction as predictors of outcome in cognitive–behavioral treatment of antisocial children. *Behaviour Research and Therapy, 33,* 271–281.

Kazdin, A.E. (1995b). The scope of child and adolescent psychotherapy research: Limited sampling of dysfunctions, treatments, and client characteristics. *Journal of Clinical Child Psychology, 24,* 125–140.

Kazdin, A.E. (1996a). Combined and multimodal treatments in child and adolescent psychotherapy: Issues, challenges, and research directions. *Clinical Psychology: Science and Practice, 3,* 69–100.

Kazdin, A.E. (1996b). Dropping out of child therapy: Issues for research and implications for practice. *Clinical Child Psychology and Psychiatry, 1,* 133–156.

Kazdin, A.E. (1997). Psychosocial treatments for conduct disorder in children. *Journal of Child Psychology and Psychiatry, 38,* 161–178.

Kazdin, A.E., & Bass, D. (1989). Power to detect differences between alternative treatments in comparative psychotherapy outcome research. *Journal of Consulting and Clinical Psychology, 57,* 138–147.

Kazdin, A.E., Bass, D., Ayers, W.A., & Rodgers, A. (1990). The empirical and clinical focus of child and adolescent psychotherapy research. *Journal of Consulting and Clinical Psychology, 58,* 729–740.

Kazdin, A.E., Esveldt-Dawson, K., Unis, A.S., & Rancurello, M.D. (1983). Child and parent evaluations of depression and aggression in psychiatric inpatient children. *Journal of Abnormal Child Psychology, 11,* 401–413.

Kazdin, A.E., French, N.H., & Sherick, R.B. (1981). Acceptability of alternative treatments for children: Evaluations by inpatient children, parents, and staff. *Journal of Consulting and Clinical Psychology, 49,* 900–907.

Kazdin, A.E., French, N.H., Unis, A.S., Esveldt-Dawson, K., & Sherick, R.B. (1983). Hopelessness, depression and suicidal intent among psychiatrically disturbed inpatient children. *Journal of Consulting and Clinical Psychology, 51,* 504–510.

Kazdin, A.E., Holland, L., & Crowley, M. (1997). Family experience of barriers to treatment and premature termination from child therapy. *Journal of Consulting and Clinical Psychology, 65,* 453–463.

Kazdin, A.E., Holland, L., Crowley, M., & Breton, S. (in press). Barriers to Participation in Treatment Scale: Evaluation and validation in the context of child outpatient treatment. *Journal of Child Psychology and Psychiatry.*

Kazdin, A.E., & Kagan, J. (1994). Models of dysfunction in developmental psychopathology. *Clinical Psychology: Science and Practice, 1,* 35–52.

Kazdin, A.E., Kraemer, H.C., Kessler, R.C., Kupfer, D.J., & Offord, D.R. (1997). Contributions of risk-factor research to developmental psychopathology. *Clinical Psychology Review, 17,* 375–406.

Kazdin, A.E., Mazurick, J.L., & Bass, D. (1993). Risk for attrition in treatment of antisocial children and families. *Journal of Clinical Child Psychology, 22,* 2–16.

Kazdin, A.E., Rodgers, A., & Colbus, D. (1986). The Hopelessness Scale for Children: Psychometric characteristics and concurrent validity. *Journal of Consulting and Clinical Psychology, 54,* 241–245.

Kazdin, A.E., Siegel, T., & Bass, D. (1990). Drawing on clinical practice to inform research on child and adolescent psychotherapy: Survey of practitioners. *Professional Psychology: Research and Practice, 21,* 189–198.

Kazdin, A.E., Siegel, T., & Bass, D. (1992). Cognitive problem-solving skills training and parent management training in the treatment of antisocial behavior in children. *Journal of Consulting and Clinical Psychology, 60,* 733–747.

Kazdin, A.E., Stolar, M.J., & Marciano, P.L. (1995). Risk factors for dropping out of treatment among White and Black families. *Journal of Family Psychology, 9,* 402–417.

Kendall, P.C. (1994). Treating anxiety disorders in children: A controlled trial. *Journal of Consulting and Clinical Psychology, 62,* 100–110.

Kendall, P.C., Flannery-Schroeder, E., Panichelli-Mindel, S.M., Southam-Gerow, M., Henin, A., & Warman, M. (1997). Therapy for youths with anxiety disorders: A second randomized clinical trial. *Journal of Consulting and Clinical Psychology, 65,* 366–380.

Kendall, P.C., & Grove, W.M. (1988). Normative comparisons in therapy outcome. *Behavioral Assessment, 10,* 147–158.

Kenny, D.A., & Kashy, A. (1992). Analysis of the multitrait-multimethod matrix by confirmatory factor analysis. *Psychological Bulletin, 112,* 165–172.

Kessler, R.C., Mroczek, D.K., & Belli, R.F. (in press). Retrospective adult assessment of childhood psychopathology. In D. Shaffer & J. Richters (Eds.), *Assessment in child psychopathology.* New York: Guilford.

Kidder, L.H., & Judd, C.M. (1986). *Research methods in social relations* (5th ed.). New York: Holt, Rinehart and Winston.

Kihlstrom, J. (1995). *From the subject's point of view: The experiment as conversation and collaboration between investigator and subject.* Keynote address presented at the meeting of the American Psychological Society, New York.

Killen, J.D., Fortmann, S.P., Kraemer, H.C., Varady, A.N., Davis, L., & Newman, B. (1996). Interactive effects of depression symptoms, nicotine dependence, and weight change on late smoking relapse. *Journal of Consulting and Clinical Psychology, 64,* 1060–1067.

Kirk, R.E. (1996). Practical significance: A concept whose time has come. *Educational and Psychological Measurement, 56,* 746–759.

Klerman, G.L., Weissman, M.M., Marakowitz, J.C., Glick, I., Wilner, P.J., Mason, B., & Shear, M.K. (1994). Medication and psychotherapy. In A.E. Bergin & S.L. Garfield (Eds.), *Handbook of psychotherapy and behavior change* (4th ed., pp. 734–782). New York: Wiley.

Klosko, J.S., Barlow, D.H., Tassinari, R., & Cerny, J.A. (1990). A comparison of Alprazolam and behavior therapy in the treatment of panic disorder. *Journal of Consulting and Clinical Psychology, 58,* 77–84.

Klusman, L.E. (1975). Reduction of pain in childbirth by the alleviation of anxiety during pregnancy. *Journal of Consulting and Clinical Psychology, 43,* 162–165.

Kohn, A. (1988). *False profits: Fraud and error in science and medicine.* New York: Basil Blackwell.

Kolvin, I., Garside, R.F., Nicol, A.E., MacMillan, A., Wolstenholme, F., & Leitch, I.M. (1981). *Help starts here: The maladjusted child in the ordinary school.* London: Tavistock.

Kopka, S.M., Howard, K.I., Lowry, J.L., & Beutler, L.E. (1994). Patterns of symptomatic recovery in psychotherapy. *Journal of Consulting and Clinical Psychology, 62,* 1009–1016.

Kraemer, H.C., Kazdin, A.E., Offord, D.R., Kessler, R.C., Jensen, P.S., & Kupfer, D.J. (1997). Coming to terms with terms of risk. *Archives of General Psychiatry, 54,* 337–343.

Kraemer, H.C., & Thiemann, S. (1987). *How many subjects? Statistical power analysis in research.* Newbury Park, CA: Sage.

Krahn, G.L., Hohn, M.F., & Kime, C. (1995). Incorporating qualitative approaches into clinical child psychology research. *Journal of Clinical Child Psychology, 24,* 204–213.

Krishef, C.H. (1991). *Fundamental approaches to single-subject design and analysis.* Malabar, FL: Kreiger.

Kroll, L., Harrington, R., Jayson, D., Fraser, J., & Gowers, S. (1996). Pilot study of continuation cognitive–behavioral therapy for major depression in adolescents. *Journal of the American Academy of Child and Adolescent Psychiatry, 35,* 1156–1161.

Kruesi, J.J.P., Lenane, M.D., Hibbs, E.D., & Major, J. (1990). Normal controls and biological reference values in child psychiatry: Defining normal. *Journal of the American Academy of Child and Adolescent Psychiatry, 29,* 449–452.

Krupnick, J.L., Sotsky, S.M., Simmens, S., Moyer, J., Elkin, I., Watkins, J., & Pilkonis, P.A. (1996). The role of the therapeutic alliance in psychotherapy and pharmacotherapy outcome: Findings in the National Institute of Mental Health Treatment of Depression Collaborative Research Program. *Journal of Consulting and Clinical Psychology, 64,* 532–539.

Kupfer, D.J., Frank, E., Perel, J.M., Cornes, C., Mallinger, A.G., Thase, M.E., McEachran, A.B., & Grochocinski, V.J. (1992). Five-year outcome for maintenance therapies in recurrent depression. *Archives of General Psychiatry, 49,* 769–773.

Kupfersmid, J. (1988). Improving what is published: A model in search of an editor. *American Psychologist, 43,* 635–642.

Kutner, B., Wilkins, C., & Harrow, P.R. (1952). Verbal attitudes and overt behavior involving racial prejudice. *Journal of Abnormal and Social Psychology, 47,* 649–652.

Ladouceur, R., Freeston, M.H., Gagnon, F., Thibodeau, N., & Dumont, J. (1993). Idiographic considerations in the behavioral treatment of obsessional thoughts. *Journal of Behavior Therapy and Experimental Psychiatry, 24,* 301–310.

La Greca, A.M., Silverman, W.K., Vernberg, E.M., & Prinstein, M.J. (1996). Symptoms of posttraumatic stress in children after Hurricane Andrew: A prospective study. *Journal of Consulting and Clinical Psychology, 64,* 712–723.

Lally, R., Mangione, P.L., & Honig, A.S. (1988). The Syracuse University Family Development Research Program: Long-range impact on an early intervention with low-income children and their families. In D. Powell (Ed.), *Parent education as early childhood intervention: Emerging directions in theory, research, and practice* (pp. 79–104). Norwood, NJ: Ablex.

Lam, D.H. (1991). Psychosocial family intervention in schizophrenia: A review of empirical studies. *Psychological Medicine, 21,* 423–441.

Lambert, M.J., & Bergin, A.E. (1994). The effectiveness of psychotherapy. In A.E. Bergin & S.L. Garfield (Eds.), *Handbook of psychotherapy and behavior change* (4th ed., pp. 143–189). New York: Wiley.

Land, K.C., McCall, P.L., & Williams, J.R. (1992). Intensive supervision of status offenders: Evidence on continuity of treatment effects for juveniles and a "Hawthorne Effect" for counselors. In J. McCord & R.E. Tremblay (Eds.), *Preventing antisocial behavior: Interventions from birth through adolescence* (pp. 330–349). New York: Guilford.

La Piere, R.T. (1934). Attitudes vs. action. *Social Forces, 13,* 230–237.

Last, C.G., Hersen, M., Kazdin, A.E., Francis, G., & Grubb, H.J. (1987). Psychiatric illness in the mothers of anxious children. *American Journal of Psychiatry, 144,* 1580–1583.

Lazarus, A.A. (1961). Group therapy of phobic disorders by systematic desensitization. *Journal of Abnormal and Social Psychology, 63,* 504–510.

Leach, C.L., Greenspan, J.S., Rubenstein, S.D., Shaffer, T.H., Wolfson, M.R., Jackson, J.C., DeLemos, R., & Fuhrman, B.P. (1996). Partial liquid ventilation with perflubron in premature infants with severe respiratory distress syndrome. *New England Journal of Medicine, 335,* 761–767.

Lefkowitz, M.M., Eron, L.D., Walder, L.O., & Huesmann, L.R. (1977). *Growing up to be violent: A longitudinal study of the development of aggression.* New York: Pergamon.

Levin, J.S. (1994). Religion and health: Is there an association, is it valid, is it causal? *Social Science and Medicine, 38,* 1475–1482.

Lewinsohn, P.M., Clarke, G.N., Hops, H., & Andrews, J. (1990). Cognitive–behavioral treatment for depressed adolescents. *Behavior Therapy, 21,* 385–401.

Lewinsohn, P.M., Steinmetz, J.L., Larson, D.L., & Franklin, J. (1981). Depression-related cognitions: Antecedent or consequence? *Journal of Abnormal Psychology, 91,* 213–219.

Lincoln, Y.S., & Guba, E.G. (1985). *Naturalistic inquiry.* Beverly Hills, CA: Sage.

Lindsay, D. (1988). Assessing precision in the manuscript review process: A little better than a dice role. *Sociometrics, 14,* 75–82.

Lipman, E.L., Offord, D.R., & Boyle, M.H. (1994). Relation between economic disadvantage and psychosocial morbidity in children. *Canadian Medical Association Journal, 151,* 431–437.

Lipsey, M.W. (1990). *Design sensitivity: Statistical power for experimental research.* Newbury Park, CA: Sage.

Little, R.J.A., & Rubin, D.B. (1987). *Statistical analysis with missing data.* New York: Wiley.

Lovaas, O.I. (1987). Behavioral treatment and normal educational/intellectual functioning in young autistic children. *Journal of Consulting and Clinical Psychology, 55,* 3–9.

Lovaas, O.I. (1988). *Behavioral treatment of autistic children* (film). Huntington Station, NY: Focus International.

Luborsky, L., Crits-Cristoph, Mintz, & Auerbach, A. (1988). *Who will benefit from psychotherapy? Predicting therapeutic outcomes.* New York: Basic Books.

Lykken, D.T. (1968). Statistical significance in psychological research. *Psychological Bulletin, 70,* 151–159.

Magnusson, D. (Ed.) (1981). *Toward a psychology of situations: An interactional perspective.* Hillsdale, NJ: Erlbaum.

Maher, B.A. (1978a). Stimulus sampling in clinical research: Representative design reviewed. *Journal of Consulting and Clinical Psychology, 46,* 643–647.

Maher, B.A. (1978b). A reader's, writer's, and reviewer's guide to assessing research reports in clinical psychology. *Journal of Consulting and Clinical Psychology, 46,* 835–838.

Manson, S.M. (Ed.). (1989). *American Indian and Alaska Native Mental Health Research, 2* (3).

Margraf, J., Ehlers, A., Roth, W.T., Clark, D.B., Sheikh, J., Agras, W.S., & Taylor, C.B. (1991). How "blind" are double-blind studies? *Journal of Consulting and Clinical Psychology, 46,* 184–187.

Marks, I.M. (1987). *Fears, phobias, and rituals.* New York: Oxford University Press.

Marks, I.M. (in press). Computerized psychotherapy. *Clinical Psychology: Science and Practice.*

Marrs, R.W. (1995). A meta-analysis of bibliotherapy studies. *American Journal of Community Psychology, 23,* 843–870.

Martin, J.E., & Sachs, D.A. (1973). The effects of a self-control weight loss program on an obese woman. *Journal of Behavior Therapy and Experimental Psychiatry, 4,* 155–159.

Masling, J.M. (1960). The influence of situational and interpersonal variables in projective testing. *Psychological Bulletin, 57,* 65–85.

Matthews, D.B. (1986). Discipline: Can it be improved with relaxation training. *Elementary School Guidance and Counseling, XX,* 194–200.

Matthys, W. Walterbos, W., Njio, L., & van Engeland, H. (1989). Person perception in children with conduct disorders. *Journal of Child Psychology and Psychiatry, 30,* 439–448.

Matyas, T.A., & Grenwood, K.M. (1990). Visual analysis of single-case time series: Effects of variability, serial dependence, and magnitude of intervention effects. *Journal of Applied Behavior Analysis, 23,* 341–351.

McCullough, M.E. (1995). Prayer and health: Conceptual issues, research review, and research agenda. *Journal of Psychology and Theology, 23,* 15–29.

McGuire, W.J. (1969). Suspiciousness of experimenter's intent. In R. Rosenthal & R.L. Rosnow (Eds.), *Artifact in behavioral research* (pp. 13–57). New York: Academic Press.

Meehl, P. (1978). Theoretical risks and tabular asterisks: Sir Karl, Sir Ronald, and the slow progress of soft psychology. *Journal of Consulting and Clinical Psychology, 46,* 806–834.

Meinart, C.T. (1986). *Clinical trials: Design, conduct, and analysis.* New York: Oxford University Press.

Meisels, S.J., & Shonkoff, J.P. (Eds.). (1990). *Handbook of early childhood intervention.* Cambridge, UK: Cambridge University Press.

Mellors, J.W., Rinaldo, C.R., Jr., Gupta, P., White, R.M., Todd, J.A., & Kingsley, L.A. (1996). Prognosis in HIV-1 infection predicted by the quantity of virus in plasma. *Science, 272,* 1167–1170.

Meltzoff, J., & Kornreich, M. (1970). *Research in psychotherapy.* New York: Aldine-Atherton.

Meyer, V. (1957). The treatment of two phobic patients on the basis of learning principles. *Journal of Abnormal and Social Psychology, 55,* 261–266.

Meyers, A.W., Graves, T.J., Whelan, J.P., & Barclay, D. (1996). An evaluation of television-delivered behavioral weight loss program. Are the ratings acceptable? *Journal of Consulting and Clinical Psychology, 64,* 172–178.

Miles, M.B., & Huberman, A.M. (1994). *Qualitative data analysis* (2nd ed.). Thousand Oaks, CA: Sage.

Miles, M.B., & Weitzman, E.A. (1994). Appendix: Choosing computer programs for qualitative data analyses. In M.B Miles & A.M. Huberman, (Eds.), *Qualitative data analysis* (2nd ed.). (pp. 311–317). Thousand Oaks, CA: Sage.

Miller, D.J., & Hersen, M. (Eds.) (1992). *Research fraud in the behavioral and biomedical sciences.* New York: Wiley.

Milner, J.S. (1989). Additional cross-validation of the Child Abuse Potential Inventory. *Journal of Consulting and Clinical Psychology, 57,* 219–223.

Moffitt, T.E., Caspi, A., Dickson, N., Silva, P., & Stanton, W. (1996). Childhood-onset versus adolescent onset antisocial conduct problems in males: Natural history from ages 3–18. *Development and Psychopathology, 8,* 399–424.

Mohr, L.B. (1990). *Understanding significance testing.* Newbury Park, CA: Sage.

Moss, M. (1996). Does annual survey of US drug use give straight dope? *Wall Street Journal,* September 18, pp. A1, A10.

Multiple Risk Factor Intervention Trial Research Group (1982). Multiple risk factor intervention trial: Risk factor changes and mortality results. *Journal of the American Medical Association, 248,* 1465–1477.

Murphy, L.L., Conoley, J.C., & Impara, J.C. (Eds.) (1994). *Tests in print. IV* (Vols. 1 and 2). Lincoln, NE: Buros Institute of the University of Nebraska. Buros Institute of Mental Measurements: University of Nebraska Press.

National Academy of Sciences, Committee on the Conduct of Science (1989). *On being a scientist.* Washington, DC: National Academy Press.

Needleman, H.L., & Bellinger, D., (1984). The developmental consequences of childhood exposure to lead: Recent studies and methodological issues. In B.B. Lahey & A.E. Kazdin (Eds.), *Advances in clinical child psychology* (Vol. 7, pp. 195–220). New York: Plenum.

Needleman, H.L., Schell, A.S., Bellinger, D., Leviton, A., & Alldred, E.N. (1990). The long-term effects of exposure to low doses of lead in childhood: An 11-year follow-up report. *New England Journal of Medicine, 322,* 83.

Neuliep, J.W. (Ed.) (1991). *Replication research in the social sciences.* Newbury Park, CA: Sage.

Newcomb, M.D., & Bentler, P.M. (1988). *Consequences of adolescent drug use: Impact on the lives of young adults.* Newbury Park, CA: Sage.

Newcomb, M.D., & Bentler, P.M. (1989). Substance use and abuse among children and teenagers. *American Psychologist, 44*, 242–248.

Newman, M.G., Kenardy, J., Herman, S., & Taylor, C.B. (1997). Comparison of palmtop-computer-assisted brief cognitive–behavioral treatment to cognitive–behavioral treatment for panic disorder. *Journal of Consulting and Clinical Psychology, 65*, 178–183.

Neyman, J., & Pearson, E.S. (1928). On the use and interpretation of certain test criteria for purposes of statistical inference. *Biometrika, 294* (Pt 1), 175–240 (Pt 2), 263–294.

Nezu, A.M., & Perri, M.G. (1989). Social problem-solving therapy for unipolar depression: An initial dismantling investigation. *Journal of Consulting and Clinical Psychology, 57*, 408–413.

Nezworski, M.T., & Wood, J.M. (1995). Narcissism in the comprehensive system for the Rorschach. *Clinical Psychology: Science and Practice, 2*, 179–199.

Noll, R.B., Zeller, M.H., Vannatta, K., Bukowski, W.M., & Davies, W.H. (1997). Potential bias in classroom research: Comparison of children with permission and those who do not receive permission to participate. *Journal of Clinical Child Psychology, 26*, 36–42.

Nunnally, J. (1960). The place of statistics in psychology. *Educational and Psychological Measurement, 20*, 641–650.

O'Donohue, W., Plaud, J.J., & Hecker, J.E. (1992). The possible function of positive reinforcement in home-bound agoraphobia: A case study. *Journal of Behavior Therapy and Experimental Psychiatry, 23*, 303–312.

Offord, D., Boyle, M.H., Racine, Y.A., Fleming, J.E., Cadman, D.T., Blum, H.M., Byrne, C., Links, P.S., Lipman, E.L., MacMillan, H.L., Rae Grant, N.I., Sanford, M.N., Szatmari, P., Thomas, H., & Woodward, C.A. (1992). Outcome, prognosis, and risk in a longitudinal follow-up study. *Journal of the American Academy of Child and Adolescent Psychiatry, 31*, 916–923.

Orne, M.T. (1962). On the social psychology of the psychological experiment: With particular reference to demand characteristics and their implications. *American Psychologist, 17*, 776–783.

Orne, M.T. (1969). Demand characteristics and the concept of quasi-controls. In R. Rosenthal & R.L. Rosnow (Eds.), *Artifact in behavioral research.* New York: Academic Press.

Orne, M.T., & Scheibe, K.E. (1964). The contribution of nondeprivation factors in the production of sensory deprivation effects: The psychology of the "panic button." *Journal of Abnormal and Social Psychology, 68*, 3–12.

Ouimette, P.C., Finney, J.W., & Moos, R.H. (1997). Twelve-step and cognitive–behavioral treatment for substance abuse: A comparison of treatment effectiveness. *Journal of Consulting and Clinical Psychology, 65*, 230–240.

Paivio, S.C., & Greenberg, L.S. (1995). Resolving "unfinished business": Efficacy of experiential therapy using empty-chair dialogue. *Journal of Consulting and Clinical Psychology, 63*, 419–425.

Palmer, A.B., & Wohl, J. (1972). Voluntary-admission forms: Does the patient know what he's signing? *Hospital and Community Psychiatry, 23*, 250–252.

Patterson, G.R. (1982). *Coercive family process.* Eugene, OR: Castalia.

Patterson, G.R., Chamberlain, & Reid, J.B. (1982). A comparative evaluation of a parent-training program. *Behavior Therapy, 13*, 638–650.

Patterson, G.R., Reid, J.B., & Dishion, T.J. (1992). *Antisocial boys.* Eugene, OR: Castalia.

Paul, G.L. (1966). *Insight versus desensitization in psychotherapy: An experiment in anxiety reduction.* Stanford, CA: Stanford University Press.

Paul, G.L. (1967). Outcome research in psychotherapy. *Journal of Consulting Psychology, 31,* 109–118.

Peterson, B.S. (1995). Neuroimaging in child and adolescent psychiatric disorders. *Journal of the American Academy of Child and Adolescent Psychiatry, 34,* 1560–1576.

Prinz, R.J., & Miller, G.E. (1994). Family-based treatment for childhood antisocial behavior: Experimental influences on dropout and engagement. *Journal of Consulting and Clinical Psychology, 62,* 645–650.

Rachman, S., & Hodgson, R.I. (1974). Synchrony and desynchrony in fear and avoidance. *Behaviour Research and Therapy, 12,* 311–318.

Reckase, M.D. (1996). Test construction in the 1990s: Recent approaches every psychologist should know. *Psychological Assessment, 8,* 354–359.

Regier, D.A., Myers, J.K., Kramer, M., Robins, L.N., Blazer, D.G., Hough, R.L., Eaton, W.W., & Locke, B.Z. (1984). The NIMH Epidemiologic Catchment Area program: Historical context, major objectives, and study population characteristics. *Archives of General Psychiatry, 41,* 934–941.

Resnick, J.H., & Schwartz, T. (1973). Ethical standards as an independent variable in psychological research. *American Psychologist, 28,* 134–139.

Robertson, R., & Combs, A. (Eds.) (1995). *Chaos theory in psychology and the life sciences.* Mahwah, NJ: Erlbaum.

Robins, L., Helzer, J., Weissman, M., Orvaschel, H., Gruenberg, E., Bruche, J., & Regier, D. (1984). Lifetime prevalence of specific psychiatric disorders in three sites. *Archives of General Psychiatry, 41,* 949–958.

Rogers, C., & Dymond, R. (Eds.). (1954). *Psychotherapy and personality change.* Chicago: University of Chicago Press.

Rosen, G.M. (1987). Self-help treatment books and the commercialization of psychotherapy. *American Psychologist, 42,* 46–51.

Rosenthal, R. (1966). *Experimenter effects in behavioral research.* New York: Appleton-Century-Crofts.

Rosenthal, R. (1969). Interpersonal expectations: Effects of the experimenter's hypothesis. In R. Rosenthal & R.L. Rosnow (Eds.), *Artifact in behavioral research* (pp. 181–277). New York: Academic Press.

Rosenthal, R. (1976). *Experimenter effects in behavioral research* (enlarged ed.). New York: Irvington.

Rosenthal, R. (1979). The "file drawer problem" and tolerance for null results. *Psychological Bulletin, 86,* 638–641.

Rosenthal, R. (1984). *Meta-analytic procedures for social research.* Beverly Hills, CA: Sage.

Rosenthal, R. (1991) Replication in behavioral research. In J.W. Neuliep (Ed.), *Replication research in the social sciences* (pp. 1–30). Newbury Park, CA: Sage.

Rosenthal, R., & Gaito, J. (1963). The interpretation of levels of significance by psychological researchers. *Journal of Psychology, 55,* 33–38.

Rosenthal, R., & Rosnow, R.L. (1975). *The volunteer subject.* New York: Wiley.

Rosenthal, R., & Rosnow, R.L. (1991). *Essentials of behavioral research: Methods and data analysis* (2nd ed.). New York: McGraw-Hill.

Rosnow, R.L., & Rosenthal, R. (1989). Definition and interpretation of interaction effects. *Psychological Bulletin, 105,* 143–146.

Ross, J.A. (1975). Parents modify thumbsucking: A case study. *Journal of Behavior Therapy and Experimental Psychiatry, 6,* 248–249.

Ross, L., Lepper, M.R., & Hubbard, M. (1975). Perseverance in self-perception and perception: Biased attributional processes in the debriefing paradigm. *Journal of Personality and Social Psychology, 32,* 800–892.

Rossi, J.S. (1990). Statistical power of psychological research: What have we gained in 20 years? *Journal of Consulting and Clinical Psychology, 58,* 646–656.

Roth, A., & Fonagy, P. (1996). *What works for whom: A critical review of psychotherapy research.* New York: Guilford.

Rounsaville, B.J., Chevron, E.S., Prusoff, B.A., Elkin, I., Imber, S., Sotsky, S., & Watkins, J. (1986). The relation between specific and general dimensions of the psychotherapy process in interpersonal psychotherapy of depression. *Journal of Consulting and Clinical Psychology, 55,* 379–394.

Rush, A.J., Beck, A.T., Kovacs, M., & Hollon, S. (1977). Comparative efficacy of cognitive therapy and pharmacotherapy in the treatment of depressed outpatients. *Cognitive Therapy and Research, 1,* 17–37.

Rutter, M.B. (1981). Epidemiological/longitudinal strategies and causal research in child psychiatry. *Journal of the American Academy of Child Psychiatry, 20,* 513–544.

Rutter, M.B., Chadwick, O., & Shaffer, D. (1983). Head injury. In M.B. Rutter (Ed.), *Developmental neuropsychiatry* (pp. 83–111). New York: Guilford.

Ryan, N.D., Puig-Antich, J., Cooper, T., Rabinovich, H., Ambrosini, P., Davies, M., King, J., Torrer, D., & Fried, J. (1986). Imipramine in adolescent major depression: Plasma level and clinical response. *Acta Psychiatrica Scandinavica, 73,* 275–288.

Ryder, D. (1988). Minimal intervention: A little quality for a lot of quantity? *Behaviour Change, 5,* 100–107.

Saigh, P.A. (1986). In vitro flooding in the treatment of a 6-year-old boy's posttraumatic stress disorder. *Behaviour Research and Therapy, 24,* 685–688.

Schlesselman, J.J. (1982). *Case-control studies: Design, conduct, analysis.* New York: Oxford University Press.

Schmidt, F.L. (1996a). APA Board of Scientific Affairs to study issue of significance testing, make recommendations. *Score, 19,* 1, 6.

Schmidt, F.L. (1996b). Statistical significance testing and cumulative knowledge in psychology: Implications for training of researchers. *Psychological Methods, 1,* 115–129.

Schmitt, N., Coyle, B.W., & Saari, B.B. (1977). A review and critique of analysis of multitrait-multimethod matrices. *Multivariate Behavioral Research 12,* 447–478.

Schutte, N.S., & Malouff, J.M. (Eds.). (1995). *Sourcebook of adult assessment strategies.* New York: Plenum.

Schweinhart, L.J., & Weikart, D.P. (1988). The High/Scope Perry preschool program. In R.H. Price, E.L. Cowen, R.P. Lorion, & J. Ramos-McKay (Eds.), *14 ounces of prevention: A casebook for practitioners* (pp. 53–65). Washington, DC: American Psychological Association.

Sechrest, L., White, S.O., & Brown, E.D. (Eds.), (1979). *The rehabilitation of criminal offenders: Problems and prospects.* Washington, DC: National Academy of Sciences.

Sedlmeier, P., & Gigerenzer, G. (1989). Do studies of statistical power have an effect on the power of studies? *Psychological Bulletin, 105,* 309–316.

Seligman, M.E.P. (1995). The effectiveness of psychotherapy: The *Consumer Reports* study. *American Psychologist, 50,* 965–974.

Shadish, W.R., Matt, G.E., Navarro, A.M., Siegel, G., Crits-Christoph, P., Hazelrigg, M.D.,

Jorm, A.F., & Lyons, L.C., Nietzel, M.T., Prout, H.T., Robinson, L., Smith, M.L., Svartberg, M., & Weiss, B. (1997). Evidence that therapy works in clinically representative conditions. *Journal of Consulting and Clinical Psychology, 65,* 355–365.

Shadish, W.R., & Ragsdale, K. (1996). Random versus nonrandom assignment in controlled experiments. Do you get the same answer? *Journal of Consulting and Clinical Psychology, 64,* 1290–1305.

Shapiro, A.K., & Morris, L.A. (1978). The placebo effect in medical and psychological therapies. In S.L. Garfield & A.E. Bergin (Eds.), *Handbook of psychotherapy and behavior change: An empirical analysis* (2nd ed., pp. 369–410). New York: Wiley.

Shapiro, D.A., & Shapiro, D. (1983). Comparative therapy outcome research: Methodological implications of meta-analysis. *Journal of Consulting and Clinical Psychology, 51,* 42–53.

Shapiro, F. (1989). Efficacy of eye movement desensitization procedure in the treatment of traumatic memories. *Journal of Traumatic Stress Studies, 2,* 199–223.

Shapiro, M.B. (1966). The single case in clinical-psychological research. *Journal of Genetic Psychology, 74,* 3–23.

Shrout, P.E. (Ed.). (1997). Special series: Should significance tests be banned? Introduction to a special series exploring the pros and cons. *Psychological Science, 8,* 1–20.

Silva, P.A. (1990). The Dunedin Multidisciplinary Health and Development Study: A fifteen-year longitudinal study. *Perinatal and Paediatric Epidemiology, 4,* 76–107.

Simes, R.J. (1986). An improved Bonferroni procedure for multiple tests of significance. *Biometrika, 74,* 751–754.

Skinner, B.F. (1957). The experimental analysis of behavior. *American Scientist, 45,* 343–371.

Sloane, R.B., Staples, F.R., Cristol, A.H., Yorkston, N.J., & Whipple, K. (1975). *Psychotherapy versus behavior therapy.* Cambridge: Harvard University Press.

Smith, M.L., Glass, G.V., & Miller, T.I. (1980). *The benefits of psychotherapy.* Baltimore: Johns Hopkins University Press.

Solomon, R.L. (1949). An extension of control group design. *Psychological Bulletin, 46,* 137–150.

Spiegel, D., Bloom, J.R., Kraemer, H.C., & Gottheil, E. (1989). Effect of psychosocial treatment on survival of patients with metastatic breast cancer. *Lancet, 2,* 888–891.

Spirito, A., Overholser, J., Ashworth, S., Morgan, J., & Benedict-Drew, C. (1988a). Evaluation of a suicide awareness curriculum for high school students. *Journal of the American Academy of Child and Adolescent Psychiatry, 27,* 705–711.

Spirito, A., Williams, C.A., Stark, L.J., & Hart, K.J. (1988b). The Hopelessness Scale for Children: Psychometric properties with normal and emotionally disturbed adolescents. *Journal of Abnormal Child Psychology, 16,* 445–458.

Spitzer, A., Webster-Stratton, C., & Hollinsworth, T. (1991). Coping with conduct-problem children: Parents gaining knowledge and control. *Journal of Clinical Child Psychology, 20,* 413–427.

Stanger, C., Achenbach, T.M., & Verhulst, F.C. (1997). Accelerated longitudinal comparisons of aggressive versus delinquent syndromes. *Development and Psychopathology, 9,* 43–58.

Stanger, C., & Verhulst, F.C. (1995). Accelerated longitudinal designs. In F.C. Verhulst & H.M. Koot (Eds.), *The epidemiology of child and adolescent psychopathology* (pp. 385–405). New York: Oxford University Press.

Statistical Solutions (1995). *nQuery Advisor.* Boston: Statistical Solutions.

Steenbarger, B.N. (1994). Duration and outcome in psychotherapy: An integrative review. *Professional Psychology: Research and Practice, 25,* 111–119.

Stein, J.A., Golding, J.M., Siegel, J.M., Burnam, M.A., & Sorenson, S.B. (1988). Long-term psychological sequelae of child sexual abuse: The Los Angeles Epidemiologic Catchment Area Study. In G.E. Wyatt & G.J. Powell (Eds.), *Lasting effects of child abuse* (pp. 135–154). Newbury Park, CA: Sage.

Sternberg, R.J. (1992). *Psychological Bulletin*'s top 10 "hit parade." *Psychological Bulletin, 112,* 387–388.

Stice, E., Barrera, Jr., M., & Chassin, L. (1993). Relation of parental support and control to adolescents' externalizing symptomatology and substance use: A longitudinal examination of curvilinear effects. *Journal of Abnormal Child Psychology, 21,* 609–629.

Strasburger, V.C. (1995). *Adolescents and the media: Medical and psychological impact.* Thousand Oaks, CA: Sage.

Stricker, G., & Healey, B.J. (1990). Projective assessment of object relations: A review of the empirical literature. *Psychological Assessment, 2,* 219–230.

Swedo, S.E., Allen, A.J., Glod, C.A., Clark, C.H., Teicher, M.H., Richter, D., Hoffman, C., Hamburger, S., Dow, S., Brown, C., & Rosenthal, N.E. (1997). A controlled trial of light therapy for the treatment of pediatric seasonal affective disorder. *Journal of the American Academy of Child and Adolescent Psychiatry, 36,* 816–821.

Szapocznik, J., Perez-Vidal, A., Brickman, A.L., Foote, F.H., Santisteban, D., Hervis, O., & Kurtines, W.M. (1988). Engaging adolescent drug abusers and their families into treatment: A strategic structural systems approach. *Journal of Consulting and Clinical Psychology, 56,* 552–557.

Tarnowski, K.J., & Simonian, S.J. (1992). Assessing treatment acceptance: The Abbreviated Acceptability Rating Profile. *Journal of Behavior Therapy and Experimental Psychiatry, 23,* 101–106.

Tarrier, N., & Barrowclough, C. (1990) Family interventions for schizophrenia. Recent developments in the behavioral treatment of chronic psychiatric illness. *Behavior Modification, 14* (Special issue), 408–440.

Thigpen, C.H., & Cleckley, H.M. (1954). A case of multiple personality. *Journal of Abnormal and Social Psychology, 49,* 135–151.

Thigpen, C.H., & Cleckley, H.M. (1957). *Three faces of Eve.* New York: McGraw-Hill.

Thompson, B. (1996). AERA editorial policies regarding statistical significance testing: Three suggested reforms. *Educational Researcher, 25,* 26–30.

Tizard, J., Schofield, W.N., & Hewison, J. (1982). Reading collaboration between teachers and parents in assisting children's reading. *British Journal of Educational Psychology, 52,* 1–15.

Tomarken, A.J. (1995). A psychometric perspective on psychophysiological measures. *Psychological Assessment, 7,* 387–395.

Toro, P.A., Bellavia, C.W., Daeschler, C.V., Owens, B.J., Wall, D.D., Passero, J.M., & Thomas, D.M. (1995). Distinguishing homelessness from poverty: A comparison study. *Journal of Consulting and Clinical Psychology, 63,* 280–289.

Tremblay, R.E., Masse, B., Perron, D., Leblanc, M., Schwartzman, E., & Ledingham, J.E.(1992). Early disruptive behavior, poor school achievement, delinquent behavior, and delinquent personality: Longitudinal analyses. *Journal of Consulting and Clinical Psychology, 60,* 64–72.

Tukey, J.W. (1991). The philosophy of multiple comparisons. *Statistical Science, 6,* 100–116.

Tversky, A., & Kahneman, D. (1971). Belief in the law of small numbers. *Psychological Bulletin, 76,* 105–110.

United States Department of Health and Human Services, National Institutes of Health, Office for Protection from Research Risks. (1983). *Code of federal regulations: Part 46: Protection of human subjects.* Washington, DC: U.S. Government Printing Office.

Verhulst, F.C., & Koot, H.M. (1992). *Child psychiatric epidemiology: Concepts, methods, and findings.* Newbury Park, CA: Sage.

Vidich, A.J., & Lyman, S.M. (1994). Qualitative methods: Their history in sociology and anthropology. In N.H Denzin & Y.S. Lincoln (Eds.), *Handbook of qualitative research* (pp. 23–59). Thousand Oaks, CA: Sage.

Vostanis, P., Feehan, C., Grattan, E., & Bickerton, W. (1996). Treatment for children and adolescents with depression: Lessons from a controlled trial. *Child Clinical Psychology and Psychiatry, 1,* 199–212.

Wainer, H., & Braun, H.I. (Eds.). (1988). *Test validity.* Hillsdale, NJ: Erlbaum.

Waldholz, M. (1996, October 30). NIH scientist says junior researcher falsified data for leukemia study. *Wall Street Journal,* Vol. CCXXVII, No. 86, p. B4.

Waldholz, M. (1997). How do we know Dolly isn't a hoax? *Wall Street Journal,* February 28, pp. B1, B2.

Walker, J.G., Johnson, S., Manion, I., & Cloutier, P. (1996). Emotionally focused marital intervention for couples with chronically ill children. *Journal of Consulting and Clinical Psychology, 64,* 1029–1036.

Wallerstein, R.S. (1986). *Forty-two lives in treatment: A study of psychoanalysis and psychotherapy.* New York: Guilford.

Walster, E., Berscheid, E., Abrahams, D., & Aronson, V. (1967). Effectiveness of debriefing following deception experiments. *Journal of Personality and Social Psychology, 6,* 371–380.

Waltz, J., Addis, M., Koerner, K., & Jacobson, J.S. (1993). Testing the integrity of a psychotherapy protocol: Assessment of adherence and competence. *Journal of Consulting and Clinical Psychology, 61,* 620–630.

Wampold, B.E., Davis, B., & Good, R.H.III (1990). Hypothesis validity of clinical research. *Journal of Consulting and Clinical Psychology, 58,* 360–367.

Watkins, C.E., Campbell, V.L., Nieberding, R., & Hallmark, R. (1995). Contemporary practice of psychological assessment by clinical psychologists. *Professional Psychology: Research and Practice, 26,* 54–60.

Watson, J.B., & Rayner, R. (1920). Conditioned emotional reactions. *Journal of Experimental Psychology, 3,* 1–14.

Webb, E.J., Campbell, D.T., Schwartz, R.D., Sechrest, L., & Grove, J.B. (1981). *Nonreactive measures in the social sciences* (2nd ed.). Boston: Houghton Mifflin.

Weber, S.J., & Cook. T.D. (1972). Subject effects in laboratory research: An examination of subject roles, demand characteristics, and valid inference. *Psychological Bulletin, 77,* 273–295.

Webster-Stratton, C. (1996). Early intervention with videotape modeling: Programs for families of children with oppositional defiant disorder or conduct disorder. In E.D. Hibbs & P. Jensen (Eds.), *Psychosocial treatment research of child and adolescent disorders: Empirically based strategies for clinical practice* (pp. 435–474). Washington, DC: American Psychological Association.

Webster-Stratton, C., & Spitzer, A. (1996). Parenting of a young child with conduct problems: New insights using qualitative methods. In T.H. Ollendick & R.J. Prinz (Eds.), *Advances in clinical child psychology* (Vol. 18, pp. 1–62). New York: Plenum Press.

Weiner, I.B. (1995). Methodological considerations in Rorschach research. *Psychological Assessment, 7,* 330–337.

Weiss, B., & Weisz, J.R. (1990). The impact of methodological factors on child psychotherapy outcome research: A meta-analysis for researchers. *Journal of Abnormal Child Psychology, 18,* 639–670.

Weiss, G., Minde, K., Douglas, V., Werry, J., & Sykes, D. (1971). Comparison of the effects of chlorpromazine, dextroamphetamine and methylphenidate on the behaviour and intellectual functioning of hyperactive children. *Canadian Medical Association Journal, 104,* 20–25.

Weisz, J.R., Walter, B.R., Weiss, B., Fernandez, G.A., & Mikow, V.A. (1990). Arrests among emotionally disturbed violent and assaultive individuals following minimal versus lengthy intervention through North Carolina's Willie M. Program. *Journal of Consulting and Clinical Psychology, 58,* 720–728.

Weisz, J.R., & Weiss, B. (1993). *Effects of psychotherapy with children and adolescents.* Newbury Park, CA: Sage.

Weisz, J.R., Weiss, B., & Donenberg, G.R. (1992). The lab versus the clinic: Effects of child and adolescent psychotherapy. *American Psychologist, 47,* 1578–1585.

Wells, K.B., Burnam, M.A., Leake, B., & Robins, L.N. (1988). Agreement between face-to-face and telephone-administered versions of the depression section of the NIMH Diagnostic Interview Schedule. *Journal of Psychiatric Research, 22,* 207–220.

Werner, E.E., & Smith, R.S. (1982). *Vulnerable, but invincible: A longitudinal study of resilient children and youth.* New York: McGraw-Hill.

Werner, E.E., & Smith, R.S. (1992). *Overcoming the odds: High-risk children from birth to adulthood.* Ithaca: Cornell University Press.

West, R.R. (1995). Cholesterol screening: Can it be justified? *Hospital Update* (May), 219–229.

Wetzler, S., & Sanderson, W.C. (Eds.). (1997). *Treatment strategies for patients with psychiatric comorbidity.* New York: Wiley.

White, L., Tursky, B., & Schwartz, G.E. (Eds.). (1985). *Placebo: Theory, research, and mechanisms.* New York: Guilford.

Widom, C.S., & Shepard, R.L. (1996). Accuracy of adult recollections of childhood victimization: Part 1. Childhood physical abuse. *Psychological Assessment, 8,* 412–421.

Wilson, G.T. (1996). Manual-based treatments: The clinical application of research findings. *Behaviour Research and Therapy, 34,* 295–314.

Windle, C. (1954). Test–retest effect on personality questionnaires. *Educational and Psychological Measurement, 14,* 617–633.

Winer, B.J., Brown, D.R., & Michels, K.M. (1991). *Statistical principles in experimental design* (3rd ed.). New York: McGraw-Hill.

Winslow, R. (1995). New pertussis vaccines by 3 companies prove effective in 2 European studies. *Wall Street Journal,* July 14, p. B5C.

Wright, K.M., & Miltenberger, R.G. (1987). Awareness training in the treatment of head and facial tics. *Journal of Behavior Therapy and Experimental Psychiatry, 18,* 269–274.

Wolf, M.M. (1978). Social validity: The case of subjective measurement or how applied behavior analysis is finding its heart. *Journal of Applied Behavior Analysis, 11,* 203–214.

Wright, L. (July 25, 1994). One drop of blood. *New Yorker,* pp. 46–55.

Wyatt, G.E., & Powell, G.J. (Eds.) (1988). *Lasting effects of child abuse.* Newbury Park, CA: Sage.

Yates, B.T. (1995). Cost-effectiveness analysis, cost-benefit analysis, and beyond: Evolving models for the scientist–manager–practitioner. *Clinical Psychology: Science and Practice, 2,* 385–398.

Yin, R.K. (1994). *Case study research: Design and methods* (2nd ed.). Thousand Oaks, CA: Sage.

Zilborg, G., & Henry, G. (1941). *A history of medical psychology.* New York: W.W. Norton.

Author Index

509

Subject Index